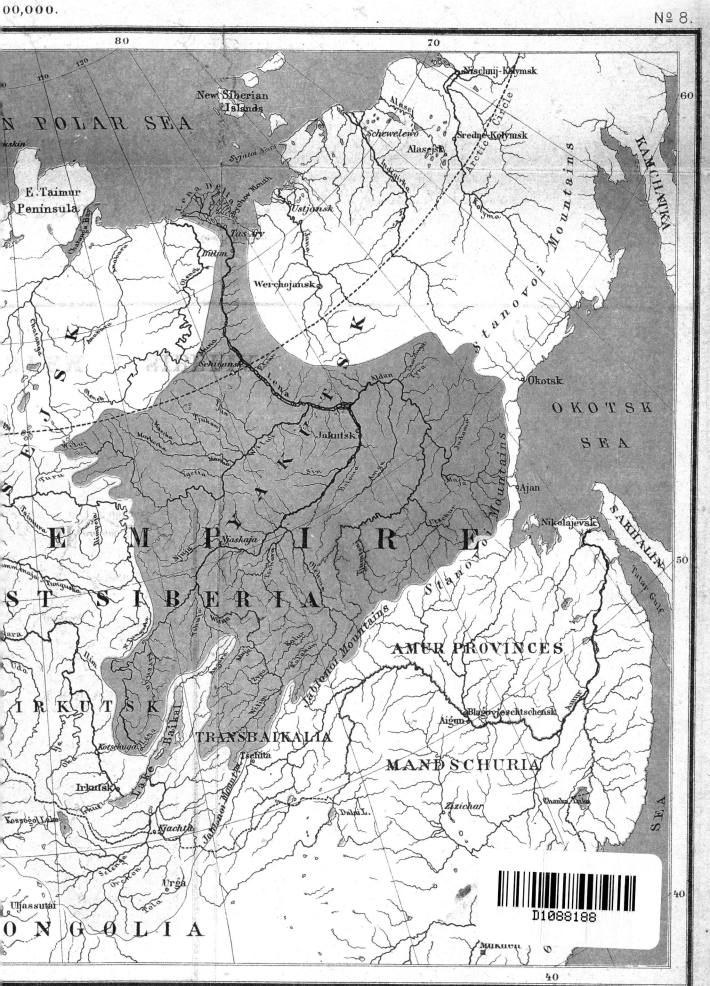

The Bark Canoes and Skin Boats of Northern Eurasia

THE BARK CANOES AND SKIN BOATS OF NORTHERN EURASIA

HARRI LUUKKANEN AND
WILLIAM W. FITZHUGH

WITH CONTRIBUTIONS FROM
EVGUENIA ANICHTCHENKO

SMITHSONIAN BOOKS
WASHINGTON, DC

Funding for this book was provided in part by Smithsonian Institution Scholarly Press.

Published by Smithsonian Books
Director: Carolyn Gleason
Senior Editor: Jaime Schwender
Edited by Martin Edmunds, Laura Harger, and Juliana Froggatt
Designed by Mary Parsons
Indexed and typeset by Scribe Inc.

This book may be purchased for educational, business, or sales promotional use. For information, please write: Special Markets Department, Smithsonian Books, P.O. Box 37012, MRC 513, Washington, DC 20013

Library of Congress Cataloging-in-Publication Data
Names: Luukkanen, Harri, author. | Fitzhugh, William W., 1943– author.
Title: The bark canoes and skin boats of Northern Eurasia / Harri Luukkanen and William W. Fitzhugh ; contribution by
    Evguenia Anichtchenko.
Description: Washington, DC : Smithsonian Books, [2020] | Includes bibliographical references and index.
Identifiers: LCCN 2015027732 | ISBN 9781588344755
Subjects: LCSH: Canoes and canoeing—Eurasia. | Skin boats—Eurasia.
Classification: LCC VM353 .L85 2020 | DDC 623.82/9—dc23 LC record available at https://lccn.loc.gov/2015027732

Manufactured in the United States of America, not at government expense.
24 23 22 21 20   5 4 3 2 1

Endpapers: August Heinrich Petermann's map of Northern and Middle Asia from *Stieler's Hand Atlas*, 1880, as it appeared in N. A. E. Nordenskjöld's 1881 *The Voyage of the* Vega *round Asia and Europe*, vol. 1, 372.

CONTENTS

4. NORTHEASTERN EUROPE:
THE EASTERN BALTICS AND WESTERN URALS   69

5. WESTERN SIBERIA:
THE OB RIVER AND YAMAL PENINSULA   93

6. CENTRAL SIBERIA:
THE YENISEY RIVER AND THE TAIMYR PENINSULA   115

7. EASTERN SIBERIA:
THE LENA RIVER BASIN AND TRANSBAIKAL   135

8. PACIFIC SIBERIA:
CHUKOTKA, KAMCHATKA, AND THE KURIL ISLANDS   155

9. THE FAR EAST:
MANCHURIA, SAKHALIN ISLAND, CHINA, AND NORTHERN JAPAN 185

EPILOGUE: ALASKA AND EURASIA—
DIVERGENCE AND CONTINUITY ACROSS THE BERING STRAIT 215

APPENDIX: LITERATURE ON EURASIAN BARK CANOES AND SKIN BOATS 233

GLOSSARY 239

ACKNOWLEDGMENTS 243

REFERENCES 247

INDEX 269

TABLES AND MAPS

TABLES

MAPS

Notes on the Text

All Finnish, German, and Scandinavian-language materials quoted in this book were translated by Harri Luukkanen (HL). As we lacked professional translators during the research phase of this project, he relied on foreign-born canoe-knowledgeable friends and machine-translation services to translate other languages. These translations were then edited for style and content. This process inevitably introduced some errors, for which we apologize.

The singular and plural names of Native peoples and groups are spelled the same way among all Russian Native groups (e.g., a Nenets herder; Nenets herders). This usage is common practice. Spellings of Native groups' names and place names in quoted texts have not been standardized to modern usage and, in quotations from original English translations, have been left as they appeared in the source documents. Some older names have been preserved (e.g., Sungari, now Songhua River) because of their prominence in old literature. In these cases, the modern name is noted at the old name's first appearance in the text.

We occasionally refer to the peoples and cultures of Arctic North America as "Eskimo," since that term—although tainted historically—is necessary when referring to all Arctic-adapted peoples, from Chukotka and Alaska to Greenland, because no other adequate collective term is available. However, this name is considered derogatory in Canada, where European explorers mistakenly applied it during the early contact period. In Canada, the proper term for the people known in the historical period is *Inuit*, meaning "real people," while their Dorset-culture predecessors are collectively known as *Paleoeskimo*. In Alaska and Chukotka (Pacific Siberia), Eskimo peoples prefer to be known by their individual ethno-linguistic names: e.g., Sugpiaq, Unangan, Aluttiq, Yup'ik, Yupik (in Russia), and Iñupiaq. Depending on chronological or former publication context, we use either older or modern names: e.g., Lapp or Saami; Ostyak or Khanty; Yakut or Sakha; Lamut or Even; Gilkak or Nivkh; Gold or Nanay.

INTRODUCTION

In 1964, the Smithsonian Institution published a pioneering book describing Native American watercraft, *The Bark Canoes and Skin Boats of North America* (fig. 0.1), authored by Edwin Tappan Adney and Howard I. Chapelle. By that time, the Smithsonian had been collecting Native American artifacts for more than a century, but except for a report by Otis T. Mason and Meriden S. Hill (1901) and a discussion of building a Chippewa birch-bark canoe (Ritzenthaler 1950), the Smithsonian's collection of bark canoes and skin kayaks remained mostly unpublished and largely unknown (as did most indigenous North American watercraft in other institutions). Adney and Chapelle described many of these boats for the first time. Their book became popular among both scholarly and amateur boating enthusiasts; it was featured in John McPhee's *The Survival of the Bark Canoe* (1975) and

is now the longest-running book in print ever produced by the Smithsonian Institution.

Adney (1868–1950), known to friends as Tappan, was a remarkable individual—an artist, naturalist, woodsman, linguist, and scholar. At age 19, while he was vacationing in Woodstock, New Brunswick, a Maliseet Indian named Peter Joe taught him how to make a bark canoe and instructed him in the Maliseet language. Adney, the son of a college professor and already a trained artist, became fascinated with Native Americans and Indian lore, in particular Indian canoes and canoe traditions. He married a woman from Woodstock, New Brunswick, moved to Montreal, and took Canadian citizenship. His interest in Native watercraft developed into a lifetime spent documenting canoes and kayaks both in the field and in museums across North America (Adney and Chapelle

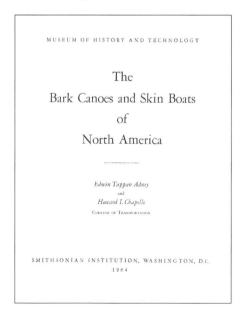 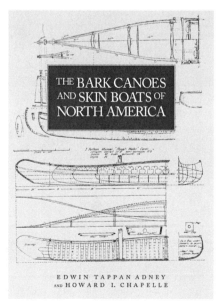

Fig. 0.1. Left: Title page of the original 1964 Smithsonian edition of Edwin Tappan Adney and Howard I. Chapelle's *The Bark and Skin Boats of North America*. In those days, Smithsonian monograph covers carried only the title and author and did not include illustrations. *Right*: Many commercial reprints of the original monograph, which continues to enjoy readership, have appeared since 1964. This Smithsonian reprinting, like most, has an illustrated cover.

1964: 4; Jennings 2004). His huge trove of collected information included tribe-by-tribe descriptions of canoe manufacturing techniques, raw materials, and vessel performance. He interviewed and photographed Native Americans making canoes; he studied, measured, and built full-size and scaled models; and he made nautical-style construction drawings of canoes' lines and details.

After his death in 1950, his models and voluminous archives were accessioned by the Mariners' Museum in Newport News, Virginia (fig. 0.2). An arrangement with the Smithsonian made it possible for Howard Chapelle, a marine architect and curator of naval history at the National Museum of History and Technology (now the National Museum of American History), to organize Adney's materials and assemble the book. Its ethnographic descriptions and photographs provide a window onto a long-neglected and mostly vanished part of North American Native life, and its construction sketches have enabled recreational boatbuilders to make and utilize authentic replicas for the first time.

More than a decade ago, the present authors began to explore the possibility of preparing a Eurasian sequel to this classic piece of North American cultural literature. From the start, we knew we could not replicate Adney's research; such a task would take a lifetime of research in Russia and Fennoscandia (Scandinavia and Finland). Even with modern communications technology, it would also require skill in Russian and several European languages as well as training in nautical engineering and drafting. Nevertheless, we felt we could make a contribution by assembling data on various types of boats from existing historical and ethnographic documents, illustrations from early explorers' journals and literature, and photographs of boats and models in Eurasian museums. Adney's professional-quality scaled nautical

drawings were beyond our capabilities, time, and finances, but we could survey the field and produce a historical "boat atlas" of the Eurasian north whose traditional watercraft were unknown to the West and even to most Russians. Such a work would provide a foundation for both amateur enthusiasts and scholars interested in pursuing future studies.

An additional goal was to make some sense, however generalized, of broad-scale patterns in the geographic distribution and historical development of boat types across Northern Eurasia and between Asia and North America. Similar questions of historical relationship motivated Mason and Hill's 1901 report, with its intriguing comparison between the semidecked Canadian Kootenai bark canoe and the Amur River "sturgeon-nose" canoe, and recent studies of North American Eskimo kayaks and open skin boats (which we discuss in chapter 10). Could these furnish evidence of long-distance cultural connections? We explore this and other issues in the history of canoe development in the pages that follow.

The response to Adney and Chapelle's book revealed wide popular interest in Native watercraft across a broad spectrum of the North American public. Besides scholars of Native American culture and maritime historians, traditional boats appeal to sports enthusiasts, wilderness travelers, craftspeople, and artists, and this is as true in Eurasia as it is in North America. Nothing had been written about the history of traditional watercraft of Northern Eurasia except a short Russian-language report—long out of print and available in only a few western libraries—written by Valentina V. Antropova in *The Historical and Ethnographic Atlas of Siberia* and published by the Russian Academy of Sciences (RAS) in 1961 (fig. 0.3). We envisioned our book as providing an introduction to Northern Eurasian traditional

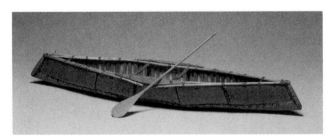

Fig. 0.2. Edwin Tappan Adney was a master craftsman who made a series of models of North American canoes and kayaks, which are now kept at the Mariners' Museum in Newport News, Virgina. This model (MP48) replicates an Evenk canoe model (MAE 334-77-R) that was collected by Richard Maak in 1891 and is now in the Museum of Anthropology and Ethnology (Kunstkamera) in St. Petersburg, Russia. Adney based this model on Otis T. Mason and Meriden S. Hill's 1901 publication of a model Yakut canoe (MAE 701-51) collected by Alexander Fedorovich von Middendorff in the Lena River valley in 1846. That Museum of Anthropology and Ethnology model was loaned to the Smithsonian to facilitate Mason's comparative study of North American canoes. (Courtesy Mariners' Museum)

Fig. 0.3. An ethnologist working for the St. Petersburg Museum of Anthropology and Ethnology, Valentina V. Antropova wrote the pioneering essay on the indigenous boats of the Siberian USSR (1961). Her classification scheme became the starting point for our study. (Courtesy Museum of Anthropology and Ethnology)

watercraft and the cultures that created and used them; we also wanted to identify the literature and institutions where researchers could find more information (see the appendix).

PROJECT RATIONALE

As coauthors, we have come together from different professional backgrounds and have had different experiences and inspirations. Our personal histories have enabled us to contribute in unique ways to a project that neither of us would have contemplated alone and which has spanned more than 15 years from inception to publication.

Harri Luukkanen: I have often been asked why I chose to cowrite a history of bark canoes and skin boats of the Eurasian north (fig. 0.4). The idea began in 2004 when my sailing canoe partner, Risto Lehtinen, asked me to contribute a short history of ancient Finnish canoes to the Finnish Canoe Union's website. I had some experience with this topic: in 1985, I had written a history of Finland's first century of modern sport canoeing and boatbuilding, which began after canoes arrived from England in the 1880s. However, Risto was asking me to write a much deeper history, one reaching

back a full millennium. I knew something about bark canoes and skin boats in North America and Greenland, but I did not know much about the traditional canoes of Northern Europe and Asia. On the other hand, I knew *modern* canoes and kayaks very well, having paddled, sailed, and built many of these kinds of boats over the past 50 years. I also knew the technical aspects of watercraft. In 2000, assisted by the Ship Laboratory at the Helsinki University of Technology, I had devised a mathematical modeling algorithm to measure hydrodynamic resistance for use in boat design. I also had experience researching complex topics, as my primary work, as an economist who forecasts the future of the electronics industry, requires such research. That and my experience as a paddler and boatbuilder gave me the tools I needed to explore ancient canoe history.

Gradually, as I began to investigate Finnish canoe history, my project expanded geographically across Northern Eurasia. At first I focused on Fennoscandia and northeastern Europe; then, after conceiving the larger project with WWF, my research spread to Western Siberia and the Yenisey River, covering all the Finno-Ugric and Samoyed language regions. (Finno-Ugric-speaking peoples include the Saami, Karelians, Khanty, Mansi, and Komi peoples of northeastern Europe west of the Urals; speakers of Samoyed include the Nenets, Enets, and Nganasan along the Arctic coast east and west of Yamal, and the Selkup and other groups around the headwaters of the Yenisey.) Later, when I became aware of the complex bark canoe history of Southern Siberia, I added Lake Baikal; finally, I expanded my study to cover not only the Lena and Amur River basins but also the rest of Eastern Siberia, including the Chukchi Peninsula, thus covering every region from Scandinavia to the Bering Strait. Most of my information was drawn from sources from medieval times to the present, but I also gained glimpses of a deeper past via researching rare archaeological finds of boats, paddles, and rock art that are as much as 8,000 years old. Besides learning about canoe regions and peoples, I discovered that experts in canoe history were willing to share their knowledge by commenting on my canoe papers (Luukkanen 2005a–f; 2006a,b; 2007) and recommending new sources (see appendix and acknowledgments). In the beginning, I did not know that my project was unique in scope and coverage, and although it was born outside the academic mainstream and was privately financed, I found that professional archaeologists, ethnologists, and historians were interested in my results.

I first became acquainted with William Fitzhugh, director of the Arctic Studies Center at the Smithsonian Institution,

Fig. 0.4. Harri Luukkanen inspects and displays plans for the Nahkasukka canoe in Lahti, Finland, 2011. (Photograph: Jorma Honkala)

in 2005 when he commented on the draft of a paper I had written on the Sintashta culture in the southern Urals and the Bronze Age Volga-Finnic peoples. In the fall of 2007, when I'd assembled a first draft summarizing my bark and skin canoe research, he proposed that we expand it to serve as a sequel to Adney and Chapelle's North American canoe history. We met to discuss the idea at a maritime studies conference in Trondheim, Norway (Luukkanen 2010; see Westerdahl 2010 for full proceedings). Then I started to collect Russian source material and illustrations. I systematically assembled this information in the "Database on Northern Eurasian Bark and Skin Canoes: An Information Guide for Bark Canoes and Skin Boats of the Eurasian North," now on file at the Smithsonian Arctic Studies Center. This database, of some 200 pages, facilitated our writing of the final manuscript. Also helping to make the book possible was the appearance of new digital technology, which enabled us to uncover information from rare old books and archival documents. Without online search tools, digital libraries, and automatic translation programs, we never could have completed this canoe history.

William W. Fitzhugh: Like Harri, I developed a love of the water and small boats in my childhood. I spent summers rowing and sailing boats in Chatham, Massachusetts, and as a teenager canoed in the Adirondacks and served as a trip guide at Keewaydin Camp in Temagami, Ontario (fig. 0.5). At Dartmouth College, I led yearly canoe trips down the Connecticut River from Hanover, New Hampshire, to Long Island Sound, a tradition begun by Dartmouth's legendary explorer John Ledyard in 1773. (Ledyard later traversed much of Siberia by canoe before being arrested on orders from the czar; see Gray 2007.) In 1964, Ledyard-inspired wanderlust led fellow student Dan Dimancescu and me to organize a 1,700-mile canoe trip down the Danube River from its headwaters in Germany to the Black Sea. The saga of this trip across a still-robust Iron Curtain was published as "Dartmouth down the Danube" in *National Geographic* in July 1965, written by William Slade Backer, one of our team members (Backer 1965). Later, my PhD studies at Harvard University took me to Labrador, where I began to use canoes, kayaks, and other boats as the logistical backbone for archaeological research,

Fig. 0.5. William Fitzhugh's introduction to the waterways of Eurasia began with Dartmouth College's Ledyard Canoe Club trip down the Danube River in 1964 (Backer 1965). In 1773, John Ledyard abandoned his studies at Dartmouth, built a canoe, and paddled down the Connecticut River to his grandfather's farm. From 1776 to 1780, he participated in Captain James Cook's third voyage of Pacific exploration. Later, at the suggestion of Thomas Jefferson in 1787, he attempted a canoe crossing of Siberia but was arrested for espionage when he reached Irkutsk on orders from Catherine the Great. (Photograph: Christopher G. Knight)

a practice I have continued for decades both there and in Quebec, Baffin Island, and Russia.

Before I met HL, my curiosity about early boat technology had been piqued by my archaeological discoveries of Inuit boats in northern Labrador, including the remains of a kayak inside a 200-year-old Inuit hut, and the remains of another kayak and a man's toolbox, still full of tools, hidden among rocks at the base of a cliff on the northern Labrador coast. Such archaeological finds on land are rare because kayaks and canoes, like most small boats, are fragile and are often not recognized or recovered when exposed by erosion or construction activity. The prehistory of boats is better discovered underwater, where cold temperatures and low oxygen levels can preserve vessels almost completely intact, as in the case of the 16th-century Basque whaler *San Juan* in Red Bay, Labrador (Grenier, Bernier, and Stevens 2007), and Sir John Franklin's mid-19th-century exploration ships *Erebus* and *Terror*, which have been discovered in the Canadian Arctic. But on occasion, ships have been recovered on land. While organizing a Viking exhibit for the Smithsonian in 2000 (W. Fitzhugh and Ward 2000), I learned about the 9th-century *Gokstad* and *Oseberg* ships buried in the anaerobic blue clay of Norway's Oslo Fjord. However, large

Viking boats, such as those studied by Ole Crumlin-Pedersen (2010), did not capture my imagination as much as the small boats that had empowered the northern cultures HL had begun to research, and together we decided to bring more of this history to light. An earlier collaboration of mine with Soviet/Russian scholars on the joint U.S.-Soviet *Crossroads of Continents* exhibition (W. Fitzhugh and Crowell 1988), and my experience as a partner in archaeological expeditions across Russia, paid dividends in the form of knowledgeable acquaintances and familiarity with Russian Native cultures, history, and boats.

In the 1990s, while I was writing up my Russian archaeological fieldwork, I realized how little English-language material was available on the history and cultures of the Russian north. In particular, the *Crossroads* project had raised many questions about connections between Northern Eurasia and North America, and boats were at the center of those questions. When HL began writing about Finnish and Scandinavian boats, I realized that by working together we could make a contribution toward filling a large gap in the history of northern peoples by extending Adney and Chapelle's work into Northern Eurasia. Such a project could lay the groundwork for a future assessment of boating history on a truly global scale.

In our early discussions, it quickly became apparent that there was no comprehensive study of Eurasian boats comparable to Adney and Chapelle's North American book. On the other hand, we discovered a large body of literature, both in print and online, on the specialized topic of Eskimo kayaks and open skin boats, including works by Eugene Arima, Sergei Bogojavlensky, Stephen Braund, George Dyson, Harvey Golden, John Heath, Jarmo Kankaanpää, Jean-Loup Rousselot, David Zimmerly, and Evguenia (Jenya) Anichtchenko, among others (see the appendix and references in Zimmerly 2010; Golden 2006, 2015; Anichtchenko 2012). Many others, such as Paul Johnston (1980), Gerd Koch (1984), Bodo Spranz (1984), and Béat Arnold (2014), have written about canoes and small boats more broadly. Rousselot's thesis (1983) and brief summary (1994) provided helpful introduction, particularly for skin boats in the North Pacific and northern North America. We decided to expand the scope of our project outward from Scandinavia to include the bark and skin boats of the entire boreal and tundra regions of the Eurasian north and to organize the study by region, river basin, and ethnic group, using Valentina Antropova's survey (1961) as both a resource and a guide. We added Mongolia, northern China, and northern Japan, as peoples in those areas used inflated skin boats and inflated skin rafts, which had a minor presence in some more northern cultures. We chose to include a few outlier stories as well. For example, we discuss the mystery of the legendary 17th-century "Finnmen" seen paddling kayaks off the coast of the northern British Isles; some of these kayaks eventually found their way into museums and even church attics. Later studies revealed the watercraft were not actually Finnish; instead they had belonged to Greenland Inuit who had been captured by whalers for sale to European circuses.

We also include the stories of naturalist Peter Kalm's 18th-century attempt to introduce American Indian canoes into (then) Swedish Finland, and the resettlement of Native Kodiak and Aleutian Islanders to hunt sea otters for the Russian America Company in the Kuril Islands. These additional topics, which link the boat traditions of North America and Eurasia, place the use of canoes and kayaks in circumpolar perspective and connect our work to Adney and Chapelle's. Likewise, we present an epilogue on Alaska's boating traditions, written by Evguenia (Jenya) Anichtchenko, a Russian American researcher of Alaskan watercraft, which demonstrates the Bering Strait's importance as a cultural and historical conduit in the transmission of boat technology from the Old to the New World, and perhaps occasionally the reverse. The many migrations across the strait brought not only people into the Americas, but also their cultures and knowledge of bark canoes and Eskimo kayaks and open skin boats.

We might ask what has changed so that we can tell the story of Northern Eurasian watercraft now. Has a wealth of new archaeological finds been uncovered? No; instead a trove of old Russian archival sources has become available on the Internet. Throughout much of the 20th century, most Russian archives were inaccessible to outside researchers due to linguistic, political, logistical, and other barriers. Before 1991, Russian museums were mainly closed to outsiders, and in the pre-Internet era, western contact with Russian scientists and curators was rare. Today, political changes have meant that Russian publications and information are widely available on the websites of local, regional, and private museums and archives, facilitating access and remote study.

As we wrote this book, we faced many complications, some intrinsic to these resources. HL, for example, has competence in European languages but does not speak Russian; thus he translated Russian canoe literature online via automatic translation services and, when possible, contacted authors directly for clarifications and for advice on where to find images. His knowledge of German enabled him to read old diaries and studies on Russia found in e-libraries (the official language of the Russian Academy of Sciences was German until the end of the 19th century). WWF's contributions came from his familiarity with Scandinavian, Russian, Mongolian, and Japanese scholars and his knowledge of Eurasian ethnography and archaeology. He took on the tasks of editing, balancing treatment across different regions, providing anthropological perspectives, and guiding the manuscript through the editing process and into publication.

When it came time to request photographs, Anichtchenko assisted with communications and provided advice and translations. She also photographed boats and models in the Museum of Anthropology and Ethnology (MAE, also known as the Kunstkamera) and the Russian Ethnographic Museum (REM) during a trip to St. Petersburg in 2014. Her research suggests that museums, archives, and cultural centers all across Russia contain boat history treasures known only to their curators and local experts, including handwritten documents and more watercraft specimens and models than we had discovered in our literature-based study. An example of the latter occurred in 2016, when WWF viewed two excellent Koryak skin boat models during a visit to the Kamchatka Regional Museum in Petropavlovsk-Kamchatsky (fig. 0.6). Similarly, we expect that still more undiscovered information awaits researchers in museums, libraries, and archives outside Russia. For instance, A. I. Savvinov (2011) provides a summary of Siberian ethnographic collections in German museums, where many of the earliest Russian collections are found.

While we have only scratched the surface of the relevant libraries and archives, our exploration provides a foundation for future studies. Our hope is that this book will stimulate researchers to dig deeper, using archaeological, ethnographic, and forensic methods to more fully understand the history of boating technology, the evolution and distribution of boat types, and their rich cultural and symbolic significance.

THE NORTHERN EURASIA SETTING

Our journey through boat and canoe history takes us across a huge area inhabited by many peoples from ancient times up to the present day. In Northern Eurasia, tundra and boreal forest (known as taiga in Russia) stretch nearly 10,000 kilometers along the 65°N parallel from the Norwegian coast to Chukotka and the Bering Strait, and from the Arctic Ocean

Fig. 0.6. Models of two Koryak open skin boats displayed in the Kamchatka Regional Museum in Petropavlovsk-Kamchatsky. The uppermost is of Koryak-Kerek design. The lower follows the Eskimo plan. (Photograph: William Fitzhugh; courtesy Petropavlovsk Regional Museum)

coast south some 2,500 kilometers to the Eurasian steppe in Southern Siberia and Mongolia. Native peoples who historically used bark or dugout canoes, dugouts with planked sides, or skin boats once occupied this entire area. Between the Saami of northwestern Eurasia and the Yupik Eskimo of far northeastern Siberia lived peoples who spoke many languages (map 1) — Finno-Ugric, Paleo-Asiatic, Tungus, Mongol, Manchu, Turkic — as well as some mixed Eurasian peoples who spoke other languages and dialects (Sillanpää 2008). For all their differences, they had some things in common: they lived as fishermen and as hunters along waterways (rivers, lakes, seashores, or estuaries) and relied on small boats or rafts for subsistence, trade, and transportation. Archaeological finds suggest that their ancient boatbuilding traditions began during the Pleistocene (also called the Ice Age) more than 10,000 years ago and persisted, in some places, into the 20th century.

This book addresses the history of two major types of indigenous watercraft: bark boats and skin boats (which include enclosed kayaks and open-topped boats of the *umiak* or *baidar* type; see the glossary). We consider boat types, design, and construction techniques found among the many indigenous societies of the Eurasian north. Because of the paucity of archaeological finds, we do not know the precise origins of these traditions, other than that they lie in deep antiquity. Like Antropova, we hypothesize that the bark canoe originated thousands of years ago in the Ice Age's birch-rich boreal forest and that knowledge of how to build it spread through migration and cultural contacts among peoples living from the Baltic Sea to the Amur River and as far south as Lake Baikal. On the other hand, we postulate that skin boats originated more recently, somewhere along the Arctic Ocean coast and river estuaries from the White Sea in Europe to Chukotka and the Sea of Okhotsk in Eastern

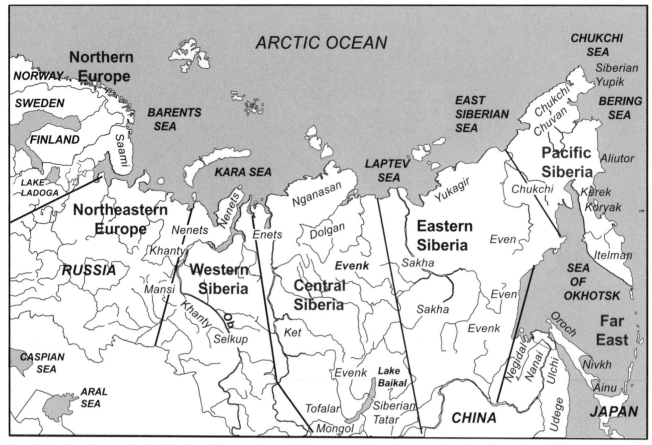

Map 1. The Eurasian north: distribution of its peoples and the geographic regions used to classify bark and skin boats. (Marcia Bakry, Smithsonian Institution)

Siberia, where water-resistant sea mammal hides were available and more suitable than tree bark for watercraft used on rocky coasts and icy seas. We suppose that these more advanced, maneuverable skin boats developed from hide-covered coracle-type "bucket boats" that had more ancient origins and were used to cross rivers and small bodies of water.

Eurasian use of birch-bark canoes and skin boats ended relatively recently. In the Upper Tunguska River of the Yenisey basin in Western Siberia, for example, the Evenk made bark canoes until the 1920s. At that time, the last Koryak kayaks were being built in Penzhina Bay, Kamchatka. Among the Amur River peoples of the Far East, bark canoes remained in use as late as the mid-20th century—longer than in other regions of Eurasia. There are indications that people used skin boats as recently as the 1700s along the Arctic coasts of Fennoscandia and Western Siberia. They are occasionally still used today in the Bering Strait.

Today, many people recreationally use modern canoes and kayaks that are the direct descendants of old bark canoes and skin boats. Many also share a keen interest in the crafts' history and construction. North America and Greenland boating history has been researched and published, but, as we have noted, the story of the early canoes and kayaks of Northern Europe and Asia has never been written in full, and even anthropologists and museum experts lack regionwide descriptive data. Researchers have explored the subject only at the very local or the very general level, and rarely from a comparative point of view.

All historical boat types have a story to tell, but the few that have served for millennia, from prehistoric to modern times, make a special claim on the history of the species whom some have called *Homo faber*, "man the builder." This is certainly the case with the birch-bark canoe, which traversed taiga waterways for thousands of years until the early 20th century. Except for simple log boats and rafts, no other boat type has spread throughout every waterway over this vast region or served all the major peoples in the Northern Eurasian forest zone for so long. A similarly deep claim exists for skin boats, which opened new frontiers in coastal

The Bark Canoes and Skin Boats of Northern Eurasia

and tundra zones thousands of years ago; they functioned well in the harsh maritime environment from Chukotka to Greenland, and Eskimo and Chukchi people still use them today for sea mammal hunting along the shores of the Bering Strait. Some craft, like St. Brendan's early-6th-century ox-hide Irish currach, were capable of sailing far into, if not across, the North Atlantic.

Thus the history of bark canoes and skin boats is not simply a history of boats; it is also, inescapably, a history of the peoples who built and used those boats for many millennia to master waterways; to migrate, fish, trade, wage war, and spear reindeer at river crossings; and to hunt seal, walrus, and whale on bays and oceans. This way of life became imperative at the end of the Pleistocene, 12,000 years ago, when forests expanded and human hunters and environmental change resulted in the extinction of mammoth, mastodon, and other tundra and taiga megafauna. No longer could people count on large stocks of land mammals for food, fuel, clothing, and construction materials. Melting permafrost and advancing forest cover required them to develop new ways of life that depended on waterways for transport, communication, and food. Fish and sea mammals became an important part of the human diet. Without the invention and refinement of the bark canoe and skin boat, hunters and fishermen, their families, and their peoples never could have survived Northern Eurasia's harsh climate and environment.

TYPES OF BOATS
Bark Canoes

This term (as well as this book itself) covers all types of canoes made with bark taken from living trees. Birch-bark canoes are the best-known type, but in the past, some Eurasian canoes were covered with the bark of elm, larch, aspen, and spruce, as there were many alternatives to birch. In small bark canoes, a wooden frame was fashioned inside a sheet of bark, and gunwales and thwarts were added to keep the boat rigid and open (fig. 0.7). In larger canoes, or where the only available bark sheets were small, the boat's cover was sewn from two or more separate sheets. Some Yenisey River (Central Siberia) and Amur River (Far East) bark canoes had rigid, self-supporting wooden frames, and the bark covers were sewn separately to fit the frames. East of the Yenisey River, the Chunya Evenk partially decked the bow and stern sections of their canoes with birch bark or deerskin (see chapter 6 and figs. 6.5–6.6, page 128). Finally, in the 20th century, people replaced the birch-bark covers of traditional Nanay canoes in the Amur River with canvas.

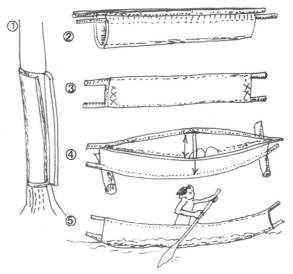

Fig. 0.7. The basic procedure for making a bark canoe is quite simple. Bark is taken from a living tree and attached to gunwales, and a third timber may be placed inside the bottom for a keelson. The hull is shaped with stone weights until ribs are installed. Thwarts are placed between the gunwales to keep the canoe open, and the bark ends and seams are sewn and caulked with larch or birch resin. The end result looks similar to boats pictured in Neolithic and Bronze Age rock art in Northern Europe. (Drawing: Harri Luukkanen)

Skin Boats

Rudolf Trebitsch (1912) defined five types of skin boats, or floating vehicles: round or oval basket boats; open, long-keeled boats; decked kayaks; inflated skin rafts or floats; and swimming vests or floats for personal use. While all five have been used in the Eurasian north, we focus on skin-covered, baidar-type long-keeled boats, decked or half-decked kayaks, and skin-covered or skin-decked boats built over self-supporting frames (see fig. 2.5, page 41). In the 20th century, painted canvas began to replace skin boat covers in coastal Western Siberia, and as late as 2008, similar crafts were still being used in the Ob River estuary in the same area.

Other Types of Boats

This book does not cover dugout log boats, log boats with expanded sides, or planked punt boats. However, we do mention them here because they were used alongside bark canoes and skin boats in Northern Eurasia for hundreds, if not thousands, of years. Log boats represent a separate tradition in canoe-building technology: people began to build them in the Neolithic—also known as the Late Stone

Age, when ground stone axes, adzes, and gouges were developed that could be used for heavy woodworking—and these boats grew larger once metal tools were developed in the Bronze and Iron ages. In medieval times, log boats began to replace birch-bark canoes in Northern Eurasia's forest zone and, in part, small skin boats on the tundra. However, studies of rock art show that log boats with expanded and planked sides appeared thousands of years earlier in the maritime regions of Northern Europe, where larger, more seaworthy boats were needed for trade, fishing, and war (Helskog 1985, 1988; Klem 2010). In the Siberian interior, away from the open sea, where the transition from bark to log and wooden boats was slower, bark and skin canoes have been better documented, both archaeologically and in historical accounts.

STRUCTURE OF THE BOOK

Because not enough archaeological evidence is available for us to construct a regional or even a continental synthesis of watercraft development over time, our study is a geographic survey of boat types and usages more than it is a deep chronology of boat history. We present information on bark canoes and skin boats in two ways: by offering both a general description of the boats themselves and by providing a regional survey of the cultures and places where they were used. Because watercraft have played an integral role in the life and survival of many peoples in the challenging environment of Northern Eurasia, they are best understood in the context of their settings: they evolved to fulfill particular uses that were determined both by the demands of the physical environment and by cultural preference.

First, to orient the reader, chapter 1 provides an overview of the book's geographical range, addressing salient features of land, climate, and biosphere and noting the major ethnic or cultural groups who lived in each area. Chapter 2 describes and compares the various types of Northern Eurasian canoes and skin boats, including their construction, and is illustrated by photos and drawings. It also situates canoes and skin boats in the context of their cultural groupings, their natural environment, and their geographic regions. After we establish these basics, we deepen our treatment by situating the major types of canoes and boats in the context of their particular tribal groups—and in relation to the neighbors of these groups—in their particular geographic regions. Thus, chapters 3 through 9 present data—people by people and area by area—on specific bark canoe and skin boat types (see figs. 2.1, page 28, and 2.5, page 41; and map 4, page 29).

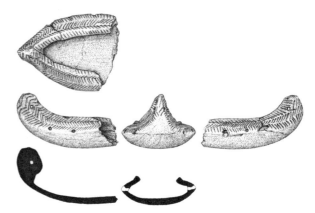

Fig. O.8. This fragment of a ceramic canoe was found in the grave of a Shagara-culture youth in the Ryazan district, near Moscow. The grave dates to the Early Bronze Age, ca. 2200 BCE. The canoe was purposefully broken at the time of burial, probably so its spirit could assist the youth as he voyaged in the upper world. The upturned bow or stern is characteristic of bark rather than dugout canoes, and the hatch-marking might indicate ornamentation on the canoe's sides. This model Shagara canoe could be the oldest-known representation of a bark canoe in Eurasia. (From Kaverzneva 2012: fig. 2)

While bark canoes and skin boats have been built and used in all areas of Northern Eurasia and by all of its cultural groups, we limit our discussion to those groups whose canoe and boat usage has been documented—some in great detail and others only vaguely—in written descriptions, drawings, and photos. Yet this remains a very broad survey: a quick sense of its scope and depth can be conveyed by stating that we have included more than 40 cultural groups and cited hundreds of geographic locations throughout the Northern Eurasian taiga, tundra, and steppe. An epilogue both extends this history across the Bering Strait into Alaska and reveals continuities and disjunctions between Eurasia and North America.

To make meaningful comparisons among boat types, we divide Northern Eurasia into seven territories (see map 1, page 8), which include the following major ethnic or cultural groups:

Northern Europe, including pre-Viking Germanic peoples, the Orkney Island "Finnmen," and the Saami (addressed in chapter 3)

Northeastern Europe, including the Karelians, Novgorod Russians, Maritime Pomors, Komi-Zyrians, and Sihirtia and Pechora Chud (chapter 4)

Western Siberia, including the Nenets, Khanty, Mansi, Selkup, Southern Samoyed, and Tatars (chapter 5)

Central Siberia, including the Nganasan, Enets, Dolgan, Ket, Yenisey River Evenk, Mongol, and Buryat (chapter 6)

Eastern Siberia, including the Yukagir, Chuvan, Lena River and Transbaikal Evenk, Even, and Sakha (chapter 7)

Pacific Siberia, including the Chukchi, Siberian Yupik (Eskimo), Kerek, Koryak, Itelmen, Kushi, and Kuril Ainu (chapter 8)

The Far East (Manchuria, Sakhalin Island, and northern Japan), including the Nivkh, Nanay, Ulch, Udege, Oroch, Negidal, Manchu, Ainu, Amur Evenk, Chinese, and Tibetans (chapter 9)

The benefits of this approach are great. When we drill down into our data, we pull up richly contextualized documentation. We sift similarities for differences, and we rake differences for similarities. For example, how does the boat and canoe use of a single cultural group vary waterway by waterway over wider territories? Which canoe and boat features are held in common by different ethnic groups living along a single river system or bay?

This book describes Northern Eurasian boat traditions from both archaeological and historical perspectives. We also adduce information from anthropological study of the indigenous cultures that have occupied these regions during the past several hundred years, when western scientists, explorers, diplomats, missionaries, and traders traversed these lands and waters. We have combined their observations on the construction and use of watercraft with Native ethnographic knowledge and language and information from archaeological contexts. Unfortunately, archaeological remains of boats and boating equipment such as paddles, being wholly organic in nature, are rarely preserved, and even when found they are often fragmentary. In most cases, their remains are found only in wet or waterlogged settings, and even there they are barely recognizable. Log hulls are often mistaken for rotting trees, and the slender frames of canoes and kayaks and their birch-bark or skin covers are rarely recognized as artifacts. As a result, few boats have been found and scientifically excavated, and rarely have there been archaeological finds of bark or skin boats more than a few hundred years old, although some ancient models and paddles have been discovered (finds of

Stone Age–era and later paddles can provide indirect proof of the former existence of bark and skin canoes in an area). For these reasons, the archaeological record of watercraft, except for some remarkable finds of Viking ships (Crumlin-Pedersen 2010), is very poor indeed, making the existing historical and ethnographic data all the more important. While we report on archaeological finds, it is the written history and observational data gleaned from administrative reports, travelers' diaries, and explorers' and anthropologists' notes that form the major substance and greatest contribution of this book.

These circumstances informed the method we employed in assembling and presenting our boat data. As noted, chapters are broken down by region and by ethnographic group, since observations from particular tribal or ethnic groups provide a baseline for studying the entire corpus of Northern Eurasia's boats. In this sense, our study is more a geographic survey of boat types and usages than it is a boat history per se; there is simply too little archaeological evidence to develop a regional or even a continental view of the development of watercraft technology over time. The most significant source of ancient data are petroglyph (rock art) images of boats, some of them as much as 8,000 years old. But even with this cornucopia of evidence—the petroglyphs illustrate scores of different types and sizes of boats, many of them shown with paddlers or rowers—severe problems of interpretation arise. For more than 100 years, scholars analyzing the prolific Scandinavian rock art record have argued over such basic issues as whether the images represent Eskimo-like skin boats (umiaks or kayaks), log-based planked boats, or other types of watercraft.

Given the lack of deep historical data, we, like Adney and Chapelle, organize our material as a distributional study of the known styles and types of boat construction that the indigenous peoples of Northern Eurasia and their known ancestors used. This cultural-geographic approach lends itself to descriptions of the basic canoe and boat types of this vast region as they are known from historical and ethnographic records, photographs and drawings, illuminations on maps and other early documents, and—where possible—archaeological evidence. We analyze these sources to discern patterns of shape and construction as they relate to boat types, and at times we reflect on how these types developed and were shared as peoples migrated from one region to another or learned from the experience of neighbors. The diffusion of boat types and stylistic features across Northern Eurasia was facilitated not only by migration, but also by the millennia-long trade and cultural contacts that have occurred throughout this huge region of interconnected waterways. In some instances, we are able to suggest specific historical events that resulted in boat types appearing outside their "home" ranges; the most conclusive evidence for such appearances is found in the case of planked boats, which spread throughout most of Northern Eurasia during the past 500 to 1,000 years, replacing bark and log canoes. However, rather than advancing conjectural evolutionary boat history, our intention is to describe the types of watercraft that can be documented and to present a historical atlas of Eurasian boat data that can be used as a baseline for more advanced study as new evidence emerges from archaeological contexts.

METHODS AND DATA

The boats presented in this book were either seen, drawn, or photographed in the field by scientists, explorers, diplomats, missionaries, traders, and travelers, or exist as full-size boats or models in museums. Very few have been measured to nautical engineering standards, and many gaps exist in information about them. Incomplete records and limited archaeological finds of these boat types present further issues. Thus, while the number of documented bark canoes and skin boats is large, detailed information on their measured lines and construction is almost nonexistent. Unlike in North America, where Adney—an accomplished nautical draftsman—compiled detailed documentation on individual boats over the span of his lifetime, only a few scaled plan drawings and detailed measurements are available for Northern Eurasian boats.

Historical sources, especially travelers' accounts, provide information about the locations of bark canoes and skin boats that outsiders encountered in Northern Eurasia, as well as details about the Native groups who used them. By comparing descriptions of canoes from many regions, we have gleaned clues about certain design types that allow us to compile a continent-wide perspective on boat type geographic distribution. In this, as noted earlier in the book, we followed the lead provided by Russian ethnographer Valentina V. Antropova, who has written on the geography of bark canoe types in Eastern and Central Siberia (1961) and identified geographic regions, principally following river courses and the borders between their basins, where certain styles or types existed. Such studies are useful for categorizing ethnohistorical boat style zones (e.g., for the North American Arctic, see Rousselot 1983, 1994) but can be misleading when applied to earlier periods for which archaeological information is scant or missing. Like Antropova, we use a combination of shape and construction to classify boat types.

Boats can have multiple functions. Ethnographic and archaeological evidence from Western Siberia suggests that in ancient as well as recent times, bark canoes and skin boats sometimes functioned as cult objects, meaning that they had a place in tribal mythology and religion. Human burials of the Nenets and other Western Siberian groups included boats as either primary burial vehicles or as components of grave offerings that enabled the deceased to travel as necessary in the afterlife; such functions are also seen in the early Bronze Age Glazkov culture north of Lake Baikal (Permyakova 2007). Boats and boat carvings, commonly found among grave offerings at ethnographic Western Siberian Yamal Nenets grave and ritual sites, were included to provide safe passage in the afterlife. Although this topic is fascinating and deserves monographic treatment, we decided not to explore the symbolic or spiritual world of Eurasian watercraft except in passing.

Canoes illustrate the skill and knowledge of their builders and have been admired by people near and far, since boats often were some of the most advanced forms of technology known in the societies that made them. To fulfill their service requirements, the boats were given various forms, sizes, shapes, construction materials and methods, and stylistic elements, and they evolved into numerous basic types. Their construction almost always reflected the environment in which they were built and used: for an Evenk hunter-fisherman in the Lake Baikal forest, a small, narrow birch-bark canoe was optimal because he had to portage it through dense forests from lake to lake (Radde 1861). Such a boat was not suited to fishing on large lakes or open river courses. Conversely, canoes used to carry warriors or large amounts of freight during the Russian fur trade era, or those used by the Canadian *courreurs des bois*, were made high and broad and required teams of portageurs.

Finally, we have assembled linguistic evidence related to canoes in the form of loanwords, which can reveal much about the history and direction of diffusion of boat types or designs that might have spread from one group or language area to another. For example, in the Amur River basin, many peoples of Tungus-Manchu origin use similar names for the birch-bark canoe (Ulch: *zai*; Nanay: *dzhau*; Manegir: *dzyau*; Manchu: *chzhaya*; etc.). Antropova (1961) noted that terms for a birch-bark boat are similar among almost all the Tungus-Manchu peoples. West of the Lena River, Sakha (Yakut) people use the bark canoe term *tyy*, which may originate from the Ket people, according to Wacław Sieroszewski

(1993), who based his conclusion on linguistic studies by Matthias A. Castrén (1858: 234). People on the Amur Peninsula once used *korevuye* larch-bark canoes, which may have been replaced by birch-bark canoes (Chepelev 2004), and these ancient boats might have been connected to the skin boats known as *kor'evye*, built for temporary use in the Lena River basin (Antropova 1961). There are reasons to believe that Karelian *kesi* skin boats may have an old ethnolinguistic connection going back to the proto-Indo-European Battle Axe people, the Late Neolithic invaders of Europe who gave the Baltic Finns the term *kesi* for "fish skin" or "seal skin" (Koivulehto 1983).

Although skin boats and bark canoes mostly disappeared in Northern Europe a millennium ago—replaced by expanded log boats, planked and punt boats, and, later, modern aluminum and fiberglass boats—the memory of those earlier watercraft lives on in tribal legends, sagas, and folk poems. People in many locations have bark- and skin canoe–related sagas and legends, including the Saami and Karelians (Scandinavia), the Sihirtia (Western Urals), the Nenets and Khanty (Western Siberia), and the Chukchi (northeastern Siberia). These memories reflect cultural life in the past, recollected now in written form, and offer important proof of the history and traditions of boatbuilding, inland and sea travel, war and peace, and the existence of various canoe types in old tribal regions. They present many variations on similar themes, which is natural for peoples who lived along watercourses in similar environments and used similar types of watercraft. Sometimes canoes are in the foreground, sometimes in the background, but for thousands of years bark and skin boats have been central to tribal and family life in the hunting and fishing societies of Northern Eurasia.

For example, Saami legends tell us that when their people's forebears entered the north, they crossed big waters in skin boats (von Diiben 1873). Legends collected from Komi-Zyrian and Nenets people go back to the origin of the semimythical Sihirtia people on the Barents Sea coast; according to the Nenets, who knew them best, the Sihirtia arrived over the sea from the west in skin boats (Castrén 1858; Chernetsov and Moszyńska 1954, 1974; Golovnev and Michael 1992; Golovnev and Osherenko 1999). The *Kalevala* saga of the Finnish and Karelian peoples tells of the construction of kesi fish-skin or seal-skin boats (Haavio 1952). Oral history and legends among the Khanty of the Ob River basin recollect Nenets wars against Khanty and Mansi peoples in the 1700s, a territorial conflict in which the Nenets paddled ancient bark canoes on their war raids; their opponents, who had expanded log boats, finally got the upper hand (Golovnev 2000; Starcev 1988). Old Khanty folk poems recall travels in birch-bark canoes, although such journeys have not happened for the past several hundred years. Reference to bark canoes is also found in the folklore of Altaian speakers, who once lived in the Altai Mountains near the Southern Samoyed, Turkish Tatars, and Mongol. Eskimo tales collected in Eastern Siberia (Bogoras 1913) include stories about Chukchi sea travels to Alaska that were told to Ferdinand von Wrangel on the Kolyma River coast in the 19th century (Krauss 2005). As we shall see in subsequent chapters, ethnographies, folklore, and early travelers' records are all boundless sources of information.

CHAPTER 1

NORTHERN EURASIA

In this chapter, we examine the environmental setting of our history of Northern Eurasia's bark canoes and skin boats from several perspectives, including descriptions of the land, coasts, waterways, and peoples. The region's physical environment—its boreal forest (taiga) and tundra zones and its climate—is central to understanding the occupations, skills, trades, and material culture involved in the development and use of these watercraft.

GEOGRAPHY AND RIVER SYSTEMS

Volume 1 of *A Handbook of Siberia and Arctic Russia*, published by the Great Britain Naval Intelligence Division in 1920, provides a useful description of the northern part of Eurasia before the Soviet era, when Native peoples who traveled along waterways in bark canoes and skin boats still economically dominated most of these lands. In broad strokes, it addresses the geography and central importance of the region's lakes, rivers, and other waterways:

> Across the plains of Arctic Russia and Siberia many great rivers drain from the highland regions in the south to the Arctic Ocean. The uniformity in the direction of flow and the other characteristics of these rivers find their explanation in the relief of the land. The largest rivers are the Ob, Yenisei, and Lena with their many tributaries. They all rise in the central high plateau and drain through the alpine foreland to the plains across which they flow with sluggish, winding courses whose length is dependent on the breadth of the plains. Further east, where the highland region trends northward towards the coast, the rivers are necessarily shorter, swifter, and more direct; but the Yana, Indigirka, Kolima, and Omolon show on a smaller scale most of the characteristics of the rivers of the west. The narrowness of northeastern

> Siberia and the proximity of the highlands to the sea cause the eastward drainage to flow in short rapid streams. The only exception is the Amur, which is comparable to the northern rivers. Like them, it drains from the high plateau across the alpine foreland and the plains. The chief respect in which it differs from the other great Siberian rivers, in addition to its Pacific outlet, is that a great part of the courses of the main river and the tributaries are on the high plains and the plateau.

> The rivers of Arctic Russia, rising in the Urals, are necessarily shorter than those of western Siberia, but in other respects the Northern Dvina and the Pechora are similar to the Ob. . . .

> Their long courses over gently sloping plains give the Siberian rivers certain characteristics which have had a great influence on the history and development of Siberia. In the first place, the absence of a very decided slope means that the rivers wind a great deal, and have ill-defined watersheds which are easily crossed. In the second place, the gentle gradient of the plains makes the rivers slow and navigable almost to their sources. Lastly, the northward course of most of the rivers results in their waters swinging to the east, owing to the rotation of the earth, and as the rivers erode easily in the soft plain, their right or eastern banks are generally high and suitable for settlements, while their left or western banks are low, ill-defined, and liable to inundation. . . . Their channels change from year to year, and their depth varies with the season. Yet despite all drawbacks the rivers form the chief highways of Siberia, and their value is enhanced by the vastness of the plains, the dense forests, and the swampy tundra, all of which make land travelling difficult if not impossible. There

are no towns of any importance in Arctic Russia and Siberia which are not on navigable waterways. Of all the physical features of Siberia, it is the rivers that have had the most progressive influence on the country, the Ob, the Irtish, and the Yenisei most, and the Lena least of all the great rivers. (24–26)

These waterways (map 2) were important to aboriginal peoples, both hunters and fishermen, whether they lived inland or along the coast, in taiga or tundra zones, because long-distance travel by foot or horse in summer was nearly impossible owing to the region's myriad rivers, streams, lakes, and bogs. Northern Eurasia covers a large part of the continent's landmass in north-south and east-west dimensions, but the continent itself, like its regions, is best defined by its sea coasts, major rivers, and largest lakes. When the rivers and seas of the northern tundra zones were frozen, people's use of boats on the waterways was limited, but the ice afforded those on foot, skis, snowshoes, or sledge unrestricted travel over rivers and lakes. Beginning about 2,000 years ago, the development of reindeer- and dog-drawn sledges greatly facilitated long-distance travel, communication, and trade in the northern regions. Yet both before and after the introduction of sledge travel,

watercraft were the only efficient method of transport along and between watercourses.

Independently of one another, coastal groups in Northern and northeastern Europe; Western, Central, Eastern, and Pacific Siberia; and the Far East developed profitable economies by hunting sea mammals. Coupled with the development of bark canoes and skin boats, these economies became the engines that joined the upper river systems to the sea through coastal estuaries, allowing navigation over hundreds of kilometers for war as well as trade and enabling migrating peoples to find new homelands. In short, the continental boat culture and the economic resources of the sparsely populated north gave its people the means to explore lands and waters both near and far. Map 4 (see page 29) shows the locations of the major bark canoe and skin boat types and the peoples who used them along the waterways of the seven Northern Eurasian territories noted in the introduction (page 8) and presented in more detail below.

Several huge rivers that flow north to the Arctic Ocean cross both Northern Europe and Asia. In Siberia, the landscape is dominated by the Pechora, Ob, Yenisey, Lena, and Amur rivers, each of which has a very large basin and hundreds of tributaries. These rivers teem with fish, which provide sustenance for human populations throughout the year.

Map 2. Rivers and seas of Northern Eurasia. (Dan Cole, Smithsonian Institution)

The Bark Canoes and Skin Boats of Northern Eurasia

The Ob and its basin have the greatest fish resources of all of Siberia's large rivers except, possibly, the Amur. Most of these big rivers also have sea mammals in their lower courses, and Lake Baikal, about 1,000 miles from the Arctic Ocean, has a naturalized population of ring seals.

The headwaters of the Ob (and its major tributary, the Irtysh), the Yenisey, and the Lena rivers are in the highlands of Southern Siberia and northern Mongolia, and all three rivers have been routes for invaders, refugees, and migrants. From their sources, people in Inner Asia could reach the huge expanses of the Eurasian north. For example, the ancestors of the Turkic-speaking Sakha probably reached their current location, in the middle reaches of the Lena River valley, from Mongolia via the Selenge River to Lake Baikal and from there to the headwaters of the Lena River, only 7 kilometers west. Many of the headwaters of the midcourse tributaries of these large north-flowing rivers nearly intersect, such that short portages connect the Pechora to the Ob in the Urals, the Ob to the Yenisey, and the Yenisey to the Lena. Thus local peoples and later explorers traversing a country with few or no roads for summer travel could piece together convenient canoe routes. Before the railway link across Siberia opened circa 1905, it could take a full year for a rider on horseback or a waterborne traveler to cross the entire territory of Russia, from the Baltic to the Sea of Okhotsk. These rivers often gave their names to the people who lived there. For example, the Ob-Ugrians were named for the river along which they lived, while the Kamas lived along the Kan and Man Rivers, in the upper Yenisey basin near present-day Krasnoyarsk. But naming got complicated with the arrival of new peoples, and sometimes the opposite took place and rivers became named for peoples. For instance, on the Lower and Stony Tunguska rivers (Russian: Podkamennaya), the Ostyak (modern Khanty) people called the people residing there the Tungus (modern Evenk), and when Russians arrived, they applied the Tungus name to both these rivers and people.

At both edges of the Eurasian continent, in Scandinavia to the west and on the Chukotka and Kamchatka peninsulas to the east, the environment is quite different from that of the middle span: the interior is mountainous and the sea coasts are rugged. But even at the continental edges, rivers played an important role, connecting inland to coast and inland hunters to sea mammal hunters and fishermen. Along the Kolyma and Anadyr rivers, each ethnolinguistic group—the Chukchi, Even, Koryak, and others—was divided into coastal and interior subgroups who kept close connections, exchanging interior and coastal products within a broad regional

cultural system. In general, people along coasts with rich marine fauna, such as the coasts of Chukotka and Alaska, developed special skills, boat designs, and construction techniques to enable them to hunt sea mammals on the open or seasonally ice-filled seas. In Fennoscandia, rivers draining into the Gulf of Bothnia and the White Sea were important conduits for communication with interior regions from ancient times onward. The rich fish and sea mammal fauna surrounding Scandinavia were instrumental, as they were in Chukotka and Kamchatka, in the life-support systems of fisher-hunter cultures from the Stone Age until recent years.

The eastern Baltic Sea region and the area between the Baltic and the White seas are connected by a dense network of waterways and large lakes that played a special role in human settlement, water transport, and fishing. Lake Ladoga is the largest lake in Europe; Lake Onega is the second largest; and Lake Saimaa—connected to Ladoga—is the fourth largest. Ladoga is connected to both Onega and the Baltic Sea by large rivers, and Onega also has river connections to the White Sea and the Volga River system, which runs into the Caspian Sea. Starting from either the White Sea in the north or Lake Ladoga in the south, a Saami, Finnish, or Karelian traveler with a small boat could cross, via rivers, lakes, and a few portages, the land we now call Finland on his way to the Gulf of Bothnia. People traveled such routes for long-range trade, war, and hunting missions for thousands of years, and these routes are the key reason for the entry of the East Vikings into Ladoga and the founding of the towns of Ladoga and Novgorod in the mid-9th century.

West of the Urals, the major rivers are the Northern Dvina, Mezen, Pechora, and Kama. All once provided fish and served as courses for inland traffic heading to the large Mezen-Pechora boreal forest hunting grounds. They connected inland populations to the northern seas for fishing and sea mammal hunting and were important elements of the network that joined the southern and northern parts of northeastern Europe. The rivers west and east of the Ural Mountains constituted a lifeline between Europe and Asia that was crucial to the Mansi and Nenets peoples who lived, hunted, and traded on both sides of the range.

Finally, the Far East—the old Manchurian territory now divided between Russia's Amur and Maritime provinces and China's Heilong Jiang Province—is dominated by the basin of the Amur River (called Heilong Jiang in China), including its large southern tributaries, the Ussuri and Songhua (formerly Sungari) rivers. To the north, the Amur basin is separated culturally as well as geographically from Siberia by the Yablonoy-Stanovoy Mountains, as the local history of canoe development reflects. Amur (or Amoor) is the name that Russians gave this river, which was called Sakhalin-Ula by the Manchu and earlier the Karamuran, or Black River, by the Mongol (Müller and Pallas 1842). The Amur is rich in fish, which in the past constituted the main economy for all its peoples, while the sea and Sakhalin Island provided hunting grounds for marine mammals. Owing to this area's more favorable maritime climate, flora and fauna are more plentiful and diverse here than in inland Siberia, and some of the Amur River basin's lowlands are suitable for agriculture.

PEOPLES AND CULTURES

For ease of reference and to render comparisons meaningful, we have, as noted on page 8, divided Northern Eurasia into seven territories and identified the major cultural groups in each territory (see map 1, page 8; see also Levin and Potapov 1964; Sillanpää 2008: annex 2 map; Wixman 1984). Our aim is to cast light on the boat traditions of major ethnic entities from all of these Northern Eurasian territories, main waterways, and regions, thus constructing a continent-wide picture from many fragments. For a broader discussion of Siberian Native material culture than we are able to provide here, and because Siberia encompasses most of the territory of Northern Eurasia, we also refer readers to the encyclopedic *Historical-Ethnographic Atlas of Siberia* (*Istoriko-Etnograficheskiy Atlas Sibiri*; Levin and Potapov 1961). This important but little-known work was published by the Kunstkamera, officially known as the Museum of Anthropology and Ethnography (MAE); it was founded by Peter the Great in 1714 and is now part of the USSR Academy of Sciences. This atlas includes Valentina V. Antropova's excellent chapter on bark, skin, and dugout boats (1961). An unpublished English translation by Henry Michael (edited by Igor Krupnik) of this monumental work is available in the files of the Rock Foundation's Edmund Carpenter Collection at the Smithsonian National Anthropological Archives, and an edited version of the work is in the Luukkanen collection files of the National Museum of Natural History's Arctic Studies Center.

The Native peoples of the Eurasian north can be classified into six main groups according to ethnolinguistic heritage:

1. the Uralic-Samoyedic-Yukagir, comprising the Finno-Ugrian, Samoyed, and Yukagir
2. the Altaic, consisting of the Tungus-Manchu, Turkic-Yakut, and Mongol-Buryat
3. the Chukotka-Kamchatkan, including the Chukchi, Koryak, Kerek, and Itelmen
4. the Eskimo-Aleut and Siberian Eskimo
5. the so-called isolated language group, made up of the Yeniseyan peoples, including the Ket and Nivkh
6. the Ainu of northern Japan, formerly of Sakhalin and the Kuril Islands

The Uralic-Samoyed-Yukagir group—or the "Finnish nations," as the Russian Academy of Sciences called them in the 1770s—once covered the northwestern parts of the continent. Finno-Ugrian peoples inhabited most of Eastern Europe's northern forest and tundra zones; the Samoyed ruled Siberian land from northeastern Europe east to the Yenisey River and the Taimyr Peninsula. Until the 1600s, the Yukagir held most of northeastern Siberia from the Lena River to the Anadyr River basin (Simchenko 1976a,b), and mixed Samoyedic-Yukagir peoples once may have lived from the Lena to the Yenisey. As we discuss later (see page 95), the tundra Samoyed and Yukagir had a shared skin boat culture that extended 120 degrees of longitude along the Arctic Ocean coast, from the Barents Sea to the Anadyr River—nearly one-third of the globe's polar region.

Beyond the scope of this book are the many Volga-Finnic peoples (the Mari, Mordva, Merya, Murom, Udmurd, and others) whose bark canoes are not known. It seems likely that these peoples, who had early access to bronze, did make bark canoes or skin boats (as did other Native groups), but these watercraft were replaced by expanded single-log boats during the Bronze and Iron ages, and evidence of the older boats has vanished (Luukkanen 2006b).

The Altaic group includes the Evenk (Tungus), the Even (Lamut), and most of the Amur peoples, such as the Manchu, who for thousands of years inhabited all of Eastern Siberia, from the Sea of Okhotsk and the Amur River north to the Arctic Ocean and west to the Yenisey River. The Turkic Tatars have occupied Southern Siberia for at least the past 2,000 years, while the Sakha (formerly called Yakut), who now are the largest non-Russian minority in Eastern Siberia, reside mostly near the confluence of the Lena and Aldan rivers. They arrived in these territories about 800 years ago, having been pushed north by Mongol invasions. Mongol-speaking groups now live in Southern Siberia and Inner Asia, but their mounted armies, from about 1200 to 1450 CE, once ruled much of Siberia, the Far East, large parts of Eastern Europe as far west as Budapest and Vienna, and north to Lake Peipus near the Baltic Sea, where they collected tax from the Novgorodians. The Mongol, as people of the open steppe, used skin boats for crossing and floating down rivers.

The peoples of the Chukotka-Kamchatkan group were proficient users of open skin boats and kayaks and must have contributed to the development of these watercraft. Great credit for boat skills can be given to the linguistically distinct Siberian Yupik, who helped shape the evolution of skin boats in the Bering and Chukchi seas and were partly assimilated—along with their boat technology—by expanding Chukchi peoples after 1500 CE. Archaeological evidence

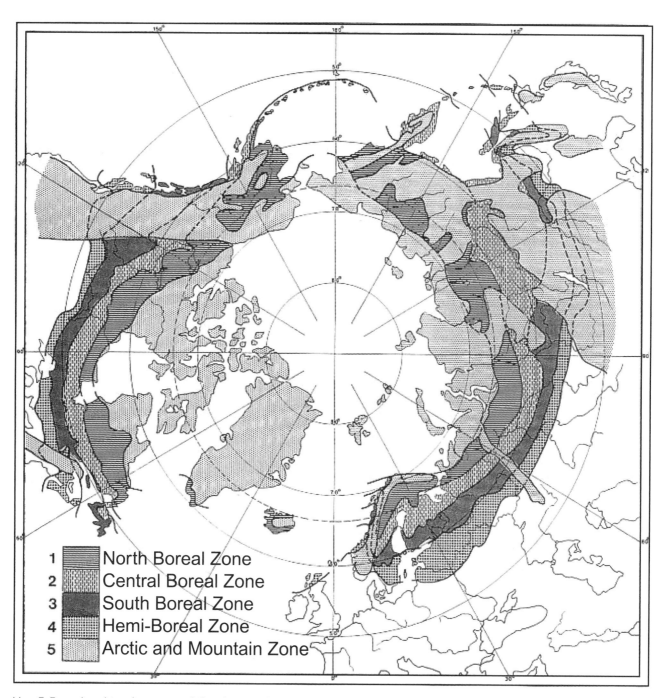

1 North Boreal Zone
2 Central Boreal Zone
3 South Boreal Zone
4 Hemi-Boreal Zone
5 Arctic and Mountain Zone

Map 3. Boreal and tundra zones of the circumpolar region. Key shows zones and growth-days (gd). 1. North Boreal Zone (100–140 gd). 2. Central Boreal Zone (140–160 gd). 3. South Boreal Zone (160–175 gd). 4. Hemi-Boreal Zone (more than 175 gd). 5. Arctic and Mountain Zone (fewer than 100 gd). (From Hämet-Ahti, Palmén, Alanko, and Tigerstedt 1989: 20)

suggests that the Ainu and Nivkh peoples on Sakhalin and the Kuril Islands may have shared skin boat traditions in the distant past with the Kamchadal (Itelmen), Koryak, and other northern groups.

THE BOREAL FOREST (TAIGA) AND TUNDRA ZONES

For the animal world, including humans, one of the most important components of our life-support system is the flora—the trees and other vegetation that offer shelter, food, and bio-organic materials that can be used to construct useful things. The hunters, gatherers, and fishermen of Northern Eurasia not only pursued its animals and its fish, but also collected edible berries, nuts, roots, and vegetation. Forest products—trees, plants, and shrubs—also provided important resources for making boats, tools, utensils, and dwelling covers.

The northern extent of any tree line, as well as the vegetation inside a boreal zone, is controlled mostly by the region's climate (see the next section). As G. M. MacDonald, K. V. Kremenetski, and D. W. Beilman note: "In northern Eurasia the treeline zone corresponds to where average July temperatures decline to 12.5–10.0°C and growing degree days [GDD; a heat index used to predict vegetation growth] drop below 800. Thus, the geographical position of the Eurasian treeline zone is controlled by a climatic gradient in summer temperatures and the length of the growing season that is related to general latitudinal patterns of decreasing northern insolation [exposure to the sun's rays], general atmospheric circulation and the location of the Arctic coastline" (MacDonald, Kremenetski, and Beilman 2007: 2288).

Boreal and tundra zones can also be defined by growth-days—the days of the year when the average (day and night) temperature is over 5°C. Growth-days are the basis for map 3. The tundra-boreal tree line—its border zone—follows the line where growth-days number 100. Where the number is lower, we speak of a tundra zone; where it is between 100 and 175, we call the area boreal forest. The boreal forest is subdivided into four zones based on the growth-day index. The Hemi-Boreal Zone (no. 4 on map 3), for example, is the transition zone between the boreal and temperate zones.

In Northern Eurasia, humans generally have settled in regions with access to forest resources. Although large regions of the colder tundra zone follow the Arctic Ocean coast, there are also large cold, mountainous inland areas, where most vegetation is similar to that of the coastal tundra but forested zones are found in protected river valleys. A rule of thumb for altitude-related climate change says that a change of 100 meters in elevation is comparable to a distance of 100 kilometers in north-south latitudinal direction and equals a temperature difference of about 1.0°C.

Birch bark, the best type for making bark canoes, is among the most useful materials found in boreal areas (Shutikhin 2003), so we are interested in where these trees grow. Just as Frederick W. Waugh (1919) showed for North America, bark canoes were built in all boreal forest zones in Eurasia wherever birch bark was available. The best canoe bark in Northern Eurasia comes from the common birch (*Betula pendula*), which grows throughout the Eurasian boreal zone. Another birch, *B. pubescens*, is a good alternative where *B. pendula* is not available. On the Eastern Siberian coast and in the Far East grows a third variant, *B. ermanii*, known as Kamchatka birch, whose smaller girth makes it less suitable for canoe construction.

In Finland, in the South Boreal Zone (no. 3 on map 3), *B. pendula* takes some 50 years to grow into a tree 25 meters high. Its trunk, of circa 30 centimeters diameter, is capable of producing a bark sheet 94 centimeters wide—a suitable size for making a bark canoe from a single sheet. In the North Boreal Zone (no. 1 on map 3), the birches are much more slender and thus less suitable, as several sheets would have to be sewn together. In Europe and Asia, birch bark was not only used for canoes; it also served as covering material for tents (*chums*) (fig. 1.1) and was made into various household objects, especially containers and decorative house and art crafts. When the bark was heated, a tar could be extracted and then used to seal canoe covers and make shoes or containers water-resistant; boiling the bark with milk produced a waterproof glue used when sewing bark sheets together. For these reasons, birch had the greatest value among all the tree species in the boreal zone.

Larch bark could also be used to cover tents and houses in tundra and mountainous regions and in the foothills of the Altai range. Larch grows in Siberia north to latitude 70°N on the Taimyr Peninsula, where no other large trees are available. From documents referred to later in this study (see page 127), we know that larch-bark canoes were constructed along the Lower Tunguska River and on Taimyr. Elm bark was also used: a late Bronze Age canoe found on the Byslätt River in Sweden had an elm-bark covering. Two species of elm, *Ulmus laevis* and *U. glabra*, grow in the South Boreal Zone (no. 3 on map 3), but only in Europe and Japan, including Hokkaido; elm was unavailable in most of Siberia.

Fig. 1.1. Throughout Northern Eurasia, birch bark was indispensable for making utensils and covers for boats, tent covers, and many household items. Birch-bark-covered *chums* (tents) such as this one, made by Dukha reindeer herders in northern Mongolia, are still used when canvas and plastic sheeting are unavailable. (Photograph: Paula DePriest)

The wood, branches, and roots of wild cherry (*Prunus padus*) were favored as canoe materials across Northern Eurasia. In Western Siberia, many groups used wild cherry for ribs, gunwales, and thwarts, and some used the tree's strong but pliant roots to sew canoe bark sheets together. Wild cherry grows in roughly the same region as *B. pendula* (Hämet-Ahti, Palmén, Alanko, and Tigerstedt 1989).

The skin and bark boats used by Alaskan Eskimo and Athapascan Indians have parallels in Northern Eurasia that raise interesting questions about these peoples' history and possible cultural relationships (see chapter 10, page 215). On one point, however, there can be no doubt: circumpolar climatic and boreal zones have played a crucial role in the habitation of Arctic and Subarctic regions, including canoe building. Climate, flora, and fauna have long been recognized as dominant factors in human biological and cultural evolution, but teams of scientists have only recently created reliable biogeography maps—such as map 3—owing to the enormous task of collecting reliable data and compositing it on a single map. These new maps

enable us to discern many things about the cultures that occupied these regions.

Canoe distribution is something else that can be mapped, as we demonstrate in chapter 3, which presents maps based on fragmentary canoe location information. Similar maps were created in North America a century ago, and with good precision. One of the first people in North America to study bark canoes and skin boats in detail was scholar Frederick W. Waugh of the Geological Survey of Canada, who published a paper on Canadian aboriginal canoes in *Canadian Field-Naturalist* in 1919. His research identified several zones of canoe-building activity, or, to be more exact, the distribution of various types of bark canoes and skin boats. Based on these data, Waugh devised a map presenting bark canoe and skin boat regions as they were then known. His map, whose canoe distribution coincides with the Canadian part of the birch-canoe zone shown on map 4 (page 29), is still considered correct, as is his discussion of the environmental factors, such as treeless tundra and availability of birch bark, that facilitated canoe use in North America. Furthermore, his map shows that the border between birch-bark canoes and skin boats areas closely follows the tundra-taiga border that Leena Hämet-Ahti and colleagues (1989) presented in their map of boreal vegetation: the southern border of bark canoe usage matches the southern boundary of birch growth. South of that boundary, canoes made of elm bark and other species replace birch-bark canoes. Waugh also noted the distribution of open skin boats and skin-covered kayaks in Arctic regions where tree bark was not available.

Our study of canoes in the Eurasian north shows the paramount importance of environmental factors in determining the zones of canoe-building activity in the boreal region. Although peoples and cultures differ across Eurasia and North America, their paths of technological development and their choices of canoe materials seem to have been much the same throughout the circumpolar Arctic and Subarctic. For that reason, the boreal-forest zone map is a good predictor of the distribution of bark and skin boat production throughout the Eurasian north and in North America.

CLIMATE AND TEMPERATURE CHANGE

Climate change—or, more precisely, long-term cold and warm swings—have had great impacts on peoples living across the boreal forest and tundra zones because of their direct effect on the environment. Archaeological evidence shows that in the past, warm weather has encouraged people to populate more northerly regions, while cold periods often forced them to retire south. Both trends are in concordance with similar movements of animals and forest boundaries. We do not know the direct impact of climate on canoe building, but there are many examples of migrations in the Arctic that were triggered by the onset of colder or warmer climates. Climate change has been the great decider, for good and ill. In recent centuries in the Eurasian north, its impacts have been most evident in the shifting northern limits of agriculture, but here we are specifically interested in long-term trends that have influenced the northern tree line and the distribution of birch, aspen, bird cherry, and other trees crucial for making boats. The Russians V. L. Koshkarova and A. D. Koshkarov, who studied the environmental impacts of cold and warm periods on Central Siberia, report:

> On the basis of geochronological and palynological [pollen and spores] materials, 25 sections of Holocene deposits and soils of northern Central Siberia were studied by paleocarpological [ancient fruits and seeds] methods. . . . The main peaks of climatic changes in postglacial history have been detected in the ranges 8,500 to 8,000 years ago (thermal maximum) and 2,500 to 2,000 years ago (thermal minimum). Importantly, the thermal maximum is characterized by warming by 3–9°C in the winter and by 2–6°C in the summer. The anomaly in moisture content was insignificant. In the middle Holocene (6,500 to 5,000 years ago), the positive temperature trend continued, but it was accompanied by a near-doubling of annual rainfall. During the late Holocene cooling (2,500 to 2,000 years ago), a negative temperature trend led to the degradation of forest vegetation, which at that time remained only in the extreme south of the territory. (2004: 717)

Fig. 1.2 illustrates temperature changes in Northern Eurasia during the past 2,000 years. Most important to this study are the Medieval Warm Period, circa 800 to 1300 CE, and the Little Ice Age, circa 1300 to 1800 CE. On the northern coast of Siberia during the latter period, temperatures dipped much more than in other regions. It seems clear that there were major shifts of vegetation across Northern Eurasia, from south to north and from north to south, following major climatic changes. During very warm periods, the northern tree line was at what is now the tundra-vegetated Arctic Ocean coast.

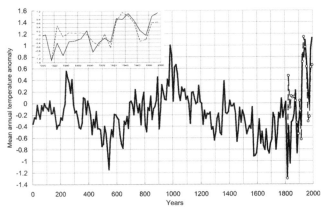

Fig. 1.2. Temperature departure from the present climate in the Arctic from 0 to 2000 CE is shown here, based on average temperature in the Northern Hemisphere, Northern Eurasia, and Northern Siberia. Compared with other regions, Northern Siberia experienced an especially large decline during the Little Ice Age, followed by a rapid rise in the 20th century. (From MacDonald, Kremenetski, and Beilman 2007: fig. 6)

These warm and cold periods must have affected the early builders of both bark canoes and skin boats. The earliest archaeological evidence of bark canoes that were made during the thermal maximum (also known as the Hypsithermal Period, circa 9000–5000 BP, or "before present," reckoned backward from January 1, 1950) has been found in the region of the West Urals Kama culture. Paddle remains dated to 8700 BP have been found at Nizhne Verete, and other paddle remains, dated to 8400 BP, have been found at Vis-I in the Vychegda River basin (Burov 1989). The Hypsithermal Period may have triggered the development of bark canoes by making water travel easier and the open-water season longer. According to Finnish conventional wisdom, a rise in average temperature of 1°C shortens the icing of the Arctic Ocean by one week, and in southern rivers and lakes across Northern Eurasia, the warming impact is even more dramatic.

The thermal minimum (known as the Sub-Boreal Period), dating from 2500 to 2000 BP, spurred a milestone in innovative boat technology, for it was in this period that the expanded dugout log boat first began to appear in the Baltic and Volga regions (Luukkanen 2006b). Over the next 2,000 years, it replaced the bark canoe throughout Northern Eurasia. Some have speculated that the development of log boat construction may have been stimulated by an insufficient supply of birch bark in the northern taiga zone (Koshkarova and Koshkarov 2004).

That climatic change had a strong impact on the development of northern cultures and their boating traditions is also seen in the White Sea region. Russian author M. I. Belov (1956) wrote about settlement of the northern Kola Peninsula from 5000 to 4000 BP by the ancient Coast Saami people, whose sites are found on river terraces on the Ter (forest) side of the peninsula in the Kandalaksha (Kantalahti in Karelian) Fjord. These early settlers hunted seals, walruses, whales, and belugas (*Delphinapterus leucas*). They also caught salmon and other fish in the peninsula's rivers, and petroglyphs carved by coastal people appear to record their use of skin boats. Beginning around 3600 BP, seals, walruses, and whales gradually declined in number and perhaps even disappeared when the channel leading to the White Sea became too shallow for sea mammals and hunters had to leave the coast. Perhaps the temperature turned colder, too, and the ice covered the sea longer than it had before, forcing the early Saami to retreat inland. This hypothesis is suggested by V. V. Klimenko, who writes that such a phenomenon occurred during the Little Ice Age (circa 1300–1800 CE), when the coast along the White Sea was gradually abandoned by the Maritime Pomors and other European fishermen and hunters. The only permanent settlement that remained there was the Solovetsky Russian Orthodox Monastery, established in 1435 (Klimenko 2010).

ARCHAEOLOGY, DATING, AND CHRONOLOGICAL PERIODS

Recent archaeological work in Northern Eurasia has greatly extended our knowledge of the history of human occupation in the Arctic and boreal regions. Less than a century ago, it was inconceivable that any human habitations in the Arctic might be traced back more than a few thousand years. But the advent of radiocarbon dating in the 1950s made it possible to determine the age of wood, bone, ivory, charcoal, hair, shell, and other organic materials, and by the 1960s and 1970s, dwelling sites once believed to be only a few thousand years old were commonly producing radiocarbon ages of 5,000 to 6,000 years. Before long, wood paddles found in marshes and peat bogs in the Arctic turned out to be 8,000 years old, providing clear evidence of ancient canoe transportation on northwestern European waterways. Some of these finds and sites, 8,000 to 10,000 years old, were located in ponds and bogs on high, raised beaches of the postglacial Baltic Sea, providing both radiocarbon and geological proof of their age. Although we still have no direct evidence of watercraft made before the end of the last glaciation (12,000 years ago), archaeological sites such as the 45,000-year-old Pechora Ice Age mammoth kill (Pitulko et al. 2016) and the nearly

30,000-year-old Yana River Rhinoceros Horn Site, near the Arctic coast east of Tiksi (Pitulko, Basilyan, Nikolskiy, and Girya 2004), are on waterways, where the inhabitants must have used boats. These people could not have survived without watercraft in a landscape full of rivers, lakes, and bogs, where even during the Ice Age summers were warm and rivers and lakes were open and teeming with fish. Perhaps in the bogs, peat, and permafrost of these tundra and northern boreal environments, we eventually may discover a boat history that leads from the present all the way back to the Neanderthal era.

The use of boats in the Arctic tundra raises a question that has intrigued northern cultural historians for more than 100 years: what was the origin of skin boats such as the Eskimo kayak and umiak? Boat models found in Old Bering Sea–culture graves indicate that Eskimo-type kayaks or open skin boats existed in the Bering Strait region as early as 2,000 years ago (see fig. 8.11a–b, page 168 a–c). Since archaeological evidence of specialized maritime adaptation and the hunting of large sea mammals has been dated as early as 8,000 to 12,000 years ago in Japan, the Amur-Okhotsk region, and the Aleutians, Kodiak, and southern Alaska, boat history in these areas no doubt will be found to be equally ancient.

Before we turn to description and classification of Northern Eurasia watercraft in chapter 2, a few words are needed about archaeological periods and terminology. Since cultural developments have not been synchronous across Northern Eurasia, it is impossible to assign tightly defined ages to archaeological complexes. What is called Neolithic in Southern Scandinavia is often called Younger Stone Age in Northern Scandinavia. For that reason, we use generalized, widely accepted cultural categories to date archaeological sites. Below are generally accepted dates for Northern European and Southern Scandinavian archaeological periods or cultures (Price 2015: 11). Dates for cultural periods in Northern Scandinavia and northeastern Europe may lag behind those in southern regions by several hundred years, while those for Northern and Eastern Eurasia require entirely different terms and periodization.

> Upper Paleolithic: 40,000 to 9,000 BCE ("before the common era")
> Mesolithic: 9,000 to 4,000 BCE
> Neolithic/Younger Stone Age: circa 4,000 to 1600 BCE
> Bronze Age: 1600 to 500 BCE
> Iron Age: 500 BCE to circa 750 CE ("common era")
> Viking period: 750 to 1050 CE

Medieval period: 1050 to 1450 CE

Early Modern period: 1450 to 1750 CE

We also mention specific cultural designations provided by the authors who reported them: for example, we discuss the Suomusjarvi culture, an early mid-Holocene Neolithic culture of the northeastern Baltic–White Sea region, in chapter 3. Throughout this book, readers also will find references to cultures and periods defined by archaeologists. The names, dates, and even the nature of these cultures often are provisional, as are the relationships between cultures, depending on the state of archaeological knowledge at the time of writing. It is not always possible to know whether one culture developed into another or whether changes in one culture resulted from new migrations, the influence of neighboring cultures, or climate or environmental change. Archaeological research, especially in Central and Eastern Siberia and the Amur region, is still a young science, and its cultural definitions and chronology change as research progresses. For that reason, our reconstructions and use of these data require what might be called reasonable speculation; terms such as *may*, *might have*, and *possibly* are a normal part of archaeological discourse, and dates for cultures and periods often have fuzzy borders.

SMALL BOATS IN NORTH AMERICA AND THEIR CONNECTION TO NORTHERN EURASIA

Scholarly interest in the history of aboriginal boats in North America began with Otis T. Mason, a Smithsonian ethnologist who wrote a 1901 paper with Meriden S. Hill comparing Northwest Coast Kootenai Indian bark canoes to canoes from the Amur River region. Mason's paper was no doubt stimulated by Franz Boas's Jesup North Pacific Expedition (1897–1903), a research program organized by the American Museum of Natural History that explored cultural connections between Siberia and Alaska (Boas 1903; W. Fitzhugh and Crowell 1988). At the time, very little was known about North American Indian or Northern Eurasian watercraft (Rousselot, W. Fitzhugh, and Crowell 1988). The first scholar after Mason who took up the challenge of documenting indigenous boats in northern North America was Frederick W. Waugh. Below, for the sake of canoe history, we quote parts of his pioneering paper "Canadian Aboriginal Canoes" (1919) because it was the first serious study to raise questions about the origins and diffusions of boat technology and to apply a scientific method to test ideas about canoe history, and because his description of the diverse types and functions of boats used by Canadian aboriginal peoples serves as a useful introduction to our study of Eurasian watercraft:

There is little doubt that, in the earlier days of French exploration and settlement along the St. Lawrence and of English settlement in New England, the birchbark canoe of Indian make was very soon adopted as the most convenient method of travel. We can readily infer, also, from early writers and other such sources, the extremely important part played by the canoe in the development of a very large portion of the North American continent.

It would obviously be most interesting to trace the canoe and other such devices to their origins, but there are indications that the problem in hand is one of the diffusion or spread of a cultural trait already elaborated, or partly elaborated, in some other region. This is in part suggested by both the extent and the continuity of the area in which canoes are used. We can see that migrations of population, or the influence of one tribe upon a neighboring one (accultural influence), would soon disseminate the canoe idea, possibly in a simple form, very widely, and that, under the influence of the varied materials at hand and diversified requirements, specialization in various directions would later arise.

Materials naturally played an important part. In areas where trees were not at hand, or were less convenient, such materials as rushes were sometimes built into a boat-shaped raft (see the balsa of California); or a skin-covered craft was employed, as in the Eskimo area, among the neighboring Kutchin of the Yukon, the Tahltan and other Athapascans of the Mackenzie region, and in some parts of the Plains (see the "bull-boat," a tub-shaped craft of skin and withes, used by various Siouan tribes, including the Mandan and the Hidatsa; also by the Arikara, a Caddoan tribe). The Omaha (Siouan) used hide-covered boats or canoes of ordinary type, but with a rude framework, indicating the slight development among them of ideas regarding navigation. In the last-mentioned craft, an oar or large paddle was used for steering, the paddlers sitting near the bow.

One of the most interesting developments in North American navigation was the canoe of birch-bark, which apparently reached its perfection in the Algonkian area, a region extending from around the Great

Lakes, and some distance westward, to the maritime provinces and the New England states, though the birch canoe area exhibits cultural extensions in various directions, but particularly northward and westward to the Mackenzie river basin. There is little doubt that this distribution was largely determined by the range of the canoe birch (*Betula papyrifera*), which extends practically from the Atlantic coast to the Rockies, as well as to some distance south of the international boundary. The disappearance of the birch southward is indicated by the fact that very inferior canoes of elm, buttonwood and basswood bark were constructed by the Iroquois of Central New York state and southward, who evidently found the materials last mentioned more plentiful. The Iroquois canoe is everywhere stated to have been heavy and logy, inconvenient for portaging and short-lived generally. In fact, so poor a craft it was in comparison with that of the Algonkians, that the Iroquois are said to have traded eagerly for the lighter and more substantial contrivance.

Bark and skin-covered canoes, however, are not the only craft which have been used by Canadian Indians, since at least two other devices—usually constructed in a very primitive style—are found side by side with considerable advancement in navigation. The dugout, for instance, which is usually little more than a hollowed-out log, is employed by a great many tribes along with canoes of a much superior kind. Another very primitive-appearing contrivance, the raft, is distributed quite widely, though employed to a greater extent in some areas than in others. . . .

The Eskimo kayak, for present purposes, may be regarded as a highly specialized canoe, differing from the Algonkian in the important, though not essential, respect of having the framework so constructed that it is held together independently of the cover; and in the superficial one that the covering is of skin instead of bark, to which we may add that of being decked over so as to accommodate, in most cases, but one person. . . . The seal-skin covering is sewn together and applied to the framework wet, so that it stretches tightly as it dries. The sewing, as in the case of the Algonkian canoe, is done by several women working together in order to complete the job at one sitting. A double waterproof stitching renders the seams water-tight.

According to E. W. Hawkes [1916: 68–73], from whose memoir on the Labrador Eskimo the foregoing description is taken, "Great speed is maintained by the Eskimo in their frail kayaks. It is said that a single Eskimo in a kayak will propel it as fast as two white men will in a canoe. The Eskimo ventures out in a sea that an Indian would not dare attempt. . . ."

The umiak, an open craft, also used by the Eskimo, presents a somewhat different appearance from the kayak due partly to its not being decked over and partly to its being rather deeper and clumsier in form. In other respects it does not differ materially, a fact which would suggest it as the form from which the kayak was derived. (1919: 1, 23–29)

Waugh's discussion of the construction details and stylistic features of North American and Siberian canoes and kayaks serves as an introduction to the description and classification of Northern Eurasian watercraft, to which we now turn.

CHAPTER 2

BOAT CLASSIFICATION, CONSTRUCTION, AND REGIONAL DISTRIBUTION

This chapter focuses on the form and construction of small watercraft in Northern Eurasia, describes boat types from various regions, and gives information on their cultural geography and history. Detailed descriptions of boats used by ethnic groups in specific regions appear in subsequent chapters. We begin with a discussion of classification systems used to identify the major types of bark canoes that once were the primary vehicles for water transport throughout Northern Eurasia. The birch-bark canoe—a frame-constructed boat without a keel—was the major boat type used before the appearance of the log boat with expanded sides in the late Iron Age, about 500 CE. Closely related to the birch-bark canoe in form and construction are canoes with elm-, spruce-, and larch-bark covers. The second major boat category is skin boats, the keeled and skin-covered open boats and decked kayaks found predominantly in the northeastern Siberian maritime region. The latter part of this chapter discusses each of these boat types individually by culture area and presents information on their geographic location, their construction materials and techniques, their use, and what is known about their history. It also serves as a summary of the findings discussed, culture by culture, in the regional chapters that follow.

CLASSIFICATION OF BARK AND SKIN BOATS

Various classification systems have been used to describe small boats. Rudolf Trebitsch's (1912) global boat taxonomy included five types of water conveyances—wicker basket boats, keeled boats, kayaks, rafts, and personal floats—all of which have been used in Northern Eurasia. However, his system did not recognize the most common type of Eurasian Native craft, the bark canoe, or the fact that kayaks are keeled vessels. Trebitsch's and Otis T. Mason and Meriden S. Hill's (1901) discussions were followed by a series of short papers by H. H. Brindley (1919a,b,c) providing further description of Siberian birch-bark canoes. Valentina Antropova (1961) developed a more accurate classification system to describe the watercraft of Russian/Soviet indigenous peoples, and our treatment employs a modified version of her taxonomy. While her outline covered much of the same territory as our work, she did not describe construction details, deep boat history as it is known from archaeology (except for the Ekven models), rock art, or environmental connections.

Antropova classified Siberian Native boats into four major groups: dugouts made from hollowed-out tree trunks; composite boats such as keeled and planked boats that did not require an outer cover; frame boats (canoes) without keels that required bark or skin covers; and enclosed or open boats, sometimes skin-covered, with both a frame structure and a longitudinal keel. Within these categories, she designated boat types on the basis of details such as bow and stern shape, overhead plan outline, breadth, sheer (degree of longitudinal curve), and construction technique (e.g., side-spreading or plank extensions in dugouts). Our study concerns her frame boats (canoes) and her enclosed or open "frame and keel" categories, but we also sometimes mention dugouts and composite types because their appearance has influenced the history of canoes and skin boats.

Frame boats, Antropova's third category, are the lightest of all watercraft owing to their latticelike structure, light outer skin, and absence of a keel (fig. 2.1). Their strength depends on their bark or skin covering and the gunwale rails that run from bow to stern along the upper edges of the boat (see the glossary for technical boat terms). Frame boats have an open top and usually have birch-bark or skin hull covers. Our classification places elm-, larch-, and spruce-bark canoes in a class of their own because their heavier coverings required structural modifications not present in birch-bark boats. The Chunya Evenk in the eastern Yenisey drainage and the Chukchi in the Anadyr River region used reindeer

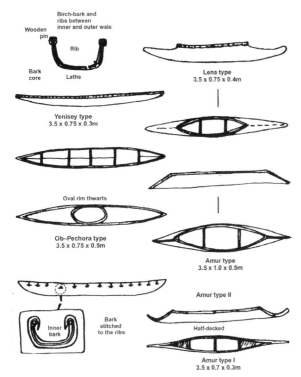

Fig. 2.1. Birch-bark canoe types of Northern Eurasia (not to scale). (Drawing: Harri Luukkanen, adapted by Marcia Bakry)

and moose hide as alternatives to birch bark and seal skin for their decked and half-decked canoe kayaks.

In her frame boat class, Antropova identified three birch-bark canoe types, which she called "versions," naming each one for the river system where it occurred: Yenisey, Lena, and Amur. The *Yenisey type* has a pointed, overhanging bow and stern. The *Lena type* has a rounded, upturned bow and stern projection, a partially enclosed cockpit, and gunwales that do not extend the full length of the boat. The *Amur type* has bow and stern projections, a narrow beam, and sometimes a partially covered bow and stern deck. Birch bark was the preferred material for all three canoe types.

Antropova's skin boat classification included two types (see fig. 2.5, page 41). The open-top skin boat has a keel running down the middle of the vessel's bottom to which ribs that curve upward to the gunwales are attached. Although it adds weight, the keel also adds the longitudinal strength needed for maritime use. The large, open-top, skin-covered *baidarka* was used by Chukchi and Pacific coastal groups in northeastern Siberia for long-distance travel and trade and for hunting whales and walrus. Such boats, depending on their size, can accommodate large loads and as many as 30 to 40 people (see fig. 8.10, page 164). Antropova recognized two subtypes in her open boat category: the Chukchi-Eskimo

angyapik (known as *umiak* in mainland Alaska and *angyak* on Kodiak Island; *angyapit* is the plural) and the broad-bow Kerek-Koryak version used in Kamchatka. Her second skin boat type was the kayak (called *baidarka* in Russian-influenced areas), which was used as a hunting craft and was propelled by single or double paddlers on both sides of the Bering Strait, where open skin boats also were used. These were the predominant boat types used in the rough waters of the northeastern Siberia coast, the Bering Strait, and Alaska.

Although Antropova was concerned primarily with the description and geographic distribution of indigenous watercraft, she also offered ideas about their history during the past 200 to 300 years. She commented on the widespread distribution of the bark canoe, which began to be replaced in Western Siberia and the Okhotsk region first by expanded log boats and later, following Russian contact with Native groups in the 18th and 19th centuries, plank boats. She speculated that the birch-bark canoe probably originated in the boreal forest zone of Southern Siberia, based on linguistic data that suggested it had spread from that area to the Sakha peoples in the middle Lena. She also commented on the northeastern Siberian distribution of skin-covered baidarkas and kayaks, which she identified as the most specialized and ancient of all known Russian indigenous boats. Citing Rudenko (1947; see also Arutiunov and Sergeev 2006), she noted that models of boats similar to modern skin-covered umiaks and kayaks have been recovered from Old Bering Sea– and Punuk-culture archaeological sites in coastal Chukotka dating to, respectively, 1,500 and 1,000 years ago. She also remarked that 16th-century exploration literature contains illustrations of what seem to be kayaklike boats used by Nenets maritime hunters around Yamal and Novaya Zemlya (e.g., Belyavsky 1833: fig. 3; see also our chapter 4).

To summarize, the classification used in this book largely follows Antropova's taxonomy but recognizes five rather than three bark canoe types: our system uses Antropova's *Yenisey* and *Lena types*, splits her *Amur type* into *Amur I* and *Amur II types* (fig. 2.1), and expands her classification by including a fifth category, the *Ob-Pechora type*, a canoe with short, overhanging ends and, when seen from above, a rounded bow and stern. We believe this latter type was similar to a postulated *Mezen-Pechora type*, employed in Northern and northeastern Europe, that ceased to be used before it could be described accurately.

Our study of keeled skin boats reveals more variation than the single kayak type and two variants of open skin boats that Antropova described. We classify the kayak group into several ethnic-based types, including *Yukagir*, *Eskimo-Chukchi*, *Koryak*, and *Kuril/Ainu types* (see fig. 2.5, page 41). Our open skin boat classification follows Antropova's two types: the *Eskimo-Chukchi type* of Chukotka and the *Koryak-Kerek type* of northern Kamchatka. Each of these bark and skin boat types is described and illustrated below with respect to its geographic and cultural region. To make this classification simple and tailor the typology to our Northern Eurasian study, we focus on the following three Native boat classes: birch-bark canoes (divided into five types); elm-, larch-, and other bark canoes; and open skin boats and kayaks.

BIRCH-BARK CANOES

The birch-bark canoe was the main watercraft in all of Northern Eurasia until the revolutionary new canoe type known as the expanded log boat began to diffuse eastward, probably from the Baltic and Volga territories, during the Iron Age (Luukkanen 2010). The expanded log boat was made from a hollowed-out log whose sides were pushed out laterally, using hot rocks, water, and spreaders, until the desired width was obtained; this increased stability and enabled the canoe to accommodate more passengers and freight. The huge cedar canoes of the Northwest Coast Indians in Canada and Alaska are the preeminent examples of this type of craft, made possible by the local availability of big trees.

All aboriginal peoples living in Northern Eurasia's boreal forest used bark canoes wherever birch or other suitable bark was available. The era of birch-bark canoes lasted until the 18th century throughout Eurasia, and a century or two longer in the eastern parts of Siberia and the Far East. Map 4 and fig. 2.1 (page 28) illustrate the major birch-bark canoe–using peoples and the canoe type associated with their culture or region. As noted originally by Antropova, the borders between canoe-type areas generally coincide with the large basins of the Ob, Yenisey, Lena, and Amur river

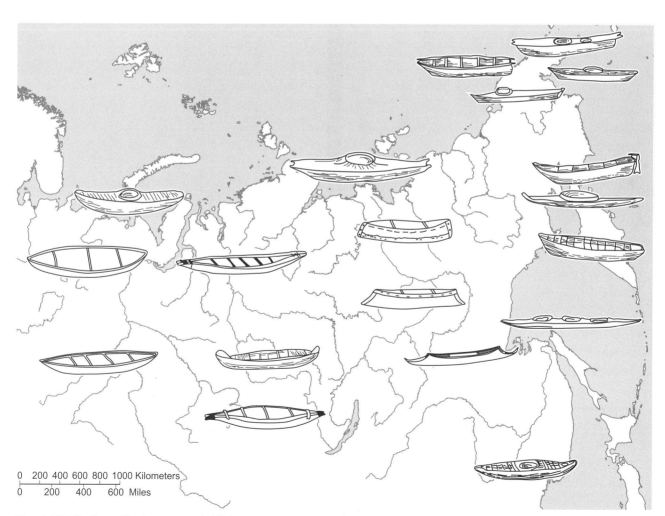

0 200 400 600 800 1000 Kilometers

0   200   400   600 Miles

Map 4. Distribution of bark canoe and skin boat types. (Marcia Bakry, Smithsonian Institution and Mapping Specialist, Ltd.)

homelands of the peoples who used these designs. Each river drainage area had its own typical canoe design or basic type, and these core types often were shared across tribal and ethnic borders. The close linguistic and cultural relations among the various groups living along a single river system facilitated this sharing, and thus their canoe traditions tended to cluster along the same drainages.

Antropova defined the regional borders among the Yenisey, Lena, and Amur birch-bark canoe types in Siberia but did not identify the Ob or Pechora River bark canoe as a distinct type. The Yenisey type had strong double gunwales on each side, sandwiching both the horizontal lath planking strips and the ribs, a technique still used in canoe construction today. This type may have been developed first by people such as the Samoyed and Ket, who lived in the lower Ob and Yenisey basins, and later by the Western Evenk along the upper Yenisey and its eastern tributaries. The Western Evenk's territory also included the Upper and Lower Tunguska rivers, the areas west of the Vitim and Olekma rivers, and the area around Lake Baikal.

The Lena type, with more or less vertical bow and stern profiles, was used by Evenk and Sakha peoples living around the eastern portions of the Vitim and Olekma rivers, both eastern tributaries of the Lena. In addition to this type, people living in the Lena basin used canoe types known from the Yenisey and Amur systems, a result of population migrations and these people's adoption of their neighbors' canoe technology.

The Amur canoes can be divided between two main forms, as we noted earlier: Amur I and II. The Amur I type had long, projecting bow and stern extensions, or "beaks," that turned upward at their ends, while the Amur II type was a short canoe with straight, pointed extensions at the waterline. The longer Amur I type typically had a beam of 70 centimeters, a strong bottom construction in which as many as five bark layers were glued together, and a keelson (an interior keel) running from end to end. In the 70-centimeter-wide boats, wooden blocks sewn into the bark sheets supported the gunwales at the bow and stern. Because its strong hull design resisted flexing, the Amur I type could be made very long, as is demonstrated by a 15-meter-long bark canoe found on the Maya River, a tributary of the Aldan.

The Amur II type canoe, originally described by Otis T. Mason (1901) as a "sturgeon-nose" canoe because its ends resembled a sturgeon's snout, was short, had rather weak gunwales, and could carry only a single person. Beyond the Amur River itself, the Amur II type was known in southern

Lena River locations where Evenk people of Amur origin resided. Most Amur basin people were Tungus-related, and all made bark canoes that varied only in local details. One type of Oroquen-Evenk canoe from this region is known only from a model: it shows an unusual method of finishing the bow and stern that avoided cutting and stitching the two sides together. Instead, the bark at the ends of the boat was folded back over itself toward the interior of the boat, a method not seen in full-size canoes.

We suggest that the Ob-Pechora type bark canoe originated in Southern Siberia, where it was used by the Samoyed and shared with the Ob-Ugrian peoples; from there, it diffused throughout Western Siberia between the Ural Mountains and the Yenisey River. Evidence of this canoe type in Western Siberia comes from five sources: Kamas canoe construction on the Yenisey River, as documented in G. F. Müller's circa 1730–40 "Description of the Siberian Peoples, 1736–1747" (2010; see also Vermeulen 2016); a drawing of a Mansi or Khanty boat in Obdorsk made by Tobias Königsfeld in 1728 (see figs. 5.7–5.8, page 106; see also DeLisle and Königsfeld 1768); a Khanty model boat, 50 by 8 centimeters, that F. R. Martin collected from the Tobol River in 1895 for the Swedish Ethnographic Museum (see fig. 5.5, page 102); a construction drawing by HL presenting the structure of a bark canoe model from the Amgun River (MAE 5333-34; see our fig. 2.3, page 39); and Samoyed oral evidence from near Narym, as documented by Galina I. Pelikh (1972).

The Ob-Pechora type occurred throughout the Ob basin, in the middle Ob-Irtysh–Tobol area occupied mainly by Samoyed people (with their subgroups, the Nenets, Selkup, and Kamas-Koibal) and Ob-Ugrian people (with their subgroups, the Khanty and Mansi). This canoe type was also a model for Turkic Tatars in the Southern Siberian taiga and was shared with Western Urals peoples in the Mezen-Pechora taiga of northeastern Europe. The Ob-Pechora type's main differences from the Yenisey type are as follows:

1. the presence of an oval rim instead of transverse thwarts (which were seen among the Eastern Khanty);

2. the presence of a single rather than a double gunwale strake;

3. a construction technique (see fig. 2.1) in which the bark was passed from the outside of the canoe to the inside, over the gunwales, and then sewn around the gunwales and ribs (rather

than being pegged between double gunwale strakes); and

4. a special way of fastening the gunwales at the ends of the boat.

The doubled Yenisey gunwales were lashed together about 50 centimeters from the ends, creating a narrow top profile for bow and stern. Ob canoe gunwales were fastened at the stern and bow with a separate piece of bent wood and thus were not pinched inward by being lashed together. This construction produced a boat with a rounder top profile that could accommodate more cargo, and it may have reduced the amount of water shipped in wind, waves, and rapids. On the middle Ob, Khanty canoe builders also doubled the birch-bark bottom by inserting a slightly smaller bark layer inside the outer shell.

The explanation for the shared features of the Yenisey–Ob-Pechora canoe types—i.e., the existence of broad similarities across vast distances and among many ethnic groups—is probably related to the migration history of the past 1,000 years and the intense interactions and cross-border activity of long-distance traders during the Russian fur-trade era. The Khanty, Nenets, and Mansi lived on both sides of the Ural Mountains, in the Ob River basin in Western Siberia to the east and in Europe to the west. These groups constantly traded and warred with one another across the low Ural passes, which were controlled mostly by the Mansi (Vogul). Until circa 1470, many Mansi lived in Europe and held lands reaching as far west as the Dvina River (Sokolova 1983), where their traders were in contact with Karelian groups; this could account for the similarity in canoe styles between the Ob and the Mezen-Pechora taiga. Archaeological, linguistic, and DNA data (Tambets et al. 2004) suggest that eastern Saami peoples who once lived along the southern White Sea coast had contacts with groups living in the Western Urals (Foss 1948). It is likely that Saami birch-bark canoes, known today from oral descriptions and from remains found in northern Sweden, also were similar to Mansi or Samoyed canoes known from the White Sea coast. Here, as in other areas of Eurasia, Antropova's and our own studies indicate that proximity along a single river system generally was a more important factor than either language or ethnicity in determining the geography of canoe types.

This principle is interesting because it confounds the usual disjunction seen across cultural-historic and ethno-linguistic borders. In his study of northeastern European paddle forms, Grigori Burov (1996; see also Kashina and Chairkina 2017) found that he could date different types of paddles to specific millennia, beginning as early as 8700 BP. In this case, chronology rather than culture seems to have been the dominant factor determining paddle form. By contrast, from 19th-century ethnographic data, Mason and Hill (1901: figs. 4–6) determined that the shapes of paddles from different Amur cultures were good indicators of which ethnic group had made them; Frederick W. Waugh (1919: 28) illustrated a similar point using North American paddles. Similarly, style shifts in Eskimo kayak and paddle types from Alaska to Greenland show strong correlations with ethnic and language areas (Rousselot 1994: fig. 13.6; see also Golden 2015; and our map 19, page 218).

Peter Rowley-Conwy (2017) reviews the scant information on bark canoes in North European prehistory while reporting on the 8500 BCE Mesolithic site at Star Carr, in North Yorkshire, England. Noting finds of birch resin and bark sheets in waterlogged Mesolithic sites, he argues that birch-bark canoes were the usual vehicles for exploiting postglacial wetland environments. Undoubtedly, this technology must have been widely available to Upper Paleolithic and post-glacial cultures in Northern Eurasia, where 8,700-year-old paddles are certain indicators of water transport.

When we began this project, we thought that care-ful comparison of boat types would enable us to make a preliminary synthesis of Northern Eurasian boat history by using a combination of form and construction details, controlled for both spatial and chronological dimensions. This approach, which is the basis of most archaeological reconstructions, had a practical disadvantage in our case: the limited state of knowledge of canoe history, even during the past 500 years. This type of historical data does exist for plank boat development in the Mediterranean and Western Europe during the past 2,000 years (e.g., Boehmer 1891; McGrail 1998; Christensen 2000; Crumlin-Pedersen 2010). Constructing such a data matrix was the goal of early attempts at a global evolutionary framework of boat development based on ethnographic data, as seen, for example, in James Hornell's 1946 *Water Transport: Origins and Early Evolution*. Hornell encountered many of the same problems we faced, including insufficient archaeological and historical data. In the case of bark canoes and skin boats, we are limited mostly to a few centuries of largely historical documentation, ethnographic boat models, rare archaeological finds, and rock art images of problematic interpretation. Our birch-bark canoe data matrix, which includes only data from the end of the 18th century onward, is not a reliable tool for understanding 10,000 years of canoe forms and constructions. Although a venerable 8,700-year chain of development is known for paddles, it does not tell us much about canoe construction or how it began and spread. At present, we know only its final stage. Nevertheless, one thing is clear: the movements of people hunting, fishing, trading, warring, and migrating in the taiga zone were hugely successful in diffusing bark canoe technology into all corners of Eurasia as well as into and throughout northern North America.

REGIONAL SURVEY OF BARK CANOE TYPES

Having laid out our typology, we now explore the regional, environmental, and cultural settings in which different bark canoe types occurred (fig. 2.2). We begin with the Far East—the Pacific coast of Siberia—where, in the Amur River basin, the bark canoe tradition continued into the 20th century. As we noted earlier in this chapter, this region had two beak-ended—or sturgeon-nose, as Otis T. Mason and Meriden S. Hill called them—canoe styles. The Amur I type had upturned, projecting bow and stern beaks, seen most notably in the watercraft of the Negidal, Nanay, and Nivkh peoples of the lower Amur River. The design was the same whether the boat was short or long (these watercraft could reach 15 meters or more). The smallest Amur I canoes, such as the Nanay and Oroch boats built

for a single person, were often decked and resembled kayaks; indeed, some Amur bark canoes were decked with skins instead of birch bark.

The Amur II type (see fig. 2.1) was usually smaller and wider, with angled or nearly vertical bow and stern ends. It was typical of the Amur Evenk peoples near the Stanovoy Mountains north of the Amur River in Russia and among peoples living along the Songhua River in China. This type also was known among the Evenk, Sakha, and Even peoples in the Aldan River basin east of the Lena River, and it penetrated the Lena valley as well.

One surprising feature of bark canoe history, as the spread of the Amur II type indicates, is that certain design or construction features that developed in one territory could spread over great distances. For example, Carl Hiekisch (1879) wrote that the Western Evenk—and presumably their canoe technology—first moved into the Yenisey River basin in the 1200s, when early Tungus-Evenk groups were fleeing the Mongol invasion of the Amur basin. Later, Evenk peoples escaping the Russian advance into the Yenisey and Baikal regions in the 1700s arrived in the Amur basin and started to build Yenisey-type bark canoes there (see chapter 9, page 208). The Yakut-speaking Dolgan now residing on the Taimyr Peninsula originally may have lived east

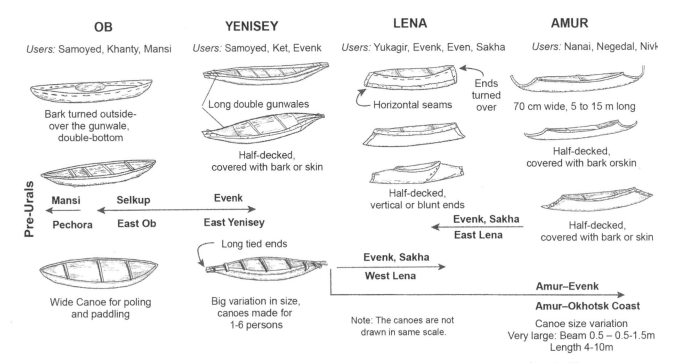

Fig. 2.2. Major birch-bark canoe types are arranged here, named for the river basins where they are found. (The canoes are not drawn to the same scale.) Overall length and width varied greatly; the shortest canoes were just 2 meters long, while the longest reached 10 to 15 meters. (Drawing: Harri Luukkanen; adapted by Marcia Bakry)

of the Lena River before their 17th-century migration west (Ushnitsky 2008a,b), when they carried their birch-bark canoes into the Taimyr tundra. Most Mansi people, as mentioned above, originally lived west of the Urals, in Europe, until their wars with the Russians caused them to retreat east of the Urals in the 1400s, when they may have introduced expanded log boats to Western Siberia. It seems likely that similar migrations changed the bark canoe typology map in many unknown ways and directions. Nevertheless, as we have noted, Northern Eurasian canoe types broadly conform to the region's major river systems and do not show a random or patchwork distribution; peoples who moved either adopted the canoe types found in their new homes or influenced their new neighbors to adopt the canoe styles they had brought with them.

The consistent homogeneity of canoe types within major river basins is remarkable. It indicates technological and stylistic persistence despite the comings and goings of specific language speakers and culture bearers, perhaps over thousands of years. Since birch bark and birch wood were present everywhere in the boreal zone, environmental factors were not prime determinants of boat types and designs (except in the Arctic zone, where bark was unavailable and was less suitable than sea mammal hide anyway). Consequently, we must wonder what conditioned various groups to adopt a common boat type throughout a given river basin. Perhaps the answer lies in the "downstream factor": people living along the lower portions of a river became aware of designs developed by people living in headwater regions via the latter's downriver travel and trade or canoe remnants that washed downstream. Conversely, in winter, rivers became frozen highways, making it easy for people in the north to travel south to trade walrus ivory and furs for metal and other southern goods, and perhaps to learn new canoe technology and styles. In fact, in the Bronze and Iron ages, peoples along the Arctic coast acquired metal and metallurgical skills almost as soon as they first appeared in the technologically more advanced and ore-rich southern Urals.

In the middle Lena River basin, we find two old and traditional birch-bark canoe types. The drawing at the top of fig. 2.2, second from right, shows a model of a small Evenk canoe collected by Richard Maak from the Vilyuy River, a western tributary of the Lena, in 1859 (MAE 334-77). The bark at the canoe's nearly vertical ends was folded over, a detail that may reflect a very old canoe construction tradition in this region, since this feature was not seen in other western or southern regions. Below it is a drawing of a very

simple, small Sakha bark canoe model from eastern Yakutia dated 1846 and collected by Alexander von Middendorff in 1856 (MAE 701-51). It had double or triple layers of bark, and apparently the bark was turned over the gunwales; the pointed or downsloping bow and stern may have been inherited from pointed or beak-ended Amur River Evenk canoe styles. Mason and Hill (1901) provided the first English descriptions of these Sakha and Evenk bark canoes made in the Vilyuy River basin.

Just as people in the eastern parts of the Lena basin "imported" beaked bark canoes from the Amur basin thanks to the in-migration of Evenk people in the 1200s, so people living in the western Lena basin may have imported Yenisey-type models when the Evenk entered Samoyed and Ket (Yenisey Ostyak) lands and Sakha peoples migrating along the Lena River crossed the lands north of Lake Baikal. While such hypothetical scenarios seem logical based on the limited historical evidence, the absence of archaeological confirmation demands caution in any attempt to reconstruct a deep canoe history from present data. Unlike many other cultural objects that archaeological preservation tends to favor—for instance, ceramics, metal tools, burials, and ornaments—very few canoe or kayak remains have been found, let alone scientifically excavated, dated, and reported. Archaeological evidence of boats from the Amur basin and the Far East is almost nonexistent.

The upper parts of the Ob and Yenisey rivers form a narrow triangle of land over which travelers could cross from one river to another. This might be one reason that the general forms of Ob and Yenisey bark canoes, such as rocker bottoms and long gunwales extending end to end, had much in common. Yet certain construction details differentiate them, perhaps because the Yenisey type persisted much longer among the Western Evenk. In the Ob-Pechora type, the rib ends were bound to a single gunwale, and the outer bark sheet was turned outside-in over the gunwale. The Yenisey type, on the other hand, had a double gunwale, and its bark cover and ribs were clamped between the inwales and outwales, as the detail view in fig. 2.1 shows.

No complete North and North-East European aboriginal bark canoes exist today, except for full-scale modern reproductions and small-scale museum models. But various languages orally document aboriginal bark canoes, and an abstract canoe "type" lives on in folk traditions and poetry, even in parts of Northern Eurasia where bark canoes have not been used for many centuries. The birch-bark canoe persisted longest as a workhorse east of the Yenisey, where it remained popular later than in Western Siberia and northeastern Europe largely because the fur trade and taiga hunting professions endured into the 20th century. Evenk and Tungus bark canoe users are well documented in Eastern Siberia and the Lake Baikal region, showing that the bark canoe was their main watercraft until the end of the 1800s; in some regions, its use into the 1930s has been documented. In fact, the bark canoe persisted as a working vessel in the Far East longer than any other traditional watercraft has done anywhere else in the northern parts of the globe. While bark canoes left few archaeological traces, many drawings and photographs show their design and construction in various regions, and descriptions remain even in areas where the boats themselves have disappeared.

Table 1 summarizes the dimensions of known birch-bark canoes, both models and actual canoes, from Northern Eurasia, arranged according to their ethnic affiliation and main territory and region. Their measurements are drawn from a variety of sources, including documents written by early travelers and explorers; scale drawings and sketches of measured boats in museums; and estimates gleaned from models, photos, and illustrations. In addition to providing the best available statistics in our study of Northern Eurasian watercraft, the table enables comparisons among cultures, boat types, and regions.

Several conclusions can be drawn from this information: (1) Most regions of Northern Eurasia had both large and small canoes. The former were used for trade and family transport, the latter for individual hunting or fishing. (2) Yenisey-type canoes from the Yenisey, Lena, and Amur rivers were large, could carry heavy loads, and presumably were built for use as trade freighters (the largest Evenk canoes could carry 10 people or a ton of goods). (3) The Amur I type was both the longest and the slenderest of Eurasian canoes, its unwieldy length suggesting that such a canoe was portaged less often and was not used for heavy transport, unlike typical Western Siberian canoes. (4) A probable factor in the difference between the larger, more heavily constructed Amur II canoe and the beamier, shorter, and lighter Ob and Yenisey canoes was their respective river geography. Most travel in Siberia proceeded from east to west and required travelers to ascend tributary streams and portage into tributaries of the next major north-south river. The Amur's east-west orientation presented a different geographical problem because its tributaries paralleled courses of the northern rivers and were separated from them by mountains or high hills. As a result, portaging was less common between the Amur and the Ob, Yenisey, and Lena: within the Amur basin, travelers tended to remain on their habitual tributaries or along the main Amur artery, so their boats could be larger and heavier.

As we stated earlier, one of our goals in this book is to provide information on bark canoes unknown in the published literature. Antropova (1961) wrote extensively about canoes and their users east of the Yenisey River, but except for the Evenk, the canoes of the Ob and Yenisey basins have not been discussed previously. Our study shows that the Samoyed and Ob-Ugrian peoples used bark canoes until the 1700s, and some Khanty and Selkup groups used canoes similar in size and shape to ones from other parts of Siberia until much later.

We must remark on an exception in the European data gap west of the Ob: the Saami bark canoe, which, although it is the canoe closest to Europe's technological heartland, lasted longer here than in other areas of northeastern Europe and Scandinavia (see chapter 3, page 61). There is some evidence that the birch-bark canoe survived as a rarity until the early 1800s in Swedish Lapland, where oral literature and archaeological sites reveal evidence of bark canoes (e.g., Westerdahl 1985a,b). In the Lake Saimaa region of eastern Finland, the remains of an undated bark canoe, perhaps of Saami or Karelian origin, were found, although not enough was preserved to determine its type classification (Itkonen 1942: 48). The Saami boats are the only examples of bark canoes known from Scandinavia, other than the failed attempt by Peter Kalm and Anders Chydenius to introduce American Indian bark canoes into Finland in the 1750s (see chapter 3, page 56).

In Europe, use of the birch-bark canoe faded early because of the appearance of the expanded log boat, which replaced it in the taiga during the late medieval period and may have superseded the skin boat in the tundra zone. In Saami territory, this phenomenon may have taken place when the Saami-Karelian people invented or adopted expanded log boats to which planks could be attached, providing higher sides (more "freeboard") to keep out water (Luukkanen 2010). In some regions such as Swedish Lapland, Saami people used bark, skin, and log canoes side by side for many centuries.

At the time when the Saami used birch-bark boats, heavy canoe traffic was underway between Europe and Asia over the low Ural Mountain passes, using traditional routes controlled mainly by Mansi peoples living on both sides. Most Mansi moved east of the Urals in the 1400s, to the western bank of the Ob River, where they opened new trade contacts

Table 1

Measured Birch-Bark Canoes in Northern Eurasia

Arranged by Ethnic Group and Region

Dimensions (overall length, beam, and depth) are in meters except where indicated, and were converted from measurements given in the cited sources.

S = small canoe, M = medium, L = large

Western Siberia and Ob River Basin

Ethnic Group	Region	Length	Beam	Depth	Source	Canoe Type
Khanty (Ostyak): 2 canoes	Narym Ob River	S 4.3 L 6.4	0.63 0.63	No data	Ides 1706: 23	Ob-Pechora
Khanty (Ostyak): model	Tobol River and Irtysh River	5.0 cm; full-size canoe would be circa 5.0 m	0.8 cm	No data	Martin 1895: model, 1892.03.0072 (catalogued in 1892), Swedish Ethnological Museum, Stockholm	Ob-Pechora
Kamas, Southern Samoyed: 2 canoes	Northern Altai Yenisey River source	S 4.1 L 5.0	0.71 0.71	No data	Müller 1957 Potapov 1957: 219–20	Ob-Pechora
Selkup (Ostyak Samoyed)	Ket River (tributary of Eastern Ob)	5.4	0.75	0.3	Donner 1979, National Museum of Finland	Yenisey

Central Siberia, Yenisey River Basin, and Lake Baikal

Ethnic Group	Region	Length	Beam	Depth	Source	Canoe Type
Evenk (Tungus): 2 canoes	Transbaikal Eastern Lake Baikal	S 2.7 L 5.4	0.46 0.76	No data	Georgi 1777: 314–15 Georgi 1775: 252	Yenisey
Evenk (Tungus)	Northern Baikal	2.7 to 3.0	0.5	No data	Radde 1861: 238	Yenisey
Evenk (Tungus): 2 canoes	Both: Lower Tunguska River	S 3.55 L 3.6	0.53 0.9	0.18 0.3	Messerschmidt 1964	Yenisey
Chunya Evenk	Ust-Uchami, Lower Tunguska River	5.0	0.7	No data	Naumov 1927: photos, Krasnoyarsk Krai Museum	Chunya-Yenisey (?)
Evenk (Tungus): 2 canoes	Ust-Ilimsk Angara River	S 1.8 L 8.2	0.7 1.8	No data	Lehrberg 1816, Geschichte der Russlands	Yenisey
Evenk (Tungus)	Lower Tunguska River	2.4	0.5	No data	Irkutsk Museum catalogue record: 1988 BC 4873-1	Yenisey

Eastern Siberia, Lena River Basin, and Kolyma River Basin

Ethnic Group	Region	Length	Beam	Depth	Source	Canoe Type
Sakha (Yakut): 2 canoes	Both: Lena	S 3.7 L 5.64	0.6 0.58	0.25 0.46	Yakutsk Museum of History and Culture and Peoples of the North catalogue record: 2011	Lena
Evenk (Tungus)	Ust-Maja, Maja River	15.0	0.7	No data	Abakumov 2001	Amur I
Evenk (Tungus)	Timpton River (tributary of southern Aldan River)	3.26	0.8	0.39	Neryungri Museum of the History of Development of South Yakutia catalogue record: 1997, 25.456 E-209	Lena
Even (Lamut): 3 canoes	Upper Kolyma River Magadan Tayi Bay	S 2.1 M 3.7 L 5.3	0.76 No data No data	No data No data No data	Sbignew 1867: 24	Lena (?)

(continued)

Table 1

Measured Birch-Bark Canoes in Northern Eurasia (*continued*)

Arranged by Ethnic Group and Region

Dimensions (overall length, beam, and depth) are in meters except where indicated, and were converted from measurements given in the cited sources.

S = small canoe, M = medium, L = large

Far East: Russia, China, and Japan

Ethnic Group	Region	Length	Beam	Depth	Source	Canoe Type
Negidal	Amgun River	9.0 to 10.0	0.7	No data	Shternberg 1933: 538	Amur I
Negidal	Amgun River	6.1	0.46	No data	Middendorff 1875, vol. 4: 1534–35	Amur I
Nanay (Gold)	Amur River	5.0 to 6.0	0.7	0.3	Antropova 1961: 127	Amur I
Nanay (Gold) (2 canoes)	Ussuri River	S 5.0 M 6.0	0.7 0.7	No data	Maak 1859: 61	Amur I
Nivkh (Gilyak) (2 canoes)	Ussuri River	S 5.3 L 6.4	0.7 0.7	No data	Przhevalsky 1869: 29	Amur I
Oroch Evenk (2 canoes)	Tugur River	S 3.8 L 5.5	0.95 0.7	No data	Middendorff 1856: drawing	Amur II Amur I
Manegir-Kumarchen	Zeya River	10.8	0.67	No data	L. von Schrenk 1881 (collected); Mason and Hill 1901 (described)	Amur I
Hezhe-Gold	Sungari (now Songhua) River, China	2.09	0.46	No data	Ling 1934: 81	Amur II
Oroch-Elunhun (3 canoes)	Songhua River, China	S 4.0 M 6.0 to 7.0 L 9.0 to 10.0	0.5 1.0 1.5	No data	Na Min 2011	Yenisey
Oroch-Elunhun	Hailan River, Inner Mongolia	7.34	0.68	0.27	Chinese Academy of Social Sciences 2014: 224	Yenisey
Ainu *yachip* canoe (model)	Hokkaido	0.288	0.085	No data	Nishimura 1931: 204–05, fig. 47	Hokkaido Ainu

as Western Siberia became a source of European-Russian wealth: the region's expensive furs were traded first by the Novgorod federation and later by the Moscow Russians. Russian customs books document evidence, dated around 1655, of Mansi, Khanty, or Komi-Zyrian hunters entering the town of Ust-Yug along the Vychegda River in bark canoes loaded with furs from the Pechora River basin and regions farther east (Shutikhin 2008).

The canoes of the eastern Ob and western Yenisey River basins conform to a single type (see fig. 2.2), within which there is significant diversity owing to the complex history of the peoples in this area, many of whom arrived here from the south and east. We know from written documents (e.g., Georgi 1776a) that Mansi hunters (known then as Yugra) on the Ural slopes and in the Mezen-Pechora River basin were bark canoe builders, but the descriptions are vague. The Eastern Khanty peoples, who lived as hunters and fishermen, seem to have built birch-bark canoes in the Narym region until the early 1700s (Ides 1706); some Western Khanty hunters, including the Tara near Omsk, may have used them in taiga forest country until 1886 (Granö 1886). Little is known about these canoes because the Mansi and Khanty, due to their proximity to sources of iron in the south and later to Russian traders, switched to expanded log boats earlier than the Samoyed, who lacked such access. But it is probable that the birch-bark canoe designs of all these groups were similar owing to close contacts among the Ugric and Samoyedic peoples.

The Samoyed of Western Siberia, inhabiting the territory between the Ob and Yenisey rivers from the Altai-Sayan Mountains in the south to the Arctic Ocean in the north, were the main bearers of the bark canoe tradition for centuries, if not millennia. From various sources, we know that the Ural Samoyed (later called the Yurak Samoyed or Forest Nenets and, later still, Nenets) originally lived as hunters and fishermen in the taiga, while the Tundra Nenets took up large-scale reindeer herding in the Arctic zone in the 1600s (Krupnik 1993; Golovnev and Osherenko 1999). During their days as forest hunters traversing streams and lakes, the Forest Nenets must have used birch-bark canoes exclusively until Russian plank boats began to replace them circa 1700.

The coming of new boat technology was part of a wave of social, economic, and political change that occurred when the Russian fur trade expanded into Western Siberia. Trade and European technology, including guns, iron, axes, and other useful goods, exacerbated longstanding regional hostilities and often led to interethnic competition. From the 15th through the 17th centuries, northeastern Europe and Western Siberia experienced recurring intertribal warfare, and watercraft played a major role in skirmishes, raids, and all-out battles. Pressure from population movements from the south and east also contributed to conflict. The arrival of Ugrian peoples east of the Ob River brought hostilities, and, according to Khanty elders' accounts of the Ob River wars between the Ural Samoyed and the Ugrian peoples circa 1500 to 1700 (Golovnev 2000), the Khanty Ugrians, with their expanded log boats, prevailed partly because their archers, who were armed with crossbows, could shoot holes in Samoyed bark canoes (Starcev 1988: 5). The Khanty replaced their bark canoes with log boats in some parts of the upper Ob before the 1700s. The Selkup (Ostyak Samoyed) also built bark canoes in the Western Siberian taiga. The Selkup bark canoe (see fig. 5.10, page 108) that Kai Donner collected at the Ket River sometime between 1911 and 1914 shows Yenisey-type construction, which also appeared in the eastern Ob basin. Distinctive features of Ob canoes included use of bird-cherry wood, double layering of the birch-bark cover, partial decking, and the use of a bent-wood oval insert instead of straight crossways thwarts.

Antropova (1961) assumed—and we concur—that the most recent major dispersion of the bark canoe occurred in late Iron Age times (circa 500 BCE to 1 CE) or even later, and probably was centered on Southern Samoyed territory around the headwaters of the Ob, Yenisey, and Lena rivers. Later, there were many other shifts in canoe types, resulting in their modern distribution. Various Samoyed groups used bark canoes, which would have been known to other people who entered their lands, including the Ket and other upper Yenisey groups. The Southern Samoyed's neighbors to the south, the Turkic Tatars, may also have adopted the bark canoe from them. Perhaps this is why Tatars called the birch-bark canoe a "Samoyed" boat (Belgibaev 2004).

Moving east, we leave the canoe traditions of the Ob-Yenisey region and come to the huge Lena River basin and its dominant people, the Sakha, formerly known as the Yakut (see fig. 2.2). The Sakha, residing at the confluence of the Aldan and Lena rivers, are today the largest Native group in Eastern Siberia. They have a mixed bark canoe history owing to their late appearance in the Lena valley in the 1300s, arriving from the Baikal region to the south, and the fact that their entry route crossed the lands of many other peoples. According to Antropova (1961), the Sakha called their Lena canoe a "Tungus" boat, while linguistic data suggest that their western bark canoe heritage is related to the Ket people and the Yenisey River (Sieroszewski 1993). On the other hand, they met Southern Samoyed, too, since the Sakha birch-bark tent is similar to the Samoyed *chum*, whose name the Sakha also borrowed. Sakha groups also settled along the upper Aldan River, where they were introduced to beaked Amur-type canoes and traded with Chinese and Manchu people by crossing the Stanovoy Mountains to the Zeya River (Mason and Hill 1901).

Environmental conditions partly dictated the origins of these peoples and the directions of their main migration routes. As this chapter notes, the Ob, Yenisey, and Lena rivers were major north-south transport corridors, but no less important were the east-west routes created by the Arctic Ocean coast and the east-west-running tributaries of the large rivers, whose headwaters nearly link up. Travel across these water routes was a routine matter by sledge in the winter and by canoe the rest of the year. In these Central Siberian regions, few mountains intervened. Finally, the open Buryat Steppe of north-central Asia, south of the Yenisey and Lena headwaters, enabled movement for horse-based pastoralists and the armies of Central Asian empires and states.

The major dynamic driving population migrations and other movements in Central Siberia, however, was the tumultuous history of cultural interactions channeled by these geographic corridors. During the past 2,000 years, many events have resulted in population movements and even major demographic disruptions in the region. The two most important were the expansion of Turkic-speaking peoples from the Altai Mountain area beginning in the 7th century, and the Mongol expansion from the same region in the 13th century. The Turkic expansion reached as far west as modern-day Turkey and north into the Lena valley, displacing some peoples into the Arctic and assimilating others. The Mongol wars and incursions caused similar disruptions as people fled or were expelled from their homelands. These migrations and displacements were not new; they were preceded by similar events linked to the expansion of militarism and pastoral nomadism, stimulated by horse domestication in the late Bronze Age and by intensified equestrian conquest in the Iron Age. These and other events undoubtedly influenced canoe history, resulting in both demographic movements, such as those of the Ket, the Evenk, and the Sakha, and cultural exchanges, seen in, for instance, the sharing of Lena traditions with Yenisey peoples and in similarities between the Lena and Amur versions of the birch-bark canoe.

The easternmost birch-bark canoe users were the Yukagir, who were in the late 19th century a remnant of a much larger people who once lived on the upper and lower Kolyma River in northeastern Siberia, where they speared reindeer at river crossings from bark canoes, skin kayaks, or log boats. They originally lived east of the Yenisey, north of Lake Baikal, next to the Samoyed, and they migrated (perhaps a millennium ago) from there down the Lena River (Ushnitsky 2015, 2016). During this journey, they would have been in contact with the Tungus-Evenk, Even, and Sakha. The Yukagir, who were still making birch-bark canoes along the upper Kolyma River in 1827, probably acquired their boat traditions from contact with the Samoyed around Lake Baikal. Later, they may have shared these traditions with other peoples they met, as they did with their decked skin kayak in the eastern Lena delta.

South of the Yukagir were the Evenk, who inhabited a large swath of territories in the Amur, Lena, and Yenisey drainages of Eastern Siberia. As might be expected from their large, dispersed territories, the Evenk have a complicated bark canoe history that includes many boat types. The origin of the western Tungus-Evenk peoples, who entered Yenisey lands from the south and east, is far from clear, but there is evidence that they learned to build Yenisey bark canoes through contacts with the Ket, the Assan, and other Yeniseyan peoples along the Angara River (see, for example, Forsyth 1994).

While these reconstructions are speculative and based on linguistic and oral-history data rather than archaeological or material culture evidence, we know for certain that Western Evenk bark canoes in the Lower and Stony (Podkamennaya) Tunguska rivers belonged to the Yenisey type. The border between the Yenisey-type and the Lena-type canoe regions ran along the Vitim and Olekma rivers, where both types were known. South of the Vitim, around Lake Baikal and along the Kirenga and Lena headwaters, the Yenisey type was dominant. Along the Lena River proper, east of the Vitim confluence, the Lena canoe was dominant (Antropova 1961). East of the Yenisey River, various Evenk hunting peoples were the main users of birch-bark canoes, and they kept this tradition alive until the early 1900s, when they adopted expanded log boats.

Canoe sizes varied considerably in these large river basins. Some bark canoes were very large, but most were small, usually only 2 to 3 meters long, and were built for one or two persons so that they could easily carry the boat over portages from lake to lake and across drainage divides. Some boats were made narrow and fast to transport hunters or warriors, while others were wide and slow, serving as freighters. The largest birch-bark canoe known in Northern Eurasia (see page 145) was built by Evenk hunters along the Maya River, the easternmost Lena tributary; it is 15 meters long and was found at Ust-Maya village in 2001, probably having been made less than 20 years earlier (Abakumov 2001). The canoe itself has not survived, but it was described as a 70-centimeter-wide Amur type I beaked canoe.

As discussed at the beginning of this chapter, many travelers and explorers documented the persistence of the birch-bark canoe in the Far East into the 20th century; chapter 9 presents illustrations and descriptions of some of these Amur canoes. In old Manchuria, in the basin of the Amur (Heilong Jiang) River and along its many tributaries in Russian, Chinese, and Outer Mongolian territory, Tungus-related peoples such as the Manchu, Nanay, and Negidal once constructed similar versions of the beaked Amur canoe. Most were small single-person vessels used for hunting and fishing. Drawings by unknown Chinese artists document canoes from the Chinese Qing (Manchu) dynasty, and, thanks to Chinese sources, we are able to present them here.

CANOES MADE OF ELM, LARCH, AND OTHER BARKS

Canoes made of barks other than birch represent another line of canoe development, but much less is known about it than is known about birch-bark canoes. It is evident from archaeological finds and documented descriptions across Northern Eurasia that other kinds of bark were used to make canoes, especially elm and larch and sometimes pine, spruce, and aspen. Probably most were used for short periods of time or distance—for instance, for a single crossing of a river—or were made in places where no other materials were available, as in the tundra. Fig. 2.3 illustrates a possible method

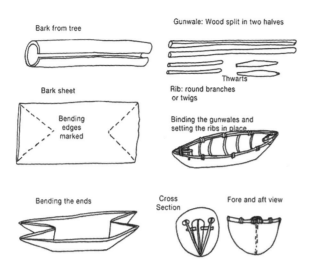

Fig. 2.3. A possible method for constructing a *korevuye*, an Orochen-Evenk larch-bark canoe. This plan is based on a model from the Amgun River in the Amur River system; the model is now in the St. Petersburg Museum of Anthropology and Ethnology (Kunstkamera) collection (MAE 5333-34). The canoe is made by folding a single sheet of bark, without seams, and attaching gunwales. (Drawing: Harri Luukkanen; based on photographs by Evguenia Anichtchenko)

Fig. 2.4. Hokkaido Ainu men forming the end of an Amur cork canoe out of Amur cork tree bark in 1937 (HUBGM 30734). (From Inukai 1939; courtesy Hokkaido University Botanical Garden and Museum)

for constructing canoes from these heavier types of bark, a method that has been documented in an extensive series of photographs showing Ainu people building elm-bark canoes in Hokkaido (fig. 2.4; see also fig 9.12a–d, page 202). Ainu bark canoes may serve as examples of some of the earliest types of expedient bark canoe technology in the evolutionary history of watercraft. This is not to say that the Ainu were not capable of more advanced boat construction; rather, they utilized very simple solutions (e.g., see fig. 9.10, 11, page 201) when they didn't require the more advanced technology seen in their seagoing log-based planked vessels.

The "alternative path" theory for non-birch-bark canoes was suggested by a unique archaeological find on the Viskan (Byslätt) River in Swedish Västergötland (see chapter 3, page 51), which may be the only elm-bark canoe known in Europe. Discovered in fragmented condition eroding from a riverbank in 1934, the canoe was estimated to be about 3 to 5 meters long, with slender ribs of hazel branches fastened into the gunwales with wooden pegs; fragments of leather were also present. Although regular stitching perforations were found in the elm-bark cover, no sewing material survived. Maria Lindberg (2012) reexamined this find, which she radiocarbon-dated to the late Bronze Age, circa 900 to

800 BCE. No birch-bark canoes (and only a handful of conventional log boats) have been recorded in southern Sweden.

Another example of canoes made from other types of bark comes from the old city of Novgorod in northwestern Russia. In 1960, archaeologists found the remains of three composite canoes under the walls of the Vladimir Tower, which dates to 1044 CE (see fig. 4.2a–b, page 79). Study of the best-preserved canoe revealed that it had an expanded log hull measuring 675 by 90 by 55 centimeters and covered with glued-on aspen-bark panels (Troyanovskiy and Petrov 2018). The Vladimir Tower canoes may be the most extraordinary small-boat find in all of Europe, since they combined all the known technologies of their day: each vessel was a very thin expanded log boat with sewn planks supported by wooden ribs, covered by an outer layer of aspen bark and an inner layer of hide. The practicality of such time-consuming construction is questionable. These canoes may not have been intended for ordinary use; perhaps they were made for some wealthy citizen or elite purpose.

Adney and Chapelle (1964) described North American Indian elm- and pine-bark canoes in addition to birch-bark ones, and some Northern Eurasian groups also used bark other than birch. Information about elm-bark canoes in Eurasia is scarce (McGrail 1998: 88). The 18th-century Swedish naturalist Peter Kalm described the use of elm bark in northeastern North America, and Adney and Chapelle highly regarded his narrative of Indians making an elm-bark canoe near Fort Anne, close to Lake Champlain, on June 28, 1749. After it was finished, Kalm and his Finnish companion used the canoe to travel by river from English American territory to French Canada (see chapter 3, page 58). The Ainu in Hokkaido also used elm-bark canoes.

Although elm was unavailable in Northern Siberia, larch was a suitable—if uncommon—alternative to birch. The first academic explorer of Siberia, Daniel G. Messerschmidt, a German traveling in 1723 on behalf of the Russian Academy of Sciences, journeyed from New Mangazeya (later renamed Turukhansk) on the Yenisey to the Lower Tunguska River, where he met small groups of Evenk and commented on their bark canoes, some of which he measured and weighed. The Evenk apparently were using larch-bark canoes alongside birch-bark ones; Messerschmidt recorded Evenk larch-bark canoes between the Uchami and Taimura rivers that were similar in both use and size (he described one as being 360 by 90 by 30 centimeters) to those made of birch bark.

In 1914, the Dolgan people in Sloika, farther north near the Golchikha trading post in western Taimyr, also were using larch-bark canoes, as recorded in the account of Maud Dorian Haviland (Haviland 1971). She and an English companion on an ornithology expedition tried to cross a flooded river with their Dolgan guides in larch-bark canoes. The Dolgan and Nganasan used similar small boats for hunting birds on Taimyr lakes, as has been documented by explorers of this northernmost land in Northern Eurasia, where birch bark is not locally available (see chapter 6, page 122). Her report from Taimyr shows that larch-bark canoes were used even in the northernmost tundra of the Russian High Arctic for spearing wild reindeer at river and lake crossings and for crossing rivers with tame reindeer during their seasonal migrations (see fig. 5.1, page 95, and the Yukagir discussion in chapter 7, page 136). These boats—as well as those used in Taimyr for duck hunting in spring—were light and small, less than 3 meters long, and suitable for sledge transport over the tundra; they were not used to carry freight.

Canoes covered with pine, larch, and aspen bark were part of a boatbuilding tradition that existed throughout Northern Eurasia. Whether they had a different developmental path than birch-bark canoes is not known; all we can say for certain today is that such canoes did exist—see the Amur Evenk larch-bark canoe in the Museum of Anthropology and Ethnology, fig. 9.19, page 209—and probably their history is as ancient as that of the birch-bark canoe.

OPEN SKIN BOATS AND KAYAKS

Fig. 2.5 illustrates the main types of open skin boats and decked kayaks, whose geographic locations are shown in map 4 (page 29). As we can see, Northern Eurasia was a skin boat region in addition to hosting bark canoes; nearly all major groups in the tundra zone probably used skin boats at some point in the past, although the intensity and purposes of that use differed, as in the case of bark canoes. Siberian Eskimo, Chukchi, and Koryak peoples have well-described skin boats, and we demonstrate here (following our study of written accounts, archaeological finds, museum collections, folk legends, and oral history) that they had a wider distribution along the Arctic and Pacific coasts in the past than is known in recent history. Open skin boats and kayaks have been reported from most coastal areas of Northern Eurasia, the Sea of Okhotsk, and even parts of the Far East. European, Siberian, and Central Asian peoples inhabiting inland regions also used skin boats and half-decked canoe-kayaks covered with seal, reindeer, or moose hide.

In Northern Europe, the Saami people probably have an early history of skin boat use, as suggested by their Stone Age petroglyphs and folk legends. For many years, Nordic archaeologists studying petroglyph images of boats here (dating between 2,000 and 6,000 years old) interpreted some as depictions of skin boats, based on their high sides and profiles, which look similar to those of Eskimo umiaks (see chapter 3, page 66). However, because heavy ground stone axes and woodworking gouges have been unearthed in the same areas as the petroglyphs, most archaeologists today interpret these images as log boats or expanded log boats, possibly with sewn plank additions. Nevertheless, some petroglyphs probably do depict skin boats, especially in areas where people once hunted seal and walrus on broken spring sea ice, where hunters would not have been able to use much heavier log boats. There are oral history accounts of Saami *skårne-väntse* skin boats in Swedish Lapland (not many, but enough to suggest that such watercraft were used there in relatively recent times), as well as legends relating how people used skin boats to cross rivers with their reindeer and to hunt sea mammals along the coast (Westerdahl 1995). Although there is no detailed knowledge of Saami skin boats, one archaeological find from Tiisteenjoki village on the Lapua River, along the western Finnish coast, dates to circa 3200 BP (Itkonen 1942). According to Mulk and Bayliss-Smith (2006), skin boats may have been used on the northern Norwegian coast, too, until circa 300 to 600 CE,

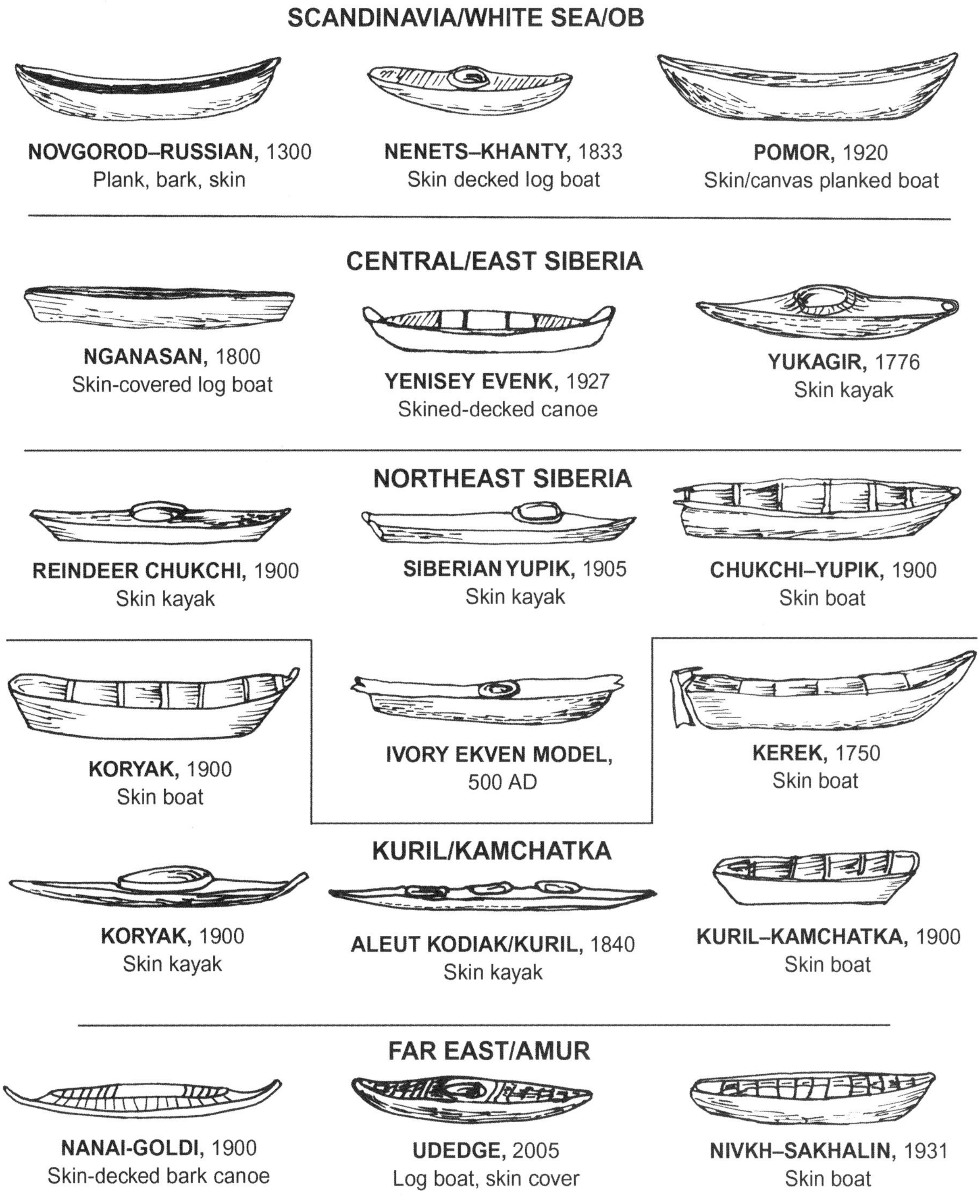

SCANDINAVIA/WHITE SEA/OB

NOVGOROD–RUSSIAN, 1300
Plank, bark, skin

NENETS–KHANTY, 1833
Skin decked log boat

POMOR, 1920
Skin/canvas planked boat

CENTRAL/EAST SIBERIA

NGANASAN, 1800
Skin-covered log boat

YENISEY EVENK, 1927
Skined-decked canoe

YUKAGIR, 1776
Skin kayak

NORTHEAST SIBERIA

REINDEER CHUKCHI, 1900
Skin kayak

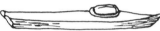

SIBERIAN YUPIK, 1905
Skin kayak

CHUKCHI–YUPIK, 1900
Skin boat

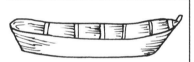

KORYAK, 1900
Skin boat

IVORY EKVEN MODEL,
500 AD

KEREK, 1750
Skin boat

KURIL/KAMCHATKA

KORYAK, 1900
Skin kayak

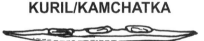

ALEUT KODIAK/KURIL, 1840
Skin kayak

KURIL–KAMCHATKA, 1900
Skin boat

FAR EAST/AMUR

NANAI-GOLDI, 1900
Skin-decked bark canoe

UDEDGE, 2005
Log boat, skin cover

NIVKH–SAKHALIN, 1931
Skin boat

Fig. 2.5. Skin boat types of Northern Eurasia. (Drawing: Harri Luukkanen; adapted by Marcia Bakry)

when they began to be replaced by "Viking" lapstrake boats. In interior regions, smaller skin boats survived in villages of the Vapsten Lapp people in Sweden until the first half of the 19th century (Whitaker 1977).

The Karelians, possibly the closest relatives of the Saami owing to mixing and assimilation, arrived on the Kola Peninsula in the 1200s. They later became skin boat users, too, especially in the White Sea region. *Kalevala* runes—epic Finnish and Saami poetry, often sung, that includes folklore, mythology, and stories of the past—collected between 1600 and 1850 describe boats covered with "fish" (i.e., seal) skin in several regions inhabited by the Finns, Karelians, and

Ingrians (people from the Gulf of Bothnia and the White Sea coast).

Russian Pomors, who arrived on the White Sea coast in the 13th century and pushed the Saami, Karelians, and Vepsian farther north, used very light canvas-covered plank boats to hunt seal amid spring sea ice until circa 1900 (see figs. 4.3–4.5, pages 82–83). This fact does not necessarily imply a prior history of skin-covered frame boats; rather, the Pomors might have used skins simply as a practical way to waterproof their leak-prone sewn or nailed plank boats. Pomor plank boats were large, some 6 to 8 meters in length, and it is likely that their construction incorporated elements of earlier Saami and Karelian technology, including seal-skin waterproofing over planks. The boat traditions of the Maritime Pomors are well documented, as is their large-scale sealing industry, which employed thousands of people and hundreds of boats for hundreds of years. Further research may show that both skin boats and sealing or whaling have a long shared history in Northern Scandinavia and north-western Russia, as M. E. Foss (1948) suggested for the second millennium BCE in the White Sea region, but the evidence to date is inconclusive. We do know that many rock engravings along several river estuaries (e.g., in Uikunjoki [Belomorsk], Dwina, Mezen, the Ter coast in Kola, and Novaya Zemlya, where beluga whales were hunted with harpoons) seem to depict skin boats.

Fig. 2.5 demonstrates the great diversity among skin boats in Northern Eurasia. Two major points can be made: first, the overriding conclusion is that open skin boats have been used widely along the continent's northern and north-eastern coasts from Europe to the Amur River and the Sea of Okhotsk. Second, skin-covered kayaks and canoe-kayaks built for individual use in a cold marine or tundra environment were widely distributed throughout these territories and were also used on inland waters for reindeer hunting in most of these same regions. These inland versions often were covered with reindeer or moose hide instead of seal skin. Although archaeological evidence is sorely needed for confirmation, historical sources documenting Stephen Burrough's voyages to the Kara Sea in 1556 and 1557 (Burrough 1567) and Pierre Martin de La Martinière's voyage of 1670 (1706) to the same area indicate that the culture of building skin boats and kayaks once had a continental scope and was not restricted to Eskimo territories around Chukotka and the Bering Strait. The widespread distribution of these watercraft raises the obvious question of their time and place of origin, which we consider in chapter 7 and the epilogue.

Table 2 lists the known skin boats and kayaks found in Northern Eurasia and notes their measurements. Northeastern Siberia and the northern Russian maritime regions are best represented in the table since skin boat use in these areas continues to the present day. Still other types of skin boats from interior regions are noted in the table as well, although details about them are often scarce.

We know little about skin boats in Western Siberia, although the Samoyed along the Arctic Ocean coast, who have long been sea mammal hunters and fishermen, reportedly used such boats. Until the late 1800s, the Nenets (Yurak Samoyed) hunted and fished in the Ob River estuary and off the Yamal Peninsula in decked composite kayaks (log boat hulls decked with seal skins). They may also have used open boats (about which we do not have details), such as the modern Nenets skin boat that Alexander Shutikhin saw in Yamal in 2008 (see fig. 5.4, page 99). For the Tundra Nenets, farther north, seal and walrus hunting was an important seasonal activity, as was hunting wild reindeer, polar bear, fox, and other fur-bearing animals. In the Ob River estuary, the Tundra Nenets shared their hunting grounds, skills, and boats with the Sea Khanty, who—according to accounts written by early polar travelers such as Alexander Schrenk (1848) and Timotheus M. Klingstädt (1769)—hunted beluga, also known as "white fish," in the lower part of the river and in Ob Bay.

East of the Ob estuary are the maritime territories of the Enets (Yenisey Samoyed), who are not well known either historically or ethnographically. Johan Balak (1581) did document their skin boats when he described the journey of polar explorer and sailor Olivier Brunel, who met Samoyed paddling skin boats on the open sea near the Taz Peninsula, east of Ob Bay, as he searched for a sea route from Europe to China in 1576. The Samoyed told Brunel to sail up the Ob River until he found a large lake (perhaps Lake Baikal), after which he would soon arrive in China. The Nganasan, wild reindeer hunters and fishermen of the Yenisey estuary, traveled in both summer and winter over the Taimyr Peninsula tundra. During the short summers, they used small open skin boats (circa 4.5 by 0.45 by 0.3 meters) for hunting duck on lakes and spearing reindeer at water crossings, as documented by Russian scholars Yuri Simchenko (1976a,b) and Andrey A. Popov (1964b).

Our study leads us to believe that in early history, a skin boat zone existed from the Barents Sea to the Anadyr River in Chukotka in which local peoples shared both boat technology and similar names for boats with one another. This zone included the regions inhabited by the Nenets,

Table 2

Selected Measured Skin Boats and Kayaks in Northern Eurasia

Arranged by Ethnic Group and Region

Dimensions (overall length, beam, and depth) are given in meters and were converted from the measurements given in the original sources.

Northern Europe: North, Barents, and White Seas

Ethnic Group	Boat Type	Region	Length	Beam	Depth	Source
Nenets Samoyed	Decked double-seater kayak	Novaya Zemlya	4.6 to 4.9	0.76	No data	de La Martinière 1706: 227–29
Nenets Samoyed	Canvas- or skin-covered open skin boat	Bolvanski Noss, Vaigach Island	2.1	No data	No data	Jackson 1895 (see chapter 5, page 97, on canvas vs. skin issue)

Western and Central Siberia: Ob and Yenisey River Basins

Ethnic Group	Boat Type	Region	Length	Beam	Depth	Source
Khanty or Nenets	Decked wood and skin kayak	Ob River estuary	4.0	0.7	No data	Belyavsky 1833: 258–59, dimensions estimated from illustration
Nenets Samoyed	Open boat with aluminum frame and canvas cover	Yamal Peninsula	2.25	1.0	No data	Shutikhin 2008, dimensions estimated from photograph
Nganasan Samoyed	Open skin boat	Taimyr Peninsula	4.5	0.45	0.3	Simchenko 1976b: 141, measurements and drawing
Chunya Evenk	Half-decked canoe-kayak	Ust-Uchami, Lower Tunguska River	Ca. 5.0	0.7	0.3	Naumov 1927, dimensions estimated from photographs

Northeastern Siberia: Lower Lena River and Chukotka

Ethnic Group	Boat Type	Region	Length	Beam	Depth	Source
Yukagir	"Two-horned" kayak	Eastern Lena sea coast	Circa 2.5	0.6	0.3	Georgi 1776b: 271, dimensions estimated from drawing
Old Bering Sea Eskimo	Walrus ivory model of open skin boat or kayak	Ekven site, East Cape, Chukotka	0.14	No data	No data	W. Fitzhugh and Crowell 1988: fig. 135; Museum of Anthropology and Ethnology, Kunstkamera, St. Petersburg, 6479/11-407; Arutiunov and Sergeev 2006: pl. 48
Old Bering Sea Eskimo	Walrus ivory model of open skin boat or kayak	Ekven site, East Cape, Chukotka	4.3	0.55	0.22	Golden 2007, reconstruction based on model
Siberian Eskimo (Yupik)	Open skin boat (angyapik)	Bering Sea	11.0 to 11.5	1.5 to 2.0	No data	Antropova 1961: 128
Chukchi	Sea kayak	Chukotka	4.63	0.53	0.26	Zimmerly 1986: fig. 10; Nordenskiöld Swedish Ethnological Museum, Stockholm, 1880.4.1255; measured and drawn in Zimmerly 2010
Chukchi	River kayak	Chukotka	4.9	0.49	0.24	Zimmerly 1986: fig. 11 (REM 2083-61a)
Chukchi	Open hunting boat	Chukotka	6.1	2.3	No data	Nefedkin 2003: 78–79
Chukchi	Open skin boat	Chukotka	10.7	1.4	0.8	Bogoras 1904–09: 127
Siberian Yupik	Open skin boat (angyapik)	St. Lawrence Island	4.6	1.3	No data	Braund 1988: 79, 87

Eastern Siberia: Kamchatka, Okhotsk Sea Coast, and Sakhalin Island

Ethnic Group	Boat Type	Region	Length	Beam	Depth	Source
Kerek	Open skin boat	Oljutorskij	4.5	2.0	0.5	Pälsi dimensions estimated from his 1917 photograph
Koryak	Open skin boat	Penzhina Bay (Kuel); Okhotsk, Kamchatka	9.0	2.5	No data	Jochelson 1908: 537, boat measured in field

(continued)

Ethnic Group	Boat Type	Region	Length	Beam	Depth	Source
Koryak	Decked kayak	Penzhina Bay	2.69	0.75	0.28	Jochelson 1908: 539; AMNH 70/3358 was traded to Museum of Anthropology and Ethnology, Kunstkamera, St. Petersburg, 956-49; Antropova 1961: 128; Zimmerly 1986
Koryak, Kushi/Ainu (reassigned as Koniag/Aleut)	Illustration of decked double kayak	Penzhina Bay	No data	No data	No data	Nishimura 1931: 101, pl. 19, fig. 8.22 (Otsuki drawing), fig. 8.23 (Utagawa painting)
Itelmen	Open skin boat	Kamchatka	< 13.0	No data	No data	Steller 2003: dimensions estimated from frontispiece
Itelmen	Open skin boat	Kamchatka	< 12.0	No data	No data	Dittmar 1890a,b
Even, Sakha, or Aleut	Open skin boat	Cape Ayan, Russian port	10.0	2.7	No data	Middendorff 1875: 1354–56
Even	Decked kayak	Cape Ayan	2.74	0.7	No data	Tronson 1859: 124–26, kayak measured in situ
Nivkh or Ainu	Open skin boat	Sakhalin Island	6.0 to 8.0	1.5 to 2.0	No data	Nishimura 1931: 236, fig. 60, dimensions estimated from photograph

Enets, Nganasan, and Yukagir and covered some 120 degrees longitude. The Nenets, Sihirtia, and Mansi peoples, all of whom lived along the Barents Sea coast, may have provided connections between the Western Scandinavian pre-Saami skin boat users, while the Yukagir east of Taimyr carried this connection to the Siberian Eskimo and the Pacific tribes as far south as the Sea of Okhotsk.

Evidence for skin boat use by the Enets and Nganasan, like the case for skin boats in the Russian Far East around the Sea of Okhotsk, the Kuril Islands, and the southern Kamchatka Peninsula, is scant compared to the rich records that exist for such use on the Chukchi Peninsula and in the Bering Strait region. In the latter area, people used skin boats and kayaks year-round to hunt sea mammals, ducks, and seabirds and to travel for trade, migration, and war. Their open skin boats, called *baidara* by the Russians, are best known among the Siberian Yupik (who called them angyapit), the Chukchi, and the Koryak, all of whom were skillful seafarers and marine mammal hunters (they are discussed at length in chapter 8). According to Antropova's (1961) classification, Siberian Yupik and Chukchi open skin boats were identical, while the Koryak boats had a different design and construction. Building a large open skin boat or kayak in the treeless tundra required lengthy preparation, including procuring wood for the frame and skins for the cover and gaining the cooperation of several builders and skin sewers.

Furthermore, skin boats needed special care and maintenance on long trips: they had to be dried nearly every day, and their skins and lashings needed constant adjustment and immediate repair when they were torn or punctured.

The close connection between the Siberian Yupik and the Chukchi since the 1600s may have resulted in transfer of Eskimo kayak and open skin boat designs to the Chukchi. Although the Siberian Eskimo ceased building kayaks in the late 1800s and switched exclusively to the large open angyapit, Chukchi inland and maritime groups continued to use kayaks for hunting on rivers and lakes into the early 20th century. Compared to the longer and more slender Chukchi and Eskimo type, the Koryak kayak was short and wide (see figs. 8.17, 18, pages 175–176); it survived as a hunting boat in Penzhina Bay, in the northern Sea of Okhotsk, until the 1920s. The Tungus-Even (or Lamut) people adopted this kayak, as well as the open Koryak skin boat, when they migrated into Koryak lands on the Okhotsk coast. In all, only a few Chukchi and Koryak kayaks have survived in museums, but Siberian Eskimo kayaks are missing from museums.

Another maritime culture, the Itelmen (or Kamchadal) of Kamchatka, employed open skin boats of both the baidar and kayak types. Like the Yukagir, they have a long history in a large and rich land, but introduced diseases and attacks by other Native groups and Russians entering their lands decimated them. The Itelmen used large skin boats for sea hunting and fishing until the 1800s, and we have some knowledge of their decked kayaks, which they might have shared with the Kushi (Kuril Ainu) and possibly the Hokkaido Ainu as well. The Nivkh, residing on the Sea of Okhotsk coast and Sakhalin Island, were probably also part of this skin boat maritime hunting culture, but they stopped using such craft before they could be documented. A photograph taken on southern Sakhalin Island, then in Japanese hands, shows what may be two large open skin boats (Nishimura 1931: fig. 60; see also our chapter 9 and fig. 9.2, page 188), but their construction details are not clear enough to describe or compare to other examples.

A drawing of a two-horned Yukagir decked skin kayak appears in a book from the 1700s (Georgi 1776b; see also our fig. 7.1, page 137), but it has escaped notice by previous boat researchers and has never appeared in the canoe literature. This kayak, from east of the Lena delta, looks similar to a miniature ivory Eskimo-Chukchi kayak model excavated from a circa 500 CE Old Bering Sea–culture site at Ekven, on Chukotka's East Cape. The model's gunwales protrude from both its bow and its stern (see fig. 8.11, page 168). The form of the two-horned Yukagir boat suggests continuities with this ancient Eskimo-Chukchi boat, and its horns are a prominent feature of modern angyapik/umiak construction as well.

Beyond the sea coast, the Evenk and Mongol peoples had a skin boat culture as well. Skin boats have been documented in the lower Yenisey and upper Lena basins (see chapters 4 and 5), and people used coracle-type skin boats for crossing rivers in Amur-Manchuria and northern Mongolia (see fig. 9.21, page 211). Most interesting from an evolutionary perspective is the skin boat type we call a canoe-kayak, which has a self-supporting structure and fore and aft decks. It was known among the Chunya Evenk people who resided between the Angara and Stony Tunguska rivers (see figs. 6.5–6.6, page 128); their version was constructed with thin, closely spaced stringers and ribs and was partially decked with reindeer skins or birch bark. The Chunya Evenk people may have originally come to this area from the Lena region, but a similar construction is seen in the Amur II type canoe, which also has bow and stern half decks covered with deerskins or birch bark (see fig. 9.6, page 191).

Manchu or mixed Evenk and Tungus-Mongol heritage could explain the presence of skin boats in the Far East—including, perhaps, the Korean Peninsula and Japan, whose skin boat history is documented in Chinese records. These records and ethnographic and historical accounts (Nishimura 1931) describe the ethnographic and probably ancient use of rafts buoyed by hides filled with straw or wool and air by horse people of the steppe, especially the Mongol and their neighbors (Sinor 1961; see our fig. 9.20, page 210). Similarly, for many years, Central Asian people used open wicker-framed skin boats, much like coracles, to cross rivers, and modern Tibetans still use yak-skin boats to fish and to transport people and freight downstream (see fig. 9.22, page 213). Air-filled skins also supported rafts used to transport cargo down the Yellow River and other large watercourses in China.

Construction and use of these rafts on Far East rivers differed completely from Northern Eurasia's framed skin boat traditions. None of the Far East rafts or coracles could be propelled efficiently, but such craft must have been used throughout the steppe, forest, and tundra zones of Eurasia as the Paleolithic prototype of all of the later, more highly engineered boats, including bark canoes and skin boats. Even in the 20th century, people caught in a pinch and lacking the time or tools to construct a more complex boat made simple coracles out of alder or birch withies covered with a couple of caribou skins to cross swollen rivers. Interesting in this regard is Denis Sinor's (1961: 167) proposal that the word *kayak* may have its origin in a Turkic word for one of these Central Asian wickercraft coracles, although this view has been critiqued as a linguistic version of an urban legend (Fuentes 2010).

In the chapters that follow, we present detailed boat data arranged on a region-by-region basis following our seven main territories (see page 8) and by the main ethnic groups living along particular rivers and coasts. We include information on these peoples' historical backgrounds, the form and construction of their watercraft, and ethnographic and linguistic data, and we make comparisons among and within regions. As readers proceed, they may wish to consult again the boat typologies and technical descriptions offered in this chapter.

CHAPTER 3

Northern Europe

GERMANY, THE SOUTHERN BALTICS, AND FENNOSCANDIA

Our regional survey of bark canoes and skin boats begins in Northern Europe. Ironically, this part of Eurasia—where historical literature extends back to the early Middle Ages, where ethnological collecting began in the 17th century, and where archaeological research has been conducted for more than two centuries—has the scantest bark and skin boat descriptions in the entire subcontinent (McGrail 1998: chs. 7, 10). On the other hand, the area is blessed with a fair number of archaeological finds—more than in other Eurasian regions—because it had larger populations, more economic activity, and a stronger tradition of historical interest than the rest of the subcontinent. Another source of information on the region's ancient boats and their development is petroglyphs, although the images' ambiguity renders them problematic. Do the 6,000 years' worth of rock art in this region actually depict Eskimo-like skin boats—as early researchers, including Gutorm Gjessing (1936, 1944) and A. W. Brøgger and Haakon Shetelig (1951), claimed—or do they simply show animal-prowed expanded dugouts with planks sewn to their upper sides? Scholars have not settled the issue, in large part because of the lack of archaeological evidence (McGrail 1998: 186).

This interpretive problem stems partly from the nature of bark and skin boats—as noted earlier, neither preserves well, and when workers excavating peat bogs or dredging lakeshores and harbors find traces of these materials, they rarely recognize them as boats or historical treasures. If such remains are noted at all, it is often too late for scientific recovery or careful description of them. For this reason, this chapter relies heavily on historical illustrations and chance recoveries, such as the Danish Hjortspring boat (page 50). Even model boats, like those found in ethnographic collections from Central and Eastern Siberia, are largely missing from Eurasia's western regions. Another reason for the absence of physical evidence is that in this region, plank boats began to replace bark canoes and skin boats centuries before the Viking era (circa 700 to 1100 CE). If bark and skin boats persisted here alongside plank ones for many years, as they did in other areas of Eurasia, few of them were recorded.

The Northern European territory covered in this section includes Germany, Denmark, the northern British Isles, and Fennoscandia (map 5). Its central geographic features are the Baltic and North seas and the surrounding coastal lowlands and rivers. Ever since glacial ice departed and humans arrived here some 10,000 to 15,000 years ago, people in this region have depended on small boats for subsistence, trade, migration, and war; this remains the case to a large degree today. This chapter outlines the history of boating traditions and technology among the pre-Viking Norrmen (Northmen) of the southern Baltic and North seas and among the Saami of northern Sweden and Finland.

We also investigate two peculiar ciphers in this region's boating history: the 17th-century appearance of Eskimo kayaks in the northern British Isles (which gave rise to the "Finnmen" misidentification) and an attempt to introduce American Indian–style canoes into 18th-century Finnish Sweden.

PRE-VIKING WOOD AND SKIN BOATS IN GERMANY AND SOUTHERN SWEDEN

Our discussion of the boats of the pre-Viking Germans, or Norrmen, focuses mainly on the period from 500 BCE to 500 CE. Early in this era, the European climate cooled, forcing Germanic agricultural societies to withdraw from their northernmost farms in Southern Scandinavia. When the climate later warmed, the agricultural frontier expanded northward again, first to Jutland and islands in modern Denmark and then to Skåne, on the Swedish mainland (Elert 1997). By 500 CE, the famous lapstrake Viking wooden boat, built with

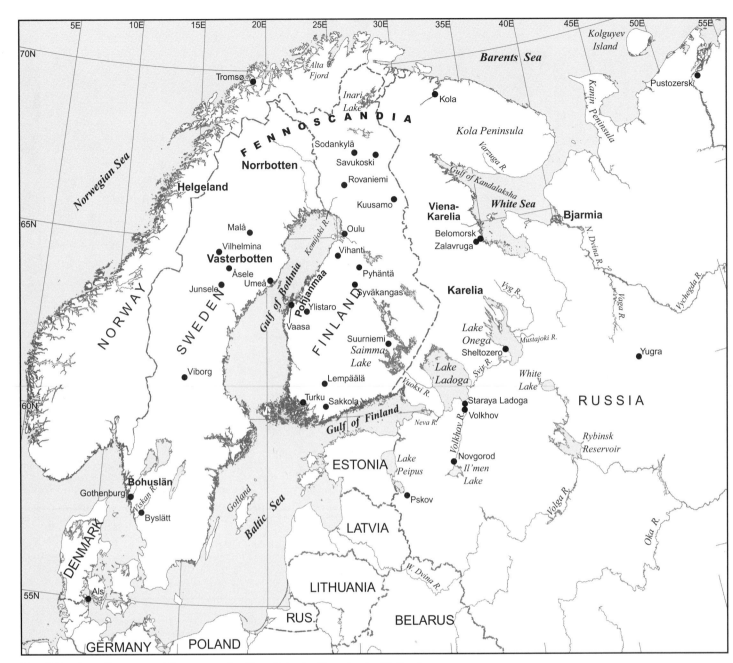

Map 5. Northern Europe and Fennoscandia. (Dan Cole, Smithsonian Institution)

overlapping planks, had been developed, but it still lacked a sail (Christensen 2000). In the 700s CE, Norrmen started raiding the European and British coasts, robbing towns and monasteries; in the following centuries, they sailed across the North Atlantic, reaching Iceland in the 870s and Greenland and America between 985 and 1000.

As Ole Crumlin-Pedersen (2004) has written, the first expanded log boats appeared in northern Germany, Poland, and Southern Scandinavia around 1 CE. Some had extra planking nailed to a single-log bottom, and Crumlin-Pedersen assumes that these became the prototypes for later Viking boats and ships (see Boehmer 1891 for an early history of naval boat development). Expanded log boats must have originated earlier on the European mainland, and they eventually replaced bark and skin boats in Northern Europe, just as they did in Saami lands, in Karelia, in areas west of the Ural Mountains, and, after the 1700s, in much of Western and Eastern Siberia.

One of the oldest wooden-plank boats known from archaeological excavations in Northern Europe is the 18-meter-long Iron Age war canoe (see below) that was excavated in 1921 and 1922 from Hjortspring, a bog in southern Denmark, and dated to 350 BCE (Crumlin-Pedersen and Trakadas 2003; Crumlin-Pedersen 2010: 28–31, 63–64). Built with thin, overlapping, sewn planks on a flat and keelless plank bottom, this slender boat continued the Bronze Age tradition of having separate keel and gunwale extensions (horns or beaks) at the bow and stern, details that are seen prominently in Bronze Age rock carvings. A cache of weapons came with the boat, perhaps indicating it was part of a sacrificial war offering, but it showed no sign of a bark or skin covering.

Skin Boats from the Elbe and Jutland

Johann (John) Reinhold Forster (1729–98) studied early northern sea explorers and is one of the sources on the Germanic Norrmen. A German scientist with English roots who was the naturalist for Captain James Cook's 1772–75 expeditions, Forster later became a professor of natural history, mineralogy, and medicine at the University of Halle in Germany and was recognized as one of the most able natural scientists in Europe. His encounters with maritime peoples around the world provided background for his study of northern people and watercraft, which was published in German in 1784. He wrote of the Norrmen: "The oldest boats that served the Nordic peoples were either large log dugouts or were made from basketwork covered with leather" (1784: 66) and noted:

> Similar skin-covered boats made of basketwork are called in England *coracles*, which are still in use in the Flüssen Sea and the River Severin; in Ireland they are called *curachs*. Julius Caesar noted their use among the British people, and his armies used them also.... The Eskimo and Greenlanders, like the Kamchadal, have boats constructed from some knees and stems [*Bögen*], made of wood and fish [whale] bones, and covered with the skin of sea animals, and the latter call them *baidars*. The Greeks and Romans even had in service some boats made of wickerwork covered with skins, which they took on the longer ships and called χαζαβια and in Latin *carabos*. It is from these craft that Russians probably took the name of their boats, which they called the *korabl'*. That the boats of the Saxon

pirates were made of leather is mentioned in "The Panegyric [eulogy] of Avitus" (Flavius Maccilius Eparchius *Avitus*, emperor of the Western Roman Empire, who died in 456) that includes a poem by Sidonius to this effect:

Quin & Aremoricus piratam Saxona tractus
Spirabat, cui pelle salum sulcare Britannum
Ludus, & assuto glaucum mare findere lembo. (1784: 66, n. 1)

[The Aremorican region too expected the Saxon pirate,
Who deems it but sport to furrow the British waters with hides,
Cleaving the blue sea in a stitched boat.] (Sidonius *Carmina* 7.369–371; W. Anderson 1936: 151)

Forster also included notes on more substantial vessels:

> Longer boats were called *chiule*, *cyule*, *ceol*, from which the German boats got their *Schifs-Kiel* [boat keel] and the English their *keelson*. . . . Those two types of boats [log boats and skin boats] gave the Nordic people their Viking expeditions. . . . Thus, as mentioned by Tacitus, the fleets of Sviones [*Svionen*] sailed from Gotland to Finland, Estonia, and Kurland. As Ottar [Othere] described, the Norrmen of Norway followed the coast of their homeland and also around [Norway's] North Cape until they reached the Kven Sea [*Kwen-See*] and the Dvina River, where the Bjarmians lived. The Danish followed the coast of the Sound of England (*die Britische Meerenge,* or English Channel) and came finally to Britain itself. (1784: 66–67)

The French doctor Jacques-Henri Bernardin de Saint-Pierre—another scientist interested in boats—referred to the Swedish military officer and historian Philip Johann Stralenberg, who wrote in 1738 of trade contacts with Asia, which he called India, and who also discussed skin boat travel in northern Germany at the time of the Romans: "The route was known to the Indians even in the time of the Romans, for Cornelius Nepos [circa 100–24 BCE] relates that a King of Suevi gave presents to Metellus Celer of two Indians, who had been thrown by the stress of weather, with their leather canoe, on the coast adjacent to the mouth of the

Elbe" (Saint-Pierre 1836: 179–80). In a history published in Königsberg (now Kaliningrad) in 1582, Maciej Stryjkowski referred to boats, made in what is now Lithuania, of *skór* (Polish: leather), which he described as coming from *zubrowych* (Polish: European bison) (quoted in Łuczynski 1986).

Perhaps the most analytical writer on boats was the Austrian Rudolf Trebitsch, who in 1912 wrote a survey and history of skin boats around the globe. His classification (see chapter 2) has a wide geographic focus, but a large part covers Western Europe. Trebitsch used Roman and later material, including illustrations of skin boats in England, Scotland, Ireland, France, and Spain and along the Danube River. He concluded that the construction of the coracle skin boat had much in common with the Eskimo kayak, but all information pointed to the fact that the English, Scottish, and Irish coracle had a Celtic origin, while in Wales, oral history tied it to the Danube (Trebitsch 1912: 166–68).

Caesar and Pliny wrote that the Angles, Saxons, and Jutes made boats with wicker frames covered with leather (see McGrail 1998: 178). Scholars who studied skin boats, such as M. Hörnes and H. Schnepper, noted that "the people of Saxony made pirating expeditions to Gallic coasts in the 4th century, but those [wicker, i.e., skin-covered] boats were used together with wooden log boats [*Kähnen*]" (1908: 11). Trebitsch thought the German skin boat tradition had Germanic-Baltic rather than Danubian roots, citing a reference to Gaius Sollius Sidonius Apollinaris in Lyon (430–90 CE) that said the pirates of Saxony (northern Germany) had ventured into the "British Sea"—the English Channel—with skin boats. Trebitsch also cited the French historian François de Mézeray, who noted in 1720 that skin boats were used in France and Germany for long journeys during the time of Julius Caesar. Around 600, Isidore, the bishop of Spain, wrote in his *Origines* (also called *Etymologiae*; book 19, ch. 1) that pirates were plaguing Germany: "The[ir] boat is made of twigs and covered with raw leather, a kind of vessel used by German pirates at the coasts of the oceans or in wetlands."

Trebitsch concluded, "As we can see from all this early information, there is a strong probability that skin boats existed in Germany itself. It also seems clear from the sources that Celtic people and related peoples, in both prehistory and the Middle Ages, built skin boats of type 1 (round and oval boats) and type 2 (long boat-shaped vessels)" (1912: 168). As for their origins, Trebitsch believed skin boats had arrived in Northern Europe in ancient times from somewhere else; although he had no specific information on Northmen/Norrmen skin boats in Scandinavia, he surmised they would

have been similar to those used by the Saxon peoples in northern Germany, near Denmark.

The Hjortspring Boat from Jutland

The Hjortspring boat, dating to 350 BCE, was excavated in 1921–22 in Hjortspring Mose, on the island of Als in southern Denmark (figs. 3.1–3.2). It is double-ended, has two-horned or bifurcated bow and stern extensions, and is made of large lime-wood planks sewn to a central plank that may have started out as a flattened log, reinforced by an internal rib structure lashed to the planks by means of raised cleats that extend from the planks. Its size is considerable: the boat is estimated to have been 18.6 to 19.6 meters in length, 2.04 meters in beam, and 0.705 meters in height amidships. A replica was built and launched in June 1999 (Crumlin-Pedersen 2010); the modern construction, built with side planks, proved the original had been a serviceable craft, even in heavy weather.

According to Ole Crumlin-Pedersen (2010), the Hjortspring boat was not a local product: it and the weapons found with it were brought here by an invading army of some 100 men, identity unknown, who attacked the residents of Als in the 4th century BCE. Images of the same type of boat in Scandinavian and Karelian bronze objects and rock carvings can be traced back to the Bronze Age. Perhaps the Hjortspring find was the result of a failed attack on Denmark by Northern Germany river tribes.

The Hjortspring boat is truly transitional between earlier Bronze Age boats and the Late Iron Age Viking boats that would emerge 800 years later. It retains a modified log bottom and the bifurcated stems so prominent in Bronze Age rock art while utilizing an early form of sewn clinker construction reinforced by rib framing sewn to the bottom planks. Some have suggested that its prototype might have been a frame boat with side-strake planks covered with leather, such as seen in Inuit umiaks (Crumlin-Pedersen 2010: 63). In an online discussion [*no longer available—Ed.*] about Hjortspring, Knud Valbjørn commented on the use of leather or wood in Bronze Age boats, noting that it would be technologically possible to make a leather-covered Hjortspring vessel with longitudinal elements continuing outboard, like those seen in rock carvings (Kaul 2003). Using hide rather than plank construction and adding stringers to reinforce its sides would have made the Hjortspring boat much lighter but perhaps less seaworthy. Many Scandinavian rock art boat images strongly resemble Inuit skin boats, but for a 19-meter-long boat like the Hjortspring

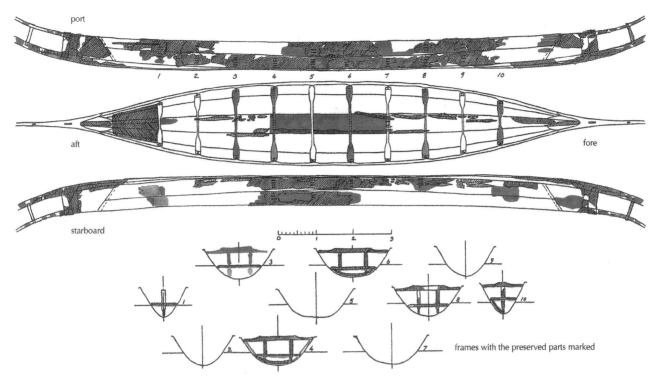

Fig. 3.1. Construction plan of the Iron Age Hjortspring planked boat, which was excavated in Jutland, Denmark, in 1921–22. Its bifurcated bow and stern follow the style seen in Fennoscandian Bronze and Early Iron Age rock art. Some experts believe such "two-horned" boats were covered with skins. (From Crumlin-Pedersen 2010: fig. 2.57, used with permission)

craft, lightness would not have been an advantage, because ballast would have been needed for stability. As we shall see in later pages, this discussion of skin versus wood has been a hot topic in Scandinavian boat history since the early 20th century. Hjortspring shows that—at least in Southern Scandinavia—boatbuilders had iron tools and were committed to wood by 500 BCE.

Fig. 3.2. Archaeological recovery of the remains of the Hjortspring boat guided the reconstruction of this model. (From Crumlin-Pedersen 2010: fig. 2.65, used with permission)

The Byslätt Elm-Bark Canoe

Christer Westerdahl (1985a), reporting on sewn boats in Nordic countries, commented on finds of Saami origin from north-central and northern Sweden. Besides the Saami boat in Lapland (see page 59), the most interesting of these was an Iron Age elm-bark canoe discovered in 1934 during a bridge excavation in the town of Byslätt, on the Viskan River in southwestern Sweden, near Gothenburg (Eskerød 1956). Yet its date (900 to 800 BCE) and location point more to a Germanic population than to the Saami. Even many decades after its discovery, according to Westerdahl, the Byslätt boat remains one of the oldest bark boats known from Europe:

> Byslätt (Viskan River, Istorp, parish of Horred, Västergötland, Sweden): A boat find, circa 3–5 meters long, of elm tree bark, with slender ribs of hazel branches with fragments of leather, was found in a riverbank in 1934. Although holes in the bark exist, no sewing is definitely recorded. The ribs were iron-nailed to the bark. This appears to be the only preserved bark boat of Europe, although the remains have not been studied and/or published in any way.

According to a geological estimation, it is possibly of Iron Age date, but hardly later. Västergötland is the only region of Scandinavia, except the Saami North, where a source, in this case a law, mentions a most probably sewn boat type, the *tagbaenda*, as late as the 13th century. Sewn birch-bark coffins have also been documented in early churchyards in this region. (1985b: 130)

J. Skamby Madsen and Kjeld Hansen (1981) demonstrated that the use of bark in Scandinavian countries goes back to the Mesolithic Maglemose culture (circa 9000 to 6000 BCE) and that bark has been used for domestic purposes at least since that time. Pine, birch, and linden bark served as coverings and insulation on the floors of houses and were used in household utensils. Until the late 1900s, Saami people in Northern Scandinavia continued to use birch bark in similar ways. At Denmark's Mullerup site, a Maglemose-culture site in western Zealand, archaeologists found rolls of birch bark stored for later use. In the 1990s, while conducting archaeological surveys in Yamal, Western Siberia, WWF found rolls of birch bark cached at abandoned 20th-century Nenets reindeer herder sites, a testament to the continued 20th-century use of this material, in this case for tent covers.

Ethnographies and modern-day craft manufacturing illustrate the importance of bark in making a variety of objects in addition to boats and houses. In northern regions, birch bark is preferred because of its lightness, flexibility, and layered, waterproof quality. But linden, aspen, and elm are also found in contemporary and archaeological contexts. Linden bark seems to have been the next best choice after birch bark; for example, among the goods buried in a woman's grave at the Egtved Middle Bronze Age (circa 1400 BCE) site in Denmark were a small box made of linden bark and a small pouch of birch bark sewn with linden bast fiber. Iron Age graves frequently contain birch-bark articles and remnants, too. In Valsgärde, Uppland, Sweden, in a pre–Viking period Vendel boat grave (a burial with a body placed in a boat or boatlike structure) dated to the Late Iron Age (600 to 800 CE), part of the boat's stern was covered with several birch-bark sheets sewn together and decorated with geometric forms. Most boat historians believe that birch-bark canoes are older than dugout log boats because birch bark is easy to peel off trees without using specialized stone tools such as axes and gouges, which are required for making dugouts or plank boats (see fig. 0.7, page 9). The most primitive bark canoe may have been simply a large sheet of bark, with its sides turned up and its ends folded or sewn and sealed with spruce or birch gum, lashed to strengthening gunwales. Covering a canoe is only slightly more complicated than making a simple bark box, grave shroud, or storage container.

Authors such as Ole Crumlin-Pedersen (2010) and Peter Rowley-Conwy (2017) have written that bark canoes are missing from the archaeological record because they were not preserved; the lonely European elm-bark canoe from Byslätt is a rarity. Even so, many parts of that canoe are missing, and thus its construction is difficult to determine. However, it quite likely followed principles used in North American Indian bark canoes because the basic principles for making birch-bark canoes are similar worldwide, although size, style, and finishing details vary among regions and cultures. When the Byslätt canoe was first found, pollen analysis suggested the boat dated between 700 BCE and 1000 CE, spanning the Late Bronze to the Viking Iron ages. Because of its fragmented state and imprecise dating, it was not possible to connect the canoe to any other boats or cultures. In January 2012, the Byslätt canoe surfaced again in a study by Staffan von Arbin, a maritime archaeologist at Sweden's Bohuslän Museum. Based on a late Bronze Age radiocarbon date calibrated to calendar years (980–810 BCE) on a sample of the bark, he found that the boat is older than was believed in the 1930s (Arbin 2012). Other than a few dugout canoes, other boat finds from this early period do not exist in Scandinavia, and until this evidence appeared, all discussion about Bronze Age vessels in the region had been based on petroglyph images carved into rock faces. A master's thesis by Maria Lindberg (2012) and a article by von Arbin and Lindberg (2017) also document the new study.

THE SCOTTISH "FINNMEN": INUIT KAYAKERS OF MISTAKEN IDENTITY

A new kind of vessel, the skin kayak, suddenly appeared in Western European waters in the 1680s: people called Finnmen (although they actually were not from Finland) were seen paddling near the Scottish coast and around the shores of the Orkney Islands. Orkney's seasoned mariners were astonished to discover that the kayakers were able to paddle in rough North Sea weather with apparent ease, staying completely dry within parkas fastened to their boats' cockpits, and that they could roll their kayaks over when they met large waves. In 1682, one of these small boats and its paddler were observed near the southern end of the isle of Eday. Another kayaking Finnman was seen and captured by shoresmen near the Aberdeenshire coast in 1688. He died soon after he was brought to shore, but his kayak was collected by the Anthropological Museum at Marischal College, University of Aberdeen (see fig. 3.3; MacRitchie 1912; Reid 1912). Soon Finnmen and their kayaks were reported in other locations in Orkney, as written testimony by Rev. John Brand recorded in 1701:

> There are frequently *Fin-men* seen here upon the Coasts, as one about a year ago on *Stronsa*, and another within these few months on *Westra*, a Gentleman with many others in the Isle looking on him nigh to the shore, but when any endeavour to apprehend them, they flee away most swiftly. It is very strange that one Man sitting in his little Boat should come some hundreds of Leagues from their own Coasts, as they reckon *Finland* to be from *Orkney*. It may be thought wonderful how they live all that time and are able to keep at sea so long. His boat is made of seal skins, or some kind of leather; he also hath a coat of leather upon him, and he sitteth in the middle of his boat, with a little oar in his hand, fishing with his lines. And when in a storm he seeth the high surge of a wave approaching, he hath a way of sinking his boat till the wave passes over, lest thereby he should be overturned. The Fishers here observe that these *Finmen* or *Finland-Men*, by their coming, drive away the Fishes from the Coasts. One of their Boats is kept as a rarity in the Physicians Hall at Edinburgh. (Quoted in MacRitchie 1890: 354)

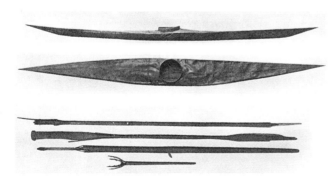

Fig. 3.3. R. W. Reid described and illustrated a Greenland or Labrador Inuit kayak and associated hunting gear in Scotland's Aberdeen Museum. This and similar kayaks and "Finnmen" finds from the 17th century had been attributed to mythological apparitions appearing in the British Isles from the European Arctic. (From Reid 1912: figs. 2, 4)

A solution to the Finnmen fantasy began to take shape in the early 1700s. Before that point, Vikings, mapmakers, and many others believed that Greenland was part of the Eurasian continent. The Russian island of Novaya Zemlya and Norse Greenland were thought to be connected to a "North Pole Land" that arced from Europe to North America. A common belief—probably stimulated by Norse tales of Icelandic volcanism—held that the Arctic Ocean had sunken islands, some of which disappeared in the 1600s; this was possibly a reference to Icelandic volcanism. Nordic folktales and legends of those days recounted that the Sihirtia, the ancient maritime-adapted people of the Kara Sea, lived on such islands. These stories were reinforced by legends about selkies (silkies), which lived as seals in the ocean but turned into humans—frequently female—when they emerged on land.

Scholars were skeptical about the possibility of Northern European Arctic Ocean kayakers reaching the Scotland coast and believed these people must have originated in Greenland, as no one previously had seen skin boats and their paddlers in Northern Europe. This assumption is not exactly correct, because Stephen Burrough and other explorers of the Barents and Kara Sea coasts encountered skin boats in the mid-16th century, as we report in chapter 4.

The major proponent of the Arctic Ocean kayak theory was David MacRitchie, a Scottish scientist who believed the Finnmen came from the European polar ocean coast and wrote several papers connecting them to the early Norse population of Orkney. His theory gained support in the 20th century when Chernetsov's excavations in 1928–30 brought to light archaeological evidence of walrus hunters on Russia's Yamal Peninsula (see the section "The Sihirtia and the Pechora Chud" in chapter 4). But there was still an absence of convincing physical evidence of Finnmen in Arctic Europe or of any extant survivals in Northern Europe of a kayak similar to the Scottish and Orkney boats.

The strongest early critique of the European Finnmen idea came from Ian Whitaker (1954, 1977), who demonstrated conclusively that the Aberdeen kayak (see below) was a Greenland Inuit boat. After studying other recorded kayaks in Europe dating to the early 1600s, he concluded that all of them had originated in Greenland or Labrador, where the boats and their paddlers were captured by whalers and transported to Europe to be sold or publicly exhibited in parks and zoos. Whitaker noted that there was no record of skin boats in those days in Norway, but he was unaware that farther east, in Russian territory, skin boat hunters had been seen in the Barents Sea.

European whalers—principally Dutch—arrived at Greenland, Labrador, and Baffin Island in the 1600s, and it was common for their captains to capture Inuit, along with their kayaks and weapons, as trophies to sell or exhibit back home. Inuit, along with "wild" Africans, were presented to European courts and to the public in zoolike contexts that showed their clothing and their boating and hunting skills. In these and other zoos, real Finnmen—meaning Saami people from Lapland—were also shown, along with their children, skin tents, and reindeer.

The Dutch anthropologist Gert Nooter (1971), like Whitaker, documented Finnmen cases and conclusively affirmed these people's 17th-century Greenland origin and that their independent appearance in the northern British Isles occurred when individual Inuit were put overboard in their kayaks as the whaling ships approached land. Nooter demonstrated that trafficking in Inuit (then known as Eskimo) and their kayaks was a lucrative side business for the whalers. Eventually the trade was outlawed; for instance, in the Netherlands, a decree was issued in 1720 prohibiting whalers from kidnapping Eskimo and enslaving other people. Faced with stiff penalties, some who continued the practice began to have second thoughts about their human cargo as they approached land, and so they set their captives overboard in their kayaks to fend for themselves. Some drowned and washed ashore, while others survived with their kayaks, creating a sensation when they reached land in Orkney or northern Scotland.

A few people have questioned this Greenland-release theory on the basis of the use of red (Scottish) pine for implements and boat parts in the Aberdeen kayak and of the usual geographic occurrence of the kayaks' appearance in Orkney. However, these issues are easily dispensed with, as it is not clear whether the "redwood" used in this kayak has been subjected to modern techniques of species identification or whether R. W. Reid used this term to refer simply to a conifer or to a specific species (see the "Aberdeen 'Finnman' Kayak" sidebar). Conifer is available as driftwood throughout the Arctic, and Northern European and Russian timber—usually Siberian larch—occurs as driftwood in Canada and Greenland, delivered there by the trans-Arctic drift (Mysak 2001; Hellmann et al. 2013). Furthermore, the location of the Finnmen finds in Orkney is easily explained by the fact that Orkney was a customary landfall for Dutch whalers returning from Greenland.

An interesting twist in this story came with the discovery of a 4,000-year-old Paleo-Eskimo microblade core in Iceland (Smith 1995: 320–21). Microblades, small but diagnostic stone artifacts, occur in abundance in ancient Greenland Eskimo cultures and raised the possibility that Paleo-Inuit kayakers reached Iceland, a distance of some 320 kilometers from the eastern coast of Greenland. Such a skin boat voyage could have been possible, especially if assisted by pack ice, but there would have been hundreds of miles of ocean to cross east of Iceland. Stormy seas and landmasses separated by 500 to 800 kilometers would have made such an unsupported voyage in a one-person skin-covered kayak almost impossible. Quite apart from being unable to hold sufficient quantities of food and water, small skin boats without wooden undersheathing would be incapable of staying afloat for the weeks required to cross these distances. The seal or walrus hides of kayaks and umiaks, even when greased, become waterlogged after one or two days and begin to stretch and leak. The only period that such a voyage in a skin boat could have been made would have been the Ice Age, when pack ice existed around the entire North Atlantic rim, onto which people could have hauled their boats to dry them or to rest or weather a storm, as the Eskimo routinely did on long voyages in the Bering and Chukchi seas.

Another argument against Eskimo trans-Atlantic voyaging is the absence of umiaks in the Scotland accounts. These larger vessels, used by all Eskimo groups, would have been the more likely vehicles for long, exploratory Inuit voyages, but none has been found in intermediate locations such as Iceland, the Faeroe Islands, or Svalbard. Finally, none of the skin boats known from the northern British Isles or English Channel Low Countries is linked by style, features, or exploring expeditions to the Barents or White seas. Only a single case is known of a White or Barents Sea skin boat and paddlers appearing in Europe: a group was presented to the Danish court in 1653 (de La Martinière 1706), but these people and their craft have never been described in detail (see chapter 4), as R. W. Reid did for the Greenland kayak in Aberdeen.

The Aberdeen "Finnman" Kayak

This kayak is well known because of papers written by David MacRitchie in 1890 and 1912 and because he asked R. W. Reid, a professor of anatomy and curator at the University of Aberdeen's Anthropological Museum, to document its construction and the tools and weapons found with it. Excerpts from Reid's "Description of Kayak Preserved in the Anthropological Museum of the University of Aberdeen" are presented below, and every feature of his description matches Otto

Fabricius's (1962) description of 17th-century Greenlandic Inuit kayaks and hunting equipment:

The general appearance of the *kayak* is well seen in the accompanying illustrations. It measures 5400 mm. (17 ft. 9 in.) in length, 450 mm. (1 ft. 5¾ in.) in its greatest breadth, and 230 mm. (9 1/8 in.) in its greatest depth. It weighs, without implements, 15.4 kilograms (34 pounds). Its bottom is flat . . . [as is] the deck . . . with the exception of the extremities, which are very slightly elevated, and it presents a little behind its middle a nearly circular aperture—manhole—measuring 400 mm. . . .

The kayak is made of four seal skins stretched over a slender framework of wood. . . . Their edges are overlapped and sewed together with strips of tendon in such a way as to produce a neat, smooth, flat, and very strong seam. The only seams in the bottom and sides of the kayak are those which join the skins transversely. . . . The framework is made of pieces of redwood, which average about 27 mm. (1 1/10 in.) in breadth by 19 mm. (19/25 in.) in thickness, and are lashed together by strips of whalebone and hide. . . . With the kayak are a paddle, a spear, a bird-spear, a throwing-stick, and a harpoon. All are made of redwood with bone and ivory mountings. (Reid 1912: 511)

AMERICAN INDIAN BARK CANOE EXPERIMENTS IN SWEDEN AND FINLAND

Peter Kalm (1716–79) was a new professor of economics at Åbo (Turku) Academy in the Swedish eastern province called Finland when, in 1747, the Swedish Royal Academy (SKA) commissioned him to travel to North America to collect information on flora, fauna, and any novelties that might be useful for the Swedish kingdom (Tsubaki 2011). Kalm's travel was funded by the SKA and promoted by his supporter, Carolus Linné (Carl Linnaeus); he had passports to enter the Dutch and French territories in North America and was accompanied by a gardener from the Botanical Garden in Åbo. Kalm was the first trained European natural scientist to study the new American continent, take notes on everything he could, and collect new plants and seeds to be grown in Sweden.

Kalm traveled via London in 1748 and settled in "New Sweden," in Pennsylvania. He remained in North America until 1751, touring widely on the East Coast and in Canada and meeting American learned men, among them Benjamin Franklin. Curious about American Indians, Kalm wrote about their crops and food, their healing methods and medicine, their hunting and fishing, their dwellings, and their material culture, including bark canoes and dugout boats. When he returned to Åbo Academy in 1752, he edited his diaries, which were printed in four volumes around 1755. In 1772, they were translated into English, published in London, and became popular in Europe and North America.

Soon after his return, Kalm and his students began constructing the sort of Indian canoes that he had documented being made in Canada in 1749. One of the American-Canadian canoes he had seen was made of birch bark, the second of white pine bark, and the third of elm bark. Swedish King Adolf Frederick is supposed to have tested one of the birch-bark canoes when he visited Åbo. The canoes were kept in the Botanical Garden, where the newly acquired American plants were being grown. Matti Leikola (2001), a professor of forestry at Helsinki University, has studied Kalm's work and found that Finnish birch (*Betula pendula*) is the tree best suited for canoes, proving to be nearly as good as American birch; he also found that spruce was a good substitute for hickory for the canoe ribs.

One of Kalm's most gifted students was Anders (Antti) Chydenius (1729–1803), who wrote a dissertation on American birch-bark canoes (Hyttinen 2001). When "Den Amerikanska Näverbåten" (American Bark Canoes) was published in 1753 (fig. 3.4a–b), the small booklet became Europe's first manual on constructing birch-bark canoes. In it, Chydenius advised Finnish peasants—including hunters and fishermen on the frontier—to build birch-bark boats to cross rivers or lakes because they were easier and faster to make than expanded log boats. Nevertheless, despite these efforts, the American bark canoe never became popular in Finland, primarily because expanded log boats were common and more sturdy, while on the coast the more durable lapstrake boat was by this time the favorite choice.

Instructions for Finnish Bark Boat Builders

In his introduction to "Den Amerikanska Näverbåten" (American Bark Canoes; 1753), Anders Chydenius described the Native American method of constructing a birch-bark canoe, which he learned from his professor Peter Kalm's studies in North America. We include excerpts here because this method is similar to that used by Eurasian canoe builders but is not well described in Eurasian sources. (See Adney and Chapelle 1964: 212–18 for a more complete construction guide.)

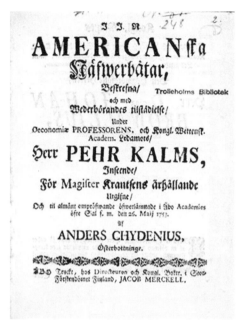

Fig. 3.4. Anders (Antti) Chydenius and his professor, Peter Kalm, promoted North American bark canoes in Finland, and they built several demonstration canoes during Chydenius's university years. *Chydenius's* master's thesis, "American Bark Canoes," presented to Åbo Academy in 1753 and later published as a book, was the first academic canoe publication to appear in Nordic countries. (From Hyttinen 2001; courtesy Pertti Hyttinen, Jyväskylä University / Kokkola University Consortium Chydenius)

They [Native Americans] make their boats from the bark of cedar or birch trees, which are huge there, and stitch them handily together . . . and when they come to some narrow bays or rivers which they want to cross, they launch the boats in the water and travel wherever they want. . . . My interest was aroused, and I wanted to know how such boats could be made. . . . The North American Natives have made bark boats from time immemorial. . . .

The bark is loosened from large, branchless trees in sheets as long as the boat is intended to be. . . . The ends of the bark sheets are layered two or sometimes four thick . . . and are sewn together . . . using thin split spruce roots. . . . The bark . . . is put on level ground, the inner part of the bark outward, and then stones are placed on the large sheet in the shape that the boat bottom will take. The ends [of the sheet] are lifted up and stakes are driven into the ground so that the bark sheet takes the shape of the boat, with two narrow ends. Then the sheet is covered inside with thin laths of a tree called *thuya* [white cedar, *Thuja occidentalis*]. . . . The ribs are also made of thuya, usually 3 inches [8 centimeters] wide and ½ inch [1 centimeter] thick, and they are set about 1–2 inches [3–5 centimeters] apart; all of them should reach up to the gunwale, which is made in the following way. . . . Two very thin strips, flat on opposite sides, are cut for both gunwales, and . . . the birch bark [is] folded over the ribs. The ends of the ribs are put between the inwale and the outwale and are shaved down narrow and thinned so as not to keep [the planks] from being lashed together. And then taking the spruce roots mentioned earlier, the inwale and outwale are fastened together by being sewn with stitches one-half inch apart, each stitch penetrating the bark. . . . Then from thuya wood two inches wide and one inch thick, thwarts are made, with their ends a little wider. At the ends of the thwart, three or four holes are drilled so they can be lashed to the gunwales some 24 to 30 inches [61 to 76 centimeters] apart, to keep the boat's shape open. . . . Finally, all the seams in the bottom are smeared with hot pitch or resin to prevent water from penetrating. (Chydenius 1753: 1–6)

Anders Chydenius and the Kemi Bark Canoe

At this point, we can ask an interesting question: did Chydenius know that in the 1750s the Saami were still building bark canoes in Swedish and Finnish Lapland? In his short dissertation, he never referred to any sources other than North American canoes and papers written about them, because the North American bark canoe was his main theme. But it is very likely he knew about Saami bark canoes, as he had grown up in Finnish Lapland. From 1743 to 1746, his father, Jacob Chydenius, was a priest in Kuusamo parish, in northeastern Finland, next to the territory called Kemi Lappmark in Sweden. When Anders was 17, he left Saami territory, as his father was transferred to Gamla Karleby Pastorat, on the western coast of Finland.

Kemi Lappmark consisted of the huge Kemijoki River basin—some 51,000 square kilometers, or one-sixth of modern Finland—and in those days, it was part of Sweden. Its river system extends to Norway and Russia and was easily traveled by boat, via portages, to the White Sea and via Inari Lake—another Saami territory—to the Norwegian coast and Arctic Ocean. Kemi Lappmark may have been the largest Saami territory in all Lapland at that time.

A. J. Sjögren (1828: 79) reported that in 1744, the Kuusamo parish population was a combination of Lapp people and peasant settlers from other regions. However, by 1750, only 13 Saami were still living in Kuusamo; the rest had retreated to Kuolajärvi Lake. According to Tapani Salminen (2003; see also Broadbent 2010), the Saami had disappeared or retreated north from these regions by the end of the 1800s. But during Chydenius's time in Kuusamo parish, several Kemi Saami villages still were engaged in wild reindeer hunting, fishing, and bird hunting (Tengengren 1952). In this respect, their economy resembled that of traditional hunters such as the Mansi in the Urals, the Nganasan and Samoyed in the Ob and northern Yenisey, and the Evenk in Eastern Siberia. All these groups lived from the forest and hunted reindeer or moose as their main occupation. Before Finnish settlers entered western Kemi Lappmark in the late 1500s and started slash-and-burn agriculture, the Kemi Saami knew no trades other than hunting and fishing. They had only a few tame reindeer, which they used to pull sledges. By the end of the 1700s, Finnish settlers had burned most of the Kemi River basin forests, and the Saami had lost both their wildlands and their hunting economy. Sjögren's (1828) study of the Kemi Saami noted that the Karelians (see chapter 4) were also moving north and west in the 1500s and migrated into Saami territory from the east. The White Sea Karelians regularly boated across Finland along its rivers and later engaged in sealing on the Gulf of Bothnia coast. These Kemi Saami were among the last Scandinavians to build bark canoes. We can deduce this from the many paddles found in Kemi Lappmark,

whose dates range from the Stone Age to 1700 CE, when these people's traditional lifestyle came to an end. The size, shape, and lightness of these paddles suggest they were used with small craft such as bark canoes or skin boats.

In Savukoski and Syväkangas, two Younger Stone Age paddles have been recovered; the Savukoski one is made of pine (*Pinus sylvestris*) and has been dated to 4500 BP. It is about 154 centimeters long, and the shaft and blade are of about equal lengths. The blade, which has a ridge running down each side, has a long leaf form, pointed at the end, and is 16.5 centimeters wide. The shaft, about 3 centimeters in diameter, has a grooved handle 6.5 centimeters wide (Kotivuori 2006). The Finnish National Museum's record on the Syväkangas Kemi Saami paddle (item no. SU5391) notes, "Saami paddle, broken, only a part of the shaft and the blade are left. The blade is long, oval [*pitkänsuikea*], very thin, especially at the edges, and decorated with grooves in the same manner as, for example, on skis." Besides these specimens, several other Stone Age paddles have been found in Sodankylä, in the center of Kemi Lappmark.

Paddle finds have also been made in Kuusamo and Pyhäntä, south of Kemi Lappmark, and at Inari Lake. Archaeologist Mika Sarkkinen provided information about the Pyhäntä paddle when he delivered it to the Northern Österbotten Museum (Pohjois-Pohjanmaan Museo), saying: "The find site is in Tavastkenkä, Pyhäntä, from the bottom of the Pyhännän River. Total length 147 centimeters, blade 17 centimeters wide; the shaft is oval and about 2 by 3 centimeters. The blade is straight, not bent, as is typical of most finds. The surface is waterworn and is not as handsome as other paddles found in Pyhäntä. No information on the age (but likely Stone Age)" (2005, pers. comm. to HL).

The Finnish National Museum in Helsinki recovered two paddles dated between roughly 1500 and 1700, one from Rovaniemi and the other from Sodankylä. The later limit of this period overlaps with Chydenius's travels, which may indicate that people in Kemi Lappmark still used bark canoes or skin boats while he was there. This was a typical taiga territory, and we may assume that at least in its southern parts, birch-bark canoes similar to those found in Vilhelmina parish in Swedish Lapland existed (see below). It is therefore likely that Chydenius had some knowledge of Kemi Saami bark canoes, and he might even have seen them. This personal experience might have inspired him to undertake his dissertation on North American bark canoes, especially as his tutor, Kalm, had firsthand information from North America.

Peter Kalm's North American Elm-Bark Canoe

Besides the birch-bark canoe, the diary of Kalm's American journey records an elm-bark canoe built at Fort Anne on the English side of the French (later Canadian) border. Kalm may never have suggested that this type of canoe be constructed in Finland, since it was heavier than the birch-bark type and thus perhaps less adaptable to Scandinavian conditions. Yet his detailed observation of an Indian boatbuilder suggests that he thought this canoe type might have some economic value for boatmen in Finland, Sweden, and the rest of Europe. As with the birch-bark canoe, Kalm's observations of American elm-bark canoes provide information not supplied by Eurasian sources.

Adney and Chapelle (1964) believed that Kalm's description of an elm-bark canoe was the best ever written. Kalm had a personal investment in the elm-bark boat because Indians built one for him, which he used to journey into French Canadian territory in 1749. During this trip, he used three kinds of bark canoes: one of white pine, a second of birch, and the third—described below—of white elm.

When Kalm left Albany with a Swedish companion in June 1749, he paddled his birch-bark canoe up the Hudson River to the then-burned fort at Saratoga on the English border, passing rapids and waterfalls along the way. He intended to continue in this way to Fort Nicholson, on the upper Hudson, but he and his companion had to leave the canoe at a waterfall portage. Carrying their bags, they followed an old path along the river, first to Fort Nicholson and then on to Fort Anne. On June 27, Kalm wrote, "About two o'clock this afternoon we arrived at Fort Anne. It lies upon Woodcreek River, which is here at its origin no bigger than a little brook. We stayed here all day, and the next, in order to make a new boat of bark, because there was no possibility of going down the river to Fort St. Frederick [in French Canada] without it" (1772: 2: 129). On June 28, he wrote about elm-bark canoe building:

> The American Elm (*Ulmus Americana Linn.*) grows in abundance in river forests hereabouts. . . . Boats here are commonly made of the bark of [white elm] because it is tougher than the bark of any other tree. They [the Indians] use the bark of hickory, which is employed as bast, to sew the elm bark together, and use the bark of the red elm to tightly join the ends of the boat to keep water out. They beat the bark between two stones; or for want of them, between two pieces of wood. Making the boat took half of yesterday

and all of today. To make such a boat, they pick out a thick tall elm, with a smooth bark, and with as few branches as possible. (1772: 2: 133)

The rest of Kalm's description is omitted here because it is similar to Chydenius's for the birch-bark canoe.

In retrospect, Chydenius's attempt to reintroduce bark canoes into Sweden was counterhistorical. Birch-bark canoes had been popular in Northern Scandinavia and Finland for thousands of years but in recent centuries were supplanted by the equally light, more durable, and longer-lived planked boat.

THE SAAMI: A TRIPLE HERITAGE OF BARK, LOG, AND SKIN BOATS

There are many reasons to believe that the Saami (also called Lapps or Laplanders in Sweden, Finns in Norway, Lopar in Russia, and Lappalaiset in Finland) or their Scandinavian ancestors contributed to the early development of skin boats and bark canoes in northeastern Europe between the Scandinavian Peninsula and the Ural Mountains (Westerdahl 1987; Crumlin-Pedersen 2010; Klem 2010; Wickler 2010). The ancestors of the Saami, who probably arrived in their lands soon after the Ice Age glaciers withdrew, left us with material evidence of skin boats and bark canoes in the form of Stone Age rock engravings and paintings, historical records and drawings, and, later, photographs. Traditional Saami beliefs and practices, including their nomadic lifestyle of reindeer herding, inland and coastal fishing, and hunting, can be traced back several hundred years. Theirs was a culture that relied heavily on boats to obtain fish, wild game, and forest and tundra products (Gjessing 1944; W. Fitzhugh 2010; Westerdahl 2010).

Originally the Saami inhabited a huge territory covering two-thirds of Norway and Sweden, all of Finland, and most of Russian Karelia (Broadbent 2010). Today Saami languages are spoken across a large territory marked by many dialect and state borders, from central Scandinavia to the Kola Peninsula (Salminen 2006). Some 40,000 Saami now live in Sweden, Finland, and Russia, but Norway has the largest Saami population, 16,000 people. Ten Saami dialects exist in Norway, Sweden, Russia, and Finland, although four of them are nearly extinct (an 11th, Kemi Saami, was spoken in Finnish Lapland in the Kemijoki River basin until the mid-1800s). The Saami language and people once extended farther east, to the White Sea coast, Karelia, and possibly the territory between Lake Onega and Byeloe Ozero (White

Lake), so it is probable that some mixed Saami-Karelians living in these regions were later assimilated by Karelian and Vepsian peoples. Starting in the 1500s, Finnish and Karelian populations settled in northern Saami lands (Carpelan 2006) and assimilated the eastern Saami populations there, leaving only the western Saami intact.

How did the pre-Saami people become the Saami, a folk speaking a Finno-Ugric language? Linguistic and archaeological researchers have debated this question widely. Ante Aikio (2006) believes that a proto-Saami language developed among a small group in southern Finland west of Lake Ladoga and expanded to pre-Saami groups in Lapland who became speakers of Saami during the Iron Age, which lasted here from circa 1 to 500 CE. The Finnic-Saami language contacts that Aikio mentions occurred during a time of dramatic technological, social, and climatic change that affected both the Saami and the Finnish populations. It has been suggested that the proto-Finnish language (the Baltic Finno-Ugrian language) may have taken root in the eastern Baltic alongside the existing Saami language during the early Bronze Age, when Finnic language–speaking peoples entered from the Volga as bronze traders and settlers (Salminen 2006; Parpola 2012). At that time, the proto-Saami people probably lived north of the Finnish Gulf, while the proto-Finnish population lived around Lake Ladoga and south of the gulf. On the other hand, a broad archaeological reconstruction of Saami origins traces their ancestors back at least 7,000 years in the northern Baltic region known as Västerbotten (Broadbent 2010: 217), and genetic data indicate the Saami have an ancient Western European ancestry, with very little Siberian admixture (Tambets et al. 2004). That these theories, based separately on archaeological, linguistic, ethnographic, and genetic evidence, do not mesh is a typical finding when one is trying to reconstruct culture and population history from different sets of evidence.

Saami people used bark and skin as materials for building boats, for covering their mobile *kota* tents, and for making a wide variety of utensils and handicrafts. Coast Saami use of skin boats to hunt marine mammals on the Scandinavian coasts and in the White Sea is known from oral tradition, but there has been only one archaeological find of their skin boat, which was discovered at Lapua River, Finland. Below we discuss this find, various theories about the evolution of boat technology, and the first appearances of skin, bark, and log boats in Fennoscandia, as informed by rock art, language, and archaeology.

Before proceeding, however, we must note the problem of using *Saami* in discussing this 10,000-year history. It is customary to extend this ethnic term into the 1500s. In 1555, Olaus Magnus (1490–1557), a scholar and the last Catholic bishop of Uppsala, published his monumental work, *A Description of the Nordic Peoples*, in which he described the "Saame" of Northern Scandinavia. They are also known from reports by northern merchants, such as Othere and Wulfstan, that date to the 9th-century court of King Alfred the Great in Wessex (England). Earlier peoples may have spoken Saami, but their ethnic and linguistic nature is not known precisely, even though Saami ancestors might have occupied this region since the Ice Age. For this reason, we either refer to the pre-1500s peoples as "pre-Saami" or use specific archaeological and culture names, such as *Stone Age, Neolithic, Bronze Age, Iron Age, Viking/Norse,* and *Medieval*. Much confusion has resulted from assumptions that certain boat types can easily be designated as Saami, as Norwegian, or as some other ethnic group. In reality, many basic technological differences, even in the recent past, have proved difficult to categorize in ethnic terms and must be studied contextually and on a case-by-case basis (Wickler 2010). Our discussion of regional differences extends to boat types found in Karelia (chapter 4) and to northern German pre-Viking boats.

The Saami Bark Canoe and Its Origin

One of the earliest references to birch-bark use in Lapland is a mention of sails on boats plying inland waters. According to Westerdahl (1999: 290), Magnus's 1555 *Description of the Nordic Peoples* does not say that birch bark was also used to cover boats (he mentions only bark sails), but that would be a logical assumption. Kristoffer Sjulsson (1843) reported that bark canoes were known to Saami elders in Sweden in the early 1800s; in the Southern Saami language, they were called *biessieråttnja, besserråjoke,* or even *biessieroådnjuo* (Westerdahl 1995). Remains of bark canoes from the 1800s have been found in northern Sweden and southeastern Finland, and wooden paddles dating to 6,000 to 8,000 years ago, and suitable only for paddling small bark or log canoes on inland waterways, have been found in the lands between Finland and the Urals.

Several birch-bark canoe finds have been made in Sweden, but these boats are known mostly from oral reports because their remains were not collected or preserved. Their locales include, per Westerdahl:

- Svartberg fäbodar, a lake chalet, similar to a Scottish shieling, in Åsele, Lapland: an oral report of a birch-bark boat found in 1889–90, based on an interview conducted by M. Möller for the Nordic Museum in Stockholm in 1928.
- Tomasflon, a bog in the parish of Junsele, Ångermanland: an oral report of a birch-bark boat found by workers digging a drainage ditch circa 1928–30. Its description is similar to those of birch-bark boats from Svartberg, for which more details are available.
- Kultsjön, a lake in Vilhelmina, Lapland: as recollected from oral tradition relating the story of a (probably birch-bark) Saami boat that was rammed and sunk by a plank boat.
- Håptjärn, a small lake, in Håptjärnlinden, Mala region, Lapland: an oral report of a birch-bark boat, almost totally preserved, found circa 1920–25. Its length was circa 2.5 to 3 meters and its breadth 1 to 2 meters. The hull had been sewn to ribs and stringers with root fibers and caulked with reindeer hair and [birch] tar. The bark was laid in four layers. There was no positive evidence that the layers were sewn together, but some use was made of birch-tar glue. (1985a,b)

Westerdahl (1999) also reported that birch-bark canoes, including those noted above, have been found or documented in five sites in Lapp territories in northern Sweden. In Mountain Saami territory bordering Norway, bark boats have been found in northern Frostensvik, southern Vilhelmina, and northern Vilhelmina. Bark boats from the Southern Forest Saami (now extinct) have been documented in northern Västerbotten. From the northern Forest Saami group in southern Norrbotten, bark boats have been found at Malå. It would appear, therefore, that birch-bark canoes once existed in most Swedish Lapp territories.

In Finland, the sole bark canoe find comes from Suurniemi, in Juva commune in the Lake Saimaa region of the country's southeast. As with many other such finds, its remains were not preserved, but an oral report on it made to the National Board of Archaeology in Helsinki stated: "Canoe covered with birch bark" (Itkonen 1942: 48). We can assume, however, that birch-bark canoes had a wide distribution in Finland, especially in northern Saami territories, and that bark canoes existed until about 1700 in Kemi Lappmark in the Kemijoki River basin, Finnish Lapland, based on its Saami population and the many paddles found there.

Although we have limited evidence of truly ancient bark canoes, it is likely that their origin is linked to the other two key inventions required to efficiently exploit the northern boreal environment: snowshoes and skis. Northern bogs and lakes have favored the preservation of ancient skis, just as they have canoe paddles. Written sources from as early as 211 BCE mention skis and skiing (Weinstock 2005: 172), and rock carvings more than 4,000 years old in northwestern Russia and northern Norway depict skiers. More than 300 skis and ski fragments have been found in peat bogs in Scandinavia and Russia, and fragments uncovered in north-central Russia have been carbon-dated to as early as circa 6700 BCE (Burov 1989, 2001). Comparative linguistic evidence also suggests an ancient origin for skiing. According to Hartvig Birkely (1994), scholars claim that the Saami word *cuoigat*, "to ski," is 6,000 to 8,000 years old. Ancient skis were also present on the other side of the world: an April 19, 2017, *New York Times* story by Kade Krichko describes a cave painting in Khom (Xinjiang), northwestern China, showing four humans on skis; it is probably at least 10,000 years old.

For many years, researchers have seen Central Asia as the original source of skis and snowshoes. Danish anthropologist Gudmund Hatt (1916) suggested that moccasins and snowshoes had a common origin in the territory between Lake Baikal and Mongolia, and the Smithsonian Institution's Otis T. Mason (1901) held a similar belief. Daniel Davidson (1937), in a comprehensive study of snowshoes, suggested that both wooden and "bear-paw" snowshoes originated in Central Asia and spread east across the Bering Strait to the Americas and west to Fennoscandia.

Archaeological finds have so far yielded little evidence of snowshoes, skis, or paddles from Southern Siberia that predate the 6,000- to 8,000-year-old Nordic and Russian ski and paddle finds. However, an early Central Asian origin for these transport systems would not be unexpected, as recent research by Alenius, Mökkönen, and Lahelma (2013) on lake sediment cores from southeastern Finland suggests: they found buckwheat pollen and evidence of landscape clearing dating to circa 5200 BCE. Unlike many other cultigens that reached Northern Scandinavia from Europe, buckwheat was not known in Europe at this early time and must have arrived in Finland from China via Southern Siberia. It is likely that bark canoes will eventually join this list.

Because they are more often preserved archaeologically, skis and snowshoes in Northern Eurasia have been researched more than the bark canoe. John Weinstock has reviewed the major literature related to skis, and his comments on the origin of the Saami people and the colonization of early Scandinavia probably represent an uncomplicated consensus view of these topics:

> The ski was invented at least eight thousand years ago in an area around Lake Baikal in southern Siberia, north of Mongolia. At that time ancestral speakers of the Ural-Altaic language family were in the area, including the forebears of the Saami. Following reindeer and other prey, Finno-Ugric peoples expanded and the forebears of the Saami eventually migrated west and north into Scandinavia and brought skis with them. Then, over many centuries, they developed and perfected skis for different types of terrain and snow conditions. (2005: 173)

Skin Boats and Saami Legends

As noted earlier, the earliest inhabitants of Fennoscandia entered the region soon after the withdrawal of glacial ice, perhaps as early as 9,000 to 10,000 years ago. Ethnic Saami people have been there at least since Viking times. The origin of their skin boat, however, is far from clear. The skin boat used to be seen as the original boat type used in the north, and it was gradually replaced by the expanded log boat with planked sides. The latter probably developed in Karelia as more sophisticated tools and fastenings evolved during the Bronze and Iron ages (Gjessing 1936; Brøgger and Shetelig 1951; Luukkanen 2010; Westerdahl 2010).

In Norway, the transition from skin boat to planked boat among the Coast Saami is thought to have occurred as a result of Nordic colonization. Mulk and Bayliss-Smith (1998, 2006), Wiklund (1947), and Nesheim (1967) studied the influence of contacts between the Saami and their neighbors on language. Nesheim suggested that the ancient Saami boats were probably skin boats with a short, broad steering oar (*maelle* in Saami, from the old Finno-Ugric *mela*). The word for "sail" (*bårjås* or *borjjas*) was taken from Early Finnish, while the transition to wooden boats and their later development were accompanied by Norse terminology. Most Saami boat terminology is of Early Norse origin. Borgos and Torgvaer (1998) suggested that in northern Norway (Helgeland), the main period for this interaction was 300 to 600 CE and that the first area in which plank boats were developed was probably the inner coastal zone, where wood was available. In Lofoten-Vesterålen, in western Norway, the oldest archaeological evidence of Nordic influence dates to 300 CE. From that time onward, either by colonization or through preexisting groups' adoption of a new culture, people of Nordic ethnicity occupied the coast, intermingled in many areas with Saami.

Although there have been no archaeological finds of skin boats in Norway or Sweden, several sources confirm Saami legends that claim the use of skin boats survived into the 1800s in Sweden. Ernst Manker (1947) wrote that the Swedish Mountain Saami, who lived in the Vapsten Lapp village and on the Norwegian side of the border starting in the 1600s, used skin boats for inland river travel through the first half of the 19th century. (Next to the Vapsten Lapp region was the Vilhelmina commune, where the majority of the last Saami-built birch-bark canoes have been found.) Sjulsson briefly referred to information about these boats from the early 1800s: "In old times Lapp (Saami) used canoes made from skin. Those skin canoes were known as *skårne-väntse* boats. The skin was stretched over a narrow wooden frame" (quoted in Drake 1918: 75). Sigrid Drake, who studied the Lapp community in the Umeå River basin in 1918, learned of the *skårne-väntse* boats from Kristoffer Sjulsson's book *Lapp Country and People*, printed in Stockholm in 1873. Baron von Diiben wrote insightfully of the same term (1873), saying that while Lapp words for sailing vessels and large boats were almost all imports, *skårne-väntse* (the only term of Lapp origin for watercraft of any kind) denoted a skin canoe propelled by paddles, without rowers' seats or a steering place.

Saami living memories and legends paint a much more colorful and broader picture of their life with skin boats. Until the 1800s, old Saami legends that narrate canoes' ancient origin and use existed only as oral literature, and stories about skin boats that were once used by their forefathers is a common motif in Mountain Lapp traditional belief. Von Diiben (1873) wrote that the Mountain Lapp assigned to their remote ancestors a home lying far to the southeast, from which, they alleged, their enemies drove them in two directions: westward and northward. The westward group eventually reached the sound separating Denmark from Sweden, which they crossed in small skin boats, and when the sea was calm, they brought their goods across on reindeer-skin floats tied together and drawn by swimming reindeer, along with the rest of the herd.

Skin boats were known in Finland and Karelia as well, not only to the Saami people there but also to the Finns and Karelians, as we can deduce from archaeology, poems, sagas, and linguistic evidence. While the Saami appear to have been the original users and builders of these craft, the Finns and

Karelians, as language relatives of the Saami living in the same territories, seem to have inherited them.

The only skin boat found in Fennoscandia was discovered in Tiisteenjoki, Finland, in the Lapua commune in the Lapuajoki River basin near the Gulf of Bothnia coast. T. I. Itkonen wrote the find report in a note to the Finnish National Museum in Helsinki, and included in it this excerpt from a letter that a Lapua primary schoolteacher, Vihtori Latvamäki, wrote to the Prehistoric Department on April 19, 1928:

> My latest information regarding the boats found in Sippola parish, [concerning] their location, the person who made the find, etc., was told to me this week by a young man named Eino Helsberg who had moved here from the Sippola church village. . . . From a riverbank of Tiisteenjoki River in Ämmälä village, Lapua, [there] was said to be found, in conjunction with the clay digging, a boat "that had ribs and that seemed to have been made of skin"; the tarred threads were visible. The parts of the boats were taken inside a farmhouse, where the remains were later burned. (Catalogue entry from 1928, handwritten note without a registry number)

Latvamäki had earlier reported two log boat finds in a letter to the museum (then the Muinaistieteellinen toimikunta), so this was perhaps a response to a request for more detailed information. Clearly this was a new find, which he was able to locate based on oral information he had recently received. The Tiisteenjoki boat remains were neither preserved nor dated, but because they were found in clay, the boat could have been well preserved at the time of its discovery, and so might have dated from an early time. We can estimate its age with the help of an ancient ski that was found in 1949 in Toijaniemi village, which is also in Lapua commune, near where the boat was found. The archaeologist E. Hyyppä studied the ski (find KM 12058), which was discovered 20 centimeters deep in clay, and recorded its location, whose land rise he measured to be 30.8 meters above modern sea level. Based on this figure, the ski was estimated to be 3,100 years old, making it a Bronze Age find. The proximity of the ski and the boat at the same old beachline elevation supports a working hypothesis of a similar age for the boat.

Tiisteenjoki village was once on an old seashore, and thus we may assume that the boat was built by Coast Saami

or their Bronze Age antecedents. According to Helmer Tengengren (1952), the Saami inhabited the eastern Bothnian seashore until circa 1200 CE. They, like the Finnish and Swedish settlers who followed, hunted seal on the winter ice. Several stone structures found on offshore islands may have been, according to Finnish National Museum records, caches used by Saami seal hunters to store meat and skins until larger boats could pick them up. The town of Vaasa and its archipelago, like the surrounding Österbotten coast, were among the favorite locations of Finnish-Swedish settlers engaged in fishing, and until the end of 1800s, all peasants and fishing families in the area participated in spring seal hunts, although they did not use skin boats. The traditional sealing conducted on Bergö Island and by other fishing communities is well known (Wetterhoff 2004). On a map drawn by Olaus Magnus (1539; shown in fig. 3.5), we see illustrations of men, perhaps Saami, in skin clothing hunting seal among the ice floes.

Among the Finnish and Karelian populations, boats covered with seal hides were known up to the 19th century. Such kesi (skin) boats are mentioned in five *Kalevala* poems describing the lives and travels of people in Lapland (Pohjola) and in the southern territories of Finland and Karelia. The oldest of these poems, a saga describing the construction of a skin boat, was recorded among the Finnish population on the coast of Bothnia and has been dated to the 1600s. The others were collected in Viena-Karelia (in the Russian Kemi district), among the Karelian population on the western coast of the White Sea, and in Kesälahti in the Lake Saimaa region. One of these poems, "The Birth of the Seal," connects skin boats to seal and was collected by the compiler of the *Kalevala* himself, Elias Lönnrot. Other poems that include information on kesi boats prove that these watercraft were also known among the Karelian and Ingrian populations around southern Lake Ladoga (see further discussion in chapter 4, page 72). Fig. 3.11 (page 68) presents an artist's view (from Mangin 1869: 572) of how a "purse-like" early Saami skin kayak might have looked based on descriptions by Pierre Martin de La Martinière (1706) and Frans O. Belyavsky (1833).

Early Skin Boats versus Log Boats: The Rock Art Evidence

Scholars have presented various theories about the origin and history of boats in Scandinavia and the White Sea region. The majority are based on interpretations of the rich inventory of rock art images, dating as early as 6,000 years

Fig. 3.5. Olaus Magnus's *Carta Marina* of 1539 illustrates events, resources, and economic activities in the Nordic region, including Saami sealers hunting in the Gulf of Bothnia. Sealing was big business in Österbotten, and *Kalevala* poems collected from the Kemi River mouth suggest people there used skin boats. (From Magnus 1555)

ago, and address questions including Who made and used these boats? Which route did their builders take to arrive here? How and when did sealing, whaling, and deep-sea fishing begin? But perhaps the most important questions are the following: Which kinds of boats does this rock art represent—dugouts, skin boats, plank boats, bark canoes, or some combination of the four? What are the relationships among them? And when did they appear here?

The interpretation of rock art boat images has a deep history in Scandinavian archaeology, having been pursued since the early 19th century (see, e.g., Christie 1837). At first scholars assumed that Viking boats must have developed from early dugout vessels, with side planking added to increase freeboard. However, in 1907, Eduard Hahn published a revolutionary idea: the Viking ship might have emerged from a sewn bark or skin boat like the Eskimo

umiak. Once postglacial land uplift began to be recognized as a way to date coastal rock art, differences in boat history were studied from the perspective of images at varying elevations. Gutorm Gjessing (1936, 1944), who spent the World War II years in the United States and became familiar with North American Inuit ethnology and archaeology, came to the same conclusion as Hahn, noting that the blocky, high-sided shapes of the highest and oldest images most closely resembled open skin boats of the Eskimo type (figs. 3.6–3.7). Although he qualified his conclusion, believing that planked dugouts could also take the form seen in the early rock art images, which show high prows, his skin boat analogy took root in Brøgger and Shetelig's (1951) influential work on Viking ship construction. This view was later supported by most other scholars dealing with this issue (e.g., Hallström 1960; Johnston 1980).

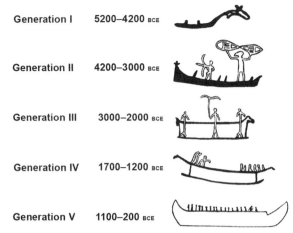

Generation I	5200–4200 BCE	
Generation II	4200–3000 BCE	
Generation III	3000–2000 BCE	
Generation IV	1700–1200 BCE	
Generation V	1100–200 BCE	

Fig. 3.6. This chronology of Nordic and northeastern European boat figures recorded in rock art from the Varanger Fjord, northern Norway, was developed by combining changes in boat design with radiocarbon dates and information on geological uplift. (From Klem 2010: fig. 47; adapted by Marcia Bakry)

Per Gierløff Klem (2010) reviews this early history in his master's thesis, taking a contrary view based on his interpretation of new boat images that came to light after 1972 at the head of Alta Fjord in northernmost Norway. The Alta rock art consists of more than 5,000 engravings, and Knut Helskog of the Tromsø Museum has extensively researched and published it. As a result of his efforts, Alta was designated a UNESCO World Heritage Site (Helskog 1988) in 1985. Among its carvings and painted images are more than 80 depictions of boats, many with human figures in them and most with animal-head effigies at their prows. The art is found from the highest shoreline elevations, at 26 meters, to as low as 8.5 meters. The carved images illustrate boats that are remarkably consistent in form for any given shoreline-elevation period. Analysis of the Alta data reveals five phases of boat images, whose calibrated (i.e., converted from radiocarbon years to earth years) ages range from circa 5000 BCE to 300 CE (Arntzen 2007; Klem 2010: fig. 47), representing boats from the Scandinavian Middle Stone Age to the Iron Age. Reanalysis of the age-elevation correlation suggests ages as much as 1,000 years older than initially believed (Gjerde 2010).

Klem argues that all the Alta boat images depict expanded wooden dugouts and that earlier interpretations stating they showed skin boats were based on superficial resemblance to Eskimo umiaks (figs. 3.7a–b). His view contradicts generations of rock art experts, including Brøgger, Shetelig, and Gjessing. The Eskimo skin boat analogy in Scandinavian rock art studies has been a particularly persuasive argument because the early archaeological cultures of northern Norway and Finland had fishing, seal, and walrus hunting economies that were similar to those of Eskimo cultures, and, in more recent times, these cultures also traded in skins and ivory. Early on, Gjessing (1936), Eskerød (1956), Hahn (1907), and others had pointed out the vital importance of skin boats to Eskimo culture and therefore to all maritime hunting and fishing cultures inhabiting the Arctic

Fig. 3.7a–b. Rock art images on Kamennyi Island, Kanozera Lake, Kola Peninsula, illustrate boats and people hunting whales and other animals. Before they were photographed, the images were temporarily darkened with watercolor. (Photographs: R. Lauhakakangas 2013, used with permission)

The Bark Canoes and Skin Boats of Northern Eurasia

zone, where sea ice can threaten wooden boats that are too heavy to be hauled out during periods of ice compression by wind and currents. These earlier scholars thought that the Arctic region of Scandinavia did not have sufficient timber for people to make large log-based seagoing boats (Westerdahl 1987; Ellmers 1996). However, pollen studies have since revealed that pine forests appeared in northern Norway by 5500 BCE (Mäkelä and Hyvärinen 2000), and although they declined due to cooling climates after 2500 BCE, even today the plundered Alta forests hold a few remaining pines large enough to make sizable dugouts. It turns out that the crucial flaw in the Eskimo analogy is that these early scholars neglected to consider the importance of sea ice. The absence of suitable trees and the long periods of winter sea ice were the imperatives that drove skin boat use among the tundra-dwelling Eskimo, and it is why log canoes eventually won out over skin boats in the more open seas and forested coasts of Northern Scandinavia.

Despite the difficulties in interpreting the boat images, Klem's argument that the Alta art shows wooden dugouts is persuasive in light of the realities described by Eskimo and Chukchi skin boat users. One cannot go to sea for more than a few hours in boats made of reindeer or moose hide before they leak and stretch; only the skins of the largest seal or walrus serve this purpose (walrus hides have to be split to be manageable because of their thickness). Ox hides also can be used, but they were not available in northern regions. These problems have been investigated experimentally by skin boat builders in Norway and Finland. Klem points out numerous construction options that could accommodate two problematic features of the skin boat interpretation: skin boats do not provide structural solutions for supporting the sizable animal-head prow-piece and keel extensions seen in Neolithic, Bronze, and Iron Age boat illustrations. Sverre Marstrander (1986) believed that the function of the projecting keel was to protect the boat's skin cover from abrasion on beach rocks and gravel. The keels and animal prows so prominent in Bronze Age carvings have elicited much discussion on both sides of the skin-versus-dugout debate, much of which revolves around the Hjortspring boat.

Since it appears that research into the early boat history of Northern Scandinavia now leans toward supporting a planked dugout scenario, we must explore the questions of how, when, and why skin boats developed there as a parallel tradition beginning in early times or were introduced during the past two or three millennia, as linguistic evidence

suggests. In principle, theories can be grouped into two types: an "eastern theory," claiming a White Sea coast route that included Lake Ladoga and the Finnish Gulf, and a "western theory," claiming that skin boats came with people who moved north along the Norwegian coast from Europe in the wake of the retreating Scandinavian ice sheet. Paul Johnston offered a summary of the proposed eastern entry of the skin boat:

> [The skin boat] cultures of northern Norway may be derived from Russia and have reached Norway via the coast of the White Sea, while Grahame Clark and Stuart Piggott regard the Lake Onega, Vyg and Karelian [rock] carvings as offshoots from the Scandinavian group. Either way, the two seem to be related, and reports of further carvings in this style on the banks of the Rivers Yenisey and Lena, which flow into the Arctic Ocean, suggest that the use of skin boats as reflected in these carvings was part of a circum-Polar tradition. (1980: 33)

The western theory claims that the roots of the Saami skin boat on the Norwegian coast can be found at the sites of Stellmoor and Husum in Germany. Grahame Clark was an early supporter of the western skin boat theory, probably because he was influenced by the old British coracle and Irish curragh, which were covered with seal skin or ox hide. Referring to Gjessing's (1936) circumpolar views, Clark (1968) wrote that at least three groups of engravings in the Arctic rock art of northwestern Norway depict skin boats: those at Forselv and at Rødøy on the coast of Nordland and at Evenhus near Trondheim. Typical of these boat images are straight keels and gunwales, steep prows and sterns, and projecting ends of the top of the wooden frame, visible in some engravings at Rødøy and elsewhere (fig. 3.8). Clark's views followed those of Gjessing (1936), Brøgger and Shetelig (1951; see also Shetelig 1903), and Marstrander (1963), holding that skin boats of the Eskimo umiak type were used during the Stone Age in Northern Europe.

Karin Hornig (2000: 22) discussed this theory with reference to possible skin boat use by the German Ahrensburg culture (circa 10,600 to 8,000 BCE), as an antler found at Husum has been interpreted as once being used as a skin boat rib. In 1993, Dietrich Evers, a German experimenting with trans-Atlantic crossings, used rock art images to build and test a skin boat, in which he used antlers for ribs (Evers 2004). He believed skin boats had reached northern Norway's

Fig. 3.8. A rock carving from Alta Fjord in northern Norway dating to 4000–2700 BCE shows a boat with an animal-headed prow, a hunter with bow, and a human brandishing a mysterious object. (Photograph: Knut Helskog)

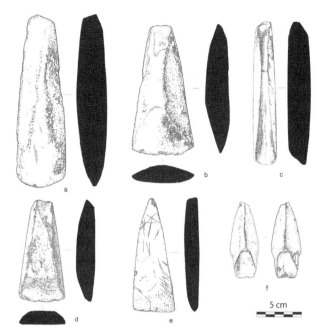

Fig. 3.9. Early Holocene Suomusjarvi-culture stone axes, adzes, and gouges from Karelia indicate people's technological adaptation to the advancing postglacial forest and their subsequent production of log boats. (From Nordqvist and Seitsonen 2008: fig. 3, used with permission)

8,000- to 9,000-year-old Komsa culture via Ahrensburg and the White Sea, whereas Helena Knutsson (2004), a Norwegian, believes that early seafaring peoples advanced up the Norwegian coast to Finnmark and the Rybachy Peninsula as glacial ice retreated. The earliest dates of rock art images from Alta (circa 5000 BCE; Arntzen 2007) suggest that the oldest depictions of boats there are about the same age as the Komsa culture. This is also about the age of the Finnish Suomusjarvi culture (8300 to 5000 BCE), an early Holocene culture of the Finnish Gulf whose toolkit included large ground stone axes and gouges (fig. 3.9). The only practical use for such heavy woodworking tools—especially gouges—would have been to fell and hollow out trees for dugout boats. This process was often assisted by fire, hot rocks, and boiling water, techniques also practiced by Indian peoples on the northwestern coast of North America in the 19th century and by 4,000-year-old Maritime Archaic boatbuilders in Maine, the Canadian Maritimes, and Labrador (W. Fitzhugh 2006). According to Grigori Burov (2000), the center of the Suomusjarvi polished tool industry was in Karelia, between Lakes Onega and Ladoga, from which the tools and technology diffused west over the rest of Fennoscandia and east toward the Urals.

In fact, we have evidence of such large dugout boats in both Finland and Karelia. Early fishing and seal-hunting people in Vihanti commune in southern Finland built planked log boats with stone tools and used early comb ware (Säräisniemi 1, or "Sär 1"), pottery decorated with comb-tooth impressions (Torvinen 2000). In Vihanti, Itkonen (1942: 51)

studied the Alpuanjärvi log boat, found in 1934 after Alpuan lake had dried up, and noted that it had sewn-on planks and the "two-horned" construction that is known from the Swedish Bronze Age and seen in rock art. The boat has been pollen-dated to 2500 BP, but a bronze medallion and a piece of asbestos-tempered ceramic found next to it in 1940 date it to the Bronze Age (see chapter 4's section on Karelia for more details). Even if it is only from the Iron Age, circa 500 BCE, this find would be older than Hjortspring boat (350 BCE) and would be one of the oldest planked boats found in the Nordic countries.

Russian studies point to more evidence of Stone Age log boats that were built using stone or early metal tools. H. V. Chernigov (2000) reported on three canoe-building sites in Karelia and the Kola Peninsula where canoe remains and stone tools have been found. One is near the ancient mouth of a river at the head of Kandalaksha (Kantalahti in Karelian) Bay in the northwestern White Sea and dates to about 1600 to 900 BCE. The second is on the shore of Sunskiye River in Raspolozhe, 30 kilometers north of Petrozavodsk on the western side of Lake Onega, and dates to about 1 CE. The third and oldest, dated to 2600 BCE, is in Sheltozero, on the southwestern coast of Lake Onega. The Kandalaksha canoe, the largest and widest (8 by 1.4 meters) of the boats found at these sites, was made using fire in addition to stone tools, and probably the Sheltozero canoes were, too.

These Stone Age log boats may also have had their sides expanded. Vilkuna and Mäkinen (1976) studied log boats made with stone tools (which therefore date to the early Bronze Age or earlier) that they believed had expanded sides. N. P. Zagoskin (1910) described the "Nordic method" used in Karelia to produce expanded log boats: first a living aspen or pine would receive a long, deep, vertical groove, into which wedges were hammered deeper and deeper every day for three to five years. Then the tree was cut down and the opening dug out with the help of fire while the builder hammered out the charred wood with large stone tools.

Considering these boat finds in Karelia and Finland alongside heavy woodworking tools, there can be little doubt that people living in northern Norway and the Varanger Fjord region, as well as in inland regions, made, knew, and used dugouts. The archaeologist Markku Torvinen has studied the first ceramics that entered Northern Scandinavia and northeastern Russia and found that they spanned the period from 4140 to 3520 BCE (2000: 32). These finds show that this early pre-Saami pottery culture (Sär 1) was distributed from the White Sea (at Belomorsk, called Sorokka in Karelian) along the waterways to the Gulf of Bothnia (Oulu region) and as far as the Varanger coast of Norway. We can safely assume that this extensive network of pre-Saami people—which, according to Torvinen, resulted in the emergence of the Saami—received stone tools traded from Karelia and shared the technology used to make large or small dugout canoes with other groups. These data suggest that the little-researched regions of Finland, the eastern Baltic, and the Western Urals may have been a place of early log boat development, if not also of skin boats. Either way, these early boats—log or skin—were important for purposes beyond travel and subsistence. Helskog (1988) and others have argued that the prominence of boats in rock art may be related to spiritual rituals connected to traveling and hunting, with boats being seen as "carriers of the gods" (Helskog 1985: 197). Given the prominence of animals and rituals surrounding the hunt in northern rock art, it is not surprising that boats are also prominent in the carvings, since they, as hunting and trading conveyances, figured importantly in both economic and ritual life.

What can we finally say about the eastern theory of skin boat entry? From the *Kalevala*, we know that the Karelian and Finnish peoples built boats covered with seal skin that they called *kesi* and which may have been of Saami origin (see above and chapter 4's section on Karelia, page 72). Which entry route might these boats have taken to reach the Nordic region? And when were they first known by people on Lake Ladoga and the White Sea? Finnish linguist Jorma Koivulehto (1983) believed that linguistic evidence shows that the Late Neolithic proto-Indo-European Battle Axe people (circa 3000 to 2200 BCE) transferred the word *kesi* (seal skin) to the Baltic Finns (fig. 3.10). We believe that the Battle Axe people, during their invasion of the eastern Baltic Sea, probably traveled in kesi skin boats and practiced a sealing economy.

To sum up, archaeological and linguistic evidence suggests that during the Late Neolithic (the Late Stone Age) and the Bronze Age, there were two parallel boat traditions in Northern Scandinavia and northwestern Russia: an inland bark canoe tradition and a maritime expanded dugout boat culture using large, heavy boats for trade and migration in open ocean waters, each employing different kinds of boats and perhaps belonging to two or more general cultural traditions. Furthermore, in coastal regions, there was a third boat tradition, consisting of skin boats that were used for marine mammal hunting among broken sea ice. This tradition paralleled the expanded dugout tradition but did not survive long enough into the era of European exploration to be documented. We might also suggest that there were

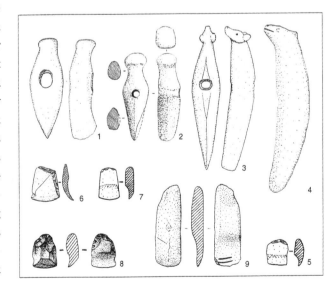

Fig. 3.10. Late Stone Age technology. Ground-stone tools of the Neolithic Battle Axe culture in Karelia, northeastern Europe, demonstrate use of harder rock types than Suomusjarvi people had used for making dugout boats with planked sides. (From Burov 2000: 25, fig. 5)

at least three regional groups of maritime people known from the forms of their boats: in Alta on the Arctic Ocean, in Belomorsk on the White Sea, and along the shores of the Gulf of Bothnia. Fig. 3.11 shows how their early skin boats might have looked, as seen in a mid-19th-century artist's reconstruction drawn from descriptions by 16th-century observers such as Pierre Martin de La Martinière, as discussed in the next chapter.

Fig. 3.11. An image in Arthur Mangin's *The Desert World* imagines a Saami scene showing a hunter in a kayaklike skin boat. The rendition was based on descriptions and illustrations in exploration literature, such as that seen in fig. 4.8. (From Mangin 1869: 572)

The Bark Canoes and Skin Boats of Northern Eurasia

CHAPTER 4

NORTHEASTERN EUROPE

THE EASTERN BALTICS AND WESTERN URALS

Our second regional chapter concerns the boat history of far northeastern Europe, from the White Sea to the Ural Mountains. This region (shown on map 6), whose eastern portion is known in European literature as the Western Urals, is dominated by tundra along the Arctic Ocean coast and by boreal forest in the Mezen and Pechora river basins in the near interior. Its eastern border is the Ural Mountain chain, which marks the boundary between Europe and Asia. The northern regions have been occupied most recently by Nenets reindeer herders, who replaced hunting and fishing peoples known in early records and oral history as the Chud or Sihirtia. Because the area's coasts were accessible to 16th- and 17th-century European exploration, voyages such as those of Stephen Burrough in 1556 and 1557 and Pierre de La Martinière in 1670 provided information on the peoples, economies, and boats they encountered along the Barents Sea coast as far east as Vaigach Island (Burrough 1567; de La Martinière 1706; Armstrong 1984; Hofstra and Samplonius 1995). These and other reports speak, and sometimes provide illustrations, of skin boats used to hunt sea mammals in river estuaries and along coasts and islands.

This chapter covers the Karelian boatmen of eastern Finland, northwestern Russia, and the early Russian trading center of Novgorod, whose fur- and fish-trading activities stimulated the rise of the White Sea Pomor and influenced the cultures of the coastal Sihirtia and Chud peoples and the Komi-Zyrians of the Western Urals forest zone. Birch-bark boats were common in forested parts of this region, but along the coasts there was a tradition, as yet poorly understood, of skin boat use, which included kayaklike vessels. Unfortunately, so little historical and archaeological evidence is available that it is difficult to determine the specifics of these skin-covered boats.

KARELIAN BOATBUILDERS AND FUR TRADERS

Anthropologists have learned that elements of culture—for instance, religion, economy, political forms, language, and technology—rarely emerge from or conform to a single ethnic or linguistic group or territory. Culture change is almost always more complicated and usually occurs for a variety of reasons. Sometimes change arises within a society, but frequently change is driven by external factors and results from new inventions, ideas, or cultural or environmental forces outside a society. For the Karelian peoples—the Korela-Karelians and the Vepsian-Karelians—changes seem to have come from within, and this may also be partly true of the ancient Finnish people who inherited boatbuilding traditions from the Saami or their predecessors over the past three millennia.

Karelia is simply defined here as the land inhabited by the Karelian peoples: a strip of Baltic Sea shore, the Karelian Isthmus, the great lakes Ladoga and Onega, and the western shore of the White Sea as far as the Kola Peninsula (map 7). The Karelian "original home" was on Lake Ladoga in the 6th century; gradually the Karelians expanded their territory over old Saami lands to Lake Onega and the western White Sea as far as the Kola Peninsula. A. M. Tallgren (1938: 9–20) interpreted archaeological evidence as showing that eastern Karelia once extended as far as the Onega River, east of Lake Onega. The broad geographical spread of the Finno-Ugrian language in northeastern Europe suggests that the Karelians may have shared their boatbuilding heritage with the Komi-Zyrians west of the White Sea (page 84).

Janne Saarikivi has written about archaeological evidence of the Karelians' origins:

In the period 600–1000 BC, there were two cultural innovation centers at the shores of Lake Ladoga. The southwestern center has been connected to the

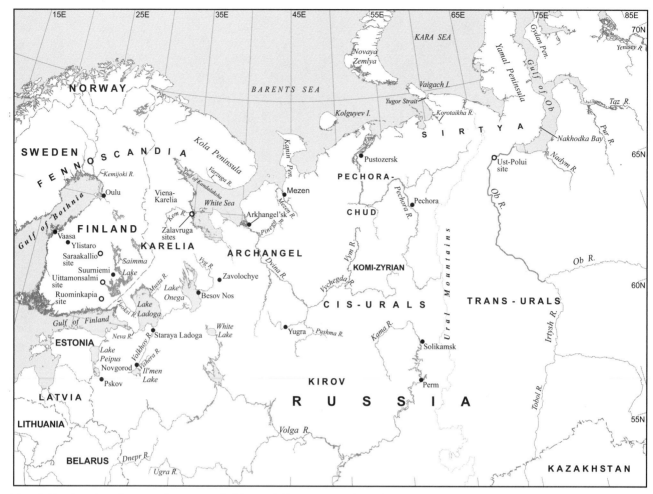

Map 6. Northeastern Europe: the eastern Baltics and Cis (Near)-Urals and territories of the Karelians, Novgorod Russians, Russian Pomor, Komi-Zyrians, and ancient Sihirtia and Chud. (Dan Cole, Smithsonian Institution)

emergence of the Veps ethnos, and the northeastern is considered to have been the original home of the Karelians. . . . In the east of the Dvina basin, the Vyčegda Perm' culture, connected with the origins of the Komi-Ziryan people, took shape, while in the Jaroslavl and Kostroma regions on the Upper Volga, an archaeological culture connected with the extinct Merya emerged. . . .

The Iron Age archaeological findings in the Dvina basin do not belong to any of these archaeological cultures but form local groups with different cultural connections. Thus, on the Middle Vaga, the findings resemble most the Karelian and Veps settlements but also include artifact types of Vyčegda Perm' origin. . . . In the Sukhona basin, the ethnical indicators of the findings relate them more to the Meryan settlements of the Kostroma and Jaroslavl regions. (2006: 32)

Farther to the north, those people living north of the Baltic Sea and west of the White Sea were, in a strict linguistic sense, not Karelians, Finns, or the Saami people whom we know today; instead they are regarded as part of a larger population called the Baltic Finns, who emerged in the eastern Baltic Sea region circa 2500 BCE (Tallgren 1931a,b). Saarikivi explains the emergence of the Karelians, Saami, and Finns in linguistic terms:

Karelian and Vepsian belong to the Finnic branch of the Uralic languages. These are offsprings of an intermediate protolanguage of the Uralic family, Proto-Finnic. This protolanguage was probably spoken approximately 500 BC–500 AD in the vicinity of the Finnish Gulf. . . . The present Finnic settlement of most of inland Finland and Karelia emerged not earlier than the Middle Ages.

The Bark Canoes and Skin Boats of Northern Eurasia

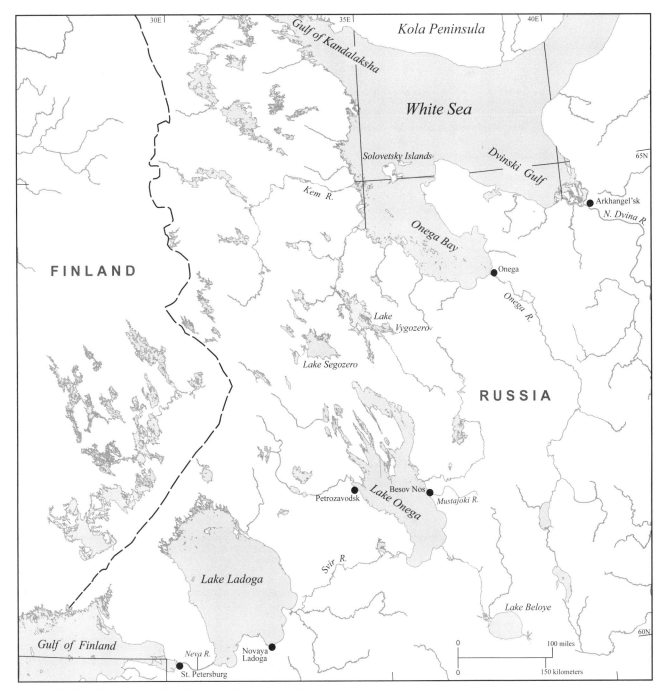

Map 7. The Karelian region. (Dan Cole, Smithsonian Institution)

The Sámi languages spoken in the Kola Peninsula and northern Fennoscandia (together approx. 25,000 speakers) are daughter languages of another intermediate Uralic protolanguage, Proto-Sámi. Proto-Sámi usually has been located somewhere in the Onega region and was probably spoken simultaneously with Proto-Finnic. Prior to Finnic, the Sámi languages were spoken in most of Finland and

Karelia. . . . Finnic and Sámi have had considerable mutual contact. (2006: 89)

Today the number of Karelian people speaking their own language is approximately 50,000 (Salminen 2003); they live in Finland and the Republic of Karelia in Russia. Nearly all ancient Karelian lands are now part of Russia, which annexed the Finnish Karelian province (Viipurin lääni)

during World War II, with the result that 400,000 Finnish Karelians fled to Finland.

Ancient Karelian Boat History

Boats and boatbuilding developed in three stages in ancient Karelia. Stage 1 began in the Stone Age with the appearance of the eastern pre-Saami population in Karelia and ended with those people's first contacts with Finno-Ugric-speaking Baltic Finns. The second stage was a time of parallel existence, when the pre-Saami population lived alongside the emerging Baltic Finnish people in southern Karelia, as well as the Neolithic Battle Axe people then entering the Baltic Sea coast and Lake Ladoga. This period, spanning mainly the European Bronze Age, ended when the southern pre-Saami population became Finno-Ugric speakers. The third stage saw the emergence of the Karelian people and their expansion to Lake Onega and the White Sea.

The archaeological history of Karelia is very complex, much more so than that of Finland or the Varanger and Alta regions of the northern Norwegian coast. Karelia was a mixing bowl of peoples entering from the upper Volga basin and from south of the Baltic, as well as Battle Axe people moving in from the German plains. All these peoples brought new technologies for fishing and sea mammal hunting, as well as agriculture, pottery, and, naturally, various types of boats. They included the Variags, the Vikings of Sweden, and the Slavic people, who, together with the Karelian people, founded the cities of Staraya (Old) Ladoga and Novgorod. All these groups depended on the expansive waterways that Karelia offered, leading to the Caspian Sea to the southeast, Constantinople and the Black Sea to the south, Gotland and the Baltic to the west, and Novaya Zemlya to the north. We should not forget the proto-Saami and their high-tech stone tool industry and boatbuilding expertise. All had special skills for producing boats made of birch bark, logs, and seal skin and the ability to use them to fish, to hunt on land and sea, and to undertake trade expeditions for stone tools, pottery, furs and skins, and bronze.

The Pre-Saami Karelian Stone Age

The Pre-Saami Karelian people who settled the western shore of the White Sea and Lake Onega were hunters and fishermen with a distinct ethnicity and culture linked closely to the region's watercourses. Their archaeological identity is based upon their early type of pottery, known as Säräisniemi 1 (Sär 1) "pit-comb" ceramics. Sär 1 pottery dates from 4000 to 400 BCE, spanning from the Finnish Neolithic to the early Iron Age, and it is ornamented with pits, incised lines, and comb-impressed decoration. Recent studies show that the DNA of these people is similar to that of the Volga and Komi-Zyrian people, with no trace of Samoyed (i.e., Nenets) admixture (Tambets et al. 2004; Torvinen 2000). According to Grigori Burov (1996), even the earliest archaeological cultures in this region used boats, as is shown by finds of short boat paddles dated to 8700 BP at the Nizhne Verete site on the upper Onega River and to 8400 BP on the Vychegda River. The canoes of these pre-Saami people were probably made of birch bark, since they had no heavy stone tools for making dugouts from logs. The Karelian sites of the pre-Saami population during the early Stone Age, as described by Mark Shakhnovich, point clearly to the use of birch-bark canoes: "Mesolithic sites are mainly represented by short-term seasonal fishing camps located on the islands and along the banks of water bodies in inland lake systems. Among them are several types of sites: multiseasonal base camps, seasonal fishing locations, hunting camps, multipurpose camps, and stone tool fabrication sites. The economy was based on hunting ungulates (reindeer, elk) and capturing spawning fish" (2007: 13). Such waterside settlements required boats, and the lightweight paddles known from this period indicate that birch-bark craft were used here.

Toward the end of the period 4000 to 1500 BCE, a heavy stone woodworking industry capable of efficiently producing dugout canoes appeared in the Ladoga-Onega region (Burov 2000). The Russian Karelian ground-stone macro-tool industry (see fig. 3.9, page 66) of about 5000 BCE, which is the earliest appearance of such technology in this region, has been studied in detail by Kerkko Nordqvist and Oula Seitsonen (2008) and by Kriiska, Tarasov, and Kirs (2013). Armed with this technology, people began to make log boats in Karelia; the oldest that has been found here dates to circa 2600 BCE and was discovered in Sheltozero on western Lake Onega. The largest (8 by 1.4 meters) is a log boat from Kandalaksha Bay, on the southern Kola Peninsula, dated to 1600 to 1900 BCE (Chernigov 2000). Both boats were made by burning out the inside of a log and removing the charred wood with ground-stone axes and gouges. These types of boats are among the earliest images seen in Karelian petroglyphs, including those at Vyg River (Uikunjoki in Karelian), near the town of Belomorsk (Sorokka in Karelian) (fig. 4.1).

The Mixed Saami and Karelian Bronze Age

The second period of Karelian boat development occurred in the Bronze Age, although according to Burov (1996), the

Fig. 4.1. Boat images in the rock art of the Lake Onega and White Sea regions. (After Savateev 1991: fig. 3; adapted by Marcia Bakry)

Stone Age continued in Karelia until circa 1500 BCE; the first copper came to the area from the Urals circa 1900 BCE. During this period, bronze appeared and fishing and sealing developed on the White Sea and on lakes Ladoga and Onega, with the help of metal technology used in boatbuilding (Savateev 1991). Metal tools made the production of wooden boats more practical and perhaps accelerated the diffusion of expanded log boat technology in the Baltic and Western Urals. Tapani Salminen believes that language change and population influx took place under the influence of the copper trade and migrations from the upper Volga (2001).

Among the animals hunted in this period were several species of seal, beluga, and walrus. The appearance of the Battle Axe people, who arrived circa 2500 BCE in the southern Baltic and circa 1800 BCE in Karelia, may have been the critical factor in the introduction of marine mammal hunting (Ravenstein and Keane 1905; Gurina 1987; Kriiska 1996). The Battle Axe people — or perhaps only their culture — expanded outward from East Prussia; they used corded-ware pottery, had a distinctive form of ground-stone battle axe, and practiced agriculture (see fig. 3.10, page 67). They also knew seal skin as *kesi* and most likely transferred that name, applying it to both seal skins and skin boats, to the Baltic Finns and Karelians (Koivulehto 1983). Seal-skin kesi are also mentioned in the *Kalevala* (see below). If this linguistic association is correct, the skin boats of the Battle Axe people probably spread to Lake Ladoga, the Gulf of Bothnia, Lake Saimaa, and the White Sea, all waters where seal were plentiful.

Along the White Sea, petroglyphs and rock paintings showing skin boats are found at Old and New Zalavruga

and date to circa 2100 to 1300 BCE. Later, toward the end of the Karelian Bronze Age, circa 1 to 500 CE, the first Southern Saami peoples along eastern Lake Ladoga became Finnic speakers under the influence of the Karelian Finnic population (Aikio 2006). During this process, these Saami likely shared skin boat and log boat production knowledge with the Baltic Finns in Karelia.

The Karelian Iron and Middle Ages

The third period of ancient Karelian boat history took place during the Iron and Medieval ages and involved mostly Karelian people. According to some theories, people from Finland, perhaps iron-using Häme fur hunters, migrated to western Lake Ladoga circa 500 CE and settled on the shores of the Vuoksi River, which flows to the Baltic Sea. These people may have formed the nucleus of the future Korela-Karelia people, and they soon assimilated the Southern Saami. The Vepsian-Karelians, the eastern people, had entered eastern Lake Ladoga as well as the Volkhov, Tiver, and Svir rivers on the isthmus between Ladoga and Onega, and they were present when the Eastern Vikings entered the region after 750 CE (Bubrikh 1947; Petrov and Petrov 2008). The Vepsians had been active as fur hunters and traders in Staraya Ladoga since 753 CE and became founding members of the Novgorod Federation some 100 years later (Stang 1980). The Korela-Karelians (later called the Käkisalmi or Kexholm) joined the federation in the 11th century. Soon they constructed their own *soima* (Viking-type lapstrake ships) in the Ladoga region, and for Novgorod they built the first Baltic Sea naval fleet. Roman Kovalev (2002) describes Karelian participation in the Novgorod fur trade and the importance of boats in its supply system; these boats, most of which were made in Karelia, were studied by Petr Sorokin (1997).

We can assume that the Karelian people, after expanding their territory first to Southern Saami lands around Lake Onega and then to the White Sea coast about 900 CE, soon were using all the boat technologies and tools available to them and that they learned to construct boats from logs, skins, and birch bark. Iron tools and nails made the work faster. The Novgorod Federation fur trade created an ever-growing demand for all kinds of portageable boats for rivers and lakes, and the Karelian people were probably the masters of that trade. Small expanded or planked log boats were practical for fur traders from Novgorod to Zavolochye (Russian for "behind the portage"), who crossed the portages to and from the Mezen-Pechora forest region. As many as 8,000 furs (mainly squirrel pelts) could be packed into a single 120-liter barrel, while perhaps three times as many could be carried in a dugout boat with a crew of one or two (Kovalev 2002: 276).

White Sea Karelian settlers began spring sealing among the pack ice and may have used skin boats, as described elsewhere (see page 81 on the Pomor). They were the people most familiar with voyaging on the White Sea and sailing to Norway and Novaya Zemlya. According to T. A. Shrader (2002), a student of Pomor pilotage, seven of the nine known early White Sea navigation charts originated on the Karelian coast.

Circa 900 CE, the Vepsian-Karelians founded a permanent settlement at Kegrela (Kevrol), a fur-trading center located where the Pinega River joins the Northern Dvina River near the White Sea coast, and they maintained it until the 14th century (Stang 1980). Some archaeologists believe this may have been where the Norwegian Viking chief Ottar (Othere) met Finnic-speaking Bjarmian hunters (Bubrikh 1947). The Vepsians founded their second fur-trading stronghold on Byeloe Ozero (White Lake), at the source of the Volga River, to push the Novgorod fur trade into the Western Urals using Komi-Zyrian and Mansi hunters and boatsmen, as is described later in this chapter.

According to Danish documents dated 1415 (see Sjögren 1828), the Korela-Karelians first entered Norwegian lands in the 1270s, in part to rob Saami people in Helgeland. Russian scientists have confirmed this early Karelian entry into the western White Sea and Kola regions. Until recently, Karelians lived around the southern end of Kandalaksha Bay (the Norse Gandvik), where they were active sea mammal hunters in winter and fishermen in summer. They also lived on the Kola Peninsula, where the majority of topographic names between Kirov and Umboy are of Karelian origin. Since medieval times, Karelians have occupied territories around Kanozera Lake, and from 1419 onward, they have been located along the Varzuga River, where they settled in Inga, Munozero, Kanozero, Poncheozero, Kovitsa, and other places.

The most remote Karelian coastal fur-trade center may have been on the Barents Sea, as suggested by documents by the Danish cartographer Claudius Clavius (Clavus) that confirm the location of Karelian people on its coast and islands. Clavius traveled extensively in the north from 1413 to 1424 and later established himself in Rome, where in 1480 he published maps covering Northern Europe and wrote about the location of peoples there. Concerning "Greenland" (here meaning Novaya Zemlya), he wrote: "It is a large land pointing toward eastern Russia. . . . the most northern part of Russia [which then meant only the European or Western

Urals Pechora part] is inhabited by the migrating Karelian people, whose land [Novaya Zemlya] points to the North Pole in the eastern parts" (quoted in Erslev 1885: 170).

Clavius's claim that there was a Vepsian-Karelian fur-trade center in Pustozersk was later confirmed by the Russian official Timotheus Klingstädt. In 1732, Klingstädt traveled for the Archangel Province government to study sea hunting and fur trade in Mezen, one of the centers of this business. The reason for a Karelian entry so far north may have been the Moscow-Russian capture of the fur town Ust-Yug in the late 1300s, which cut the Karelian trade route from Byeloe Ozero (White Lake) to Yugra. From Pustozersk, Karelians could navigate safely on the Barents Sea to their bases on the White Sea.

Boats in Karelian Petroglyphs

A rich trove of boat images in ancient Karelian rock art is found on the southwestern White Sea near Belomorsk, on the Vyg River (Uikunjoki in Karelian), and on Lake Onega. The images most relevant to our study are those depicting skin boats from New Zalavruga and those showing bark canoes from Besov Nos (see fig. 4.1). Table 3 summarizes known boat images in Karelian rock art, arranged according to the presumed age of the figures. The upper Vyg River figures, found near the town of Belomorsk (Sorokka in Karelian), seem to be the oldest, dating to the late Stone Age (Neolithic). Next in age are the engravings and paintings in Old and New Zalavruga, near the White Sea shore, estimated as dating to the Bronze Age. Rock art on Lake Onega, mostly at Besov Nos, is found around the lower part of the Karelian Mustajoki River; the age of these images is much discussed, but scientists mostly agree that they were created later than those in the Vyg and White Sea regions and perhaps were made by different people. Some date the Onega images to the Early Bronze Age, but most are more recent, from the Late Bronze Age, perhaps circa 1000 to 500 BCE. A. M. Tallgren estimated they were made circa 1700 BCE.

Yuri A. Advinatee (1966), who studied the Karelian petroglyphs in Belomorsk, in Old and New Zalavruga, and on Lake Onega, discussed the controversy over whether the images illustrate real boats or are simply symbolic. He mentioned A. M. Linevski (1939) and A. J. Bryusov (writing in the 1930s) as being among those who thought they depict actual boats; their opponents, including V. I. Ravdonikas (1936) and K. D. Lauskin (1959), suggested they are images of solar rooks (crows) who, after retiring into the next world, were transported to earth. In addition, some assume that

Table 3

Boat Images in Karelian Petroglyphs and Rock Paintings

Location	Number and Percentage of Boat Images Compared to All Figures at This Location	Height above Modern Sea Level (meters)	Date before Present
Upper Vyg River	29 10%	19.5–20	5180–4500 BP
Old Zalavruga	32 15%	15.6	3500–3300 BP
New Zalavruga	428 36%	15.3	4100 BP
Lake Onega	40 5%	At current lake level	4500–3000 BP

SOURCE: Autio 1981.

the Karelian rock art figures belong to a single tradition, while others believe the Belomorsk images depict boats too large to have been constructed with the technology available in the Neolithic. The most recent English-language discussions of these issues are by Poikalainen (1999) and Poikalainen and Ernits (1998). The modern consensus is that the images of larger boats—those containing as many as 24 paddlers and fitted with animal-effigy prows—might represent log boats with sewn plank sides, while the smaller images could depict either skin boats or log boats (*dolblenka* in Russian) with sewn planks.

Vyg River Log Boats

In all, only 29 boat images are found in rock art on the Vyg River, the smallest number at any of the three petroglyph locations in this area. Nevertheless, these images are interesting because they might be the oldest stone art in Karelia, possibly dating to the Neolithic. The types of boats in these images look different from those seen in other rock art images in this area, and some scientists have suggested they are log boats. Like Linevski and Bryusov, Advinatee believed these images do illustrate log boats, some possibly with outriggers. When fitted with a balance pontoon, such a craft could be sailed or paddled long distances; this technology was part of the Karelian boating tradition as recently as the 20th century (Advinatee 1966) but is almost completely unknown to experts on Arctic and North Atlantic regions.

The best archaeological option to match the White Sea boat figures is a Vihanti planked dugout boat unearthed in Finland in 1934 and studied by Itkonen, who published its details in a book on Finnish log boats (1942: 51). The Vihanti boat was discovered at Alpuanjärvi (Alpuan Lake), some 100 kilometers south of Oulu near the Gulf of Bothnia (64.41.66°N, 25.21.66°E). Today Alpuanjärvi is 40 kilometers

from the gulf and perhaps 500 kilometers from the White Sea and Varanger Fjord via river and lake connections. Here, near Oulu, old log boats were called *lapinvene*, "the boat of Lapp people" (Itkonen 1942: 32). Itkonen, then a curator at the National Museum in Helsinki, wrote:

> In Vihanti, an Iron Age log boat [later dated to circa 500 BCE/2500 BP by pollen analysis conducted by the National Museum of Finland] was found in the bottom of an artificially dried-up lake buried 113 centimeters deep in peat. The log canoe, probably of aspen, was rotten and discolored by peat such that the aft and middle parts were destroyed. The next summer, a circa 120-centimeter-long rotted front part was discovered and soon disintegrated. It seems that it had extra boards, one on each side (sewn into the log). A circa 10-centimeter-long "horn" projecting from the bottom . . . appeared like [those of] the Scandinavian two-horned canoes seen in Bronze Age rock engravings. Also present were conifer strips (10 by 19 millimeters thick and 4–9 millimeters wide) wrapped with birch-bark strips about 100 centimeters long. . . . It is possible that the bark-wrapped wooden strips had sealed the seam of the boards sewn to the log boat. (1942: 51–52)

Later excavations at the Vihanti site revealed a bronze figurine and a piece of asbestos ceramic, indicating that the boat was older than originally thought, dating to Neolithic times and thus one of the oldest planked boats found in Fennoscandia. Vihanti-type boats may have been used in the White Sea, too, as Russian scientists such as Bryusov assumed, and might be documented in the Vyg-Belomorsk rock art. These findings support Klem's (2010) claim that the Alta boat images represent wooden dugouts, and it seems likely that part or a large share of the Alta and Vyg-Belomorsk rock art images show wooden boats.

New Zalavruga Skin Boats

New Zalavruga has the largest set of boat figures known in Karelia—a total of 428. These images appear in scenes of sea hunting, with men harpooning beluga and angling with hooks and lines. Researchers have suggested that these depictions resemble skin boats, and Advinatee (1966) and the Karelian professor Yuri Savateev (1991) believed that the rock art depicts real boats, or at least realistic images of them. Savateev, who studied fishing and sea mammal hunting in Karelia, including boat use in the Neolithic and early Bronze and Iron ages, viewed the White Sea petroglyphs as portrayals that fit well with interpretations of archaeological finds. Marine hunting and fishing were central features of the early Karelian economy, providing fat and skins for trade and boatbuilding. Hunting of ring, bearded, and harp seal, beluga, and walrus began along lakes Onega and Ladoga and the White Sea in the Neolithic and the Bronze Age, between the 4th and 1st millennia BCE. The intensification of maritime hunting during this period must have been accompanied by an explosion in boat technology, which would not have been restricted to the sea coasts, since fish and seals were found in all the major rivers and lakes as well. Zalavruga, one such site, is located in the estuary of the Vyg River. Savateev (1991) believed that the images here represent Eskimo-type skin boats because of their slightly curved bottom keels, suggesting skeletal frames, and angled sterns. He noted that while some were small, carrying one to six people, others could accommodate 12 to 24 (some skin-covered North American Eskimo umiaks could accommodate 30 to 40 individuals). More recently, Martynov (2012) also has expressed the view that these images depict skin boats.

Boat Images at Besov Nos, Lake Onega

Only a few of the rare Lake Onega petroglyphs show boats. In contrast to rock art on the White Sea, which shows short boats with high freeboard, the Onega images show long and low boats. Archaeological evidence suggests that the Neolithic and Bronze Age people of southern Onega might have differed from those on the White Sea coast: sites east of the lake contain Sperrings fish vertebra–impressed ceramics, while those in northern Onega and on the White Sea coast have Sär 1 pit-comb ceramics (Autio 1981). These petroglyph sites (circa 4500 to 3000 BP) are on sandy terraces in

convenient locations for launching boats, often by a small lake or in the narrow bays of Lake Onega, but rarely on riverbanks (Vitenkova 2003). Savateev (1991) believed the low-freeboard Onega images depict birch-bark canoes and that these images were created later than the rest of the Karelian rock art.

In his classic book *The Circumpolar Stone Age*, Gutorm Gjessing discussed Karelian petroglyphs from Lake Onega and the Vyg River in Russia, near the southwestern shore of the White Sea. He believed that the Vyg River and White Sea images illustrate skin boats, while those at Lake Onega show bark boats, writing that bark canoes had been in use mainly in "Sweden, southernmost Finland, and south of Lake Onega. . . . And whereas the boats in the carvings at the White Sea clearly were skin boats, those in the contemporary carvings at Onega are of quite another form" (1944: 15). But, on the other hand, he argued that skin boats were the most important means of transport along the Arctic coasts and that together with stone lamps, toggling harpoons, and *ulu* knives, they were among the core elements of what he called the Circumpolar Stone Age. Ella Kivikoski (1944) came to a similar conclusion in her study of Russian Karelia, conducted in 1942–43, finding a qualitative difference between the Onega boat figures and the White Sea ones. As Gjessing suggested, the White Sea images show boats that are wide and short and have a high freeboard, whereas the long, low Onega boats have animal figureheads that rise directly from the bow. In her view, the birch-bark canoe zone continued from Onega to central Finland, where similar boat figures are seen in rock art in Myllylampi, Viittamosalmi, Saraakallio, Uittamonsalmi, and Ruominkapia.

An earlier researcher, Walther Vogel (1912: 4–6), believed that the rock engravings here show bark canoes. The two-horned type of boat image is found on the northern Swedish and Norwegian coasts, especially in rock art in Swedish Bohuslän, on the coast of the Skagerrak north of present-day Gothenburg, and in Denmark, where bronze figures of these boats have been discovered. Vogel referred to Eduard Hahn's (1907) theory that sewn-bark canoes came first and later led to the construction of sewn planked boats in Scandinavia. In 1938, the remains of an undated canoe was discovered in Suurniemi, Juva commune, in the northern Lake Saimaa region of Finland not far from Ladoga Karelia. According to an oral description (Itkonen 1942: 48), it was covered with birch bark. This might have been one of the birch-bark canoes—*tuohine veneh*—of the Karelian or Saami people. Christer Westerdahl (1985a,b) documented other bark canoes in Swedish Lapland, which perhaps is the westernmost limit of the inland boreal forest bark canoe zone that once spanned Eastern Siberia, crossed the Ural Mountains, and ended in the Karelian and Saami communities in Fennoscandia.

Skin Boats in Kalevala Poems

Martti Haavio wrote in *Väinämöinen* (1950) that the *Kalevala* tradition originated in southwestern Finland and accompanied Finnish people as they migrated to the western coast of the White Sea (Finnish Viena-Karelia in the Russian Kemi district), carrying their runic alphabet and poems with them. The *Kalevala* poems gradually became part of the Karelian Finnic tradition. The verses were collected by many people in many parts of Finland, notably in Karelia, where Elias Lönnrot gathered the major part of the poems and where the songs, as oral tradition, survived longer than in other Finnish regions. Some of the old southwestern Finnish poems, he discovered, still existed among the Karelians, documenting everyday life and traditions, including the use of boats between 1600 and 1850 CE.

Kalevala poems present the ancient Finnish worldview with much action and fiction, but they also present Middle Ages life and crafts; they speak both of large matters, such as the creation of the universe, and of smaller ones, such as the making of beer, fishing, metalworking, and boatbuilding. Boat themes are present in nearly all *Kalevala* poems because Karelia (like Finland and Lapland) has the most extensive inland and coastal waterways in Europe and because its people had to use boats to travel both short and long distances.

One of the oldest *Kalevala* songs describing boat construction is an archival fragment with a 23-line rune in the handwriting of Christfried Ganander, who published the first *Kalevala* compilation, *Mythologia Fennica*, in 1789. It presents us with a sketch of skin boatbuilding in 17th-century written Finnish (the manuscript dates from the 1760s, but Haavio [1950] believed the orthography is from a much earlier period). Apparently Ganander had notes at his disposal that were recorded, perhaps in the 1600s, on the northeastern Gulf of Bothnia, maybe in Kemi parish, at the inflow of the Kemi River to the sea. The first part of the poem, rendered here in English, captures the basic principles of skin boat construction:

> Smith Ilmarinen made a boat with his knowledge,
>> built a boat by singing.
> When he got it ready, he covered it with fish skin,
>> greased it with scales of the rudd.
> When he had to make the gunwale,
>> he lacked three [charm] words.
> He went to look for them
>> from the mouth of Andera Vipunen,
> That Vipunen had been dead a long time,
>> long gone,
> long had Andera been missing,
>> a great ash tree on his shoulders,
> on his knees a squirrel hill,
>> on his jawbone an alder,
> a bird cherry for the collar-bow [wood]
>> at his beard. (Haavio 1952: 110)

In the Finnish-Karelian *Kalevala* language, the poem's first lines are as follows:

> Teki Seppoi Ilmarinen,
>> teki tiedolla venettä.
> Latoi purtta laulamalla,
>> jonga satti tehnehexi.
> Sen ketti kulun kädellä,
>> voiti sorvan suomuxella.
> Puuttui colmia sanoa,
>> paras puita pannesahan. (Haavio 1952: 134)

Haavio discussed the connections among Ganander's reference to fish skins, boats, and the origin of the name of the Finnish people, *Suomi*:

> These lines [in Ganander's poem] may contain recollections of an ancient skin boat; the boat-maker covers his boat with fish skin (*kesi*). The word *suomus* is a derivation of the word *suomi*, originally meaning "fish skin," as Lauri Hakulinen has shown; "Suomi" also has become the word for Finland and its people. There is some evidence that the Lapps in old times used a skin boat like a kayak, as certain information about the Lapps in Sweden would seem to prove, but we have no knowledge of their having boats of fish skin. (1952: 110)

In fact, there is archaeological evidence of skin boats in Pohjanmaa (in Swedish Österbotten), where Ganander collected this poem. In Itkonen's book on Finnish log boats, he reported that in Lapua commune, near the present-day town of Vaasa, remains of an as-yet undated skin boat were found; their "ribs and thread seams [were] visible" (1942: 48; see also page 62). Two light Stone Age paddles also have been found in this coastal region, in Kemi and Ylistaro; other old paddles were recovered in northeastern Finland, at the sources of Kemijoki River in Savukoski commune (Kaarlo Katiskoski, pers. comm. 2005), and were possibly connected to inland birch-bark boats (Itkonen 1942: 48). HL has two replicas, measured and made by Harri Mäkilä, of Savukoski paddles dating to 3500 BP. Furthermore, 16th- to 18th-century literature commonly refers to seal skins as "fish skins," and thus poems that mention canoes covered in fish skins are not controversial, given our knowledge of boatbuilding. Such usage also appears in the incantation "The Origin of the Seal," which the rune singer Juhana Kainulainen dictated to Lönnrot in 1828, in Kesälahti commune on northern Lake Saimaa. It runs as follows:

> Little Väini, son of Mauni, made a sailboat, with his wisdom made a little boat by singing. The boat got ready. He covered it with fish skin, greased it with fat of the seal, furnished it with scales of the rudd [a fish]. He rowed slowly along the Neva River and circled the Neva Peninsula [*neva* = swamp]. Huiko [a bystander on the shore] shouted from the neck of the land, beyond the hill, crying: "Whose boat on the water, whose boat on the waves?" Old Väinämöinen's boat, swishing ripples of water, a little ripple of the north, ripple of the bark on the water. A man rose from the sea, came up from the waves, one who counted the little islands of the sea, a watcher of the fishes of the water. In his hand he had six flowers, at the tip of each flower are six more, all full of seal fat. From them it congeals into a seal. If you have done evil, come confess your work, better your evil deed. Take hence your hatred—into yellow lungs, into sweet liver. (Quoted in Haavio 1952: 110–11)

As this story indicates, early Saami and Finnish literature includes frequent references to boats made of fish (seal) skin and allusions to seal, seal skins, and seal oil in the spiritual and economic life of these people. The end of this passage suggests the role of sea creatures in spiritual cleansing rituals. (Väinämöinen, also mentioned in this excerpt, is an ancient god or hero and the main figure in early Saami and Finnish folklore, including the *Kalevala*.)

Parallel poems describing skin boat construction have been found in many old Karelian, Saami, and Ingrian locations and may be evidence that such boats were built across a wide territory, from the White Sea and Gulf of Bothnia coast to lakes Saimaa and Ladoga. Besides the northwestern coast of Finland, similar poems mentioning boats covered with fish skin have been collected from the south, on the Karelian Isthmus (Sakkola and Lempaala), and from northeastern Karelia (Vuokkiniemi), in Viena-Karelia, on the Russian east coast of the White Sea.

These *Kalevala* poems also cast light on skin boats' wooden structure and construction. The poem that Ganander collected mentions various trees, such as ash, alder, and bird cherry, that were used in canoe construction. Bird-cherry wood also was used in Finland to make parts of horse harnesses (*luokki*) because it is elastic and bends easily. In Western Siberia, the Samoyed, Khanty, and Turkic Tatar (Chelkan) used bird-cherry branches for gunwales and ribs in birch-bark canoes (Belgibaev 2004; Pelikh 1972). *Kalevala*-related runes also tell us about the use of fish bones and teeth as pins or nails in boat construction: a rune collected in Lempaala commune, a region inhabited by the Ingrian people on the Karelian Isthmus (on the Russian side of the old Finnish-Russian border), tells us, "He made it [a boat] with suomi scales [fish skin], of the pike-fish's teeth" (Haavio 1952: 110). This idea seems novel but is eminently practical, for pins such as these would long outlast iron nails.

In his *Kalevala*, Lönnrot included another song (number 16) about boatbuilding, which contains information on the construction of a planked boat. He may have had at least two reasons for this selection. First, the main figure, Väinämöinen, is building the boat himself—not Ilmarinen, the folkloric *Kalevala* blacksmith, who makes the boat in Ganander's poem. Second, the lapstrake boat (a planked expanded log boat) was more common in Karelia and Finland in those days than the skin boat and thus would have been more familiar to Lönnrot's readers.

In summary, in the collected and interpreted *Kalevala* runes, we find mention of skin boats, expanded log boats (*haapio*), and sewn and nailed lapstrake boats. (We have not located a reference to birch-bark canoes in the *Kalevala*, but we might if we investigated all the handwritten *Kalevala*-related poems; as noted earlier, a term for the birch-bark canoe, *tuohine veneh*, does exist in the Karelian language.) Thus we can say with confidence that the *Kalevala* provides evidence of a long period of boatbuilding history that includes nearly all the major boat types known from ancient times.

NOVGOROD: A BALTIC RUSSIAN TRADE FEDERATION

The Novgorod Federation was founded in 862 CE on the northern shore of Ilmen Lake (Ilmajärvi), the source of the Volkhov River, which flows to Lake Ladoga, 200 kilometers inland from the Finnish Gulf. More than a century earlier, in 753, Eastern Vikings from Sweden had established a trading post, known later as Old (Staraya) Ladoga, on Lake Ladoga's southern shore, on the route to Novgorod, so that they could pursue the fur trade and expand their military ventures farther east to the Volga and south to Byzantium and the Black Sea. According to legends and the Novgorod chronicles (Walsh 1948), the federation was established by three Finnish-Karelian peoples and two Slavic peoples. After long quarreling, they invited Prince Rurik, the Varangian chieftain of the Slavic Rus people, to rule Novgorod, while the prince's brother, Sineus, became the master of the Byeloe Ozero (White Lake) region around the headwaters of the Volga River, ruling the local Vepsian-Karelian people. As a result, Novgorod originated as a Finnic-Baltic-Slavic confederation with a Varangian Rus superstructure and an early democratic society (Lind 2004). As C. Raymond Beazley wrote in the introduction to his translation of *The Chronicle of Novgorod, 1016–1417* (Royal Historical Society 1914), the Novgorod Federation was a trading entity whose power stemmed from alliances that forced peoples under its dominion to pay taxes, usually in fur. The Novgorod trade was based on two entities: the Novgorod settlement area and its tributary states, and a huge adjacent region that it dominated colonially.

In time, the role of northern Finnish peoples in state affairs declined, and Novgorod's business connections with the Volga Finnic Merja, Murom, and Moscow Russians increased. These connections followed two transport routes: one from Lake Onega to Byeloe Ozero and then to the Volga headwaters, and another from Ilmen Lake via the Musta (Msta) River eastward and across a portage into the Volga basin. The major route to the most important fur-supply territory in the Mezen-Pechora forest region was over portages in the lands behind the Northern Dvina River, inhabited by the Komi-Zyrian, Mansi, and Samoyed peoples (Kovalev 2002). Boat transport was the key to Novgorod's hegemony. Below we describe a unique Novgorod contribution to the story of canoes: a most unusual composite boat made of wood, bark, and skin.

The Swedish naval officer Philip Johann Stralenberg's *Historico-Geographical Description of the Northern and Eastern Parts of Europe and Asia* (1738) mentions pirates who used skin boats to prey on commercial boats plying the eastern Baltic Novgorod trade. Stralenberg was familiar with the Russian Empire because he was sent as a prisoner of war to Siberia, which he explored as a member of the D. G. Messerschmidt expedition of the 1720s. A few years later, Stralenberg, while searching for trade connections to the east, learned that Pechora fur traders knew about Asia, which they called "India." The Pechora traders had reached the White and Baltic seas before Novgorod rule began in the Western Urals and in the Pechora basin circa 1150.

A Late Iron Age Composite Aspen-Bark Canoe

In 1960, the remains of three similar boats were found under the walls of Vladimir Tower of the Novgorod Kremlin (fortress), built in 1044 (fig. 4.2a–b). The boats were likely made when Novgorod was emerging as a major Baltic power. Their highly unusual construction combines all the technologies known in their day. The vessel studied in most detail is an expanded log boat that has sewn planks held up on the inside by wooden supports. A layer of skin was fastened to the interior planks with tree nails (wooden nails), and a layer of aspen bark was glued to the outside of the planks.

According to James Hornell's (1940) paper on canoe history, bark canoes emerged first, followed by dugout canoes

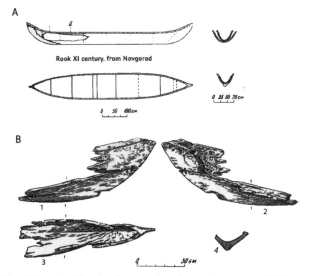

Fig. 4.2. a. Architectural reconstruction of an unusual 11th-century planked log canoe excavated in 1960 from beneath the Vladimir Tower in Old Novgorod. *b.* Fragment of the planked side that had a skin covering on the inner surface and sheets of aspen bark glued on the outside. (After Troyanovskiy and Petrov 2018)

and expanded dugouts. The Novgorod boats defy this conventional evolutionary classification. According to Hornell's taxonomy, the Novgorod canoe would be called a bark canoe with dugout reinforcing. But it also has a skin component, since its structure includes a layer of leather. Ole Crumlin-Pedersen might call it an expanded planked log boat, and Christer Westerdahl might say it is a sewn boat, since the frames and planks are all sewn. In fact, it is a composite of all three types. The Russian scientists S. V. Troyanovskiy and M. I. Petrov, who studied the Novgorod boats, give a detailed description of the best-preserved one:

The dimensions of the ancient boat are 6.75 meters length, 90 centimeters width, and 55 centimeters height. In the center there [was] a place for a small mast. . . . The mast and sail [would have been] fastened with ropes to the bow and the stern. The log hull was extended by eight ribs, whose ends are tapered. . . . Judging by the marks on the boards and the sizes of the frames, they extended up to 5–7 centimeters short of the upper edge of the side-board. . . . The upper edge of the board has a small protrusion with small rectangular openings containing oak nails 3–2 millimeters in diameter. These nails are about 18–20 centimeters apart and encircle the entire boat. . . . There is another series of oak nails not on the log base but on the board. . . . In the bow and the stern is an additional row of nails. The nails on both the log base and on the board are not flush but rise 0.3–0.4 centimeters above the surface. Consequently, the nails must have fastened a 0.3- to 0.4-centimeter-thick skin that has not been preserved. This skin covered the entire exterior of the boat. . . .

Traces of different organic matter were identified by conservator G. N. Tomashevich as pine tar, chalk, and animal glue. Pine resin was present on all surfaces of the boat, while animal glue was only on the exterior, mixed with chalky putty. Glue and chalk have also been found on the remains of the other boats. . . . The skin was firmly fastened to the log bottom with chalky animal glue and wood nails. This skin protected the thin wood hull of the boat. . . . In the bow, a board fragment was attached to the body of the boat with bast fibers. To keep water out, a skin patch covered the joint between the two. (2018, paragraphs 6–10)

The authors wrote that the Novgorod chronicles describe three varieties of 11th-century boats: simple, *naboynoy* (planked), and seaworthy. The naboynoy variety had additional boards mounted to its hull, and this is the vessel type found in Novgorod. Until this recovery, such finds had never been discovered in the Novgorod 11th-century cultural layer or in other Russian cities. There are no similar finds from Western Europe; the log boats that are known there do not have bark or skin coverings.

The complexity of the small sailing vessel described above is quite amazing: its outer bark and skin inner layers, the detail of its construction and assembly, the precise arrangement of its pins and nails, and the use of different tree species—aspen for the hull, fir for the frames, oak for the nails, and linden for the lashings. All these details testify to the shipbuilding skills of the Novgorodians and the complex construction technology available to them in the 10th century in the upper reaches of the Volhov River. Petr Sorokin (1997) has shown that during the Viking Iron Age and into the Middle Ages, expanded log boats with sewn planks were preferred over nailed boats and canoes in Novgorod. For hundreds of years, no iron-nailed boats were built there. It would appear that the Novgorod boats were part of a long tradition of building log canoes with sewn plank sides fastened with glue and tree nails, rather than iron nails as in the coeval Northern European Viking tradition. In the context of these more common boats, whether the extraordinary Novgorod bark-and skin-covered planked log boat was an aberration or a major technological line of medieval boatbuilding remains a question that only future archaeological finds can resolve.

THE MARITIME POMOR: RUSSIAN HUNTERS OF THE WHITE SEA

A. J. Sjögren (1828) studied the Finnish, Saami and Karelian, and Russian (Slavic) populations in Lapland and the White Sea region and wrote about the movement into the north of the Russian Pomor (in Russian, *Pomor* means "living along the sea coast"). This migration began when Tatar (Mongol) invasions in the 1240s forced people into northern forests inhospitable to Mongol horses. Among the migrants were Volga residents who came to settle south of the White Sea (map 8), where they mixed with the local Finnic "Chud" population (Spörer 1867). Over time, the definition of *Pomor* spread to cover all Russian nonindigenous settlers, while the Natives east of the White Sea were still referred to as the Chud or, on the eastern White Sea shore, as the Komi-Zyrians. Toward the end of the 15th century,

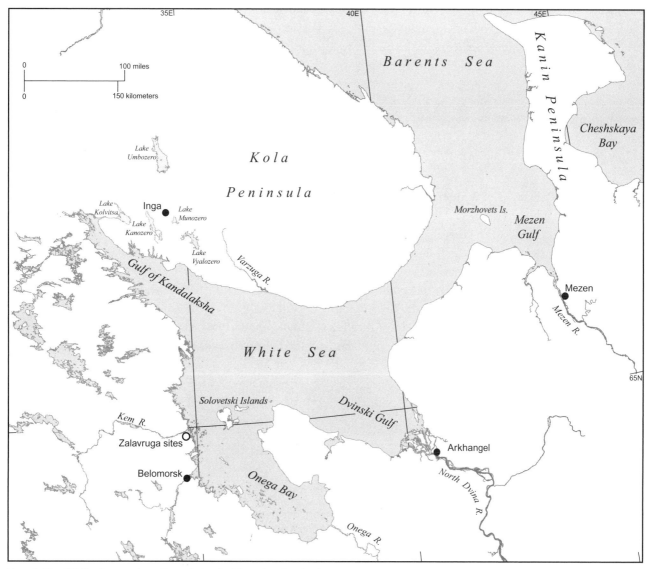

Map 8. The White Sea region. (Dan Cole, Smithsonian Institution)

the Pomor discovered Svalbard (Spitsbergen), which they later occupied, 100 years before Willem Barents named these islands in 1596. In the early 17th century, the Komi-Zyrians and Russians mixed and became known as "Pomor" fur hunters, a trading people who then pioneered the Northern Sea Route along the Arctic Ocean coast to Yamal and eventually reached the Bering Strait (Black 1988).

The White Sea Fishery

Early Pomor settlements on the southern White Sea coast owed their economy to fishing, seal hunting, salt production, and fur trading (Jasinski and Ovsyannikov 2010). The thick forest provided fuel that the Pomor used to boil seawater in large metal cauldrons, extracting salt for pickling

fish and curing sea mammal hides. Salmon, herring, cod, and other marine fish were abundant, and freshwater fish populated the lakes and rivers. Sea mammals, including harp and ring seal and walrus, were also plentiful in coastal waters, and beluga ascended the lower reaches of the rivers in the summer as they chased fish, including sturgeon. Of these, the harp seal (*Phoca groenlandica*) was the most economically important. Its blubber and hide were highly sought after, and the annual return of thousands of individuals to give birth and wean their young on the spring ice made this species a target for maritime hunters from Mesolithic to modern times.

In 1867, the Russian Pomor operated 41 stations for fishing cod, herring, and salmon and hunted seal along the

Murmansk coast of the Kola Peninsula (Tengengren 1965). There were still more in the White Sea, on the Kanin Peninsula, and along the Barents Sea coast as far as Novaya Zemlya and Vaigach Island (fig. 4.3). They fished in the summer. As winter closed in, most of the fishermen withdrew to their homelands on the southern White Sea to sell their sea mammal hides and dried and salted fish to merchants, who transported it to Moscow, Scandinavia, England, and Western Europe.

Seal hunting in the White Sea was a large-scale enterprise for which thousands of hunters, including Pomor, Karelians, and Saami, gathered from their inland locations in Norway, Sweden, and Russia (Tengengren 1965). If the hunting and fishing localities were far from home, men had to overwinter in outpost stations, which they used as staging grounds for other expeditions. In the early 19th century, hunters spent the winter in Kola and put to sea to catch whale and walrus early in May. Those who voyaged to Novaya Zemlya and Spitsbergen hunted polar fox, Arctic reindeer, polar bear, walrus, and beluga, leaving in their ships in June or July and arriving on the hunting grounds weeks later. The voyages of these Arctic fishermen were astonishingly long, sometimes exceeding 1,900 kilometers. Such trips may have begun as early as the 15th century.

There is a 1588 reference, written by Giles Fletcher, an English ambassador to Russia, to seal hunting on ice floes in the White Sea. Fletcher was one of the first Western Europeans to sail there, visiting Archangel soon after it was

Fig. 4.3. Pomor men outfitted for the harp seal hunt among the floating White Sea spring ice in 1899. (Photograph: Leitzinger of Archangel; courtesy Taras Tyupko)

founded in 1584. His report, reprinted in Samuel Purchas's encyclopedic work *Purchas His Pilgrim* (published in London in 1625), provides documentation of the seal hunt in the Gulf of Bothnia in earlier times. Referring to Fletcher's descriptions, Tengengren noted:

One of Russia's most important articles of trade is oil recovered from seal blubber. Seal hunters collect in great numbers in late summer when the innermost part of Dvina Bay becomes frozen; here they drag up their sealing boats and store them for the winter. In the late winter or early spring, before the ice has broken up, the hunters return to their boats and start to hunt. They drag the boats with them over the ice, sleeping in them during their hunting expeditions. As the number of the seal hunters is large, the sealing boats form 17 or 18 fleets, which they divide into several teams or gangs of five or six boats each. . . .

When a boat crew has discovered the seals, which lie sunning themselves on the ice in massive groups of 4,000 or 5,000 animals, the men light a beacon, whereupon other crews hasten to the spot. The seals are surrounded and killed with blows on the muzzle with a club. When the animals notice that they are surrounded, they crowd together in order to break the ice with their weight. The hunters must often wade into the pools of water that form on the ice. After the slaughter, the quarry is divided among the boat crews. The skin with the blubber is removed from the bodies, which are left behind on the ice, and the pelts are taken to land. They dig pits 1.5 fathoms deep on the beach and free the skin from the blubber by placing the pelts in the pits in alternating layers with red-hot stones. In this way the blubber melts. The oil rising to the surface is of varying quality and is sold for different purposes at trading stations. (1965: 450–52)

Fletcher's description of the seal hunt and the huge skin-processing industry provides context showing the importance of boats in the sealing economy of the White and Barents seas region, an industry that was practiced for thousands of years. It also explains why boats are so prominent in ancient rock art in this region. Beyond the pragmatics of the seal hunt, the pursuit of seal among the floating spring sea ice was a dangerous enterprise and for this reason was given protective and spiritual expression in religious ritual, which included rock art representations.

As Germanic farmers, the Iron Age ancestors of the Swedes, expanded north along the western Baltic, they displaced Coast Saami fishermen and seal hunters, and earlier boat types—perhaps skin-covered—disappeared (Broadbent 2010). In Österbotten in northwestern Finland, people began to keep cattle and cultivate land as maritime fishing and hunting declined. In the White Sea region, agriculture was not an alternative; it was feasible only on the coast west of the Dvina River. Here sealing persisted for much longer in the White Sea than in the Gulf of Bothnia. Tengengren suggested that White Sea fishery was more profitable, larger, and better financed and may also have benefited from a deeper pool of natural resources. The more restricted resources of the Baltic and Bothnian Gulf rapidly declined due to overexploitation in the 1600s. Here the Lapp, Karelian, and Finnish peoples turned to inland fishing on lakes and rivers, but these resources also were depleted under voracious western market pressure. This was also a time of Saami reindeer herding expansion, which required a strong inland focus for the herders.

Pomor Boats

The attention to boats in prehistoric rock art on the White Sea demonstrates that the fishery has drawn people to these coasts for thousands of years. Although discussion continues as to whether prehistoric boats were skin-covered frame watercraft, expanded dugouts, or planked boats, rock art carvings clearly demonstrate an ancient boat ancestry in the area (see chapter 3's section on the Saami). These petroglyphs show that some boats were small, while others were larger and had crews of 6 to 10 oarsmen. By the Middle Ages, the boats used by Pomor seal hunters were planked and fitted with sledge runners so that they could be dragged over the ice by manpower. The Pomor used canvas-covered boats as late as the early 20th century; a photographer known only as Leitzinger of Archangel may have taken photos of these boats (figs. 4.4–4.5) in 1897 or earlier, since similar shots—which might even the same canvas-covered boats and Pomor men—illustrate a book on Mezen seal hunters by Alexander Engelhard (1899: 297).

Using these and other photos, we can estimate that the typical Pomor boat was about 6 to 8 meters long, 2 meters wide, and 1.2 to 1.5 meters high. Under the gunwales, oars were inserted through small ports in the uppermost plank. These wooden boats may have been made of very thin boards or stringers, and the photos suggest they were covered with

Fig. 4.4. A postcard from 1899 shows Russian Pomor circa 1920 dragging their canvas-covered plank boats over the frozen ice near Mezen to reach open water and the sealing grounds. (Photograph: Leitzinger of Archangel; courtesy Taras Tyupko)

Fig. 4.5. Pomor hunters worked in teams when hunting harp seals on the dangerous ice front; this picture was taken in spring 1899. (Photograph: Leitzinger of Archangel; courtesy Taras Tyupko)

canvas, perhaps sail-quality canvas coated with seal oil or oil mixed with tar.

The hull form may not have been much different from that of the boats that sailed these same waters 500 or 1,000 years earlier, although their construction and materials were different. The same can be said of the open skin boats and kayaks of the Eskimo and Koryak. Whenever a good boat form has been created—in this case by the Saami-Karelian-Chud sealers—there is a strong tendency to maintain it from one generation to the next. Karelians were skilled boatbuilders who made boats for themselves as well as for sale; many worked in the Dvina estuary as shipwrights for the Russians, building both large ships and small boats. These traditions continued even when they built ships for the White Sea and Arctic Ocean; as late as the 1800s, they were making these ships with planks sewn with *vitsa* spruce roots, since flexible lashings are better at withstanding ice impacts than iron nails, which are too rigid and prone to breaking under cold conditions (Sorokin 1997).

THE KOMI-ZYRIANS: FUR HUNTERS AND TRADERS OF THE MEZEN-PECHORA FOREST

The ancestors of the Komi originally inhabited the middle and upper Kama River region west of the Ural Mountains in the Mezen-Pechora-Kama taiga, the largest forest territory in northeastern Europe. According to the *Academic Dictionary of Komi People* (Komi People 2014), the Komi were closely related to the Udmurd (Votyak), but around 2,000 to 1,500 years ago they split into several groups, one of which migrated into the Vychegda River basin. Here they mixed with other groups and began acquiring their ethnic identity as Komi (or Komi-Zyrians), while those who remained in the Kama basin became known as the Komi-Permians. Their neighbors were the Mansi to the east, the Nenets Samoyed to the north, and the Vepsian-Karelians to the west. The Komi-Zyrian language is close to the Komi-Permian and Udmurd languages, and all are part of the Permic subbranch of Finno-Ugrian.

From the 10th to the 15th centuries, before Russians inhabited the Northern Dvina River basin, the Komi lived in contact with Karelians in the basins of the Northern Divina and Vym rivers. The Komi language has many loanwords from and cognates with Karelian, including terms relating to agriculture, spinning, house building, food, crafts, and clothing. The Komi have also adopted Russian loanwords over many centuries. The modern Komi, comprising some 345,000 people, generally live in Russia's Komi Republic, whose population is roughly one-third Komi and two-thirds Russian.

The Komi-Zyrians were among the most outstanding fur traders in all of Northern Eurasia. Their trade networks ranged from the White Sea to Western Siberia and the Tunguska rivers. As A. M. Tallgren (1934) noted, during the Iron Age fur trade in the Kama-Pechora region from 400 to 500 CE, the Kama River Perm-Zyrians (Zyrians living in the Perm region) sold sable and other furs taken by the Mansi and Nenets in Urals-Pechora territory. The Komi-Zyrians probably had a stake in the great fur-trade center Ust-Yug on the upper Northern Dvina (J. Martin 1983) and may have partnered with Karelians in the fur-trade center in Pustozersk beginning in the mid-1400s. The Komi helped in the early phase of the Russian subjugation of Siberia and played a role in fur-trade activities with the Khanty, Mansi, and Nenets-Samoyed at the Khanty fortress of Obdorsk (modern Salekhard). In the White Sea region, the Komi-Zyrians operated mainly from the town of Mezen and participated in commercial fishing and sea mammal hunting, known later as the Pomor trade.

In the latter part of their history, the Komi-Zyrian people were land and maritime hunters and skilled fur traders along the polar sea coasts and across Western Siberia. Their primary conveyances in these later years were expanded log boats and planked wooden boats, but their earlier heritage was connected to skin boats and birch-bark canoes. They probably acquired expanded log boat technology while living as part of the Udmurt people in the Perm region. In the large spring sealing operations near Mezen, the Komi used boats that they could drag over sea ice to reach open water or leads. Russian sources often describe the Komi-Zyrians as Pomor, and Pomor sealing practices, including the boats they used, were similar to those of the Komi-Zyrians as well. But here our main interest is the Komi birch-bark canoe and its construction and use, as gleaned from old documents and later studies. Most of the Komi-Zyrians' and Komi-Permians' neighbors—such as the Mansi, Khanty, and Nenets, whom they met regularly in the Pechora-Kama area while trading furs—used bark canoes, so it is likely that the Komi did, too.

Komi Birch-Bark Canoes

The best descriptions and history of Komi bark canoes are found in the work of Alexander Shutikhin (2008), who is from the Komi Republic. Our present work owes much to his scholarship and to his generosity in sharing his experience in building replica birch-bark canoes.

Komi and Russian Slavic boat terms can be misleading, since some are not original, others have been corrupted over time, and sometimes bark canoes, planked boats, and log boats carry the same name, depending on time, place, and speaker. Thus, according to Shutikhin, the ancient bark canoe was known in Komi lands by the Russian loanwords *ushkuem*, *korab*, *kayuchok*, and *syumodpyzh* in Komi and Mansi, although the major Russian term for a birch-bark canoe is *berestyanka*. In the Pechora woods lived not only Komi people but also Mansi, whose earliest means of water transportation was the *syumodpyzh* birch-bark canoe (Shutikhin 2008: 6). As discussed below, the word *uskuem* or *ushkuy* implies a skin boat. Even so, the Russian researcher A. N. Plastinin, who has written about the language, terminology, and analysis of boat types in the Western Urals, doubts that skin boats ever were used on Komi inland waters:

The reflections of D. Zakharov, a Kirov student of local lore, about the origin of the word *ushkuy* directed him to the thought that ushkuy boats are canoes over which cattle hides were stretched (*ya'sh*—bull, bull calf; *osh*—bear; and *ku*—skin in the Komi language). This may be true from a linguistic point of view, but historical information tells us that the ushkuy is an expanded log boat [*odnoderevka*], such as can be reconstructed under modern conditions by finding an aspen tree 1 meter in diameter. Probably the presence of suitable logs is one of the reasons for the disappearance of the ushkuy. By the middle of the second millennium CE, intensive forest harvesting led to the exhaustion of old timber and it many have become difficult to find aspen of sufficient diameter and 18-meter length. Now, for the building of an expanded log boat, one can only find an aspen trunk with a diameter of 30–40 centimeters and a length of 6–7 meters. . . .

On the origin of the Slav name *ushkuy* one can make a daring and simple assumption, as one can see under the porch of the house of Boris Nikolayevich Nemdinova in upper Ust-Yug the dried-out shape of a "carved" expanded log boat, which strongly resembles the convoluted ear of an animal. Descriptively thinking, the Novgorodians probably could not but note the similarity between a cartilaginous ear and the aspen canoe preform when it is dried over a fire during its construction. In Vladimir Dahl's Russian-language dictionary there is an old word for "boat," *ushkuy* or *ushkol*. In the same dictionary, the expanded log boat is called in Archangel Province *ushkan*, while in Pskov it is called *ushan*. . . . There are also small birch-bark or aspen expanded log boats [*dolblenye*] of the Komi people, called *syumya* or *dpyzh* [birch-bark boat] and *pipupyzh* [aspen boat], but there is no information about Komi skeleton [frame] boats covered over by the skins of animals. (2008: 5)

Other suggestions about the possibility that skin boats with skeletonlike frames were once used on the White Sea have been inspired by Karelian, Onega, and Belomore (White Sea) rock art, as we have recounted earlier (Poikalainen 1999: 64–67; see also fig. 4.1, page 73). In these images, depictions of boats show 3 to 24 rowers (Shutikhin 2008). The Archangel archaeologist A. Martynov (2012), who has studied navigation with rafts, expanded log boats, and skin boats in the

Solovetsky Monastery archipelago, considers skin boats the type most likely to have been used in the White Sea region in early times, while canvas-covered planked boats have been used there for seal hunting during recent centuries. But the smoking gun—an intact Komi bark or skin canoe—is still missing, and there is neither a description in the literature nor an illustration of one, as far as we know. A likely conclusion is that the Komi people, from very early times onward, used expanded log boats for their inland trading expeditions and later adopted planked boats for maritime ventures.

However, we do have a description of a Mansi birch-bark canoe from the western side of the Urals that may be relevant to Komi boat history. Long ago, Antropova's (1961) research demonstrated that the bark canoes used by a given people usually resemble the canoes of their close neighbors, especially if there is no pronounced cultural or geographic border, such as a large river or mountain range, between them. There were no such barriers between the Komi and the Mansi, who lived in the Mezen-Pechora-Kama taiga between the Urals and the White Sea. It is therefore likely that the Komi and the Mansi shared birch-bark canoe technology, as Shutikhin and others assume, and that both built nearly identical boats along the tributaries of the Pechora and Kama rivers. The general rule of thumb can be reduced further: people on the same shore or in the same forest tend to make similar boats. The principle operates equally well in the North American Arctic, where kayak types change only gradually from region to region from southwestern Alaska to Greenland and Labrador (Rousselot 1994: fig. 13.6; see also our map 19, page 218).

Thus the following description of the Mansi birch-bark canoe by Johan Gottlieb Georgi, who wrote about the boats in Solikamsk, on the upper Kama River, may also be valid for the Komi: "They make fishing boats from birch bark, which they sew with sinew taken from moose, and treat the seams with larch resin" (1776a: 66). Additional information comes from an old Moscow customs book that described traders appearing in the fur town of Ust-Yug along the Vychegda River in 1655–56 in 5- to 7-meter-long birch-bark canoes, each carrying three to six paddlers and a heavy load of furs (Shutikhin 2003; see also our chapter 5's section on the Mansi).

Based on what he learned about bark canoes, Alexander Shutikhin (2008) built a Mansi-style bark canoe in August 2007 on the Pushma River in the Podosinovskiy District of Kirov Oblast (figs. 4.6–4.7). He used two large birch-bark sheets and made ribs from spruce branches fastened with pine roots, working with only a knife, an awl, and an axe.

Fig. 4.7. Alexander Shutikhin paddling his Komi canoe replica in 2008. (Photograph: Alexander Shutikhin)

Fig. 4.6. Alexander Shutikhin with a birch-bark replica canoe he made in Kotlas, Komi Republic, in 2008. (Photograph: Alexander Shutikhin)

Measuring 4.5 by 0.90 by 0.30 meters and weighing 35 kilograms, the boat has a rather large volume and can carry two people and a load of 150 kilograms. He and A. Martynov successfully tested the canoe by paddling it on rivers and even used it in a 40-kilometer trial voyage from the Solovetsky Islands to the White Sea mainland (Martynov 2012).

THE SIHIRTIA AND THE PECHORA CHUD: PRE-SAMOYED PEOPLES OF THE BARENTS AND KARA SEA COASTS

When the Russian archaeologist Valerie N. Chernetsov went to the Yamal Peninsula in 1928–29, he discovered remains of a sea mammal–hunting people who had lived there some 500 to 1,500 years earlier. Later, when he expanded his studies to the Nenets, they told him about an ancient pre-Samoyed people called the Sihirtia who once inhabited the lands that the Nenets appropriated. Their legends about the Sihirtia—perhaps the same semimythical people referred to as the Chud (a term meaning "alien" or "fiend"

in Russian)—were informative, and soon Chernetsov connected his coastal archaeological finds of a late Iron Age maritime-oriented culture of circa 500 CE with the legendary Sihirtia people. Could these people be the sea mammal hunters in skin boats whom early European explorers had described meeting on Vaigach and Novaya Zemlya islands? he wondered.

The Sihirtia are described in numerous Nenets legends. As recounted by Andrei Golovnev and Gail Osherenko: "Sihirtia, the legendary small people once gone and still living underground, are considered to be the Nenets' predecessors on the tundra, sometimes hostile but more often friendly. They can appear on the earth only at night or in a mist. Underground, they pasture earthen reindeer, whose 'horns' are used for the door handles of their pit houses. They seem to be skillful blacksmiths and magicians, presenting iron or bronze objects to people" (1999: 28). Such Sihirtia stories helped explain mammoth tusks and metal artifacts eroding from shorelines and archaeological sites.

Chernetsov's discoveries inspired his theory that the Sihirtia might be related to the Siberian and Alaskan Eskimo. In the 1920s and 1930s, archaeological work in North America had defined Thule (Inuit) and other prehistoric Eskimo cultures but had not yet solved the problem of Eskimo origins. The idea that a proto-Eskimo-like culture might have originated in the European Arctic and spread to the Bering Strait and North America resonated with 19th-century theories that the Eskimo had originated from European Upper Paleolithic cultures. Although Chernetsov's hypothesis of an Eskimo-like culture in Western

Siberia has since been disproved (W. Fitzhugh 1998, 2010), similarities do exist, as he and later researchers pointed out, especially in the areas of skin boats and maritime subsistence technology.

Skin Boats in Yamal: Local Origins or Circumpolar Eskimos?

The facts and theories first presented by Chernetsov convinced scientists in many countries to consider the supposed Sihirtia-Eskimo link and the wider issue of circumpolar and circumboreal cultural connections promoted by Gjessing (1944), Spaulding (1946), W. Fitzhugh (1975), and others. Since the 1930s, scholars had investigated the past two millennia of Eskimo development in the North Pacific and the Bering Sea. The Eskimo question required research into the relationship between the Nenets and the Sihirtia (Erichsen and Birket-Smith 1936; Vasiliev 1979; Golovnev 1995; Khomich 1995), Sihirtia archaeological identity (Pitulko 1991; Fedorova 2003; Kosintsev and Fedorova 2001), and their circumpolar connections with the Eskimo, maritime hunting, and skin boats.

Much of this research revolved around skin boats and the hunting of marine mammals. The earliest description of a kayaklike boat in the Barents Sea was by the British captain Stephen Burrough in 1556. On August 1, Burrough learned that "there were people called Samoeds [Nenets] on the great Island [Vaigach] . . . who have no houses, but only coverings made of Deerskins." On August 2, he visited a Samoyed ritual site, where he saw hundreds of figurines stained with the blood of sacrificed reindeer. And August 3, he noted, "Their boates are made of Deerskins, and when they come on shoare they carry their boates with them upon their backs" (Burrough 1567 in Hakluyt and Goldsmid 1903: 338–39). More detail was reported by Pierre Martin de La Martinière on a voyage to the Barents Sea around 1670:

> We brought them [people from Novaya Zemlya] to our ship together with their boat made in the form of a gondola. It is 15 to 16 feet [5 m] long and 2 and a half feet [0.76 cm] wide and is made very skillfully of fish [whale or walrus] bones and hides. From the inside, the skins are sewn in a form of a bag that extends from one side of the boat to the other. When sitting in such a boat, the people were protected up to their waistlines, since the water did not penetrate inside the boat. Such a construction allowed people to sail [travel] safely in any weather. (1706: 91)

A description and a picture of similar kayaklike boats appeared in Frans O. Belyavsky's *A Trip to the Arctic Sea* (fig 5.2, page 96):

> The Ostyak [Khanty] and Samoyed [Nenets] boats are similar to regular Russian boats, with the differences that they do not distinguish between the head and the stern; and on the top, the boat is covered with cleaned whales' intestines, which are gathered in the middle of the boat similar to [the closure of] women's purses. During floods and storms and whale and seal hunting, which requires highly skilled actions, the natives get in the boat, tighten the rope of the gathering [spray skirt] around their waistlines, and off they go not only along rivers, but also into the Ob Bay and along the shores of the Arctic Ocean, where they dive similar to dolphins, chasing whales and hunting young walruses, and feeling perfectly safe. (1833: 258)

Following publication of Gjessing's 1944 *Circumpolar Stone Age* monograph and its identification of the shared chacteristics of northern maritime cultures, knowledge of Chernetsov's earlier 1935 report in *Sovetskaya Etnografiya* became known and began to provide the first archaeological data from the vast, unknown Russian Arctic. Chernetsov's work was a watershed event that caught the attention of scholars in Europe and North America who were beginning to try to resolve the "Eskimo problem" (see further discussion in chapter 6, page 165). Nineteenth-century theorists had proposed that the Eskimo originated from European Mesolithic reindeer hunters who had migrated to the Arctic coasts following the receding glaciers and began hunting sea mammals at the end of the Ice Age. If this theory was correct, there should be a chain of archaeological evidence across the Russian Arctic to the Bering Strait and North America; but other than Eskimo-like Upper Paleolithic technology and evidence of Mesolithic reindeer and sea mammal hunters in the Nordic region, no evidence from the vast expanse of the Russian Arctic was found until Chernetsov began his studies in Yamal. His 1935 report, identifying an Iron Age Eskimo-like sea mammal–hunting culture, appeared to provide the missing link.

> As we [can] see from these [archaeological] records, skin boats manufactured on the coasts of the Barents and Kara seas were absolutely similar to the Chukchi and Eskimo kayak. The presence of such boats indicates a high level of sea mammal

hunting.... Relying on excavated and literature data [from Yamal], we can identify major traits that are characteristic for the ancient maritime culture.... Judging from the abundance of walrus bones ... I suggest that walrus was one of the most important game animals.... It is important to mention harpoons that were widely used there and were typologically similar to Paleo-Asiatic and Eskimo specimens.... [Together these data indicate] developed sea mammal hunting in the open sea ... [and] a highly sophisticated level of sea mammal hunting. (1935: 131)

Chernetsov also pointed to specific parallels between Yamal and the recently identified Thule (Inuit) culture of Arctic North America: "One cannot but infer that the main features characterizing the [Barents Sea] culture are also characteristic for the so-called Thule Culture identified by Therkel Mathiassen from the data collected by the [1921–24 Fifth Thule] expedition of Knud Rasmussen in the North American Arctic and in Greenland" (1935: 132). He also speculated on the problems inherent in identifying an archaeological link between the Yamal finds and the Eskimo:

The extreme scarcity and patchiness of data from the coasts of the Kara and Barents seas does not allow me to fully reconstruct all the forms of the Western Maritime Culture and to talk about its similarity to the Thule Culture in any detail. However, some issues identified by Frederik Schmidt in both cultures, such as use of harpoons and similarities in lithic industries and in many other types of tools and implements, as well as in ornamental motifs, could be now complemented with additional data: use of long arrowheads in the Yamal similar to those described by Schmidt [at Bolshoi Olenyi Island]; a type of ornamentation that is close to Proto-Eskimo but which does not occur in the Nenets bone industry; and finally the tattoos among Novaya Zemlya women as reported by Martinière, which are surprisingly similar to the [tattoo] pattern used by contemporary Chukchi women. Unfortunately, the vast territory of the Arctic coast from Ob Bay to the northeastern tip of the [Eurasian] continent is almost totally unknown from an archaeological viewpoint. This [geographic separation] does not allow us to cover the area of the ancient maritime culture that existed along this territory and to

speak more or less convincingly about the connections between its two most distant versions—eastern and western. To determine the ethnic background of these bearers of the ancient Yamal culture does not seem possible at this time. (1935: 132–33)

The present authors do not fully trust these early descriptions, and as reported by Erichsen and Birket-Smith in their summary of Chernetsov's findings, even Chernetsov was cautious about them, noting, "Whatever the old descriptions may have said, that may not be always true, especially regarding Martinière" (Erichsen and Birket-Smith 1936). Other scholars agree that de La Martinière's descriptions are problematic. Some seem to be fantasy, and he may have described locations and things he had never seen. Even reliable written sources from the 1600 and 1700s are rarely free of errors. Nevertheless, his 1670 accounts (see page 69) of skin boats and clothing conform to Burrough's earlier reports. A trained surgeon, de La Martinière served in an expedition of the Danish Northern Trade Company in 1653, financed by King Frederick II of Denmark, to discover natural resources and trade opportunities. On returning to Denmark, the fleet reported on lands visited and presented four Native people from Novaya Zemlya to the king. The captives were two women and two men, who probably were Nenets but might have been the mysterious Sihirtia, the Nenets's predecessors (figs. 4.8–4.9).

New excavations in Yamal by Russian archaeologists Leonid Khlobystin (1990), Vladimir Pitulko (1991), William Fitzhugh (1998), and Natalia Fedorova (2003) at sites Chernetsov studied have clarified these issues. Their finds confirm that pre-Nenets Sihirtia people hunted seal and walrus during the spring and summer with harpoons and intercepted migrating wild reindeer at river crossings, but the Kara Sea sites show no specific types of Eskimo harpoons or other artifacts. These authors date the Yamal sites to Late Iron Age and Early Medieval times, circa 500–700 and 1100–1400, before the spread of intensive reindeer herding made maritime hunting and long-term coastal settlement obsolete. What is certain today is that an Iron Age Yamal people and their Sihirtia, Khanty, or Nenets successors once hunted sea mammals along the Barents and Kara sea coasts and among the islands in skin boats. However, the chimera of a Nordic or Western Siberian proto-Eskimo culture has vanished. The Sihirtia, Chud, and other early peoples of these regions did indeed develop ancient maritime hunting and fishing

Fig. 4.8. The French doctor and explorer Pierre Martin de La Martinière illustrated his exploration report with this image of a Kara hunter on Novaya Zemlya, fleeing from Europeans with his harpoon and boat. (From de La Martinière 1706: 151)

Fig. 4.9. These 17th-century Novaya Zemlya hunters, armed with harpoons and bows, wear bird-skin garments. Europeans exploring the Northeast Passage were eager to cash in on the abundance of seal, walrus, and polar bear in the Barents and Kara seas, resources that were already being exploited by the indigenous people, who were perhaps Sihirtia or Nenets. (From de La Martinière 1706: 151)

adaptations, but without any connections to the Eskimo and their highly engineered kayak.

As a coda to this story, a new page of the Sihirtia story emerged in 2011 when Oleg Kardash published his excavations at the Sihirtia hillfort in Nakhodka Bight. Here in southeastern Yamal, he found remains of a large pithouse settlement dating to the 1220s. The village was occupied for a long period by coastal people who were hunters and fishermen and had no reindeer (Kardash 2011: 11). For the first time, scientists might have found a "Sihirtia" village

whose inhabitants hunted sea mammals and did not herd reindeer. Perhaps from the permafrost of this site will come the evidence of their boats.

The Sihirtia-Chud Connection

Much of the preceding description also applies to a people known in early literature as the Chud, who in fact may have been the same people as the Sihirtia. Ivan Lepekhin and a missionary known only as Veniamin collected some of the earliest information on the Sihirtia and Chud of the Western Urals boreal zone. According to L. P. Lashuk:

> Academician I. Lepehkin (1806 [see Lepekhin 1774]), knowing the legends of the European north about the "Chud people," attempted to find their traces in the form of archaeological sites. Based on local information, he made the following statement: "The entire Samoyed land in the Mezen region is filled with the rude dwellings of ancient people. These are found in many places: near lakes, in the tundra, in the forest, along rivers, in the mountains and hills, and in caves [pithouses] in the earth with openings similar to doors. The hearths in these caves contain fragments of iron, copper, and clay domestic wares."
>
> Nenets stories about the Bol'shezemel' Sihirtia were not missed by the observant missionary Veniamin (1855), who wrote, "The Korotaikha River is remarkable for its abundance of fish and the Chud earthen caves, into which, according to Samoyed legends, the Chud retreated in antiquity. These caves are located 10 *versts* [11 kilometers] from the mouth, on the hillsides of the right bank, which since ancient times the Samoyed have called Sirte-sya—'Chud mountain.'" (1968: 180)

More detailed information on the Sihirtia and Chud was collected by the German-born Alexander Gustav Schrenk, botanist for the Imperial Garden in St. Petersburg. In 1837, he journeyed across the Russian Western Urals region from Archangel to Mezen, and then to the Pechora River and Pustozersk. As a natural scientist, he studied flora and fauna as well as people whom he met on his route across taiga and tundra coast and on the islands of Novaya Zemlya and Vaigach. He also collected information on the ancient people called the Chud and Sihirtia by locals in these regions from Komi-Zyrians, Samoyed, Russians, and other people he met, including descriptions of their archaeological remains that he, the Samoyed, or other locals had studied or seen. He also gathered Samoyed legends on the Sihirtia and others, and his journal (1848) is a major account of the history of the Chud and Sihirtia people.

Schrenk (1848) found that the people whom the Samoyed called Sihirtia, who were "living (or gone) underground," and the people whom the Russians called Chud were one and the same. He noted that the Kara River has a tributary named Siirteta, which may point to the original Sihirtia location. The Sihirtia appeared in Komi-Zyrian legends, and the Samoyed living in northern Yamal knew them as well. Further, Schrenk thought the Pechora River's name was related to *peschmera* ("cave" in Russian), perhaps a reference to Chud "caves" or underground dwellings.

Schrenk described ancient Chud sites and subterranean dwellings stretching from the Mezen region to Pustozersk and the banks of the lower Pechora River and estuary, and farther east to the Kara River, next to the Yamal Peninsula. Most were located on river estuaries where fishing and hunting could be conducted year-round. Schrenk learned that many Chud families had lived near Mezen long ago but were killed by Novgorod troops. Novgorod-Russian rule brought war over hunting, fishing, and fur-trapping rights from the 11 to the 15th centuries, during which the Chud and Sihirtia declined in numbers. But east of Pustozersk, in the coastal fur-hunting villages that the Finnic Chud established in the late 1400s (Klingstädt 1769), Schrenk met people who claimed to be descendants of the Finnic Chud.

On the coast, Sihirtia houses were not built underground but were made from driftwood and had doors opening to the east, according to local Nenets. Their fishing and hunting camps contained remains of seals and fishnets made of nettle (*urtica*) fiber, some with sinkers of lead or walrus tusk. The Nenets knew the Sihirtia by reputation, and Schrenk reported the Nenets' views: "We can assume with certainty that the Sihirtia, like the Samoyed [Nenets] today, were located at the coast and engaged in fishing and hunting sea animals" (1848: 377). The Samoyed also assumed that the Chud, who were not Samoyed and spoke a different language, had a life similar to theirs: the Chud were nomadic, as they themselves were, had reindeer, and even then the Samoyed could still find old Chud places on the tundra where a bark- or skin-covered tent had been erected. Schrenk also gave an account of the sea mammal–hunting tradition on the shore and on Vaigach and Novaya Zemlya islands, including the hunting of beluga, a Sihirtia trade carried on by the Samoyed and later by Russian and other commercial hunters in Pustozersk.

The most ambitious and far-reaching explanation of Sihirtia and Chud origin was made by the Finnish scientist Matthias A. Castrén. Traveling on a Russian Academy of Sciences mission in the late 1830s in the Western Urals from the Mezen to the Pechora River along the Arctic coast, he remarked on "Chud caves" and heard Komi-Zyrian and Samoyed legends of Sihirtia people. But his main mission was the linguistic and ethnological study of the Finno-Ugric-speaking people. Castrén's (1844) publication on the Zavoloch'e Chud, who were Finno-Ugric people living in the Novgorod domain, proposed that Karelian territory once had covered the southern part of the White Sea and the Northern Dvina River and that the ancient Sihirtia people might have been a Karelian- or a Komi-Zyrian-related people, like the Chud.

However, modern linguistic studies by Eugene Helimski (2001, 2006) and ethnographic studies by Andrei Golovnev and Gail Osherenko (1999: 28) and others claim that the Sihirtia and Chud people were not Saami-related but very likely were Finno-Ugrian or, more precisely, Ugrian people connected later to the Nenets (Tapani Salminen, pers. comm. to HL). This is also the conclusion of Vladimir Pitulko (1991), who excavated archaeological sites on Vaigach Island and the on the opposite shore of Yugor Strait that contained bone, stone, pottery, metal, and wood implements from two or more sea mammal–hunting cultures. These sites and their multiple occupation layers reach back nearly two millennia, and the similarity of their finds to others in Western Siberia, such as those discovered in 1949 by Chernetsov at Ust-Polui near Salekhard, also suggests that these peoples were Ugrian, not Saami (Chernetsov and Moszyńska 1974: part III).

Based on archaeological evidence, Pitulko (1991: 33) wrote that the history of Yamal and Kara Sea sea mammal hunting is much older, beginning in the second millenium BCE. Around 1000 CE, there is a cultural change in the Yugor Strait sites: artifacts connected to Nenets culture increase. Pitulko assumed that the Ugrian and Nenets cultures lived side by side for a long time in the lower Ob River and on Yamal Peninsula. The Nenets eventually adopted a seasonal maritime hunting economy from the Ugrian people, perhaps by assimilating them, since sea mammal hunting in more recent times became part of the Nenets economic system.

These linguistic and archaeological studies validate Chernetsov's original assumption that the Sihirtia people were probably Ugrian. Most evidence from the coast and mainland points in this direction. We might also conclude that the Pechora Chud were the same or a related Ugrian people, and, since is there is some continuity in settlement areas, the Mansi or the Khanty or some of their maritime groups probably were involved as well. This history was repeated in the Ob River estuary, where the Khanty carried out maritime hunting (see chapter 5's section on the Khanty). It is also clear, as Vladimir Vasiliev demonstrated (1979), that the Yurak Samoyed (Nenets) later became engaged in the sea trade that the Sihirtia had practiced earlier along the Barents and Kara coasts and on Vaigach and Novaya Zemlya islands. So, in the end, it seems that Nenets reindeer herders assimilated the Sihirtia and continued their tradition of seasonal sea mammal hunting on Yamal Peninsula, in Ob Bay, and in the Western Urals (see chapter 5's section on the Nenets). The Nenets also most likely assimilated part of the Chud population as Nenets occupations expanded west of the Urals.

CHAPTER 5
WESTERN SIBERIA

THE OB RIVER AND YAMAL PENINSULA

East of the Ural Mountains lies the vast territory of Siberia, whose Russian name—Sibir—probably originated from the name of the town or fort on the Irtysh River where the famous Russian Cossack leader Yermak defeated a local Mongol khanate in 1581, opening the way to Russian conquest east to the Pacific Ocean. The Irtysh is the major left-bank tributary of the great Ob River, which drains the entire region of Western Siberia (map 9) from Kazakhstan to the Arctic Ocean and from the Urals to the Altai Mountains. One of its most important features is its navigability; its flow is virtually unimpeded by falls or rapids for hundreds of miles. The Ob basin covers nearly 3 million square kilometers, and its 15,000 kilometers of waterways are mostly navigable in summer; in winter, they provide ice transport for half of the year. The basin's surrounding lowlands and swamps harbor huge quantities of fish, including sturgeon, prized for its flesh and black caviar, and its forests and tundra zones are rich in fur-bearers as well as deer, moose, bear, and other creatures.

The huge Ob basin has been the home of many indigenous cultures, including those discussed in this chapter: the Nenets, Khanty, Mansi, Selkup, several Southern Samoyed groups, and Turkic Tatars in the northern Altai Mountains. Because the middle and lower Ob basin is low and marshy, water transport historically was a virtual necessity. Boat technology here, as known from the 16th century onward, reflects both the cultural diversity of the region and the influence of European and Russian technology, which resulted in a shift from traditional bark and dugout boats to plank boats and barges after 1500. Bark canoes were used throughout the Ob basin, except along the Arctic coast. There and in the tundra regions, the Nenets and other reindeer herders used both bark and skin boats to fish and to cross rivers during the annual northward and southward migrations of their herds. Like Barents Sea coastal people (see Chapter 4), Ob River people used simple coracle skin boats for river crossings and

kayaklike boats to hunt sea mammals along the Kara Sea coast. Today Russian researchers do not share the belief of early anthropologists—including Gutorm Gjessing (1944) and Valerie N. Chernetsov (1935; see also Mozhinskaya 1953)—that Eskimo-like kayaks and umiaks were ever used along the Kara Sea coast (see the Sihirtia section, page 86). This chapter explores these and other issues in detail, providing information on the history of Ob River cultures and languages (G. Anderson 2004) as well as technical features of their canoes and other watercraft.

THE NENETS: REINDEER HERDERS AND SEA HUNTERS OF THE LOWER OB RIVER

The Nenets live mainly in the tundra, forest tundra, and northern taiga belt of the European and Western Siberian part of Russia, and they are the largest of the so-called Small Nations of the Russian north, totaling some 41,500 people (Janhunen 1996). Traditional Nenets subsistence combined reindeer breeding, hunting, trapping, fishing, and gathering. The reindeer economy intensified during Russian colonization from the 16th to the 20th centuries, largely replacing the Nenets' earlier, semisedentary marine mammal–hunting and fishing economy and the hunting of wild reindeer, which became locally extinct owing to competition with domestic reindeer (Krupnik 1993). For the past 300 years, reindeer breeding and fishing have been the Nenets' main occupational focus.

Reindeer breeding today is a seminomadic occupation for many Nenets, although a number of families continue a fully nomadic way of life. Tundra Nenets and Forest Nenets differ mainly in the economic cycle of reindeer breeding and its attendant migration pattern. The nomadic Tundra Nenets undertake long-distance seasonal migrations of 200 to 300 kilometers (and sometimes as far as 600 kilometers) with large reindeer herds that travel from wintering grounds at the northern forest fringe through calving grounds at the

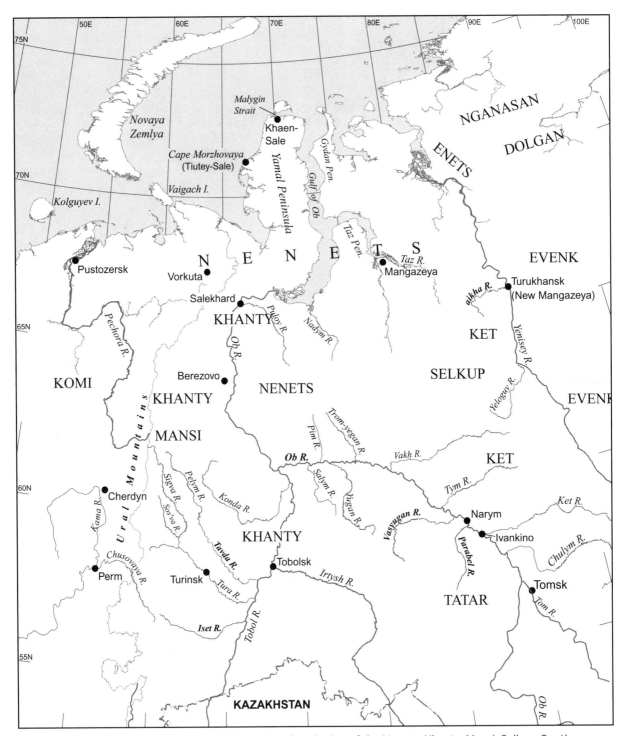

Map 9. Western Siberia: the Ob River Basin and Yamal and territories of the Nenets, Khanty, Mansi, Selkup, Southern Samoyed, and Turkic Tatars. (Dan Cole, Smithsonian Institution)

forest-tundra transition in May to tundra pastures near the Arctic coast in the summer. They use boats to cross the Ob and other rivers along their route (fig. 5.1). Tundra Nenets usually winter at the northern forest edge, close to Russian villages, where they have relatives and economic exchanges.

Forest Nenets (who number about 2,000) have smaller herds and shorter migration routes and spend more time in their base camps or seasonal settlements. Forest Nenets also spend significant time fishing in the summer and fur trapping in the winter.

Fig. 5.1. Throughout Northern Eurasia, small boats are still used to ferry camp gear and lead migrating reindeer herds across waterways. These boats were originally simple bark- or skin-covered canoes but have been replaced by aluminum or fiberglass boats in recent decades. This photograph (RV-0144-28) shows a Nenets reindeer brigade with loaded sledges in tow crossing the Syoyaha River on the Yamal Peninsula. (Photograph: Bryan Alexander, used with permission)

Fishing, still an important element of the Nenets economy, became a key commercial activity when the Soviet government established a network of fish factories in settled villages on Ob Bay. In the post-Soviet era since 1990, the decline of state-sponsored reindeer and fishing industries has resulted in hunting and gathering regaining some of their pre-Soviet importance, although the Nenets' reindeer-herding economy is now being challenged by immense hydrocarbon development throughout Yamal. Animals hunted and trapped by the Nenets include wild reindeer, moose, wolf, otter, muskrat, fox, polar fox, weasel, sable, hare, wolverine, and brown bear. Their new economic interests include fur, vegetable, and livestock farming in the lower Pechora, where the Nenets mingle with Komi and Russian people (Golovnev and Osherenko 1999).

Nenets boating and bark canoe history probably began thousands of years ago, when their ancestors lived in the taiga zone farther south. After adopting reindeer breeding and losing taiga territories to the Khanty, the Nenets expanded to the lower Ob River and the Yamal Peninsula, where they may have encountered the Sihirtia people, known from early mythic stories (see chapter 4, page 86), who used skin boats for hunting marine mammals. Reindeer sledge transportation made it possible for the Nenets to expand their coastal tundra territories east to the Yenisey River and west across the Ural

Mountains to the Barents Sea, adding a sea mammal–hunting component to their economy that included seal, walrus, and beluga.

The Nenets Birch-Bark Canoe

Not much is known about the canoe history of the Nenets people, who appear in early literature as the Stony or Ural Samoyed. Most information comes from documents describing encounters with their neighbors (and sometime enemies) the Khanty and the Mansi, and from the early history of the Samoyed, who, in the distant past, inhabited southwestern Siberia between the Ob and Yenisey rivers (see the discussion of origins in the Southern Samoyed section, page 124).

In the Siberian taiga, one cannot survive without a boat, and the birch-bark canoe was crucial for hunting, fishing, and trapping as well as trade, migration, and war. The Nenets depended on it until circa 1700, after which they adopted the expanded log boat, although they transitioned to that technology later than other groups in Western Siberia. From Selkup, Southern (Altai-Sayan) Samoyed, and Khanty birch-bark canoe construction, we can learn much about Forest Nenets canoes. According to Pelikh (1972), the birch-bark canoes of the Selkup and the Khanty were similar to those used farther north by the Nenets. Belgibaev writes that the Turkic Tatars learned to build bark canoes from the Samoyed and Khanty and that the Khanty called the birch-bark canoe a "Samoyed boat" (2004: n. 37, online version).

In 1928, Georgij Starcev published a study on the Vakh River Ostyak (Khanty) in Western Siberia in the 1500s and afterward (1988). From a bark canoe perspective, the most interesting information relates to how the Nenets waged war against the Khanty using birch-bark canoes. When the reindeer and Russian fur-trade economy intensified in Western Siberia in the 16th century, wars over pastureland and fur territories broke out among the peoples previously engaged, relatively peacefully, in fishing, hunting, and gathering, and these wars continued into the 18th century. The Nenets attacked the Khanty and the Mansi, who had expanded their territory north and east into Samoyed lands in the Ob River basin and along its tributaries leading to the Yenisey River. Most battles took place in summer near or on taiga rivers and lakes. Andrei Golovnev (2000) writes that the warlike Nenets living in the northern taiga zone and the wooded hills of the Urals used birch-bark canoes to raid Mansi peoples living along the Konda and Tavda rivers, burning their villages on the left bank of the Ob. Their light bark canoes were a crucial part of the Nenets' mobile warfare strategy, which emphasized raids followed by rapid retreat. The tactic worked because bark canoes were faster than the heavier expanded log boats used by their Mansi pursuers and could be carried quickly over portages that their pursuers could not cross. In the end, however, the Nenets lost the war against the Khanty and had to give up lands from the eastern bank of the Ob to Surgut, which included major villages, according to a map by Finnish scientist T. V. Lehtisalo (1959: 32) that locates old Yurak Samoyed regions. "According to living Khanty today," Starcev wrote in his summary of the taiga war, "birch-bark canoes are to blame for the fall of the Nenets, for the Khanty could shoot holes in them and the Samoyeds would drown" (1988: 5).

Nenets and Khanty Kayaks in Ob Bay

Having lost the taiga war to the Khanty, the Nenets retreated with their reindeer to the Yamal tundra and expanded along the Barents Sea coast west of the Urals. There they continued to hunt walrus, beluga, and seal in the Ob River and Ob Bay, as did the Khanty after they gained access to the coast. Elena Perevalova's (2003) history of the formation of the Northern Khanty people discusses their maritime and river economies and the mixing of Khanty and Nenets groups in the Ob River estuary. Their marine hunting tradition probably continued the pre-Nenets and pre-Khanty economic pattern established by the coastal Sihirtia and their predecessors. The Khanty penetrated Nenets territory along the northern Ob River, reaching Nadym River in the 1700s. Gradually, Nenets and Khanty mixed along the lower Ob, sharing customs, technology, and language, partly through marriage. Thus Nenets of Khanty origin, as they were called by Matthias A. Castrén (1844), may have inherited skin boats from earlier Samoyed residents.

In the long-term competition for coastal hunting grounds, the Nenets got the upper hand when they assimilated many Northern Khanty, as Perevalova (2003) explains. When Lehtisalo (1959) studied the region from the Kanin Peninsula to the Taz River and Bay in 1910–11, there were no Khanty-speaking coastal people; instead he found mainly Samoyed-speaking Yurak Nenets. Thus it seems likely that coastal Khanty became Samoyed speakers during the latter half of the 1800s; when travelers such as Castrén and Belyavsky met them in the early 1800s, Nenets and Khanty were still separate language groups.

When Belyavsky visited the Northern Khanty and Nenets areas in the early 1800s as a member of the Tobolsk Medical Commission, his principal objective was to stop syphilis and other diseases. He met both Nenets and Khanty people

and noted their similar kayaklike skin canoes in the lower Ob River and estuary (fig. 5.2). He also found rock art showing pre-Nenets kayak paddlers. Reflecting on Belyavsky's illustration, Antropova writes, "In some of the early drawings and engravings the skin boat of the Nenets externally gives the impression of a kayak" (2005: 33). Furthermore, she adds, "Apparently skin boats were once known to the Nenets in the past as reported by some early narratives." Belyavsky noted some details of the skin-covered Samoyed-Ostyak log boat: "In the middle of the canoe on both sides, rings of whale gut woven into a rope are firmly attached to the wood. Short, wide paddles are inserted into these rings and tied to them. The natives paddle with only one of them; the second serves for changing hands when one hand gets tired, because they don't find it necessary to use both paddles at the same time" (1833: 259). This description suggests that the craft was propelled with oars rather than paddles, but the description or the observation appears flawed. Either the craft was rowed with both paddles through the oarlocks, or it was paddled like a canoe with a single-bladed paddle.

Fig. 5.2. This watercolor from the early 1800s, published in Frans O. Belyavsky's book *Poezdka k Ledovitomy Moryu* (A Trip to the Arctic Sea) in 1833, illustrates daily activities of an Ob Bay Nenets reindeer-herding family: tending their herd, returning with fish, and cooking a meal. The skin-covered canoe-kayak in front of their *chum* (tent) has an oval cockpit with a combing for attaching a spray skirt. The Khanty, Nenets, and other Barents and Kara Sea peoples used similar canoe-kayaks for marine mammal hunting. (From Belyavsky 1833: fig. 11; courtesy National Library, Helsinki)

The Nenets of Vaigach and Novaya Zemlya

Most Russian experts believe that the Ural Samoyed (Nenets) had crossed the Urals and entered the European tundra by at least 1000 CE, after they had learned to harness reindeer and could rely on sledge transport over the tundra between the taiga and sea coast in summer and winter. Willem Barents and Jan Huyghen van Linschoten's 1595 map shows the Samoyed east of the Pechora River, a century after they began attacking the Pustozersk trading post at the Pechora mouth (Linschoten 1598; A. Schrenk 1848). Archaeological research suggests that pre-Nenets maritime hunters were present along the Barents Sea and Kara coast much earlier, during the warm "Viking Age," circa 1000 CE, before the adoption of intensive reindeer herding (Pitulko 1991). Whether these people were Sihirtia or Chud is not known.

Nenets skin boats were first described on the Barents Sea coast. The British navy captain Stephen Burrough, who was exploring and mapping northern waters, might have been the first European to meet Nenets face to face, in 1556. Along with a Russian, Captain Loshak, who knew the place and its people, he landed on Vaigach Island (called also Waigat, Waigatz, or Weygats in European sources) to inspect the wooden human figures that the Nenets erected at sacrificial reindeer sites. Loshak told him about Samoyed who paddled between the mainland and the island. "Their boats are made of deer skins, and when they land on shore, they carry their boats upon their backs," Burrough wrote in his logbook on Monday, August 3, 1556 (1567: 77).

In addition to the Nenets, European explorers of Vaigach and Novaya Zemlya islands and the Barents Sea coast as far east as Yamal met Sihirtia people (see chapter 4, page 86). Vaigach Island became a sacred place for the Nenets because of its remoteness and rich animal resources. Nenets winter hunting expeditions to Vaigach Island were carried out with reindeer sledges over the ice, but they traveled to more distant Novaya Zemlya mainly with dog-driven sledges because there was not enough lichen there to nourish reindeer (Lehtisalo 1932). In summer, a boat could quickly cross the short distance between the mainland and Vaigach. Because of these islands' excellent hunting grounds for walrus, seal, beluga, and whale, other groups, including the Pomor and Karelians and Norwegian and Dutch hunters, regularly visited them and the nearby mainland.

A document written by Jan Huyghen van Linschoten, a lieutenant on Barents's 1595 expedition, tells us something about Dutch encounters with the Nenets (see Linschoten 1598; Zeeberg 2005). Illustrations in van Linschoten's documents show people whaling on the shores of Novaya Zemlya and Vaigach with small boats that were probably skin canoes (fig. 5.3). When the Dutch encountered sea ice in Yugor Strait in August 1595, they established contact with the local people and went ashore. On the beach, they found five whales that Nenets people had killed. The Nenets themselves had fled, leaving their sledges behind, when they saw the fleet—some seven ships and 180 men—entering the bay. Another time, the Dutch found nine Nenets armed with bows and arrows, and later the same nine people paddled their small boats alongside the Dutch ships and climbed aboard to trade.

Not much is known about Nenets sea mammal hunting on the Barents Sea coast and islands. However, Aleksander Gustav Schrenk provided some information on beluga hunts on Vaigach Island:

> At Novaya Zemlya, the [Russian] hunters traditionally go to the southwest coast to Kostin Mar, or still farther north. On Vaigach Island, they go every year to Lamchina Bay, where belugas are hunted, and for which purpose the hunter, who has a camp at Yugor Strait, visits the island. . . . Hunters catch them with nets stretched across the channel or spear them with lances from the shore or from boats. . . . Now [in 1837], while the beluga hunt is the business of Pechora (Russian) hunters, the Samoyeds (if they are not working for Pechora men) concentrate on fishing

Fig. 5.3. Jan Huyghen van Linschoten and William Barents's report of a 1595 voyage to Novaya Zemlya illustrates whaling operations on Vaigach Island, between the Barents and Kara seas, carried out with Samoyed help. (From Zeeberg 2007: 145; courtesy JaaJan Zeeberg)

for *omyl* [a species of whitefish] and seals, mainly owing to their lack of larger boats and equipment for a larger-scale venture. (1848: 367–68)

The Northern Sea Route

After Burrough (1567), van Linschoten (1598), and de La Martinière (1706) visited Vaigach and Novaya Zemlya, where they met Sihirtia, Saami, and Nenets maritime hunters with skin boats, we have to take a long leap forward in time before new accounts appear. This is because after 1619, Russia banned European navigation between the White Sea and Ob Bay in order to block European competition with Russia's fur trade and its expansion into Siberia.

In 1600, not long after the Russians had advanced east across the Ural Mountains and appropriated the land they called Sibir (now Western Siberia), Komi-Zyrian traders founded the fur-trading center of Mangazeya on the estuary of the Taz River (Vizgalov 2005, 2006). Later, Mezen Pomor operated it for the Archangel government, using the maritime passage along the Arctic Ocean coast that became known as the Northern Sea Route. The fur trade proved to be a source of great wealth for the Russian state and private traders. However, their advantage soon became a liability. The income gained from furs and from taxes imposed on local Enets (Yenisey Samoyed) and Khanty people, and the encouragement they received to trade more furs with Archangel, eventually led to a Nenets rebellion (Golovnev and Osherenko 1999).

To understand these developments, it is important to remember that all traffic between Mezen and Mangazeya had to be made during the short summer season, when the Northern Sea Route was ice-free. From Mezen, people sailed small open boats to the Kanin Peninsula, where, using a small river and a portage running across its base, they dragged the boats to the Barents Sea. From there, they sailed along the coast to the Yamal Peninsula, where they were portaged to Ob Bay. This route was vulnerable to the Nenets, who robbed or killed boat parties along the way, and to Dutch and English interference in the most profitable fur trade ever. When Russian authorities banned the sailing of foreign ships along the Arctic coast to the Ob, it became a capital offense for any Russian citizen to travel with or pilot a foreign ship along this route. However, soon the walrus ivory and later the sable resources of the Mangazeya region were exhausted, and Nenets resistance to Russian trade policies led them to burn Mangazeya town and its fortress in 1678. Later, a new fur-trade town named New Mangazeya

(later renamed Turukhansk) was founded farther south at Turukhan River, near the confluence of the Tunguska and Yenisey.

The restriction on European vessels and trade sharply limited early documentation of the Nenets and their maritime hunting and skin boat use along the Arctic Ocean coast. Only after Russian Pomor began voyaging beyond the White Sea and the trade companies, which had monopolies on White Sea hunting and fishing until 1757, established fishing and hunting stations farther east did information on the Nenets on the Barents Sea begin to appear again. At that time, most of the Nenets mentioned in Russian documents (which called them Samoyed) were working for the hunting and fishing companies.

English Journeys with the Nenets

Samoyed boat information is not completely missing in later years. The British polar explorer Frederick Jackson may have been the last European to document a Samoyed skin boat on the Arctic Ocean coast. In the winter of 1893–94, he traveled from the White Sea to the Kara Sea, living among local Samoyed; in the summer, he crossed Yugor Strait to Vaigach in a 2.1-meter-long canoe. It is unclear whether this was an imported canvas or local skin boat.

Jackson was not the only English traveler in Samoyed lands in 1894. Aubyn Trevor-Battye, an English gentleman on a hunting excursion on Kolguev Island, lived with Samoyed people and wrote about his experiences (1895). On his return to the mainland east of the Pechora River estuary, he took note of the small, light Samoyed skin boats that could be carried on one's back after crossing a river, and in nearly the same place as Jackson, he met Samoyed with these small boats. This suggests that local people on the Barents Sea coast in the 1890s regularly used skin- or perhaps canvas-covered boats, some of which are still being made today (fig. 5.4).

THE KHANTY: OB-UGRIAN INLAND AND COASTAL FISHERMEN

The Khanty people were organized into northern, southern, and eastern groups, as documented by Chernetsov and Mozhinskaya (1974), Sokolova (1983), and Perevalova (2003). They inhabited large regions of Western Siberia, along the Ob (from the Tom River) and Irtysh from the eastern slopes of the Ural Mountains north to the Arctic Ocean, and in the lowlands between the Ob and Yenisey rivers. Their large territory and their mixing with neighboring groups

Because of this chain reaction of migrations and because they occupied a large territory surrounded by Nenets and Turkic groups, the Khanty were, after 1500, constantly involved in conflicts over hunting and fishing grounds and control of waterways. Because all travel took place on the network of rivers that traversed the flat, frequently marshy Ob basin, the Khanty protected their villages by placing sharpened poles underwater at the shore to defend against Samoyed raiders in birch-bark canoes. Khanty legends tell of "artillery" consisting of large, strong bows—possibly crossbows with heavy arrows—that could shoot holes in attacking canoes from a great distance (Starcev 1988).

The Khanty (and to a lesser degree the Mansi, who were mainly Ural hunters and horse breeders) have been at the forefront of boat development and use in Western Siberia. The reasons for this phenomenon are many, not least being their location along the Ob River, the most productive river for fishing in all of Siberia. Fishing was a primary Khanty trade along the small tributaries of the Ob and Irtysh, with hunting being a supplementary profession. Their lives were tuned to the seasonal migrations of fish and land animals. As a result, these Khanty lived a seminomadic lifestyle, and their dwellings reflected their need for seasonal movement. Throughout the summer, their lives were connected

Fig. 5.4. A Nenets man and his son with a plastic tube-framed, canvas-covered boat they constructed in Yamal in 2008. (Photograph: Alexander Shutikhin)

make their tribal definition difficult; adding to the confusion is the fact that in the early days of the Russian Empire, most people in this region were called Ostyak. Only after the distinctions among the Khanty, Mansi, and Samoyed languages were established in the 1700s did people who were actually Khanty become better known (Donner 1933a).

Scholars believe that the ancient homeland of the Ob-Ugrian Khanty lay on both sides of the Ural Mountain slopes, where a Permian population spoke a Uralic language. Those people who became Ob-Ugrian speakers mixed circa 400 CE with Iranian cattle-breeding people migrating from the southern grasslands to the northern taiga. In the later stages of this amalgamation, the Khanty settled along the western banks of the Ob and Irtysh rivers, expanding north, south, and west until they encountered Samoyed peoples in the north and Turkish Tatars in the south. In the early 1500s, the Mansi resettled east of the Urals after a war with Moscow Russians (see page 105) and pushed the Khanty to the east bank of the Ob, into Nenets lands (map 10).

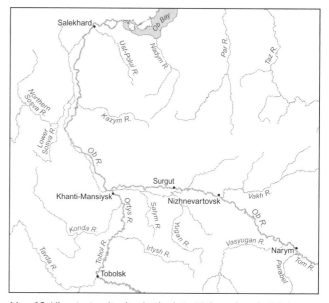

Map 10. Khanty territories in the late 19th and early 20th centuries, including the Northern Sea Khanty in Ob Bay, the Southern Khanty between Tobolsk and the Ob River, and the Eastern Khanty from Surgut to Narym, along the Vah and Vasyugan rivers. (After Kulemzin and Lukina 1992; adapted by Marcia Bakry and Mapping Specialist, Ltd.)

to the water and water transport; in winter, they used dog traction for transport in their southern lands and reindeer sledges in the north, a technology they acquired from the Nenets. The Finnish scientist U. T. Sirelius, who studied Khanty fishing in the late 1800s (1906), noted that they had more than 200 types of fish traps and other methods of catching fish. Without boats, such an economy would have been impossible. Unfortunately for boat historians, while Sirelius studied Khanty domestic birch-bark handicraft (1904), he did not mention their canoes.

The Khanty's geographic location—between the Permian peoples west of the Urals and the Nenets to the east and north, and between the Arctic Ocean to the north and the Turkic peoples to the south—is important in their boating history. In Western Siberia east of the Urals, the Ob-Ugrian peoples had bark canoe traditions similar to those of Nenets and Yeniseyan peoples such as the Ket. On the lower Ob River and Bay, the Ob-Ugrians had deep roots, as demonstrated by the rich Ust-Polui culture studied by Chernetsov and Mozhinskaya (1974), Moberg (1975), and Fedorova (2003). Conflicts with the Nenets over marine resources occurred between 1500 and 1700, when the Northern Khanty extended their seal and beluga hunting on the lower Ob to the maritime region (Golovnev 2000; Golovnev and Osherenko 1999: 51).

Living on the eastern and western slopes of the Urals meant that the Khanty traded with the Volga River Finnic and Permian peoples, from whom they learned about expanded dugout boats; this technology gradually replaced their birch-bark canoes, perhaps beginning among the Northern Khanty. Skin boats, which the Northern Khanty used until the 1800s, are better documented than bark canoes among the Southern and Eastern Khanty fishing people; traces of bark canoes are difficult to find, although documents attest to their existence. After the 1600s, the Khanty primarily used expanded log boats made of aspen, poplar, elm, or larch. Larch boats were favored where forest portages were required because of their more durable hulls. For long trips, the Khanty used large planked log boats, partly decked with birch bark, which they propelled with oars or sails or had towed from shore by people and dogs.

The Northern Sea Khanty and Their Skin Boats

V. N. Chernetsov and W. I. Mozhinskaya (1954, 1974), who studied the archaeological ancestors of the Khanty and Mansi, wrote about their traditional boats:

There is no doubt that the Ust-Polui culture [circa 2000 BP, lower Ob River] had boats. The most archaic form . . . was a small, narrow birch-bark canoe, known from folklore and descriptions by 18th-century travelers. [Peter Simon] Pallas [the German 18th-century naturalist] wrote of Mansi on the right side of the southern Sosva River that they have Russian canoes made from hollowed-out trees or their own birch-bark boats, which they sew with spruce roots and whose seams they treat with larch tree resin. . . . In some places on the lower Ob, the *berestyanka* [bark canoe] was preserved until the mid-19th century. In the lower reaches of the river, furthermore, there was a skin or hide boat. (1954: 170)

The French mapmaker Joseph-Nicholas DeLisle traveled close to the northern Sosva River in 1728 in the service of the Russian Academy and saw in Berezov both Khanty and Mansi bark canoes, which his assistant Tobias Königsfeld documented in a drawing (see figs. 5.7–5.8, page 106).

Some scientists, including Golovnev, Fedorova, and Krupnik (pers. comm. to WWF, 2014), have questioned Chernetsov's statements about Khanty skin boats on the grounds that few seal bones have been found in old Khanty settlement middens and that Burrough's and de La Martinière's reports were vague or untrustworthy. Nevertheless, there is sufficient evidence to conclude that skin boats were used in the Kara Sea and Ob Bay, where the Nenets and Khanty hunted beluga and seal. It seems likely that they would have used these animals' skins for boat covers, since they are more durable and waterproof than deer hide, but the matter will have to remain for future archaeological investigation to solve.

Matthias A. Castrén visited the Obdorsk (Salekhard) region in 1847 and 1848. A highly reliable source who studied the nomadic habits of the Khanty and Nenets, he wrote that the Obdorsk Khanty were divided into two groups, reindeer herders and fishermen (1967: 223–24). The fishermen lived along the Ob and Nadym rivers, while the reindeer herders migrated north during the summer into the tundra and maintained close contact with the Nenets. Castrén said that some Khanty fishermen also had small reindeer herds. These herder-fishermen divided their households in the summer between those who looked after the reindeer and those who resided at fishing grounds. In the summer, reindeer migrated to the coast to find cooler weather and avoid mosquitoes. While at the Arctic Ocean coast with their reindeer, the Khanty began fishing and hunting seal, walrus, and polar bear, as did the Russians and Nenets in this area. Only a few Khanty hunted on the open sea, Castrén wrote, but he did not describe their boats.

Chernetsov and Mozhinskaya wrote about mammal hunting and fishing on the Ob River and Ob Bay circa 1850:

The Ob River is divided into countless small rivers, which contributed to the development of lock fishing where waterways discharge into Ob Bay, which is rich in marine animals, especially seal and beluga that prey upon the river's abundant fish resources. According to Ivan Lepekhin, in the past the beluga ascended the river as far as the birch forest zone near the mouth of the northern Sosva River. Beluga appear annually in mid-June, as described by the well-known mid-19th-century French traveler Eyriye, and sometimes advance like a wave spreading across the entire width of the river, circa 5 versts [5 kilometers] in width. The Khanty know how to process the hides of these animals to make belts for reindeer harnesses. (1954: 167)

Lehtisalo, who traveled in 1910 and 1911 along the Barents Sea coast and the Ob River estuary and visited the Taz River in summer, never met Nenets of Khanty origin, but he described the Yurak Nenets he met at the coast (1932). It seems likely that the Tundra Nenets had fully assimilated the coastal Khanty by the early 1900s. Additionally, although Lehtisalo described seal and beluga in the Taz estuary, no Nenets fishermen were hunting them. Samoyed boats, which hundreds of years earlier still had been made of skin (Balak 1581), were by then expanded log boats or planked dugouts. While at the Taz River, Lehtisalo found on the shore a small birch-bark canoe that had floated downriver, which a local Nenets told him was an Evenk boat.

The Southern Khanty: Under the Pressure of Many Neighbors

The Russian scientists Vladislav M. Kulemzin and Nadezhda V. Lukina, who wrote about Khanty history and economy, also described the making of an expanded log boat and provided a few comments about birch-bark canoe construction. They observed bark processing in the Tobolsk region:

The Tobolsk ethnographer Natalya Dmitrieva-Sadovnikova wrote an article at the beginning of the 20th century about women harvesting and processing birch bark for utensils and men preparing bark tent covers. They selected a birch growing deep in the woods among high aspen, where the birch have tall, slender, smooth trunks. Initially, one makes a vertical incision as deep as the bast layer. Then two horizontal cuts are made for the desired length and a cut between the bark and the bast, and then they tear the bark out by hand. . . . For utensils, hunting decoys, floats, etc. . . . they cut the bark into pieces of the desired shape. For tent covers and boats, you need large, flexible pieces of birch bark. To [prepare the bark], boil it in water and fat (fish oil)—fold the pieces, and put them into a large pot and cover the pot with moss and fir bark. Boil on a fire for at least several days without burning. . . . Birch bark was originally sewn together using bone awls made from the ribs of a young deer or elk and later on by the usual [metal] awl. Seams are sewn using strips of bird-cherry bark. (1992: 35)

We have found only two descriptions of birch-bark canoes among the Southern Khanty, both from the same location near Omsk. In June 1886, the Finnish Lutheran priest Johannes Granö, attending to Finnish citizens who were Russian political and criminal prisoners deported to Western Siberia, traveled near the town of Tara in the Khanty region north of Omsk, where the wild, endless Siberian forest begins. From the banks of the Irtysh, he wrote, could see nothing but trees. Granö composed "A Letter to Finland from Tomsk, Siberia" for the August 29, 1886, edition of *Finland's Morning Paper* (Helsinki), remarking, "In this forest . . . the Ostyak migrates seasonally, still carrying his birch-bark canoe over his head, out of reach of civilization . . . where the animals of the forest have their peace."

In 1892, the Swedish archaeologist Fredrik Robert Martin (1895) collected hundreds of Khanty material-culture items from the Tobol and Irtysh rivers in the Tiumen region. One was a model birch-bark boat measuring 50 by 8 centimeters (fig. 5.5a–b). Now in the collection of the Museum of Ethnology (Värdskultur) in Stockholm, it provides evidence of how to construct a blunt-nosed boat: cut the ends of a bark sheet, fold the bark over at the ends of the canoe, and sew the overlapped layers together. Other than gunwales, the model maker did not bother to fashion the usual inner structure. This is a novel and simple construction, unique for the forest zone. If this model accurately reflects Khanty

A

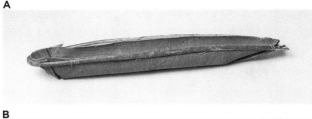

B

Fig. 5.5a–b. This model Khanty (Ostyak) birch-bark canoe (SEM 1892.03.0075), 50 by 8 centimeters, was collected on the Tobol River in 1892 by Frederick Robert Martin. The design and method used to cut and sew its bark could also be used to create elm- and larch-bark canoes. (Courtesy Martin Schultz, Swedish Ethnological Museum, Stockholm)

Fig. 5.6. In a 1706 book documenting his travel from Moscow to China in the 1690s, Russian ambassador Evert Ysbrants Ides included this illustration of a Khanty family near Narym showing a sturgeon, a dead bear, a summer tent camp, and a canoe. (From Ides 1706: fig. 5)

canoe construction, it might suggest the persistence of an early, primitive type of bark canoe construction.

The Eastern Khanty and Their Bark Canoes

More than the Southern or Northern groups, the Eastern Khanty maintained their Northern Siberian forest traditions, including their use of dugout canoes. They continued to use bark canoes well past 1700, perhaps due to the influence of Ket and Tungus peoples from the Yenisey River and the southern Forest Nenets, all of whom also still traveled in bark boats.

In the late 17th century, Evert Ysbrant Ides, the Danish-born Russian ambassador to China, left Europe on the Chusovaya River and arrived in Siberia via the Tobol River, proceeding by barge on the Irtysh until he came to Narym. There, in July 1695, he met Khanty people wearing fish-skin clothes and shoes who inhabited most of the Ob River basin from the Arctic Ocean to the Tom River in the south. Ides wrote about their bark canoes, which he illustrated in his book (fig. 5.6), and their houses:

> Their boats on the outside are [covered with] the bark of trees sewn together, and the inside ribs [are] of very thin wood; they are two or three fathoms [4.25 to 6.40 meters] long and but an ell [71 centimeters] broad. And yet in them they can be safe in great storms, until they reach shore. . . . In winter, these Ostyak live entirely underground, there being no other entrance

to their caves except a hole left open on the surface of the earth to let the smoke out. If, as occurs frequently, a heavy snow falls, it often happens that, according to their customs, they lie asleep naked around the fire, and the parts of their bodies that lie away from the fire may become covered two or three fingers deep in snow. When they feel cold, they turn over to warm the cold part of their body a little while, and so take no more notice of it, being very hardy people. (1706: 19–23)

Some years later, another Russian ambassador heading toward Peking (Beijing) and China traveled along the Ob, accompanied by Lorenz Lange, a Swedish officer in Russian service. While returning from China to Russia, Lange kept a diary, writing in autumn 1721 about the same Khanty people near Narym whom Ides had seen: "We always had a number of them in canoes around our barge, supplying us with plenty of fish and wild-fowl, of various sorts, at an easy rate" (Lange 1806: 142–43). It seems that birch-bark canoes were the favorite watercraft of the Narym and Ket River Khanty, whose boating habits D. G. Messerschmidt also documented. However, the identity of the people Lange saw may be questioned, as the people called Ket River Ostyak in the early Russian literature might, in fact, have been Selkup (Ostyak Samoyed).

During his travels of 1721 to 1725, Messerschmidt covered a large part of Western and southeastern Siberia in winter and summer and met Khanty on several occasions. He noted the self-designation Ysstiack or Asstiak (Ostyak) for a people living along the Ket River near Narym, as well as Native words for the Ostyak paddle (*luhp*) and canoe (*re'eth*), the latter likely made of bark (Messerschmidt 1964: 243, 247). His two descriptions of Khanty birch-bark canoes were very short but mentioned the ancient bark boat tradition still known on the Ket River near Narym. "The Ostyak [arrived] in their small canoe made from birch bark, in which they sit cross-legged . . . and bring me for sale two grouse, which I measure with the scale and prepare later for a meal." The second noted that upon reaching the Ob River, his Khanty guide found a birch-bark canoe and paddled away toward Narym, the guide's home (1964: 231, 242).

A Russian anthropologist in Tomsk, Galina I. Pelikh, wrote about the Khanty, Selkup, and Nenets peoples and their relations and material culture. Her work contains a chapter devoted to the birch-bark canoes used by the Khanty and Selkup and some of their neighbors on the middle Ob. Summarizing her findings, she wrote:

> Our reconstruction of the birch-bark boats is based on oral descriptions received from various districts of the middle Ob River. This information has been communicated by the Khanty on the Vasyugan and the lower reaches of the Vakh and by the Ob River Selkup and was obtained during archaeological excavations in the basins of the Tom and Chulym rivers. However, all these sources reflect the same type of birch-bark boat. Therefore, we can assume that the boat, whose skeleton was covered with birch-bark *pachzha*, was used in ancient times by native inhabitants of the whole middle Ob. Around Narym, it has been preserved in the lands of the Khanty and Selkup until relatively recently. (1972: 67)

Until the 1950s, according to Pelikh (1972), people in this area could still describe Khanty and Selkup bark canoes they themselves had seen. One interesting point was the form of the Khanty birch-bark canoe, which had a double-shell construction, with a small bark canoe inside a larger one. This may also have been the template for the Ket canoe—which has a similar shape and construction method but is not double-hulled—since the Sym River Ket call the birch-bark canoe *hap-hap*, corresponding to the Ob-Ugrian bark canoe name (Verner 1977: 160).

Pelikh (1972: table 32) provided a description of the Khanty canoe and drawings of other middle Ob River bark canoes, which must have appeared nearly identical to the boat described by E. A. Belgibaev (2004) among the Chulym Tatars, the southern neighbors of the Selkup. Based on their descriptions, the Ob River birch-bark canoe differed from the canoes of the Yenisey, as seen in figs. 2.2, 5.10a–b, and 5.11 (pages 32, 108, and 109). The Ob basin canoes used by the Selkup, Khanty, Mansi, Forest Nenets, and Tatars are regionally related, and thus they probably share both a common birch-bark canoe history and a common origin in this region.

THE MANSI: MOUNTAIN HUNTERS OF THE URAL FORESTS

The Mansi people, formerly known as the Vogul, have lived on both the western and the eastern slopes of the Urals, partly in Europe and partly in Western Siberia. The Mansi were a much larger nation in the past than today and were divided regionally into northern, eastern, southern, and western peoples or language groups. The Ob-Ugrian Mansi are part of a larger Permian people speaking a Uralic language, and they, like the Khanty, came under pressure from the Komi-Zyrian expansion in the Perm area and migrated east after 1000 CE. As discussed above, after the Moscow-Russian fur wars in the late 1400s, most Mansi peoples settled east of the Urals, west of the Ob and Irtysh rivers, next to the Khanty. As a consequence, the Khanty peoples moved east of those rivers (Lehrberg 1816), as map 11 shows.

Julius von Klaproth (1823) wrote in *Asia Polyglotta* of the borders of the Vogul people in the 1700s, noting that their settlements were found west of the Ural Mountains in the upper reaches of the Vishera River at Kama and near Solikamsk, and in the territory south of the upper Kosva as far as the sources of the Chusovaya rivers. On the Siberian side, they lived on the southern Iset, upper Tavda, Konda, and greater and smaller Vogulka rivers; in the north, their region reached Sosva.

August Alhqvist, a Finnish expert on the Mansi, wrote a description of their territory in 1859 that provides insight into the life of the last European fur hunters at the border of Northern Asia. He reported that their numbers were few compared to the large territory they inhabited, since in Tobolsk province there were only 900 Mansi men and perhaps some 5,400 souls altogether. In Perm province, in Europe, they

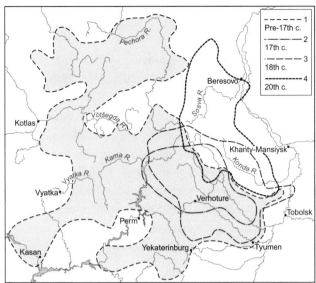

Map 11. Mansi territorial change. Pressure from Russians and other native groups resulted in Mansi territory shifting east from Europe to the Urals from the 17th to the 20th centuries. (After Sokolova 1979: 47; adapted by Marcia Bakry and Mapping Specialist, Ltd.)

totaled fewer than 900 people; thus, in those days, the total number of Mansi amounted to fewer than 7,000 people. Now only the Northern Mansi group exists, also with a population of about 7,000 (Salminen 2012). The reasons for such a small number were many, according to Ahlqvist: the climate and lifestyle were difficult, especially for forest hunters when game was decreasing; venereal disease was common; and living near Russian villages meant that vodka took a heavy toll.

Mansi Taiga Hunters

In late June 1854, Ahlqvist traveled through Tobolsk and Turinsk to Pelym Church, near the mouth of the Tavda and Pelym rivers, and then via the Tura and southern Sosva rivers to find taiga people and study their language. He noted (1859) that the Sosva and Losva river names are of Komi-Zyrian origin and that this region became known to the Russians through Zyrian guides.

The land between the Tura and southern Sosva rivers was then a forest wilderness with extensive marshes. The most common tree species were spruce, birch, pine, silver fir, cedar, larch, and willow. The greatest commercial asset of this region was its fur fauna: beaver (seldom seen now), fox (including gray and Arctic), sable (still abundant), and squirrel. There were also Eurasian elk (moose) and the usual forest birds, including hazel hen, black grouse, and wood

grouse, which were hunted for food. The rivers, especially the northern Sosva and the Ob, had so many kinds of fish that Ahlqvist found it impossible to name them all.

The Mansi were a settled hunting people, and in their southern lands, along the Losva and Pelym rivers, agriculture and cattle raising played a secondary role. Along the northern Sosva River, fishing was important. Hunting was the best trade a Mansi man could have, and he hunted from his home yurt or from small birch bark–covered tents one or two days' distance from home. Ahlqvist (1859) recounted his arrival, after a week's travel, at a busy hunters' village that had more than 50 birch-bark tents. The hunting season began in late summer, targeting moose, which grazed in the marshlands. Sable was hunted all winter until the spring snow became too soft to support a man or a dog. The price for sable varied between 4 and 10 silver rubles per pelt, according to its quality, and the Mansi hunter had to pay a Russian tax, known as *yassak*, of one sable for every three people in his household. It was largely income from the yassak tax, which was levied across all of Siberia, that powered imperial Russian expansion. Another important game animal, the squirrel, was hunted year-round with the assistance of dogs. Fox, bear, and forest birds were caught with traps, the last usually by women. In spring, waterfowl were taken in large numbers with bow and arrow.

Fishing was not very profitable on the Tavda or smaller rivers, where it was conducted in winter, usually by women, who set traps in the water. To the north, in the Sosva, where fishing was more productive and began as soon as the ice was gone, Mansi people fished until September; for this reason, autumn moose hunting was less important. The usual method was to fish with a seine, and he who has never seen Sosva fishing, Ahlqvist (1859) said, could hardly believe the huge numbers caught. What the Mansi could not eat on the spot was dried or smoked for winter.

Besides fur, the Mansi collected pine nuts, both for themselves and as a cash crop, which they sold at markets in Kazan for 7 or 8 silver kopecks per *pood* (1 Russian pood = 16.4 kilograms). All Mansi hunters communally owned the forest hunting territories, and thus all had access to game. On the Pelym River, local Mansi people often refused to let Russians hunt alone on Mansi lands. By agreement, a Russian hunter had to give half of his game to a Mansi, who would follow him into the forest. Rules to protect Mansi fishing grounds were even stricter, and Russians could fish only if they rented a waterway.

Mansi Canoes

The Mansi were the last large Native group to survive as a major hunting people in the northeastern European forest, and some Mansi people continue that hunting tradition today. According to Zoya Sokolova (1983), who studied their past territories as reflected in toponyms, they once lived as far west as the Northern Dvina River. The Mansi supplied sable, beaver, fox, bear, and moose fur first to Komi-Permian merchants and later, after 1096, to Novgorod traders in Ust-Yug. In their final stage, after circa 1450, they provided these goods to Moscow-Russian traders in Cherdyn (Tallgren 1934), after Moscow had captured the trade from Novgorod. As the Mansi were bark canoe users, their presence in northeastern Europe can provide clues about canoe history in that region. The bark canoe was the principal conveyance of taiga fur hunters, and the Mansi were its last major users in Europe and Western Siberia, although it persisted longer in the east.

The Mansi also used expanded log boats and large planked log boats, which they sometimes doubled by connecting them together, but they seem to have used birch-bark canoes longer than the Khanty did. Living in a heavily forested taiga environment laced with small rivers kept their bark canoe tradition alive, as it did among the Evenk peoples of the Yenisey River. When the migrating taiga hunter's life ended in the latter half of the 18th century, the era of the bark canoe ended as well; the portion of the Berezov District along the northern Sosva River might have been the last place in Western Eurasia to see regular use of bark canoes.

Mansi Bark Canoes in the Fur Trade

Janet Martin (1978, 1983) discussed Moscow's northeastern expansion into new lands between the 1300s and 1600s, including the wresting of the fur trade and its market from Novgorod. The importance of those lands was twofold: first, they increased the tax-paying population and the number of men in arms; second, in northeastern Europe, Barmia and Yugra were the major sources of furs. Until the road to Siberia opened in the 1600s, these were the only sources of fur available to exchange for foreign imports. Controlling these lands thus offered new trade opportunities. The early Russian state of Muscovy expanded in two stages. During the first, in the war against Novgorod in the last quarter of the 14th century, it absorbed the Vychegda Perm (Komi-Zyrians). In the second stage, competing against the Vepsian fur-market town Ust-Yug a century later, Muscovy turned its attention to the Permian Velikayans (Komi), the Yugra

(Khanty), and the Mansi and subjugated peoples dwelling as far east as the Ob River.

The Mansi were active players in the fur wars described earlier and in trade connections west of the Urals. They controlled the land passages over the Urals from Europe to Siberia, by which furs from the Ob River and Western Siberia came to European markets. The Mansi, and later the Komi-Zyrians, inhabited the territory as far north as Obdorsk (Salekhard) on the Ob River estuary, where Nenets lands began. During the 17th and 18th centuries, most long-distance trade between the Ob and northeastern Europe was conducted in birch-bark canoes, as it had been earlier. Alexander Shutikhin studied Mansi and Komi contacts and fur-trade links and found a constant stream of fur traders traveling to the Ust-Yug market in birch-bark canoes:

> The customs book at Vychegda River, in collecting duties from boats arriving from the Vychegda, Pechora, or Northern Dvina in 1655–56, states, "September over three days from Archangel Permian in the *bereshchanom* [bark canoe]. . . ." Birch-bark boats from the upper Pechora were large-capacity. *Osnachikh* [rowers] on the vessel were three to six people. Plus the cargo. Most likely fur. During the period from September 22 to 30 in 1655, 15 birch-bark *kayukov* [Russian/Siberian: boats] came from the Pechora, probably with fur. The crew of a *kayuchka* [small boat] is composed of two to four people. (2008: 8)

Ob River Mansi bark canoes appear in a book printed in Paris (DeLisle and Königsfeld 1768) with illustrations by Tobias Königsfeld, a student at the Geography Institute of the Royal Academy in the French capital. An assistant to French cartographer and mapmaker Joseph-Nicholas DeLisle, Königsfeld was employed to draw maps of Western Siberia for the Russian government on a 1740 astronomical expedition to observe the transit of Venus in Berezov, and he documented his journey through Mansi and Khanty lands. His drawing *View of Berezov from the South Shore* (fig. 5.7) shows Khanty/Ostyak bark canoes near the confluence of the Ob and Sosva rivers. A more detailed view of canoes is seen in an earlier illustration (fig. 5.8) that he drew on May 28, 1728, with a note in French describing the scene (Zarisovski 1949). Berezov was one of the few locations where Mansi inhabited the western Ob River shore and Khanty lived opposite them, on the eastern shore, which may explain why the illustrator was uncertain as to whether they were Khanty or Mansi.

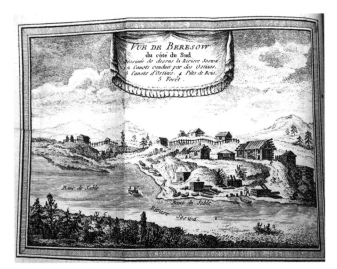

Fig. 5.7. *View of Berezov from the South Shore*: Tobias Königsfeld's 1740 view of Beresov village, at the confluence of the Ob and Sosva rivers, shows the town and Khanty/Ostyak bark canoes on the river and shore. (From DeLisle and Königsfeld 1768: 113)

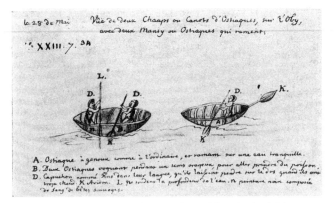

Fig. 5.8. A May 28, 1728, drawing by Tobias Königsfeld, with notes in French: "Two *chaps* (Ostyak canoes) on the Ob River, with Mansy or Ostyak paddlers. (*a*) An Ostyak kneeling and paddling on still water. (*b*) Two Ostyak fishermen navigating through stormy weather. (*c*) A cap (*kus* in Khanty) that can hang down the wearer's back when he is too warm. (?). Oar. (?) Using a pole to sound the water. (?) Black paint made with wild animal blood." (From Zarisovski 1949: 131)

Königsfeld's journal contains the statement "On the 12th of May, the ice being melted, several Ostiacks were seen paddling canoes in the Soswa [River]" (DeLisle and Königsfeld 1768: 118). The bark canoes depicted in the illustration have rather wide ends, as was typical of the Ob River and similar to both Khanty and Selkup designs; each boasts a strong gunwale and eight ribs, which would make them 3 or 4 meters long. The boat on the right shows the paddler in a

kneeling position; in the other, one man sounds the depth with a long pole while another paddles. The wide blades are characteristic of Mansi paddles. The bark cover is painted red with animal blood mixed with seal oil.

Ahlqvist (1859) noted that the fur trade had been practiced in Yugra since ancient times. Before the arrival of the Russians, it was controlled by the Komi-Zyrian people, who were forced to begin sharing profits with Russian traders in the 1850s. Until then, the Komi-Zyrians traded furs that came from two routes across the Urals, from the Obdorsk and Berezov markets. The southern route went from Berezov along the Sosva River and then the Sigva tributary before crossing the Ural Mountains, which are rather narrow at the source of the Sigva. In one day's travel from the Sigva, a reindeer sledge could reach the Pechora River. All trade in Siberia was by barter, with the common currency being squirrel skin. In the 1850s, when the fur trade between the Zyrians and Russians began to be handled via moneylending in order to make advance payments, the use of money had a destructive effect on Mansi incomes because of devaluation, and they lost the advantage of the barter system, which had provided them with material goods in exchange for their furs.

THE SELKUP: FOREST HUNTERS OF THE MIDDLE OB

According to Kai Donner (1933a), the Selkup people, sometimes referred to as the Ostyak Samoyed, spoke a Samoyed language but had a Khanty material culture. Today the Selkup are the only Samoyed people living on the upper Ob River; another group lives in the far north around the Taz River. In 1989, these two groups together numbered roughly 3,600. They live in the northern parts of Tomsk Oblast, Krasnoyarsk Krai, the Yamalo-Nenets Autonomous Okrug, and the Nenets Autonomous Okrug (Norwegian Polar Institute 2006: Nenets).

Anton Schiefner, who edited Matthias A. Castrén's collected early-19th-century works at the Russian Academy of Sciences, wrote a summary of the Samoyed people in *Grammatik der Samojedischen Sprachen* (1969). In his introduction, Schiefner described the Selkup and their territories, writing that they belonged not to the tundra zone but to the forest region on the Ob and its tributaries between the Tym and Chulym rivers. Castrén noted that the Selkup population could be divided into three groups by dialect: the northern (or lower) dialect, covering the Tym and upper and lower Narym rivers; a middle, or Ket, dialect; and a southern, or upper Chulym, dialect (cited in Schiefner 1969). All these rivers run on the right, or eastern, side of the upper Ob north of the present city of Tomsk.

The best-known of the Selkup watercraft are their expanded log boats and larger planked river boats with sails (Donner 1915), but they also used two types or variations of birch-bark canoes. The first was related to the boats of the middle Ob River, while the second, found on the Ket River (which a short portage connects to the Yenisey basin), most likely developed via contact with the Yenisey people or the Southern Samoyed living on the opposite side of the upper Yenisey River (see page 108). In this respect, the Selkup resemble the Evenk peoples, who had one type of bark canoe typical of the Lena while living by that river and later developed a new style after migrating to the Yenisey (see below).

Selkup Birch-Bark Canoes

The Origins of the Sel'kup (1972), by Galina I. Pelikh, comments on Selkup birch-bark canoes and cites evidence from people who had used or seen them. She recounted stories by three tradition-bearers from the Ob River villages of Ivanka and Kolpashevo about bark canoes called *pachzha* (coffers) that were used into the 1950s. In Kolpashevo-on-Ob, a local man, B. A. Potapov, made her a drawing of such a boat he had seen in a shed at his grandfather's home. Its dimensions were the same as those of a small *oblaska* (expanded log boat). Pelikh noted this birch-bark boat's form and construction. Its frame was made of bird cherry, and its gunwales were bent into an elongated oval, tapering toward bow and stern. Cherry ribs, semicircular in cross section, were tied to the upper gunwale to form the boat's hull. The bow and stern were not sharp but rounded. Bark strips were attached to the larger, upper gunwale and hung free beneath the ribs for reinforcement. A "duplicate hull" had been inserted into the first to insure that the boat would not sink if the outer layer of bark was torn. Thin wooden planks were laid over the bottom frames. There were no seats; the paddler sat in the middle and paddled on both sides (Pelikh 1972: 16, 269). Paddles were made of spruce and pine, in two types: simple paddles (*lappu*), both single and double bladed, and oars (*moga-lappu*) for larger boats. Pelikh quoted one of her informants, Boris Tabolgin from the Aleksandrov yurts on the Ob River, in one passage describing these boats:

> "In the past the Samoyed had birch-bark boats. What can you expect from the single[-hulled] boat [if it rips]? But if you make it doubled—it is strong and light." [Pelikh continued:] If you see such a

[double-hulled] boat from the distance, it looks like two bows and two sterns protruding from the water—one above the other. N. Shahov's drawing of ancient Khanty boats published by V. N. Chernetsov shows a similar arrangement, with a double bow and stern resembling the pachzha described above. (1972: 16–17)

In essence, the Selkup birch-bark canoe may have been of the typical Middle Ob River type, the dominant design in the Ob basin. It was built in two versions, single-hulled and double-hulled. The first was a canoe covered with a single sheet of bark. In the double-hulled version, a second canoe was inserted inside the first (fig. 5.9). The Samoyed used both types on the middle and northern Ob River. According to Pelikh (1972), the Selkup birch-bark canoe was nearly identical to that of the Khanty, owing to their Ostyak Samoyed heritage, and was similar to the boat used by the Chelkan Tatars, the Selkup's southern neighbors.

Pelikh's descriptions (1972: table 32) are nearly identical to those of E. A. Belgibaev (2004) of the Chulym Tatar boat.

A Ket River Selkup Bark Canoe

Historically, one group of Selkup lived on the Ket River, west of the Yenisey, in the easternmost corner of the Ob River basin, adjacent to the Khanty, Ket, and Evenk peoples. To differentiate them from other peoples and other Ostyak, this Selkup group was sometimes called the Ket River Ostyak in old Russian books. There is only one surviving Selkup birch-bark canoe from the Ket River. Kai Donner collected it during his fieldwork from 1911 to 1914, brought it to Finland,

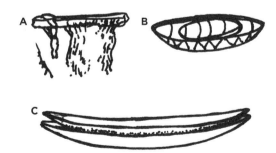

Fig. 5.9. This sketch of a Selkup birch-bark canoe (A) described by B. A. Potapov had rounded ends and an internal oval hoop that served as thwarts; B is a side view showing the double birch-bark hull, the upper one resting in the lower; C shows the ribs turned around both the outwale and inwale gunwales and the bark sheet turned from the outside inward and down between the two gunwales. (From G. I. Pelikh 1972: plate XXXII)

and in the 1920s donated it to the National Museum of Finland in Helsinki as a rare example of the Ob-Yenisey canoe tradition from Samoyed lands. The Donner canoe (National Museum of Finland KM 4934: 256) is shown in photos by Henry Forssell (fig. 5.10a–b), the photographer, illustrator, and author of many books on early boat history. It measures approximately 5.4 by 0.75 by 0.3 meters, a long boat that would have been good for running both smaller and larger rivers, even upstream, although the fast flow of the Yenisey, at circa 10 kilometers per hour, exceeds the capability of light paddling craft; the slower Ob is easier in this respect. Bark canoes and expanded log boats, like all small watercraft propelled by paddles, were used along the smaller tributaries of these rivers, where most people lived in villages consisting of just one or two families.

The boat has three sections, each one-third of the total length. Three thin planks on the bottom provide strength for supporting the weight in a fully loaded boat. The greatest beam (75 centimeters) is in the center, where the bottom is flat; from there the bilge takes a gentle round turn to the gunwales. From the middle of the boat, the bottom gradually rises toward the bow and stern, where the bark cover is neatly sewn. The depth-to-beam ratio gives the canoe a rather flat look, much like a kayak. Donner's Selkup canoe is equipped with two double-ended paddles, each approximately 270 centimeters long. The canoe has 25 half-round ribs set about 22 centimeters apart. They are rather thin but many in number, imparting a smooth, curving shape to the craft. The ribs are a little wider in the stern than in the bow, giving the former more volume and buoyancy but making the hull slightly asymmetric. The ends of the boat are sharp at the gunwale level (fig. 5.10b). The gunwales are nearly horizontal, and the in- and outwales are single pieces lashed together at the ends, perhaps with spruce root. Each gunwale has one large lashing hole at each end; a lashing binds the gunwales at each end and is wound several times around the gunwale ends. The bark sheet and the rib ends are clamped between the in- and outwales and fastened with wooden pins bolted from the outside in. The canoe has five thwarts evenly spaced along the boat's length. The whole bark surface under the ribs is covered with thin, narrow laths up to the gunwale, providing extra strength and stiffness.

Although the canoe is long, it is made of one large sheet of birch bark. This is rather unusual, as bark canoes of this size are usually sewn from two or more sheets. Bark canoes sometimes had to be made quickly to cross a river or lake or for other types of travel, and in such cases fresh birch bark was used. But if a canoe or chum (tent) cover was to last longer than one season or one journey, the bark had to be prepared carefully. Ket people boiled birch bark for canoes or chum covers in large vats for two or three days, then rolled it, bound it with rope, and placed the bundle back into the vat, stuffing the upper part of the roll with moss to keep the steam inside. Every few hours they turned the roll over to submerge the previously uppermost part. Such boiling makes bark pliable and easier to sew. After boiling, it was smoked, making it resistant to water and rot (Alekseenko 1976).

THE SOUTHERN SAMOYED: HUNTERS AND HERDERS OF THE ALTAI AND SAYAN MOUNTAINS

The Southern (Mountain) Samoyed, including the Koibal, Mator, Karagas, Soyot, and Kamas peoples, are all almost extinct as ethnic groups; few remnants are extant today in Western Siberia. Juha Janhunen and T. Salminen have written (2000) that the Kamas-Koibal and Mator are often

Fig. 5.10a–b. Two views of a Selkup Yenisey-type canoe (FNM KM 4934: 256) collected by Kai Donner on the Ket River in 1911–14, which was made from a single sheet of bark. (Photograph: Henry Forssell, 1975; courtesy Henry Forssell)

The Bark Canoes and Skin Boats of Northern Eurasia

considered to be a special sub-branch, known as the Sayan Samoyed. The Mountain Samoyed, as the Southern Samoyed were also called, used to include the Mator and Kamas peoples. Although their original language is extinct, these people still survive among the modern Khakass and Tuvan ethnic groups of the Sayan-Altai mountain region. A notable descendant group of the Mountain Samoyed is the culturally unique northeastern Tuvan group known as the Tofalar (Janhunen 2000).

Until Turkic peoples entered the northern Altai-Sayan Mountains and areas farther north circa 400 to 600 CE (Tomilov and Friedrich 1996), Samoyed land extended from the Yenisey and Ob river headwaters, near what is now the Mongolian-Chinese border in the south, to the Arctic Ocean in the north. The Samoyed are one of the oldest aboriginal peoples in Western Siberia, making their boating history important because they shared much of their knowledge of bark canoes, rafts, and log boats with other groups, including the Yukagir, Khanty, Ket, Turkic Tatar, and Evenk, who invaded or bordered their territory. We can assume that bark canoes were in use very early in forested southwestern Siberia and that such boats were built and used by the Samoyed, whose lands extended from the southern steppe-taiga border zone over the whole northern taiga, where birch bark was available. The ethnic diversity and complicated history of this region can be seen in differences in the details of their canoe construction (fig. 5.11).

Cultural Contacts in the Yenisey River Basin

One of the first descriptions of Samoyed groups was recorded in 1775 by Johan Gottlieb Georgi, who wrote about all the peoples in the Russian Empire in a multivolume series (1776a, b, 1777). He told of some very small (and now extinct) groups of Samoyed peoples in southwestern Siberia who still spoke their own languages. They included the Koibal, a society of sheep, goat, and cattle herders living a Mongol-style life with horses, on the upper Yenisey in the Sayan Mountains around modern Krasnoyarsk. There were also the Soyot, hunters, fishermen, and reindeer breeders living in northern Sayan and around Lake Baikal. Third were the Mator, a people living in the Sayan on the right bank of the upper Yenisey, who until Russian entry into the region in 1609 had been dominated by the Mongol Golden Horde. Finally, there were the Kamas, another group living on the eastern bank of the Yenisey along the Kan and Man rivers near Krasnoyarsk. All these peoples used birch-bark canoes before Russian contact. Their

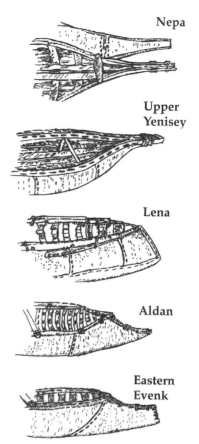

Fig. 5.11. Central and East Siberian canoe variation. The Sayan-Altai Mountain region has been the birthplace of many cultures, and its canoes are more diverse than those of any other location in Northern Eurasia, as evidenced by the bow styles of canoes from Nepa (Lower Tunguska), Tulum Dyav (the Upper Yenisey source), Vilyuy (a Lena tributary), Uda (Santarsky Bay), and regions near Lake Baikal and the headwaters of the Yenisey and Lena Rivers. (Drawing: Harri Luukkanen)

diversity, concentrated in a relatively small area, demonstrated both the ethnic variety of the Altai-Sayan mountain region and the impact of Turkic and Mongol expansion on what were once larger populations occupying much larger territories.

Jaakko Häkkinen (2010), among others, has discussed the Ural origin of Samoyed languages, Samoyed genetic markers, and the Samoyed's contacts with other peoples in Southern and Western Siberia. He believes that the emergence of the Proto-Samoyed language resulted from the expansion of the Uralic language into the northern Sayan Mountains. The time, place, and direction of this expansion point to the mid-2nd-millennium BCE Seima-Turbino Bronze Age culture and its trade network, which reached east of the

Urals. This culture was largely in the region of the East Uralic dialect, and a smaller center existed in the Proto-Samoyed area of the western Sayan Mountains between the Irtysh and Ob rivers. Besides adopting bronze, and perhaps because of western migration, people east of the Urals adopted Uralic language as well. In Häkkinen's view, the Proto-Samoyed language started to disperse, as new dialects or languages north of the Sayan Mountains between the Ob and Yenisey sources, around the beginning of the Christian era. The Samoyed-speaking peoples then existed as three macro-groups, defined mainly by geography: Northern (Nganasan, Enet, Yurak, Nenets), or Forest and Tundra Samoyed; central (Selkup), or Forest Samoyed; and Southern or Mountain Samoyed (Kamas, Koibal, Mator, Taigi, Karagas, and Soyot).

Eugene Helimski (2008) has written a review of Samoyed studies, mainly from the linguistic point of view, in which he discusses the likely location of the Proto-Samoyed homeland. Based on language and archaeology, he points to the triangle of land formed by the cities of Tomsk, Yeniseysk, and Krasnoyarsk. If this is correct, then the proto-Samoyed people later divided into three groups, one settling to the north along the Yenisey and Ob rivers, another—the Southern Samoyed—taking up life in the Altai and Sayan mountains, and the third—the Selkup—remaining in their original territories between the Ob and the Yenisey. Their migrations might have been instigated by pressure from the Khanty from the west and the Turkish Tatars from the south or southwest. The impacts of the Mongol, the Ket (Yeniseyan), and others may also have been important. Here, too, near the Yenisey River, the Samoyed may have met the proto-Yukagir before the latter (see page 136) retreated east to the Lena. Although these reconstructions of ancient times by scholars rarely mention canoes, it seems likely that birch-bark canoe technology, which became an enduring tradition of all later Samoyed peoples and remained strong into the 1700s, originated in their ancestral home between the Ob and Yenisey rivers.

The Kamas Birch-Bark Canoe: Shared Samoyed and Yeniseyan Heritage

In his manuscript "Description of the Siberian Peoples," the German historian G. F. Müller, employed by the Russian Academy, wrote about the Kamas people, remarking that they used birch-bark canoes, which in the Koibal language were called *kimä* or *tos kimä* (Castrén 1857c: 137). The same canoe may have been used at that time, and earlier, by all the Altai-Sayan Samoyed—the Mator, Karagas, Soyot,

and Koibal—and possibly the Tavgi Samoyed people on the Taimyr Peninsula as well. Müller gave the best description of the Samoyed bark boat, which seems to have been a prototype for the canoes of the Yeniseyan peoples:

They have a length of 4.5 *segnes* [4.1 meters]; the width in the middle is about 1 *arshin* [71 centimeters], and on the bottom they are flat. Their maximum length is five and a half hands [manual *segnes*, or 5.5 meters]. The birch bark is sewn together, and the seams are greased with spruce resin. The white part of the birch-bark cover is sewn to the ribs, [which are] made of birch or cherry tree, connected to form a boat, and where it is pierced, it is also greased with resin. There are three poles along the length [gunwales and bottom keel], then 6 or 8 ribs in the width direction, so that they are separated from each other by more than a *polsazheni* [1 foot, or 30 centimeters]. Then there are two more curved pieces of wood [stems] at both ends. Their paddles have only one blade. (Quoted in Potapov 1957: 219–20)

Mikhail Batashev, an expert on the history of southwestern Siberia at the Krasnoyarsk Krai Museum of Local Lore, refers to Müller's description in a private letter to HL of May 11, 2011:

The people living east of the upper Yenisey River (in the taiga and mountain-taiga zones) used a birch-bark boat in the 1600s and 1700s. Moreover, the ethnicity—Tungus, Samoyed, Yeniseyan—of the people played no role in their canoe styles; the main factor was the regional cultural tradition. The Samoyed in Western Siberia made a *dolbleniki* [expanded log boat] and the Sayan Samoyed made a bark canoe. The Tungus on the eastern bank of the Yenisey made bark canoes, and on the left (western) side, a dolbleniki. The Kets make a dolbleniki and the Koibal a bark canoe.

Here we can point to the Koibal. In the first half of the 17th century, the Koibal were part of the Kott tribal region at the Kan River; in other words, they were Yeniseyan people. In the second half of the same century, they moved to Arin tribal land. The Arin also spoke a Yeniseyan language, similar to Ket. Currently they are part of the Khakass, as they were Turkicized from the second half of the 18th century to the early 19th century. Thus we can assume that the Koibal and the Kott tribe, who occupied the territory from the foothills of the eastern Sayan in the south to the Angara Tungus region in the north, and from the Yenisey River west to the eastern Buryats, used a birch-bark boat for river transport. The Mator and Koibal tribes occupied the basins of the Kazyr, Kizir, and Amur rivers. The Karagas [modern Tofalar] resided in the upper reaches of the Uda, Oiá, and Oka rivers.

Information on the Koibal confirms our assumption that the Samoyed shared their bark canoe tradition with the Yeniseyan-speaking peoples (see chapter 6). When these peoples—the Ket, Kott, Assan, Arin, Yugh, and Pumpokol—entered Southern Siberia from Inner Asia somewhere between the Ob and Yenisey river sources, they must have crossed Samoyed lands. Like the peoples of the southern steppes and mountains—the Ket, for example—they did not have bark canoes of their own and probably adopted them to use in their new taiga environment.

THE TATARS OF THE NORTHERN ALTAI: MOUNTAIN HUNTERS OF THE SIBERIAN FOREST

The northern Altai Mountains lie in the southernmost part of Siberia. South of the Altai, Russia borders China, western Mongolia, and eastern Kazakhstan. This region has been inhabited longer than any other part of Southern Siberia; during the coldest periods of the last Ice Age, it was a refuge for the cultures and peoples who would later expand into Northern Siberia as the tundra and forest zones advanced to their present positions. During the past 1,500 years, Altai Mountain peoples such as the Turks and the Mongol created huge empires or, alternatively, were subjugated by the Chinese, Manchus, or Russians. Part of this region—the Republic of Tuva—was independent from 1911 to 1944.

Soviet and Russian scholars agree on the multiethnic composition of the "Siberian Tatars," who live between the Ural Mountains and the headwaters of the Yenisey River. Nikolai A. Tomilov (2000) writes that in the most general sense, the ethnogenesis of the Siberian Tatars resulted from a blending of Ugric, Samoyed, Turk, and, to a lesser degree, Iranian and Mongolian peoples. The Ugric group (ancestors of the Hungarians, Mansi, and Khanty) and the Turkic-speaking Kipchaks were central to the formation of the Baraban (a small group) and the Tobol-Irtysh Tatars, as the Samoyed and Kipchak were to the coalescence of the Tomsk Tatars. Turkic-speaking peoples penetrated the Western Siberian

plain from the Altai and Sayan mountains between the 5th and 7th centuries; a later influx of Turkic groups from Central Asia and Kazakhstan occurred in the 13th century following Mongol invasions. Thus, by the 14th century, the basic ethnic constituents of the Siberian Tatars were in place. According to Tomilov and Friedrich (1996), there were some 500,000 Tatars in Siberia at the time of their writing, of whom only 200,000 were Siberian Tatars, whose ancestors were living in Western Siberia before the appearance of Russian immigrants at the end of the 16th century.

The boat history of the Turkic Tatars is interesting but obscure. The birch-bark canoe was widely used by the Turkic Tatars in the northern Altai Mountains and probably arose from a much more ancient Samoyed bark canoe tradition. Two varieties are known, one in the eastern and another in the western Altai. The far-traveled 10th-century Arabic scholar Ibn Fadlan entered Turkic Tatar lands on his expedition to the Volga Bulgars and described crossing the Ural River, also called the Yaghandi, in a coracle-like boat:

> We traveled forth until we came to the Yaghandi River. There the people took their skin boats, which had been made from camel hide, spread them out, and took the goods from Turkish camels; and as the boats are round, they put the goods inside them till they spread out. Then they filled them up full with garments and wares. When each skin boat was full, the group of five, six, or four [sic] men, more or less, sat in them. They took in their hands birch wood and used it like oars and kept rowing while the water carried the boat on down, and it spun around until we got across. (Fadlan quoted in Sinor 1961: 159)

Chelkan Birch-Bark Canoes

The Chelkan (Chelkantsy) people's culture and boats have been studied by E. A. Belgibaev (2004) of Altai State University, who has written that they, along with the Kumandin and Tube (Tubalar), form a single cultural area. Their life was once based on a fundamentally different economy than that of the southern Altai peoples. Ethnic groups in the northern foothills of the Altai are defined largely by the mountain and valley landscape they occupy and by their local economic activities, which include hunting, fishing, gathering, farming, forging, weaving, and sheep, goat, and horse breeding. The homeland of the Chelkan in the 17th century was a place called Shchelkany or Shchelkanskaya Volost. In 1642, part of the Chelkan population moved to the Sayan Mountains.

According to Belgibaev, the Chelkan hunted bear, elk, maral (Altaian mountain deer), wild goat, deer, fur-bearing animals, and wild birds using a variety of tools, including loops, traps, self-triggered arrows, and muzzle-loaded guns. They caught fish, including perch, bream, and pike, with fishing tackle, nets, traps, and other tools. Practicing slash-and-burn agriculture with mattocks, they cultivated millet, wheat, barley, rye, flax, and hemp. Horse breeding was a part-time activity. The Chelkan adopted beekeeping in the 19th century and vegetable gardening in the 20th. Their housing was similar to that of other people in the region: dugout shelters with two-sided birch-bark roofs, conical yurts, barns, and summer kitchens. Their means of transportation included skis of the Sayan-Altaian type, sledges made of skins and birch bark, canoes, dugouts, and other types of boats.

In 1998–99, Belgibaev conducted fieldwork among the Chelkan people in the towns of Biyka, Kurmach-Baigol, Suranash, Maisky, and Turochak in the Turochaksky District of the Altai Republic, where, along with the Cygnus River area, the birch-bark canoe was used. He writes:

> During the flood season, hunters used birch-bark canoes [tos keve] to overcome obstacles. The design of the canoe can be determined from stories about a famous hunter known as Chemuka Kandarakov. In mid-April [in the 1920s], this hunter crossed the flooded Sadr River in his canoe, which he made in the forest "in haste." The canoe had bird-cherry gunwales to which cross thwarts were attached. Prior to attaching the thwarts, the ribs were warmed over the fire. From the top, the boat looked like an elongated semioval skeleton. The birch-bark sheets were sewn with bast stripped from the bird-cherry tree. The edges of the birch-bark sheet cover were turned over from the outside to the inside over the gunwales and sewn in place with bast. In order not to make holes with one's feet, shingles or tree branches were placed in the bottom. The boat was propelled with a single-blade paddle or a pole. The Chelkan hunter used the bark canoe for some two or three seasons and then abandoned it in the taiga. (2004)

Chulym and Shor Bark Canoe Heritage

The Chulym and Shor Tatars resided in the eastern part of the northern Altai Mountains, between the upper Ob and Yenisey rivers. According to Antropova (1961), the Shor (Shortsy) used birch-bark canoes, which played a major role in their heritage as fishermen and hunters. The same can be said about the Chulym people, close relatives of the Shor, who lived along the Chulym River where the Yai and Kii rivers join it in Tomsk Oblast and Krasnoyarsk Krai. According to the census of 2002, the Chulym people numbered 700.

Nikolai A. Tomilov reports that the Chulym "traveled on horseback and on carts and sleighs, sometimes using one or two dogs, and in expanded log boats [dolblenki], plank boats, and birch-bark canoes [kem]" (2012a: 221). That their bark canoe was called kem is revealing, as the word might connect the Chulym-Shor people to the Samoyed: kem may be a Southern Samoyed word for "bark canoe." In 1781, Finnish-born professor Erik Laxman of the Russian Academy wrote in "Sibirische Briefe" that "the Koibal [Mator] folk called the upper Yenisey Kem, meaning 'river'" (1793: 12). This might reveal a relationship between this river and the bark canoe, whose designation the Chulym Tatar later adopted. On the other hand, Tomilov has written in another paper that the Omsk Tatar, living north of the Altai near the source of the Ob River, called their expanded log boat kama, keme, or kim (2012b). Linguists may one day help to resolve the connections here among boat names, languages, and peoples. In the meantime, we hypothesize that kem, as an early name for the bark canoe, came from the name of the great river Kem (Yenisey), where the bark boat might have been first built, used, or encountered. When bark canoes vanished, the name kem was given to the type of boat that replaced them: the expanded log boat known as kim, keme, or kama.

The connection between the Chulym-Shor's bark canoe and the term kem might be explained by their location and origin as remnants of the Ugrian, Samoyed, and Ket peoples of Western Siberia before they became part of the greater Turkic Tatar community. Leonid P. Potapov, who studied the ethnic composition of Altai peoples south and north of the mountain range, saw a clear difference between the two cultures: "In the southern Altai, the main means of transport was horse and packhorse, while in the north it was the raft and bark boat in summer and skis in winter" (1969: 19). The oral folklore of the southern Altai people was the typical epic, reflecting their hunting lifestyle, and for the northern it was tales about domestic life heroes and stories about animals. As in the case of the Finnish Kalevala poems, we can learn about boats and their uses from Altaian oral literature: Northern Altai legends and tales provide evidence of bark canoes, including the epic Alyp-Manash, in which a traveler uses a birch-bark canoe during his wanderings (Legends of Altai 2010). Alyp-Manash poems have been collected from the Oirot, a northern Altai people; the poems and prose have been dated to the 7th and 8th centuries, and similar legends and tales are known in all Turkic regions (Kuusi and Pertti 1985: 76).

Tatar-Samoyed Contacts in Southwestern Siberia

It is likely that birch-bark canoe technology, as represented by the boats we have described for the Ob River, originated in southwestern Siberia, developed by the ancient ancestors of the Mansi, Khanty, Ket, Samoyed, and Turkic Tatars, among whom this craft was widely known. In a paper on Chelkan landscape and culture, Belgibaev writes:

> In ethnographic and folkloric literature, bark canoes are known among the Turkic-speaking Shor, Tomsk Tatars, Ket, Ob-Ugric groups, and Nenets, as well as among a number of peoples of Eastern Siberia and the Amur River. The Narym Selkup navigated the taiga rivers in bark canoes or *dolblenki*, making frequent portages between waterways. This same method of travel through the taiga was known to Chelkan hunters. In the 18th century, the Kumandin used to hunt in the bark canoe. . . . Among the Turkic-speaking peoples and the Tatars of Southern Siberia, the frame of the bark canoe was made of bird cherry. . . . Among the Narym Selkup and the Chelkant, boats were made of bird-cherry frames and birch bark. For the basic frame of a Selkup boat, long branches were bent into an oval and fixed to the bottom by ribs, the bent staves that formed the skeleton of the boat. Birch bark covered the frame on both the outside and the inside: the Selkup produced a birch-bark canoe with a double bark cover. At the bottom of the boat, thin wooden boards were put under the ribs for protection. Comparing the bark boats of Narym Selkup and Chelkan, we find many similarities. In addition, one should bear in mind an important fact: the Narym Selkup bark boat was designed for prolonged use, while the Chelkan bark canoe was made for only two or three river crossings. (2004)

Yet Belgibaev also presents evidence that the taiga bark canoe could have originated among the Khanty people: "In folkloric material, the Vakh and southern Khanty people regard the dolblenki as their own, as opposed to the 'Samoyed' birch-bark canoe" (2004). However, such reconstructions based on ethnographic, folkloristic, and linguistic analyses rely on relatively recent data, from perhaps the past 1,000 to 2,000 years, and archaeological evidence of bark canoes is similarly time-constrained. Paddles and rock art dating to 6,000 to 8,000 years ago suggest truly ancient origins but do not provide us with scientific evidence for the origins of canoes, although we can assume they were widely used in the forested regions of Eurasia well before the last Ice Age ended.

CHAPTER 6

CENTRAL SIBERIA

THE YENISEY RIVER AND THE TAIMYR PENINSULA

The second of the great north-flowing rivers transecting Siberia is the Yenisey, which rises in the Altai and Sayan mountains of northern Mongolia and reaches the Arctic Ocean through the Yenisey Gulf west of the Taimyr Peninsula. Its basin covers a huge territory in the center of the continent (map 12). Major tributaries drain the region west of Lake Baikal. Like the Ob basin, the Yenisey basin is a vast lowland bowl, with few geographic barriers other than bogs, swamps, and thick forests restricting the movement of people and land animals. Below its mountain headwaters, the river and its tributaries are easily navigable by small boats except during spring ice breakup. In winter, the Yenisey system is a virtual ice highway; for millennia, its main stem and east-west tributaries have been routes for migration and trade. In some cases, the headwaters of its tributaries are only a short portage from corresponding rivers in the Ob or Lena basins. Such proximity has also facilitated the sharing of boat styles and technology.

The major cultural groups of the Yenisey described in this chapter are the Nganasan, Enets, Dolgan, Ket, Yenisey River Evenk, and Mongol-Buryat. Their cultures range from Arctic tundra reindeer herders and hunters to river-based fishermen in the middle Yenisey and steppe pastoralists in the Altai-Baikal region. Despite the economic and cultural diversity of the basin, all these groups used a single Yenisey bark canoe type. As in other large Siberian river systems, a shared connection to the river produced a shared technology of bark canoe styles. When new peoples appeared in these basins, they generally discontinued use of the canoe forms of their old homelands in favor of styles prevalent in their new territory.

THE NGANASAN: ARCTIC TUNDRA HUNTERS OF THE TAIMYR

Also known as the Tavgi Samoyed, the Nganasan are the northernmost people living north of or on the eastern

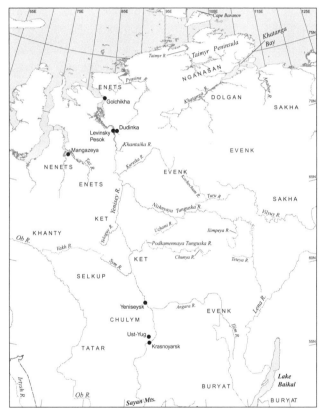

Map 12. Central Siberia: the Yenisey River basin, Taimyr Peninsula, and territories of the Nganasan, Nenets, Dolgan, Ket, Yenisey Evenk, Mongol, and Buryat. (Dan Cole, Smithsonian Institution)

tributaries of the Yenisey River. As a result of their location on the Taimyr Peninsula in the northernmost part of the Asian continent, they were, until the 20th century, one of the most isolated people in Northern Eurasia, although they were taxed by the Russians as early as circa 1650 because of their proximity to the Russian Northern Sea Route. Johan G. Georgi wrote one of the first descriptions of this group, calling them Tavgi and locating them between the Yenisey and the lower

Lena (1777: 277). They are one of the few Northern Eurasian peoples for whom wild reindeer hunting continued to be a major element of their economy after Russian contact, and it has remained important to the present day (Chard 1963). Their reindeer economy, which they shared with the Yukagir, was the last predominantly hunting and food-gathering way of life practiced in the Siberian tundra. Major changes in their traditional culture began in the 1920s, when other groups, such as the Dolgan, Evenk, Yakut, and Russians, began settling in their Taimyr territory.

The Nganasan hunting culture of the Russian High Arctic has been a prominent feature in circumpolar scientific literature. The American Arctic archaeologist Chester Chard (1963) thought the original prehistoric populations of Taimyr were ancestors of the western Yukagir. This kinship has recently been supported by Volodko and colleagues (2009), who linked Nganasan DNA to that of the forest Yukagir living in western Chukotka. These peoples might have been part of the same population in the distant past before separating in the Yenisey River valley and taking different routes north—the Nganasan to Taimyr and the Yukagir to the Lena basin and eventually Chukotka. This shared history might include the use of similar canoe types and boat terminology (Simchenko 1976b). On the other hand, recent research in Taimyr (Khlobystin 2005) shows that this region's cultural history is complex, so it is highly unlikely that continuity exists between the Nganasan or Yukagir and the Early Holocene pioneers, who must also have been boatbuilders, and the region's modern residents.

The Nganasan comprise two closely related groups, the Avam and the Vadeyev, both of whom speak a Samoyed dialect. The Avam people inhabit the western part of the Taimyr Peninsula, from Yenisey Bay and its rivers to Taimyr Lake, while the Vadeyev settled the eastern part of the peninsula along Khatanga (Chatanga) Bay and the opposite shore as far as the Anabar River. In 1989, the total Nganasan population consisted of 1,280 people, of whom 83 percent had some knowledge of the native Samoyed language (the others spoke another native language or Russian). They belong administratively to the Taimyr Autonomous District of Krasnoyarsk Krai.

From a boating perspective, the Taimyr Peninsula is a rather hostile environment: it is in the permafrost zone and entirely above the Arctic Circle, where the ice-free summer season is short and cool. Nevertheless, the Nganasan used log and skin boats for spearing wild reindeer at water crossings in spring and fall, much as the Yukagir did (Gracheva 2012);

they even employed boats as sledges towed by domesticated reindeer, a practice known also to the Nenets and Saami. For these reasons, their boat history has differed from that of other Siberian peoples.

Skin Boats for Tundra Hunting and Fishing

As far as we know from the limited records, the Nganasan used two kinds of dugout boats for hunting reindeer and fishing. They obtained these boats from Khanty and Yakut (Sakha) people, as there were no trees for boatbuilding in Taimyr. Andrey A. Popov (1966) wrote that the Nganasan did not like the Khanty's Ob-type log boat, however, preferring the lighter Yakut model supplied by the Russian Trade Commission in the 20th century. Wacław Sieroszewski (1993) believed that the Yakut log boat (*vetki, vetka; anabuska* in the Yukagir language) was actually a Yukagir type. Thus it seems likely that the Nganasan, who are related to the forest Yukagir, adopted their log boat, too.

In use until the 19th century, the Nganasan skin boat called the *kukhungondu* was studied first by A. A. Popov and later by Yuri B. Simchenko (1976b: 138), who contended that the boat might have been similar to a skin boat known as *kubaodu*, made with reindeer skin and built by the Enets. Popov had a rather poor view of its construction: "Nganasans say they borrowed their dugouts [vetki] from their neighbors, the Dolgan and the Yakut [as opposed to the Khanty, noted above]. This confusion about boat history probably reflects the diverse origins of the Nganasan people. According to their oral history, Nganasan did not travel much by water; instead of wooden boats, they used skin ones, but the latter were so dangerous that people would not launch them during windy weather because even a small wave could bend them in two" (1966: 50).

Simchenko (1976a) included a drawing of a combination Nganasan skin-covered boat-sledge (fig. 6.1) and noted that the construction of framed skin boats (kukhungondu), which had completely fallen out of use by that point, was much more complicated than Popov reported:

Until recently these boats had a ritual dimension. They were used to cross rivers in the places where reindeer were hunted and were also placed at these locations as objects of veneration (*fala-koika*) for good luck. The boat frame in this case performed the role of a magical object. These ritual boats were not as poorly made as Popov's informers claimed. They were, of course, not as sturdy as wooden vetki but could nevertheless serve

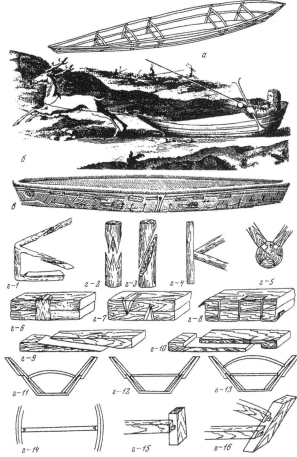

Fig. 6.1. The Nganasan *kukhungondu* reindeer skin–covered boat (circa 450 by 45 centimeters) of Taimyr was made to accommodate sledge runners on its bottom. The Enets, Nenets, and Yukagir made similar skin boats. (From Simchenko 1976a: 141)

their primary purpose—transporting hunter spearing deer at water crossings.

The building of a boat frame began with the keel timber. The Nganasan canoe did not have a keel in the proper meaning of this word. The keel consisted of two halves: the stem and stern parts. These timbers looked similar to contemporary cargo sled runners (*balki*). They were joined slightly aft of the middle with a plain scarf or rabbet joint. Regardless of the type of scarf, the stern half of the keel member was laid over the stem half. This was because the boat's center of gravity (with the paddler) was closer to the stern and the keel timber was under vertical pressure while in motion.

The bottom of the boat was usually made in two halves. This construction, which caused complications when attaching both halves to the keel timber, resulted from the fact that the reindeer hunters lacked both enough trees large enough to make the entire bottom and the tools needed to work large surfaces. The size and proportions of the bottom (and the wood available) determined the shape of the entire boat. The traditional ratio of a boat's length to its maximum breadth was 10:1. Thus, a 4.5-meter-long boat would be 45 centimeters wide at the place where the paddler sat. The paddler's seat was about two-thirds of the boat's length from the stem. This allowed the boat greater maneuverability. It could turn around on the spot, which was necessary when hunting reindeer at a river crossing. The Nganasan attached the bottom of the boat to the keel with either sinew lashings or pegs. . . .

The edges of the bottom were perforated with openings for vertical frames [ribs]. The classic construction consisted of five symmetrical pairs of vertical frames. The vertical frames were inserted into the openings in the bottom, then wrapped and tied with sinew. Sometimes additional vertical support members were inserted at the stem and stern of the boat. . . .

The most important detail of the "framed" boat was the V-shaped stem post. It connected all the most important parts of the kukhungondu and was believed to house the soul of the boat. The stem post was connected to the keel timber with a plain scarf or notched joint. The V-shaped stem post was made of larch root stumps that had symmetrically placed angled roots to which one could attach stringers. . . .

The gunwales were connected to the stem and stern posts with diagonal joints, without any specific scarfs. The joints were wrapped with leather belts and sinew and covered with fish glue, and fat was applied after they dried. The inner side of the gunwale was flattened and received shallow notches for the vertical frames. Stringers were inserted into the notches in the stem and stern posts and were tied with belts that fixed them in place. This created sturdy triangles at the front and the aft ends of the boat that were flexible enough to withstand tension [as the boat flexed]. The horizontal bottom stringers gave the frame rigidity. . . . The ratio between the maximum breadth at the bottom and at the gunwales was

1:2. The hull gradually narrowed from the cockpit toward the stem and stern. . . .

The frame was covered with skins of wild reindeer. The covers were made exclusively from the best, sturdiest fall skins. To make the cover, skins were removed in one piece. The skin removed in this manner looked like a sack, with holes where the animal's front legs and neck had been. Skins of two large bucks were needed for one cover. They were soaked and scraped with special care so as not to be cut through. Skins with unpatchable holes and other imperfections were discarded. A layer of subcutaneous fat was left on, and the skin was thoroughly oiled after drying. Both skins were sewn together in the middle and folded over the central vertical frames. Some sources state that the cover was doubled. These boats were also used as sleds (or carried on sledges) during hunting expeditions. (1976a: 35–37)

The Nganasan skin boat was rather small, perhaps owing to its use in tundra transport, and one obvious weakness was the seam along its bottom plank. The question remains of whether they built larger skin boats, as the Enets, their close cultural relatives, had done in the past in Taz Bay. The use of strong knees connecting the bottom keel plank and stringers, as in the Chukchi open skin boat, would have made a larger skin boat feasible.

The skin boat never dies, at least not in legends and rituals. Simchenko wrote that these boats, in the form of models and replicas, were still used in ritualistic contexts until recent decades. Since boats were conveyances used for travel and hunting, they needed ways to communicate with spirits; sometimes this was done by painting images of people and animals on the sides of boats or by including human-shaped spirit figures of carved wood or stone at ritual sites on land. Believed to assist in hunting, some of these spirit figures were placed inside sacred "ritual boats" (1976b: 139–40). Interestingly, the designs painted inside these boats imitated stringers and ribs, perhaps to replicate the skin or frame boats of their ancestors. In modern times, these ritual boats were carved from a single piece of wood and painted in the same manner as cradles for infants, with black and red vertical lines. Inside were crossbeams, which had no functional use in a dugout but could have been vestigial features from some ancestral craft. The Nganasan also had ritual boats made with skins covering the entire length of the craft, including the deck. A idol in the shape of a human figure was placed in the cockpit-like opening in the center of the boat.

A boat model in the Museum of Anthropology and Ethnology (MAE 6724-3), collected by Simchenko in 1975 from a ritual site in Ust-Ava, Taimyr (fig. 6.2), is a dugout covered with deerskin and decorated with images of sledges, deer, arrows, people, and eyelike motifs. Small ivory boats found in a 1,500-year-old Old Bering Sea–culture grave at the Ekven site near East Cape, Chukotka (see fig. 8.11, page 168) are probably also ritual models rather than representations of real boats.

Goose and Reindeer Hunting with Boats

The Russian anthropologist Boris O. Dolgikh described Nganasan hunting methods as being similar to those of the Tungus, Yukagir, and Eskimo:

During the summer, they nomadize to the tundra on the interior of the Taimyr Peninsula, returning south for the winter to the northern limit of the forest. Their main occupations were the hunting of wild deer, polar fox, and geese, reindeer-breeding, and fishing. Like the Olenek Tungus, the Anadyr and Lower Kolyma Yukagir, the Caribou Eskimo, and others, the Nganasan formerly hunted for wild deer mainly in the fall, gathering collectively at river crossings to slaughter them with spears (*fonka*) from boats. Until recently, they also used special leather nets, into which the deer were driven by the hunters. During summer and fall, the Nganasan hunted wild deer on foot, both alone and in small groups. (1962: 220)

Boats were important in capturing and retrieving these game animals.

A. A. Popov also studied the communal hunting of wild reindeer and geese. His research on the Dolgan, published

Fig. 6.2. This skin-covered ritual model (MAE 6724-3)—possibly a shamanic object representing a Nganasan skin boat—was found in a sacred cache in Ust-Ava, Taimyr, in 1975. Its markings include black and red images of sledges and reindeer as well as obscure motifs and notations. (Photograph: Evguenia Anichtchenko; courtesy Museum of Anthropology and Ethnography)

in Russian in 1937 (Popov 1964a, 1966), contains a drawing of boats that people are using to drive flightless geese on a pond, a method also used by the Nganasan and other northern peoples (fig. 6.3). In addition, dogs assisted in hunting geese and reindeer in Taimyr. Popov wrote:

Certain types of collective hunting that had in the not too distant past great economic significance have been preserved until our times among the Nganasan. This includes the penning and slaughter of wild reindeer in nets. Flags (*labaka*) were indispensable in this hunt. These included long strips of painted skin and white partridge wings hung on the ends of long sticks. Hunters following a herd of wild reindeer would plant the flags in the form of two converging rows, leaving an opening of 4 to 6 meters at the narrow end. Signalers (*seriti*) would hide near one row of flags at the wide end of the lane.

The cleverest hunter, in a sledge drawn by two domesticated reindeer, would drive a herd of wild reindeer into the converging funnel. The signalers then would spring up, shouting and waving garments, thus driving the reindeer further into the trap. At the narrow end of the lane, the reindeer would be met by the arrows of two or three hunters armed with bows. The flags served as a hedge keeping the reindeer from running outside the flag line. This method of hunting was called *ngatangiru*. If the reindeer were near a lake, then the flags were planted in a single row. Opposite from this line, at some distance, people would station themselves along a second row of flags. The reindeer would be driven into the water

by dogs along the lane thus formed. Then hunters on the other side of the lake would at once go out in their canoes to kill the swimming reindeer with long-shafted spears. This method of hunting was called *suodisiti bantanu*. (1966: 34–35)

The same dog-driving method was used to hunt molting geese, Popov wrote:

When there are only a few geese on hand, they are driven and hunted down by dogs along a lake or river-bank. Using this method, several men with dogs hide around a lake where geese had gathered. One or two hunters would paddle around the lake in canoes and drive the geese to the far bank. . . . When the geese reached the bank, the hunters lying in wait would hunt them down with dogs. Usually such hunting does not produce great results, since some of the geese almost always get away. (1966: 35)

Speculation on Early Taimyr Boat History

One might ask if the Nganasan used skin boats for fishing and hunting in the Yenisey estuary, where the Avam group resided. The Avam lived next to the Enets, who, according to the Finnish explorer Matthias A. Castrén, were closely related to the Tavgi. The Enets were sea fishermen of the Yenisey and Taz river estuaries who used skin boats before Europeans appeared. There could be a rich reward, since in the springtime, beluga traveled inland 200 kilometers from the Yenisey mouth as far as Levinsky Pesok (Levinsky Sands), opposite Dudinka, as reported by Fridtjof Nansen (1911). As chapter 5 notes, the Samoyed and Khanty hunted beluga in the Ob and Taz estuaries, so they were likely hunted in the Yenisey as well. Nganasan skin boats certainly would have been sufficient for this purpose.

Did the early Nganasan have bark canoes before they appeared in the Taimyr tundra? A. A. Popov believed they previously lived in a more southern location, the Yenisey forest zone, a supposition reinforced by trade records. Popov wrote, "This is evident from the fact that the 'extracts' from the yassak (fur tribute) book of the city Mangazeya speak of tribute payments by the Nganasan made in sable, an animal that does not dwell in the tundra and had to come from the forest" (1966: 11).

Matthias A. Castrén, who visited the Samoyed camps in Taimyr on his route up and down the Yenisey, noted Tavgi locations and speculated on this people's former territories:

Fig. 6.3. In the 1930s, the Dolgan used boats for hunting moulting birds, driving them across lakes into nets. (From Popov 1964a: fig. 38)

At the Tura River, which drains into the Pyasina where the Karassina group of Yenisey Samoyed live, the Tavgi Samoyed are also present. Two other Tavgi tribes are found at the Pyasina River proper, and at the Taimyr River no fewer than five tribes of Tavgi folk are present. . . . Looking at those facts and the region of the Bai Samoyed tribe gives us reason to believe that the Tavgi, [among] whom we also have to include the Yenisey Samoyed, [formerly] lived much farther west; also the Yenisey Samoyed lived and hunted in the past much farther south than in 1846. Farther west lived the Yurak Samoyed (Nenets), as well the Southern Samoyed who had entered the Yenisey River region. (1856: 236)

Early reports such as this one suggest a complicated ethnic history for Taimyr, one in which at least some peoples here used skin boats. The Khatanga River in eastern Taimyr was the traditional home of the Vadeyev group of Nganasan and later became a favorite location of the Evenk, Sakha, and Dolgan as well. In their annual subsistence cycle, the Vadeyev Tavgi migrated across a large territory as far as the upper parts of the Anabar and Olenek rivers, close to the Lena River basin. Khatanga Bay was rich in fish and sea mammals. As reported by Nils Adolf Erik Nordenskjöld (1881), Lieutenant Khariton Laptev, the Russian maritime explorer on the Great Northern Expedition who spent a winter in the Khatanga Bay region in 1739, met an Evenk people called the Irvin. The Irvin-Evenk people, Laptev said, did not have reindeer; they used dogs for sledge travel, and they lived from maritime hunting, as did the settled Chukchi. It seems likely that the Irvin people had simple skin boats, which other tundra groups commonly used for hunting reindeer and crossing lakes and rivers. Laptev's reference to contact with "settled Chukchi" is interesting, since some of the Chukchi people, who were originally inland reindeer herders, came to settle on the coast and adopted skin boats and marine mammal hunting from the Eskimo (see pages 158–164). The same process of adaptation to the coast, including the use of skin boats for hunting caribou in rivers and lakes, may have taken place among the Nganasan and other groups that historically inhabited Taimyr.

Other evidence of possible Nganasan-Chukchi contact was provided in 1882 by Franz R. von Monnier, a scientist from Vienna. He wrote about a Nganasan legend telling how starving Chukchi had first appeared in Taimyr in the 1600s on a desperate flight from wars on the Kolyma River (see

page 157 in chapter 8). Farther east, von Monnier said, on the lower Yenisey and Taimyr rivers, the Samoyed once did not hunt at sea, instead following the reindeer only as far north as Lake Taimyr to avoid waking up the "sleeping" people (meaning the dead Chukchi refugees).

THE ENETS OF THE TAZ AND YENISEY ESTUARIES

The Enets, formerly called the Yenisey Samoyed, are relatively poorly known because they were assimilated by the Nenets and Nganasan in the mid-19th century. One of their subgroups was the former Taz Samoyed people, whose language and culture were studied by Castrén (1856) between November 1846 and February 1847 in Yenisey Bay and estuary. Although they were a small group living at the Arctic Circle, documented references to their use of boats give them a place in this canoe and boat history.

The first record of Taz River skin boats—perhaps one of the earliest records of any skin boat in Siberia—is a 1576 report by the explorer Olivier Brunel, who arrived in Western Siberia with European ships (see Spies 1997). He worked for Russian and Dutch commercial groups searching for a sea route to China via the Northeast Passage. In that same year, Martin Frobisher sailed from England to Arctic Canada to search for a northwest passage to the same destination. In a 1581 letter that the explorer Johan Balak wrote to the famous mapmaker Gerardus Mercator, Balak said that Brunel had entered Ob Bay in 1576 and landed near the Taz River mouth, where he met Samoyed people paddling skin boats on their way to the Ob River estuary. They told him about a route southward toward China that followed the Ob River. This encounter indicates that the Samoyed (who might have been Enets or Nenets at that time) built and used skin boats capable of extended voyages. Their boats, manned by many paddlers and able to carry heavy cargo, could also be used for maritime hunting on the large Ob and Taz bays and in their estuaries, which were rich in fish, seal, and beluga. A Russian map of 1745 (map 13) illustrates the extensive network of Enets villages along the Yenisey estuary during the peak of the fur-trade era.

Enets Migration Routes between the Taz and Yenisey Rivers

From 1845 through 1848, nearly 300 years after Brunel's journey, Castrén explored Western Siberia and studied Samoyed language, peoples, customs, and trade from the Arctic Ocean to Mongolia. In 1846–47, he traveled from Turukhansk

Map 13. This Russian Academy of Sciences map from a 1745 atlas shows settlements in the Yenisey River estuary at the height of the fur-trade era. (From Nordenskjöld 1881: 192)

to Tolstoi Nos, visiting the wintering peoples and clans in the region and interviewing their chiefs. Castrén met Enets people living on the Yenisey River and estuary, in the Pyasina tundra of the southern Taimyr Peninsula, and along the Taz River and its estuary and bay, which were their customary territories, and which they navigated via boats and canoes on rivers and lakes. Based on firsthand information, Castrén wrote:

> The Yenisey Samoyed are primarily a fishing people who reside mostly on the left [western] side of the lower Yenisey River and estuary from June to August before retiring to winter quarters near the Yenisey. The left bank of the Yenisey is better for fishing and boating because the water is shallow and runs slowly.

Only the Karassina Samoyed come in large groups to the eastern side of the Yenisey—to the Pyasina tundra at the Tura River—for hunting fox, sable, and wild reindeer, together with the Tavgi Samoyed [Nganasan] and the Sakha.... The Enets tribes or clans are grouped along the rivers in their old wintering quarters, where they pay tax, or yassak, to the Russians. These include the Khantaika River (Khantaika Samoyed, or the Samatu group in the Yenisey-Samoyed language), Karassina River (Karassina Samoyed, or Mungandji, Mogadji, or Mokase group), and Bajicha River (Bai or Podgorodnyje Samoyed [Selkup])....

The Karassina Samoyed are mostly tundra hunters, while the entire Bai tribe and the larger part of the Khantaika tribe are fishers who live at the Yenisey River during summer and winter.... Some tens of years back, the Yenisey Samoyed lived during winter on the Khantaika River and paid tax in their winter camp—thus the Khantaika name for the tribe. The Bai tribe remained during winter near Turukhansk and received its name from the Bajicha village and river. (1856: 236)

At the time the first Russians appeared in Siberia, Castrén wrote that "we have historical notice that the Mogadji (Mokase) Yenisey Samoyed tribe lived at Taz River, farther west" (236). This record comes from the founding of the great Mangazeya trading town, the largest and richest fur-hunting center in all Siberia, located on the lands of the Mogadji (Mokase) people, who named this fur entrepôt (G. P. Vizgalov, pers. comm. to HL, 2012; see also page 98). One result of the establishment of Mangazeya was that the Enets and Nganasan gradually lost their native boat traditions and adopted Russian vetka planked boats.

Castrén arrived in the autumn of 1846 at Turukhansk on his expedition to the northern Yenisey and recorded the various groups who traveled there to market their furs in May and June. Here on the northern Yenisey, fishing was the main occupation. Castrén provided some information on the Tazow (Taz) Samoyed (who are not the Yurak Samoyed or Nenets) and the Karassin Samoyed. He noted constant interaction between the nomadic groups of the Ob/Taz region and those of the Yenisey River basin: "The Tazow [Taz] Samoyed travel from the Taz to the Yenisey, then along the Kundasei River and its tributaries and portages, and make their way to Bajicha Lake and then to the upper Bajicha River to Turukhansk. The northern route goes from Mangazeya to the Wolotshanka

River and Ratilicha River. . . . Sometimes the Samoyed travel from the Taz over Lake Nalymye to Turukhansk and the Yenisey" (1856: 236–37).

Castrén's observations make it seem likely that at the time of Russian contact, the Yenisey and Taz Samoyed (Enets) peoples were using boats and canoes similar to those of the Nganasan and that they were engaged mainly in sea and river fishing. In the previous section on the Nganasan, we discussed Simchenko's (1976a) observation that they used small skin boats until the early 19th century and that the Enets and Yukagir used similar skin boats. Thus we can suggest that the Enets, whose skin boat was first documented in 1576, were part of the Samoyed-Yukagir "skin boat belt" that ran along the Arctic Ocean coast from the Barents Sea in Europe to the Anadyr River in Eastern Siberia. The Enets eventually suffered the fate of many other small folk: they were decimated by invading peoples, died of hunger or disease, or were assimilated by their neighbors or conquerors. Many of them mixed with the Nenets when the latter expanded their tundra territory east from the Ob River to the Yenisey.

THE DOLGAN: MIXED SETTLERS OF TAIMYR

The Dolgan, who historically lived on the Taimyr Peninsula between the Yenisey River estuary and the Khatanga River next to the Nganasan, Enets, Nenets, and Sakha, today number some 5,300 people, composing the largest Native group in this tundra territory. This Yakut-speaking people arrived here in the 17th or 18th century after they had amalgamated with Evenk, Yakut, Russian, and Enets people. Their reindeer herding, wild reindeer hunting, fishing, and trapping economy was similar to that of neighboring groups in the tundra and northern forest fringe. They migrated seasonally across the northern border of the forest, and most wintered in the Khatanga forest from Lake Pyasina in the west to the lower reaches of the Anabar in the east. In the summer, they moved north into the tundra on skis or sleds drawn by dogs or reindeer, and they rode reindeer and used bark boats for crossing rivers and lakes (Antropova 1961). In both winter and summer, they lived in conical tents and wore mostly fur clothing.

The most common boat type in Taimyr in the 1800s was an expanded log boat derived from the Sakha in the southern taiga territory. Antropova (1961) thought canoe use among the Nganasan, Enets, and Dolgan was quite similar. Their canoes, usually propelled by a double-bladed paddle, were used for fishing, for crossing rivers, and, to a limited extent,

for trade and travel. They were also used to hunt birds: as noted earlier, A. A. Popov (1964a) included a drawing of Dolgan using canoes to drive flightless geese into nets (fig. 6.3, page 119). Geese and other waterfowl are vulnerable when the adults molt their wing feathers and the young have still to fledge; both can be captured in great numbers during this flightless period.

It is interesting that in this treeless polar tundra, a territory with no resources for birch-bark canoes or log boats, knowledge of the larch-bark canoe persisted. In 1723, D. G. Messerschmidt saw an Evenk-built larch-bark canoe on the upper Lower Tunguska River at the confluence of the Taimyr River, some 400 kilometers south of the Arctic Circle. Larch is the only tree that grows in Taimyr. Larch-bark canoes, called *irakta-djau* by the Tungus, were used as recently as 1914 for crossing rivers and perhaps for hunting. In July of that year, the English traveler Maud Dorian Haviland made a trip from Krasnoyarsk down the Yenisey, passing Dudinka and ending at Golchikha, a seaport on the Yenisey estuary. In Golchikha, she conducted ornithological research and collected bird skins and eggs and then made an inland trip to Sloika, in Tundra Enets land, in company with some Dolgan people. She wrote an account of her travels in reindeer-driven sledges over frozen tundra and told of an unsuccessful river crossing in a bark canoe:

Towards six o'clock in the evening we descended a long gradual slope from the higher tundra into a river valley. . . . The river, though shallow enough, was wide, and the wind, blowing with the current, drove long white tongues of foam down the channel. Vasilii [her guide] shook his head as he dismounted from the sledge, and drew a little bark canoe from under the overhanging bank. He first tried the ford with Miss Czaplicka, the lightest of our party, behind him in the boat. "Sit still, or death!" was his dramatic and rather disquieting command in broken Russian to his passenger as he cautiously pushed off in his little craft. But it was soon evident that it would be hopeless to try and cross. The current was so strong that even Vasilii, with all his skill with the paddle, could do no more than keep the canoe's head to the wind, and so prevent it from drifting broadside and over-turning in the water. He was soon obliged to give up the attempt and return to the bank. (1971: 210–11)

THE KET (YENISEY OSTYAK): BOAT PEOPLE OF CENTRAL SIBERIA

The Ket are perhaps the most mysterious group in Central Siberia. Their roots are unknown, although their language and other connections might suggest a distant affiliation with the Alaskan Na-Dene people (Vajda 2010; Kari, Potter, and Vajda 2011). They were called the Ostyak before their language and culture became better known, and then they were designated the Yenisey Ostyak to differentiate them from the Ostyak (Khanty) of the Ob River. The Ket inhabit the Yenisey basin on the Sym, Kureika, Yeloguy, and Podkamennaya Tunguska rivers. This middle section of the Yenisey River valley is administratively in today's Turukhansky and Baikit districts of Krasnoyarsk Krai. When Russians first arrived in the Yenisey River basin in the 1600s, the Ket inhabited a much larger territory, and some peoples lived east of the river.

The original area of the Ket seems to have been farther south than their present location. They probably emerged as a discrete cultural entity from mixed peoples originating in the Sayan Mountains and the indigenous groups of the Yenisey valley (Flegontov et al. 2016). Ket tradition has it that their ancestors were driven north by "mountain people" and had to cross ranges of mountains before they arrived in Siberia. The Ket language belongs to the Ket Assan (Yenisey) group of Paleo-Asiatic languages. The Kott (Kot), Arin, and Assan (Asan) languages also belong to this Paleo-Asiatic group, but the Khakass, Evenk, and Russians assimilated the people of Southern Siberia who spoke them. The Ket are the only surviving people of the western Paleo-Asiatic group. The origin of the Ket language is not clear, but it is thought to be related to the Sino-Tibetan languages (Austin and Sallabank 2015). There are now only some 1,000 Ket, of whom only a minority speak their native language.

Until the middle of the 20th century, the Ket lived in permanent summer camps in bark-covered chums and log dwellings; during the winter, they lived in temporary camps. Their main subsistence activities were fishing in summer and hunting moose, deer, and fur-bearing animals in winter. For fishing, they used large, flat-bottomed boats, which also served as summer shelters. Reindeer breeding (now abandoned) was subordinate, with reindeer serving mainly as transportation. The Ket's modern economic activities are animal breeding, small-scale gardening, and dairy farming.

Ket boat history is not well known but is nonetheless important because it demonstrates the mixing of traditions in the Western Siberian taiga. The Ket—and other Yeniseyan peoples—might have learned to build birch-bark canoes from the Samoyed after the Ket entry into the Western Siberian taiga and the Yenisey River valley. When the Evenk (Tungus) entered the Yenisey River valley from the east, they adopted the Yenisey-type bark canoe from the Ket and other peoples. In later days, the western Yakut on the Lena River also built similar bark boats. Ket groups were also in contact with Khanty people on the Ob River tributaries. All these groups used a similar Yenisey-style canoe. As noted earlier, the Sym River Ket group called their bark canoes *hap-hap*, the Khanty term for their own bark boats (Verner 1977; Khelimski 1982).

Bark Boats of the Ket and Other Yeniseyan Peoples

The Ket lived along the 1,500-kilometer length of the Yenisey River from Krasnoyarsk nearly to the river's mouth, in a territory that was both rich in fur, a major source of income for the Russian government, and served as a vital east-west transport link. As a result, they were exempted from military service during Russian rule in exchange for transporting official travelers and goods along the river. Demitri Shimkin wrote:

> Accounts from the 1770s relate that the Arin [Ket] lived in birch-bark tipis in the summer and felt tents in the winter. They traveled upstream twice a year in birch-bark canoes for hunting and trapping. Ski-shod, they took moose, reindeer, and sable in their great February rounds. In the summer they primarily fished, but a few were small-scale farmers with horses and oxen. Accounts from 1790 report that the now-Christianized Yenisey Ket migrated with portable birch-bark tipis for hunting and fishing, wearing Russian clothing in the summer and reindeer fur in the winter, and traveling by canoe in summer and dogsled in winter. Those living on the Keti River kept horses. Yenisey Ket betrothals included offerings of bride-gifts in Russian trade items, notably copper kettles. Betrothals, once agreed upon, were sanctioned in church rituals (today all the Ket are Christian). The Turukhansk area included 1,205 Ket (652 males, 553 females) of a total population of 4,878. Some Ket lived near the town and others in remote camps, in harmony with each other and Russians. They traded furs for grain and other needs, and paid tribute. (1996: 1)

James Forsyth discussed the Yenisey Evenk people and referred to a study by V. A. Tugolukov noting that Evenk who entered the Yenisey via the Angara River from Lake Baikal adopted elements of Ket culture, including bark canoes:

> While the central Siberian larch forest was the classical setting of Tungus life, their mobility in search of hunting grounds took them in every direction from their presumed place of origin east of Lake Baikal. In the region of the middle Angara, the Evenk went naked in summer apart from a fringed deerskin loincloth, painted their faces with various colors, sacrificed dogs, and used birch-bark canoes in which they knelt while using two-bladed paddles. These features, which are atypical of the Tungus, have been attributed to their predecessor in this region, the Asan and Kott, who were related to the Ket, and whom the Evenk presumably assimilated or drove out to the west, beyond the Yenisey. (1994: 52–53)

In his manuscript "Description of the Siberian Peoples," G. F. Müller remarked that the Kamas people had birch-bark canoes similar to those of the Yeniseyan Kott and Arin peoples (see chapter 5, page 110).

Ket-Samoyed Contacts in Southwestern Siberia

Where and when did the Ket and other Yeniseyan peoples learn to build birch-bark canoes? And what was the likely source of this common boat technology? As far as we know, these peoples were not originally taiga dwellers or even from the southern plains of Western Siberia. Kai Donner (1930) argued that they entered Western Siberia from the south along the Tom River, and that much of their material culture probably originated from the Inner Asian steppe and mountains. This assumption is based on the Tibetan roots of their language (according to Castrén's 1858 grammar and dictionary), on archaeological evidence of their material culture and livestock breeding, and on their physical appearance, which differs from that of their neighbors. Modern DNA studies make a compelling argument for inner Asian Altaian origins (Flegontov et al. 2016). As horse-riding people of both mountains and plains, they could not have had birch-bark canoes when they first entered Western Siberia near the headwaters of the Ob and Yenisey rivers. No other peoples of the plains and mountains—not the Mongol, Turkic Tatars, or Buryat—had had bark canoes in their earlier homelands,

so Turkic peoples learned of them only after entering the Western Siberian taiga.

Thus we have to take a step back and focus on early Yeniseyan-Samoyed contacts if we want to study the bark canoe origin of the Yeniseyan people. As discussed previously, the Ket and other Yeniseyans crossed the lands of the Samoyed peoples, so they may have learned to build birch-bark boats from them, just as the Turkic Tatars had done (see page 113 in chapter 5). Donner (1930) wrote that in the 1600s, Samoyed influence was still strong on the Ket, who had close contacts with the Selkup residing in the same region; although they spoke different languages, their material cultures were similar.

N. P. Makarov and M. S. Batashev (2004) studied the migrations in the Yenisey River valley and wrote a paper that casts light on the early life of the Ket and other Yeniseyan peoples and on their contacts with the Samoyed and other peoples at the time of the former's appearance in Western Siberia, likely during the Iron Age. Since we know that the Samoyed north of the Altai and Sayan mountains made birch-bark canoes from early times until the appearance of Russians in the early 1600s, this paper is a valuable source on the possible origin of Ket bark canoes. According to Edward Vajda and Andrei P. Dulzon (1962), Yeniseyan-speaking people entered the mountain taiga regions of Southern Siberia about 2,000 years ago. He dated the Ket's northward migration into the Irtysh-Vasyugan watershed to the next few hundred years. Makarov and Batashev (2004) believe that other Yeniseyan groups, notably the Pumpokol and Kott, likewise moved north along the Yenisey during this time. Other Yeniseyan-speaking groups, such as the Arin, were also present in the Yenisey and Angara watershed at the time of Russians' arrival in the 1640s (Flegontov et al. 2016).

In the 9th and 10th centuries, Turkic expansion dislodged the Ket-speaking population—like their Samoyed-speaking neighbors—into the Ob and Tom river watershed. There was a second northward Yeniseyan migration in the 13th century as the Mongol conquest forced the Ket farther down the Yenisey River. The entry of the Evenk peoples from the east turned the tables again in the 1600s, decreasing the territory inhabited by resident Yeniseyan peoples. Forsyth (1994) wrote that when Russians arrived, bringing diseases such as smallpox in addition to valuable trade goods that were exchanged for furs, the Ket were living around the confluence of the Stony Tunguska, having moved there under pressure from the Evenk, while the Evenk had moved into the Yenisey under pressure from the Buryat Mongol expansion from the Lake Baikal region to the east. East of the Yenisey River, the Ket had become culturally dominated by the Evenk in the 1680s and were reduced as a distinct ethnic group. According to Forsyth, Evenk, Ket, and Samoyed clans originally lived on the forested northern slopes of the Sayan Mountains.

Birch-Bark Canoes of the Imbat-Ostyak of Bahta River

There is little direct evidence of any Ket birch-bark canoes; the Ket turned to expanded log boats and planked log boats in the 17th century, as did the Khanty on the Ob River (see chapter 5, page 100), and afterward they did not often use bark canoes for hunting and fishing in the Yenisey taiga. However, we have found one model that might represent a Ket bark canoe from north of the Angara River in the eastern Yenisey taiga. It was collected by G. Gut in 1897 and is now in the collection of the Museum of Anthropology and Ethnology (fig. 6.4; MAE 382-21); documentation from its former owner indicates that it is "Ostyak or Tungus." Gut worked in the gold mines north of the Angara and might have had contacts with Ket there, as this area was where the Imbat-Ostyak (a Ket people) lived, at Imbatsk on the Bahta, a tributary of the Lower Tunguska River. They were the last remnants of the Ket on the eastern side of the Yenisey River before they were assimilated by Evenk or forced to migrate to the western bank.

This birch-bark canoe model has features typical of Yenisey construction, such as the gunwale made of two inwale and outwale strips with the bark sheet pressed between them. The "buckle," or higher ends fore and aft, is also typical of Lower Tunguska canoes in the Uchami region, especially those built later by the Chunya, a Western Evenk people.

Fig. 6.4. This model birch-bark canoe (MAE 382-21) is from the taiga north of the Angara River, east of the middle Yenisey. G. Gut collected it in 1897, and although it is documented as being "Ostyak or Tungus," it might have been made by the Imbat-Ostyak, the last Ket people living here before they were assimilated by the Western Evenk. (Photograph: Evguenia Anichtchenko; courtesy Museum of Anthropology and Ethnography)

The buckle is made when a stringer at the bottom is bent upward to form the bow or stern. But in this canoe we also find something atypical of Evenk bark canoes: a waterline that turns up vertically at the ends. Inside, on the bottom of the canoe, several long, wide, thin planks (instead of the many thinner and shorter laths found in other regions' boats) are inserted, running from end to end. Those planks run beneath the ribs and were assembled on the bark before the frames were inserted. Perhaps the form and construction of this rare bark canoe mark the last trace of the ancient Imbat-Ostyak hunting canoe.

In the Siberian bark canoe classification, this design, with a flat bottom rising up gently to the gunwales at both ends, is a Yenisey type, since it is typical throughout the Yenisey River basin (Antropova 1961). As noted, we assume that the Samoyed influenced the Ket bark canoe, called in the Ket language *ti* or *tii* (Castrén 1858: 234), while, as noted earlier, the Southern Samoyed called their similar birch-bark canoe *kem*, which was also their name for the Yenisey River (see page 112 in chapter 5). We might perhaps freely translate *kem* as "Yenisey canoe."

In turn, Ket canoes may have had an influence to the east. According to Sieroszewski (1993), the Sakha (Yakut) people in the upper Lena valley had contacts with Ket groups east of the Yenisey and learned from them to build Yenisey-type bark canoes. As a Polish exile in Yakutia, Sieroszewski studied the construction and origin of the Sakha canoes and reported that the Sakha had had no boats of their own when they entered the Lena basin. He proposed that the Sakha bark canoe and its name west of the Lena, *tyy*, had a Ket origin, based on Castrén's linguistic evidence: "The Yenisey Ostyak use this same word *ti* with a drawn-out *i* on the end for a boat of medium size, which has the same meaning as the Yakut *ty* [sic]" (Castrén 1858: 234). This assumption of boat name transfer, and perhaps of boat technology and type, too, was confirmed by Antropova, who wrote, "The birch-bark boat with pointed, undercut ends (the 'Yenisey type') was used among the southwestern Yakuts (Sakha) people . . . and was called *tuos tyy*" (1961: 110).

THE YENISEY RIVER EVENK: TUNGUS IN THE WEST

In Kai Donner's *Siberia: Present and Past Life* (1933b), a chapter describes the culture and history of the Evenk (formerly called the Tungus, and now alternately known as the Western Tungus). The Evenk once inhabited much of Siberia from the Yenisey River to the Sea of Okhotsk, including

Transbaikal and Manchuria, areas thought to have been their original homeland (Levin and Potapov 1964; Albova 1968a). The Evenk have a deep history along the eastern tributaries of the Yenisey, including the Lower (Nizhnaya) Tunguska, Upper Tunguska, and Southern Tunguska (now called the Angara). The name of the Yenisey, which the Evenk once called the Jelissee, might have originated with them as well. Prior to the appearance of the Russians on the Angara River in the early 1600s, the Evenk paid tax to the Mongolian-Turkic Buryat; afterward, they paid it to the Russians.

Movements of other peoples probably triggered the Evenk's territorial expansion. Based on information in Russian Academy of Sciences archives, Carl Hiekisch (1879) stated that the largest Evenk migration took place after circa 1200, when the Mongol dominated Manchuria and Dauria (the eastern part of Inner Mongolia). At that time, the Buryat and Turks who were allied with the Mongol invaded Southern Siberia, and the Sakha (Yakut) moved into the middle Lena River basin circa 1300, taking Evenk lands and cutting Lena Evenk territory in two. As a result, the western Evenk moved toward the Yenisey valley.

Going west was not easy: the Yukagir were also on the move, and in the Yenisey basin, the Evenk found Yeniseyan and Samoyed peoples occupying the main river valley from the Sayan Mountains north to the Arctic Ocean. As Kai Donner wrote, there was a constant "silent war" between the Evenk and Ket-related peoples on the eastern side of the Yenisey and Angara river valleys. By the time the Russians appeared, the Evenk were occupying most of the eastern shore of the Yenisey (Donner 1979: 210).

The Yenisey Evenk Bark Canoe

The first general description of Siberia, published in 1673 by Albrecht Dobbin, a Swedish officer in Russian service who lived in Siberia for 15 years, reported on the Evenk living along the Yenisey River: "Tungus [Evenk] live along the large Jelissee River as fishermen; their boats are made of birch bark, which they know how to tar so they do not leak. These boats can travel very fast" (1702: 294). The Evenk bark canoes from each of the river systems on Yenisey's eastern side differ slightly in form and construction. These canoes are fairly well known and are documented in museums thanks to their persistence into the 1930s. Below we describe these different bark canoes, as well as some of skin boats found between the Lower and Stony (Podkammenaya) Tunguska rivers. We begin, however, with Russian scientist G. M. Vasilevich's general description of Evenk canoe construction on the Lower and Stony Tunguska, Olekma, and Vilyuy rivers west of the Lena:

The birch-bark boat (*dyav*) was small (for one to two persons) and was for fast river transportation and portaging as well as hunting on the water. It was also used for spear fishing. The methods of preparing the bark, sewing bark strips, frame building, and fitting the bark over the frame were the same among all Evenk. Traditionally the bark preparation and sewing were women's work, while the frame construction and fitting of the bark cover over it were jobs for men. In spring, people (mostly women, but sometimes men) cut the bark from trees. The cleaned and steamed bark was hung to dry. Using thin wooden stakes, they sewed together three strips of bark to form a so-called *tiska*. Two strips of bark were pegged together along the seam with these stakes, which were removed as the seam was sewn with thin bird-cherry tree roots or, if these were not available, with sinew. . . . Three to six such tiskas were needed for a boat cover. . . .

For the frame, they prepared in advance ribs made of naturally bent branches, thin strips of split wood for inwale and outwale, thwarts, and laths for sheathing. Wooden pegs attached the ribs to the gunwales, and one or two of these strips were laid on the bottom of the boat. Three or four ribs (thin sticks with a natural curve) were inserted into the holes in the inwale. After this, they put on the bark cover made of tiskas, attaching it to the inwale of split wood strips along the sides. The Evenk laid the edges of the bark cover between the inwale and outwale strips at the stem and stern and then sewed them together (on the middle and lower part of the Lower Tunguska River); or connected the ends of the inwale and outwale strips 0.5 meters from the bow and stern and sewed them together (on the upper and lower parts of the Lower and Podkamennaya Tunguska rivers); or bent the split wood strips inward and attached them to each other (east of the Olekma). Then long, narrow strips of sheathing were inserted between the bark and the ribs. After this work was finished, all the seams and small holes were pitched with heated larch gum. Vilyuy Evenk sew tiskas for their boats with horse hair and pitch them with a glue made of birch gum, soot, ashes, and a small amount of water. (1969: 105)

Birch- and Larch-Bark Canoes on the Lower Tunguska River

The Lower Tunguska River is the longest tributary of the Yenisey River, with a mouth at Turukhansk, some 1,000 kilometers south of the Yenisey mouth. The source of the Lower Tunguska is about 300 kilometers north of Lake Baikal, where the river nearly meets the upper Lena River. Although the Lower Tunguska runs through some of the most remote regions in Siberia, it was (and remains) an important east-west waterway linking the Yenisey and Lena basins via the portage at its headwaters near the town of Nepa. It was famed as a rich fur-trapping territory after sources west of the Yenisey became trapped out after the Russians established New Mangazeya (Turukhansk) in 1620: the Lower Tunguska remained an important fur-trading zone for the Ket, Evenk, Zyrians, and others until the early 1900s.

Messerschmidt sailed upstream along the Lower Tunguska in 1723 as part of his exploration of Western, Southern, and Eastern Siberia from 1720 to 1725. He commented in his diary on the local Evenk bark canoes as well as those of the Khanty and other peoples. He had the distinction of being the only trained scientist to describe larch-bark canoes in Siberia, and his diary is one of the best early sources on this remote region. Other Russian Academy of Sciences members exploited his findings because his diary was never published in full in Russia; even today it is available only in a German edition printed in five volumes in East Germany in 1964, and for this reason, his work is underappreciated.

In volume 2, Messerschmidt's party travels from July to August 1723 in two *kajuk* (partly decked planked boats) along the Lower Tunguska River, upstream from New Mangazeya to the mouth of the Ilimpeya River and on to the Vasil'eva Podvolocnaja *volok* (portage) between the Yenisey and Lena river basins, where they meet Evenk in bark canoes:

> July 11, traveling on the Lower Tunguska between the Uchami and Taimura rivers: We reached about 4 p.m. some Tungus yurts situated on the Irkutsk (left) side where we had a rest. . . . Two Tungus boys and an elderly mother, two young women, and one bald, manlike girl came to take me across [the river] in a canoe [*Nahen*, in German], 2 *klafter* long, 0.5 klafter wide, and 1/6 klafter high or deep [360 by 90 by 30 centimeters]. Some of the canoes of birch bark are called *dschlban-djau* while others are made of larch bark and are called *irakta-djau*. One of those canoes

> may carry three men at most, although there are seats for only two people.

> July 12, Taimura River mouth: A rather big river, something like the Turuhan near [New] Mangazeya, running from the Irkutsk (left) side, lived in by Tungus.

> July 16, location 64°7' north, at Buhr Ostrov (also Sazin Ostrov or Sasin *byk* [stone]). I sat down in a very small Tungus boat of sewn birch bark which was 5 arshins long, ¾ arshins wide, and ¼ arshins deep [circa 356 by 53 by 18 centimeters] and paddled with my Tungus [guide] a little more than 1 verst [1 kilometer]. You have to sit as though frozen just like a log, without moving, to maintain balance and not turn over, while the Tungus keeps his balance easily. When getting out I raised my weight with one hand while maintaining the boat's balance with the other.

> August 21, location 61°43' north, a river mouth between the Tavlonka and Vechnajaja Kocoma Rivers. About 4 p.m. a Tungus appeared who had built his *yugil*, or what Russians call a chum, and a light boat of birch bark (like the one I saw on July 11), which can float three persons and one child. I weighed that boat on a Russian scale and found it to be 55 Russian *funt*, or on a medical scale 22.619 kilograms. Owing to this, it is no wonder that the Tungus can carry the boats on their backs for several miles.

> August 26, mouth of the Novatskaja (Ungatka) River on the Samoyed (right) side and the Teteya River on the Irkutsk side. Here on the right bank of the Lower Tunguska River there is a mountain range trending to the southeast: About 6 p.m. we found a Tungus boat, or Nahen, at the shore in which there was a *halma* (or *palma*), a Tungus hunting lance. The Tungus was off in the forest. I had the halma taken from the canoe and put a birch-bark notice near the boat to indicate that they should follow the river upstream to get their palma back.

> September 16, at the Vasileva Podvolochnaja portage. This was the *volok* [portage], the watershed between the Yenisey and Lena rivers, the customary travel route from the Vasilev volok to the Lena, some 20 versts [21 kilometers] between the rivers. (Messerschmidt diary, July–September 1723, quoted in Messerschmidt 1964: 86–135)

Chunya Evenk Bark and Skin Boats

The terrain between the Lower and Stony Tunguska rivers is typical of much of the Siberian taiga. Situated between 60°N and 64°N, two boreal subzones sit between these two major east-west-running rivers in the western Yenisey River basin: a northern boreal zone with pine, spruce, and larch, and a midboreal zone to the south with various hardwoods and softwoods, like that of central Scandinavia. In the eastern area of the two major rivers, the mountain tundra rises to 2,000 meters; there, boreal forest is found only in the deep river valleys. This region, called Ilimpeya after a river farther east, was termed the most desolate and least-known area of the Yenisey basin by the 1926–27 Polar Census Team members when they counted and described Evenk people living there. Its remote location, its mixture of forest and mountain terrain, and its Evenk residents, with their ancient traditions as foot hunters and fishermen, all contributed to the development of the most interesting inland canoes in all of Siberia, which remained in use nearly into modern times.

When Russians first visited the area, they met Chunya Evenk people near the Uchami fur-trade station and saw deerskin canoe-kayaks built by local squirrel hunters. These half-decked boats of the fur-trade stations on the Lower Tunguska River's southern tributary (fig. 6.5), documented in the 1927 photos of N. P. Naumov, were some 5 meters long and well made, and they had a skin cover over a self-supporting, kayaklike wooden frame. In 1932, a man known to us only as Kalashnikov took photographs in a nearby location of several canoe-kayaks partially covered with birch bark. These boats had a structure that could accommodate either skin or bark covers, according to need and available raw material. In the tundra, the canoes had deer- or elk-skin covers; in the taiga, they used birch bark. This versatile method of construction

was not unique to Siberia: boats of this type also were made in the Amur region.

A 1932 Kalashnikov image (fig. 6.6) shows several nearly identical birch-bark canoe-kayaks on the Niblet River, a right (northern) tributary of the Stony Tunguska River. As on the Lower Tunguska, the resident group here is Chunya Evenk, according to Mikhail Batashev of the Krasnoyarsk Krai Museum (pers. comm. to HL, 2012). The respective locations of the Naumov and Kalashnikov photographs are only 100 to 200 kilometers apart. We have no information about photographer Kalashnikov, but Batashev assumes that he worked with a team of Western Evenk; from the late 1920s to the early 1930s, they were employed in land cultivation, transport, and medical duties. Batashev (pers. comm. to HL, 2011) also writes that the Chunya Evenk people lived in the middle Chunya River area, now in Evenkia District. The first permanent settlement of the Chunya people was established in the fall of 1925 in an area controlled by the Chunya Taymura Evenk, who lived in the middle and upper Chunya and Taymura river basins (both tributaries of the Lower Tunguska River). The Evenk population there consisted of only 179 people in 1989.

The shape and construction of the Chunya canoe-kayak (circa 500 by 70 by 30 centimeters) differ greatly from those of the rest of the Evenk canoes east of the Yenisey (fig. 6.7). Its wooden frame is self-supporting, making it more like a kayak than a bark canoe. The wooden structure is made first and is then covered with skin or bark. The frame has

Fig. 6.6. These seven Chunya Evenk half-decked bark canoes were photographed in 1932 by a man known to us only as "Kalashnikov," after a group of people on the Niblet River, a right (northern) tributary of the Stony Tunguska River (KKM 028-009-2107). (Courtesy Krasnoyarsk Krai Museum)

Fig. 6.5. Members of the Chunya, a Western Evenk group, seen here in deerskin-covered canoe-kayaks on the Uchami River, a left (southern) tributary of the Lower Tunguska River. N. P. Naumov took this photo in 1927 (CMC7930-1-25-08). (Courtesy Krasnoyarsk Krai Museum)

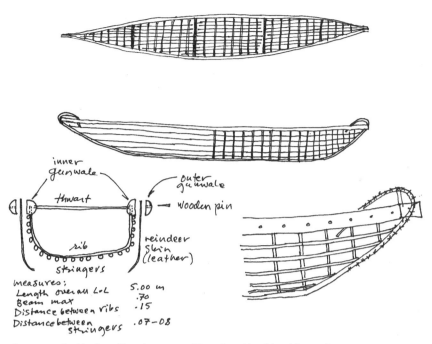

Fig. 6.7. Construction diagram of a Yenisey Evenk canoe. (Drawing: Harri Luukkanen)

an inwale and an outwale, between which the skin or bark is clamped. The frame has ribs about 15 centimeters apart, and several longitudinal stringers run the length of the boat, some 7 to 8 centimeters apart. The hull is half-decked fore and aft, and the deck cover can be raised in the bow by placing a deck stringer through a notch in the forward thwart. The boat is designed with a rising bow and stern for better performance in waves, adding to its kayaklike profile. A similar construction style was known on the Katanga River, where a canoe without half-decking was collected in 1907–08 by A. A. Makarenko (REM 1211-56; fig. 6.8).

In the constructing the frame of Chunya canoes, the inwale with thwarts was probably made first, then the

Fig. 6.8. A. A. Makarenko collected this Yenisey Evenk canoe (REM 1211-56) from the Katanga River Evenk circa 1907–08. (Photograph: I. Tkachenko; courtesy Russian Ethnographic Museum)

narrow ribs were fastened into holes drilled into it. The stringers were fashioned from thin wood splints or branches split in half, lengthened as needed by joining. They were then lashed or sewn to the ribs. The keelson-like stringer in the center of the bottom was turned backward over the bow and stern and sewn into place, forming an upturned bulge at both ends, as seen in fig. 6.7. Finally, the frame was covered with deerskin or birch bark fastened to the inwale, which was then nailed to the outwale with thin wooden pins, as seen in fig. 6.7. Excess skin or bark was trimmed flush to the gunwale.

Unlike Eastern Evenk canoes, the Chunya canoe-kayak has an asymmetric hull with a wider and more buoyant stern and a narrower bow section. Both of these give the boat good hydrodynamic performance and the speed needed when hunting wild reindeer with spears at water crossings. The half decks in the stern and the bow are fixed to the gunwales, providing strength to the hull and helping to shed water. The vessel has very thin ribs and stringers and no wide laths, as seen in Evenk bark canoes; however, it probably had a plank or two on the bottom for seating to even out the load across several ribs, especially when more than one person was inside. The gunwale line is not straight from bow to stern but has a slight rocker, and the ends turn up a bit.

The Chunya Evenk prepared reindeer and moose skins for canoe covers in the same way as skin covers for winter tents. The hides were left to ferment until the hair was loose and could be removed with a scraper. Then the skin was cured in a bark solution, tanned with smoke, and treated with animal or fish oil. David Anderson describes the Evenk use of skin covers for tents in southern Taimyr:

> In the Putoran region, most people spoke of conical lodges being covered with smoked moose hide or smoked [wild or domestic] reindeer hide. Both types of covering are properly called *niuk* [*niukil* plural] in Evenki, while in Russian some people would use the term *rovduga* to speak of leather made from moose-hide and *zamshcha* to speak of leather made from reindeer skins. The reindeer hide coverings were by far the more common type in old stories, while the moosehide coverings represented the entire collection of coverings in the Evenki District Regional Museum save one. (2007: 54)

Preparation of birch bark for boats and conical summer tents followed a boiling process that was similar to that described previously for other groups (see page 101).

A common theory holds that the maritime skin boat or kayak developed from a much older bark canoe tradition (Zimmerly 1986; Jensen 1975). The versatile Chunya canoe-kayak might be a survival of such an ancient prototype and could shed new light on this idea. Perhaps both canoes and kayaks were used in some inland territories, and the deerskin version became the usual form on the tundra and coast, where it was later developed into Eskimo-type skin boats. The Chukchi (and probably also the Siberian Eskimo) used kayaks both on the coast and in the interior. It seems likely that the Siberian canoe-kayak had a wider distribution in the past in both inland territories and the rivers running to the Arctic Ocean. According to Mikhail Batashev of the Krasnoyarsk Krai Museum, the Chunya group from the Lower and Stony Tunguska once resided on the Chunya River, a tributary of the Vilyuy River running east to Lena. Thus the half-decked and skin- or bark-covered canoes probably were known in the middle Lena basin as well. The Chunya canoe-kayak resembles the Pacific Northwest American Athapascan birch-bark canoe in Alaska and the British Columbia Kootenai canoe described by Otis T. Mason (1901), both of which have half-decked bows and sterns. While these correspondences could be coincidental, a linguistic connection between Na-Dene Athapascan and Ket, whose speakers once lived on the Bahta River near the

Chunya before retreating to the western side of the Yenisey, has been proposed (Vajda 2010; Vajda and Dulzon 2004), although recent DNA studies do not support a link between their speakers (Scott and O'Rourke 2010).

Nisovian Tungus on the Angara River

James Forsyth discussed the Evenk and their movements and contacts (see pages 151 and 204), and Evert Ysbrant Ides (1706) also met Evenk people along the Angara River in 1693. After leaving the town of Yeniseysk in January that year, Ides entered the Angara River, passing Rybnoi, or Fish Island. One week later, he came to the Ilni (Ilim) River and reached Shammanskoy or Negromantick Rapid (which took its name from a famous Evenk shaman who lived some miles upstream), where the boats had to be towed or winched for more than half a mile. The birch-bark canoes of the people here, known as the Nisovian Tungus, were designed for rapid rivers and were propelled by double-bladed paddles, as seen in his illustration of a large canoe displaying birch-bark panels and carrying several paddlers and a large, smoking firebox (fig. 6.9). This illustration records a period at the height of the Siberian fur trade when boats were large and fast and could carry heavy payloads—a time and scene not unlike the great fur-trade era of mid-17th-century Canada,

Fig. 6.9. In an illustration from Evert Ysbrant Ides's *Three Years' Travel over Land from Moscow to China* (1706: plate 7) reminiscent of scenes of the French Canadian *coureurs des bois*, an Evenk paddler and a bark trade canoe are shown at the Nisovian rapids on the Angara River.

with its *coureurs de bois*. Ides described these boats, calling their makers the "Downstream Tungus":

> Their canoes are made of sewn birch bark and can carry seven or eight people. They are long, slender, and without any seats, and they sit in them upon their knees. They use a double-bladed paddle, expanded at both ends, which they hold in the middle and paddle, first with the one blade and then with the other, and when they row all together the canoes travel at a great speed. With these light canoes they can weather violent storms. They generally subsist by fishing in summer and hunt all kinds of furred game, bucks, and does, etc., in winter. (1706: 28)

Sym River and the Narym Evenk

The Sym River is a left-hand tributary of the middle Yenisey and one of only a few locations west of the great river where the Evenk peoples had a permanent foothold. With the Vah and Ket rivers, it formed two water routes between the Yenisey and Ob rivers. The area functioned as a transport hub for the Evenk, Ket, Selkup, Khanty, Turkic Tatars, and Russians throughout the 1800s.

Antropova (1961: 109) wrote that the Sym River Evenk did not have bark canoes and instead used log boats. This idea, often quoted in Russian literature on bark canoes, has led many Russian museum curators to believe that bark canoes were not present west of the Yenisey during the past 200 to 300 years. However, this view is not correct; the Sym River Evenk might have had log boats, but they also used birch-bark canoes, at least until the 1820s.

On one excursion from the Ob to the Vah River in the 1840s, Matthias A. Castrén (1967) joined the Sym River at Yeniseysk, where Evenk and Ket people were assembling to pay tax to Russian officials and to sell their furs at riverside trade markets. He described their two large camps, some distance from each other, where the people, accompanied by their respective chiefs, lived in tents made of birch bark or skin. Near the marketplace, small native boats were stored upside down on the bank, and at the riverside, a large number of Yenisey-type boats, *lodyas* (Russian for large plank boats) and *soima* (smaller planked boats), could be seen. The Evenk canoes were made of birch-bark sheets sewn together, contra Antropova, while the Ket had dugout boats.

From Russian sources (e.g., Forsyth 1994), we know there was a small permanent settlement of Evenk in "Sibir" in the late 1500s after Russian military power had opened the path to the Sibir Khanate, the first Russian Siberian colony to be taken from the Mongol. The new Russian administration in Siberia employed Evenk hunters as scouts, and they guided the first Russian military and fur-hunting parties to the Yenisey River and farther east toward the Lena, discovering new peoples to trade with, tax, or rob. The Evenk also traveled as far west as Narym on the Ob River and even to Pustozersk, probably because some of them worked as guides for Russians. Donner (1933a), referring to old English printed documents, wrote that western Evenk groups may have lived in the 1600s in Narym on the Middle Ob and could have participated in the European fur trade. According to him, Evenk fur hunters crossed the Ural Mountains and reached the Pechora River system, probably to access the Zyrian-Chud fur-trade center in Pustozersk, where they sold furs to English merchants.

THE MONGOL: SKIN BOATS, RAFTS, AND FLOATS FOR HORSE PEOPLE

Discussion of Mongol boats introduces a problem of definition: should we include all the territories that were once under Mongol rule or focus only on Mongol people or culture in their pre- or postempire homelands? The first option would be too large a task, for circa 1300 the Mongol ruled most of the Eurasian continent north of India and east of Budapest. So we focus here on postempire Mongolia and nearby regions.

Lev Gumilev (1997) has studied the history of the Mongol-related peoples who migrated from the Amur basin west into northern Mongolia in the middle of the 8th century, perhaps in response to a war with the Manchu. Present-day Mongolians arose from a small group connected to the clan of Genghis Khan (known originally as Temüjin) and peoples of Khalkha Mongol ethnicity (see articles in W. Fitzhugh, Rossabi, and Honeychurch 2013). Today there are more than 2.3 million Khalkha Mongol in Mongolia, whose total population is about 3 million, and Khalkha Mongol dominate many small minority groups who live in the northern and western parts of the country. More than 300,000 Mongol known as Buryat (who speak a similar language; see the next section) live in the Russian Buryat Republic, east of Lake Baikal and bordering northern Mongolia. Besides these, 25 million Mongol live in Inner Mongolia, an autonomous region in northern China, along with many other peoples, such as the Khitan and Daurian, who have Mongol roots and speak variants of Mongolian. All were once part of the Mongol Empire, which was multiethnic, including Turks and Turkic Tatar as well as Khitan and Daurian. Today a large population of ethnic Mongolians live in Western Asia, including the Kalmyk and other Mongol-related peoples who were driven west by the 13th-century Mongol invasions or who remained behind when the Mongol Empire collapsed.

Inner Mongolia West of the Amur

The Mongol appear for the first time in Chinese books of the Tang period (7th–10th centuries), under the ethnonyms Menu and Menva, but their origins are clearly much deeper, and their place of origin is much debated (Atwood 2004; Gumilev 1997). Some writers assume they originally lived in the Lake Baikal region and northeastern Mongolia; others cite the southern bank of the Amur River, west of the confluence with the Songhua, in the upper reaches of the Amur near the inflow of the Shilka and Argun rivers in Inner Mongolia, near Manchu and Chinese lands. The *Xin Tang Shu* (Old records of the Tang dynasty) mentions them as part of the Shivei, a Khitan people who lived on the northern bank of the Yaoyenhe River (Gumilev 1997).

The Mongol term for a skin boat, *tulum*, literally means "leather bag or skin filled with air"; this kind of boat was widely known in Southern Siberia, Manchuria, Tibet, and China (see figs. 9.19–9.21, pages 210, 211, and 215). How frequent was Mongol skin boat use, and what kind of boats did they build for themselves? Denis Sinor (1961: 158–63) answered both questions: it seems that the Mongol, like their Turkic horsemen comrades, used skin boats primarily for crossing streams and rivers but rarely needed boats for other purposes such as transport, hunting, or fishing (there are few references to any larger Mongol boats, either). Both these groups built coracle-type skin boats with wicker or wooden frames and makeshift boats or rafts of inflated skin floats. Their coracle boats were probably similar to Tibetan yak-skin boats, since these areas shared Buddhist faith, which reached Mongolia from Tibet along with cultural beliefs and technology. Sharaf al-Zamān Ṭāhir Al-Marwazi, writing in the 12th century, mentioned a Furi (or Quri) people living east of the Kirghiz in impenetrable forests: "The boats they employ for the transport of their loads consist of the skins of fish and wild animals" (quoted in Sinor 1961: 161).

Mongol activities near the Amur River, which put them in touch with Evenk and Manchu peoples, cast light on the general use of skin boats and rafts in Central and Eastern Siberia. F. B. Steiner (1939), who studied Yakut skin boats, wrote that both the Mongol and their Xiongnu predecessors of circa 200 BCE to 100 CE used skin boats. Matthew Paris (Mathaeus Parisiensis), writing in the mid-13th century, mentioned that "they [Mongol] have boats of ox-hides, which ten or twelve of them own in common; they are able to swim or to manage a boat and can cross the largest and swiftest rivers without trouble" (quoted in Sinor 1961: 160). Steiner said the Chinese *Tsin Shu* history mentions one people (between 644 and 646 CE), perhaps Turkish-speaking and living in northeastern China and Manchuria, who had made boats of inflated ox hide. These boats were for temporary use and employed almost exclusively for crossing rivers. Steiner, referring to this boat, concluded that

> the Amur skin boat, like the Sien-pi [people's] boat, is not related to the umiak; it is a cultural element of Central Asiatic horse and horned cattle breeders, and it must have passed to the northeastern regions with other elements of the late and hybrid stage of Mongol cattle breeding. Fishing gear used in the Yakut [Sakha] territory shows Mongol influence, as is proved by the Mongol name of the fishing-net itself. If the Mongolian ox-hide boat penetrated as far northeast as the Amur Evenk, we must assume that this boat made its way through Sakha territory. (1939: 180)

This last comment is interesting, considering Denis Sinor's observation that the Turkish word *kayik* may be an Eskimo loan word stemming from a Turkic term for a small boat. If this linguistic link is valid—and it has been contested (Fuente 2010)—a likely route of transmission to the Arctic coast could have been the Baikal-Lena corridor, which later experienced Turk and Mongol incursions. However, chronology is not in favor of this transfer, as it would have had to occur during the second or first millennium BCE to account for the fact that advanced kayaks were present around the Bering Strait well before the time of Christ.

A general absence of information makes it impossible to know if the Mongol peoples used bark canoes. In the upper Amur basin, it is known that they lived near the Zeya River mouth next to pastoral, horse-breeding Evenk peoples—the Birar and Manegir—who had birch-bark canoes, so some Mongol must have known of bark canoes even if they did not use them. Shinji Nishimura (1931) noted the use in Manchuria of skin-covered wicker boats like those used in Mongolia, but probably they were employed only for expedient purposes.

A magic boat mentioned in a Mongolian myth translated by Jeremiah Curtin (1908: 131) was made of the bark of the tamarack tree (larch, *Larix laricina*). Nishimura (1931) thought the tamarack was native only to the American continent and did not grow in Mongolia, so he presumed the boat must have been made of the bark of another species, such as osier. However, Mongolia does have an abundance of both larch and bitter willow (purple osier), and their wood and bark are used in a variety of objects, probably including boats. A Russian study (Chepelev 2004) has reported that people on the Amur used to build *korevuyu* (bark boats) covered with larch bark (*L. sibirica*).

THE BURYAT: SKIN BOATS FOR CATTLE BREEDERS AND FOREST HUNTERS

The Buryat, a Mongol subgroup numbering more than 500,000 today, live east of Lake Baikal in Russia, around Lake Khovsgul in northern Mongolia, and north to the Angara River mouth and on Olkhon Island. Traditionally the Buryat, like their Mongol relatives to the south, were mainly cattle breeders for whom hunting and fishing were secondary economies (Khanturgayeva, Khankhunova, and Zhilkina 2003). Their culture and lifestyle blend the traditions and technologies of the Mongolian steppe and the Siberian taiga.

When Gustav Radde (1861) traveled in the Baikal region from 1855 to 1859, the Buryat were using planked boats, perhaps of Chinese origin. The large Buryat boat was called *oŋogo*, while in the Karagas language it was *oŋota* (Castrén 1857b: 232; Castrén 1857c: 137). There is some evidence that the Buryat also used skin boats. On their trading expeditions, they made long voyages along the upper Lena River, where they came in contact with the Yakut. Waldemar Jochelson wrote of a Yakut legend about an encounter with a Buryat man paddling a skin boat: "Many many years ago there lived a rich Yakut named Ohonom who had two daughters, only one of whom he loved. A Buryat named Elyai (Elliei) used to ascend the Lena River in a skin boat to visit Ohonom. They were excellent friends. Ohonom offered him one of his daughters. Elyai selected the unloved one" (1933: 52). The story goes on, but the salient fact is that according to this legend, the Buryat used skin boats in the past. These might have been made of yak, camel, or horse skins; seal skins also would have been available from the large population of *Pusa sibirica* (a freshwater species closely related to the ring seal) in Lake Baikal.

If the Buryat were paddling along the Lena River in skin boats, as Jochelson reported, then they might have used similar boats on other rivers and on Lake Baikal. The Buryat were in close contact with Mongol groups living south of Lake Baikal, and they could have learned this craft from Mongol herders, who used skin boats to cross rivers. Mongol skin boat influence might also extend to the Evenk and Sakha peoples living south and east of Baikal; G. A. Albova (1968a) proposed that the Oroch Tungus learned from the Mongols both how to ride reindeer—or at least the concepts of riding and harnesses—and the technique of building skin boats to cross water:

> The North Amur Tungus, who mastered the terrain of Oro, have long been called the Oroch (i.e., residents of Oro). According to a legend, some of them taught wild reindeer to stand by the fire to escape flies, which was how the early domestication of reindeer began. . . . These stories circulated among the Evenk and Even of Edzhen [near Ust-Maya on the Aldan River]; however, to the east of the Aldan-Uchur line, the Selemdzha-language data [from people on a tributary of the Zeya River] show that Evenk riding was inspired by the pastoral Mongolian tribes. . . . The Mongol supplied textiles to the Evenk, who originally used only deerskin *rovduga* clothes. . . . When they became reindeer breeders, the Transbaikal Evenk began to hunt on horseback and lost the *ponyagu* [backpack] board and skis used formerly by the pedestrian Evenk. From their southern (Mongol) neighbors, the Oroch borrowed a leather covering that was stretched on a wooden frame to cross rivers, and crossed rivers in a leather boat. (1968c)

Such stories might be apocryphal, but they do provide interesting material for studies of boating history.

CHAPTER 7

EASTERN SIBERIA

THE LENA RIVER BASIN AND TRANSBAIKAL

The Lena is the third and the easternmost of the great north-flowing Siberian rivers, and the only one completely within Russian territory (map 14). Rising only a few kilometers west of Lake Baikal at an elevation of 1,800 meters, it runs 4,400 kilometers northward, reaching the Laptev Sea at one of the largest river deltas in the world. Its major tributaries are the Kirenga, Vilyuy, Vitim, Olyokma, and Aldan, the last draining the mountainous territory west of the Sea of Okhotsk, making it a travel route from the Pacific to the Eastern Siberian interior. However, because much of the Lena drains upland regions, its flow is faster and its bed shallower than the Ob's or Yenisey's, which has limited its importance as a transport corridor in both ancient and modern times. Northeast of the Lena, the Verkoyansk Mountains have been a hindrance but not a formidable obstacle to overland travel into Chukotka; nevertheless, the rugged terrain traditionally tended to channel communication along the lowland Arctic tundra belt and the coastal routes east of the Lena delta.

The traditional cultures who occupied the Lena basin during the historic period, circa 1600 to the present, include the Yukagir, Chuvan, Lena and Transbaikal Evenk, Even (formerly called the Lamut), and Sakha (formerly known as the Yakut). The Yukagir and the Chuvan are Eskimo-like cultures who were much reduced in population and territory over the past millennium as their tundra hunting, fishing, and sea mammal economies came under pressure from expanding Chukchi reindeer herders. Chukchi expansion resulted in part from the expansion of Turkic Mongol and Sakha cattle breeders who had originated in the Baikal region. The Lena Evenk, part of the much larger Evenk ethnolinguistic group, has practiced low-intensity reindeer herding, fishing, and fur hunting in the mountains east of the Lena over the past 1,000 or more years. The Even, closely related linguistically and culturally to the Evenk, practiced reindeer herding and

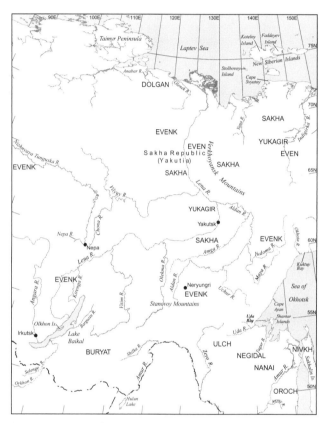

Map 14. Eastern Siberia and territories of the Yukagir, Evenk, Even, and Sakha. (Dan Cole, Smithsonian Institution)

hunted in the mountainous territory between the Sea of Okhotsk and the Lena River, east of the Turkic-speaking Sakha.

In the Lena River basin, we find a greater variety of birch-bark canoes than anywhere else in Siberia. The Lena-type canoe in general constitutes a third basic Eurasian canoe type, differing considerably from the neighboring Yenisey and Amur types, although there are large variations in its form and construction. One very archaic model, collected by Richard Maak in 1891 in the Vilyuy River, is sewn from

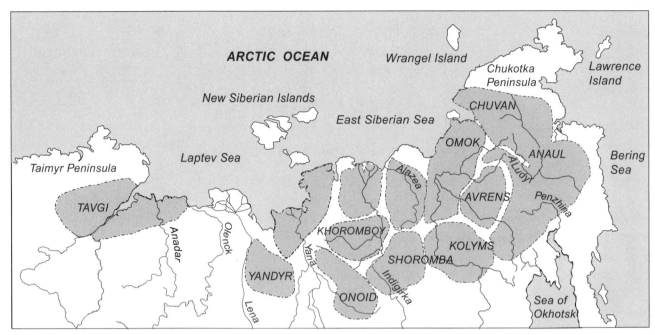

Map 15. Yukagir tribal regions circa 1700. (After Volodko, Eltsov, Starikovskaya, and Sukernik 2009: fig. 1; adapted by Marcia Bakry)

many bark sheets and has simple turned-over ends with weak multipart gunwales (see fig. 7.2a–c, page 143). Another type, perhaps developed as a result of the influence of kayaks or "pointed" bark canoes, is longer and has closed ends and a partially enclosed cockpit, giving it a kayaklike form (see fig. 7.1, page 137). At the Lena's source near Lake Baikal, the Yenisey-type bark canoe was used by the Evenk and Sakha peoples, while the Transbaikal Evenk, who lived east of the Vitim and Olekma rivers, preferred small bark canoes similar to those in the Amur basin.

THE YUKAGIR AND THE CHUVAN: ESKIMO-LIKE PEOPLES OF DIMINISHED FORTUNE

The Yukagir are of interest to anthropologists because of their cultural similarity to the Eskimo and their probable contributions to the development of Eskimo culture. Their territory once covered much of the Siberian taiga and tundra zone from Lake Baikal to the Arctic Ocean (map 15), and their culture included dog sledges, harpoons, and kayaks but not reindeer breeding. Waldemar Jochelson (1910, 1924, 1926), who studied the Yukagir as part of the Jesup North Pacific Expedition (1897–1902), recorded their rapid population decline and loss of territory to the reindeer-herding Chukchi in the 17th and 18th centuries. Today Yukagir speakers are a very small group, and we know little of their early history. Yet their once-powerful ancestral position

would have made them influential in the boating history of northeastern Siberia.

A paper by Natalia Volodko and colleagues (2009) provides an overview of Yukagir history from archaeological, ethnological, and genetic perspectives. The Yukagir descended from Late Iron Age hunters of reindeer and moose who had Mongol and Turkic genetic, linguistic, and cultural heritage. Archaeological evidence suggests that a proto-Yukagir people inhabited the tundra and taiga from the Yenisey to the Anadyr River in western Chukotka. When Russian colonists first counted the Yukagir in the mid-1600s, they numbered about 5,000 and were distributed among some 13 groups north of the Arctic Circle. Their lands extended from the Anadyr River in the east to the Taimyr Peninsula in the west, where their closest biological relatives, the Tavgi (now called the Nganasan), resided. The coastal tundra Yukagir, known as the Vadul group, hunted mostly wild reindeer, while the taiga people hunted mainly moose.

The Yukagir's later population history is grim owing to epidemics of smallpox and measles contracted from Russians, which caused a rapid reduction in their numbers. Their misery was described by the Russian naval lieutenant Gavril A. Sarychev, who took part in the Joseph Billings Expedition (1785–95) and met Yukagir people on the upper Kolyma River in October 1786 (Sarychev 1805: 67). By the early 1900s, the Yukagir comprised only a few residual groups from the interfluves of the Yana and lower Indigirka rivers like the Alazeya and the lower and upper Kolyma, together numbering—including the Chuvan (Krupnik 2019)—no more than 1,000 people (Jochelson 1910: 2). Yukagir lands in Taimyr were taken, and the Yukagir who remained have been assimilated by neighboring Yakut, Evenk, Even, Samoyed, Chukchi, and Russians. Today there are fewer than 100 Yukagir speakers left.

Canoes were a vital part of Yukagir history, as they were a culture of hunters and fishermen. Yuri B. Simchenko (1976b) wrote that the Yukagir of the late 19th and early 20th centuries had three types of traditional boats: expanded log boats (*ekchil*), birch-bark canoes (*khotan*) similar to the Sakha boat, and plank *karbas* borrowed from the Russians. The last boats used by the Taiga or Forest Yukagir were probably log boats, which were also adopted by the Sakha and in the west by the Nganasan in Taimyr, who made narrow log boats from poplar trunks. Simchenko suggested that the words for "boat" in the Nenets (*ngano*), Nganasan (*ngondui*), and Yukagir (*ngolde*) languages come from the same root and that in ancient times all these people used skin boats of the same type, similar to the kukhungondu of the Nganasan (see chapter 6's section on the Nganasan, page 115). For most of their recent history, the Yukagir lived in the forest zone, and they used birch-bark canoes until the 1860s.

Skin Kayaks on the Arctic Coast

When the Yukagir originally spread north along the Lena River and into the tundra region, the climate may have been warmer than it is today, but they still had to adapt to the new environment. According to Simchenko (1976b), they used a small, versatile open skin boat there, but until recently no early description of a Yukagir skin-covered kayak has been found. However, an illustration in Johan G. Georgi's expedition report (1776b: 271) most likely illustrates Yukagir kayaks (fig. 7.1). The scene includes three boats on a lake or river and shows a man with a double-bladed paddle in a short skin-covered kayak that has a double-pronged bow and stern. Two other kayakers in similar boats are setting nets or seines in the distance. On the far shore is a Native village with conical tents, and in the foreground an ox pulls a sledge while a man rides another ox, suggesting these people might be Sakha or Yukagir influenced by Sakha cattle breeders. All three individuals in the foreground wear similar clothes and three-pointed hats. Since a group of Yukagirized Yakuts called the Yandyr lived east of the Lena delta in the 1700s (Willerslev 2007: 5), this illustration (despite the artist's inclusion of exotic vegetation and animals) suggests a location near the forest edge east of the lower Lena.

The illustration is interesting but difficult to interpret, as it may represent an amalgam of places, peoples, and times. Drawings from the 1700s often do not accurately show technical details; they idealize subjects and settings and portray

Fig. 7.1. Johan G. Georgi included this illustration of two-pronged kayaks in his discussion of the Yukagir, although it might represent the Sakha. The romanticized scene shows conical tents, domesticated cattle, and people with distinctive headgear paddling and fishing in kayaklike skin boats that have the same type of bifurcated bow and stern seen in modern Inuit umiaks and ancient ritual boat carvings (see fig. 8.11, page 168) found at the 1,500-year-old Ekven Eskimo site near East Cape, Chukotka. (From Georgi 1776b: 271)

local peoples with a European aspect. One cannot assume that this scene is "real" since it was probably drawn by an illustrator based on a traveler's written or verbal description or field sketch, and it might have nothing to do with the Yukagir. It is important, however, that these three kayaks are shown with forked ends similar to the extended gunwale rails seen on Chukchi and Eskimo open skin boats. This same bifurcated construction feature is seen on the bows and sterns of Old Bering Sea–culture archaeological model kayaks, dating to 500 CE, that have been found on the Chukchi coast of the Bering Strait (see fig. 8.11, page 168). The Georgi illustration is the only known image of a boat of this type from the historical era.

Some indications of direct Eskimo-Yukagir contact in the Kolyma River estuary and nearby regions (see below) mention Yukagir and related peoples living between the Lena estuary and the Anadyr River. We know from Yukagir ethnography that their culture was similar to that of the Eskimo and that both groups used skin-covered kayaks (Jochelson 1926: 375). Information from Boris O. Dolgikh convinced Mikhail Batashev that a string of skin boat–using Yukagir groups once lived along this coast, including the Yandyr, Khoromboy, Olyuben, Alai, Omok, Chuvan, and Anaul (M. Batashev, pers. comm. to HL 2013). According to Rane Willerslev (2007), the Yukagir living in this region mixed with other groups over time, and we can assume that they also used skin kayaks. These groups had diverse origins and histories but shared technology, including harpoons and skin boats, for maritime mammal hunting. The Yandyr were Yukagirized Yakut, as mentioned previously; the Khoromboy were Tungus-Yukagir; the Alai were Yukagirized Evenk; and the Chuvan were Russianized Yukagir. Igor Krupnik (1993) wrote that the Chuvan were mixed with a few families of Even, Koryak, and other Yukagir ethnicities as well as people of Russian peasant and Cossack descent. (We have no information about the Olyuben, Omok, or Anaul.)

Whatever the source of the information for Georgi's kayak, its short, blunt form might not have been an inferior design. Harvey Golden, an expert in early boat design, comments, "It looks like a modern river kayak, a play boat, or rodeo kayak" (pers. comm. to HL, 2015). This type of kayak would be very stable in waves and capable of making fast turns in strong river currents. Thus, like its modern equivalent, the Dagger G-force slalom kayak, it would be especially good for spearing reindeer at river crossings, hunting ducks, or conducting other riverine or maritime tasks, but slow and of limited use in an open-ocean setting.

Reindeer Hunting on the Anyui River

The Russian naval lieutenant Ferdinand P. von Wrangel and his travel companion, midshipman F. F. Matyushkin, met Yukagir people during a lengthy expedition to the Kolyma and Chukotka regions of Eastern Siberia in 1820–24. Wrangel's book about the experience (1839) included some 20 references to skin boats, kayaks, and bark canoes. One passage written by Matyushkin gives a fine account of a reindeer hunt in August and September in Plotbische, on the Anyui (Anyuya) River east of the Kolyma; it does not describe the Yukagir's boats but does provide a description of how they were used:

When we arrived in Plotbische, the gathered population there was in agony waiting for information on the deer. Finally, the rumor spread that the first reindeer herds had appeared in the valley north of the Anyui. Instantly all who could manage a paddle ran to their boats and hastened to hide in the [river] bends and [beneath] the high [river] banks, where hunters waited for their prey.

River crossings of deer deserve comment. In the best years their number can be in the many thousands over a territory 50 to 100 miles [80 to 160 kilometers] wide. Although the deer, as it always seemed to me, keep themselves in smaller herds of 200 and 300 animals each, these separate groups often follow in close succession, creating a huge herd. The route the deer take is almost always the same. . . . To cross, deer usually descend to the [Anyui] river bed, where it is dry or shallow, choosing a place where the opposite shore is not too steep. First, the whole herd is shy and in one dense crowd; then the lead deer, with a few followers, advances, raising his head high, observing the surroundings. When reassured, the advance company enters the water, followed by the whole herd, and in a few minutes the entire surface of the river is covered with swimming deer. Then the hunters pounce, emerging in their boats from behind rocks and bushes, usually upwind of the deer, and surround them and try to keep them moving. Meanwhile, two or three of the most experienced hunters, armed with long spears and *pokolyugami* [a long knife connected to one end of the double-ended paddle], burst into the herd and stab the swimming deer with incredible speed. Usually, one strike is enough to kill an animal or cause him to be so severely wounded he can only swim to the opposite shore.

Pokolka [reindeer] spearing puts the hunters in great danger. A small boat is in danger every minute of tipping over in the dense, chaotic crowds of deer, which try in every way to protect themselves against their persecutors. Males bite, butt, and kick, while females try to tip the boats over using their front legs. If they manage to overturn a boat, the hunter's death is almost inevitable. He can be saved only if he grabs a strong, unwounded deer and gets carried to shore. However, accidents are rare, because the hunters display great dexterity in keeping their boats upright despite the exertions of the animals. An experienced hunter can kill a hundred or more deer in less than half an hour. When a large herd arrives in smaller groups, pokolka spearing is more convenient and safer. Other hunters secure the dead or dying deer and bind them to the boats, and each hunter gets his share. (1948: 185–86)

The High Arctic Islands

The Yukagir once inhabited islands in the Arctic Ocean where marine mammals were more abundant than they were near the shallow, muddy mainland coast. Sledges and skin boats helped the Yukagir negotiate the mixed conditions of pack ice and open water between the islands and the mainland. There is some evidence that the Yukagir made hunting expeditions to the New Siberian Islands in the Laptev Sea north of the Lena delta and among the Bear (Medved) Islands outside the Kolyma estuary. Jochelson cited the shallow coast as a reason for the lack of intensive maritime hunting near the Siberian mainland: "The ocean between the mouth of the Kolyma River and the Sviatoi Cape to the west is only 7 meters deep at a distance of 10 or 20 miles [16 or 32 kilometers] from the shore" (1910: 4). About the Bear Islands, he wrote: "The geodesist Andreyev found in 1763 on the third Bear Island the remnants of huts belonging to ancient Yukagir. . . . The polar bears on the islands and Arctic Ocean ice are hunted occasionally by the Russianized Yukagir and other inhabitants around the mouth of the Kolyma River, who go to the Bear Islands to hunt seal for dog food. This occurs in winter, when the summer catch of fish have run out" (1910: 347, 382).

Yukagir occupation of the Bear Islands raises questions regarding the origin of maritime hunting and the skin boats that later became a central feature of Eskimo studies. The westernmost prehistoric Eskimo settlements are at Cape Baranov, east of the Kolyma River. These sites were first explored by Gavril Sarychev in 1790 and more recently by Alexei Okladnikov (Sarychev 1805; Okladnikov and Beregovaya 1971). Based on their reports, Albova (1968a) wrote that two cultures met there in the early Iron Age. One group, the pre-Yukagir, had since ancient times inhabited the Yakutia forest and tundra as hunters and fishermen. The other group, ancestral Eskimo, who were at this time already fully maritime-adapted sea mammal hunters with skin boats, were expanding west along the northern coast of Chukotka. It is therefore possible that Eskimo contact with the Yukagir gave rise to the Yukagir kayak, which explains the similarity of the Georgi kayak illustration to the ancient Old Bering Sea boat models and the capability of the Yukagir and the Eskimo for periodic occupations of High Arctic islands, including Wrangel Island, where prehistoric sites nearly 4,000 years old have been found (Dikov 1988).

The Swedish-Finnish polar explorer N. A. E. Nordenskjöld (1881) wrote, in his account of the *Vega* expedition, that Michael Stadukhin had acquired Native information in 1644 near the Kolyma River about the existence of large islands, later named the New Siberian Islands, in the Laptev Sea that were rich in fossil walrus tusks and mammoth bones. Stadukhin also learned that Chukchi people had reached this place in sledges from the Chukotka coast. Russians finally reached the New Siberian Islands in April 1770, when Ivan Lyakhov followed the tracks of an enormous reindeer herd approaching from the north, which led him to the two southernmost islands, Little and Great Lyakhovsky. These islands held great numbers of mammoth tusks and were rich in foxes and other fur-bearers. Between 1800 and 1805, the hunter Yakov Sannikov discovered the northern New Siberian Islands, now named Stolbovoy, Kotelny, and Faddeyevsky.

In March 1809, the Russians dispatched Matvei Hedenström to study the islands, accompanied by Sannikov and another hunter known to us only as Koschevin (Mills 2003). On Faddeyevsky, Sannikov found a Yukagir sledge, stone skin scrapers, and a mammoth ivory axe, and he concluded that the island had been visited before Russians introduced iron into Siberia. In 1811, a new attempt to study the New Siberian Islands was made, again involving Sannikov. This time the party ventured over the ice in reindeer sleds to Kotelny Island and found skulls and bones of extinct animals, including mammoth, horse, oxen, and sheep that had lived there in a warmer climate in ancient times. Sannikov also discovered the remains of what he called "old Yukagir dwellings," indicating that people from the mainland had visited the island, using watercraft and sledges. His scientific and geographic contributions became eclipsed when a "blue haze," which he speculated was another island, was sighted northeast of the New Siberian Islands in 1811. It was only a mirage, though, and instead of attaching his name to a new piece of real estate, Sannikov become perversely famous when this "Sannikov Land" entered the popular Russian vocabulary as shorthand for all manner of illusory schemes and promotions. Today his legacy fares better: "Sannikov" has found a niche in popular-culture references to romantic illusions in song, theater, and film.

Wrangel, who began his expedition to Chukotka to map its territory and people in 1820, was aware of the New Siberian Islands but never visited or described them directly. During his travels, he met a British Royal Navy captain named John Dundas Cochrane, an adventurer who offered his service in Eastern Siberia and published a lively diary of his experiences (1829). Cochrane reported that the Kolyma Yukagir, who lived on the border between the Russians and the warlike Chukchi, occupied neutral ground where both groups laid aside their weapons aside to trade. He learned about the New Siberian Islands from the Yukagir and Chukchi, noting, "New Siberia has been inhabited, without doubt; many huts or yurts still exist, and there are traditions in Siberia of tribes having been compelled, due to persecution, small-pox, as well as other diseases, to quit their lands for those beyond the seas" (1829: 328).

In North America, Wrangel Island (between the Chukchi and East Siberian seas) is famous for Robert Bartlett's rescue there of the crew of the *Karluk*, which was marooned on the island in 1914 during an oceanographic misadventure in the Arctic Ocean (Bartlett and Hale 1916). More recently, in the 1990s, it became famous for its mammoth remains. The animals became isolated on Wrangel Island by sea level rise and survived there into the mid-Holocene, evolving into a pygmy form. The last mammoths on Earth, they went extinct 4,500 years ago (Vartanyan, Garrutt, and Sher 1993).

Birch-Bark Canoes of the Upper Kolyma River

In his book on the reindeer hunters of Northern Eurasia, Simchenko (1976b) wrote that the Yukagir of the upper Kolyma forest zone had a birch-bark canoe that they called *khotan*; it was similar to the Yakut canoe, making it a Lena-type bark canoe in our classification. Since the last Yukagir lived on the upper and lower Kolyma east of the Lena River, his observation probably is drawn from that region. The Russian poet

and popular writer Alexander Bestuzhev-Marlinsky, who was exiled to Yakutsk in 1826, also mentioned Yukagir birch-bark canoes in a work written in 1827 and published in 1838 in Germany, noting their location (the upper Kolyma) and the use of dozens of birch-bark canoes in a hunt. This is the only known reference to Yukagir birch-bark canoes being used in a reindeer hunt:

The inhabitants of the Kolyma River, who know the habits of reindeer, gather from the nearby camps in small boats made of birch bark, called "vetka," on the Kolyma River where the reindeer swim across and wait for them covered in grass or in their boats. . . . At first light in the morning the rumors spread that the animals are nearing in large herds and are coming closer and closer. The reindeer in the front row rush alone into the water while the others look around, move their ears, and sniff the wind—meanwhile the hunters stay still and dare not move. When the reindeer are reassured, the leading deer turns around toward the herd, and this is the signal for the river crossing. Down the animals spring into the water and start swimming, without fear, the backs down and the heads up, looking proud[ly] toward the opposite shore. When some 2,000 reindeer are in the river, the hunters enter the scene with loud shouts, causing the animals in the rear to try and turn back, but all are pushed into the water. . . .

Now the slaughter begins: the light boats attack the herd, cutting off their way to the shore, and the hunters in boats try to get the herd to turn and swim upstream. The skillful hunters mix themselves in the middle of the swimming animals and spear them right and left in the body, just behind the fore leg, in the lungs and liver, with a small sharp spear. The stream carries the killed animals away, and auxiliary boats downstream collect the bodies and take them to shore; the wounded animals drag themselves to the opposite shore and collapse. (1838: 426)

The Kolyma certainly was not the only region where the Yukagir built birch-bark canoes, but it might have been the final location where they were used before people switched to plank *karbas*. When Bestuzhev-Marlinsky was there in 1827, birch-bark boats were more common on the middle and upper Lena River, before the Sakha and Evenk took those lands. Both birch-bark and wooden boats were in use when Jochelson visited the Yukagir and copied a charcoal drawing provided by one of his informants (Okladnikova 1998: fig. 8.18).

Birch-Bark Canoes of Lake Baikal

Genetic, linguistic, and archaeological evidence shows that the pre-Yukagir people originally lived in Southern Siberia on the Yenisey River north of Lake Baikal before they migrated east and north, finally ending up at the Kolyma. This evidence is of utmost importance when we try to establish the Yukagir connection to the Yenisey River birch-bark canoe, which, as we will see, was used in most of the southern regions that the Yukagir and Samoyed inhabited in earlier times.

Some of this evidence is linguistic. Jaakko Häkkinen of Helsinki University has discussed the emergence of the Proto-Samoyed language in the Sayan Mountain region of Southern Siberia and proposed that early Samoyed-Yukagir contacts took place there, likely a few thousand years ago (2010: 3). He writes that the Proto-Samoyed language displays an East Uralic construction, shown in loanwords in the Yukagir language, and that the pre-Samoyed and pre-Yukagir had later contact, dating to the Bronze Age, somewhere between the Yenisey and Lena watersheds. Additional proof that the pre-Yukagir language was spoken in a more western region comes from its older loanword substrate.

In summarizing early Yukagir history, Vasily V. Ushnitsky (2008a) refers to Valerie N. Chernetsov, who believed that pre-Yukagir culture formed at the end of the Neolithic somewhere on the eastern bank of the Yenisey between the Angara and the lower Stony Tunguska rivers. This timing and place are in line with Häkkinen's proposed Yukagir-Samoyed contacts. Under pressure from the expanding Evenk and Sakha, the reindeer-hunting Yukagir eventually reached northeastern Siberia. On the other hand, archaeological evidence led M. A. Kiriak to conclude that the more ancient foundation of Yukagir ethnogenesis was farther east, in the Ymyyakhtak Late Neolithic and Glazkov Bronze Age cultures of the Lena valley and surrounding regions (Kiriak 1993). More recent information comes from research on the Glazkov culture, located north of Lake Baikal:

> The Baikal taiga was the territory of the Bronze Age Glazkov culture of the 17th to 13th centuries BCE. Their name comes from a suburb of Irkutsk where the first burials with copper and bronze were found. Fishing had a great significance for the Glazkov-culture people. They learned to make a boat from white birch bark that could be carried under the arm; furthermore, it was considerably faster than the heavy expanded log boat [doblenki].
>
> Funeral rites changed in many respects. Earlier burials were oriented in the direction of the sun (from the east to the west), whereas now burials were oriented downstream. This testifies to the exceptional role of rivers in the life of Glazkov-culture people. Rivers not only provided food but were, according to these people's ideas, the road along which they swam after death, downward into the unknown country of the dead. It is interesting that some of the burials of this period take the form of *omorochki* [birch-bark canoes].
>
> The Glazkov culture is connected with one of the complex problems of the ancient ethnic history of Siberia—the Tungus [Evenk]. Scientists assume that Evenk culture has its roots in Glazkov times and monuments [a term that in Russian means all sorts of cultural constructions].... All Tungus tribes shared specific elements . . . like the birch-bark boat, fitted out for hunting from the water and for floating on mountain streams, and birch-bark wooden cradles and plates. (Permyakova 2007: 1–2)

The Yukagir and Samoyed peoples, who were, in part, inheritors of Glazkov traditions were not alone in Southern Siberia. Beginning in the 4th century CE, groups from Transbaikal (east of Baikal, and also known as Dauria), the Baikal area, and the Amur River who spoke Tungus, Mongol, and Turkic languages penetrated the Lena, Aldan, Vilyuy, and Olekma river basins. When the Yukagir retreated north under Evenk, Mongol, or Turkic pressure along the Lena River circa 1000 CE, some were assimilated by Tungus people later known as the Even or Lamut, while others in the Yenisey River basin may have been assimilated by the Tungus Evenk. Later the Sakha people assimilated some Yukagir groups in the Lena River basin. Thus, over time, all newcomers to the Eastern Siberian taiga inherited Yukagir bark canoe technology and culture.

Based on place names and linguistic data, Russian scholars have identified ancient southern locations of proto-Yukagir peoples at Lake Baikal; on the Yenisey, upper Stony Tunguska, Angara, Lena, Vilyuy, Olekma, Aldan, and Amur rivers; and even on the Sea of Okhotsk coast. There is information about birch-bark canoes in most of the places where Yukagir mixed with Sakha or Tungus peoples. Even though Yukagir origins are still uncertain, their ancestors must have lived with birch-bark canoes in Southern Siberia in the Yenisey or Lena river basin before they moved north as a result of Turkic or Mongol expansions.

THE LENA RIVER AND THE TRANSBAIKAL EVENK: NOMADIC TUNGUS IN EASTERN SIBERIA

The Evenk, previously known as the Tungus, are one of the most successful peoples in Eastern Siberia if we consider the large territory they once occupied around the Lena River basin (Tugolukov 1963). Their borders extended to the Yenisey River, Transbaikal, the Amur River, the Sea of Okhotsk, and the Arctic Ocean coast. No other Native group had such a broad territorial range or the capacity to adapt to such diverse environments and neighbors. Since the early 18th century, scholars have theorized about Evenk origins and how and when they reached their present locations. These are important questions for canoe history because the birch-bark canoe played a crucial role in Evenk life and is found throughout their homelands. Most of these proposals point toward the lands between Lake Baikal and the Amur (Pakendorf 2007), while a few suggest a more western location. Vasilevich (1969) assumed their ethnogenesis and language origin was between the mountains south of Baikal and the Lower and Stony Tunguska rivers, while others argued for origins in the Transbaikal region between Lake Baikal, the Upper Angara River, and the Vitim and Olekma rivers. Perhaps the soundest view is that of Carl Hiekisch (1879), who argued that Evenk- and Manchu-speaking peoples originally lived in the Amur River basin and from there shifted to Transbaikal and the Lena when Mongol armies began to plunder Amur villages in the 1200s. Some Evenk, known in old Russian literature as the Oroch, could have entered Transbaikal much earlier.

The early history of the Evenk is difficult to pinpoint archaeologically because nomadic reindeer-riding hunters and fishermen leave few material traces. Most historians (e.g., Duggan et al. 2013) see their origins in the territories around Lake Baikal and the middle Amur River and assume that when the Evenk entered the Lena River basin about 1000 CE, they assimilated some Yukagir people in the middle Lena valley, while the rest of the Yukagir retreated north. Then, when the Turkic Sakha people entered the basin from Baikal, the Evenk peoples either mixed with the new arrivals or retreated north to the Lena River estuary, west toward the Vilyuy and Yenisey rivers, or east to the Aldan-Maya basin. As nomadic forest people, the Evenk in the Lena River basin and along other rivers running to the Arctic Ocean relied heavily on birch-bark canoes for summer transport. Below we describe their boats west of the Lena along the Vilyuy River and east along the Aldan and Maya rivers before we move south to the Lake Baikal region. Like their cousins on the Olenek and Anabar rivers, some of the Lena Evenk also used skin boats.

The Lena Birch-Bark Canoe

The Lena River basin covers most of the Eastern Siberian interior, from the Arctic Ocean to Lake Baikal in the south and to the Stanovoy Mountains in the east. In the west, the Vilyuy River parallels the Lower Tunguska River and partly overlaps it adjacent to the Yenisey River basin. The Lena and its many tributaries are the traditional home of the Eastern Evenk peoples, who as forest hunters and fishermen were still using birch-bark canoes as late as the 19th century. The Evenk were the last large group in Siberia north of the Amur River to turn to expanded log boats or planked boats, and for this reason their bark canoes are the best known of all the Native peoples of this vast region.

Both the Evenk and the Sakha used the Lena bark canoe. The Eastern Evenk used all three major bark canoe types found in Eastern Siberia, as Antropova (1961) noted: the Yenisey, the Lena, and the Amur versions. The pointed Lena-type canoe, with its long bottom line, was most typical of the Eastern Evenk in the Lena River basin. She believed that the Lena-type birch-bark canoe probably diffused from the Lake Baikal region to the Lena, Vitim, Olekma, Vilyuy, Aldan, Maya, and other rivers in the Lena basin.

Across the area occupied by the Eastern Evenk, a birch-bark boat is called a *dyav* (Vasilevich 1969). The typical Evenk canoe had pointed ends, but unlike most Western Siberian canoes, these were formed by extending the lower part and lengthening the bottom, while the upper stems sloped inward toward the center of the boat. This feature probably reflects the influence of Amur-style canoes' more accentuated inward-sloping bow and stern design. This same Lena-type boat also dominated the regions inhabited by the Sakha people, who lived next to the Evenk along the Lena River and its eastern basin. The Sakha called their boat *Tungus tyyta*, "Tungus boat," reflecting its origin. In the Yenisey River basin, the Yenisey-type bark canoe used by the western Evenk was typical of that territory and differed from the Lena canoe, which was called *djau* on the Lower

Tunguska (Messerschmitt 1964) and *jau* on Lake Baikal (Georgi 1775: 252).

According to Antropova (1961), in the Far East (Manchuria), the border between the Lena- and Amur-type bark canoes ran approximately along the watershed between the Lena and Amur rivers until the 1800s: north of the Stanovoy Mountains, Lena canoes were found, while south of them, Amur bark canoes were used. To the west, the border between canoe types followed the Vitim and Olekma rivers, with the Yenisey-type bark canoe dominant to the west and the Lena type to the east. Later, especially in the Amur region, when the Baikal Evenk migrated to new regions in the east, the border between bark canoe types changed accordingly (see chapter 9's section on the Amur Evenk, page 204).

The Vilyuy River Bark Canoe

The Vilyuy River is the largest west-bank tributary of the Lena River, flowing some 2,600 kilometers from the west, where its source, the Chona River, nearly reaches the Stony Tunguska in the Yenisey basin. In 1889, the German scientist Otto Herz traveled 30 kilometers up the Chona River by land on an insect-collecting trip to Yakutia, but for the return trip to the Lena, his party needed boats. A local Evenk man residing in Buja-ssura built birch-bark canoes for them. Herz wrote in his diary one of the few reports on bark canoes on the Chona and Vilyuy:

> No day passed without rain, and we [would not have] stayed here (30 versts [32 kilometers] to Vilyuy on the Chona) if we had not had to wait for the Tungus birch-bark boat to be made for our return tour. We were thus glad when our Yakut guide delivered notice that the boats and all were ready for our travel. In a short time we and the 10 small boats made of birch bark [were] ready to set out on the Chona River, and on August 28 [1889] at 10 a.m. the small fleet began to move. (1898: 230)

A Baltic-German scientist, Richard Maak, later explored the region's flora and fauna. One outcome of his travel was the deposit in the Museum of Anthropology and Ethnology of a model Tungus birch-bark canoe that he collected on the Vilyuy in 1891 (fig. 7.2a–c). Perhaps one of the oldest bark canoes from the Vilyuy and the Lena basin, it shows the persistence of an ancient form of construction that might have dominated this region for centuries. Otis T. Mason and

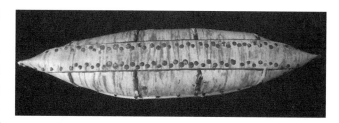
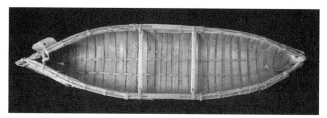
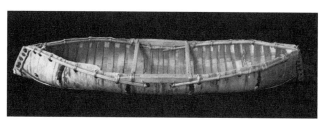

Fig. 7.2. Richard Maak explored the Lena River region in 1891 and collected this birch-bark canoe model (MAE 334-77) from the Vilyuy River Evenk. A few years later, Smithsonian ethnologist Otis T. Mason borrowed the model from the Museum of Anthropology and Ethnology and described it in his comparative study of canoes and kayaks. Although models often reveal few details, this one faithfully illustrates construction details such as the detailed sewing of the bark. (Photograph: Evguenia Anichtchenko; courtesy Museum of Anthropology and Ethnography)

Meriden S. Hill compared the bark canoes of the Kootenai in North America to ones found on the Lena and Amur rivers, including Maak's Evenk model:

> The Tungus model, though clumsy-looking, is built in five sections. Five strips of bark are bent in the middle and united at their edges to form the hull. The four seams extend all around the craft and are sealed tight with pitch. The canoe is kept in shape by a series of flat ribs, almost touching one another and extending along the inside from one end of the canoe to the other. On the outside, along the bottom, a wide strip of bark is sewed neatly, the stitches long on the inside of the boat and short on the outside, passing through two thicknesses of bark, including the flat ribs on the inside, holding it all together. At the ends the canoe line is straight, sloping inward

a bit, creating a slight point at the bottom. The bark is doubled over at the ends and sewed down. Strips of wood are sewed on both sides of the bark to form the inwale and outwale. There is no top piece except along a short space between the thwarts. Here the side strips for gunwales are indented to make space for the cap-piece along the middle. . . . Two solid pieces near the middle of the canoe serve as spreaders. The ends of these thwarts are perforated and lashed to the gunwale at the ends of the cap pieces to hold all parts firmly together. The Tungus canoe is wide and shallow and is an excellent freight boat. (1901: 536–37)

The Evenk canoe was similar in design to the Sakha bark canoe but had a single birch-bark sheet covering the whole bottom from end to end instead of several smaller sheets sewn together.

Olenek and Anabar River Skin Boats

Some Evenk groups inhabited the tundra-taiga border zone between the Yenisey and Lena rivers along the upper Olenek and Anabar rivers, probably the same Evenk who had once lived along the Vilyuy River. Their origin is obscure, but they seem to have used skin boats to cross rivers during reindeer migrations. As Antropova wrote:

At the end of the 19th century, the Evenk still used a peculiar skin boat called *mereke*, which was made as follows: Two poles were tied together at the ends and formed the rim of the frame. They were spread in the center by several transverse thwarts. A covering of sewn moose hide was stretched over the frame to form a shallow boat. Boards were placed inside, resting on the ribs, to support the cargo and crew. Such boats were made as needed, and after the use the frame was discarded and the moose hide was recycled or used as a tent cover. Similar boats were also used by the Aldan, Zeya, and Uchur River Evenk east of the Lena River and by the Ilimpeya Evenk living along the headwaters of the Olenek and Anabar rivers. (2005: 9)

During the 1950s, there was a lively discussion in Soviet anthropology about the origin of the Olenek and Anabar River people, who were shown on ethnological maps as Evenk mainly because they bred and herded reindeer

(Michael 1962). Boris O. Dolgikh (1960), Ilya S. Gurvich (1963), and Hiroki Takakura (2012), who did fieldwork on the upper Olenek and Anabar rivers, strongly disagreed, writing that these people were Sakha—making them the only reindeer-breeding Yakut in Asia. They had moved to the Olenek and Anabar rivers after most of the reindeer-breeding Evenk had died of smallpox, and they assimilated the remaining Evenk, taking over their identity and reindeer economy before the mid-1800s. These Sakha spoke Yakut but identified themselves as Tungus. But that is not the end of the story. Dolgikh and Gurvich assumed that the original skin boat–using population in the Olenek and Anabar river basins was Yukagir and that they were later assimilated by the Evenk. Future DNA studies certainly will clarify the genetic history of these groups.

Aldan and Maya River Bark Canoes

Following the Evenk and subsequent Sakha incursions, the Yakut groups inhabited the eastern Lena basin as far as the Sea of Okhotsk, while Evenk who had mixed with the Yukagir retreated into mountainous terrain some 500 meters above the Lena valley, where the plateau was a good hunting ground for these reindeer-riding people. To the south, a portage via the Aldan and Zeya rivers over the Stanovoy Mountains connected the Lena and Amur basins for Sakha traders doing business with the Manchu and Chinese.

For trade and movements between the Lena and the Sea of Okhotsk, the Evenk and Sakha peoples living in the Aldan basin (along the Aldan, Amga, and Maya rivers) used bark canoes of the Lena River type, while those living farther south used the Amur River type, both built mainly by Evenk groups. These boats might have been much like the Amur Evenk canoes (see fig. 9.17, 18, page 208). However, because the Sakha people were the main operators of the Aldan-Zeya portage to the Amur, their Lena-type canoes were known there as well. This commerce is confirmed by Manchu-Chinese border-control documentation of Yakut who reached the Amur River in birch-bark canoes in the late 1600s.

The Ust-Maya Canoe

We have two descriptions of bark canoes at a village on the Maya River, one early and one late. The first comes from the Russian naval officer Gavril Sarychev, who traveled from Yakutsk to Okhotsk in the supply train of Captain Billing's expedition in June 1788. Where the Aldan reaches the Maya, Sarychev encountered Tungus or Yakut hunters:

Here we found some River Tungus people, called by this name because they had no reindeer and traveled on the river in small birch-bark canoes [*Kähner von Birkenrinde*], inhabiting similar bark homes and living totally from fish. They were called Tungus, although they are not; instead, they belong to the Yakut folk, while we found very seldom among them people who spoke the Tungus language. I took one of them as my guide, to learn from him the names of all the rivers, riverbanks, and islands.

Their birch-bark canoes are very small and are used by Yakut on rivers and lakes. They are made from thin wicker branches, which serve as ribs, and long rods; this makes the basis for the hull, which is then covered with birch bark. To treat the holes, the Yakut use some sort of milk-based putty. (1805: 125)

In September 1788, Sarychev traveled north in log boats along the Maya and the Yudoma rivers and portaged across to the source of the Okhota River at a place called Veta. From there, he wrote, "we made our way in a pair of birch-bark canoes down the Okhotsk River. The current was so fast that in six hours we came 70 versts [75 kilometers], reaching the sea coast close to Okthosk [town]" (1805: 134–35).

The following report concerns the remains of a large birch-bark canoe discovered in June 2001 near Ust-Maya village at the mouth of the Maya River on the Aldan by Sergey Abakumov, a student and amateur archaeologist working under the direction of A. N. Popov. This boat is remarkable because of its length; it is probably of Evenk origin, since these rivers and the western slopes of the Stanovoy Mountains were mainly Evenk territory. Abakumov writes, "During our expedition we found fragments of an old . . . boat, 15 meters long, made from birch bark and wooden rods. The boat was for transporting cargo along the river. Its width was 70 centimeters, and could travel very rapidly along the river" (2001: 5).

This is the largest birch-bark canoe known in all of Northern Eurasia and represents an achievement akin to the great French and Indian *voyageur* birch-bark canoes of the 18th- and 19th-century Canadian fur-trade era. Its 70-centimeter beam shows that it had a typical Amur-type construction: Amur canoes were made in various lengths, but all were about 70 centimeters wide. We may assume its builders entered the Aldan and Maya rivers from the Amur basin in the late 20th century; otherwise its frames would

have rotted (although a birch-bark cover can last a long time). Unfortunately, no drawing or photo was made.

The Iengra Canoe

In the archives of the Neryungri Museum of History of South Yakutia (Sakha Republic) is a description of a birch-bark canoe (fig. 7.3), built locally in 1997, that is unusual among Lena or Amur versions: its bow and stern ends terminate in a convex taper when the craft is seen from above and a squared profile in side view. The museum's description reads:

Evenk boat [dyav], length 326 centimeters, beam 80 centimeters, height 39 centimeters, made of wood, birch bark, resin, and wicker. . . . Assembled from two separately manufactured parts: a frame consisting of longitudinal laths and transverse ribs, and a birch-bark cover. Bow and stern ends converge and are elevated above the line of the bottom boards. The cover is made of sewn bark sheets whose seams are sealed with resin. The top edges of both sides are strengthened with a wooden inwale and outwale. Inside, at the bottom of the boat, are two broad planks cut to fit the boat's shape. Across the top of the boat's midsection are two wooden thwarts attached to the gunwales with lashings threaded through holes in their ends. The canoe is made for rapid movement on rivers, for hunting birds and other animals, or catching fish. Purchased by the museum in the village of Iengra in Neryungri District. (Neryungri Museum of History catalog entry, September 8, 1997, CP 25 456 E-209)

The birch-bark bottom of the Neryungri Museum canoe consists of one long sheet of bark sewn to the bottom of the bark forming the canoe body, as in the boat studied by Mason in 1899 (see fig. 7.2, page 143; Mason and Hill 1901). Thus this bark boat follows the tradition of old Lena-type canoes, although its bow and stern shapes are different.

Fig. 7.3. This recently made birch-bark canoe (NMCP 25-456 E-209) was collected in Iengra village in the Neryungri area of the southern Sakha (Yakutia) Republic and was catalogued by the Neryungri Museum of History in 1997. It has the full-length double bark layer typical of Lena Evenk canoes but lacks the usual pointed ends. (Courtesy Neryungri Museum of History of South Yakutia)

Baikal Evenk Canoes

The Lake Baikal's outlet is the powerful and swift Angara River, which runs to the Yenisey River. For this reason, we could have considered the lake and its Evenk peoples in chapter 6. But Lena basin rivers surround Lake Baikal on two sides: to the northwest, the Kirenga River flows so close that some maps show it starting from Baikal, and to the northeast, the Vitim River, another tributary of the Lena, drains a mountainous landscape. Owing to its dual connections to the Lena and Transbaikal, Lake Baikal has generally been regarded as part of Eastern Siberia. We also consider the Evenk and Baikal to be vital parts of Eastern Siberian bark canoe history, so we will address it here.

Which people claims Lake Baikal as their home territory? Which group or people has the strongest ties to this lake? These questions are not easy to answer: many peoples and groups have resided here since ancient times. The multidisciplinary Baikal-Hokkaido Archaeological Project (Weber, Katzenberg, and Schurr 2011) has researched the prehistory and skeletal biology of the area; however, as usual, the archaeological and biological evidence has not resolved the complexities of historical ethnicity. During the early part of their history, the Yukagir reportedly lived along the southern Yenisey and Angara rivers, and they might have been involved in the Glazkov culture, as the Evenk might also have been. The Samoyed's early home might have been west of the southern Yenisey; later, the Southern Samoyed resided in the eastern Sayan Mountains, west of Lake Baikal. Johan G. Georgi wrote that the Samoyed, after they became Tatars, regularly visited the western shore of Lake Baikal: "To the Tunkiskoi Ostrog [fort] comes also one tribe of Sayan Tatars, who call themselves Soyot and who belong to the pagan Tatar sat the upper Yenisey" (1775: 153). On the other side of the Altai Mountains, in the Tom River Valley, lived the Shor people, who were later assimilated by expanding Turkic groups. According to L. P. Potapov, the Shor here made birch-bark canoes called *tos kebe* (1936: 82–83).

It is hazardous—to say the least—to attempt ethnic constructions from these snippets of information, especially in the absence of definitive archaeological data. But we can cautiously suggest that Lake Baikal has been a mixing bowl of peoples and cultures for millennia. Turkish Tatars must have known the route to the Baikal shores. The Buryat, who live west and south of Lake Baikal in the Republic of Buryatia, are the largest minority group in Russian Siberia today, and as a people they represent the northern Mongol; Mongol and Daurian people have long lived in the northern plains and mountains of present-day Mongolia, south of Baikal. Then there are the Yeniseyan peoples, among them the Ket, Kott, Assan, and Arin, who have lived in the Yenisey River basin, especially in the Yenisey-Angara-Baikal delta, since they arrived from their presumed original Central Asian locations. Finally, there are the Sakha (not considered a "minority" in Russia), who rafted to their future home along the middle Lena River; the Chinese, who called the western Angara the Nana-ga-la; and the Uighur people, who, according to written sources, crossed this Southern Siberian hub on war and trade missions.

Owing to its central location and to the many peoples who have resided in or crossed the region, Lake Baikal has raised more interest among scientists than any other inland area in Eastern Siberia. Anthropologists have theorized that Baikal was the cradle of innovation from which important inventions such as skis and snowshoes originated and where reindeer breeding began and spread throughout Siberia (Vainshtein 1980) and perhaps even to Europe. Baikal may also have been the place from which the birch-bark canoe spread outward on its way to the Pechora, Ob, Yenisey, Lena, and Amur river basins via trade contacts or migration. The strategic cultural geography of the region was recognized early by researchers such as Johan G. Georgi and Gustav Radde.

Georgi explored the Lake Baikal region in the summer of 1772, beginning his trip from the town of Irkutsk and traveling in a sailing and rowing boat around the lake to map the rivers running into it. He described the harsh climate at the shore, the cold summer nights, the morning fog, and the first frost in August. In some ravines deep in the forest, he found permafrost and ice that never melted during the short summer. By April 1773, the lake was still covered with 100 to 140 centimeters of ice. Most Evenk gathered in large fishing camps at the outlet of the Upper Angara River at the northeastern end of the lake, north of Olkhon Island, which the Buryat occupied. Georgi visited many of these camps, and in June and July 1772, he wrote a description of their sledges and bark canoes:

> Their hand sledges (*tolgoki*) are narrow and up to 5 feet [1.5 meters] long, similar to Ostyak *nartta*. They pull them themselves, or hitch a reindeer or dogs to tow them. . . . All forest and fisher Tungus [Evenk] people are equipped with small boats (*jau*) made of birch bark. They are narrow but up to 3 klafter [5.4 meters] long. To reinforce the bark cover, the

sides and bottom have thin laths. The bark is strong, sewn by the Tungus, and the seams are caulked with coniferous tree resin. The paddle is 1½ klafter [2.7 meters] long, with two blades, with which a Tungus paddles on one side and then on the other with such speed that he looks like a rotating windmill. . . . The boat carries up to four men and equipment. They [Tungus] go up to 3 or 4 versts [3 to 4 kilometers] in them, including directly across large bays. One man can carry such a boat. . . . In Lake Baikal there are also many small wooden boats built according to Russian models. (1775: 252)

After traveling around Lake Baikal, Georgi described Transbaikal Evenk hunting and fishing and their bark canoes:

For fishing, the Tungus [Evenk] move in summer from one river, lake, or other waterway to the next, and they engage in hunting only briefly. For fishing, they stay longer in one place than they do while hunting, and they have certain territories allocated to each family. For water travel, they use small boats (*jau*), built with light wooden structures fastened by roots and covered with birch bark, which is sewn so tightly that it will not leak. One such boat is flat-bottomed and pointed at both ends, 1½ to 3 klafter [2.7 to 5.4 meters] long, 1½ to 2½ feet [46 to 76 centimeters] wide at the top, and only some 30 to 50 pounds [13.3 to 22.5 kilograms] in weight. Yet it is still strong enough to carry four or five men on a swift river or a reasonably large lake, or venture on Lake Baikal far from shore. . . .

They catch fish with hooks hanging overboard, and with a forked iron spear (*keronki*) that has [three] finger-long points 1 inch [3 centimeters] apart and is fastened on a wooden shaft 1 klafter [1.8 meters] long. They fish during the night from the shore or in ponds with the help of burning pine splints, or move in their bark boats here and there over the water. Their skill is such that the fish they see cannot easily escape their iron spears. In springtime when the *omuln* (*Salmo gregarious*) ascend some rivers running into Baikal, they assemble a fence near the shore in the path of the teeming fish and stand in the water where the fish swim by, and owing to the huge number passing by, they can catch them with their bare hands and throw them onto the shore. (1777: 314–15)

We also have a description of a different kind of Baikal economy nearly a century later, documented by Gustav Radde (1861), who met two Evenk families on the lake's eastern shore in August 1855; they were hunting seal, which provided their entire sustenance. Sealing was popular among the Evenk and Buryat, and both enjoyed seal meat as a luxury food. Most seal were found south of Olkhon Island and migrated in summer to the lake's southern shore. In the 1850s, the Evenk inhabited the eastern side of Lake Baikal as far as the Barguzin River mouth, and the area north of the lake, where they had a regular seasonal migration. They were fully nomadic, living in the forest and migrating from place to place on their hunting and fishing trips, setting their camps in different locations. The husband hunted and the wife took care of everything else: the household, the reindeer, and the fishing near the camp. Without a wife, a hunter could not survive.

From the birch tree and its bark, the Evenk made all the household items they needed, large and small, including covers for canoes. Their tents (Radde 1861: *haran*; Georgi 1775: *aran*) consisted of some 15 to 20 poles arranged to form a cone at the top and covered with birch bark. Birch bark was called *tischa* (Georgi: *tisa*), and Georgi recorded that some sheets of it were as much as 5 *faden* (10.7 meters) long and 1 to 1.5 *arshin* (0.7 to 1.4 meters) wide. Usually three boiled, soft, single sheets were sewn into a single long sheet to cover a canoe.

Radde (1861: 236–38) wrote about the seven items of equipment the Evenk needed when hunting or traveling: a bear lance (*gidda*), a flintlock rifle (*pakterauen*; Georgi: *pokterahon*), a horse-tail flyswatter (*arpuk*; Georgi: *arpok*), a Chinese tobacco pipe (*ulla*) with a flint-and-steel fire kit, a thin board (*panange*; Georgi: *ponagna*) to support a backpack, a three-pronged iron harpoon (*keronki*; Georgi: *heronki*) for fishing, and a birch-bark canoe (*tschauf*; Georgi: *jau*). Radde described this last item as a sewn birch-bark boat, 3 meters long, propelled with a "balancing pole" that had narrow blades at each end. Most of these canoes had only one long seam and three cross seams in the bottom, fixed with pitch or treated with a paste that made the seams water-resistant. The ends of the canoe were fastened together with birch branches. New, such a watercraft cost some two rubles. It provided an essential service in all the local terrain, where the swamps turn into small lakes and then to swamps again. The Evenk had acquired special skills for traveling safely and speedily in spite of fast currents in the rivers; sometimes Radde saw three men in one small, fragile canoe, standing upright and paddling in unison.

Nepa and Kirenga: A Portage to the Lena River

Ferdinand F. Müller, a scientist in the Russian Academy, made a long journey in Eastern Siberia in 1873, traveling from the Yenisey to the upper Lena along rivers and over portages, ending his trip at the Yana River in northeastern Yakutia, now known as the Sakha Republic. One leg of his journey began at the Kirenga River, north of Lake Baikal, and on May 31, he reached Nepa village, on the Lower Tunguska River. In the early 1700s, the Lower Tunguska had been a busy gateway to the Lena. A Russian village near Nepa, Preobrazhenskoe, was a trade center that supplied all kinds of manufactured goods to nearby people, who traded furs, fish, and moose and reindeer meat for them. Likewise, most of the villages at the headwaters of the Stony Tunguska River owe their existence to the region's rich fur and game, including Yerbogotan, established circa 1800 to trade sable.

Müller traveled in flat-bottomed Russian boats similar to those he had seen on the Western Dvina and in Riga, Latvia, his hometown. Before his departure from Eastern Siberia, he had a birch-bark canoe built—or, rather, the parts for one that could be assembled later:

> For a smaller boat used for fishing, we had a canoe made of birch bark that could carry four to five persons if necessary, for which we had brought the materials from the Tiniguska [Tunguska] River, from Monjerosh village. The bark canoe was assembled by Gele and Uwotgcliän [his Evenk guides] and made ready for use. The Evenk know well how to do this work, since they use bark boats on the Tunguska, although they are much smaller; our boat was made especially [large] for our expedition team. One man with a double-bladed paddle was enough to propel this boat. (1882: 84–85)

Nepa village continued to be an important location even much later because of the two-way traffic between the Yenisey and the Lena and the freight and fur trade connected to it. Evenk birch-bark canoes continued to be made there as late as 1930, when Pavel Khoroshikh photographed them (fig. 7.4a–b). The Nepa village Evenk birch-bark canoe shown here may have been one of the last of its kind, but as we can see from the photographs, it was still a masterpiece among the bark canoes in this region. From Müller's description above, we can reconstruct the process of building this sort of canoe. It was made of three sheets of birch bark, which likely had been boiled for two days in large metal vats and perhaps smoked for a long time to give them leathery properties. The sheets were sewn together using wooden pegs to keep them in proper position before they were sewn with bird-cherry roots to make one large canoe cover, and the seams were waterproofed with pine or larch pitch. There was perhaps an extra sheet of bark inside the boat to give it additional strength. The wooden inwale and outwale, as well as the wide laths, were prefabricated before assembly. The inwale was made first, and its ends were bound with a wide bark band. A thwart was added in the middle to give the bow and stern their typical shape. Then the ribs were set in holes bored in the inwale. The frame was then covered with bark and clamped between the inwale and outwale, and the ribs were put in place and fastened to the gunwale at their upper ends with wooden pins. Finally, thin laths were slid under the ribs on the bottom and sides of the boat for added strength. The result was a fine bark canoe in classical 1:5 form, about 1 meter wide and 5 meters long. The wide canoes Khoroshikh photographed had a flat bottom, indicating river service, and probably they were used to transport goods between Nepa village and the trade stations.

Fig. 7.4. Constructing a birch-bark canoe at Nepa village on the Lower Tunguska River in 1930. (*a*) Staking out the bark cover. (*b*) The finished canoe, showing internal construction. (Photographs: Pavel Khoroshikh; courtesy Krasnoyarsk Krai Museum)

THE EVEN: LAMUT-TUNGUS PEOPLE
OF THE OKHOTSK COAST

The Even (formerly called the Lamut, after their word for "big water or lake") are the second-largest Manchu-Tungus-speaking group in Russia, today numbering some 17,000 people, about half of whom live as a scattered minority in the northeastern Sakha Republic. The remaining Even live in the western Chukchi Koryak and Magadan *okrugs* (political districts) and the northern part of the Khabarovsk region; a small enclave also exists in central Kamchatka (Norwegian Polar Institute 2006). It is difficult to draw a boundary between the Even and their relatives, especially the Oroch Evenk, who lived south of them along the Sea of Okhotsk from the Ayan River to Sakhalin Island. Leopold von Schrenk called these Tungus-related people the Orotschen or Orochen (1881: 21–23). Most Even in the mountainous regions were nomadic reindeer-herding hunters, fishermen, and trappers; however, a small number were seminomadic, living along the river courses and sea coasts.

Early Even history might have begun in the upper Lena River basin, where the proto-Tungus Even lived circa 1000 CE. After around 1500, when Mongol and Yakut peoples of Turkic origin entered the Lena region, the ancestors of the Even were pushed to the Sea of Okhotsk. On 17th-century Russian maps showing the distribution of Siberian peoples, the Even territory is on the Sea of Okhotsk coast, extending approximately from the Amur River estuary to the present town of Magadan. The Even competed for this land with the Koryak, who tried to block their advance into their traditional hunting grounds. In the south, their neighbors were the Evenk in the interior, as well as the Nivkh, who fished and hunted sea mammals north of the Amur River estuary in the Shantar Islands and on the coast and on northern Sakhalin Island. Later the Sakha also gained access to the Sea of Okhotsk coast (Levin and Vasilyev 1964).

Archaeologists have discussed the Even's history in relation to the prehistoric Okhotsk maritime culture (circa 800–1300 CE) and the ethnographic Koryak, Yukagir, and Siberian Eskimo. A. A. Burykin (2001) writes of Even appearing on the Okhotsk coast circa 1700, later than was earlier believed, where they encountered remnants of the Okhotsk and Old Koryak maritime cultures (see also Duggan et al. 2013). Some Even maritime hunting equipment, including their harpoons and oil lamps, is similar to that used by the Eskimo and Koryak and by the Nivkh on Sakhalin Island. It seems likely that the Okhotsk coast was Old Koryak territory before the appearance of the Even,

and after the Even arrived, they mixed with the southern Koryak in the middle of the 17th century while maintaining a boundary with the northern Koryak south of the Motykley River (Lebedintsev 1998).

In 1860, Aleksander Sbignew (1867) studied the Even of the Okhotsk coast. He noted that they included both nomadic reindeer herders and settled coastal fishermen and sea mammal hunters and that the nomadic group was larger and hunted in the taiga and mountains throughout the year. There was no permanent boundary between the two groups, since the coastal group consisted of individuals and families who had lost their reindeer and were forced to make their living from the sea. Hunting provided the inland people with food and skins for clothes and for paying the fur tax to the Russians. What furs were left they sold to traders. They used reindeer for riding and as pack animals, and a wealthy man might own hundreds. The reindeer people traveled in groups of two to three families and rarely remained in one location more than two or three days.

When a family was traveling in the taiga, the man usually walked first, on foot, making a path that the pack animals followed. When crossing a river, the family built a log raft or vetka, according to Sbignew (1867). The vetka is a flat-bottomed boat made of birch bark, supported inside by a row of thin ribs. It is very light and easy to paddle, 1 to 2.5 *sajen* (2.1 to 5.3 meters) long. A vetka 1.75 sajen (3.7 meters) long and 2 1/2 feet (76 centimeters) wide could carry four people. The heaviest boats weighed no more than 2 poods (33 kilograms) and could be carried by one man. Considering the Even's location in the taiga between Magadan and the Kolyma River, their vetka was probably similar to the Yukagir or the Sakha canoe (see their sections in this chapter). It probably also had pointed ends, bark turned outside-in over birch gunwales, and bottoms and sides sewn from several sheets of bark, owing to the shortage of large birch trees.

Keyukey *and Kayaks*

In the 1860s, around the time of Sbignew's study, the number of settled Even was rather small, and they lived on the Sea of Okhotsk coast between Tayi Bay in the south and the town of Gizhiga in the north (Sbignew 1867). Because an Even man's wealth was measured by the number of reindeer he owned, the sea people were considered very poor; they had few or no reindeer and subsisted on fish, birds, seal, and sea lion. They also ate the skin and other parts of the beluga. Settled Even did not usually engage in inland hunting, as they were too poor to own guns; when hunting land animals, they mostly used traps. After Russians began to settle on the coast, they partly assimilated the Even. Sbignew noted one exception: the Even living in the villages of Ola and Arman on Tayi Bay. This harbor, some 100 kilometers from Magadan and called Tausk in American literature, was a base for American whalers visiting the Siberian coast in the 1800s. On a busy day, as many as 30 whalers might be present. The Even living there became Americanized, adopting western clothing, hats, footgear, stoves, domestic equipment, and plank housing. The other settled Even kept one house for summer, next to a small river, and another for winter, set in some sheltered place hidden from the wind.

Not much evidence of Even skin boats survives. Pre-1800 oral history tells of a tribe called the Heyeki who resided on the Okhotsk coast before the arrival of European whalers and were associated with the settled coastal Koryak (Burykin 2001). They might have been Even. The Even folklore expert Vassa Yegorovna Kundyr had this to say about the Heyeki in an interview with Burykin conducted in the summer of 1988 in Gizhiga, an Even village north of Magadan:

The Heyeki lived on the shore in houses whose frames and rafters were made of whale ribs and bones. They hunted marine animals and sewed clothes from their skins. To worship and to sacrifice to the sea, they piled the bones of dead whales on the land for a special ceremony. . . . The dead are not burned but are buried along the coast among the rocks. The Heyeki made from the skins of sea animals very good boats, which they brought to their neighbors in exchange for reindeer. They called these boats *keyukey*. (Quoted in Burykin 2001: 3)

The Heyeki may have been a remnant group of the sea mammal–hunting Okhotsk-culture people. Burykin (2001) believes the name *keyukey* relates to the Eskimo word for a skin boat, *kayak*, and below we will see that the Even had skin kayaks as well. While this testimony does not specify the type of skin boat they used, two extant descriptions do provide clues. One, from Cape Ayan in 1854, details the construction of a skin kayak and its equipment, and the other tells about the use of hundreds of small Native boats for goose hunting in an Okhotsk coastal town in 1785. These examples show that skin kayaks used by early Okhotsk coastal peoples conformed to the later boating traditions of the region and that their use was extensive and shared by all local coastal inhabitants, including the Even and Sakha.

On July 7, 1854, during the Crimean War, British Royal Navy officer J. M. Tronson was sailing with his squadron along the Okhotsk coast toward Cape Marie, the northwestern point of Sakhalin, on a blockade mission. The fleet proceeded to the port of Ayan, where Tronson came across an Even or Oroch hunting camp that had been abandoned hastily when the Europeans approached. In addition to camp gear and food remains, Tronson found an old rifle, a spear, and a "canoe," which from his description we recognize as a version of an Eskimo or Koryak kayak:

The canoe, a perfect model of neatness, was constructed of a light framework nine feet [3 meters] long, sharp at both ends, and covered with the skins of some animal; the hair being removed. A circular aperture in the centre surrounded by a narrow ledge was adapted to encircle the waist of the fisher as he squatted in the canoe. Two loops were attached to the sides for spears, and for a double-bladed paddle with which it is propelled. . . .

The spear was a curious instrument of destruction. A light shaft, 2 inches [5 centimeters] in circumference, and four feet long, was tipped on one end with bone, having a slit in the centre for the reception of a small barbed point. The latter was of copper, about 2 inches in length, wedge-shaped at one extremity, and barbed at the other; it was connected in the middle by a double line of gut, which diverged from the attachment; each end being neatly bound to the shaft, about a foot [30 centimeters] from either extremity. A hand-board [throwing stick], which measured a foot in length, completed the apparatus, the base fitted to the hand, and had a hole for the thumb; a shallow groove ran along the centre, with an ivory stop projecting. In throwing the spear, the hand is held horizontally over the head. The spear fits in the groove close to the stop and is balanced by the thumb when thrown. The hand-board acts as a lever. The barb, in striking a bird, leaves the end of the shaft, which is dragged by the wounded animal or bird, till caught against the ledge of a rock, branch of a tree, or some other obstacle. (1859: 125–26)

If this was a typical Even maritime craft, rather than an exceptional case of a boat left by a wayward Koryak individual hunting in Even territory, then the regular use of short, Koryak-type skin kayaks and hunting gear must have extended as far south as Ayan Bay. What is most surprising about Tronson's encounter is that the technological assemblage he described in great detail—the kayak, harpoon, and throwing board—are "Eskimo" in every detail, and the interpretation of how the harpoon functioned is consistent with Eskimo technology.

The presence of kayaks on the western shore of the Sea of Okhotsk also makes sense of a duck hunt observed in 1785 by Martin Sauer (1802), who served as the secretary for the Billings expedition. During this hunt, 50 boats went to sea to drive molting ducks into the shallows and ashore, where hunters in 200 more craft slaughtered them. Sauer's colorful description of the hunt does not provide details on these boats, but this drive on the open sea could not have been conducted in open canoes.

THE SAKHA: TURKIC CATTLE BREEDERS IN THE YAKUTIAN SUBARCTIC

Today the Sakha, known as the Yakut until the mid-20th century, are the largest group in the Lena River basin. They comprise some 478,000 people (per the 2010 Russian census) centered around the city of Yakutsk in Eastern Siberia. In the 1600s, when the Russians appeared there, the Sakha mostly lived on the Vilyuy River, part of the Aldan-Lena river system, with smaller groups around the mouth of the Olekma and on the upper Yana River. The Sakha are of Turkic origin, having migrated from central Western Asia during the 5th through the 8th centuries CE and expanding to their present limits in the 1300s, when they floated on rafts down the Lena until they reached the mid-Lena region, then inhabited by the Yukagir and Evenk. According to James Forsyth, Yakut cattle and horse breeders found an ideal home "in the lowlands around the northern bend of the Lena and the lower reaches of its eastern tributary, the Aldan, where amid the larch forest were areas of meadowland providing grazing and hay for their horses and oxen" (1994: 55). After mixing with Yukagir, Evenk, and Even people and acquiring their current name, the Sakha now live in the central part of the Sakha Republic, in the eastern portion of the Taimyr Peninsula, on the Lena delta and the Olenek, Anabar, and Yana rivers, west along the Vilyuy River, and on the Okhotsk coast. Before the 18th century, the Yakut used the same types of bark canoes and skin boats as neighboring groups, mainly those they inherited from the Yukagir and Evenk, and in later days they used dugout boats and planked boats, some of which they adapted from Russian designs.

Sakha Bark Canoes in the Lena Basin

In 1899, Otis T. Mason studied a model of a Yakut Lena-type birch-bark canoe (MAE 701-51) collected by Alexander von Middendorff in East Yakutia in 1846, which he had borrowed from the Museum of Anthropology and Ethnology (fig. 7.5). Mason wrote:

> The Yakut pointed canoe is . . . made in sections of birch bark, of which, in the model here studied, there are four in number, passing around from gunwale to gunwale, overlapping and stitched together. The bottom is strengthened by adding broad strips of bark from end to end and sewing them down at their edges. At the ends the Yakut canoe is shaped like a snout, the line from bottom upward being incurved. The joint at the ends is a very simple one, the edges of the bark cut to shape and sewed together. The gunwale is formed by a binding of bark turned over and hemmed down: the edges showing on the outside and inside. Two thwarts are held in place by lashing through both ends of the thwart and fastened through the bark sides. The canoe is held in shape by means of flat, wide ribs, whose ends are concealed under the bark binding of the gunwale. The Yakut canoe is a wide craft, better suited to freight than to speed. As the model here described is rougher than the others shown, it is possible that the larger ones have better elements of construction. (Mason and Hill 1901: 537)

We should here remark on one detail mentioned by Mason: the gunwale, whose construction by this hemming

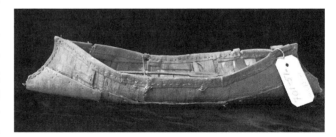

Fig. 7.5. Another Kunstkamera model (MAE 701-51) that Mason and Hill (1901) illustrated is a Yakut Lena-type specimen that Alexander Fedorovich von Middendorff collected in the Lena valley of East Yakutia in 1846. This model has the pointed ends typical of Amur-style canoes, although its shape among the Sakha, who live well north of the Amur, is less pronounced. (Photograph: Evguenia Anichtchenko; courtesy Museum of Anthropology and Ethnography)

method, rather than by turning over one of the gunwales, weakens the canoe's resistance to longitudinal tension, restricting both the volume of the load that can be carried and the size of the canoe. It is likely that only a rather short canoe could be constructed in this way; larger ones would collapse. In the old Lena-type Tungus pointed bark canoes, the gunwales were made stronger to avoid such problems. On the other hand, the small Middendorff model in the Museum of Anthropology and Ethnology may not have been an accurate replica; the Sakha were known to build strong bark boats. Mason's little model is amplified by Antropova, who studied Sakha culture and canoes in the mid-1950s and wrote:

> In the southern part of Yakutia, the birch-bark boat had a wider distribution [than in northern Yakutia]. It was often called *tuos tyy*, "birch-bark boat," or *tongus tyyta*, "Tungus boat"; sometimes it was also called *omuk ongochoto*—"strange boat," according to Andrei Popov. Its form and construction were like those of the Evenk boat. A birch-bark boat with pointed, undercut ends was used among the southwestern Sakha people, similar to the boat type common in the Yenisey region; but more characteristic for the Yakut was a birch-bark boat with an elongated bottom from which the pointed ends sloped upward, familiar in the Lena region. (2005: 9)

In 1896, Wacław Sieroszewski (1993: 526), a Polish anarchist exiled to Yakutia, studied the construction of Sakha boats and speculated on their origin. He wrote that the Sakha might have learned how to build the western Yenisey birch-bark canoe from the Ket people. His conclusion was based on language studies by Matthias A. Castrén (1858: 234) proposing a borrowing of boat names: the Sakha name for a bark canoe was *tyy* or *ty*, while the Yenisey Ostyak (Ket) name for the same boat was *tii* or *ti*. On the other hand, Sieroszewski found that the Sakha expanded log boat was based on the Yukagir model.

The proto-Yakut people—that is, their immediate Turk ancestors—migrated across the lands of the Southern Samoyed as they entered the Lena River basin from the south. A label accompanying a 2009 Yakut exhibition at the Museum of Anthropology and Ethnology in St. Petersburg presented the idea that the Yakut learned to make their *urasa*, a conical tent covered with birch bark, from the Sayan Samoyed. This connection also suggests that the Yakut birch-bark canoe

might have originated in early Samoyed lands; not only is it of the Yenisey type, but the Sakha took their word for "bark canoe" from the Yeniseyan-speaking Ket.

Baron Gerhard Maydell, working first for the Yakutian governor and later for the Russian Academy of Sciences from 1868 to 1870, mapped the wide Yakutian administrative territory, which started east of the Yenisey River and stretched north to the Arctic Ocean and the Sea of Okhotsk. He also wrote about the history of the Russian explorers of Yakut lands, the armed gangs and hunters who were there first, and the Native people, publishing his studies in three volumes (1896). Maydell documented all he saw in Eastern Siberia, including manufacture of the vetka, which was still in wide use in those years because of its light weight and easy handling. A single man could carry one of these birch-bark canoes made for three people on his shoulders, and it could be navigated by a single man with a double-ended paddle in whitewater streams where even the lightest wooden boat could not be used. North of the Verkhoyansk Mountains, bark canoes were not used because there were no trees large enough to make them; to build a vetka, one needed a large sheet of birch bark without branches. If multiple sheets were used, the boatbuilder sewed them together with long pieces of larch root, covering holes and weak spots with patches. Once the bark cover was prepared, the maker began to build the frame. Two straight 5-centimeter-thick poles of birch formed the gunwales, bound together at their ends with larch roots; between them were set 71-centimeter-long horizontal thwarts in two places, opening the frame into the shape of the canoe. The maker then sewed the bark sheet to the gunwales. Then thin 8- to 10-centimeter-wide laths split from pine or spruce were bent to support the round bottom of the canoe, with their ends fastened beneath the gunwales. Once complete, the canoe required caulking with a resinous mixture; the Sakha boiled thin slices of birch bark in milk to create a waxy-looking black pitch that they used to seal seams and holes.

Maydell (1896) also informs us that during his extensive travels along the Yakutian rivers and lakes, he frequently found canoes left in the bushes at crossing places. These abandoned boats were usually in reasonable condition and needed only treatment with "birch wax" to make them watertight. Only once during his travels in the Eastern Siberian forest did Maydell need to have a bark canoe made; his three Sakha companions completed it in a single day. Figs. 7.6 and 7.7 illustrate two large Sakha birch-bark canoes in the collection of the Yakutsk Museum. In locations where suitable

Fig. 7.6. This large birch-bark canoe (no. 2) in the Yakutsk Museum follows the Yenisey style: it is long and narrow, and its gunwales extend straight out beyond the bark hull. (Courtesy Yakutsk Museum of History and Culture and Peoples of the North)

Fig. 7.7. Unlike Yakutsk canoe no. 2 (see fig. 7.6), this canoe has curved stem posts that rise from the keel and project above the bow and stern, as do the Amur and half-decked Chunya Evenk canoes on the Lower Tunguska River in the Yenisey River system. Before this photo was taken, the canoe was moved outdoors onto the snow from its tight storage location. (Photograph: Yakutsk Museum of History and Culture and Peoples of the North)

birch bark was unavailable, Maydell found people using a flat-bottomed three-plank boat: one plank formed the bottom and the other two the sides. These plank canoes existed all across the Verkhoyansk and Kolyma regions.

Skin Boats in the Lena Basin and on the Sea of Okhotsk

The Yakut were cattle and horse breeders and active traders and middlemen who traveled widely in Eastern Siberia. They lived in yurts covered with birch bark, skins, or felt, and likely always had horse, cow, and yak skins available, as well as skins from other mammals such as seal, reindeer, and moose, which they acquired through hunting, trade, or war.

In written sources, we find many references to Yakut skin boats, mostly from inland regions near the Lena River, which was their major population base. We know of one skin boat east of the Lena, among the Yakut-influenced Yukagir tribe called the Yandyr; to the west, on the upper Anabar and Olenek rivers, the Sakha used skin boats in conjunction with reindeer breeding. Finally, coastal Sakha who lived on the Shantar Islands in the Sea of Okhotsk, which were formerly Nivkh land, might have used skin boats for sea hunting and trade. In 1844, when Middendorff (1856) reported seeing thousands of migrating whales in Okhotsk—perhaps one of the richest hunting places for sea mammals on the entire Siberian coast—he was traveling from Ayan to Uda Bay, opposite the Shantar Islands, in a large open skin boat (10 by 2.7 meters) built by Yakut or other Native seamen in Ayan. The origin and construction of Middendorff's boat were explained in a contemporary diary written by Karl von Dittmar, who wrote that when he visited the Russian port of Ayan circa 1855, he found among the marine and naval officers and sailors there a company of Tungus, Yakut, and Aleut men, who had been brought there with their baidars to catch fish for the Russians (1890b: 54). Thus Midderdorff's large skin boat was of either Tungus, Yakut, or Aleut origin.

In the travel diary of Evert Ysbrants Ides, a Russian ambassador to China, compiled and edited by the Dutch traveler, mapmaker, and author Nicolas Witsen, we find a summary of the regions and peoples of much of Northern Eurasia. Ides's contacts ranged from the Samoyed at the Barents Sea coast to the Evenk, Yukagir, Sakha, Mongol, Tatars, Chukchi, and Koryak in Eastern Siberia and along the Amur coast. Ides noted many Native boats, including skin boats on the Lena River, about which Witsen remarked, "The neighboring heathens, or Tatars, make use of little leather boats . . . which are very swift" (1706: 105). The Tatars in this reference could be non-Christian peoples, such as the Yakut, Yukagir, Evenk, or Mongol. If Johan G. Georgi's (1776b: 271) drawing (see fig. 7.1, page 137) is correct, the Yukagir and Yakut used a small kayaklike skin boat in the Lena River basin. By the 1600s, the Yakut had reached the Lena River estuary and the Arctic Ocean region, where they mixed with the Yukagir-speaking Yandyr, who lived between the Lena and Yana rivers (Willerslev 2007). Georgi's Yukagir skin kayak could be from this location, since some features in the drawing link it to the Yakut—including the man riding an ox, which would not be likely for a Yukagir.

Waldemar Jochelson (1933) wrote about a Yakut legend telling of a Buryat or Mongol man who appeared on the upper Lena River in a skin boat and met a rich Yakut, with whom he became friends. This could indicate that skin boats were found along most of the river, from the south to the north, and used by the Yakut as well as the Evenk, Yukagir, Mongol, and Buryat in this inland region. The southern connection was of particular interest to F. B. Steiner, a scientist in Prague who wrote a paper exploring the origin of Yakut skin boats. In his paper, he explained that "the original Tungus birch-bark vessel is the only Yakut boat whose design shows an adaptation to Subarctic hunting culture; that skin boats, if present in the area, have come from the southwest; and finally, that the Yakut word *xayik*, if [referring to] anything other than a European boat, certainly did not mean a skin boat" (1939: 183).

CHAPTER 8

PACIFIC SIBERIA

CHUKOTKA, KAMCHATKA, AND THE KURIL ISLANDS

In his introduction to a translation of Georg W. Steller's 1774 account of discoveries during Vitus Bering's Second Kamchatka Expedition (1740–42) in the North Pacific, the American anthropologist James W. VanStone (1959) summarized the German naturalist's ideas about the peopling of the Americas from Asia. Steller was one of the first to propose Asian origins for North American Indians based on similarities between Siberian Natives he was familiar with (including Chukchi, Koryak, Itelmen, and Siberian Yupik Eskimo) and the Eskimo and Aleut he met in Alaska. His theory of connections across the Bering Strait proved to be correct (see chapter 10, page 215), and one of his supporting observations relates to skin boats—kayaks and the open skin boats that Russians called baidars—which were used by peoples living on both sides of the Bering Strait. Regarding Eskimo boats, Steller wrote:

> Their canoes (kayaks) are of a construction very suitable to their needs, easy to carry on land and fast in the water. They are made of wood or of extremely thin whale ribs covered with seal skin, with the exception of an opening in the middle which has a raised rim made of whale bone or wood to prevent water from entering. This hole is made in such a way that only one man can get in and seat himself in the canoe, stretching his legs in front of him. The man seated in the canoe ties around his body a piece of skin fastened to the rim that protects him completely from the water. They place on the seams a kind of tar or paste, it is claimed, made of seal oil. In these canoes they carry all the equipment they need for fishing for whales, sea horses [walruses], narwhals, seals, etc. These small canoes are only for the men; they are pointed at both ends and are approximately 20 feet long [6 meters] by 18 inches [46 centimeters]

or 2 feet [61 centimeters] wide. The man who is within has only one paddle, but it is flattened at both ends and is used for paddling alternately, first on one side and then on the other. Besides these small canoes, they have others which are much larger and more unprotected, and in these the women are obligated to paddle. These canoes (baidar or umiak) are constructed with the same materials as the others and are large enough to carry more than twenty persons at a time. (Quoted in VanStone 1959: 102)

Far northeastern Siberia is a mountainous region that bears little resemblance to the lowland river basins of Central and Western Siberia (map 16). Its fast-running streams and rivers are relatively short and steep, and there are few lakes or large areas of bog or swamp. The mountainous terrain resulted in low population densities for its interior peoples, while the coasts and the near-coast Arctic tundra regions allowed for larger concentrations of people owing to productive reindeer-herding pastures and an abundance of sea mammals. The main north-flowing rivers here are the Yana, Indigirka, Omolon, and Kolyma. The Chukchi Peninsula has a few medium-sized rivers, such as the Anadyr and Penzhina, but they are short and have steep gradients, making river travel less common than river crossing; only during the winter could the lower portions of these rivers be used as highways.

Unlike the forested regions of Siberia, the open country of the tundra coasts and mountain regions was suitable for reindeer sledge travel, enabling the Chukchi to cover long distances with great speed. Before reindeer sledging began about 1,500 years ago, the sea coasts and rivers were the major communication and transport corridors and offered access to maritime resources and trade for cultures with maritime capabilities. It is there that we find the most technically advanced watercraft in Eurasia: skin-covered kayaks

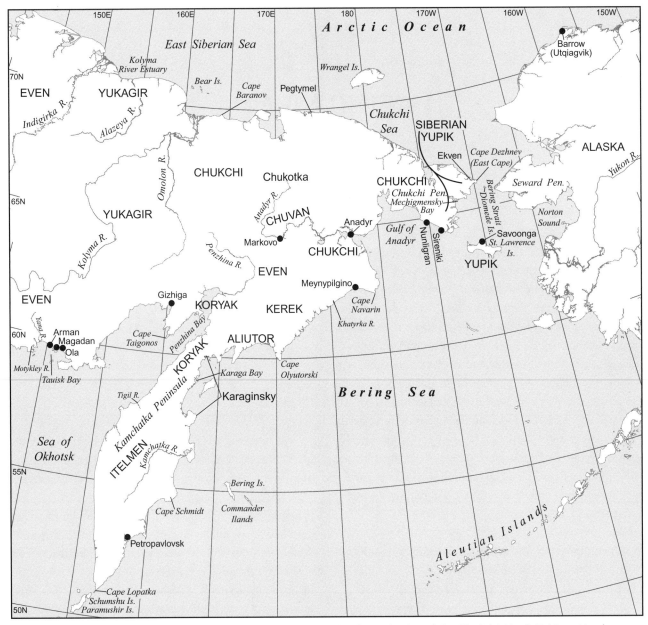

Map 16. Pacific Siberia and Chukotka, Kamchatka, and the Kuril Islands: territories of the Chukchi, Yupik Eskimo, Kerek, Koryak, Itelmen, and Kushi Ainu. (Dan Cole, Smithsonian Institution)

and open skin boats that were perfected over thousands of years by people whose survival depended on light, efficient, easily repairable boats that could operate in rough and seasonally icy seas.

Contact between Asia and Alaska has taken place since the first Siberians entered North America, about 15,000 to 20,000 years ago. Prehistoric contacts between Kamchatka and the Aleutian Islands may have occurred as early as 5,000 years ago, and archaeologists have found Asian iron and bronze on St. Lawrence Island and mainland Alaska that dates to the 3rd or 4th century CE. The peoples whose boating

traditions this chapter documents—the Chukchi, Yupik Eskimo, Kerek, Koryak, Itelmen, and Kushi/Ainu—were in contact with Russian explorers, Pomor sailors, and Cossack military cadres beginning in the 16th century. Evidence of these connections comes from Alaskan archaeological sites in the form of glass beads, tobacco, and other goods from Russian, Manchu, and Chinese sources that were exchanged for Alaskan fur, jade, ivory, and other products. The ancestors of these northeastern Asian peoples were deeply involved in this early trans-Beringian trade, which was made possible by centuries of development of both seagoing boats and navigational skills. Because Alaska was a market destination as well as a source of the trade goods, people, and technology that crossed the 90-kilometer- (56-mile-) wide Bering Strait, we extend our discussion of Eurasian boating history into Alaska in an epilogue. Much of the instigation for these contacts during the past millennium came from Chukchi and Siberian Yupik middlemen.

THE CHUKCHI: REINDEER-HERDING WARRIORS AND TRADERS

The Chukchi live on the Chukchi Peninsula in the Russian province of Chukotka in northeastern Russia. They were the last indigenous group in the Far East to succumb to Russian power—but only after a long history of repulsing military attacks, first by Russian-backed Cossacks and later by the Russian army and navy. Even in the 1820s, when the Russian naval lieutenant Ferdinand P. von Wrangel explored the Arctic Ocean coast, Russia did not have full access to Chukchi lands. Before this period of Chukchi domination, the Yukagir had prospered as middlemen between the Chukchi and Russians, but the Russian advance and Chukchi competition soon decimated the Yukagir. The Chukchi were both respected and feared by their neighbors—the Siberian Eskimo, Even, and Koryak as well as the Yukagir—for their trade and military capabilities, which brought them wealth, territory, and prestige. In the 19th century, under Russian rule, the Chukchi created a wide-ranging trade network in northeastern Siberia based on reindeer sledge travel in the interior and voyaging along the coast that took them as far as Alaska.

Waldemar Bogoras (1904–09), Nikolai Dikov (1977, 1978), Sergei Arutiunov and William Fitzhugh (1988), Anna Kerttula (2000), Igor Krupnik (1993), Krupnik and Mikhail Chlenov (2013), and Bogoslovskaya, Slugin, Zagrebin, and Krupnik (2016) all have described the cultures and history of Chukotka. The Siberian Eskimo preceded the Chukchi by at least two millennia in the Siberian sector of the Bering and Chukchi sea region. The Chukchi expansion into the Anadyr lowland probably began in the latter part of the first millennium CE and, aided by rapid reindeer sled transport, resulted in a long history of armed confrontations with their neighbors between 1100 and 1700. Dikov believed climate change stimulated the development of the Eskimo maritime economy, especially whaling, at the same time that Chukchi reindeer herders began to move into the northeastern Siberian tundra and Arctic Ocean coast. The Medieval Climate Optimum may have made reindeer herding chancy along the forest-tundra fringe due to winter rain, which can cause reindeer pasture to ice over. As the Chukchi reached the Arctic coast, they found a new Yukagir and Eskimo market for their Russian and Chinese metal, beads, tobacco, and other trade goods. They began to diversify their technology and economy, adding Eskimo adaptations to their herding, trading, and warfare skills and adopting elements of Eskimo culture such as waterproof gutskin clothing, oil lamps, toggling harpoons, kayaks, and large, light, open skin boats. Once introduced to the cultural and natural resources of the Beringian region, the Chukchi became a transformative force, mastering most of Chukotka in the centuries before Europeans arrived and initiating trade directly with Asian Pacific coast and Alaskan tribes.

Scientists today find Dikov's climate-stimulated theory simplistic, but excavations in Alaska and northeastern Siberia have substantiated his broad outline of Chukchi expansion and diversification and Eskimo maritime intensification during the past 1,500 years (Bronshtein, Dneprovsky, and Savinetsky 2016). By the 1800s, Chukchi tribes had replaced or assimilated many Eskimo settlements on the Bering Sea coast and on the Chukchi Sea coast between the Kolyma River and the Bering Strait. For example, the Chukchi displaced the so-called Shelagi people who lived east of the Kolyma River, who were probably the westernmost Eskimo-like tribe known. Archaeological evidence of former Eskimo occupation has been found as far west as Cape Schmidt and the Bear Islands near the Kolyma River (Okladnikov and Beregovaya 1971; Dikov 1977). Added support for the existence of these former western Eskimo territories comes from oral history of a legend recorded by Wrangel (1839) about a sea voyage to Alaska circa 1650 by Siberian Eskimos called the Onkilon, presumably before the Chukchi arrival on the Siberian coast (Krauss 2005).

An Ancient Maritime Adaptation

After settling on the Chukotka coast, the Chukchi adopted Eskimo maritime hunting technology, including their large skin boats and sea kayaks. The Chukchi might not have built maritime skin boats before circa 1500, so they did not contribute to the development of early Eskimo boats; later, the increasingly mixed Chukchi-Eskimo population made both large open skin boats and kayaks following Eskimo styles. Antropova (1961) found the Chukchi and Eskimo open boats similar in design and construction, and the same holds for their inland and maritime kayaks, according to Eugene Arima (1987) and Jarmo Kankaanpää (1989).

A remarkable series of petroglyphs at Pegtymel on the Arctic coast of Chukotka provides a visual record of the ancient coastal hunting economy and mode of life there. Dikov (1999, 2004) assumed the carvings date from the late Bronze Age to the 1st millennium CE, while Vladimir Pitulko (2016) dates them to about 1000 CE. Pegtymel rock art (fig. 8.1) depicts people hunting reindeer in the spring, using skis and accompanied by dogs; fall hunting at river crossings using kayaks with double-bladed paddles; and whaling with skin boats and harpoons. Prominent among the carvings are images of people with large mushroom shapes atop their heads, which Dikov interpreted as evidence of a hallucinogenic mushroom cult. This notion is not as fanciful as it might appear: the Chukchi and other Arctic Siberian peoples practiced rituals that included trances brought on by drinking reindeer urine after the animals had gorged on hallucinogenic *Amanita muscaria* mushrooms, which sprout in great quantities on the tundra in midsummer. However, rock art showing similar "mushroom people" has been found in Central Asia, far south of the range of this mushroom species, so it is more likely that the Pegtymel images simply portray a widespread headdress style.

Chukchi Skin Kayaks

Tappan Adney had an interest in Siberian as well as American boats and constructed a few models of Siberian boats that

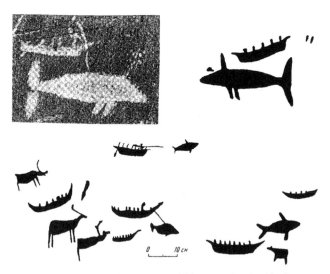

Fig. 8.1. Rock art at the Pegtymel River on the Arctic Ocean coast of Chukotka depicts hunters spearing caribou and hunting whales in open skin boats (*angyapit*). Other images show humans wearing mushroom-shaped headdresses, which are common in northeastern Siberian Iron Age rock art. (From Dikov 1999; composite image adapted by Marcia Bakry)

are now in the Mariners' Museum in Newport News, Virginia. Because kayaks were a sideline for Adney, the part of his book that discusses them was written by Howard Chapelle, but it does include a few words about Chukchi kayaks:

> The Chukchi on the Siberian side of Bering Strait use a kayak that is on the same model as the one found at Norton Sound, in Alaska. The Chukchi kayak differs only at the ends, which are wholly functional and without the handgrips that distinguish the Alaskan type [*incorrect; Chukchi kayaks do have hand grips—Eds.*]. There is also a crude Chukchi river kayak covered with reindeer skin, but its design is not represented in an American museum. (Adney and Chapelle 1964: 195)

Antropova (1961) noted that skin boats with keels had a more limited range than other types of boats and canoes and were used only in the northeastern part of Siberia, principally along the coast from the Kolyma River to the Sea of Okhotsk. Both types of boats—the kayak and the larger open skin boats—existed in the same area. However, she remarked on the spotty distribution of the kayak; by the beginning of the 20th century, it had disappeared from all the major whaling areas and was used only in the Sea of Okhotsk, Kamchatka, the middle reaches of the Anadyr River, and the western Chukchi Sea. Because of its rarity by the early 1900s, the Siberian (Yupik) Eskimo skin kayak is not well known, although it was used throughout Siberian Eskimo lands in earlier times. One of the few depictions of the Siberian Eskimo kayak is a sketch (fig. 8.2c) published by Waldemar Bogoras based on a 1901 photograph (1904–09: fig. 47c) taken in the Chukotka Eskimo village of Wute'en, now known as Sireniki. Bogoras's brief comment said it was 15 feet long and was similar to Chukchi kayaks (135), and his illustration shows a round cockpit placed well astern of the kayak midpoint.

The Chukchi used to build two types of kayaks, one for hunting marine mammals and the other for spearing wild reindeer at river or lake crossings. Bogoras also provided information on a Reindeer Chukchi kayak he measured and illustrated, along with its paddle (fig. 8.2b). This craft was made of deerskin rather than seal skin, had a teardrop-shaped cockpit, and, since it was used on rivers and lakes, was used without a spray skirt. The double-bladed paddle had round "poplar leaf" blades with a deer spear attached at one end. Kankaanpää discussed Bogoras's drawing:

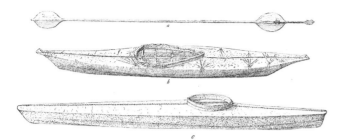

Fig. 8.2. Waldemar Bogoras's Chukchi monograph illustrates (*a*) a Reindeer Chukchi paddle/spear; (*b*) a kayak of reindeer skin drawn from models; and (*c*) a rare Siberian Eskimo (Yupik) seal-skin kayak drawn from field photographs. (From Bogoras 1904–09: fig. 44)

The drawing [Fig. 8.2b] . . . shows a fairly short, wide, and high craft characterized by a teardrop-shaped cockpit and very steeply rising prow and stern, which meet the keelson at an acute angle. The gunwales seem quite stout, the ribs and stringers fairly thin. The number of bottom stringers is not evident from the drawing, but the chines [the longitudinal stringer that causes the angle change in the hull when the boat is seen in cross-section—see glossary] on the cover suggest three were used. The deck is flat,

and there seems to be almost no sheer; the shape of the keel line is not discernable, nor is the number of deck stringers. According to the text, the cover is of reindeer skin. The stem and stern are oddly flattened; however, the drawing is based not on a full-size kayak but on a model, so the structural details and proportions may not be represented accurately. (1989: 18)

Reindeer Chukchi kayaks are also known from two full-size examples. One was collected by N. I. Sokolnikov for the St. Petersburg Russian Ethnographic Museum between 1904 and 1907 (fig. 8.3a). Rousselot (1994: 250, fig. 13-5) described and provided a line diagram of a second full-size Reindeer Chukchi kayak, also covered with reindeer skin, in the Museum für Völkerkunde in Munich (no. 99-120), which was probably collected at about the same time. David Zimmerly's documentation of the Sokolnikov kayak (1986: fig. 11), shown as fig. 8.3b, indicates that these kayaks resembled the Chukchi maritime version but had features that made them more suitable for river and lake use, especially for portaging and for spearing swimming caribou. Made of deerskin, which is lighter but less waterproof than seal skin, these kayaks could be used for only short periods before they had to be dried out, because their covers became water-soaked and stretched.

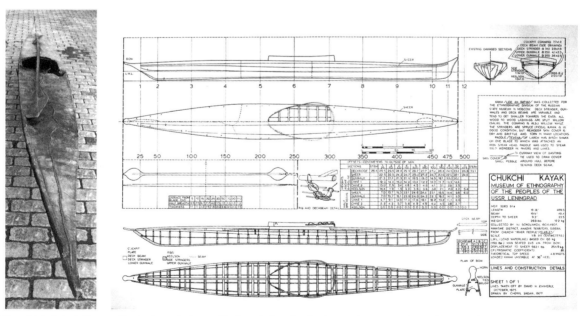

Fig. 8.3. a. N. I. Sokolnikov collected a reindeer-skin kayak for the St. Petersburg Russian Ethnographic Museum between 1904 and 1907 while he was working among the Reindeer Chukchi. (RME 6779-46) *b.* David Zimmerly's documentation (1986: fig. 11) shows the Sokolnikov boat's bow and stern handle projections, V bottom, and teardrop-shaped cockpit. This type of kayak was light and maneuverable, but the reindeer skin quickly became waterlogged, so the craft could be used for only a short period before it had to be dried out. (*a*: photograph by I. Tkachenko; courtesy Russian Ethnographic Museum; *b*: illustration by and courtesy David Zimmerly)

The design of the Chukchi inland kayak preserves some of the features seen in the Georgi illustration of a possible Yukagir kayak on the Arctic Ocean coast east of the Lena River (Georgi 1776b; see also see fig. 7.1, page 137). Both are fully decked, have a small manhole, are covered with deer or seal skin, and are rather short, no more than 3 or 4 meters long. These similarities suggest, if not a common origin, then at least a degree of design continuity. Possibly the resemblance is explained by the Yukagir's westward migration along the Arctic Ocean coast from an earlier homeland in the region of the Lena, Kolyma, and Anadyr rivers (see chapter 7's section on the Yukagir, page 136). Yukagir, Eskimo, and Chukchi kayaks show that the East Cape Old Bering Sea–culture model from the Ekven site (see fig. 8.11a, page 168) was not a fanciful creation but a representation of an ancient tradition of Chukotka kayak building.

A rare example of a Maritime Chukchi kayak was collected by the Swedish explorer N. A. E. Nordenskjöld during the winter of 1879 while he was on the Swedish *Vega* expedition of 1878–80. Now in Stockholm at the Swedish Ethnological Museum, this kayak was called *ana'kua*, and Zimmerly later photographed and measured it and recorded its vital statistics (fig. 8.4a–b). It is unique among Beringian kayaks for its square cockpit, flat deck, and absence of cockpit combing. Another unusual Bering Sea Eskimo kayak, in this case a model (MAE 20-22; see fig. 8.21a–b, page 178), was collected circa 1840 by Ilya Vosnesenskya, a Russian ethnographer of Russian America, in Mechigmensky Bay on the Chukotka coast of the Bering Strait. Vosnesensky described it as Koryak, but its collection location suggests it might be a rare example of a Siberian Yupik Eskimo kayak, made before kayaks passed out of use there.

Inflated *Pyg-Pyg* *Skin Floats*

The Chukchi and Yupik people had other types of water transport besides the kayak. Some rafts and floats they probably inherited from southern peoples, while others, such as rafts made from reindeer sleds, they might have invented themselves. Traveling in Chukchi territory in Anadyr in 1915–16, Sakari Pälsi recorded skin boats and saw inflated seal skins being used as floats; they were known as *pyg-pyg*. Tied together, several pyg-pyg could float a sledge, a man, and his dogs to safety when the sea ice began to melt. A similar skin float was used to cross rivers (Nefedkin 2003: 78). Pälsi photographed a dog sledge being paddled in open water, buoyed by skin floats, after an unsuccessful hunting excursion on the ice (fig. 8.5). This simple inflated raft resembles Mongolian and Chinese skin rafts (discussed in chapters 6, page 132, and 9, page 210). Similar floats used by the 19th-century Canadian Sadlermiut (Inuit) in the Canadian Arctic appear in a famous illustration from George Francis Lyon's 1824 exploration in northern Hudson Bay (Lyon 1825).

Ludmila Ainana wrote of old Naukan Eskimo traditions, including the use of skin boats and pyg-pyg floats, in the Smithsonian's *Crossroads Siberia/Alaska* exhibition:

> Our entire life comes from the sea. Eskimos settled where the water remained ice-free in winter, where

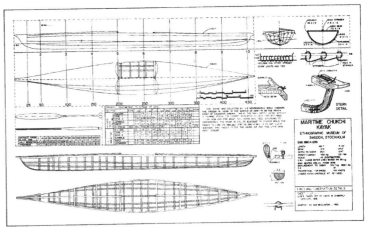

Fig. 8.4. a. This Maritime Chukchi kayak (SEM 1880.4.1255) was collected on N. A. E. Nordenskjöld's *Vega* expedition in the winter of 1879. If complete, this kayak is notable as the only known Arctic kayak lacking a cockpit combing or a way to secure a parka or spray skirt to the hull. Like the inland versions, it has bow and stern handle extensions and a V-shaped hull. *b.* David Zimmerly's documentation of this kayak. (*a.* Photograph by David Zimmerly [75ZM32-22]; courtesy Swedish Ethnological Museum, Stockholm; *b.* From Zimmerly 1986: fig. 10, used with permission)

Fig. 8.5. When proper skin boats were unavailable, Siberian Eskimo and Chukchi people, as well as Canadian Inuit, used *pyg-pyg* seal-skin floats, such as this one that Sakari Palsi photographed in 1915 or 1916 among the Chukchi on the Siberian coast (1917-VKK157). (Courtesy Finnish National Board of Antiquities)

trade venture could turn into an armed raid. Later, when he became an admiral and the head of the Russian-American trade company in Alaska, Wrangel (1839) wrote an account of the Alaskan territory and its people in which he described Chukchi trade between the two continents.

The Chukchi open skin boat (fig. 8.6) varied in size to suit local needs. As seen in fig. 8.7a–b, the construction of Chukchi and Eskimo angyapit were almost identical, although the Chukchi boat seen in these two models was more streamlined and made for a smaller crew. The lattice-like frame was made of driftwood, sometimes supplemented with whale bone, and the cover was of split walrus hide. Judging from archaeological finds (see below), its techno-logical development over the past 2,000 years was slow, and today's skin boats are not significantly different from their ancient prototype. Large open boats were used for hunting whale and walrus on the open sea and for camp moves and

walruses, whales and seals came close to the shore, and where there was a fishing stream or a bird colony nearby. Even if a place was not very convenient for humans but was rich in game, they would settle there. . . .

Winds, currents, ice floes, fog, storms, tides—all of this is Eskimo life, and at its heart there are sea mammals, fish, and birds. Everyday life, culture, and language of the Eskimos are saturated by an under-standing of their unbreakable ties with the sea. The toggling harpoon is one of the elements upon which our sea culture is based. Two other elements are inflated seal skins used as floats (*pyg-pyg*) and the *angyapik* (Russian, *baidara*), a boat with a wooden frame that is held together by sinew lashings and cov-ered with split walrus hides. These inventions, which undoubtedly date back more than two thousand years, have shaped the history of Asiatic Eskimos. (Ainana, Archirgina-Arsiak, and Tein 1996: 22–23)

Open Skin Boats in Chukchi Warfare and Trade

When Wrangel made his expedition from Kolyma to Chu-kotka in the 1820s, he entered Yukagir lands west of Chukchi territory. Until that point, Russians did not have safe access to Chukotka, and the Yukagir region was regarded as neutral territory between Russians and Chukchi where both parties interacted and traded. The Chukchi also made long sea voy-ages to trade goods between Alaska and Siberia, and often a

Fig. 8.6. This detailed illustration was prepared by an American Museum of Natural History artist for Waldemar Bogoras's Chukchi monograph. Its style set an example followed by many other authors and artists reporting on Chukchi and Eskimo open skin boats. (From Bogoras 1904–09: pl. 44a–c)

Fig. 8.7. These open skin boats were called *baidaras* or *baidars* by Russians, *iygytvet* by Chukchi (A), and *angyapit* by Siberian Yupik Eskimo (B). Both are nearly identical in design, probably because the Chukchi boat design (MAE 407-20) was copied from the Siberian Yupik version (MAE 4211-28) when the Chukchi came to the Arctic coast from the interior about 1,500 years ago. Both are nearly identical to Eskimo boats on St. Lawrence Island and the Alaska mainland. Nikolai L'vovich Gondatti collected the Chukchi model angyapik in 1898. (Photographs: Evguenia Anichtchenko; courtesy Museum of Anthropology and Ethnology)

trading voyages. Smaller boats were used for fishing and hunting birds and seal in drifting pack ice, which sometimes required the hunter to bring his craft singlehandedly onto the ice floe.

Antropova (1961), relying on Bogoras's documentation, described Chukchi open skin boats in the 19th century and their recent use. These boats, known in Chukchi as *lygytvet* (common vessels), were the coastal Chukchi's major means of ocean transport until the early 20th century, when planked wooden boats became available after the arrival

of whalers, metal axes, and planning tools. Larger versions were equipped with sails; sometimes they also had rudders, and later, in the mid-20th century, inboard and outboard motors were added.

A construction diagram for a Chukchi open skin boat and its rigging was illustrated by Sergei Bogoslovsky (fig. 8.8). Aleksandr Nefedkin describes such boats in his book on Chukchi warfare:

> The Chukotka boat [baidar]—light, portable, strong, and stable on the water—is made from walrus skins stretched over a wooden frame, with oars and a slanting sail. The wooden frame consists of thin . . . poles covered by the skin of a walrus. The hunting canoe for eight people was 6.1 meters long and 2.3 meters wide, and the weight was 130 to 160 kilograms. . . . A large boat, seating 20 to 30 people, was 15 meters long. Making a baidar on average takes between four and six skins, depending on its size. The skins are specially treated, dried, and then softened and wrapped around a wooden frame, then redried so they fit tightly to the wood. The bottom of the dried, ready-to-use canoe is slightly translucent and makes a sound like a tambourine. The thickest part of the walrus skin—its dorsal portion—is used for the keel of the baidar. . . . The skin covers have to be changed every year or, with careful use, every 2 to 3 years, because they become brittle. In general, it was easy to disassemble the canoe and even, if necessary, to reduce its size. These boats were used from the 18th to the beginning of the 20th century and are still in use in some Chukotka villages today.
>
> The crew were positioned as follows. The owner of the boat sat in front with a hook [to fend off ice]. The rowers used short single-bladed paddles. Discipline was strict in a baidar, and the men rowed synchronously and rested 5 to 10 minutes each hour. . . . [In times of war,] soldiers sat on the floor and helped row by pulling ropes tied to the ends of the oars. . . .
>
> By the end of the 18th century, baidars began using square sails of skins, but the main propulsion was still paddles. Hide boats of this type (called *angyapik* by Eskimos) were intended primarily for the hunting of large marine animals. For long-distance sea travel, [the Eskimos] used a special type of baidar. By the end of the 19th century, rectangular sails began to be

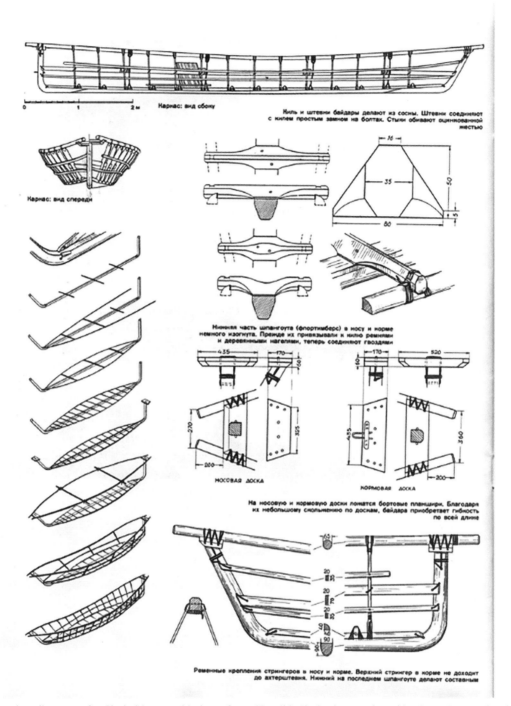

Fig. 8.8. Construction diagram of a Chukchi open skin boat from Sireniki, Chukotka, produced by Sergei Bogoslovsky. (From Bogoslovskaya 2007: 233)

used. For comparison, Eskimos had used large skin boats with sails as early as the 1830s. . . .

The Chuckhi often took fire into their canoes, keeping it in a box of sand or sod. When traveling upstream, the boat could be pulled by dogs or reindeer. For military travel, judging by documents, the

Chukchi used, along with baidars, an *odnoderevki* [expanded log boat] . . . , whose length was 3.7–5.8 meters, width 53–70 centimeters, and height 53–62 centimeters, and which was designed for movement on shallow rivers and lakes. . . . This boat was unstable, and when there were waves it could swamp;

consequently it could be dangerous for the hunter, who normally could not swim. (2003: 78–79)

The skin covers of Chukchi and Eskimo umiaks had to dry out after a day or two in the water. Fig. 8.9 shows a group of Chukchi resting or camping overnight under their upturned boat, waiting for it to dry and tighten before they continue their voyage. Fig. 8.10 is one of Pälsi's photos of 13 Chukchi paddlers at sea off Chukotka in 1917. While conducting ethnographic work in Chukotka in 1898, Nikolai L'vovich Gondatti collected a model of a Chukchi angyapik with a skin sail; the model is kept at the Museum of Anthropology and Ethnography in St. Petersburg (fig. 8.7, MAE 407-20).

THE SIBERIAN YUPIK: ESKIMO SKIN BOAT MASTERS OF THE BERING STRAIT AND CHUKOTKA

The Russian naval lieutenant Ferdinand P. von Wrangel, Baltic-German by origin, was the first to explore the Arctic Ocean coast from the Kolyma River to Chukotka during a long journey there in 1821–24. Along the coast he found remains of old stone and earth houses built by the ancient "Onkilon" (Eskimo) people. Nordenskjöld (1881) documented similar remains during the *Vega*'s voyage of 1878 through the Northeast Passage, where he met Chukchi people, then rapidly becoming the new masters of the Arctic coast. Wrangel's and Nordenskjöld's findings and later information on the Onkilon

Fig. 8.9. Boats covered with sea mammal skin (ideally split female walrus hide) can be used for only two to four days before the skin becomes waterlogged and begins to stretch and leak. On long voyages, the boats were taken out of the water to dry and became impromptu shelters (REM 318-297). (Courtesy Russian Ethnographic Museum)

Fig. 8.10. Chukchi and Eskimo open skin boats were highly seaworthy and could carry many people and goods along stormy coasts or across the Bering Strait for trade, war, and migration. Most new populations migrating from Siberia to Alaska probably arrived in skin boats. Sakari Pälsi photographed this Chukchi boat (VKK157_60) carrying 13 people off Chukotka in 1917. (Courtesy Finnish National Board of Antiquities)

suggest that the early pre-Chukchi settlers were Eskimo or Eskimo-like people who had vanished or been assimilated by the coastal Chuckhi.

As Robert Ackerman (1984) noted, the Bear Islands, in Kolyma Bay, were the western limit of the Siberian Eskimo, who had used open skin boats and dogsleds to hunt marine mammals since at least 500 CE. Archaeologists understand Siberian and Alaskan Eskimo history as a sequence of distinct cultures that evolved in the North Pacific and Beringian region over the past 3,000 to 4,000 years (Fitzhugh and Crowell 1988; B. Fitzhugh 2016; see other articles in Frisen and Mason 2016). This area was large and diverse enough—ranging from open-water Subarctic coasts to seasonally icebound Arctic shores, with great differences in ecology, animal species, weather patterns, and neighbors from region to region—that several Eskimo-related cultures and language groups could occupy the Bering Strait area at any given time, creating a multistrand historical web rather than a single evolutionary sequence of cultures (W. Fitzhugh 2009). The earliest evidence for indisputable Eskimo occupation of northeastern Siberia dates to the Okvik–Old Bering Sea period. By this time, about 2,000 to 1,000 years ago, all the major technologies needed for efficient sea mammal hunting—principally toggling harpoons, harpoon float gear, and skin boats—were available for people to use at the ice edge or in open or icy seas. For maritime hunting, the Eskimo employed various types of harpoons, spears, floats, nets, and other gear; for land hunting and fishing, they had bows and arrows, multipronged bird and fish spears, and hand- or dog-drawn sledges.

The Siberian Eskimo, whose culture and language properly are known as Yupik, once lived on the Chukotka Peninsula from the Kolyma River on the Arctic Ocean to Cape Navarin, and possibly farther south on the Bering Sea coast. These same people, sharing the same language and culture, also now occupy St. Lawrence Island in Alaska, and they have much in common, culturally and linguistically, with the Central Yup'ik people of southwestern Alaska and the Iñupiat of the Seward Peninsula and northern Alaska. These cultural, linguistic, and biological bonds point toward a common origin—as yet still unknown—in the Beringian region.

Many changes occurred during the past 3,000 years as these cultures developed their "Eskimo" character. New types of harpoons and boats were created, providing a stable economic basis for Eskimo culture. Then Eskimo traders introduced ceramics (and later bronze and iron) from Siberia. Still later came glass beads and tobacco, also via Siberia, but this time brought by Chukchi who had outmaneuvered Eskimo middlemen. Transberingian warfare became endemic as Siberia-Alaska trade intensified. During the past several hundred years, the territory and population of Yupik-speaking Siberian Eskimo has declined, due both to these conflicts and to assimilation by the Chukchi. Since the mid-1800s, climatic, economic, and political changes also have eroded the Siberian Eskimo's sea mammal–hunting way of life, while whale and walrus populations were decimated by American and, in the 20th century, Russian commercial hunting. Finally, the introduction of European diseases by traders and whalers took a toll on both Yupik and Chukchi populations.

Of all the Eurasian peoples, the Eskimo have been the ones most closely connected to skin boat and harpoon technology, which made their maritime economy possible. The Siberian Eskimo built both large open skin boats and skin kayaks but did not always use them concurrently during the past 2,000 years. Building and operating large open skin boats for hunting walrus and whale required specialized boat design and carpentry skills accrued over hundreds of years; equally important, boat owners needed detailed knowledge of marine conditions and navigation, as well as the leadership ability to successfully manage hunts for large sea mammals and to prosecute trading and warfare ventures across the Bering Strait.

Theories of Eskimo Skin Boat Origin

The "Eskimo problem"—meaning the question of the origin and development of Eskimo culture in Siberia, Alaska, Canada, and Greenland—has been a subject of international research for more than a century (Krupnik 2016; W. Fitzhugh 2016). The quest has produced hundreds of scientific papers and scores of theories about development stages, large-scale migrations across vast polar territories, the evolution of hunting methods and tools such as the toggle harpoon, and, of course, the Eskimo's skin boats and kayaks. There are far too many theories to review here, so instead we present a brief summary of the most viable ones.

A popular theory of Eskimo origins assumes that proto-Eskimo people moved into northeastern Siberia from Inner Asia—perhaps Mongolia or Southern Siberia, the region around Lake Baikal, or the early Holocene shores of the Sea of Okhotsk (H. Collins 1940; Rudenko 1961; Arutiunov and W. Fitzhugh 1988; W. Fitzhugh 2008; Dikov 2004; Rubicz and Crawford 2016). These ancestral Eskimo, like the Chukchi, Koryak, Itelmen, and Ainu, were at first inland people engaged in fishing, hunting, and gathering, just as their Stone Age ancestors had been. They fished in rivers and lakes, hunted elk and moose, and pursued wild reindeer at river crossings, perhaps with the help of birch-bark canoes. On Lake Baikal and along the coasts, they hunted seal.

The earliest known toggling harpoons were found at 6,000-year-old coastal sites in Northern Japan, suggesting technological development toward Eskimo culture and technology. Their first appearance in an archaeological context that can be considered as proto-Eskimo is at the 1500 BCE Chertav Ovrag site on the southern shore of Wrangel Island, 150 kilometers off the northern coast of Chukotka, where an Eskimo-like life would have been impossible without skin boats (Dikov 1988). Such boats, along with toggling harpoons, seal-thong lines, floats, and spear-throwers, were technological necessities for efficient maritime hunting. Over time, the proto-Eskimo became specialized marine mammal hunters, and as their technology improved, they were able to secure larger game such as walrus and eventually whale. Concurrently, their skills in building skin boats and kayaks improved until by 700 to 800 CE, the Eskimo of the Bering Strait Punuk culture had become efficient hunters of bowhead and gray whales. With these technological developments, Eskimo culture spread south into Kamchatka and the Okhotsk, west along the Arctic Ocean coast to Kolyma, across the Bering Strait to southern and northern Alaska, and, after 1200, to Canada and Greenland, making the Eskimo the second most widely distributed people in the world after Europeans (W. Fitzhugh 2008).

Skin boats were a crucial part of this phenomenal cultural and population dispersal. The Smithsonian's Paul Johnston, in his comprehensive *Seacraft of Prehistory*, noted that "some sort of pattern [can] be seen in the variety of boats used in Russian Siberia.…The skin boat—*baidar* or *baidarka*—seems to have been used by the so-called paleo-Siberians, the Chukchi north of the Gulf of Anadyr, the Koryaks and Kamchadals of the Kamchatka Peninsula, the Aleuts and Eskimo of many island groups (Kurils, Pribilof, Nunivak, St. Lawrence, Kodiak, and the Aleutians) around or near the Bering Strait and Alaska" (1980: 33). In keeping with early Scandinavian interpretation, Johnston considered Samoyed and Lapp skin boats in the Barents Sea to be a separate tradition from Beringian skin boats, one that might or might not have been associated with bark canoe building; he believed that these western two peoples first used skin boats and later turned to bark boats.

Theories are fine, but what evidence do we have about how and when northeastern Siberian peoples acquired their large open skin boats and kayaks? Below we present evidence for three scenarios dealing with the origin of skin boats in Arctic North America; on the Chukotka (Chukchi) and Kamchatka peninsulas; and in Okhotsk Sea environs, including Sakhalin Island and the Amur River estuary.

The Russian archaeologist Nikolai Dikov and others assumed that the Arctic maritime economy in Chukotka began with an inland hunting and fishing culture, based on caribou hunting on lakes and at river crossings, that in time was adapted for hunting sea mammals on the coast. This idea is based on late Stone Age finds on the lower Lena River that extend toward the Chukchi Peninsula. Dikov (1979: 157–59) believed that after interior hunters and fishermen became familiar with sea mammals in the Anadyr-Main-Penzhina river valley lowlands, they expanded their hunting grounds to the open sea, where they applied their technology to capture seal and walrus. This theory has much to recommend it, since it is known that skin boats were used on all the major Siberian rivers, usually in tandem with bark canoes.

The second theory posits that northern maritime adaptations began as incremental adjustments in warmer southern waters. Alexei P. Okladnikov (1959), the pioneering Russian archaeologist of Siberia, proposed that advances in open-sea hunting on the Sea of Okhotsk near or in the mouth of the Amur River, around Sakhalin Island, and perhaps in the

Japanese archipelago preceded northern maritime hunting in Chukotka. Many types of sea mammals and small whales, in addition to myriad anadromous fish species, migrated in and out of these rivers. As noted in chapter 9, the Nivkh along the Amur River and the Ainu on Sakhalin Island used harpoons to hunt seal, sea lion, and small whales and might have had skin boats. However, as Ackerman (1984) noted, the ethnographic cultural models on which this theory is based are too recent to illuminate the origins of Arctic marine mammal hunting, which can be traced back 8,000 years in Scandinavia; in Kodiak, Alaska; and in Hokkaido, Japan, where Jōmon-culture people began to use toggling harpoons 6,000 years ago (Yamaura 1998). On the other hand, the existence of open skin boats and kayaks from Chukotka to Sakhalin underlines the likelihood of early north-south cultural contacts along the shores of the Bering and Okhotsk seas. A study showing that the DNA of Koryak and Itelmen populations in Kamchatka is closest to that of a small population in the Amur-Sakhalin region reinforces the idea of a north-south cultural and biological continuum along the northwest coast of the North Pacific (Schurr, Sukernik, Starikovskaya, and Wallace 1999).

A third theory, citing Eskimo origins in Alaska, is based on the work of the American archaeologists Henry Collins, William S. Laughlin, and Don Dumond in the Aleutian Islands, southwestern Alaska, and the Bering Strait. Collins (1940) was able to reconstruct 2,000 years of continuous Eskimo cultural development on St. Lawrence Island in the strait and found that Eskimo culture was already fully developed by 1 CE, thus showing that sea mammal–hunting technology and skin boats had much earlier origins. The date of the Chertov Ovrag site on Wrangel Island, north of the Siberian coast of Chukotka, pushes back the date for harpoon-based Arctic marine mammal hunting another 1,500 years, to 3,500 years ago. Laughlin (1963) believed that the missing early stage of Eskimo maritime adaptation occurred along the southern edge of the Bering Land Bridge and southwestern Alaska when sea levels rose at the end of the last ice age, causing proto-Eskimo groups, with their skin boats and harpoons, to move north along the Alaskan coast into the Bering Strait. Dumond (1977) had similar ideas but believed that Eskimo culture originated in Southwest Alaska around the Alaska Peninsula and Kodiak Island, based on evidence of the early development of sea mammal–hunting technology and maritime adaptations in early Ocean Bay cultures by circa 5000 BCE.

Hans-Georg Bandi (1969) elaborated on Collins's and Laughlin's ideas by proposing that specialized Eskimo culture developed in the Bering Strait, with influence from Siberian Neolithic and Bronze Age cultures, 4,000 to 2,000 years ago. Along the strait, this population learned to hunt large sea mammals, especially walrus and sea lion, in icy waters, and by the early centuries of the Christian era, the Okvik and Old Bering Sea cultures were flourishing (Bronshtein, Dneprovsky, and Savinetsky 2016). By Punuk times, circa 600 to 1200 CE, Bering Strait Yupik Eskimo were hunting large whales from umiaks with toggling harpoons and floats. The earliest physical evidence of skin boats in this development sequence comes from 500 CE Old Bering Sea–culture grave finds of ivory models that probably represent kayaks (see below, page 168). By 800 CE, large open skin boats similar to the historic Eskimo umiak—called *baidara* in the Aleutian Islands and *angyak* in Kodiak—were being used; otherwise, those islands could not have been discovered and occupied. Recently, umiak boat parts have been found among remains at a Birnirk-culture site near Barrow (now named Utqiagvik), Alaska, dating from circa 800 to 1000 CE (Anichtchenko 2013; and see our epilogue, page 215). The problem with the Alaska origin theory is that the Eskimo are the most Asian-looking people in the Americas, and their biology has its roots in Asia 6,000 to 8,000 years ago, long after the ancestors of the American Indians had arrived in North America. Eskimo culture, on the other hand, could well have developed in southwest Alaska along with a new influx of Asians, followed by Neolithic, Bronze, and Iron Age influences from East and northeastern Asia.

Valentina Antropova, writing more than 50 years ago in her history of skin boats, turned this question in a different direction, away from generalized theories of Arctic adaptation and toward detailed archaeological studies of evolving boat construction:

> The issue of the origin of the various types of boats used by native Siberians and of their classification has almost never been dealt with in anthropological literature. Let us consider some of the knotty problems and attempt a preliminary conclusion. . . . It can be concluded that only the keeled boats of the native Siberian people were associated with the development of specialized sea transport and sea mammal hunting. . . . The origin of the keeled boat is manifestly associated with a coastal or littoral culture. Remains or pieces of kayaks are known on the Chukotka Peninsula from as early as Old Bering Sea sites (around 100 CE), and remains of skin boats are known from

early Punuk sites (around 1000 CE). In the past the distribution of keeled craft in Siberia was apparently wider than at the beginning of the 20th century. There are reports pointing to skin boats in the past farther west along the coast of the Arctic Ocean, but their construction has not been described. In some of the early engravings the skin boat of the Nenets externally gives the impression of a kayak. (2005: 33)

This type of technical boat study is now being pursued by Evguenia Anichtchenko (see epilogue, page 230).

The problem with Antropova's proposal is the continuing scarcity of early boat remains or detailed models or imagery. The absence of archaeological evidence and the ambiguity of rock art figures are daunting barriers to resolving the question of skin boat origins, both in the White and Barents seas region and along the North Pacific, Bering, and Chukchi sea coasts (but see Pegtymel circa 500–1500 CE; and our fig. 8.1, page 158). At present, we have no obvious signs of connections between the cultures of these two sea mammal–hunting regions (W. Fitzhugh 1998). Nordic skin boat development appears to have been truncated 2,000 years ago by the shift to planked boats during the Iron Age and by the absence of a long winter pack ice season that would necessitate use of skin boats. The North Pacific arena, including its northern seas, was far more permissive for sea mammal–hunting developments, as is evidenced by its 6,000 years of toggling harpoon use, plentiful stocks of large sea mammals, and skin boat technology sufficient for people to populate the Central Aleutian Islands circa 4000 BCE and even the remote western Aleutians by 2500 BCE (Veltre 1998). Therefore, it seems likely that open skin boats and kayaks developed in the broad arc of the North Pacific, between Amur, Chukotka, and western Alaska, where sea mammals were plentiful and icy sea conditions were present for long periods of the year. Development of decked skin boats from the bark canoes used for reindeer hunting at northern river crossings and for hunting sea mammals in river mouths is a viable pathway for the kayak's development. As open sea travel and the hunting of larger sea mammals became feasible given advanced harpoon technology, large open skin boats with heavy keels, frames, and gunwales were developed.

All these discussions about development of the skin boat assume that it evolved in the North Pacific and Chukchi and Bering seas regions, where the tradition continued into the historical and modern era. Recent scholarship has neglected to consider the possibility that skin boats developed in Northern Europe or on the coasts of Western Siberia. Given the evidence of Neolithic log boat development and reevaluation of early ideas about Eskimo-like boats in White Sea petroglyphs, recent critical thinking on boats has emphasized the need for more scientific evidence and more skepticism about 16th-century explorers' observations of skin boats. Perhaps future archaeological finds in Western Eurasia (such as the discovery of the ivory Ekven boat from Chukotka, described next) will produce a new generation of thought about skin boat origins east and west.

The Ekven Kayak Model

The history of the Siberian Eskimo kayak is almost completely unknown. In the case of the Yupik kayak, we do not have even a good description from early explorers because the Siberian Eskimo economy had shifted away from hunting seal with kayaks toward hunting walrus and whale with large, open, multiperson angyapit during the Thule-culture period (circa 1000–1500 CE). The study of kayaks and open skin boats from earlier times has also been hindered by the difficulty of identifying boat parts among the many wooden artifacts found in ancient, frozen Eskimo village sites, such as those excavated by Henry Collins, Froelich Rainey, and Otto Geist (see chapter 10, page 226). On the other hand, recent excavations at the circa 1600 CE Nunaleq Yup'ik site in Quinhagaq, on the Bering Sea coast of southwest Alaska, are producing large amounts of boat parts and numerous models made as children's toys (Knecht 2019).

Nevertheless, an important archaeological find proving that the Eskimo kayak existed at least 1,500 years ago appeared during excavations by Soviet archaeologists in the 1960s. While working at a 1,500-year-old Old Bering Sea–culture site at the Ekven site, near Cape Dezhnev at the northwestern corner of the Bering Strait, excavators found a 14-centimeter-long ivory kayak model in one of the many burials in the cemetery (fig. 8.11a–c). A masklike human face appears in the place of the cockpit, and two whales (or inflated drag floats) are shown on the deck, perhaps

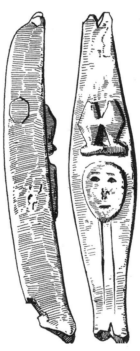

Fig. 8.11. This 14-centimeter-long ivory model of a spirit boat was recovered in a 1,500-year-old Old Bering Sea–culture grave at the Ekven site near Cape Dezhnev (formerly East Cape), Chukotka, in the 1960s. It and a second example from Ekven are the earliest three-dimensional renderings of Eskimo skin boats known to date. Whether it represents a kayak or an open boat is debatable because it shares features of both: the two-pronged gunwale extensions and general proportion suggest an angyapik (umiak) while the covered deck, human face in place of the cockpit, and two sea mammals that look like whales (but might be inflated sea mammal skin floats) make it look like a kayak. It was found as an offering in Ekven Grave 10/11, so its purpose was probably symbolic, not realistic. (Photograph: Evguenia Anichtchenko; from Arutiunov and Sergeev 2006: plate 48)

The Bark Canoes and Skin Boats of Northern Eurasia

signifying animals that were magically "caught." The carving was certainly not intended as a toy but rather as a ritual offering, probably to ensure good hunting in the afterlife. More important in terms of boat history is the shape of the boat: its flat hull is similar to that of Chukchi and Yupik kayaks (see fig. 8.3–8.4, page 159), while its bifurcated bow and stern recall a design feature of Eskimo open skin boats. One has to ask, "What is this model supposed to represent? An umiak (angyapik) open skin boat, or a hunter's enclosed kayak?" It has features of both. It is probably significant that whaling harpoons have been recovered at Ekven, so the capture of large whales had begun here at least by 500 CE. We also see this double-pronged type of boat 1,000 years later in Georgi's 18th-century illustration of a 17th-century double-pronged Yukagir kayak (see fig. 7.1, page 137).

Siberian Yupik Skin Boats

Rock art at Pegtymel and other locations on the northeast Asian coast suggests that the history of systematically hunting whales from open skin boats is ancient. However, the dating of this development is clouded by the absence of archaeological data earlier than 500 CE; whaling harpoons, float gear, and open skin boat parts only later begin to appear in Punuk and Thule archaeological sites on both sides of the Bering Strait (see chapter 10). So far, earlier evidence of whaling and skin boats has been found only at the Un'en'en site near the village of Nunligran, Chukotka, at the southwestern corner of the Bering Strait. Russian archaeologist Sergei Gusev was excavating a house full of whale bones there in 2007 when his team found a whale-bone artifact engraved with a depiction of five hunters in a boat that resembles an open skin angyapik or umiak, which is being towed by a harpooned whale (fig. 8.12; University of Alaska, Fairbanks 2008). The scene is repeated on both sides of the bone, which was found on the floor of the house, which itself was radiocarbon-dated to 1000 BCE. Archaeologists have questioned that date and context, however, because engravings of a similar style have been found in Bering Strait and Canadian Punuk- and Thule-culture sites of 1000 CE and because the whale bone itself has not been dated. While questions remain, the Un'en'en engraving might document the hunting of large whales from open skin boats (the defining characteristic of later Eskimo cultural tradition) 1,500 years earlier than we have previously realized.

The development of skin boats certainly was not limited to Siberian shores; we can expect that western Alaska peoples, too, were important players in the emergence of

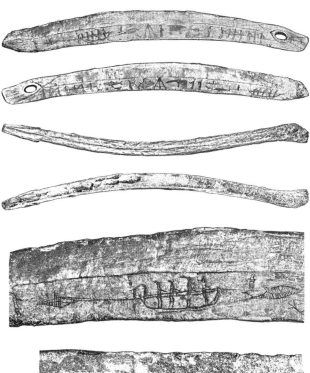

Fig. 8.12. This engraved whalebone artifact, found in 2007 at a 3,000-year-old Eskimo site at Un'en'en, Chukotka, shows whalers harpooning a whale. Similar scenes can be found on Okhotsk-culture needlecases (see fig. 9.3, page 189) and on Punuk- and Thule-culture artifacts of circa 1000 CE in Alaska and Canada. Presumably, all depicted skin boats, because the tundra environment was treeless. If the engraving on the Un'en'en bone is as old as the site, it could demonstrates whaling technology and the use of open skin boats 1,500 years earlier than at the 500 CE Ekven site (see fig. 8.11). (Courtesy Sergei Gusev)

this technology. The Eskimo and their predecessors in northeastern Siberia and Alaska were in close contact across the narrow, seasonally ice-covered Bering Strait, and peoples on each side demonstrated advances in sea mammal–hunting technology as early as 4000 BCE, as evidenced by toggling harpoons from Jōmon Japan and *atlatl* throwing boards for hunting sea mammals from Kodiak Island (W. Fitzhugh 2008). Siberian Yupik walrus and whale hunters using open skin boats resided on St. Lawrence Island for at least 1,500 years, and they could easily move back and forth between this island and Chukotka in their boats since they spoke the same language as their neighbors and shared relatives with them. There were fewer contacts between the Yupik and the Iñupiaq Eskimo of northern Alaska, but the past 500 years have seen wars, raids, and trade sporadically conducted between them, mostly initiated by the Yupik or the Chukchi.

Bogoras (1904–09) and Antropova (1961) studied keeled boats (open skin boats and kayaks), and both also wrote about open skin boats, which were made with a frame composed of a longitudinal beam (the interior keel), ribs, side arches, and complementary parts (fig. 8.13). They were covered with the skins of sea mammals—usually split walrus hides—and were propelled by several paddlers or, after European contact, by sail. Differentiated by the construction of their bow and stern ends, there are two Siberian types of skin boat: Chukotka and Kamchatka. Antropova's classification recognizes the cultural bases for these variants. The Chukotka type, with bifurcated ends (extended gunwale rails), was used by the Eskimo and later by the Chukchi, whereas the Kamchatka type had a broad, low bow with a curved gunwale rail bent around the bow (see page 176).

Nearly identical types of Eskimo open skin boats were used on both sides of the Bering Strait. Fig. 8.14, a photo taken by Finnish anthropologist Sakari Pälsi on the Siberian coast of the strait in 1917, shows two large Naukan Eskimo skin boats on a beach near East Cape (Cap Dezhnev), at the northwestern edge of the strait.

Antropova described Asiatic Eskimo open skin boats:

The skin boats of the Asiatic Eskimo . . . represent the highest technical achievement of the native people of Russia. In construction, the skin boat and kayak are close to a keeled vessel. . . .

The base of the lattice frame of the [open] skin boat was a long beam with upturned ends [*the keelson—Trans.*]. The bottom of the craft was formed by the straight part of the beam and curved planks on either side, the ends of which were fastened to the center beam at the point at which they began to curve. To these planks were secured transverse ribs that formed the sides of the frame. . . . All the parts were lashed together with thongs.

The frame was covered with walrus hide. On the outside of the skin cover, a platelike bumper made of a piece of whale rib [or jawbone] was fastened along the bottom to protect the hide from being abraded when the boat was dragged in and out of

Fig. 8.13. This full-size Yupik Eskimo open skin boat or *angyapik* (REM 8412-1), which Dorian Sergeev collected in Sireniki village on the Siberian shore of the Bering Strait in 1974, displays the simple yet sturdy design and the engineering of skin, wood, and lashings that allowed these boats to flex rather than break under heavy loads and sea stress. (Photograph: I. Tkachenko; courtesy Russian Ethnographic Museum)

Fig. 8.14. This photograph (VKK157_155) shows Nome Inupiat Eskimo from Alaska landing at Cape Dezhnev (East Cape), Siberia, on a trading expedition in 1917. Migrating, trading, and raiding had been taking place across the Bering Strait for thousands of years before Europeans arrived. For travel in rough seas with heavy loads, the Eskimo lashed skin freeboard extenders above the gunwales and tied inflated seal skins outside the gunwales. (Photograph: Sakari Pälsi; courtesy Finnish National Board of Antiquities)

the water. . . . The dimensions of the skin boat varied, from a small one for two people to large ones up to 11 to 11.5 meters long and 1.5 to 2 meters wide, with a cargo capacity of 2 metric tons. The thwarts of the large boats could accommodate six to eight oarsmen [*the largest skin boats often carried as many as 15 to 20 people, plus cargo—Eds.*]. At the end of the 19th century, oars of two kinds were used: wide and short, and long and narrow. The latter appear to be imitations of whaleboat oars; the Eskimo often acquired them ready-made from American whalers and traders. The steering oar had a wide blade; at the end of the 19th century it was replaced with a crude rudder.

The skin boat was provided with a mast to support a rectangular sail; sometimes two sails were used, one above the other. At the end of the 19th century, [imported] triangular sails also came into use. The sails were made of cotton twill but formerly they were prepared from carefully worked reindeer skin. To steady the boat in a high wind, inflated seal skins were tied to the sides.

The skin boat had great advantages over many of the wooden vessels used for offshore travel. It was light yet stable, and its frame, held together with thongs, was quite resilient, making it easy to maneuver among ice blocks and avoid damage when an ice floe was struck. Its shallow draft enabled it to traverse shallow waters even with a heavy load and to approach the shore in a running surf. Under the conditions of a subsistence economy, these qualities made the skin boat indispensable for hunting sea mammals. (Antropova 2005: 14–15; see also Bogoras 1904–09)

The Siberian Yupiit (the plural of "Yupik") used angyapit throughout the 20th century for hunting walrus, seal, and whale and traveling along the shores of the Bering Strait. By midcentury, these boats were being modified; rudders were added, as well as internal wells through the boats' bottom where outboards could be installed. Researchers have studied the construction and use of these angyapit in detail since the 1960s (Ainana, Tatyga, Typykhkak, and Zagrebin 2003; Bogojavlensky 1969; Braund 1988), making the Yupik open skin boat one of the best-described traditional vessels in the northern world. One example of such work is Stephen Braund's *The Skin Boats of Saint Lawrence Island, Alaska*

(1988), the most extensive study of the construction, use, and social context of the Yupik open skin boat. It documents these craft in Savooga, St. Lawrence Island, Alaska, and provides details of their framing and changes in hull design from precontact to modern times (fig. 8.15a–b). Collecting and maintaining skin boats in museums is always a challenge, but in 2017, the Smithsonian National Museum of Natural History acquired a 8.5-meter (28-foot) angyapik that was built and used by St. Lawrence Island Yupik in the 1950s (see fig. 10.15, page 231).

Although the Siberian Yupik Eskimo had abandoned kayaks by the mid- to late 19th century, one example of them might remain: the model (discussed earlier in this chapter) collected circa 1840 by Ilya Vosnesensky from Mechigmensky Bay, on the Siberian side of the Bering Strait (MAE 20-22; see fig. 8.21a–b, page 178). As noted earlier, though Vosnesensky described the model as "Koryak," its location suggests it is Eskimo. If so, and if it was accurately rendered, it is the only known representation of a Bering Strait Yupik/Eskimo kayak before such boats were abandoned in favor of open skin boats more suitable for hunting walrus and large whales.

THE KEREK: COASTAL DWELLERS OF THE WESTERN BERING SEA

The Kerek, now a small and almost extinct Native group, lived along the western Bering Sea coast and on islands from the Geka Spit in the north to Cape Oliutorsky in the south, an extent of more than 900 kilometers. Their recently extinct language belonged to the Chukotko-Kamchatkan (Paleo-Asiatic) family, whose speakers also include the Chukchi, Koryak, and Itelmen, and their traditional culture has largely disappeared. Originally the Kerek were probably inland hunters and fishermen who adapted to a new economy on the coast, including maritime hunting and skin boat use, while surrounded by larger population groups. Unlike more northerly peoples, they might not have had a long history of open skin boat use and probably learned the necessary skills from the Koryak, their southern neighbors, or from the Eskimo to the north.

Because their culture already was in decline when ethnographers arrived in the mid- to late 19th century, we know little about their life and customs. The major source is the Russian-language *Ethnography and Folklore of the Kereks* by Vladilen Leont'yev (1983), excerpts of which were published in the Norwegian Polar Institute's summary of Russian indigenous peoples:

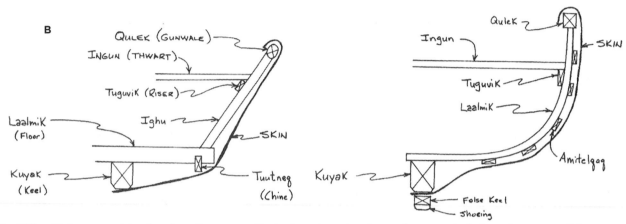

Fig. 8.15. *a*. St. Lawrence Islanders from Savoonga, Alaska, have been hunting walruses and whales using *angyapit* for more than 1,500 years. When not in use, boats are stored on racks to dry, which also keeps dogs from eating their skin covers. *b*. Spruce driftwood framing of the traditional flat-bottomed *angyapik* (left; see fig. 8.13, page 170) from St. Lawrence Island and Chukotka, with its angled chine on the sides, was suitable because the boat was still propelled by paddle or oars. *c*. But in the 20th century, stronger fore and aft stringers and bent-wood oak ribs obtained from European or American visitors produced the rounded hull needed for outboard motor propulsion. (*a*: From Braund 1988: plate 10, photograph: Lee Spears; *b* and *c*: from Braund 1988: fig. 24; both courtesy Stephen Braund)

Their traditional culture involved . . . fowling, fishing, land hunting, sea mammal hunting, fur trapping, and reindeer breeding. . . . According to the census of 1897, the Kerek numbered about 600. By the beginning of the 20th century, many groups of Kerek had been assimilated, mostly by the Chukchi. The Kerek consisted of two territorial groups: Yjulallakku ("Upper Kerek," of Navarin Bay) and Iutylallakku ("Lower Kerek," of Khatyrka River). Today the remaining people live in the Mys Navarin area in the village Meynypilgino and other villages of the Chukotka Autonomous Okrug. . . .

Fowling and hunting for small animals traditionally started in spring. Birds were caught with bows and arrows and with nets made of whale sinew [*paynintyn*], which were lowered down over cliffs where birds were nesting. In summer they caught red salmon, humpback salmon, Siberian salmon,

loach, etc., using harpoons, hooks, and clubs. In autumn they hunted wild reindeer, wild sheep, and bears and along the coast, seals and walruses. In winter fur-bearing animals like fox, wolverine, Arctic fox, and others were the main quarry. Gathering food, such as sea cabbage, algae, clams, cedar nuts, and berries, was a subsidiary occupation. . . . The principal means of water transport was the skin baidara, which was shorter and broader than the Chukchi and Yupik Eskimo boat. They also used dog sledges, and their snowshoes—called "crow's skis"—were similar to those of the Chukchi. . . . Kerek interactions with the Chukchi and Koryak and, to a lesser extent, Yupik [Eskimo] resulted in considerable linguistic borrowing. (Norwegian Polar Institute 2006: Yupik)

Kerek Origins

Alexander Orekhov's research on the prehistoric Lakhtina culture of the southwestern Bering Sea coast provides information on what probably was a proto- or early Kerek culture there (1998). He believes Lakhtina is typical of the changes that usually occurred when inland hunting and fishing people (the Chukchi, for instance) began adapting to coastal conditions, economies, skin boat use, and trade. In the Kerek case, he sees the process as beginning more than 3,000 years ago and continuing into the 17th century:

> There is no evidence of maritime transportation in the early stage [of Lakhtina culture, circa 3,000 years ago]. Baidars of the Koryak type, covered with walrus skins, are known among the Kerek ethnographically and probably were a late borrowing from the Siberian Eskimo. However, the possibility of their independent, convergent appearance [in Kerek culture] cannot be excluded. During these early years, the exploitation of walruses, seals, and sea lions was limited to procuring them at haul-outs. . . . However . . . whale hunting is not possible without water transport. Although ethnographic data for Koryak-type baidars appeared late in Kerek culture, the prehistoric evidence of whale hunting indicates [that baidars must have made] an earlier appearance. (1998: 184)

Michael Fortescue of Copenhagen University has studied the Eskimo language and language relationships in the Chukotka Peninsula. In 2004, he documented linguistic contacts between the Kerek and their neighbors and explained regional similarities, including the use and form of skin boats and maritime hunting technology:

> The specific effect of [Eskimo] presence down the Kerek coast on the Chukotian population there can be seen most clearly in the phonological traces they left behind in the Kerek language. . . . The variety of Kerek that has survived . . . may thus have been in large part the result of [Bering Sea] Punuk Eskimos shifting language as they mixed with the Chukotian population already occupying the coast. . . . All we know for sure is that Eskimos traded "in earlier times" (Bogoras 1904–09: 12) as far south as Cape Navarin, where the northernmost Kereks lived. Could relatively small numbers of powerful Central Siberian Yupik–speaking whale-hunters thus have settled along the northern part of the Kerek coast of the Bering Sea, intermarried with and subsequently been absorbed linguistically by autochthonous Kereks such that only their distinctive (and prestigious) accent remained in the manner in which Kerek came widely to be spoken?

> As for that autochthonous population itself, its origin is a more complex matter: the archaeology of the area tells of an unbroken tradition from the Old Kerek (Lakhtina) culture some 4,000 years ago up to modern times, so it could hardly have been "Eskimo" in any direct ethnic or linguistic sense (Orekhov 1998: 166ff). This population was during long periods isolated from events farther inland, and its roots seem to be shared with those of the bearers of the Kamchatkan Tarya Neolithic culture. [This culture is] believed by Dikov [1979, 2004] and others to represent the ancestors of the Itelmen, with a later overlay of Koryak from farther west breaking their connections with the south around 500 BC. . . . These [Tarya] newcomers may have brought the basis of the language that developed into Kerek since it is far closer to Koryak than to Itelmen. Much later, in the far north of their territory, Orekhov (1998: 166ff) notes strong influence from the technologically more advanced Punuk culture. . . . The Kereks, inhabiting their steep, rugged coast, were almost as thoroughly orientated towards marine mammal hunting in their subsistence patterns as the Eskimos and coastal Chukchis of the far north. . . . The last chapter in their history, leading up to the final extinction of the language . . . was the encroachment on their territory by inland Chukchis from the north and west. (2004: 179–80)

The Kerek Open Skin Boat

The Kerek open skin boat is part of the Koryak-Kamchatka tradition, and this relationship is seen in the design and construction of a Kerek boat that Sakari Pälsi photographed in 1917 (fig. 8.16). This boat is similar to boats from Karaga Bay, on the eastern coast of Kamchatka, where the population might have consisted of mixed Itelmen-Koryak (or Apuka) people. In Karaga, the open skin boat had a reasonably wide bow, as can also be seen in boat models in the Russian Ethnographic Museum and the Museum of Anthropology and Ethnology (see figs. 8.18a–c and 8.19, pages 176–177), unlike the typical Koryak boat, which had a more symmetrical hull form. In the Kerek boat, this wide bow was very dominant. The boat that Pälsi documented in the Alyutor region in the southern

Fig. 8.16. This 1917 photograph (VKK157_57) of a Kerek skin boat on the Aliutor coast between Kamchatka and Anadyr reveals design departures from Chukchi and Eskimo skin boats. Especially notable is the wide, rounded bow, which facilitated launching and landing in the surf on Bering Sea and North Pacific beaches. (Photograph: Sakari Pälsi; courtesy Finnish National Board of Antiquities)

Fig. 8.17. This model (BM 2-715) shows a group of Kerek or Koryak in an open skin boat that has a V-shaped stern, a European rudder, and the wide, low Kerek bow. By the mid-19th century, most open boats were also equipped with sails. (Courtesy Burke Museum, University of Washington, Seattle)

part of Kerek lands in 1917 is circa 4.5 by 2.0 by 0.5 meters and has a beam-to-length ratio of 1:2.8, making this type unusual among all of the large open boats known in northeastern Siberia. As figs. 8.16 and 8.18 show, the internal spreader boards keep the bow open. The reason for the unusual expanded bow shape was experienced dramatically by Pälsi himself when he came ashore on a sandy beach through heavy surf at the mouth of the Alyutor (Oliutorsky) River. The wide bow and 0.5-meter height kept the boat from swamping. A similar boat is seen in a model with finely costumed paddlers in the collection of the Burke Museum at the University of Washington, Seattle (fig. 8.17). The model is documented as being Koryak, and it has a European rudder. If the documentation is accurate, its wide, low bow and teardrop shape suggests it is Kerek or Kerek-influenced. The Kerek and Koryak shared a boundary in the Alyutor region north of the Kamchatka Peninsula and probably shared boat styles as well.

THE KORYAK: PEOPLE OF PENZHINA BAY AND KAMCHATKA

The Koryak, numbering about 9,000 today, live in Kamchatka along the shores of the Okhotsk and the Pacific Ocean. Their language is part of the Paleo-Asiatic group, and their DNA reflects early contact with the Amur River basin (Schurr, Sukernik, Starikovskaya, and Wallace 1999; Rubiscz and Crawford 2016). In the 17th century, when Russians first arrived in their lands, some of the Koryak, who called themselves *chav'cu*, or "reindeer herders," lived in nomadic camps, while other Koryak, called *nymol'o*, resided in small sedentary

villages. When the Even people appeared at the Okhotsk coast from the Lena River, they mixed with the Koryak, forming new groups that shared boatbuilding traditions and technology connected with decked kayaks and large open skin boats (Burykin 2001; Tronson 1859). It is difficult to trace this part of Koryak history in the historical literature, since Russian sources of 150 years ago refer to most people living on the northern Sea of Okhotsk and in the Kamchatka region as Koryak. The same is true for the Kerek, who were often confused with and described as Koryak.

Referring to the work of Aleksandr Lebedintsev, Waldemar Jochelson, and Alexander Orekhov, Ben Fitzhugh, of the University of Washington, Seattle, has written about the emergence of Lakhtin- and Old Koryak–culture maritime adaptations 3,000 to 4,000 years ago on the northern Sea of Okhotsk:

On the northern Sea of Okhotsk, near Magadan, interior populations settled the sea coast and offshore islands only around 3,000 years ago, where they appear to have developed unique maritime traditions (Lebedintsev 1998). Eventually this group expanded around the northeast Sea of Okhotsk to settle northern Kamchatka, establishing the earliest archaeologically visible maritime tradition in that region: Old Koryak (Jochelson 1905).

North up the western coast of the Bering Sea, between Kamchatka and the mouth of the Anadyr, the first coastal and maritime living also appears around 3,500 cal. B.P. (Orekhov 1998). . . . In overview, the earliest evidence of coastal and maritime adaptations around the Subarctic Northwestern Pacific signals a significant age difference between southern and milder coasts of the southern Sea of Okhotsk, with early Holocene maritime use, and the more northern regions, including the remote Kuril Islands, where maritime foci emerge—apparently independently—in several locations only after 4,000 cal. B.P. (2016: 258)

If the development of maritime adaptations in these regions did not begin until 3500 BP, that suggests 3500 BP was when kayaks and open skin boat became functionally sufficient, a time matching the dating of the Chertov Ovrag site on Wrangel Island. One suspects, however, that archaeological work will discover still earlier evidence of maritime life, as it is known to have existed in northern Japan and southeast Alaska 3,000 years earlier.

The Koryak Open Skin Boat

Antropova and Jochelson are the basic sources for information on Koryak skin boats. Antropova provided a rough comparison of the Koryak open skin boat to those of the Eskimo and Chukchi:

> The principal hunting boat of the Koryak (*kultaytvyyt*, Korsakov 1939), literally a "boat made out of bearded seal skins," was structurally similar to the Eskimo and Chukchi umiak but differed in important details. The Koryak boat was considerably shorter but wider than the Eskimo umiak. Its length rarely exceeded 10 meters, and its width was about 2.5 meters. Thus the Koryak length-to-width ratio was 4:1, while for the Chukchi or Eskimo umiak this relation was 11.5:1.5, or about 8:1. The ends of the gunwales were supported with additional braces that formed a semicircular bow and stern. In Eskimo umiaks the ends were pointed [each gunwale protruding separately]. . . . The skin cover of the Koryak boat was made from bearded seal (*Erignatus barbatus*) skins, which are thinner than the skins of walruses [used by Eskimo and Chukchi]. . . . Large boats were manned by eight rowers and a man on the steering oar. The boat was propelled by single-bladed oars that passed through loops acting as oarlocks. The steering oar had a wider blade than the rowing oars. When traveling downwind, the boats used a sail. (2005: 16–17)

The large Koryak skin boat could travel long distances and was very fast, as we learn from a 1790 letter written by Lieutenant Adam Laxman to his father, the Finnish-born Erik Laxman, who was a professor at the Russian Academy

and a board member of the Russian Geographical Society when it financed the Billings expedition (Lagus 1880: 209–11). Before traveling to Japan as a trade negotiator, Adam Laxman had been garrisoned in the town of Gizhiga on Penzhina Bay, in the northern Sea of Okhotsk. In the summer of 1789, he took a boat trip along the coast with three Cossacks in a large skin boat paddled by seven Koryak, two of them women. The Penzhina Peninsula, at the northern end of the Sea of Okhotsk, was in those days the center of the Koryak population. Among Laxman's tasks were observing nature and searching for minerals. After several days' travel, during which the Koryak paddled 50 to 70 versts (53 to 75 kilometers) per day, living on seals, they landed west of a peninsula near Cape Taigonos. The Koryak led Laxman to a rocky seashore where there was a deposit of crystal cinnabar, which he called quicksilvermalm. He reported that the Koryak collected this mineral to color their spears after the fall storms had crushed the rocks on the shore.

The best description of the Koryak open boat is by Waldemar Jochelson, who conducted ethnographic research among as part of the Jesup North Pacific Expedition. His monograph "The Koryak" (Jochelson 1908) is a tour-de-force in field ethnography and devotes several pages to Koryak skin boats, including a detailed description of the open boat, known to the Koryak as the *matyv*. His description was condensed and paraphrased by Adney and Chapelle:

> The Koryak umiaks illustrated by Jochelson show a highly developed boat, rather lightly framed compared to boats on the American side. In profile, the bow has a long raking curve and the stern much less; as a result, the bottom is rather short compared to the length over the gunwales. Viewed in plan, the gunwales are rounded in at bow and stern to form almost a semicircle. At the bow, the gunwales are bent around a horizontal headboard tenoned over the stem head, but at the stern there is no headboard. The sheer is moderate and very graceful. The flare of the sides is great, and there appears to be a little V in the bottom transversely. There is also a slight fore-and-aft rocker on the bottom. The construction is similar to that of the Alaskan umiaks except that the Koryak umiaks have double-chine stringers and a double riser, or longitudinal stringer, halfway up the sides. The riser is not backed with a continuous stringer, as is the chine; instead, three short rods are lashed inside the side frame members. The

side stringers do not reach bow and stern. The four thwarts are located well aft, and between the first and second thwarts is a larger space than between the others, for cargo. The boats are rowed, two oarsmen to a thwart. The cover was formerly walrus hides split and scraped thin, but more recently the skin of the bearded seal has come into use [*because walruses were being extirpated locally by Europeans and Russians—Eds.*]. A rectangular sail of deerskin is sometimes lashed to a yard and set on a tripod mast about amidships. Two legs of the mast are secured to the gunwale on one side; the remaining leg is lashed to the opposite gunwale. Judging by the drawing made by Jochelson, this umiak is perhaps the most graceful of all those known today. (1964: 182)

Jochelson obtained a detailed model of an open boat (fig. 8.18a) that he shipped back to the AMNH in New York City along with hundreds of other Koryak ethnographic items, including scores of beautifully embroidered Koryak funeral robes that he had commissioned. After cataloguing and describing the model for his monograph, the model was transferred to the Kunstkamera, known widely as the Peter the Great Museum of Anthropology and Ethnography, in St. Petersburg, along with a sample of other Koryak and Chukchi objects that Jochelson acquired. Jochelson had conservators at the AMNH replicate the wooden frame of the boat and for his monograph described the function of all the key elements (fig. 8.18b–c). Among the interesting features was a Y-shaped chock at the bow used for cradling the harpoon before striking a whale. On some boats, this yoke carried a human image that provided spiritual protection

for the boat and crew. A similar whaling charm was used on Alaskan umiaks, demonstrating a wide distribution of ritual beliefs related to whaling across the North Pacific and Bering Sea (W. Fitzhugh and Crowell 1988: fig. 210).

F. M. Golyushkin also collected a curious open skin boat model in Karaga in 1913 for the Russian Ethnographic Museum (REM; fig. 8.19). Its provenence is listed as "Koryak" in the museum records, and its features suggest a blend between Koryak and Kerek boats, not doubt due to Karaga region being on the border between Aliutor/Kerek and Kamchatka Koryak territory. Its bow is very wide (making a 1:2.5 beam-to-length ratio) compared to those of typical Koryak boats, which are more symmetrical at both ends. The odd thing about the Karaga model—if it reflects actual boat construction—is its raw skin cover, with hair remaining on the outside. This model appears unique, and we are not aware of any descriptions of skin boats with fur covers. A. A. Popov collected a similar model of a Koryak boat (with fur removed) from the Karaginsky region of Kamchatka for the REM in 1910 (REM 2246-91).

The Koryak Kayak

Like the Koryak open skin boat, the Koryak kayak differed from the Eskimo version in some of its details (Antropova 1961), although its construction made it suitable only for short open-sea travel. Like the Eskimo version, it had a lattice frame with a circular opening in the middle and was covered with bearded seal skins. The Koryak kayak was shorter and wider than the Eskimo and Chukchi kayak, and the circular manhole had a wider opening. Like the Eskimo, the Koryak kept water out of their boat by attaching a skin spray cover, or the hem of the paddler's waterproof parka, to the rim

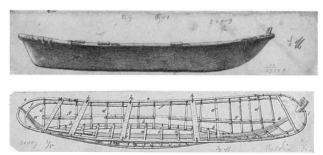

Fig. 8.18. Waldemar Jochelson collected this 105-centimeter-long model from the Koryak circa 1900 while on the Jesup North Pacific Expedition. Its broad bow, tapering to a narrow V-shaped stern, is likely an adaptation to the open sea and surf conditions of the Kamchatka Pacific coast (*a*, MAE 956-263). Jochelson illustrated a drawing of this model and reproduced a skeletal version to reveal its framing (AMNH 70/3756). (Photograph: Evguenia Anichtchenko; Jochelson 1908: figs. 80, 81; courtesy American Museum of Natural History)

Fig. 8.19. This open skin boat model (REM 3964-113), which F. M. Golyushkin collected in the Karaga region in 1913, has an unusual feature: seal fur was retained on its exterior. The fur's function has never been explained. (Photograph: I. Tkachenko; courtesy Russian Ethnographic Museum)

of the hatch. The Koryak kayak that Jochelson collected (fig. 8.20a–b; Jochelson 1908: fig. 83) was 255 centimeters long by 72 centimeters wide by 19 centimeters high and was paddled with a double-bladed paddle or two single-bladed one-handed paddles. Such paddles were also used in small bark canoes on the Amur River when a hunter needed to quietly approach his prey.

Antropova (1961) noted that the kayak on the western coast of Kamchatka appeared more primitive than the version on the eastern coast. At the beginning of the 20th century, when the Karaga and Alyutor and Apuka Koryak started using rifles instead of harpoons for hunting seal, they stopped using nets and kayaks. However, in Penzhina Bay, traditional seal-hunting equipment and kayaks were still used at this point; even in the early 1930s, the Penzhina Koryak were employing nets for sealing. The persistence of traditional technology had its logic: harpoons don't scare basking seals the way that gunshots do, and hunters preferred quieter kayaks for pursuing seal at their breeding grounds. While skin boats were favored along the coast, log boats were preferred for fishing, travel, and hunting on the Kamchatka River.

The kayak used by the Koryak of the Gulf of Penzhina represents an extreme example among kayak types, at least as concerns measurements. Jochelson's Jesup North Pacific Expedition kayak is 2.69 meters long, only 28 centimeters high, and 79 centimeters wide. The hull has a very shallow draft and a V-shaped bottom. A carrying handle is at the bow and stern. The weakly curved flat ribs support three similarly flat bottom stringers; of these, however, only the keelson is full length. There are three deck stringers fore and aft, but only two deck beams. Other published descriptions of this boat have stimulated discussions about the internal structure of the Koryak kayaks in New York and London (Birket-Smith 1929: 5, pt. 2: 78; Adney and Chapelle 1964: 195; Arima 1975: 67–69; Kankaanpää 1989: 16). Adney and Chapelle wrote, "The Asiatic kayaks, curiously enough, exhibit the construction of both eastern and western Arctic

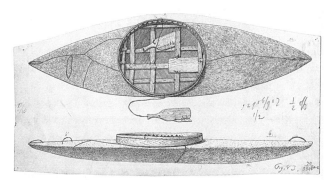

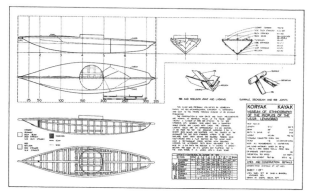

Fig. 8.20. While on the Jesup Expedition, Waldemar Jochelson collected a Koryak seal-skin kayak that the American Museum of Natural History (70/3358) later traded to the Museum of Anthropology and Ethnology, where it was recatalogued as MAE 956-49a–c. His published illustration shows its short length, width, and depth (255 by 72 by 19 centimeters), making it the smallest traditional hunting kayak known. The kayak was documented by David Zimmerly. (*left*: From Jochelson 1908: fig. 83; courtesy American Museum of Natural History; *right*: from Zimmerly 1986: fig. 7; courtesy David Zimmerly)

kayaks, the crude, small Koryak kayak having a 3-batten V-bottom, while the Chukchi kayak is built like the kayaks on the east side of the Bering Strait. The decking of the kayaks is of very light construction; usually there are two heavy thwarts to support the manhole and from one to three light thwarts afore and abaft these" (1964: 192). It seems that the Koryak kayak followed the general pattern but had a local expression. The wide cockpit, reminiscent of the Alaskan Nunivak Island kayak, seems to have been a recent innovation, judging from the Koryak model kayak, dating to 1840, with a narrow manhole and a rear handle, that Vosnesensky collected for the Museum of Anthropology and Ethnology (see fig. 8.21). However, as noted previously (page 171), the source of this model—Mechigmensky Bay, Chukotka—means it is likely Yupik/Eskimo, not Koryak.

The small Koryak kayak was known not only from Penzhina Bay to eastern Kamchatka but also on the southern Sea of Okhotsk near Nivkh territory. The British naval officer J. M. Tronson (1859) saw Even people in Cape Ayan using similar boats for bird hunting (see chapter 7's section on the Even, page 149). Thus the Koryak kayak might have been used over a wider geographic range than the larger Eskimo-Chukchi kayak.

Generally, it has been thought that the Koryak had only a single-seat kayak. Yet Shinji Nishimura (1931: 158–59) noted that Bansui Otsuki, a noted scholar in Sendai, described the voyage of a Japanese ship to "Ondereitske" (possibly near Anadyr) in June 1794. This ship became disabled and was rescued and returned to Anadyr with its crew, who mentioned a double-seated kayak called a *kaitara* (baidara) while they were describing the customs of the Naatska people on islands near Anadyr. Otsuki illustrated such a boat in his work *Kwan-Kai-Ibun*, and Nishimura reproduced it as plate XIX in his *Study of Ancient Ships of Japan*, part 4: *Skin Boats* (1931: 192) (fig. 8.22; see also fig. 8.23, and fig. 8.25). The illustration shows two bearded hunters in a double kayak wearing parkas with spray skirts. The man in the bow casts a spear at a sea mammal, probably an otter. A quiver of additional missiles is fastened to the side of the boat. Nishimura attributed this boat to the Koryak, believing its location might have been between Anadyr and southern Kamchatka. However, the content of the image has a distinctly Aleut flavor, since double kayaks were never part of the northeast Asian sea mammal–hunting complex, and the Koryak did not use spears in quivers, all of which are instead part of Alaskan Aleut and Kodiak Island hunting technology (see chapter 10, page 226). Thus, instead of Koryak hunters, this image probably represents Aleut (Unangan) or Kodiak (Alutiiq) hunters who were imported by the Russian American Company (RAC) from Kodiak Island and the eastern Aleutians, beginning as early as 1774, to hunt sea otters in the Kuril Islands.

Valerie Shubin (1994) described this history and his excavation of an Aleut/Koniag-Ainu village on Urup Island in the southern Kurils. His report noted the sporadic importation of Koniag (Kodiak, now Alutiiq) people from Alaska; however, from 1828 to 1868, the RAC made a concerted

Fig. 8.22. This Japanese illustration appeared in Bansui Otsuki's *Kwan-Kai-Ibun* with the title "An Old Japanese Picture of the Koryak Kayak." It was later reproduced in Shinji Nishimura's 1931 book *Study of Ancient Ships of Japan*. The painting raises many questions, including the caption's identification of the kayak and paddlers as Koryak, because double kayaks traditionally were not used by northeast Asian people. Beards could signify either Ainu or Kodiak Alaskans, but the double kayak and dart bundle confirm these people were among the hundreds of Kodiak or Aleutian Islanders whom the Russian American Company imported to the Kurils in the early 19th century to work as commercial sea otter hunters. (From Nishimura 1931: plate 19)

Fig. 8.21. The origin of this model kayak (MAE 20-22), collected by Ilya Vosnesensky circa 1840 for the Museum of Anthropology and Ethnology, is documented as being Mechigmensky Bay on the Chukchi Peninsula, far north of Koryak territory. This is among the oldest model kayak in any museum. If its source location is accurate, and if the model faithfully represents its type, it is probably not Koryak but rather a rare example of a Bering Strait Yupik/Eskimo model kayak. (Photograph: Evguenia Anichtchenko; courtesy Museum of Anthropology and Ethnography)

effort to colonize the Kurils, resulting in trading-post settlements that included Koniag and Ainu people. It seems likely that the Otsuki image illustrates this little-known story of Koniag Eskimo history in the Kurils a century before Roman Hitchcock began anthropological investigations there (1891).

More definitive confirmation of this interpretation is seen in an illustration in *Dai-Nippon Busson Zue [Products of Greater Japan]* (1887), a book of paintings made in the late 1870s by Hiroshige Utagawa. One painting (fig. 8.23) shows two three-person Aleutian-style kayaks paddled by men wearing the flat-topped woven spruce-root hats characteristic of the Alaskan Koniag (Alutiiq) people of Kodiak Island and the Sugpiaq of nearby Prince William Sound. Uzumi Koide of the Shibusawa Foundation believes this book was published in conjunction with a large industrial trade fair held in Ueno (Tokyo) in 1877 (Koji Deriha, pers. comm. to WWF, 2018). The painting's original caption describes "native people" hunting sea otters and their hunting methods but does not discuss whether the paddlers' ethnicity might be Kuril Ainu, Unanagan (Aleut), or Koniag (Alutiiq). Shavings are attached to the bows of the kayaks, suggesting that these Alaskan hunters adopted the Ainu custom of using *inau* (wood shavings) on boats to honor gods and spirits and provide spiritual protection at sea. The rocky coast suggests the Kuril Islands environment, and the presence of Russian ships is a clear indication that the sea otter hunt was conducted under the supervision of the RAC, likely in the area of Urup Island, an RAC base. Nishimura also described and illustrated both Jochelson's open skin boat model and a single kayak that he attributed to Koryak and Kamchadal (Itelmen) peoples (1931: figs. 42, 43; see also our fig. 8.25, page 183).

THE ITELMEN: FISHERMEN AND HUNTERS OF VOLCANIC KAMCHATKA

The Itelmen, known to the Russians as the Kamchadal (Georgi 1777), inhabited most of the Kamchatka Peninsula before Russian colonists first appeared there, circa 1690. Their territory extended from southern Kamchatka (which Ainu people also occupied or visited at this time) to the Uka and Tigil rivers in the north, bordering Koryak lands. Their main population was concentrated in the Kamchatka River basin, in the east-central part of the peninsula. Kamchatka is rich in sable and other furs and has highly productive salmon and marine fisheries, including sea mammals. Historically, people living along the rivers running into the sea were mainly fishermen, while on the eastern and western

Fig. 8.23. This image (1-4265-2) makes it possible to deconstruct the unusual features of Nishimura's problematic illustration (fig. 8.22): a two-man kayak, spear-throwers (*altatls*), and wooden quivers of darts. This image shows men in three-holed Aleut-style kayaks (the rear boat is missing its middle paddler) wielding spears and wearing flat-topped woven hats typical of the Koniag (Alutiiq) people of Kodiak Island, Alaska. The image comes from *Dai-Nippon Bussan Zue [Products of Greater Japan]* (1887), a series of paintings made in the 1870s by the Japanese artist Hiroshige Utagawa (1842–94). Russian American Company ships lie at anchor in the background. The location is likely near the RAC's establishment on Urup Island in the southern Kurils. (Courtesy Waseda University Library)

coasts, the Itelmen hunted whale, as did the Itelmen and Ainu at the southern tip of Kamchatka.

The Itelmen language is considered to be part of the larger Paleo-Asiatic group known as the Chukotko-Kamchatkan language family, but its exact relations are unknown because the language is nearly extinct and relatively unstudied. According to Schurr, Sukernik, Starikovskaya, and Wallace (1999), Itelmen DNA is closest to the Koryak's and dissimilar to that of the Chukchi and Eskimo. Their study also indicated that the expansion of continental Evenk and Even tribes into the northern Sea of Okhotsk region probably gave rise to the ancestral Koryak and Itelmen populations, while movements from the lower Amur River and Sakhalin played a secondary role.

Itelmen boats, too, are poorly known. They can be understood best in relation to their neighbors, the Koryak and Ainu, owing to both proximity and similar economic pursuits. As a starting point, we can take the situation at the time of the Russian entry into Kamchatka, when contact among the Itelmen, Koryak, and Ainu might already have been underway for centuries. In 1697, the Kamchatka Itelmen comprised almost 12,000 people, of whom the Burin made up 6,900; the Itelmen-Koryak group about 1,200; and the rest, some 3,800, belonging to the Itelmen-Ainu group living near the Kuril Islands (Zuev 2012: 16). In the late 17th and early 18th centuries, the Even, under pressure from expanding Chukchi populations, crossed Koryak lands and entered Kamchatka as inland reindeer herders and hunters. Later in the 18th century, when many Itelmen on the Kamchatka River died in Russian-introduced epidemics or were killed in wars following their unsuccessful 1770–71 rebellion against the Russians, the mixed remnants of various Native groups on the peninsula came to be called the Kamchadal or Itelmen ("those who live here"). According to the 2002 Russian census, the total number of Itelmen was 3,180, of whom only a handful still spoke the Itelmen language.

Early Descriptions of the Itelmen

When the German naturalist Georg W. Steller (2003) visited Kamchatka on Vitus Bering's 1733–43 expedition, organized by the Russian Geographic Society, he explored the entire peninsula and visited Alaska and the Commander Islands. While returning to Kamchatka, the voyage's origin, they shipwrecked on Bering Island, where many of the crew, including Bering, died of scurvy and starvation. The survivors built a smaller ship and returned to Petropavlovsk, where Steller continued his earlier observations of the Itelmen, Kamchadal, and Koryak. He took special interest in Kamchatka's natural history and peoples and described their travels, hunting trips and methods, and use of boats. He noted that the Itelmen of Kamchatka, the Kushi (Ainu) of the Kuril Islands, and some Koryak in Penzhina Bay were seasoned sea mammal hunters who traveled in baidars, the largest of them 13 meters long.

When another German, Karl von Dittmar, explored Kamchatka in 1851–55 to search for mineral resources for the Russians, he met Itelmen and observed skin boats in many locations. In 1890, he wrote that some of these boats were 12 meters long. We have no illustrations of these baidars, but we can be rather confident that they resembled Koryak boats, owing to proximity and the close ties between the two peoples. When Jochelson studied the Kamchadal in the same location in 1909–11, he did not find many people, and he noted that their skin boats and ancient sea hunting traditions had disappeared.

Boats in Central Kamchatka

The use of boats differed among various groups of Itelmen according to their economies and locations, and all the standard boat types were known here: log boats, plank boats, bark canoes, and, in northern Kamchatka, perhaps open skin boats and decked kayaks as well. The Kamchatka forests provided all the northern types of trees needed to build log and bark boats. Our limited knowledge of these watercraft is primarily a result of early, heavy Russian contact, which decimated the Itelmen population and economies, especially the maritime economy, before their boat traditions could be carefully documented.

For interior river fishing, hunting, and travel, the Itelmen used log boats, called *bat*; for heavy-duty river transport, especially in rough water, they built paired or trimaran log boats. While we have some information on the use of log boats on the Kamchatka River in the 1700s, our knowledge of the Itelmen's birch-bark canoe use is almost totally lacking, although such boats must have been part of the old Itelmen forest culture. One historical reference (Woss 1778: 188) said that the Itelmen filled small birch-bark canoes with fish offal and set them out as decoys for catching seal.

Not much more is known about Itelmen use of skin boats. Benjamin Fitzhugh (2012) writes that in central and southern Kamchatka, an indigenous transition to maritime economies emerged between 4000 and 3500 BP, as is suggested by sculpted stone images of marine animals. Log boats would have been ideal for Itelmen maritime use in river estuaries, as they were for Ainu and Amur groups to the south, who used planked log boats for ocean travel and trade. The Itelmen were in regular contact with the Kuril Ainu, who used conventional log boats with planked sides and possibly also skin boats, as discussed below, but we have no direct documentation of the existence of expanded log boats before the Even (Lamut) entered the area.

The Ainu occupied the Kuril Islands and the southern tip of Kamchatka, where they mixed with and might have influenced the Itelmen. Known in old German Kamchatka studies as the Kushi, they engaged in sea trade and hunted sea animals. The Ainu-type log boat, as we know it from illustrations from Hokkaido and the Kuril Islands (Ohtsuka 1999: figs. 53.2, 52.3), had a high, upturned bow and stern and rather low freeboard, and thus it was not similar to the Itelmen's traditional low-sided boat, used on inland rivers and in estuaries. Ainu log boats without planked sides were not intended for long-distance sea travel and were instead used mostly for coastal trips and fishing in rivers running into the sea (see the discussion of the Ainu in chapter 9, page 200). For long-range travel, the Ainu used a large log boat with planked sides and sails.

Fig. 8.24 shows an Itelmen decked log boat, a kind of canoe-kayak, which might have been equipped with a spray skirt and a double-bladed paddle, illustrated on the frontispiece of Georg W. Steller's *History of Kamchatka* (2003). The depiction was based on his observations as part of the Bering expedition of 1741–42. However, the image lacks detail and might be only an artist's fanciful reconstruction that blends canoe and kayak elements. Another image of what might be a skin-covered boat (see below) is seen in a drawing published by Nishimura illustrating an artist's sketch of a "Koryak" man, with long hair and a beard, rowing a skin-covered boat in Kamchatka.

THE KUSHI AND KURIL AINU: ISLAND DWELLERS OF THE NORTHWEST PACIFIC

References to the Kuril Ainu (see also the Ainu section in chapter 9, page 200) reveal a degree of confusion about the identity of the peoples who historically occupied the southern tip of Kamchatka and the northern Kuril Islands. Southern Kamchatka was a region where the Kuril Ainu were present as seasonal settlers and visitors during the heyday of Kuril Ainu-Kamchatka trade in the 17th and 18th centuries. Early explorers of the area were not ethnographers and could not converse directly with most of the people they encountered, and this difficulty, especially profound near cultural boundaries, is clearly reflected in the case of the Kushi.

At the southern tip of the Kamchatka Peninsula and in the Kurils, the chain of islands stretching between Kamchatka and Japan, there lived in the early 1700s, according to Boris O. Dolgikh's (1960) estimate, a few thousand seagoing people whom old Russian records call the Kushi or Kuril

Fig. 8.24. Georg W. Steller's *History of Kamchatka* illustrates a dramatic scene from the Kamchatka interior, with a smoking volcano, native huts, and a man in a canoe or planked boat using a double-bladed paddle and possibly wearing a spray skirt. (From Steller 2003: frontispiece)

(and later the Southern Insulaners). Not much is known of these people, who were almost certainly Ainu, in part because when Dittmar (1890b) encountered them in the 1850s, they had retreated from the Kamchatka mainland to the more remote Kurils, seeking refuge from Russian invasions. Most interesting for their boating history was their command of the sea and use of large open skin boats—perhaps of the Koryak-Kamchatka type—and of skin-covered kayaks different from those of the Koryak. The life of the Kushi-Ainu Kuril Islands population was much different from that of other tribes and peoples living on the mainland sea coast and might have most closely resembled that of the Itelmen or the Aleut living on the Aleutian Islands, which arc from Alaska toward Kamchatka.

Steller in 1774 (2003) and later Dittmar (1890b) documented the peoples of southern Kamchatka. The Insulaner, according to J. G. Georgi (1777), included the Southern Insulaner of the Kurils and the Eastern Insulaner, a maritime people living on the islands between Siberia and America from the Bering Strait to the Aleutians; the two groups had a similar lifestyle, living from the sea, inhabiting isolated islands, and using skin boats.

The Kuril Maritime Environment

When Dittmar explored Kamchatka, he found large open skin boats belonging to the Kushi (perhaps mixed Itelmen-Ainu people). These vessels enabled them to travel from island to island trading furs with Russians. Although the Kuril-Kushi (i.e., Ainu) and Itelmen had no firearms, they were warriors feared by their enemies because they possessed poisoned arrows that caused a painful death. As Dittmar wrote:

> The Kuril Islanders are a nearly extinct race whose small remnants roam the chain of islands in their baidars. They have no fixed settlements but live from the earth and build driftwood yurts as long as the hunt in one location requires, or stay over the winter, leaving a place when they wish. They are nomadic peoples in baidars. They often visit Paramushir Island, the largest of the Kurils. Every year they capture [sea otter] furs for both branches of the Russian-American Company: in the north on Schumshu and in the south on Urup. (2004: 17)

Georgi described the Kuril-Kushi (Ainu), who then still occupied the southernmost tip of the Kamchatka Peninsula:

The inhabitants of those islands do not all themselves by the same name, and they are in outlook and language different from each other. Most call themselves Kuschi, from which Kushi, the name from which "Kurili" (the name for the people and their islands) may originate, while the most Southern Insulaners were usually called Kikkurilen. Some islanders resemble the Japanese in language, outlook, and lifestyle; others are close to the Kamchadals (Itelmen), while some other islands are inhabited by both groups. The northern islands recognize Russia as their ruler, the southern recognize Japanese rule, and many others are independent. . . . Those under formal Russian or Japanese rule are that in name only. They do not pay [yassak] every year, and when they do pay tax, the number of people represented varies, and for this reason their population is not known. In 1776, all people living under Russian rule paid yassak only for 262 people [family heads]. . . .

The proper Kuril people are similar to the Japanese: they are small and have round, somewhat flat faces [and] black hair [but] very hairy skin. They behave in a very humane way. They are friendly, honest, steadfast, and always polite . . . but with a tendency to suicide. . . . The men catch sea animals, birds, walruses, etc., as well as hunt and fish. Their kayaks (nahen) are built from wood from their forest and driftwood, and their paddles have a blade at both ends. The women prepare food, make clothes, etc., and the northern population spins and weaves nettle thread [for clothing]. . . . The Southern Insulaners, who are more intelligent than the northerners, trade in whale oil, furs, eagle feathers [for arrow fletching], and pipe shafts with Japan. In exchange, they receive Japanese metal, lacquer cups, pots, harpoons, and different things like bracelets, knives, and tobacco. . . . They live in underground huts like the Kamchadal, but cleaner, [which] are partly furnished with Japanese household items. Their food consists entirely of wild animals—sea animals, birds, and fish—wild roots and fruits, and seaweed (Fusi sp.), and in the south they enjoy Japanese delicacies like sugar. . . . The clothes of the Northern [Insulaners] are similar to the Evenk and are made of swan, waterfowl, and seal skins and of sea and land animal hides. Their hair is not cut and hangs down to their necks. Their hats are woven from reeds. The Southern

Insulaners have large beards and do not cut their hair, and their lips are [painted] grey. Their clothes are long and follow Chinese style, decorated with furs. (1777: 354–56)

Steller provided more information on Kuril Ainu sea hunting and whaling:

Whales are caught in many surprising ways in Kamchatka, considering the large size of these marine animals. Around Cape Lopatka and the Kuril Islands . . . the natives go to sea in their baidars, searching for locations where whales sleep. Wherever they find these animals, they shoot them with bows armed with poisoned arrows, which soon make the animals swell, screaming and thundering in a terrible way, and force the whales into deep water, and after a while some of them, but not all, may be thrown ashore by the wind and waves. (2003: 71)

Kushi Ainu Skin Boats and Kayaks

Steller's description quoted at the beginning of this chapter grew out of his observations of Eskimo kayaks and umiaks in the Aleutian Islands and southern Alaska and others he had seen in Kamchatka. As we have noted, the Itelmen built large skin boats, but their kayaks are nearly unknown. However, a Japanese warrior named Morishige Kondo wrote a book on the geography of Kamchatka in 1804 that included a description of a skin boat used by Native peoples there, and Nishimura included his report in his own Study of Ancient Ships of Japan:

The skeleton [of the skin boat] is covered with, or rather wrapped in, a sheet of skin. With the boat's frame put inside this spherical skin cover, which in appearance somewhat resembles a money pouch with its neck open or closed by means of string, the opening at the top is closely shut so as to prevent the inrush of water in rough weather. Ainu call the boat tondo-chip, while the Russians call it maitare (baitara [baidara—Eds.] is the correct name).

According to the Ainu, the Kurumusé, or natives of Kamchatka [Kurumusé was the Japanese name for Kamchatka and its people used by the people of Yeso (Hokkaido) during the Tokugawa (Edo) period, 1603–1868—Eds.], when hunting birds in Urup Island [southern Kurils] in this boat, are in the habit of paddling the oars to right and left and thus pushing the craft hither and thither while chasing game with bows and arrows in hand. It is supposed that they paddle the oars with their feet by means of some device set on a string. (Quoted in Nishimura 1931: 107; also footnote 126)

But Nishimura went on to correct this description of the method of propulsion, writing about the image seen in fig. 8.25:

As shown in the picture, the boat is paddled by *kuruma-kai* (perforated oars) and not by means of any other device or mechanism. The skin boat shown in the picture can accommodate only one person and has one manhole. In shape, the boat resembles the Koryak skin boat. The man in the boat is apparently Ainu [because of his long beard], but this is a case of the painter's ignorance or the deceptiveness of pictures. A Kamchadal ought to have been represented here. (1931: 167)

Fig. 8.25. Like Nishimura's illustration of a two-man kayak (fig. 8.22), his illustration of a man with a full beard—and therefore ostensibly Ainu—rowing a skin-covered boat raises questions. The drawing seems to be a crude rendition of a Koryak kayak whose cover is gathered around the man's waist in the fashion of a spray skirt. Unlike the boats shown in figs. 8.22 and 8.23, this one is propelled by oars. Like the early Saami renditions (see fig. 3.12, page 68), this type of evidence for skin boats poses more question than it resolves: are the man and kayak Kushi Ainu, Itelmen, or Koryak? The artist probably never saw the subject and instead created the picture from second- or third-hand knowledge. (From Nishimura 1931: fig. 43; adapted by Marcia Bakry)

Nishimura provided little information about the provenance of this image, which would be revolutionary to scholars if it does in fact show an Ainu in a skin boat. Yet the fact that this illustration is not known outside of Nishimura's book and has not been researched by recent Japanese scholars makes an Ainu identification unlikely. Among the image's inconsistencies are the unlikely physical appearance of this "Ainu" in a Kamchadal boat and the use not of a paddle but of oars, which would be impractical in a small kayak. More likely, this is an artistic creation based on imperfect descriptions of Koryak, Itelmen, or Kushi Ainu boats (Koji Deriha, pers. comm. to WWF, 2018).

We also should point out here the relevance of the foregoing discussion of figs. 8.22 and 8.23 on pages 178–179 and the importation by the Russian American Company of Aleut (Unangan) or Kodiag (Kodiak, now Alutiiq) people from Alaska to the southern Kuril Islands during the late 18th and 19th centuries to serve as indentured sea otter hunters. Some of these Alaskan Natives resided in villages alongside Kuril Ainu (Shubin 1994). Their appearance in the Kurils explains unusual images painted by Japanese artists of double kayaks and hunters using Alaskan costumes and technology.

The End of Traditional Boating in the Kurils

One of the best sources on the Kuril Islands and their people during the late 19th century is a book by the American whaling captain Henry James Snow, who sailed for many years in Russian and Japanese waters and knew their peoples and islands, including Sakhalin. He also had the misfortune to be shipwrecked on one of the Kuril Islands and spent months among the Ainu.

Snow (1897) described how the northern Kuril Islanders, the Kushi, used skin boats, while the Ainu of the southern Kurils had larger planked log boats rigged for sailing. He wrote about attempts by the Russian American Company to profit from Kuril fish, sea mammals, and forest products by using imported Native workers from Kamchatka and Aleut (Unangan) from the Aleutian Islands. This enterprise lasted until 1875, when the company abandoned the Kurils after an agreement was reached under which Russia gave the Kurils to Japan in exchange for southern Sakhalin. Most of the Kuril population was deported to Kamchatka with what little they could carry aboard Russian ships; others retreated to Hokkaido or Alaska. Snow, an eyewitness to this sad event, reported that their homes, boats, and fishing gear were abandoned, bringing an end to the thousands of years during which the users of traditional boats lived on this volcanic island chain.

The answer to the question of whether skin baidars and kayaks were present in the Kurils in the historical era, or even earlier, remains equivocal. The very sparse Japanese information on these boats, as well as Snow's tangential account, is suggestive but allows us only to speculate plausibly about skin boats, at least for the northern Kurils and possibly also for the Itelmen of Kamchatka. Skin boats of the Koryak type were in common use in Kamchatka, and they would have been as useful to the Ainu and Itelmen as they were to the Aleut in the Aleutian Islands. It seems likely that Kuril-Kushi open skin boats did exist, but convincing historical and archaeological documentation remains absent for the moment.

We do know that when the Russians imported Aleut people to the Kuril Islands to work as loggers and hunters, the Aleut brought along their skin boats, which they needed for seal and sea otter hunting. In 1892, Hokkaido's Hakodate museum had a three-hole decked "Kamchatka kayak" (measuring 6.5 by 0.55 meters) collected from Shekotan (Shikotan) Island, adjacent to Hokkaido. Similar to the case of the Greenland Inuit paddlers (and their kayaks) who turned up as "Finnmen" in Scotland (see chapter 3, page 52), the Aleut-Eskimo kayak and its paddlers took passage, via the Russian American Company, to the Kurils and to Japan, as documented in a photo taken by Scottish missionary-ethnologist John Batchelor (1892: 184). Unfortunately this pattern of ambiguity in Kamchatka and the Kurils regarding skin boats continues as we follow the story into the maritime region of the Far East, where bark canoes were abundant in interior settings but where skin boats, if they ever were present, disappeared in coastal waters before they could be described, owing to the early appearance of log and plank boats.

CHAPTER 9

THE FAR EAST

MANCHURIA, SAKHALIN ISLAND, CHINA, AND NORTHERN JAPAN

The final chapter of our Eurasian survey is devoted to the region surrounding the lower Amur River and the southern shores of the Sea of Okhotsk (map 17). Archaeological evidence indicates that as early as 14,000 years ago, even before the end of the last ice age, people were living in large semiunderground houses in settled villages along the lower Amur, making pottery, fishing for sturgeon and other fish, and hunting river-run sea mammals. By 13,000 years ago, settlements at the Ushki site on the Kamchatka River were concentrated at salmon-fishing locations (Dikov 1996; Goebel, Waters, and Dikova 2003). Sites of comparable age exist on Honshu and Hokkaido, where maritime resources were abundant, and by 8,000 to 9,000 years ago, the peoples of the lower Amur and Jōmon Japan, and probably others, had developed harpoons for

securing large fish and sea mammals (Yamaura 1978, 1998; Habu 2004, 2010). All these developments required the use of boats for river or coastal navigation. By 2,000 years ago, trade along the Okhotsk and northwestern Pacific coasts had connected the ivory-rich Bering Sea cultures with East Asian metal-using agricultural societies and their elites. Soon after the arrival of early explorers such as Vitus Bering, Georg W. Steller (2003), and Stepan Krasheninnikov (1755), the Native societies of Kamchatka and the Bering Sea began to suffer the ravages of European diseases. However, enough is known to indicate that these peoples were experienced boatbuilders and navigators accustomed to traversing the Bering Strait and perhaps even the passage from Kamchatka to the Aleutian Islands (although recent DNA studies do not support a Kamchatka-Aleut connection).

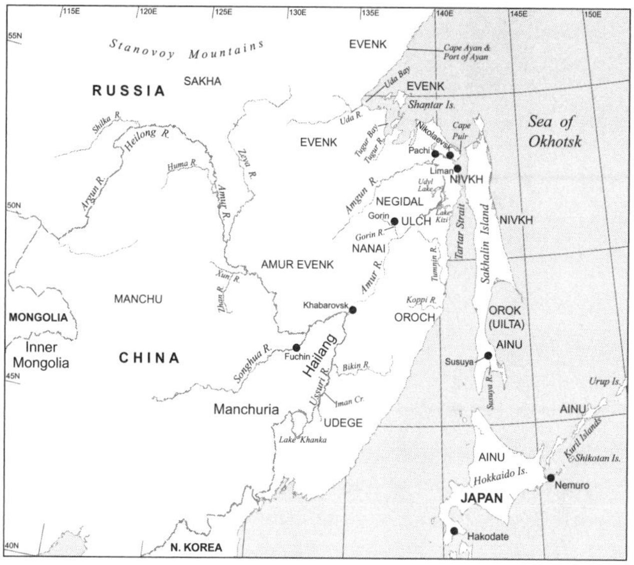

Unfortunately, documentary evidence of boats in this region comes almost exclusively from ethnographic museum objects, photographs, and post-1700 exploration reports that contain ambiguous illustrations. The only traces of archaeological data known to the authors are two 1,500-year-old ivory kayak models (discussed previously; see fig. 8.11, page 168) and the 1,000-year-old images of whale hunters carved on Okhotsk-culture bone needlecases (see fig. 9.3, page 189). These finds indicate that skin boat technology was already well advanced by this period and that early Okhotsk hunters were capable of hunting large whales, probably with skin boats. Historical accounts speak of skin boat use among the Kerek, Koryak, and Itelmen peoples of Kamchatka (see the previous chapter), and Japanese reports and old illustrations hint at skin boat use in the Kuril Islands and Sakhalin, where the maritime-adapted, Eskimo-like Okhotsk culture flourished until circa 1200 CE. These data are insufficient to establish the existence of an indigenous skin boat tradition in southern Okhotsk waters, although one might have been present before the Russians, Chinese, and Japanese

Map 17. The Far East and Manchuria, Sakhalin Island, and northern Japan: territories of the Nivkh, Nanay, Udege, Oroch, Negidal, Manchu, Ainu, Amur Evenk, Chinese, and Tibetans. (Dan Cole, Smithsonian Institution)

introduced plank boats and the double kayaks used by Alaskan sea otter hunters.

The following sections describe the boat traditions and uses of the Nivkh, Nanay, Ulch, Udege, Oroch, Negidal, Manchu, Ainu, and Amur Evenk, as well as Chinese and Tibetan groups who used skin rafts and ox-hide boats for river transport. The last section is admittedly thin, since we have not been able to access the voluminous Chinese literature that exists on indigenous watercraft. Nevertheless, it is clear that the Amur region has a distinctive boat history and that the Amur I and II birch-bark canoe types constitute a fourth bark boat tradition in the boreal regions of Eurasia.

THE NIVKH: MARINE HUNTERS OF THE SOUTHERN OKHOTSK SEA AND SAKHALIN

The Nivkh (formerly called the Gilyak, and who call themselves the Grimin; Lattimore 1962: 351) are thought to be direct descendants of the Neolithic populations of their present residence areas close to the mouth of the Amur River, on the Sea of Okhotsk coast, and on the northern half of Sakhalin Island (see papers in S. Nelson 2006). Although Sakhalin had early Holocene occupations, Russian archaeological finds suggest that the ancestors of the Nivkh on Sakhalin arrived in two waves around 3,000 and 4,000 years ago (Kuzmin et al. 2004). Formerly, Nivkh territory on the Siberian mainland extended to the Uda River in the northwest and included the Shantar Islands before the Amur Evenk and Negidal took over these lands. Salmon and freshwater fish were central to Nivkh subsistence and were caught with nets, seines, pole barriers, and traps. The Nivkh on Sakhalin and in the Amur River estuary also hunted seal and sea lion with harpoons and clubs from boats, from shore, and from winter sea ice. In the 1897 Russian census, the Nivkh numbered 4,649 people, of whom 1,744 lived on Sakhalin (VanStone 1985). Near the Nivkh on the Uda River estuary, the Oroch-Evenk lived along the Tugur River. To the north lived the Even, in the territory around Cape Ayan that they had taken from the Nivkh. The Nivkh are the only large group in the lower Amur-Sakhalin region unrelated to the Tungus or to Manchu-speaking peoples; instead their DNA discloses a close relation to the Ainu, who dominated the Amur delta region in medieval times. The primary ancestors of the Nivkh were the maritime Okhotsk culture of the southern Sea of Okhotsk and Hokkaido.

Fishing and Hunting in the Amur Basin

Finnish natural scientist Arthur Nordmann visited the Amur region from 1857 to 1860 to continue the work of Leopold von Schrenk, a Baltic-German naturalist who had stayed at the Amur on a Russian Academy of Sciences mission from 1854 to 1856. While there, Nordmann (1867) studied Nivkh fishing and hunting and gathered information on birch-bark canoes. The Nivkh are usually described as maritime hunters of the Okhotsk coast and Tatar Strait, between Sakhalin Island and the Asian mainland, who used boats for hunting, fishing, and trade. Nordmann contributed information on their inland economy as well and, like Schrenk (1881: 207–08), believed they were originally inland people who displaced and partly merged with Ainu from northern Sakhalin. Birch-bark canoes were central to Nivkh transport, as they were for the Nanay and Oroch (see this chapter's section on the Amur Evenk, page 204). In the Russian Ethnographic Museum collection, the remains of a large Nivkh birch-bark canoe from the village of Pachi, on the lower Amur (fig. 9.1), reveal that it had very strong double gunwales and was wider

Fig. 9.1. Some Amur River bark canoes were extremely long and could accommodate several people. V. N. Vasiliev collected a Nivkh paddle and the middle part of a birch-bark canoe (REM 6762-50) from the lower Amur River village of Pachi in 1910–11. This was an important find because Lev Shternberg, who studied the Nivkh earlier, claimed they had no bark canoes. (Photograph: I. Tkachenko; courtesy Russian Ethnographic Museum)

than the typical Amur bark canoe, whose width was circa 70 centimeters.

In the 1920s, some 60 years after Nordmann's visit, the Russian ethnologist Lev Shternberg arrived on Sakhalin as a political exile to continue Nordmann's studies. He found that the Nivkh no longer used or knew how to make bark canoes. It seems that in the interval, planked boats, acquired through contact with the Chinese and Russians in the late 19th century, had replaced bark canoes. A similar change occurred among the Nanay, as Owen Lattimore, the cultural geographer of China, reported (1962). The last Nivkh or Ainu bark boats on southern Sakhalin Island were seen in the 1920s. The shift from bark to plank boats also may have precipitated the disappearance of skin boats in coastal regions.

The Amur and its tributaries are famous for their great quantities of fish. During the summer season, the Nivkh used bark canoes for fishing, principally with nets made of nettle fiber, which they set at fixed locations or let drift in the current. Winter fishing involved stretching nets beneath the ice. The Nivkh used one species of salmon for dog food, and dried others for human food in winter. Salmon were caught with traps, hooks, and harpoons as they traveled up the Amur and its tributaries and were dried in shelters roofed with birch bark. Pike were also caught with harpoons from canoes, as Nordmann described in a colorful passage:

> During the hot clear summer days, when the Gilyak [Nivkh] has nothing else to do, he takes off in a so-called *omorochka* made of birch bark, which is thus very light to steer, to the quiet side streams, where the river bottom is decked with water plants. Here he tries to get some pike and other large fish that sunbathe close to the water surface. The Gilyak will be armed with a three-bladed harpoon fixed to a long shaft. As soon as he gets close to the sunning fish, the latter will slowly move away, indicating its location and direction with a small swell or wave on the surface. From the small surface wave on the calm water, the Gilyak knows exactly where the fish is hiding, without seeing it, and he can harpoon it with great precision. (1867: 338)

Nordmann also saw people harpooning fish from a bark canoe that had a burning birch-bark torch in an iron holder projecting from its bow. The Nivkh inhabitants of Bai, on the coast of the Tatar Strait, practiced this method in small sea bays.

The Nivkh also hunted moose and reindeer in spring, especially in the mountains near the Amgun, Gorin, and Ussuri rivers. When the snow was deep, hunters on snowshoes or skis could outrace the animals and kill them with a spear or gun. They also hunted with dogsleds in spring, when icy crust impeded the prey's escape. In autumn, when moose gathered in shallow water to feed on grass and water plants, the Nivkh hunted them with boats. On dark nights, hunters in canoes could approach through the tall grass until they were close enough for a shot or spear thrust when the moose had its head underwater, feeding on plants.

Nordmann (1867) and Watanabe (2013) described beluga—an important source of meat, leather, and oil—on the coast and their seasonal visits to the Amur as they chased fish as far as 400 versts (427 kilometers) upriver. When the animals entered the Amur in large pods in spring, the Nivkh harpooned them with hooked spears connected to ropes and skin floats. Hunters would follow a wounded beluga marked by a float until it weakened; then they killed it with a spear and, attaching more floats, towed it home. After the village gave the animal a welcome ritual, they held a feast and sent the beluga's spirit off to the sky. Similar "sending rituals" were practiced by many North Pacific peoples in the belief that honoring the animals' spirits would ensure a plentiful supply of prey in the future. After the arrival of the Russians, the Nivkh began to use planked boats rowed by half a dozen men to hunt beluga in the open sea, and by 1860, the Russians had begun their own beluga fishery, competing with the Nivkh, by establishing a company on Cap Puir that hunted with nets, as the Pomor were doing in the White Sea. Needless to say, the Russians did not honor the spirits of the animals they caught, an affront that the Nivkh and other Native groups saw as the reason for the subsequent depletion of the animals.

Sealing, however, was more important than beluga hunting to the Nivkh, and it was conducted in Liman and along the Tatar Strait. They hunted seal with nets and ambushed them with clubs and spears on rocky shores. Another favorite prey animal was the sea lion, which they hunted on the spring sea ice, approaching in boats and killing them with spears or guns, just as the Pomor did in their spring harp seal hunt.

Skin Boats on Sakhalin Island

Descriptions of Nivkh canoes and boats vary according to sources and time periods. For example, Shternberg (1933: chap. 12, 538) thought they did not use bark canoes. Historical and archaeological sources provide information on skin boats because the Nivkh used them for hunting the rich marine fauna of the Amur estuary and the Sea of Okhotsk. But Antropova evidently did not know or did not believe that skin boats had been used in southern Sakhalin, offering this blunt opinion of Nivkh and Ulch watercraft: "As far as the seagoing boat of the Nivkh and Ulch is concerned, it is actually a river boat, only partly fitted out for use in the coastal zone. In this case a change in function was not accompanied by a change in construction" (1961: 112).

One of only a few Japanese sources on skin boats written in English is Shinji Nishimura's *A Study of Ancient Ships of Japan*, part 4: *Skin Boats* (1931). Nishimura was a professor of ancient Japanese history at Waseda University who, between 1928 and 1931, published a series of books on boat history, including skin boats. He believed a chain of skin boat users once stretched from Sakhalin to Kamchatka, and probably throughout the Sea of Okhotsk and northern Japan as well, before western contact. Jochelson (1928: 57–60) was inclined toward a similar conclusion regarding the Nivkh after he had studied Koryak skin boats, but he never found material evidence for his supposition, or for their use by the Ainu (see the Ainu section, page 200). While traveling in Sakhalin, Nishimura came across two old skin boats that provide rare material evidence of their use in the southern Okhotsk Sea. His skin boat volume included a photograph (Nishimura 1931: fig. 60, 157, 236) of these boats that is too murky to see clearly; however, an interpretation of their structure suggests a construction and skin covering similar to those of other North Pacific open skin boats (fig. 9.2a–b).

Ancient Boats on Sakhalin Island

As in Chukotka, archaeological finds on Sakhalin have provided tangible evidence missing from historical records and ethnographic objects, this time from the Okhotsk culture, which existed from 700 to 1200 CE on the southern shores of the Sea of Okhotsk. In 1907, while excavating a large Okhotsk-culture shellmound on the Susuya River on southern Sakhalin Island, Shogoro Tsuboi found 21 bird-bone needlecases, some of which were engraved with navigation and fishing scenes. One showed a boat manned by seven paddlers who had captured a rorqual whale with a harpoon and a drag float (fig. 9.3; see also Nishimura 1931: pl. XVIII). From these illustrations, Tsuboi drew conclusions about the nature of Okhotsk-culture people's boats, harpoons, and maritime capabilities (discussed in Nishimura 1931: 154–56). In the summer of 1924, Nishimura traveled

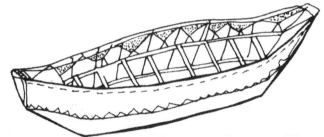

Fig. 9.2. Studying Shinji Nishimura's poorly printed photo (*a*) of two skin boats he photographed on Sakhalin Island enabled HL to reconstruct their general features (*b*), which resemble those of open skin boats of North Pacific peoples, including the method that was used to lash the boat's skin cover over the gunwales. (*a*: From Nishimura 1931: fig. 60; *b*: drawing: Harri Luukkanen)

to Sakhalin, which was called Karafuto by the Japanese, to collect anthropological data for his book. Revisiting the Susuya River site, he excavated pottery, stone implements, and animal bones but was disappointed at not finding engraved needlecases. However, the presence of whale vertebrae confirmed Tsuboi's idea that Okhotsk was a fully maritime-adapted culture with deep-sea hunting capabilities. Later, researchers found whaling scenes carved on needlecases at other Okhotsk-culture sites and determined that Okhotsk-culture territory once included northern Hokkaido, Sakhalin, and the southern Kuril Islands (B. Fitzhugh, Shubin, Tezuka, Ishizuka, and Mandryk 2002; W. Fitzhugh and Dubreuil 1999: fig. 3.19). Nishimura praised Tsuboi's insights into Okhotsk whaling but thought he had not paid sufficient attention to the needlecases' boat images. He pointed particularly to the large crews shown in the carvings, noting that the boats could not have been bark ones and instead must have been open skin boats,

Fig. 9.3. In 1907, Shogoro Tsuboi excavated the Okhotsk-culture Susuya site on Sakhalin and found this needlecase with an engraving of people hunting whales from boats using harpoons. Tsuboi and Nishimura assumed Japan's early people were ancestral Japanese. Later, archaeologists uncovered engraved needlecases in Okhotsk-culture sites at the Bentento site near Nemuro, Hokkaido. Like the Susuya find, they also showed whaling scenes and could be dated to 700–1300 CE. Their age and northern distribution showed that the Okhotsk people were in fact ancestral Ainu, not Japanese. (From Fitzhugh and Dubreuil 1999: fig. 3.19; courtesy Hokkaido University Botanical Garden and Museum)

like the ones he had seen on Sakhalin, which he thought resembled Eskimo angyapit and umiaks.

The Susuya finds fascinated the Japanese because it confirmed stories about a people known in Ainu mythology as Koro-pok-guru, legendary "little people" who made pottery, used flint tools, lived in underground houses, and traveled in skin boats light enough to carry on their backs. Tsuboi did not believe the Koro-pok-guru were Ainu ancestors because none of their maritime characteristics matched those of the impoverished, landlocked 20th-century Ainu of Hokkaido. Rather, he saw the skin boat–using Koro-pok-guru as possible ancestors of the Eskimo. Nishimura did not see a direct Okhotsk-Eskimo connection, but he supported Tsuboi's idea that they had used skin boats, and he became an early proponent of the idea that the Japanese once were a skin boat–using maritime people. Nishimura wrote:

It is rather clear that the pottery found in Susuya is decidedly quite different from the Stone Age pottery occasionally found in Hokkaido or Hondo [Honshu]. However, considering the fact that the Gilyaks living in Sakhalin have a kind of skin boat and are skilled in the art of processing fish skins and making various things of them; that Koryak dwelling north of Kamchatka possess skin boats [ma'to]; that Aleuts have the custom of making boats of animal skins; and that Eskimos have their kayak, . . . it may be conjectured that the people who left behind the engraved artifacts in the shell-mound at Susuya must have been one or other of those tribes and that the boats

etched on one of the bone tubes represent one of the boats that belonged to them. (1931: 151–53)

Despite sharing features with ancient Eskimos, including whaling, open skin boats, pithouses, sedentary coastal life, and intensive maritime economies, there is no archaeological, DNA, or linguistic evidence of direct Okhotsk-Eskimo contact. This is not surprising considering the two peoples were separated by 2,500 kilometers, with many other cultures between them. Nevertheless, Tsuboi's and Nishimura's views find more support today than they did 100 years ago. Most archaeologists who have studied northeastern Asia's prehistory now see evidence of widespread interactions between the Amur-Okhotsk and Bering Sea regions for thousands of years (Chard 1974; Ackerman 1984; Arutiunov and W. Fitzhugh 1988; Dumond and Bland 1995; Habu 2004, 2010; S. Nelson 2006; Vasilevsky and Shubina 2006; B. Fitzhugh 2016; Cooper et al. 2016). If not the peoples themselves, at least some of their maritime technologies spread north to the Eskimo peoples living around the Bering Sea.

THE NANAY AND ULCH: RIVER PEOPLE OF THE AMUR, USSURI, AND SONGHUA BASINS

As Berthold Laufer, an ethnographer of the Amur peoples, wrote after researching this culturally complex area for the Jesup North Pacific Expedition: "None of the tribes mentioned can [be] thoroughly understood by its own culture alone, for the single tribes have influenced each other to such an extent that, generally speaking, all of them show at present nearly the same state of material culture. The principal differences between them lie mainly in their physical types and intellectual life" (1900: 297; see also Laufer 1898, 1917). In similar fashion, we can say that if one studies a single Amur people's bark canoes in detail, one can gain a general sense of the canoes of the entire Amur region, but to understand their differences, one must study them all.

This statement relates well to the Nanay groups along the lower Amur (Heilong Jiang) River and the Ussuri and Songhua (formerly known as the Sungari) rivers in the Russian Amur Oblast and in China's Heilong Jiang Province. In the past, these groups went by ethnonyms or tribal names given to them by Russians, Evenk, or Chinese, and the resulting naming intricacy complicates our study of watercraft, making it difficult to correlate boat types with ethnic groups, which usually have been defined by their language affiliations.

The Ulch and Oroch peoples are also closely related to the Nanay, who include a group called the Samagir, who live in the Ussuri-Girin region. In the Manchurian part of China, the Nanay live where the Ussuri and Songhua (Sungari) rivers join the Amur. Here several subgroups compose the larger Nanay people, who in the early 19th century lived principally as settled fishermen and cultivated ginseng root for sale to the Chinese. At that time, the Nanay were known by their Russian name, Goldi (or Golde or Gold), an ethnonym that was also often used to describe the Ulch, Oroch, and Negidal. The Russians and Chinese also colloquially referred to the Nanay as "Fish Skin Tatars" (Lattimore 1962), owing to their use of tanned salmon skin for bags, clothing, summer raincoats, and sails for their canoes. Properly scaled and processed, fish skin is waterproof, durable, and decorative; when fish scales were retained on the soles of fish-skin boots, the boots acted like skis when people walked downslope and provided traction going up. Ancient Chinese documents such as the *Shūjīng* note the Nanay penchant for using fish skin as early as 2,000 years ago.

Today the Nanay and closely related groups number about 16,000 people, of whom some 2,500 belong to a group in Russia called the Ulch; about 9,000 Nanay live in the Russian region of Khabarovsk and between 2,500 and 4,000 live in China. In the Amur region, the Nanay are the most numerous aboriginal river people and the best known. They called their canoe *dhzai* (*dsai*); the Ulch, *zai*. Since the Nanay have a close relationship with the Manchu, this chapter also includes an introduction to Manchu *chzhaya* bark canoes.

Nanay Canoes North of the Amur River

Referring to Leopold von Schrenk's (1881) documentation of peoples and boats in the Amur region and his own observation of several boat models that the Smithsonian borrowed from St. Petersburg, Otis T. Mason and Meriden S. Hill described the Nanay (Gold) and Ulch Amur bark canoes thus:

> Canoes made of a wooden interior structure covered with birch-bark are more commonly in use than dugouts among the Oltscha [Ulch] and Golde on the Lower Amur, and are employed also by the Tungus on the Amur tributaries and throughout the streams of the Stanovoy Mountains. In general, of like type everywhere, having the two ends similarly pointed, these bark canoes called *dsai* by the Oltscha and Golde, in their outlines and proportions, as in individual traits, present many peculiarities. However, corresponding nearly to the *gulba* and *otongo* dugouts of the Oltscha and Golde, there are two forms of

> bark canoes, one deeper and narrower in proportion to the length, generally decked a little with bark at bow and stern [Amur type II canoe]; and a broad, flat, and open form with ends strongly upcurved [Amur type I canoe]. Of the former, von Schrenk furnishes a lithograph and of the latter a woodcut, showing a Golde man at the mouth of the Ussuri River sitting in his *dsai*. The former, through its light form and the deck over the bow to keep off the spray of the turbid waters, is better adapted for use on the upper streams. The latter, on the contrary, furnishes more room for the fishing and hunting outfit and for game. The handling of the canoes is precisely the same as that of the dugouts, the *otongo* and the *gulba*.

> The measurements of the Oltscha canoe were 18½ feet [5.64 meters] long, 2½ feet [0.76 meters] broad in the middle, depth 11 inches [28 centimeters]. In operating these frail and light canoes, the Amur-Tungus, Oltscha, Golde and other tribes, like their Siberian congeners, developed skill and dexterity which, at times, in the mad rush of the swollen streams, recalls the hardihood and readiness of the Aleuts in their baidarkas and is in strong contrast with the clumsiness and prudent foresight of the Giliak [Nivkh] at the Amur mouth and on Saghalin [Sakhalin] Islands.... Also, the Birar and the Manegir have bark canoes of the form and structure of the *dsai*, but twice as long, while the width is the same. Schrenk saw among the latter an example 35½ feet [10.8 meters] long and only 2 feet 2 inches [0.66 meters] wide. Such a boat is like the Aleut baidarka with several holes and more like the great *mango*. These are propelled with poles or with two or three double paddles, and are worked by men paddling first on one side and then on the other, shooting forward with great velocity.

> The pointed dugouts, as well as the birch-bark canoes, are found also among all the aboriginal tribes of the Upper Amur. Since these are chiefly nomads living by the chase who only occasionally go down from their hunting grounds and the tributaries to the main stream in order here to prosecute their fishing, these simple, easily repaired, and, on occasion, readily transported craft, which are also available in rapid as in still water, suffice for all their needs. Not only the narrow types, like the *otongo* or the *dsai*, are seen, but also those of large dimensions. In such boats they migrate from winter to summer quarters

and back, transporting not only women and children, but a multitude of tools and utensils. In the museum of the Imperial Academy of Sciences of St. Petersburg are three models of pointed canoes, all made of birch bark. (1901: 535)

Of the three Nanay birch-bark models that Mason and Hill noted, the earliest, collected by Leopold von Schrenk in 1840 (MAE 36-241), is damaged and has lost its pointed ends. A second model (MAE 313-2), collected in 1896, is also damaged. The third (MAE 1765-281a), collected with its double-bladed paddle and a trident fish spear by Lev Shternberg in 1910, is complete (fig. 9.4); it shows the classic Amur type I form, with the upturned bow and stern projections seen in M. G. Levin's 1927 illustration (fig. 9.5) and in a type I canoe replica in the Khabarovsk Regional Museum (fig. 9.6).

Circa 1870, Thomas W. Knox, an American traveler, visited the Amur during an expedition across Asia and made some interesting comparisons between Nanay and North American birch-bark canoes:

Besides their boats of wood the Goldees make canoes of birch bark, quite broad in the middle and coming to a point at both ends. In general appearance, these canoes resemble those of the Penobscot and Canadian Indians. The native sits in the middle of his canoe and propels himself with a double-bladed oar. . . . The canoes are flat bottomed and very easy to overturn. The canoe is designed to carry but one man, though two can be taken in an emergency. When a native sitting in one of them spears a fish, he moves only his arm and keeps his body motionless.

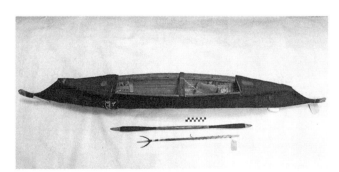

Fig. 9.4. A Nanay birch-bark model (MAE 1765-281a) collected by Lev Shternberg in 1910 displays features typical of the Amur type I canoe: upturned keel projections, a partially decked bow and stern, and a double-bladed paddle. (Photograph: Evguenia Anichtchenko; courtesy Museum of Anthropology and Ethnography)

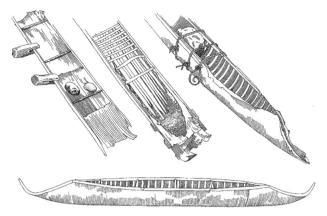

Fig. 9.5. In 1927, M. G. Levin studied the construction features of an Nanay Amur I type bark canoe, including the method used to construct the pointed ends, with curved, bark-covered wood supports attached to keel extensions. Long bottom stringers reach from end to end. Most Nanay canoes are narrow, only about 70 to 80 centimeters wide. This illustration is part of Levin's 1927 drawing, later published in Thiele (1984: fig. 6). (Courtesy Museum für Völkerkunde, Berlin)

Fig. 9.6. A different method of making boat ends is seen in this Nanay Amur type I replica canoe, displayed in the Khabarovsk Regional Museum (KP-6623). Its upturned bow and stern projections extend from the gunwales at the top of the deck, where they join the upturned keel. Strong gunwale rails provide rigidity for such a long canoe. Like most Amur canoes, its bow and stern ends are decked with birch bark. (Courtesy Khabarovsk Regional Museum)

At the Russian village of Gorin there was an Ispravnik [*a local administrator—Eds.*] who had charge of a district containing nineteen villages with about fifteen hundred inhabitants. . . . The Ispravnik was kind enough to give me the model of a Goldee canoe about 18 inches [0.46 m] long . . . made by one Anaka Katonovitch, chief of an ancient Goldee family. . . . The canoe was neatly formed, and reflected favorably upon the skill of its designer. I boxed it carefully and sent it to Nicolayevsk for shipment to America. (1871: 155–56)

Knox was off-base here in his comparison of Nanay and Penobscot birch-bark canoes. While they do share birch-bark covers, gunwales, ribs, and floor lathing, their bows, stern decks, and ends are radically different. However, Schrenk's and Knox's observations are supported by Antropova (1961), who said that the Nanay bark canoe differed from that of the Amur Evenk mostly because of its sharply upward-bent ends. The Nanay used a two-bladed paddle for normal propulsion and smaller single-bladed hand paddles when they needed to travel silently; in shallow water, they punted with poles. Sails were rarely used on rivers, although the Ulch people used fish-skin sails. The sizes of their bark canoes varied, but a length of 5 to 6 meters, a beam of 0.7 meters (with the greatest width in the middle), and a depth of 0.3 meters predominated. Russians called the Nanay birch-bark canoe *omorochek* or *omorochka*.

V. R. Chepelev (2004), a Russian Academy of Sciences researcher working in the Russian Far East, describes the planked boats, dugout boats, birch-bark canoes, and skin boats that the Nivkh and Nanay once used on the lower Amur and Sakhalin Island. In addition to log boats, lower Amur peoples used birch-bark canoes and skin boats. Chepelev notes that the birch-bark boat might have replaced the more ancient *korevuye*, made from the bark of coniferous trees by ancestors of the Tungus-Manchu (Evenk) people (see more on larch-bark canoes in this chapter's section on the Amur Evenk). Birch-bark boats were distributed mainly on the left-hand, or northern, tributaries of the Amur, which had the relatively calm rivers needed for such fragile boats. Chepelev describes the building of one of these Amur birch-bark canoes in detail:

> From a birch tree, usually in July, the bark is removed with a sharp knife and dried under a canopy [as in figs. 1.1 and 9.12a, pages 31 and 202]. Then from spruce or larch wood, long thin strips are planed out, which, after being soaked in water, are fastened to the edge of the canoe with a very durable adhesive—*kaluzhego*, made from fish bladders—and after they have dried, a trimmed bark sheet about 1 meter wide is glued in two layers. For a more lasting bond between the layers, strips of birch bark are fastened with small wooden or metal pegs. In the middle of the boat, an extra strip of bark, going the full length, is added to give additional strength to the bottom. On the bottom of the boat, for the same purpose, they place rows of single wood strips, usually made of larch, and then install curved ribs [inside the boat] made from spruce soaked in water for half a day. To make the omorochka slide noiselessly on a glassy river or stream, the rough bottom of the boat is burned over a fire of pine shavings. After this fire treatment, the bark becomes brown and shiny, as if varnished. The sides of the boat are sometimes decorated with images of fish and animals. The paint is made from grasses and the dark blue "chachaka" flower. Pigments are mixed with fish glue to make the paint durable, and the color can last as long as the omorochka itself. (2004: 151)

Chepelev also writes that Nanay birch-bark canoes had many forms: most had an open top, but the Nanay also made some with decked bow and stern sections, almost like the Eskimo or Aleut kayak (fig. 9.7). The ends of the omorochkas were usually somewhat raised so the boats could slide easily over the water's surface. Sometimes the top had only a small, square hole, nearly as wide as the boat, to accommodate a man. Chepelev notes that in times of danger, a hunter could roll his boat over and breathe the air trapped inside it. The Nanay had birch-bark boats for heavy-duty jobs as well. Despite the boats' apparent fragility, some could carry one or two moose carcasses. Chepelev reports that those who lived on the banks of the Songhua River in Manchuria used a willow-twig wicker-frame boat covered with animal skins, whose shape was similar to that of the bark boat.

Fig. 9.7. This poplar-framed birch-bark Amur II type canoe, of the type that the Hezhe (Goldi) people used for hunting and fishing in the Songhua (formerly Sungari) River, is a smaller craft built for one or two persons and measures 209 by 46 centimeters. It is similar to the craft shown in fig. 9.8 (page 194), an old Qing-dynasty drawing. (From Ling 1934: fig. 101)

While many Eurasian peoples made birch-bark boats, the Nanay were the unsurpassed masters. Using the birch-bark canoe, the Nanay hunted, fished with hooks and spears, and traveled between camps. For the Nanay, the bark canoe was equivalent to the horse for a Mongol warrior or Russian peasant. Almost every family member had an omorochka custom-made for his height and weight. The Nanay treated their fragile omorochkas carefully but used them everywhere. They were famous for the carvings and designs they used to decorate their canoes, which they made more comfortable with reed and cane mat seats. The hunter and his boat were inseparable: he fished and hunted with it, slept under it while traveling, and used it as a roof in the rain. According to eyewitnesses such as Owen Lattimore (1962), sometimes a whole fleet of Nanay traveled in birch-bark canoes on forest streams. Today, Chepelev says, omorochkas are difficult to find because the Nanay have replaced them with frame boats covered with canvas.

Nanay Canoes on the Ussuri River

The Ussuri River runs south to north before entering the Amur River near the Russian city of Khabarovsk, and it marks the border between the Russian Primorsky Krai (also known as Primor'e, which translates as Maritime Province) and the eastern part of China's Heilong Jiang Province. In its upper part, the Ussuri has two eastern tributaries, the Bikin and Iman rivers, which have important archaeological sites. Nikolay Kradin and colleagues (2009) write that in the 18th century, Nanay and Manchu peoples settled on the lower reaches of the Bikin and Iman, whereas the Udege people (see this chapter's next section) lived on their middle and upper reaches. These peoples were not numerous, consisting of only a few hundred members, but nonetheless the region once was a center of early habitation.

Settled life in the area of today's Primor'e, south of Sakhalin and the Amur mouth, began around 16,000 BCE, when fishing villages first appeared on these rivers. Several Iman and Bikin sites date to the Neolithic and many more to the Bronze and Iron ages (A. N. Popov and Yesner 2006). The medieval period is also well represented, and one can trace hunters, fishermen, and farmers from that time up to the modern age. Such a rich archaeological history leads to the assumption that the birch-bark canoe must have a deep history in this region. Chepelev (2004), citing the work of Anatoli Derevyanko, Alexei P. Okladnikov, and Klavdia Mylnikova-Forshteyn, maintains that birch-bark

canoes were used here starting in the 1st millennium BCE and might have been present even earlier, during the Neolithic (5000–2000 BCE). In actuality, their history must reach back into the late Pleistocene to account for the area's riverine fishing sites that date to this time; fishermen at these sites must have used canoes, and they likely were made of birch bark, as it was available throughout the Amur region and was the easiest type of bark to work, and because woodworking tools, such as axes and gouges, were not yet available to make expanded log and plank boats.

The Russian naval officer Nikolai Przhevalsky was one of the explorers who documented birch-bark canoes sailing along the Ussuri River. He traveled in the Far East in 1867–69 and gathered information about the new Russian-Chinese border after the 1860 Peking Treaty had annexed the eastern Ussuri region to Russia. In his 1869 book about the mapping expedition and the Chinese, Nanay, Oroch, and Koreans he met in the Ussuri valley, he commented on the Nanay bark canoe:

> Spending a large part of his life on the water, the Gold [Nanay] devised for himself a special boat called the omorochka. This boat is 2½ to 3 *segnes* [5.3 to 6.4 meters] long but only 1 *arshin* [0.7 meters] wide, and both its ends are highly bent above the water. The frame of the omorochka is made from thin wood strips and strong gunwales and is covered with sewn white birch bark so that this boat is featherlight and obedient to the smallest motion of the paddle, but it is also necessary to have decks for spray covers so that it is safe to use. Under the skillful hand of the Gold, who with one long paddle rows on both sides, the boat flies like a bird. But if it is necessary to not make noise, then he puts away his long paddle and, taking in his hands two small paddles whose blades are made of planks, carefully paddles with them, and slips over the mirrored surface of the water as quiet as a whisper. (1869: 29)

Przhevalsky stayed at Lake Khanka (Hanka), one source of the Ussuri River, in 1868 and 1869, giving him the opportunity to observe Nanay birch-bark production there: "The bark of the white birch is of great help in building different items. The bark, after the usual preparation (soaking in hot water and then smoking over fire), is used to cover temporary dwellings like yurts, bark boats, and different utensils, etc." (1869: 14) (fig. 1.1). He also documented hunting methods, describing how the Nanay stalked in bark canoes near the shore until flocks of mountain sheep crossed, at which point the hunters would attack them with spears.

Two interesting details appear in Przhevalsky's story. One is the Nanay's use of small hand paddles (noted above) when silence was required in maneuvering a boat, reminiscent of the Koryak's propulsion of their short-decked kayak (see fig. 8.20, page 177; and chapter 8, page 177). The Negidal and Amur Evenk also employed hand paddles (fig. 9.8). The other is the technique of soaking bark in hot water and then smoking it over a fire (something done by most birch-bark canoe makers), a tanning process that took several days but made the bark water resistant.

Fig. 9.8. This drawing from a Qing-dynasty (1644–1912) book shows a Qiahala Nanay man paddling a birch-bark canoe in rough water. Notable are the boat's short length (typical of Sungari Nanay), the two short paddles, and the harpoon, used for fishing in the Heilong Jiang (Amur) and Songhua river basins. (From Ling 1934: fig. 103)

The Ulch Bark Canoe

Antropova (1961) wrote that at the beginning of the 20th century, the Ulch had boats similar to those of the Nanay: a birch-bark canoe (*zai*), two types of dugouts, a boat made of three planks, and a larger planked boat rigged with a sail, similar to a Nivkh boat. Unlike the Nanay, the Ulch engaged in sea travel and sea mammal hunting. Today they number some 3,200 people, living mainly along the lower Amur River. The Norwegian Polar Research Institute database on Russian ethnic groups describes them thus:

The Ulch led a sedentary mode of life based on fishing and, secondarily, hunting and trapping.... Fishing was a year-round activity with its climaxes during the salmon migrations. The migratory routes of the salmon also determined the distribution of Ulch villages along the right bank of the main channel of the Amur River. Traditional fishing tools included nets, *zaezdkas* (fishhooks on long shafts), and various types of spears. Fish was not only the main food for people, but also for dogs, which they kept in large numbers as draught animals.

Hunting was of secondary importance. They mostly hunted fur animals—mainly sable, but also weasel, squirrel, otter, fox. Prior to the introduction of guns, weapons were bows and arrows and spears. Pelts were in great demand among Russian and Chinese merchants. When sables became rare in the Amur area at the end of the 19th century, the Ulch hunters would leave for long expeditions to Sakhalin, to the basins of the Amgun, Gorin, and Tumnin rivers, in order to find them. Moose and wild reindeer were hunted throughout the year. Marine mammals, especially otter and sea lion, could be taken on the coast of the Tatar Strait. The Ulch travelled there in small groups across Lake Kizi....

The main means of summer transport were boats: plank punt boats, *ugda*, canoes, omorochki, and small birch-bark boats; in winter, the Ulch used skis and dog sleds of the Amur type, which were narrow and light and had bent runners. (Norwegian Polar Institute 2006: Ulch)

Western literature offers only a few remarks on the bark canoes of the Ulch (also written as Ulcha, Ulchi, and Oltscha) or their measurements. Leopold von Schrenk wrote that the Ulch birch-bark canoe was 5.4 meters long, 0.76 meters wide, and 0.28 meters deep—about average for an Amur River canoe (1881; also repeated by Mason and Hill 1901: 535). Antropova (1961) cited it as being 5 to 6 meters long and 0.7 meters wide.

Nanay and Manchu Canoes South of the Amur

In the state of Manchuria (today's northeastern China) in the early 20th century, most of the Nanay population lived between the Amur and the Songhua, its main tributary. In general, the old literature assigns most peoples in China to the greater Nanay (Gold) group. Their birch-bark canoe, called *umurchen*, was small, fast, and double-ended. By 100 years ago, not much was left of the Nanay birch-bark canoe tradition, wrote Owen Lattimore, who in the 1920s met Chinese scientists documenting this rare boat heritage:

> On this second visit to Fuchin I found that two Chinese ethnologists had arrived and were undertaking an intensive study of the Goldi: Drs. Shang and Ling [Chungshen] of the National Research Academy in Nanking were making a splendid collection of specimens, including so large an object as a birch-bark canoe. No birch-bark canoes were then in use, but they had found an old man who knew the art of making them, and were dispatching him to the nearest forest with large birches, where he was to make a canoe for them. (1962: 340)

During his travels in Heilong Jiang Province, Lattimore searched for the Nanay people, also known in China as the Fish Skin Tatars and the Yii-p'i Ta-tze people. He found little of their bark boats, since the Nanay were by then building log boats and plank canoes under Manchu and Chinese influence. According to Lattimore, the bark canoe "is no longer to be seen along the lower Sungari, but there are men who remember it. They say it can still be seen on the Amur and Ussuri, where it was used when spearing fish and propelled with a double paddle. The canoe that replaces it is of three-plank construction" (1962: 364).

In the early 20th century, the Nanay had more people and boats on the Songhua (Sungari) River. Chepelev observes of their skin-canoe building in Manchuria in those years: "One should mention that among the Nanay people who lived on the banks of the Sungari River, there was in use another type of skeleton boat, which was manufactured from willows and the skin of domestic animals, and also the skin of deer,

elk, or moose. Apparently, in their construction they differed little from the birch-bark canoe" (2004: 152).

Perry McDonough Collins, an American businessman, was the driving force behind an ill-fated attempt from 1865 to 1867 to construct a telegraph line from America to Europe via Bering Strait (see P. Collins 1962). He had been inspired to this cause by a journey he made across Russia from the Finnish Gulf to the Pacific coast in 1856–57. The Collins Overland Telegraph Project failed when the trans-Atlantic line was completed in 1867. However, Collins's trip, on which he traveled via a Russian log raft along the Shilka and Amur rivers to the town of Nikolaevsk on the Amur River estuary, accompanied by Finnish-born Russian army captain Karl Harald Felix Furuhjelm, yielded useful observations on the Nanay birch-bark canoes he saw on both banks of the Amur between the Zeya and Songhua river mouths:

> The natives use here, as well as all along on the Amoor, the birch-bark canoe, very lightly and beautifully made, which they use in hunting and fishing excursions. They usually carry but one person and can be readily transported over portages. They sit in the centre, flat on the bottom. . . . These canoes are like those used by our Indians on our northern lakes and rivers, only these are mostly for a single person, or two at most, while those of Michigan, Huron, and Superior, are frequently constructed to carry the whole family, their provisions, and lodges. They are constructed like those of our Indians. (1962: 265)

The Chinese also knew the small Nanay bark canoes. In 1934, Ling Chunsheng, whom Lattimore (1962) met in Fuchin, published a book about the Nanay people on the lower Songhua River that is regarded as the first ethnological study of a Native culture in China. Fortunately, Ling documented their boats, including their birch-bark canoes (fig. 9.8) and a skin boat covered with ox hide, in what may be the only extant description of native Nanay boats in China:

> In summer, for water travel the Hezhe (Gold) [Nanay] people mainly used a birch-bark boat, called *wumirichen*, which is usually . . . about 209 centimeters long and 46 centimeters in beam. The boat's wooden structure, which is covered with birch bark, is made of poplar. The bow and stern are pointed like needles, and the boats are light and fast. Two kinds of paddles are used [for different purposes]. One is

some 284 centimeters in length, with double-ended blades. The shorter paddle is circa 161 centimeters in length [and has a single blade]. . . . The longer is used in the deeper water away from the shore. The shorter paddle is for navigation closer to riverbanks. Birch bark is very light, so the boat can be moved by a single man near the shore and along the river, but it is very fragile and not durable, and recently birch-bark boats have fallen out of use as people have turned to wooden boats. (1934: 81)

Ling noted other old Nanay boats then in use, the most interesting of which were the skin-covered bull boat, also mentioned by Chepelev (2004), and the *weiyihu* (or *weihu*) punt made of boards, which was the latest model to replace birch-bark canoes on the Amur and in many other parts of Eastern Siberia:

> According to the folktales of the Hezhe, there were other methods and means of water transport. The other kinds of watercraft used by the Hezhe include the *temoken* [*temchien* in Antropova 2005: 21], a small boat made of three wood planks, large enough for seven or eight people; the *weiyihu*, made of three boards, smaller than the *temoken*, for one or two people; the "bull boat," whose keel (structure) is made of wicker and whose frame is covered by ox hide that has been made impermeable to water; the *jilachuan*, 3 *zhang* [about 10 meters] long and 6 *chi* [2 meters] in beam, with 16 people rowing in the front and one man steering in the rear, a very fast boat named after the *jila* worm; the *feichuang* [fly boat], a sailing boat with a sail; and finally the Russian steamships. (1934: 82)

THE UDEGE AND THE OROCH: PEOPLES OF THE USSURI RIVER AND TATAR STRAIT

The Udege (Udehe) and Oroch are two closely related peoples living in the seaside mountain territory between the Ussuri River valley and the Tatar Strait. In this section, we first describe the Udege, whose boats are nearly identical to those of the Oroch; the major difference between the two peoples is that the Oroch are more or less settled coastal people, while the Udege engage in forest hunting and fishing in the Ussuri basin. They share boatbuilding traditions with many other language and ethnic groups with whom they have been in contact.

Our previous discussion of Nanay origins applies equally to the Udege and Oroch, whose particular ancestry is mostly unknown apart from the general outline for the Amur region as a whole. Like most ethnic groups, the Udege have a multi-layered culture whose traditions reach deep into ancient history. Some anthropologists, such as Leopold von Schrenk, believe that they originated from Manchuria or farther south, while others argue for a northern origin, with influence from Evenk/Tungus peoples (Nikolaeva and Tolskaya 2001: 12). The medieval Tungus-Manchu states of the 8th, 9th, 12th, 16th, and 17th centuries also influenced the ethnic history of the Udege. In 2002, the Udege population was 1,665, while the Oroch numbered 884. Today only a small portion of the Udege still speak their native languages, and it is likely that Russians or other Amur peoples soon will assimilate these groups.

On inland Ussuri waters, small planked punt and log boats gradually replaced bark canoes, as happened in Western Eurasian territories. On the Primor'e coast and in the Ussuri and Amur basins, the advances in Manchu and Chinese technology that led to the development of larger planked boats during the past millennium might have had an important influence on local traditions as well. During this period, long, narrow Chinese-style plank boats replaced the Nivkh's large baidar skin boats on Sakhalin Island. Similar vessels also might have been part of Udege and Oroch tradition, for the coastal Oroch fished and hunted sea mammals and might have operated in Sakhalin waters.

The settled Oroch have been much more involved in fishing than the Ussuri Udege, since they live in the coastal zone along the Tatar Strait, along the rivers running into it, and on the western shores of Sakhalin Island. According to the Norwegian Polar Institute synopsis:

> The Orochi live dispersed in the southern part of the Khabarovsky Kray, particularly on the lower reaches of the Tumnin River (Usjka, Usjka-Russkaya), but also on the Amur and Kopp rivers. In the wide area between the Lower Amur and the Tatarsk Strait there used to be numerous small Orochi settlements for winter and summer use, divided into five territorial groups. In a search for better fishing grounds and hunting forests, there were migrations to the River Amur and Sakhalin Island in the 19th century. . . . The traditional means of subsistence for the Orochi has been fishing and hunting. In coastal regions the Orochi have also practiced hunting sea animals. . . . The Orochi are a more or less settled people among

whom only the hunters led a more nomadic life. This differentiates them clearly from their nomadic kindred people, the Udege. Formerly, the seasonal nature of fishing and hunting necessitated shifting between summer and winter settlements. (Norwegian Polar Institute 2006: Oroch)

By the end of the 19th century, both the Oroch and the Udege had abandoned the open-topped birch-bark canoe that was most suitable for mountain rivers (Antropova 1961). Instead they were using skin- or bark-covered half-decked canoe-kayaks in both coastal and river settings. Their single-paddler canoe-kayak resembled a river kayak, although it followed the form of the Amur-type birch-bark canoe.

THE NEGIDAL: CANOE FISHERMEN OF THE AMGUN RIVER

The Negidal (or Negital, Negda, or Nigidalza) are a Manchu-Tungus-speaking Evenk people who live in the Amgun River valley in the Khabarovsk region, where they mixed with Nivkh, Ulch, and Nanay peoples. In Russian censuses, their numbers were sometimes fewer than 1,000 people, and now fewer than 500 Negidal remain. They were first studied by Alexander von Middendorff, the famous Russian researcher of German origin who explored northeastern Siberia in 1844. He described the Negidal, collected some of their stories, sketched some of their decorative handicrafts, and was the first to measure and write about their birch-bark canoes, which Shternberg described more completely in 1933.

In 2006, the Russian scientist Dmitry V. Yanchev also studied the Negidal, who hunt and fish mostly in ponds in the Nikolayevsk region of the Amur River and on Udyl Lake. These people earlier resided on the Okhotsk coast, fishing and hunting sea mammals, as their neighbors the Nivkh did. Yanchev reports that E. P. Orlova's article "Negidals," published in the late 1960s (which we have been unable to access) described the making of traditional omorochki used on the Negidal's collective Soviet hunting and fishing farms. Concerning their inland and coastal hunting and trade, Yanchev wrote:

The Negidal economy was based on hunting fur animals, an activity that had deep ancient roots, as indicated in China's medieval *shi* (history) chronicles. After the Amur region joined Russia in the mid-1800s, the market value of furs increased. In pre-Russian times, much attention was paid to hunting birds. In the taiga, [the Negidal] hunted upland game:

grouse, Siberian spruce grouse, and black grouse; on rivers and lakes, they caught wild geese and ducks. At the beginning of the 20th century, they traveled to the Okhotsk coast and returned with valuable trade goods. Sea hunting was important in the southern Russian-governed area, mainly among the Nizovsk Negidal. Sea mammal skins were made into clothes, footwear, headgear, and pack bags, and meat and fat were cached for winter use. The Negidal targeted mainly the sea lion [*ontanat*] and a small seal [*dyauhta hutanyn*]. In late spring they created a cooperative for fishing and hunting and came to the Okhotsk coast or to the mouth of the Amur River to hunt seals with guns and harpoons [*pelaha hoe*]. (2006: 12)

Shternberg (1933) claimed that the Negidal learned to make the birch-bark canoe by themselves. Their omorochki were 9 to 10 meters long and large enough to carry 300 chum salmon plus an entire family and all their belongings. He said that their neighbors the Evenk made omorochki badly but made them by themselves, while the Nivkh never made them at all. This latter point, however, was not true: the Nivkh had made bark canoes, as had other Amur peoples, but discontinued the practice when they turned to building Chinese-style planked river boats.

Little is known of Negidal boats, but probably they were similar to Nivkh canoes and to more recent planked boats. When Middendorff studied Negidal bark canoes, he described craft much smaller than Nivkh canoes: "The canoes of birch bark were 20 feet [6.1 meters] long and only 1½ feet [0.46 meters] wide and had the upper ends decked, for two reasons: to deflect incoming waves and to keep things dry in the boat. Simple but practical was their method of clamping the bark between two thin split wooden laths [the inwale and outwale] rather than sewing it around the frame" (1867, vol. 4 [2]: 1534–35). The fore and aft decks were fitted to the gunwale in the same way. The bark canoes that Middendorff saw were very narrow but long, similar to the Negidal Amur II bark canoe (fig 9.9). This boat, for one or two persons, would have been very fast, approximating the speed of a kayak. Shternberg witnessed the construction of such an omorochka, and while his description has ambiguities, this is what he reported:

Three pieces of birch bark, each up to 6 meters long, were rolled out flat; only the edges of the middle piece were inserted into the gunwales (*sim*) with the help of wooden pegs (*tipkyn*). Elders prepared sulfur [not

Fig. 9.9. A 2008 exhibition at the Museum of Anthropology and Ethnography included this photo, taken by A. Polezhaev, of a Negidal fisherman employing a spear with a mechanical hook to fish in the Amgun River beside his narrow Amur type II canoe. (Courtesy Museum of Anthropology and Ethnography)

pitch]. After that they smudged this sulfur over the holes and less sturdy places and covered them with thin pieces of birch bark. The bottom was covered with long planks, laths made of larch known as *chully*. Then they inserted cross ribs made of pine that had been soaked overnight and bent with the help of special clips (*z:awannga*). After this, the middle part of the omorochrka is pulled together with belts. . . . The next stage is inserting bow planks (*chilyhi*) between the side planks. The ends of the bow planks are brought together and tied; the bark is folded at the bow and fixed with clips. Then, 15 to 20 centimeters past the ends of these planks, the bark is cut in a straight line. This long overhanging end is fixed in the middle with the bow protrusion (*a[r]inga*), which ends with the split end protruding for 2 meters. The split end is wrapped and secured with wooden pegs that penetrate the split end and both pieces of bark. Then the split planks are inserted inside the hidden edge of the side planks, and nearly broken, are bent back and laid along the outside surface of the boat sides. The birch bark at the bow is heated with birch kindling and the entire bow assembly is fixed on with a series of clips and wooden pegs. (1933: 538; trans. Evguenia Anichtchenko)

The author's description is less than satisfactory, especially as it lacks illustrations and suitable boat terminology, but it is the only one we have found.

THE MANCHU: MASTERS OF MANCHURIA AND THE AMUR RIVER BASIN

Manchuria is a region of northeastern China bordered by Korea to the south, the Primor'e region of Russia to the east, Mongolia to the west, and Russia and the Amur River to the north. The Manchu are the largest minority in Manchuria, some 10 million strong, although few still speak the Manchu language (Janhunen 1997). Originally, Manchuria was a powerful multicultural state society that dominated Mongolia and much of northeastern China, but it fell under Chinese power early in the 20th century. Owing to the Manchu's complicated recent relations with today's majority Han Chinese, Manchu history is not well studied or published, but fortunately there are many old sources that cast light on their boats, which are similar to those of the Nanay.

Carl Hiekisch, a German-Baltic scientist working for the Russian Academy of Sciences, wrote in his ethnological study of the Evenk (1879) that according to the history of the Manchu people, their common ancestor was a large group called the Niutschi or Ju-tchi (Jurchen), better known in Russian history as the Diucher and in English literature as the Dutchery. Their original home was in "the long white mountains" near the Korean Peninsula, near the sources of the Sungari (Songhua) River and next to the coastal Jalu and Tumen rivers, where most Manchu lived. During the 10th century, when several regional dynasties ruled what is now China, the Niutschi became subservient to the Khitan-Liao, their western neighbor. In 1125, the Khitan-Liao defeated the Khitan and got the upper hand over the Western Liao dynasty. Then, the Niutschi established, in the Amur-Sungari-Ussuri basin, the short-lived Jurchen Jin dynasty, which in 1234 came under the rule of Genghis Khan and the Mongol Empire.

In 1625, a people who called themselves the Manchu (and who regarded the Niutschi as their forebears) united the smaller tribes in eastern Manchuria; their chief, Thai-tsou, took the Mongol title of *khan*. The new khan called all the peoples under his rule Manchu, which became the general name of all Amur peoples as well. Successive Manchu rulers expanded their territory to the Amur River and to the Songhua (Sungari) River basin by 1635. In 1644, the combined Manchu army marched into China after a Chinese military leader asked them to help crush rebels in Beijing. However, the tables turned and the Manchu became the new rulers of China, consolidated their power, and created the long-lasting Qing dynasty (1644–1911). During the Qing dynasty, as many as 40 percent of all Chinese official documents and books were written in the Manchu language, and among those papers, now in Chinese archives, we might one day discover a detailed Chinese history of bark and skin boats. For the time being, however, we have had to rely on secondary European sources.

Manchu Bark Canoes

Many boat types were in use in the 18th and 19th centuries in Manchuria, as water transport was the backbone of the Chinese economy. Most Manchu boats today are made of wood and metal and are built in Chinese styles, including big planked boats, small punts, and the long, narrow planked river boats that gradually replaced birch-bark canoes in the Amur basin, the farthest corner of Chinese Manchuria (fig. 9.11).

The Manchu had many names for their bark canoes. Antropova (1961) cited *chzhaya*, similar to the Nanay word for canoe, *dhzai*. Lattimore (1962) said that the Nanay sometimes called a bark canoe *weihu*, which indicated any small boat and, according to him, was probably a Manchu word modified by Chinese pronunciation. The Manchu used *tolhon weihu* for bark canoes. The same term for a birch-bark canoe is also found in a Manchu-German dictionary (Hauer and Corff 2007), which explains it as a combination of *tolhon* (meaning birch bark) and *weihu* (boat).

Hiekisch's (1879) compiled information on early Russian encounters with Manchu peoples helps us to pin down some locations where Manchu birch-bark canoes were used. Various Manchu peoples, including the Diucher (Niutschi) and Natki, inhabited a large region south and north of the Amur River and along the Songhua (Sungari) and Ussuri rivers up to Dauria (now Inner Mongolia), just as Boris O. Dolgikh (1960) confirmed. They were settled river peoples who practiced agriculture, raised cattle, and engaged in mining and trade; fishing and hunting were a smaller part of their economy. They might have had many kinds of boats, but they certainly knew the bark canoe, as did their close relatives the Nanay and Ulch. Hiekisch wrote that some Solon people (also relatives of the Even/Tungus and Manchu) left their settled homes after the 13th-century entry of the Mongol, took refuge in the northern forest zone, and began a new life as hunters. When the Russians entered their lands in the 1890s, the same migration took place in reverse: most of the Solon, as well as the Daur (near the Zeya River) and the Natki, as Hiekisch wrote, "preferred to live with their tribal brothers rather than to meet their fate under the foreigners" (1879: 40) and so took refuge in Manchuria.

Were the Manchu Skin Boat People?

The history of the Manchu has involved many geographical dislocations in response to Mongol, Russian, and Chinese interventions. Their migrations could explain why so little has been written about Manchu bark canoes. But several hundred years before these incursions, they might have used skin boats. Nishimura (1931) studied bark canoe users on inland waters in the Amur basin before the wide diffusion of advanced dugout and planked boats. He reasoned that because the Korean and Japanese peoples can be linked to the Evenk of Manchuria, the bark canoes of the Japanese islands likely were also linked to the Evenk. He assumed that before the appearance of planked wooden boats in about 1000 CE, Manchu people used skin boats for sea trade, as did the Nivkh and possibly the Ainu. Evidence of Manchu skin boats is found in old annals relating to Korea and the Amur River, as reported by Nishimura:

> One old Korean annal has a record concerning the invasion of Korea by Nyö-chin (Manchurian people), who, according to it, arrived in Korea in *pi-sun* (skin boats). Whether the material of the skin boats in which the invaders came was vegetable substance [birch bark] or animal skins is unknown, but probably the boats used by the Manchu invaders were of wickerwork covered with animal skins, because in Manchuria hide boats are more common than bark boats. Hsi-Ching, a Manchu of the Ching dynasty and the author of *Ho-lung-chiang-Wai-Chi* (*Journal of Travel in the Amur*), writes as follows: *Cha-ha* is a small boat carrying two or three persons, it can sail faster than the *wei-hu*. It is told that a prefect of Mo-erh-ken, while journeying through the country, came upon the river (the Amur), which was flooding and could not be easily crossed. Thereupon a junior officer named Na made a small boat (*cha-ha*) from horse skin, in which the party crossed the swollen stream and reached the far shore. Afterward, a man named Yü made a small boat with the bark of the birch tree exactly after the style of *cha-ha* made by Na. (1931: 134–35)

Clearly Manchu influence on Eastern Siberian canoe building has a long and deep history. All the aboriginal Amur basin peoples have been the beneficiaries of their Manchu ancestors, as can be seen in their sharing of similar bark canoes; whether these peoples also shared skin boats, however, is less certain and will require new evidence from documents or archaeology.

The Qing dynasty had a huge impact on the non-Manchu Amur and northern Chinese tribes. Besides unifying China under one central administration, the Manchu ruling class adopted Chinese culture and technology; as a result, after they were in large part assimilated by the Han people, one result was the loss of the bark canoe. After the Nerchinsk Treaty of 1689, the Nanay lost a large part of their northern hunting lands and fishing rivers north of the Amur—the Argun, Shilka, and Ussuri rivers—leading many tribal people to migrate to Manchuria south of the Amur. In the 18th century, to resist Russia's influence and army and to increase the population base south of the Amur, the Manchu allowed Han Chinese to settle in ancient Manchu lands, which Manchu authorities earlier had forbidden. This influx of people changed the population mixture and accelerated changes in boat technology south of the Amur.

THE AINU: MARITIME HUNTERS, FISHERS, AND TRADERS OF YEZO AND SAKHALIN

The Ainu have the distinction of being the only ethnic group in Northern Eurasia to have lived on islands for many thousands of years (W. Fitzhugh and Dubreuil 1999; B. Fitzhugh, Shubin, Tezuka, Ishizuka, and Mandryk 2002; B. Fitzhugh 2016). Their large maritime territory around the southern Sea of Okhotsk once included southern Kamchatka, the Kuril Islands (see chapter 8, page 183), much of Hokkaido, northern Honshu, and the southern portion of Sakhalin. Beginning in early Jōmon times, 12,000 years ago, their life came to depend on the region's rich fisheries. Their maritime capabilities included the boat construction and navigation skills needed to harvest fish, marine mammals, seaweed, shellfish, and other aquatic resources. Most of these skills began to develop after Upper Paleolithic people arrived in these territories about 35,000 years ago, when sea levels were as much as 92 meters lower than they are today and these islands were an amalgamated arcing landmass connected to the Asian mainland via Sakhalin.

Sea level rise beginning 12,000 years ago isolated the Japanese archipelago, so that the only way for people to move among the islands or reach the mainland was by boat. Physical isolation stimulated the development of maritime resource economies, boatbuilding and navigational skills, and maritime trade with the continent. These achievements—culminating in an Ainu cultural florescence

circa 1200–1800 CE—took place in a cold terrestrial and maritime climate. Winter sea ice appeared annually on the Sea of Okhotsk and reached southern Sakhalin and northern Hokkaido, and Ainu territories often accumulated deep winter snow. In these respects, Ainu territories presented conditions for life and culture similar to those found in Scandinavia and Finland, at the other end of the Eurasian continent.

These early Paleo-Siberians—including the ancestors of the Ainu and their Jōmon predecessors—engaged in maritime hunting; built elm-bark, skin, and log boats; and later dispersed in different directions and regions, creating the various Ainu groups known in this region in recent centuries. Archaeological, genetic, and linguistic data suggest that the Ainu people have a deep history in northern Japan and the southern Sea of Okhotsk, reaching back as far as the inception of Jōmon culture, more than 12,000 years ago. Genetic data point toward connections to the Nikvh on Sakhalin Island (Tajima, Hayami, Tokunaga, and Juji 2004). More recently, the specific formation of Ainu culture took place on Hokkaido around the 12th century from a fusion of the preceding Satsumon and Okhotsk cultures (Irimoto 2012). From the 15th through the 18th centuries, the Ainu occupied the entire Kuril island chain and the southern regions of Kamchatka (B. Fitzhugh, Shubin, Tezuka, Ishizuka, and Mandryk 2002; B. Fitzhugh, Gjesfjeld, Brown, Hudson, and Shaw 2016; Takase 2016), necessitating open-sea capabilities. They used planked boats built on log bottoms (described below) and, in the northern Kurils, possibly open skin boats as well.

The Ainu Yachip Birch-Bark Canoe

Nishimura (1931) noted that the basic Ainu boat, a dugout craft known as a *chip*, closely resembled the dugouts of the ancient Evenk-related Japanese. Besides log chips, the Ainu used built-up versions called *mochips*, hollowed-out tree trunks to which planks were stitched on either side to provide greater freeboard (Ohtsuka 1999); larger seagoing versions were called *itaomachips*. These Ainu log and planked boats existed on Sakhalin Island into the 19th century; Chepelev (2004) studied them and other wooden boats of the Far East. Nishimura (1931) also wrote that the Ainu had bark canoes (*yachips*), in addition to log and plank boats, before they began to be influenced by Japanese culture after 700 CE. In 1931, the Hokkaido University Natural History Museum (now the Hokkaido University Botanical Garden and Museum), part of Hokkaido Imperial University in Sapporo, exhibited a model of an Ainu birch-bark canoe (fig. 9.10) that looked

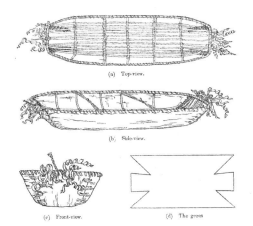

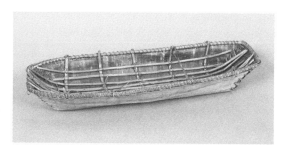

Fig. 9.10. In 1931, Shinji Nishimura published this sketch of an oval-shaped Ainu birch-bark canoe (HUBGM 9633; Nishimura 1931: fig. 47, plate XXII) that he saw on display in the 1920s at the Hokkaido Natural History Museum in Sapporo, Japan. It is still on exhibit there today, although the craft has since lost the ritual *inau* (ritual wood shavings). (Courtesy Hokkaido University Botanical Garden and Museum)

very different from other boats of its era known in Japan; the full-scale boat was used to cross lakes or rivers while traveling in the forest:

> The canoe [model] is made of tree bark chiefly of *tat-ni* (birch tree) and measures 0.95 *shaku* [28.8 centimeters] in length, . . . its breadth ranging from 0.28 shaku [8.5 centimeters] at the middle to 0.17 shaku [5.2 centimeters] at the stern. The boat is made of a single sheet of birch bark, with gores cut at its four corners [see fig. 9.12a–b]. The bark seams are caulked with bog mosses stuffed in the gores, which then are sewn together with cord made of the fiber of the inner bark of *ohiyo* [Japanese elm], the same material as used in making "attush," the clothes worn by the Ainu. Then, to provide the boat, which is frameless, with proper longitudinal as well as transverse tension, it is lined with the stems of osier [willow], interlaced vertically and horizontally so as to form a lattice, while outside, the boat is made tight and strong by means of bamboo canes lashed on the top of gunwales. Further, to keep the boat in shape or, more precisely, to secure it from gaping and collapsing, the top of the gunwales, left and right, are bound with a piece of strong cord ("rope-thwarts") at two places. (Nishimura 1931: 204–06)

The Hokkaido University Botanical Garden and Museum has a second Ainu birch-bark boat of even simpler construction (fig. 9.11). It has no rib framework; rather, there is a square frame atop the boat, which is attached to a gunwale-like oval hoop of robust bent sticks. Bark sheets are fastened to the oval at several points. A mat of parallel sticks serves as flooring to protect the bark bottom. This is the simplest type of bark boat we have seen in Northern Eurasia, and it can be imagined as an early prototype in the evolution of the framed bark canoe.

An extensive series of photographs from the 1960s, held in the archives of Hokkaido University Botanical Garden and Museum (fig. 9.12a–d; Inukai 1939), documents the process of constructing an Ainu bark canoe: felling a large tree and stripping its bark, inserting ribs and gunwales, finishing its ends, caulking, and decorating its bow and stern with ritual *inau* shavings. Although this construction probably produced a less well-finished craft than would have been

Fig. 9.11. This small early 19th-century version of an Ainu elm-bark canoe (note that this model is actually made of birch bark). This model (HUBGM 9634) has a square frame supporting an oval gunwale of bent poles to which the bark is secured. (Courtesy Hokkaido University Botanical Garden and Museum)

Fig. 9.12. This series of photos taken by Tetsuo Inukai in 1937 documents the construction of a bark canoe by an Ainu craftsman named Kaba from an Amur cork tree (*Phellodendron amurense*) in Hokkaido. Stages include (*a*) stripping bark, (*b*) inserting ribs and gunwales, (*c*) finishing, and (*d*) displaying the two finished canoes, fitted with ritual *inau* shavings. (*a*: HPN-30734, *b*: HPN 50097, *c*: HPN 50087, *d*: HPN 61028; all courtesy Hokkaido University Botanical Garden and Museum)

created by a 19th-century Ainu boatbuilder, it is likely the only extant detailed photographic record of the manufacture of an elm-bark canoe.

Finally, we call attention to an unusual source of data for Ainu boats: the miniature carvings that are found on Ainu *ikupasuy*, called "mustache sticks" by 19th-century collectors but today known as prayer sticks or libation wands. Ikupasuy are used in the Ainu sake prayer ritual to fling drops of sake in the air for the gods, and to lift a man's mustache as he sips sake from a lacquer cup. They are adorned with elaborate decorations, including sculptural carvings of important objects and animals such as canoes, bears, and sea mammals. Hundreds of ikupasuy—some dating to the early 19th century—show illustrations of log and plank boats. One (fig. 9.13; HUBGM-09512) appears to show a boat with upturned, rounded ends and internal frames, suggesting a bark canoe; however, upon obtaining detailed photographs of it from Masaru Kato of Hokkaido University, we agreed with our Japanese colleagues that this vessel is not a canoe but a square-sterned planked boat.

The Question of Ainu Skin Boats on Sakhalin

Because of the Ainu's extensive trade with Amur groups before 1600 CE, Ainu boats might have been similar to those of the broader continental bark canoe tradition of the Amur Basin, as well as to those of skin boat users who lived earlier on the Okhotsk coast and in Kamchatka. The best example of a skin boat connection might be a boat—possibly skin-covered—documented in a photo Nishimura took in 1924 in the Nivkh part of Sakhalin Island. It was of a type that the Ainu, too, might have used during and before Japanese rule of this area (see fig. 9.2, page 188; see also Nishimura 1931, fig. 60). We know little about this period because from 1643 to 1853, the Japan shogunate had a closed-door policy toward European nations and refused to trade with them. No foreigners were allowed to come ashore. While the Russians explored the Sea of Okhotsk near the Japanese islands, the Japanese government was collecting information in or near Russian waters and around Sakhalin Island.

Takashi Irimoto (2012) notes the mention of Sakhalin in the *Hokuidan*, or *Record of Ezo* (Hokkaido), written by Matsuda Denjuro between 1799 and 1822. This work reported

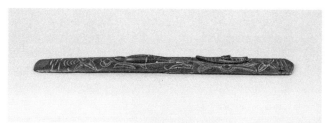

Fig. 9.13. Among hundreds of Ainu *ikupasuy* ("mustache sticks") held in museum collections around the world, this one, at Hokkaido University Botanical Garden and Museum (HUBGM-09512), bears a carving that looks like a bark canoe with upturned ends. However, close inspection reveals that it is a square-stern plank boat with rib framing. (Photograph: Masaru Kato; courtesy Hokkaido University Botanical Garden and Museum)

that the Orotsuko-jin (Uilta or Orok) raised *tonakai* (reindeer) for riding and to carry loads, and that the Sumeren-guru (Nivkh) kept dogs to pull boats from the sea onto the shore in summer and to pull sleighs on the snow in winter. The Santan-jin, a Tungus-speaking Evenk people in the Lower Amur coastal area, visited Sakhalin and Soya on Hokkaido every year to trade with the Ainu, while the Ainu on Sakhalin and the Santan-jin who hunted in the mountains went by boat to Deree (Deren) near the Amur River, where the Manchurian government maintained a station. There they traded river and sea otter and fox fur for foxtail millet, rice, sake, and tobacco. At Soya, the Ainu received silk brocade, blue glass beads for neck ornaments, tobacco pipes, lacquer cups and bowls, and other goods in exchange for otter, fox, and raccoon dog fur. Again according to Irimoto, these records reveal not only the status of fur trading in the coastal area of the Asian continent and Sakhalin (areas connected to the Qing dynasty), but also that the Santan-jin and the Ainu on Sakhalin acted as middlemen in trading with the Ainu of Hokkaido. Much of this trade was conducted by canoe.

In 1905, when the Russians established their hold on Sakhalin and the Amur and Ussuri basins, wresting them away from the Chinese, Japanese expeditions into these territories became rare. Only after the Russo-Japanese War of 1904–05—when Japan annexed southern Sakhalin up to latitude 50°N—could Japanese scientists enter the island to study its Ainu people. As we have recounted above, Nishimura was convinced that Sakhalin was populated in ancient times by a people who lived from the sea, hunted whales, and traveled in skin boats. His views were based not only on archaeological finds of engraved needlecases, as reported earlier, but also on information about hide-covered boats made by the Koro-pok-guru people, who are mentioned in Ainu folklore (see the section on the Nivkh, page 186, and fig. 9.3, page 189). Nishimura thought these people were ancestors of the

Japanese, but most scholars today see them as Okhotsk-culture ancestors of the Ainu (Hanihara, Yashida, and Ishida 2008).

In his book *The Ainu of Japan*, John Batchelor, an Anglican missionary who lived among the Ainu in Hokkaido from 1877 to 1941 and was a strong proponent of their culture, provided a rare record of Ainu trade with the Amur region using skin boats:

> In later times, trade with northern countries [north of Hokkaido] has been broken off, and barter has been carried on with the Japanese in Japan; and, still later, after the Japanese pushed their way into Yeso, Hakodate and Matsumaye, in this island, have been the chief centres of trade by barter. The Ainu traded with the Manchurians when they were at war with the Japanese, and with the Japanese only after they were subjugated by them. Manchurian cash is the only relic of Manchuria to be found amongst the Ainu of the present day. Siberian dog-sleighs and canoes, made of seal and sea-lion skins, and which were used in trading with Manchuria, may still be seen in the Kurile Islands and Saghalien. Specimens of these are to be seen in the Hakodate Museum. (1892: 182)

Batchelor's information provides the strongest evidence available of the Kuril Ainu's use of skin boats. The Okhotsk bone needlecases depict whales being hunted by people in boats that could carry five to eight persons, but there is no assurance these boats are *skin* boats; they instead could be planked dugouts like those Ainu used in historical times. Further, the shellmound sites in which the engraved needlecases were found date to the Okhotsk culture, circa 700–1200, whose northern descendants probably became Nivkh, while its southern stock became Ainu. The proximity, similar environments, and trading relationships of the Nivkh of northern Sakhalin and the Ainu of southern Sakhalin suggest that there were close ties between these peoples, and, as discussed previously, there is reason to believe the Nivkh used bark or skin boats before they acquired planked boats. Until more data are available, it would be premature to state unequivocally that the Ainu had a skin boat–building tradition similar to that of the Nivkh; but figs. 9.10–9.12 (page 201) clearly illustrate their use of birch- and elm-bark canoes for transport on inland waterways.

Contrary to Tsuboi and Nishimura, modern archaeology and DNA studies demonstrate a close historical and biological relationship between the Okhotsk and the Ainu following the Okhotsk decline that began around 1200 CE. Archaeologists no longer see the absence of pithouses or a maritime economy in Ainu culture, or the fact that they did not use large boats, as indications of a lack of cultural continuity. Rather, as Okhotsk culture began to collapse, the Ainu emerged in a fusion with Satsumon immigrants from northern Honshu. After several centuries of dominance as middlemen traders between the Japanese and the Amur Manchurians, the Ainu were overwhelmed by Japanese encroachment. Subsequent military defeats and losses of population, land, trade, and marine resources to the Japanese led to the marginalization of the Ainu people and massive changes in their material culture, forms of settlement, trade connections, and boating traditions. Nevertheless, in their 15th- to 16th-century heyday, the Ainu ranged from Honshu to the Amur, the Kurils, and Kamchatka in plank boats built up from a log base, and they plied rivers in elm- or birch-bark canoes. Whether they also used open skin boats or kayaks in Hokkaido and the southern Kurils remains an open question, although it is highly likely that they did so in the northern Kurils.

THE AMUR EVENK: TUNGUS WHO RETURNED TO THEIR MANCHURIAN HOMELAND

When discussing Evenk bark canoes in the Amur basin (see also the discussion of the Yenisey and Lena Evenk in chapters 6 and 7), one must be mindful of the problem of source material concerning the Oroch, who inhabited a large region of the Amur basin and Eastern Siberia. In pre-1917 literature (e.g., Hiekisch 1879), Evenk hunters and reindeer herders in the Transbaikal in today's Amur Oblast and the southern portion of the Yakut Oblast are also called the Oroch, or Orochen as they are known in China (Tugolukov 1963). As a result, there is confusion about who is portrayed in early illustrations depicting bark canoes in these regions. Although

it is not a watertight distinction, one can consider the Evenk to be the "mother culture" of a large number of subsidiary groups, one of which is the Oroch or Orochen. The same problem exists in Chinese literature, which calls some Evenk peoples in Manchuria and present-day northern China the Oroqen or Elunchun.

The Amur Evenk today live in a well-defined region bordering Transbaikal to the west, the Stanovoy Mountains to the north, the Amur River to the south, and the Okhotsk coast to the east. They might have migrated here late in the 19th century, after the Even, their linguistic relatives, had expanded to the Okhotsk coast a few hundred years earlier (see chapter 7, page 149). Nadezhda Ermolova (1984) wrote that most of the Amur Evenk came from southern Yakutia, where they received many elements of material culture from the Yakut. James Forsyth (1994) said that the Amur Evenk and other groups came to the Amur region from Transbaikal and the Yenisey basin to escape Russian rule and fur taxes before 1850.

The Evenk lived mostly on the left-bank (northern) tributaries of the upper Amur rather than on the main stream, where the Nanay, Ulch, and Manchu lived. On the Okhotsk coast, they lived between the Uda and Tarda rivers, across from the Shantar Islands. Forsyth (1994) noted that there was a strong Mongol component among the Evenk beginning in the 17th century, mainly Dahur Evenk people, who were Mongolized Tungus and spoke Mongolian. The Dahur living at the Zeya-Amur junction and the Manchu-Tungus-speaking Jurchen might have had hunting rights on the Aldan River to the north in Yakutia. With the appearance of Russians in the mid-1600s, some Evenk peoples migrated to the south side of the Amur River, to the Manchu-Chinese state, where they were called the Orochen or Elunchun.

Most Amur Evenk were horse breeders who practiced agriculture supplemented by hunting and fishing. Only the Evenk living in the Stanovoy Mountains had reindeer. After arriving in the Amur drainage, the Evenk learned hunting and fishing practices from their neighbors, mainly the Nanay and Nivkh on the coast. These coastal Evenk numbered some 1,000 people by the end of the 1800s. Another Evenk group, known as the Manegir Evenk (called the Kumarchen in old books, owing to their residence on the Kumara River), were a horse-breeding people, as were the Birarchen Evenk, their close relatives. The Manegir Evenk lived mainly in the Zeya River valley next to the Oroch Evenk, and south of the Amur River in Manchu-Chinese territory.

The Amur Evenk made birch-bark boats similar to those of other Amur peoples, which they called *umurechun* (fig. 9.14) and used for fishing on small tributaries. They also continued to make the Lena-style pointed bark canoes that they had made in Yakutia along the Aldan and Maja rivers. There is some evidence that they also had larger baidars, based on documentation gathered by Alexander von Middendorff, who explored this region in 1844; he sometimes traveled in one of these boats, which was built by Yakut men in the Russian port of Ayan (see page 206).

Oroch Bark Canoes on the Tugur River

At the Tugur River, south of the Stanovoy Mountains on the Sea of Okhotsk coast, Middendorff had an opportunity to study birch-bark boats used by the Amur Evenk (who were more specifically known as Oroch). He described two kinds (fig. 9.15) of the boats, one with a narrow beam and

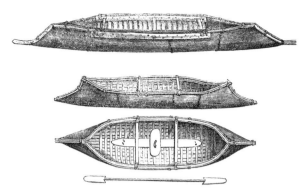

Fig. 9.15. Alexander von Middendorff's 1856 report described and illustrated two Oroch or Amur-Evenk birch-bark canoes from the Tugur River. One, long and narrow, was used for transporting people (Amur I type); the other, short and wide (Amur II type), carried freight. (From Middendorff 1856)

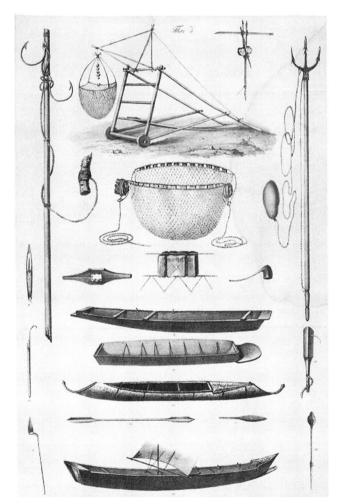

Fig. 9.14. Richard Maak's 1859 illustration catalogues key features of Manegir Evenk boats and fishing gear common in the Amur River Basin and nearby Manchuria. No. 15 shows a Manegir Amur type I canoe (1629036). (Courtesy New York Public Library)

high sides for fast water, and another with lower sides and a wider beam for greater stability and carrying capacity. "We do not know whom we should admire most, the Tungus (Evenk) [as] a son of the mountains when he shoots the rapids with paddle in hand in deep valleys, or when he is punting the boat against the current using two short poles (*muketschi'*)," Middendorff wrote (1856: 1357). He also provided details on the construction of the fast-water Evenk birch-bark canoe:

> Still more light construction is seen in the Tungus watercraft. The frame of a bark canoe [*Nahen*] is built from flexible but strong wood and the cover is made of birch bark, prepared like that for a chum. . . . [The bark] . . . is first boiled, after which it is like leather and has a smooth surface, and then pieces are trimmed and sewn together with thin cedar and spruce roots. . . . The bark from three birch trees is enough for one canoe. Canoes are made watertight with putty made of fat and clay. Such a canoe, which weighs not more than 50 pounds [23 kilograms] but can carry a reasonable load, is paddled by the Tungus with great skill on rivers and over fast-running rapids; the paddle . . . has blades at both ends. In wider waters these watercraft are not used, because they cannot maintain course, owing to their light weight. (1856: 1357)

Manegir Bark Canoes in the Zeya River Valley

S. M. Shirokogorov, an early-20th-century Russian ethnologist who studied Tungus peoples in Manchuria and taught at

Japanese and Chinese universities, documented the Manegir people and provided a good overview of bark canoe heritage in Manegir Evenk (Tungus) society:

The [Manegir] Tungus canoe made of birch bark is one of the remarkable inventions of the populations living in the regions rich in birch bark. In fact, most of the rivers in the regions inhabited by the Tungus are not good for navigation. They are very often interrupted by cataracts difficult to cross. However, with the exception of short distances where the cataracts are, the rivers may be quite good for shallow canoes. The birch-bark canoe is so light that one capable of carrying three men and some cargo may be easily transported on the shoulders of two men when it cannot be used. The Tungus who know perfectly well all conditions of the rivers, the rapids, the cataracts etc. may thus quite safely use the birch-bark canoe. Despite the antiquity of this type of canoe, it has survived amongst the Tungus groups living in the regions where other methods of communication are difficult. For instance, the Kumarchen use the birch canoe along the rivers, such as the Kumara and the Taga rivers, but their neighbours, the Birarchen, do not use it because the Amur River is too big a river for such a canoe. The Reindeer Tungus of Manchuria use birch-bark canoes only for hunting, crossing rivers and when they go to visit the banks of the Argun and the Amur rivers, in which case they go on, leaving the reindeer behind. Yet many groups prefer the birch-bark canoe for hunting elk [moose] often found feeding on the hydrophites [water plants]. The hunter may approach very near the animal without any noise in a very small canoe for one person. The survival of this form of the canoe is conditioned thus by considerations of utility. (2010: section 27)

Leopold von Schrenk saw umurechun and wrote about them in his book published in 1881. He said that the Birar and the Manegir (see fig. 9.14, page 205) had bark canoes with a form and structure similar to the Nanay *dsai*. The Manegir canoe was twice as long as the Nanay one, while the width was the same: Schrenk saw among the latter a canoe that was 35½ feet long and only 2 feet 2 inches wide (10.8 by 0.67 meters). A similarly large (8-meter-long) Amur Evenk bark canoe collected in 1864 is at Copenhagen's Danish National Museum (fig. 9.16).

Fig. 9.16. This huge Amur Evenk type I canoe, collected in 1864 for the Danish National Museum, appeared in a 1981 publication by Ole Crumlin-Pedersen (1981: 6). It is 8 meters long; some Amur canoes might have reached more than 10 meters in length. This canoe might be one of the largest birch-bark canoes in existence today. (Courtesy Ole Crumlin-Pedersen)

Open Skin Boats on the Okhotsk Coast

As he traveled to the Shantar Islands, north of the Amur River estuary, while exploring for the Russian Academy, Middendorff came to the Port of Ayan, on the Okhotsk coast, in July 1844. There the Russian commander (later admiral) Sawojko (Savoiko) loaned him a large baidar covered with sea mammal skins and measuring some 10.0 by 2.7 meters. He also loaned Middendorff Yakut mariners to paddle the baidar; they might have built this the boat for Sawojko (Middendorff 1856: 1354–55). They traveled south along the coast until they reached Uda Bay, opposite the Shantar Islands. The Russian ambassador Evert Ysbrant Ides (1706) had written in his journal that these islands once might have been the territory of the Nivkh but were later occupied by Yakut from the Lena River, who hunted sea mammals and fur animals.

What makes the skin boats of Uda Bay so interesting is the fact that the bay might have been one of the most productive hunting grounds for whales in the northwestern Pacific. To hunt whales with harpoons or poison arrows, one needs a boat, and most peoples in the North Pacific used skin boats for the purpose. Middendorff (1867: 930) wrote that when he entered Uda Bay from the Uda River in early July 1844, he saw hundreds of whales (likely humpbacks, *Megaptera novaeangliae*); in a single day, he counted 30 to 40 groups, together numbering some 800 animals, passing to the northwest. This rich concentration of large whales prompted Sergei A. Arutiunov and Dorian A. Sergeev (2006: 205) to suggest that the Sea of Okhotsk coast near the Shantar

Islands might have been the earliest home of the Eskimo or Eskimo-like peoples, who learned to hunt large whales there before crossing the Kamchatka Isthmus to settle along the Bering Sea (see page 165).

On the Tugur River at the shore of Tugur Bay, Middendorff had his Yakut mariners build him a skin boat measuring only 3.4 by 0.9 by 0.4 meters, which he said rode the waves "like a nutshell" (1867: 1354–56). He and an officer named Waganov used it to explore Tugur Bay, where they soon found themselves in grave danger in a heavy sea some 5 versts (5 kilometers) from land. The boat's lightness saved them, and they were able to reach the shore. When Middendorff explored the Lena River estuary a year later, he had people build him skin boats from 60 ox hides from Yakutsk, following the model of the boat he had used in the Port of Ayan. Unfortunately, these boats could not be used because of the hides' poor quality. Instead, he built himself a single small skin boat, in which he paddled far to the north.

Such reports raise numerous problems of interpretation. Middendorff's, Nishimura's, and Tronson's observations (see pages 188–206) of skin boat use among the peoples of the southern Sea of Okhotsk might lead one to believe that baidar-type skin boats or kayaks existed on the coast from Cape Ayan south to the northern branches of the Amur, on Sakhalin Island, and on Kamchatka. Unfortunately, the documentation for this idea is difficult to assess. It is possible, given the mixing of peoples, as well as Russian expeditions' and naval forces' use of Koryak and Eskimo skin boats, that such craft might have been seen occasionally as far south as the Shantar Islands and Sakhalin, owing to the ivory trade with northern peoples who hunted walrus along the Bering Sea coast. In a similar way, Aleut kayaks and open skin boats from Alaska were paddled as far south as Fort Ross, California, as part of the Russian America Company's sea otter quest. Until detailed information becomes available from Chinese-Manchu archives or archaeology, it would be prudent to view these appearances as isolated cases rather than as evidence of an indigenous southern skin boat–building tradition.

The Elunchun-Oroch in the Songhua River Basin

Richard Noll and Kun Shi write that the Chinese Oroch historically lived "in the forests and on the rivers of the Lesser and Greater Khingan (Xing'an) and Ilkhur (Yiehuli) Mountains of northern Manchuria" (2004: 142). In terms of culture and ethnicity, the Chinese Oroch are similar to the Evenk (Janhunen 1997: 130–33). The Elunchun-Oroch—a mixed group probably formed by members of both peoples who merged and were described with this hyphenated name starting in the 1800s—who lived south of the Amur River in China's Heilong Jiang Province built birch-bark canoes as late as the 1990s, in part as a tourist attraction.

The life of the Elunchun-Oroch people has undergone a major transition in China, as has that of the Evenk north of the Amur in Russia. Jade Lee-Duffy (2005: 13–14) describes the Oroch people of a generation ago as the last hunters in the forest region of China's Inner Mongolia. Traditionally, they were forest people who made birch-bark canoes and herded reindeer (Oroch means "people of the reindeer"). "In the 18th century," Lee-Duffy writes, "the tribes adapted to herding horses, which were more prized during the Manchurian period. . . . However, in the past five decades the Orochen have been pushed towards modernization and forced to settle in ethnic townships and villages in Heilong Jiang province and Inner Mongolia." According to Lee-Duffy, "as the Orochen traditionally relied on the forest for their existence, birch bark was integral to their lives. They built everything out of the material, from canoes and water containers to fishing baskets." The importance of birch-bark boats was evident when Noll arrived in the village of Shibazghan (location uncertain, but probably Inner Mongolia) in 1994 and found the Oroch shaman Chuonnasuan building birch-bark canoes with his mother and brother in their front yard. They had an order for 100 boats (at a price of 1,500 yuan apiece), which they would send to "ethnic villages" as tourist displays.

Today, construction of canoes for tourist purposes continues the long tradition of canoe building by the Oroch. A study by the Chinese Academy of Social Sciences' Institute of Archaeology (2014) describes the heritage of Oroch-Elunchun people in Inner Mongolia and in the Hailan region in the northwesternmost part of China, and documents Chinese Evenk birch-bark canoes. One of the canoes it describes is a five-section craft measuring 7.34 by 0.68 by 0.27 meters whose design is similar to that of the Yenisey-type bark canoe, suggesting a recent cultural connection (fig. 9.17).

Oroch birch-bark canoes have been documented in another book (Na Min 2011), which was dedicated to the master canoe builder Guo Bao-Lin, who lives on the Huma (Kumara) River (fig. 9.18). Here in Heilong Jiang Province on the upper Amur River, the Elunchun-Oroch are also known as the Kumarchen or Manegir (Noll and Shi 2004). As in other regions, here the birch-bark canoe was used for hunting, fishing, and crossing rivers; its silence and ease of portage

Fig. 9.17. Similar in size to other large Amur canoes, this Oroch (Oroquem) Evenk birch-bark example (7.34 by 0.68 by 0.27 meters), from Hulan-Buir west of Nen Jiang in Inner Mongolia (Chinese Academy of Social Sciences 2014: image 9385), takes the form of Yenisey and Baikal-style boats in its bow and stern construction. (Courtesy Chinese Academy of Social Sciences, Beijing)

made it preferable for people fishing with nets and hunting with harpoons. The Oroch canoe had a different shape from other Amur basin bark boats. It had a wide, open central body,

with the bow and stern tapering slightly upward. It also had a very low profile: the center depth was only some 25 centimeters, and the bottom was nearly flat, making it suitable for slow-running rivers. Otherwise, the Oroch canoe was similar to that of Hulunbuir, in the Hailan region.

A video clip taken by Ferdy Goode in 2009 (now offline) showed an Elunchun-Oroch man cutting a large sheet of bark from a birch tree and splitting a log to make gunwales and thin, flexible stringers using little more than a knife, an axe, and a saw. He set the 6-meter-long, 1-meter-wide bark sheet was set on the ground, inside up, and pinned it with stones and wood stakes to keep it flat. Then he fastened the bark cover between the inwale and outwale with wooden pins or pegs from the inside out, starting at the center and working toward the ends. To finish the bow and stern projections, he heated the birch bark to make it flexible and then folded it into the upturned ends. Finally, he covered the inside of the bark with long wood strips from end to end and set wide ribs between the inwale and the outwale. This technique—folding the bark in against itself at the ends of the canoe—also can be seen in a detail

Fig. 9.18. Chinese scholarship has provided some documentation of its disappearing canoe traditions, as in this publication featuring Guo Bao-Lin, an Oroch (Oroquem) Evenk canoe-builder from the Huma region in Inner Mongolia (Na 2011). A similar canoe (REM 28-2009-36) is in the collection of the Russian Ethnographic Museum, but its source location is not known. (Photograph: I. Tkachenko; courtesy Russian Ethnographic Museum)

picture of a model Amur Evenk larch-bark canoe (fig. 9.19; MAE 5334-34) from the Amgun River and an accompanying construction sketch (seen in our book as fig. 2.3, page 39).

The size of the Elunchun-Oroch bark canoe on the Huma (Kumara) River varied from large trading boats to small boats holding a single person (Na Min 2011). The large canoes, 8 to 10 meters long and up to 1.5 meters wide, required many sheets of bark, had a big carrying capacity, and were paddled or punted by several men. The medium-size boats, 6 to 7 meters long, were suitable for use on narrow rivers and fast water. The small bark boats, only 4 meters long, were slow and thus were used for local traffic, crossing rivers, and for children's play and training. Each bark canoe had one or more double-ended paddles and two short poles for use in shallow water. The use of short poles similar to those of the Oroch is a trademark feature of Evenk canoeing in the Amur basin.

The most interesting feature of the Elunchun-Oroch canoe is its unique design, which is unlike that of the typical Amur- or Lena-type canoes found among other Amur Evenk. It resembles Yenisey canoes and probably originated from an earlier prototype shared by both the Yenisey and the Amur Evenk before the Western Evenk migrated into the Yenisey Valley from the Baikal/Amur region in the 17th century, as Ides noted (1706) during his journey from Moscow to Beijing. Later, when Russia annexed the territory north of the Amur, many Evenk peoples retreated south to Chinese soil. Most likely, it was remnants of those Evenk people who built canoes some 300 years ago in the Yenisey region and became the Elunchun-Oroch of the Sungari (now Songhua) basin, living south of the Amur in northeastern China and keeping the old Yenisey birch-bark canoe tradition alive.

Fig. 9.19. This rare larch-bark canoe model (MAE 5334-34) was collected by Forshtein-Mylnikova in 1935 from Amur Evenk people on the Amgun River. The model resembles Evenk canoes from the upper Lena and Lake Baikal region. (Photograph: Evguenia Anichtchenko; courtesy Museum of Anthropology and Ethnography)

THE CHINESE AND TIBETANS: SKIN RAFTS AND CORACLES FOR RIVER TRADERS AND TRAVELERS

The influence of China's cultural, political, and economic practices on the smaller peoples and cultures of northeastern Asia hardly can be overstated. The hundreds of millions of Han people, and the members of the 55 minority groups who live mainly in the border territories of this vast empire, make up a diverse pattern of patchwork and blending. China's Great Wall historically provided a modicum of protection from northern Mongolian raiders, making the country's waterways even more important as arteries for trade and transport of goods and armies. It was along these waterways that the major centers of Chinese civilization developed; its river systems connected to a network of artificial channels and ditches used for both irrigation and transport. China's waterways drove the early development of boatbuilding and seafaring that eventually culminated in Admiral Cheng Ho's huge naval expedition of 1421, which explored nearly half of the globe to the west (but never reached the Americas, as Gavin Menzies [2003] claims).

All the larger Chinese rivers have their sources in the Himalayas and the other mountains of the Tibetan Plateau. The Yangtze and Yellow rivers (Huang He) run in deep valleys in their upper courses and become very wide as they enter the Sichuan basin, Central China Plain, and coastal flatlands before they reach the sea. This geography required people to develop a dual system of river boats. Large, bargelike planked boats dominated the navigable lower river courses, alongside small, flat-bottomed planked punts for individual use, but people also used small skin rafts or boats for mountain river travel and crossings. For this reason, Chinese skin rafts and boats were found mainly in the border regions, where fast-running rivers dominate and most Chinese minority peoples historically lived. As we describe below, this river geography explains the presence of yak-skin rafts in Tibet as well.

The division between lowland and highland is not the only distinguishing feature of boat use in China. Not very long ago, the Chinese expanded into the Siberian taiga. Between the Nerchinsk Treaty of 1689 and the Treaty of Aigun of 1858, the Chinese-Manchu state dominated Southern Siberia as far as the confluence of the Irtysh and Ob rivers in Transbaikal and the northern Amur and Ussuri valleys, reaching to the Sea of Okhotsk. Thus, the peoples of the Amur basin who engaged in birch-bark canoe building were within the Chinese sphere of influence. A number of

Chinese ethnic groups, in addition to the Manchu, lived in the Amur forests and mountain regions alongside Tungus-Manchu peoples (such as the Nanay, Oroch, Ulch, and Negidal) and were familiar with Udege-Oroch, Nivkh, and Ainu visitors. Chinese boatbuilding technology had a major impact on these forest and coastal peoples, who over time adopted log boats or the more popular planked boats of Chinese design.

The previous section concerned watercraft of the Amur area in the China-Russia borderlands. Now we turn briefly to the skin rafts and boats used in China proper and among the more southerly Chinese minority peoples. In general, these watercraft resemble the skin boats that the Mongol built (see chapter 6), but some types found only in these southern regions are similar to boats once used in Japan and Korea.

Skin Rafts in the Yellow River Valley

When Swedish archaeologist J. G. Anderson (Chen 2003: 170) made his surveys in Gansu Province, China, in 1923, excavating, collecting, and purchasing thousands of ancient artifacts, including painted ceramics, he assumed there was a close relationship between the Near and the Far East during the Neolithic and that the Yellow River valley had experienced strong Western Asian influence. To transport his collections to the nearest city, he commissioned large skin rafts. There were many to choose from, because several types of skin rafts have been used in China. Some were simple wooden structures supported by inflated sheepskin bags (fig. 9.20), while others were ox hides filled with wool and sewn water-tight. The latter had a solid wooden platform resting on large airbags and was steered by long oars at each end. Chunsheng Ling described both of these craft:

> Chinese skin boats are most famous from the Yellow River valley. The Yellow River is more than 2,500 English miles [4,023 kilometers] long, and the leather vessels may be used on the river between Xining and Baotou, a distance of about 700 English miles [1,127 kilometers]. There are two kinds of skin rafts on the Yellow River: rafts carried by sheepskin bags filled with air, and ox skins filled with wool. The sheepskin rafts have from 12 to 15 sheepskin bags, while larger rafts for carrying heavy cargo may have as many as 500. The ox-skin rafts may have as many as 120 skin floats. (1934: 82)

Fig. 9.20. Inflated animal skin rafts were common conveyances for goods and livestock on the Yellow River until the early 20th century. This large skin raft used a dozen sheepskins, filled with wool and air and attached to a wooden frame. (From Forbes 2008)

Why use wool- or straw-filled ox- or horse-skin floats? Small sheepskin airbags had to be filled by air pumps and had a tendency to leak, especially under heavy loads, and needed frequent refilling, but large skin bags filled with wool or straw kept their shape and did not need high pressure, so rafts supported by them could float long distances and carry large loads.

As we discuss on page 131 in chapter 6, the Mongol exported thousands of skins of many kinds—sheep, horse, camel, and ox—to China, mostly to the Yellow River valley, for the raft industry. Along the Yellow River, skin rafts with wool-filled floats traveled great distances, after which the skins and wool were reused or sold. In a sense, these rafts constituted a water caravan, supplying hides, wool, and other products from the Mongolian steppes to cities in the Chinese lowlands. In fact, the Silk Roads connecting the West and China were both land and waterway caravan routes.

Old Chinese records usually mention skin boats, inflated skin-bag boats, and rafts without elaboration (Herron 1998). Xingcan Chen believes that most of these rafts originated in the deep river valleys of western and southwestern China. Even observations on boats made of wood or bamboo and covered with skins or "leather sewn together to make boats" (2003: 178) also derive from these regions. Similar observations come from Baoan in Yunnan Province, and others from a locality called Fuguo, between present-day Sichuan and

Qinghai, or from Dongnüguo, in the modern Qamdo area of Tibet. Similar boats are used along the Yellow River's and the Yangtze's upper reaches. In all these highland regions, land transportation is difficult and the rivers are fast, making skin boats useful.

Skin rafts were especially popular in the Middle Ages, but raft builders on the upper river courses needed a steady supply of skins to build them. A raft carrying passengers or goods down the river for several hundred kilometers would be lost to the raft builders forever, since only the pilot would return home upstream to guide other rafts downriver. To solve the skin supply problem, the Chinese turned to their northern neighbors, the Mongol, who had vast numbers of cattle, sheep, goats, cows, yaks, camels, and horses.

Throughout much of the past 2,000 years, including the Yuan dynasty (1271–1368) established by Kublai Khan, Genghis Khan's grandson, Mongol have found themselves within the Chinese sphere of influence. Although the Mongol were able to offer only a limited variety of useful raw material items to the Chinese, such as horses, wool, cashmere, and animal skins, they desired in return a wide range of Chinese commercial products, including cloth, metal goods, weapons, furs, and prestige items. Other than the land-based Silk Road caravan routes to the west, river transport was the preferred means to transport goods into China, which had much difficult terrain where roads were poor or dangerous. One might go east on the Wei or Yellow River in Gansu, where inflated goat-skin rafts are still used today, or west on the Oxus (Amu Darya), in the region of Termez. Among the goods transported over these river routes were prized furs, including sable, ermine, fox, and marten, as well as rhubarb, whose root was highly regarded as a bowel tonic. Less valuable but also transported east from the Hexi Corridor and Mongolia were horse hides, used in making armor, and small coraclelike craft, used on the Huang He and other rivers in northern China. Sacred objects, such as Buddha images, relics, religious treatises, and of course books of secular knowledge, also entered China by caravan from the west as well as via the passes across the Pamirs from India.

Skin Boats at the Sichuan-Tibet Border

Nishimura's 1931 publication again helps us with information on China. He believed that boats covered with animal skins have deep roots in Manchuria, Korea, and Mongolia and that skin boat technology was transferred to Japan by the Evenk, whom he considered distant Japanese ancestors.

Archaeologists and linguists today describe Evenk influence as resulting from Turkic expansion around 700 CE, but the development of boats—including skin varieties—in Japan must have occurred much earlier, in the Early Jōmon period (Habu 2010), and certainly before the arrival of the proto-Japanese from the Korean Peninsula during the mid-1st millennium CE. Nishimura also believed that Tungus (i.e., Turkic) peoples from Mongolia and Manchuria had introduced skin-covered boats to Tibetan peoples. He recalled a Chinese dictionary from the Ming dynasty (1368–1644) that mentions a skin boat of the coracle type: "*Pi-chuan* is a boat made of the hides of ox or horse which are stretched on the framework of bamboo or wood, shaped like a case or box. The boat thus made is dried over fire and then floated on water. A one-hide boat can carry only one person, and a two-hide boat, three men" (quoted in Nishimura 1931: 137). Xingcan Chen (2003) also has written about coracle- or curragh-type basket boats covered with skins or hides, which were used by local people in the borderlands between Tibet and China's Sichuan Province. Such boats also have been studied by Chensheng Ling, one of the pioneers of Chinese ethnology.

Joseph Needham and Gwei-Djen Lu (1962) studied the evolution of sailing craft in China and surrounding western territories, and they supposed the coracle came into existence when a basket frame was covered with skin or hide (see also Sinor 1961). They also believed the distribution of this craft

Fig. 9.21. Impromptu crafts for crossing rivers in the form of round coracle boats made from bentwood frames covered with the hides of cattle or buffalo (known in the North American plains as bull boats) are found in many places in the Northern Hemisphere. This example, from the Sichuan-Tibet border, was photographed by ethnographer Ling Chunshen in 1970. (From Chen 2003: 188)

was much wider in both time and space than has been noted, since it likely emerged early in Assyria and Mesopotamia and is the characteristic vessel of the rapidly flowing headwaters of the great rivers that rise in Tibet:

Skin-covered coracles are found near Batang, on the Yalungchiang, the upper Yangtze and the upper Mekong. Travellers both Western and Chinese have often described them, e.g. Yao Ying in 1845 and King-don Ward more recently. In China they are known as "skin boats" (*phi chhuan*), but apart from the Tibetan borders [they are] now used only in Manchuria (*chaha*) and Korea. Nishimura supposed they were the *kagami-no-fune* (berry-boats) mentioned in a Japanese legend. There is also a reference in *Pao Phu Tzu* of the [late 4th century] to a man paddling himself across a broad river in a "wickerwork boat" (*lan chou*); somewhat earlier in the 4th century Chuang Chou spoke of a boat a man could carry away, thus probably a coracle. Not long after Ko Hung's time cowhide coracles were used in considerable numbers by the first king of the Later Yen dynasty, Mujung Chhui, for diversionary attacks during military operations along the Yellow River in 386. Three coracles are depicted on the walls of a Sui cave at Chhien-fo-tung. And there is much evidence that boats of this type were used by Mongol in their 13th-century conquests. But in the Chinese culture area such craft never developed into the elongated skin-covered and decked boats of the Eskimos and northern Siberian peoples. (Needham and Lu 1962: 386)

F. B. Steiner (1939), who wrote about skin boats among Central Asian peoples, was interested in Chinese skin boats (although the Yakut in Siberia were his primary focus). He found old references to Mongol and Xiongnu (also known as Hunnu) people using such watercraft; the latter were a Turkic people related to the Mongol who created a powerful empire 2,000 years ago that extended from the Great Wall north of Beijing to eastern Kazakhstan. Matthew Paris (Mathaeus Parisiensis) reported in the mid-13th century that Xiongnu boats were made of ox hide and owned in common by 10 or 12 men, information led Steiner to assume that the boats were made for only temporary use. On Chinese and Manchu skin boats, he remarked: "In *Hou han shu*, Nan Hiung nu chuan speaks of the horse-skin boats of the southern Xiongnu (1st to 2nd centuries AD). From *Tsin shu* (*History of the Tsin*), written

between 644 and 646: Mu jung ch'ui tsai chuan mentions the Sin-pi, another people, probably Turkish-speaking and living in northeastern China and Manchuria, as having boats of ox hide during a campaign" (1939: n. 23). More detail on these ancient references to coracles and hide boats is found in Denis Sinor's 1961 article "On Water Transport in Central Eurasia."

Tibetan Yak-Skin Raft-Boats

Among Asian skin boats, Tibetan rafts deserve their own category. They are unique among those we have described, but in a sense they should be grouped with Northern Eurasian boats, since Tibetan rafts—or some sort of coracles, as Diana Altner has said (pers. comm. to HL 2008)—are used at an altitude of some 4,000 meters, in a climate resembling Northern Siberia's. Tibetan Buddhism diffused to Mongolia and Inner Mongolia after the 8th century via missionary monks, and perhaps it was accompanied by technology for Tibetan rafts or for similar craft made of yak skin, which were used on the Selenge River headwaters, and thus in the Yenisey River basin (see chapter 6, page 132).

Little is known about the ancient skin boat tradition in Tibet. In her 2008 letter, Altner wrote that she was looking for fishing communities in southern and central Tibet and was interested in their everyday life, their material culture, and their position in Tibetan society. She found only one remaining fishing community in that region, and focused her research on that village. She found that its residents depended in many ways on yak-skin boats and that the decline of Tibetan coracles, which these people traditionally had used to transport food, themselves, and building material as well as for fishing, was a key indicator of change in the community's economy over the preceding decade.

According to Altner Lange (2009), there are several skin boat types in Tibet. Many medium-size round boats, used by two or three people to cross rivers, are made of a framework of sticks connected to a ring-shaped wooden gunwale and covered with several yak skins. Some larger boats have four-cornered wooden frames covered with skins, with wooden plank flooring sewn to the ribs, whose ends are mortised to the gunwales. When these boats are in the water, their sides bend inward because they lack horizontal thwarts. As the drawings and pictures in Altner's book demonstrate, these boats vary greatly in size, construction, and form because every boat is built according to the user's individual needs and preferences (fig. 9.23).

Tibet is the world's highest mountain territory; numerous fast-running rivers cross the land in deep valleys

Fig. 9.22. Tibetans fashioned their rafts, made for river crossing, traveling, and fishing, from wood lashed together in a square framework, over which a cover of yak skins was stretched and fastened to the gunwales. This raft was light enough to be carried easily by the daughter of Diana Altner of Berlin, who studied Tibetan rafts for her PhD dissertation in 2009. (Photograph courtesy Diana Altner)

without many roads or bridges. In the countryside, travel often follows the rivers, and rafting has been an attractive means of transport since early times; historically, rafts could carry people, animal products, and fish in a fraction of the time and with a fraction of the wear caused by land transport. Altner describes the life of a Tibetan riverman who combined rafting with subsistence and trade, using a yak-skin boat for river travel or fishing that he steered with one or two paddles or oars. During his journeys, he would fish with a line or net until he reached a village or marketplace. Once there, he sold his fish, lifted the skin boat onto his back, and carried it back to his home, a journey that could take a day or more; for this reason, Tibetan fishermen

made their skin boats as small and light as possible (Altner 2009: 43–47).

SUMMARY: EAST MEETS WEST

We end this chapter with a question: Why is the history of bark and skin boats in northeastern Eurasia and the Far East so different from their history in the continent's northwestern extremes, around the Baltic and White seas? To put it another way, why have so few of these highly serviceable craft been documented during the past 1,000 years in Northern Europe, with virtually none persisting into the recent historical era, while in the east, bark boats and rafts dominated coastal and interior waterways into the 20th century?

The answer lies partly in the types of available records. Written records in Fennoscandia date back only to medieval times, and archaeological finds consist mostly of paddles. Here, bark and skin boats were largely replaced during the Iron Age, and few excavated boats have been found dating to the next 1,500 years. In Eastern Siberia and along its Arctic and Subarctic coasts, bark canoe and skin boat use continued into modern times; both have been studied and documented, and skin rafts persisted into the 20th century. In Europe, skin rafts, too, disappeared during the Iron Age, replaced by wooden barges. A wealth of data no doubt exists in Chinese and Manchurian literature dating back to the Iron Age, but this information has not been accessible to researchers who lack Chinese or Manchurian language ability.

In both areas, poor preservation has been a major factor, as bark and skin boats are usually preserved only underwater or in wet soils. However, factors other than archaeological preservation are involved. In Northern Europe, planked boats built with iron nails on a keel rather than a log base were introduced 2,000 years ago, stimulated by developments in Western Asia and the Mediterranean (Crumlin-Pedersen 2010). Lapstrake boats with overlapping planks (fastened first by sewing and then, in Viking times, by nails) were strong and light and could be built in all sizes following a single basic hull design. The smaller versions, for one or a few people, were more durable, and therefore safer, than bark or skin boats and quickly replaced them. Once iron nails and iron cutting tools became available, plank log boats and clinker boats supplanted birch- and larch-bark canoes in the Baltic region by 1500, and soon afterward they replaced skin boats along the Arctic coast of Western Eurasia.

In the quieter waters of the Amur basin, unlike in Northern Europe, bark canoes continued to be used regularly for hunting, fishing, and travel into the 20th century. Birch bark was readily accessible and could be fashioned into a hunting or fishing craft with just a few days' work, and efficiency and the ongoing existence of small-scale tribal economies were the dominant factors in the canoes' continued use. Their persistence in the Far East also resulted from social, economic, and political factors related to the maintenance of traditional lifeways and settlement patterns, and especially the absence of industrialization and commerce in areas away from the coast and the main rivers. As in Europe, boats with nailed or stitched planks began to supplant bark canoes in the flat-water parts of the Amur system, but these changes did not reach the northern interior peoples until the 19th century. In the meantime, wherever hunters in the forests north of the steppe had to navigate rapids and portage between lakes and tributaries, the bark canoe—easy to build, requiring few tools or nails, made of zero-cost materials, and extremely light—remained the work boat and travel vehicle of choice until, in the 20th century, plank boats replaced them.

Bark canoes have been an influential factor uniting peoples from Northern Europe to Chukotka and the Far East. They probably spread throughout Northern Eurasia even before the final retreat of Ice Age glaciers, more than 10,000 years ago, and must have accompanied the first Asian immigrants to North America. Life in the Eurasian taiga, with its extensive swamps and waterways, was impossible without the bark canoe. Its success continued until canvas, fiberglass, and aluminum replaced bark and wooden frames. Yet even with new materials, canoes following the age-old design pattern remain an integral part of modern life in the boreal and northern temperate forest zone, and even far south of the northern forests.

Skin boats and kayaks had the same level of importance for northern coastal peoples that canoes had for boreal peoples. From a construction point of view, the skin boat must have evolved from the skills people had learned earlier while building bark canoes in the forest zone. The skin boat was the only feasible means of travel, migration, hunting, and fishing in the rough, ice-infested waters of the northern marine environment. It is unclear whether a single skin boat technology was shared throughout the Eurasian Arctic, but there is no doubt that after its refinement by Eskimo cultures in the Bering Sea, more than 2,000 years ago, it spread as a single tradition throughout the North American Arctic and Greenland. This technology represents one of the finest examples of nautical design (especially as seen among the Alutiiq and Unangan) known in the preindustrial world.

Today bark canoe craftsmen such as Henri Vaillancourt (featured in John McPhee's *The Survival of the Bark Canoe*) and a host of skin boatbuilders—as well as researchers James Hornell, Harvey Golden, David Zimmerly, Christer Westerdahl, George Dyson, Valentina Antropova, Ole Crumlin-Pedersen, Alexander Shutikhin, Mikhail Batashev, and Evguenia (Jenya) Anichtchenko, among others—continue to produce, describe, and promote the study and use of bark canoes and skin boats following traditional indigenous designs. The continuing success of Adney and Chapelle's North American treatise attests to the undying interest among scholars, enthusiasts, and canoe/kayak builders who celebrate the ingenuity of northern craftsmen and the profound influence their boats had on human history. Their revolutionary technology, originally inspired and made possible by the birch tree and by animal skin, turned rivers and oceans into highways, made possible the discovery and exploitation of new lands, and connected peoples and cultures long before most conveyances other than human feet existed. Two facts guarantee the legacy of Eurasian canoes and skin boats: they were instrumental in the settlement of the Americas, and they have continued to be a vital means of transport and recreation in the years since, as they likely will be far into the future. Together, these small boats are a technology that, just as surely as the horse and the internal combustion engine, changed the world.

EPILOGUE

ALASKA AND EURASIA—DIVERGENCE AND CONTINUITY ACROSS THE BERING STRAIT

BY EVGUENIA (JENYA) ANICHTCHENKO

Only 85 kilometers separate northeastern Asia and North America at the narrowest point of the Bering Strait (map 18), a distance that people can cross in a relatively short time using any of numerous forms of transportation. Modern oceangoing ships cover it in less than three hours. An experienced kayaker can reach the far shore in a day or two, and it is possible to make a dangerous crossing over the frozen strait by foot in two weeks' time.

Historically, however, this geographical proximity did not result in lasting cultural unity between the two continents. Instead, the Bering Strait was and continues to be a transitional and transformative zone that both connects and divides the cultural and political entities on its two shores. On the one hand, it fostered a number of important intercontinental population migrations and cultural exchanges, including the initial peopling of the Americas; on the other, with the exception of the Siberian Yupik population, the Native peoples inhabiting the strait's Asian and American shores belong to different culture groups and speak different languages (Krupnik and Chlenov 2013).

The similarities and differences between the archaeological and ethnographic cultures of northeastern Asia and North America have generated a wealth of scholarship focusing on various aspects of material culture, folklore, and linguistics (W. Fitzhugh 1994; W. Fitzhugh and Crowell 1988). Few of these studies specifically undertake comparative analysis of the indigenous boats of the two continents, although a number of perceptive observations and interesting theories have been put forward, especially regarding kayak technology. Yet one might argue that as one of the predominant modes of transportation, indigenous boats may be a key to our understanding the relationships between different cultures. Designed for travel, boats are a means of mobility and important evidence of exchange. An understanding of boat technology and use in prehistory and

ethnographic times can and undoubtedly will shed light on the processes leading to the establishment of common traits in Beringia and beyond. This field of study is still young, and few conclusions can be reached with certainty. This epilogue summarizes some observations and hypotheses regarding the relationship between the indigenous boats of northeastern Asia and those of North America, and it outlines promising directions for future research.

COMPARISON BASELINE

Similarities between the skin boats of northeastern Eurasia and Alaska were noted by the very first Russian and Western European explorers in the North Pacific region (fig. 10.1). The earliest written record of open skin boats, or umiaks, in the Bering Strait is the report by the Russian trader Kurbat Ivanov, who met a party of nine Chukchi umiaks between the Anadryr River mouth and Kresta Bay in the Gulf of Anadyr in 1659 (Vdovin 1965: 108). Since most Chukchi expeditions were maritime ventures, indigenous knowledge of both coastal and intercontinental marine routes was of crucial importance for western "pioneers." Explorers mentioned the skill of Native mariners, and the ingenious design of the boats in which they negotiated these waters long before the arrival of European ships, with both frequency and admiration. Martin Sauer, observing the kayaks of Unalaska Island, remarked:

> If perfect symmetry, smoothness & proportion, constitute beauty, they are beautiful; to me they appeared so beyond anything that I ever beheld. . . . The natives, observing our astonishment at their agility and skill, paddl[ed] in among the breakers, which reached to their breasts, & carried the baidars quite under water, sporting about more like amphibious animals than human beings. It immediately brought to my

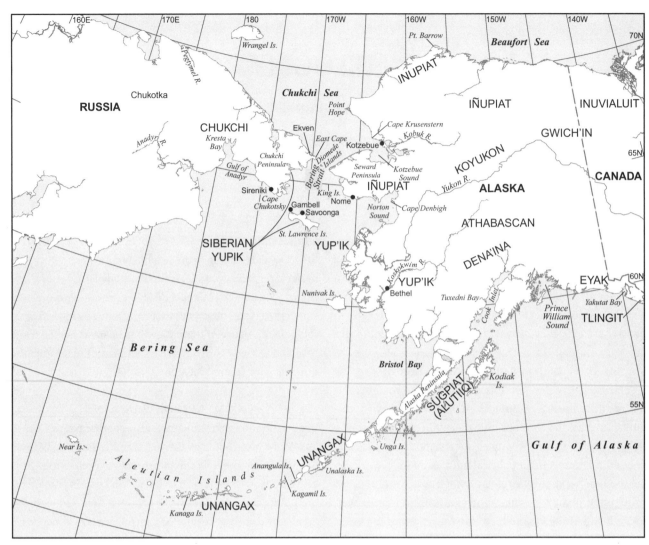

Map 18. Alaska Native group locations. (Dan Cole, Smithsonian Institution)

recollection, in a very forcible light, Shakespeare's expression [from *The Tempest*]—

He trod the water,
Whose enmity he flung aside, and breasted
The surge most swoll'n that met him. (1802: 157–58)

Russian interest in exploring the lands beyond the Bering Strait was inspired by, among other factors, stories of the skin boat voyages that Chukotka natives had taken. In 1711, the Russian Cossack Petr Popov, sent to collect taxes from the Chukchi, interviewed the local elder Makachkin, who told him about the "great land" (a nickname for present-day Alaska) directly due east of "Anadyrsky Nos" (Cape Chukotsky), which could be reached in a day's boat travel. This land reportedly had abundant fur-bearing animals and

was inhabited by people with ivory "teeth" inserted in their cheeks (a reference to the use of labrets), with whom the Chukchi were at war (Timofeev 1882: 458–59). The promise of these rich and seemingly accessible fur grounds prompted Russian exploration and ultimately led to Vitus Bering's "discovery" of Alaska in 1741.

In addition to placing a portion of the Alaska coast on the map, the second Bering expedition (1741–42) initiated the first attempts at comparative analysis of Siberian and Alaskan Native cultures. Again, indigenous watercraft played a prominent role in this process. Contributing to the fashionable debate on where America got its inhabitants, Georg W. Steller, a naturalist on the expedition, was the first to point out the proximity of the strait's Asian and American shores and the role of indigenous watercraft and skilled paddlers in connecting these lands. "One would long ago have learned

The Bark Canoes and Skin Boats of Northern Eurasia

Fig. 10.1. Yupik Eskimos at St. Lawrence Island, Alaska, butchering a small whale alongside the shore ice in the mid-20th century (UAF 4393-223). Although they live in a U.S. territory, St. Lawrence Island people are closely related to the Siberian Yupiit, with whom they have closer geographic, linguistic, and cultural connections than they do with more distant Alaska Natives. Their boat culture is the best studied of all Arctic peoples. (Courtesy University of Alaska, Fairbanks)

this [the proximity of Chukotka and Alaska] if the pluck and curiosity of the seafarers in their large vessels had been as great as the clamor and courage of the Chukchi, who row from one part to the other in their baidaras and skiffs." He then offered seven observations that to his mind confirmed that the Americans were descendants of Asians, and of the Koryak people in particular, the very first of which was that "Americans use the same kind of boats at sea as we found with the Koryaks" (2003: 191).

Twenty years after Steller's untimely death, the Moravian priest David Crantz published his *History of Greenland*, in which he recorded detailed descriptions of Greenlandic umiaks and kayaks (1820: 148–50; see also Gessain 1960: 19) and suggested that the Greenland Inuit are related to the Mongol of Central Asia and had arrived from Asia via the Bering Strait. This book became a standard item in the ships' libraries of 18th- and 19th-century Arctic explorers and proved to be a lasting influence on the perception and representation of circumpolar Native cultures in general and skin boats in particular. In 1778, Captain James Cook

left the following description of his first encounter with the Chugach Sugpiaq people of Prince William Sound:

> The Natives who left us yesterday when the bad weather came on, paid us another Visit this Morning; the first came in small Canoes, others afterward in large boats, in one were twenty women and one man besides children. I attentively examined these boats with Crantz's description of the Women's boat in Greenland before me and found these were built and constructed in the same manner, parts like parts with no other difference than the form of the head and stern; particularly in the first, which bears some resemblance to the head of a Whale. (Cook 1967: 348–49)

Cook's observation was the first published comparative analysis of two geographically removed skin boat traditions, and owing to the popularity of the accounts of his third voyage, this approach could hardly have had a more illustrious start. The perceived similarity between different circumpolar skin boat traditions is cited in almost all 19th-century accounts. Sauer's account of Billings's 1785–93 expedition contains an example of such a generalization: an image of an umiak illustrating one of his chapters is titled "Baidar Used by Natives of Both Continents of the Bering Strait" (1802: pl. IX).

In reality, the circumpolar north is home to dozens of Native nations, and their watercraft, although similar, also exhibit diversity, as studies of indigenous kayaks demonstrate. To give just a few examples: James Hornell's comprehensive study listed six main kayak groups (1946: 166–74); Eugene Arima distinguished nine variants (1975: 67–86); David Zimmerly lists 11 groups for Alaska and Siberia (2000); Jean-Loup Rousselot divided all the kayaks of the American Arctic coast into 28 "ethnographic" types (1994: fig. 13.6; see also our map 19); and Harvey Golden identifies 13 types in Greenland alone (2006: 26). The body of work dedicated to umiaks and birch-bark boats, though significantly smaller, also reveals a wealth of regionally specific features.

The variety of boat forms goes beyond the ethnic breakdown, reflecting the wealth of boats' economic and cultural meanings. In the past, the boat repertoire of many cultural groups included a number of different designs, many of which were gone before they could be recorded. Some of these boat forms evolved in response to specific subsistence and transportation needs. The 19th-century Iñupiat

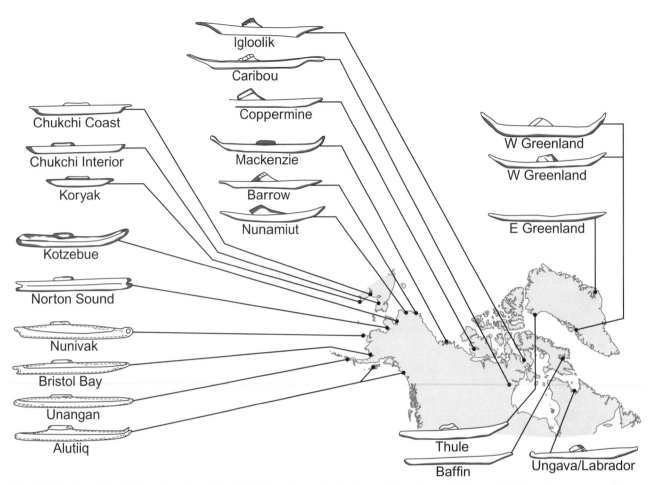

Map 19. Kayaks of the Bering Strait and the North American Arctic. Boat styles, like artifacts or clothing, change over time and space. Jean-Loup Rousselot's diagram shows a gradual shift in 19th- and early-20th-century kayak styles from Bering Strait to Greenland. Their distinctive shapes made it possible to identify, at a safe distance, friend or foe. (From Rousselot 1994: fig. 13.6; used with permission)

communities of the Chukchi Sea, for instance, made and used two types of umiak: a smaller and more maneuverable boat for whaling, and a larger and heavier one for trading and long-distance traveling. Other watercraft variants owe their existence to certain beliefs and cultural practices. In southern Greenland, a special kind of kayak, called *piaaqqiiaq*, was built for boys whose older brothers had died (Petersen 1986: 51). It had distinctive upturned ends and was constructed of *qassallak*, a "red, soft wood," which was not normally used in the construction of kayaks or their gear. It was believed to have the power to resist malevolent spirits, and a piece of the wood was often tied to the framework as an amulet (18).

Finally, the same indigenous groups often had regional variants in their boats. Even in the surviving ethnographic record, which likely represents only a portion of past traditions, the Yup'ik kayak has two variants, Nunivak–Hooper Bay and Norton Sound. The Iñupiat kayak survives in three

distinct types: King Island, Chukchi Sea, and inland Nunamiut (Zimmerly 1986). Fine differences, often inconspicuous to outsiders, emerge when the boats are discussed with the Native people of those communities that still practice traditional boatbuilding. People of Point Hope, for instance, consider their umiaks distinct to be from those of Barrow because of slightly different dimensions and the way the bearded seal skins are sewn for the umiak cover. The features that distinguish the boats of a particular community are cherished and emphasized by its members as a part of their unique identity, and one might assume that they played an even more important role in the past, when this identity had stronger political implications.

This juxtaposition of regional diversity and overreaching similarities makes the study of Arctic and Subarctic indigenous boat technology both fascinating and challenging, particularly when the traditions of different continents are

The Bark Canoes and Skin Boats of Northern Eurasia

compared. Intercontinental comparison reveals two kinds of cultural affinities. The first is between groups that shared a large array of cultural traditions because of their historical ties and adaptations to similar environmental conditions, both fostered by geographic proximity. Given the history of military and trade exchange between the Siberian Yupik and Chukchi peoples of Eurasia and the Iñupiat of Alaska (Bogoras 1904–09: 126; O. K. Mason 2009), as well as their mutual subsistence focus on organized crew whaling, it is not surprising that their open skin boats are similar. Interestingly, the kayaks of these groups lack any close resemblance to each other. More suitable for one-man subsistence hunting, these small boats might not have been involved in trading or raiding expeditions and thus were less influenced by these exchanges.

The second kind of cultural affinity encompasses more enigmatic cases of similarity among the boats of geographically distant groups. The resemblance between the open skin boats of the Aleutian Islands and those of the Koryak people of Kamchatka, the implication of a possible connection between Koryak and East Greenlandic kayaks, and the similarity between some bark boats of the Amur River region and those of British Columbia are all examples of such affinities. What produced these similarities? Did they occur in the process of adaptation to similar environmental conditions and resources? Or do they represent historical relationships between peoples? While the remarks of the first explorers were based largely on cursory observations and reflect generic characteristics, such as construction material, size, and general shape of the hull, more recent skin boat research looks at finer details and attempts to incorporate both ethnographic and archaeological evidence.

ETHNOGRAPHIC EVIDENCE

Modern Alaska comprises nine Native nations: Iñupiat, Yup'ik, Siberian Yupik, Unangan (Aleut), Sugpiaq, Athabascan, Eyak, Tlingit, and Haida (see map 18, page 216). The Iñupiat homeland includes the Alaskan coast of the Beaufort and Chukchi seas, extending southward to Norton Sound, where it borders the land of the Central Yup'ik people. King and Diomede islands are also populated by Iñupiat people, while St. Lawrence is home to the Siberian Yupik, who maintain close ties with the Siberian Yupik people of Chukotka. The Iñupiat, Siberian Yupik, and Central Yup'ik are genetically related.

South of St. Lawrence Island and the Central Yup'ik territory lies the Aleutian island chain, the windswept home

of the Unangan (Aleut) people since circa 9000 BP. Although linguistically removed from other Eskimo groups, the Unangan shared a number of subsistence techniques and material culture trends with the Sugpiaq people of Kodiak Island and Prince William Sound (Dumond 1977: 55). Genetic and archaeological evidence suggests that following a westward population movement from the Alaska Peninsula, an ethnic unity of the ancestral Unangan and Sugpiaq peoples might have existed around 6000 BP (Crawford, Rubicz, and Zlojutro 2007: 713; Zlojutro, Rubicz, Devor, and Spitsyn 2006; Dumond 1977: 59). Alternatively, these cultural and genetic connections might have been the result of a long history of trade and warfare.

The Sugpiaq nation consists of two major groups: the Alutiiq (formerly known as the Koniag) of Kodiak Island and surrounding smaller islands, and the Chugach of Prince William Sound (Crowell, Steffian, and Pullar 2001: 30). Closely related, each group traditionally maintained its own sovereignty and engaged in both trade and military exchanges with the other. Both the Alutiiq/Koniag and the Chugach Sugpiaq had regular interactions with the Denai'na Athabascans, who also resided in Cook Inlet. Farther south, around Yakutat Bay, the Chugach bordered the Eyak and the Tlingit, both of whom who neighbored Haida people—the southernmost Native group of Alaska, who migrated to the coast from the Canadian interior only around 300 years ago.

Owing to its history and geographical and cultural diversity, the indigenous boat tradition of Alaska is both rich and complex. In general, skin boats are the main traditional form of marine transportation for the Inuit, Iñupiat, Central Yup'ik, Siberian Yupik, Unangan, and Sugpiaq peoples. Athabascan groups used bark canoes, while the Eyak, Tlingit, and Haida used dugouts. There were, however, a number of exceptions to this delineation, and the three types of boats—bark canoe, skin boat, and dugout—often overlapped (fig. 10.2). Bark canoes were known to the Iñupiat of Kotzebue Sound because the Kobuk River connected them with inland Athabascans. South of the Bering Strait, the Yukon and Kuskokwim rivers provided similar links between the Athabascan bark canoe tradition and the skin boat legacy of the Yup'ik people. Both groups used a birch-bark boat with a partially covered deck and a frame that closely resembled that of a kayak (fig. 10.3). Chunya Evenk canoe-kayaks of the eastern Yenisey River basin had a similar construction (see figs. 6.7–6.8, page 128).

The Dena'ina Athabascans had both kayaks and open skin boats that closely resembled Sugpiaq skin watercraft

Fig. 10.2. People used both skin umiaks and birch-bark canoes for seasonal migrations in the Yukon Delta. This stereo-pair (1975-0178-34) from the mid-20th century, titled "Malemut Indians Moving Camp" (the people were actually Inuit, not Indian), shows a birch-bark canoe next to a small skin-covered umiak. Impromptu umiaks or coracles often were made from fresh moose hide when hunters needed to transport their meat downstream from an interior kill site. (Courtesy Stereographic Library Collection, University of Alaska, Fairbanks)

(fig. 10.4). Linguistic data and oral lore suggest that although the form might have been borrowed, the Dena'ina built these boats themselves rather than obtaining them through trade (Kari and Fall 2003: 102–04). A legend recorded in the early 20th century tells the story of the great Dena'ina chief Jaconestus, who built a dam at Tuxedni Bay to catch seals, whose skins were used to make skin boats 30 feet (9 meters) long. According to this legend, Jaconestus and his men painted the

Fig. 10.3. Yup'ik people sometimes made birch-bark canoes like this model boat, which were quite similar to the Athabascan (Kootenai) birch-bark canoes. This model (IVX57), collected in Alaska in Bethel or Quinhagak, between 1907 and 1917, has fancy ornamented gunwales and a Yup'ik Eskimo circle-dot motif painted on the bow deck. The patterns on the paddle are ownership marks. (Courtesy Sheldon Jackson Museum, Sitka, Alaska)

Fig. 10.4. This circa 1800 Denai'na Athabascan double kayak (CCM 1984.48.1) has the bifurcate bow and other construction details of Alutiiq and Unangan kayaks and umiaks, demonstrating one of many shared traditions characteristic of neighboring Native and other Eskimo cultures in western and southern Alaska. (Courtesy Canadian Canoe Museum)

rock art of Tuxedni Bay, which features multiple boat images, to capture their "deeds and exploits" (Alexan, Chickalusion, Kaloa, and Karp 1981: 49).

The boat tradition of the Chugach Sugpiaq, in turn, was not limited to their skin boats. Both oral tradition (Birket-Smith 1953: 110–11) and archaeological evidence indicate that they also employed dugouts. Several such canoes were discovered in the Palutat burial cave (De Laguna 1956: 239, 245–49), and their similarity to Eyak canoes suggests that the latter might have inspired Chugach dugouts (Birket-Smith 1953: 50).

There might also have been reciprocal influence between Eskimo skin boats and Indian watercraft traditions. One Tlingit legend tells a story of a cannibal who lived in Yakutat Bay at the time when "raven taught the people to make canoes out of skins." The cannibal's sons, appalled when he massacred his own brothers, made a large canoe out of his victims' skins, sewn with human hair, and went in it to avenge their uncles: "It was the first of the skin canoes.... Nowadays these canoes are made of all kinds of skins, but the hair used is always human hair" (De Laguna 1972: 330).

Traces of skin boat use among the Native groups of the Pacific Northwest are found as far south as British Columbia. Some construction features and ornamentation details of the whaling dugouts of the Makah people of Nootka Sound indicate these boats' connection with open skin boats. Unlike other dugouts, the Nootka canoe has a flat bottom, vertical stern, outward-flaring sides, and gunwales that do not meet at stem or stern, giving it a shape that, according to Wilson Duff, bears a strong resemblance to "Eskimo" umiaks (1981: 201). This canoe is decorated with sinuous grooved or painted lines, which lack functional meaning but are "an important element of a good canoe" (201). Positioned on the inside surface, just below the gunwales, and on the stem and stern, these lines resemble the lashings of a skin boat cover (fig. 10.5). Duff saw similarities in the shape of the Nootka canoe's stern, which to his mind resembled the vertical stern post of the umiak with the headboard fitted over it. Likewise, he thought the stem of the Nootka canoe referenced the protruding gunwales and harpoon rest of an umiak. Duff also pointed out that both umiaks and Nootka canoes were used in whaling and "frequently bore painted designs on their sides depicting a supernatural creature that combined attributes of the serpent and the wolf" (203). To him, these similarities suggested that the umiak was an ancestor of the Nootka canoe and that both were elements of the same ancestral whaling complex, transmitted from Alaska to the Pacific Northwest coast as a result of an umiak-borne migration (206). Although access to wood changed the material from which the boats were made, "the conservatism of culture" ensured that some characteristics of the ancestral form were retained.

Specific design features of the Nootka canoe are strikingly similar to those of Yup'ik and Unangan umiaks of western Alaska and the Aleutian Islands. The vertical stern,

Fig. 10.5. Wilson Duff (1981) reported on one of the strangest remote connections in indigenous boat technology: the striking design similarities between the Eskimo umiak of western Alaska and this Nootka dugout canoe of southern British Columbia. Similarities include general vessel shape, upright stern line, gunwale extensions forward, a prow support serving as a harpoon rest, and, most convincingly, a zigzag design painted beneath the Nootka gunwales that mimics the lashings used to keep the umiak skin taut. Both boats served as whaling crafts. The similarities remain unexplained; somehow key elements of the Alaskan whaling complex found a new home in a distant geographic setting and a different culture. (From Roberts and Shackelton 1983: 105)

divided gunwales, and the serpent- or dragonlike creature painted on the sides are especially strong indicators of a cultural connection, since they are not functional aspects of boat technology per se (fig. 10.6). However, it is important to note that the home coasts of the Yup'ik people are at a considerable distance from whale migration routes, and as far as historic and archaeological records can tell, whaling has never been a major part of their subsistence economy.

Another interesting case of a presumed connection between geographically removed boat traditions is the similarity between Unangan and Koryak open skin boats. Unlike most umiaks of the circumpolar north, which have straight gunwales separated at both ends by headboards, the gunwales in Unangan and Koryak boats are bent to form a rounded bow and stern. However, Koryak boats have a semicircular board attached to the stem post (see fig. 8.18c, page 176), while the Unangan umiak lack headboards altogether (fig. 10.7).

Neither Koryak nor Unangan umiaks have proper stem posts: the timber serving in their place is a continuation of the keel, bent in a long upward rise starting about three-quarters of the way from the stern. The chine (bottom stringer) frame members that form both boats' bottom are notched into the keel at the same point. As a result, the front quarter of the boats has a sharp V-shape that contributes to the vessels' speed and agility (Durham 1960: 21). At the same time, the bent gunwales give the upper part of the boats a wide oval shape, aiding buoyancy and increasing cargo capacity. The Unangan umiak reportedly could accommodate up to 60 people and move 10 tons of cargo over the turbulent waters of the Bering Sea.

The frames of the Koryak and Unangan umiaks, as we know them from 19th- and early-20th-century records, were constructed of carved, slender pieces of wood. Some of the

Fig. 10.6. Side view of a Yup'ik umiak model (AMHA 1983.152.100) collected circa 1910 from the Bering Sea coast of Alaska. Note the upright stern post and skin cover lashings painted under the gunwales of the Nootka canoe shown in fig. 10.5. (Courtesy Anchorage Museum of History and Art)

Fig. 10.7. Although lacking bow and stern head boards, the high sides, flaring bow, and absence of a stern post makes this late-19th-century Unangan umiak (NMNH E73019) from the Aleutian Islands resemble a Koryak or Kerek boat more than a Bering Sea umiak. Was there a sea connection between Kamchatka and the Aleutians via people or floating boat wrecks (Quimby 1947)? (Courtesy Smithsonian National Museum of Natural History)

ribs appear to have been bent, which is also unusual for umiak construction. All the timbers were lashed together with sinew or baleen to create a light, flexible structure. One noteworthy detail of Unangan open skin boat construction is that all the bottom cross timbers were lashed together by a pair of rawhide lines running parallel to the chines along the boat's entire length. Structurally, this reinforced the bottom of the boat and served as an antihogging device (to prevent longitudinal flexing) by tying together the boat's stem and stern. The rawhide lines functioned as a second pair of chines; a second pair was also present in the Koryak umiak, but there they were made of wood. Interestingly, this construction element is not found in any other circumpolar umiaks known to the authors, which strengthens the connection between these boat forms.

The resemblance between these boat traditions has puzzled researchers since it was first pointed out. Bill Durham suggested that since the Koryak were "comparatively un-maritime," they probably borrowed the design of their boats from the Unangan (1960: 25). Waldemar Jochelson described Koryak umiaks in the early 20th century as being cumbersome and not very seaworthy (1908: 534–36). However, Yakov Lindau, in his *Description of the Peoples of Siberia*, observed that Koryak open skin boats were used for whaling, trading, and even long-distance travel that took them as far as the Near Islands of the Aleutian chain (1983: 103–04). A "genetic connection" between Unangan and Koryak boats prior to these peoples' contact with Russians is, however, problematic owing to the lack of precontact archaeological sites on the Near Islands and the absence of genomic connections.

An alternative explanation was offered by the Russian anthropologist Roza Liapunova, who suggested that Russian traders and colonizers introduced the Koryak type to the Aleutians in the second half of the 18th century and that the precontact Unangan umiak resembled Sugpiaq umiaks, with their characteristic split bow. Indeed, Koryak frequently served as deckhands on Russian voyages to the Aleutians, and Russian fur traders used indigenous skin boat technology for their operations in the Aleutians (Liapunova 1975: 98), but the complete replacement of one indigenous boat form with another appears too dramatic and perhaps unnecessary, since it was equally possible for Russians to use the traditional Unangan open skin boat for their purposes, as they did with the Sugpiaq *angyat* (open skin boat) around Kodiak Island (Anichtchenko 2012: 168–69). Furthermore, a fragment of an umiak timber from a precontact cave site on Kanaga Island in the western Aleutians, which likely represents the stem post, has no sign of bifurcation but was notched for a headboard, thus showing some affinity with the Koryak form (W. Nelson and Barnett 1955). To further complicate the issue, the kayaks of the Unangan and Koryak were very different from each other but exhibited some affinity with those of other groups. The Unangan kayak, with its multichined hull, ridged deck, and split bow, was closely linked to the Sugpiaq kayak, while the flat-decked Koryak kayak, with its single pair of stringers, had some affinity with the kayaks of the eastern Arctic, as will be discussed later.

Similarly complicated is the case of the "sturgeon-nose" canoe—a peculiar form of bark boat with a characteristic ramlike stem and stern. It was longer at the bottom than at the gunwales, which gave it a distinctly trapezoidal shape. According to John Jennings, this form of canoe was "fast, though rather unstable, and was used in rivers and lakes where rapids were not an issue" (2002: 20). As observed originally by Mason and Hill (1901), in North America, boats of this type were made and used exclusively by the Kootenai and Salish Native peoples of southern British Columbia and northern Washington and had no analogues among the bark watercraft of North America (fig. 10.8). However, the Nivkh, Nanay, Sakha, and Evenk peoples of the Amur River region in Siberia had boats of essentially the same shape and construction (see fig. 9.14, page 205). The only major difference was that the Kootenai and Salish boat makers used spruce, white pine, or cedar bark, while the Amur River boats were made of birch bark (Mason and Hill 1901: 525–37).

On the same parallel but on opposite sides of the Pacific, thousands of miles separate the homelands of the Amur

Fig. 10.8. In this photograph (L97-25.45), Kalispel men are seen fishing from a birch-bark canoe on Cee Cee Ah Creek, Pend Orielle River, Washington, in 1908. The canoe's "sturgeon-nose" construction, which differs from that of other North American canoes, follows the style of the Amur type II canoe, a similarity first explored by Otis T. Mason in 1901, prompting questions about Athabascan-Amur connections. (Courtesy Northwest Museum of Arts and Culture)

River Natives and the Kootenai and Salish Indians. Their recorded and oral histories contain no indications of immediate interactions, but a broader and older relationship might have existed through the Dene-Yeniseyan connection, which might have linked the ancestors of the western neighbors of the Kootenai and Salish to the ancient population of Southern Siberia (Potter 2010: 1–24).

The similarity could be based not on genetic connection or ties to an ancestral prototype, but rather on adaptation to similar environmental conditions across the coastal North Pacific. Some elements of boat design can travel from one culture group to another and even cross the boundaries among bark canoes, dugouts, and skin boats. An interesting analogy to the "ram" bows of Salish and Kootenai bark boats, for example, exists among the indigenous groups of southeastern Alaska. The lower portion of the bow of the sealing dugout canoes of the Tlingit and Eyak of Yakutat Bay had a similar shape extending forward below the waterline. The forked bow of these boats was said to be useful in averting icebergs (Grinnell 2007: 161–62). Furthermore, the open skin boats of the Sugpiaq people, whose land borders Yakutat Bay, also had an extended prow, but instead of being triangular, the prow had a discoid shape recalling a whale's head, as

mentioned in the above-cited note in Captain Cook's journals (fig. 10.9).

The relative fluidity of borders among the skin, bark, and log boat traditions of the Native peoples of Alaska and the North Pacific demonstrates that indigenous boatbuilding was highly dynamic and open to both internal innovation and external influences. This, in turn, invites consideration of the idea that indigenous boats perhaps continually changed through time (Dyson 1986: 5) and that "cultural conservatism" or "tradition" did not prevent boatmakers from creative rethinking and ongoing fine-tuning of their watercraft. Native lore contains many references to such experimental attitudes toward boat making. In the Siberian Yupik village of Sireniki on the Chukchi Peninsula, for instance, a newly made umiak was tested by chasing a least auklet. If the boat was not fast enough to match the little bird's speed, it was reportedly reassembled and improved until it could keep up with the auklet (Bogoslovskaya, Slugin, Zagrebin, and Krupnik 2007: 166). An Athabascan story recorded in Ruby village on the Yukon River tells about the set of trials leading to the creation of the first canoe by "the man who went through everything":

He came to a place where the river makes a circle and there is short portage between the bends. He took a piece of spruce bark, threw it in the water,

Fig. 10.9. This Sugpiaq (formerly Prince William Sound Eskimo) open skin boat, known as an *angyaq* in Kodiak, southern Alaska, and the Near Aleutian Islands, has the bifurcate bow also seen on Sugpiaq and Unangan kayaks. This exquisite model (NMNH E1130) is one of the earliest artifacts accessioned in the Smithsonian's collection. Its paddlers are dressed in ceremonial garments, and the boat is ornamented with colored yarn. (Courtesy Smithsonian National Museum of Natural History)

and walked the portage. He waited for the piece of bark, and waited, and waited. It didn't float down. It must have sunk. So he sat down and thought. Then he took cottonwood bark. He threw it in the water and walked the portage. He waited for it. He didn't get that, either. It didn't float. He has done that to lots of trees that got long bark. Finally he came to the birch tree. He barked that. He threw that in the river and walked the portage. Then it floated down. So he thought, that's the kind of material to make a canoe. So he got some bark long enough to make his canoe. He got some spruce roots. But he didn't know how to make the front turn up. So he killed a hawk and took off the lower jaw and measured that. But it didn't fit. He did the same with an owl. So finally he got a spruce hen and took off the lower jaw, and then made a pattern from it that fitted. (Quoted in De Laguna and DeArmond 1995: 190)

A number of regional watercraft studies have shown that some significant changes in boat construction occurred over comparatively short time periods. Tlingit and Haida dugouts, for instance, underwent a major changeover at the end of the 18th century, when their large-head canoe, with its square bow profiles, upswept stern, and V-shaped cross section, was replaced by boats resembling southerly Nootkan and Coast Salish canoes (Holm 1987: 145). Similarly, a comparative analysis of 18th- and 19th-century images and models of the Unangan kayak revealed significant changes in the shape of its bifurcated bow (Heath 1987: 94–95).

In northern Alaska, contact with commercial whalers and experimentation with the outboard motor inspired first King Islanders and later the St. Lawrence Yupiit to shift from their traditional flat-bottomed umiaks to round-bottomed skin boats that resembled wooden whale boats (Bogojavlensky 1969: 215; Braund 1988: 112–13; see also fig. 8.15b, page 172, and fig. 10.14, page 231). The introduction of firearms had even more dramatic consequences, particularly for the Chukchi Sea Iñupiat's kayaks. Designed for speed, traditional kayaks provided a good platform for precontact hunting methods, allowing a hunter to approach the animals to the distance of a harpoon throw. The head of the harpoon was attached to a line so that the prey could be retrieved. After firearms were introduced, traditional kayaks lost their primary stealth purpose. The animals could now be shot from much greater distances, so there was no need for a speedy, silent approach. Consequently, by the 1920s, the traditional

long and slender "old-timer" kayak had been replaced with a shorter and lighter kayak whose main purpose was to provide an effective means of retrieving seal shot in open water before the animals sank (R. Nelson 1969: 307). By the 1960s, the advent of the aluminum skiff made even these retrieving boats obsolete, and kayaks disappeared from everyday use.

These ongoing changes complicate the attempt to reconstruct the history and prehistory of indigenous boats, especially when such an attempt is based solely on surviving ethnographic data, for which the temporal depth in Alaska and northeastern Asia rarely exceeds 200 years. Additional understanding of the relationship between different indigenous boats can be gathered from the archaeological record. Although fragmented and incomplete, such data exist for skin and log boats, but they are lacking for bark canoes. This is both lamentable and surprising, as some birch-bark artifacts do survive in archaeological records. Future finds might elucidate some aspects of deeper bark-boat history.

ARCHAEOLOGICAL EVIDENCE

Owing to the perishable nature of both skin and bark boats, as well as postglacial flooding of coastal regions in the Alaskan Arctic, the earliest history of boat use in North America likely will remain the subject of speculation. A key element of Subarctic maritime subsistence, boats might have accompanied people on their first entry into North America. Recent maritime migration theories suggest that instead of walking across the Bering land bridge between 20,000 and 10,000 BP, the first migrants from Eurasia might have moved along its southern coastal margin in boats (Fladmark 1979; Dixon 1999; Fagundes et al. 2008), but direct archaeological evidence of these early watercraft has never been found.

By circa 10,000 BP, people had settled in areas of Alaska that would not have been accessible without watercraft, such as Anangula Island in the Aleutian chain (Aigner 1977; Laughlin, Heath, and Arima 1991: 187) and Prince of Wales Island, where the second-oldest human remains in Alaska were found (Kemp et al. 2007). At 3000 BP, the presence of maritime transportation is indirectly suggested by toggling harpoon points found at the Cape Denbigh archaeological site in Norton Sound, a find that, according to J. Louis Giddings, carries "a strong implication of boating skill while hunting among masses of floating ice" (1964: 241). The use of umiaks circa 1800 to 1500 BCE might be inferred from the Cape Krusenstern site, where large whaling harpoons and lance blades and large quantities of whalebone, combined with permanent settlement, indicate communal whaling (Giddings

1967: 242). A toggling harpoon found at the 3,500-year-old Chertov Ovrag site on Wrangel Island, 140 kilometers off the coast of Chukotka, indicates sea mammal hunting (Dikov 1988: 85), which, along with the insular location, might signal the presence of seaworthy boats.

The earliest direct archaeological evidence of skin boats in the circumpolar north, however, comes from neither northeastern Asia nor Alaska. A 4,300-year-old wooden rib from a flat-bottomed vessel was found at Qeqertasussuk, a Saqqaq-culture site in southeast Disko Bay, West Greenland (Grønnow 1994: 19, 221). This U-shaped fragment is only 35 centimeters across and 22 centimeters high, with a triangular cross section that aided its identification as a kayak rib (Arima 2004: 49; fig. 10.10).

In northeastern Eurasia, the earliest representation of the boat found to date comes from the Tokarev-culture site on Spafar'ev Island, 1.5 nautical miles (2.8 kilometers) off the northern coast of the Sea of Okhotsk. This site dates to the second half of the 1st millennium BCE and has yielded a 15-centimeter-long bone boat miniature with a protruding bow and incised marks in a dot-and-line pattern. The Russian archaeologist Aleksandr Lebedintsev interpreted it as representing a kayak (1998: 300, 302), although its overall shape is more suggestive of a dugout (fig. 10.11).

Another object serving as evidence of skin boats on the Russian side of Bering Strait is an engraved whalebone artifact found in a 2007 archaeological excavation at the Un'en'en site, near the village of Nunligran on the Russian side of the Bering Strait. The artifact, excavated from the floor of a house radiocarbon-dated to circa 1000 BCE, is engraved with pictures of hunters in a boat harpooning large whales

Fig. 10.11. This representation of what might be an early boat from northeastern Asia is an enigmatic round-bottomed carving with a flat top, pronounced sheer, and a bow projection, and it is covered with incised decorations. Found in a circa 500 BCE–0 CE Tokarev-culture site on Spafar'ev Island in the northern Sea of Okhotsk, it might be either a kayak or a dugout. Its decoration recalls the ritualized markings on the Taimyr boat model in fig. 6.2, page 118. (From Lebedintsev 1998: 300, 302)

(Witze 2008; see also fig. 8.12a–c and discussion on page 169). Given the site location—a treeless Chukotka coastal environment—the supposition that the artifact shows a skin boat is reasonable but not certain, given the controversy over wood versus skin boats in Scandinavian and White Sea rock art (see page 73). Dating 1,500 years before the appearance of whaling harpoons and the first direct evidence of skin boats at the Ekven cemetery near East Cape (see fig. 8.11, page 168), indirect evidence of skin boats in the form of ivory harpoon cradles like those used on later skin umiaks has been found at 3,500-year-old Choris sites in Alaska. Some have questioned if the Un'en'en find might be intrusive, since similar scenes of boats and harpooned whales have been found only at Okhotsk-culture, Punuk, and Thule Eskimo sites dating after 500 CE, and also since the Un'en'en bone itself has not been radiocarbon dated. If the find context is secure (see discussion on page 169), the image is the earliest evidence of open skin boat use and the systematic hunting of large whales, dating back 1,500 years before the Ekven site.

Interesting pictographic evidence of boat use in Chukotka is seen in rock art on cliffs along the Pegtymel River, 60 kilometers southeast of its mouth (see fig. 8.1, page 158). The complete body of pictographs there includes 76 images of single-person boats and 32 watercraft with large crews (Kiryak 2007: 246). Some images show scenes of deer, goose, and sea mammal hunting. Both the date and the ethnic authorship of these images remain speculative; Nikolai Dikov suggested that they were created by the ancestors of the Chukchi between 1000 BCE and 700 CE, but he also noted that some of the images might have been added later, dating to the 1400s CE (1999: 86, 53). M. A. Kiryak, basing his theory

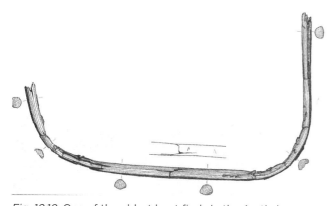

Fig. 10.10. One of the oldest boat finds in the Arctic is represented by this wooden rib from a flat-bottomed kayak excavated from the frozen 4,300-year-old Saqqaq-culture Qeqertasussuk site in Disko Bay, West Greenland. (From Grønnow 1994: 19, 221)

on a stylistic comparison with more modern Eskimo art, extends the Pegtymel art's upper chronological boundary to the 1600s CE and suggests that the images reflect three ethnic components: Yukagir, Chukchi-Koryak, and Eskimo-Aleut (2007: 256–63). While no definite proof can be produced, it is likely—given the treeless environment and implied availability of marine mammal skins—that these images depict skin boats, but some have claimed that they show plank and dugout boats (Kiryak 2007: 257). Ivory and wooden boat miniatures found at the Ekven site (see fig. 8.11, page 168; Arutiunov and Sergeev 2006; Bronshtein and Dneprovsky 2009) attest to the use of both umiaks and kayaks on the Chukotka Peninsula by the first centuries CE. Boats were likely used in whale hunting, which reached peaks at least twice, in the 2nd to 4th and the 6th to 7th centuries CE (Savinetsky 2002). Images of people whaling from what might be skin boats are commonly found on needlecases of the circa 1000–1200 CE Okhotsk culture (see fig. 9.3, page 189).

Ivory kayak models and umiak harpoon rests found in Choris sites on Kotzebue Sound and dated to approximately 3,000 years ago constitute some of the first hard evidence of skin boat use in Alaska (Giddings 1967: 214). The presence of kayaks and umiaks is inferred from ivory deck fittings, harpoons, and harpoon rests from the western Alaska Norton and Okvik cultures (Giddings 1967: 126; Bandi 1969: 69–70) and was established with even more certainty by models and frame and paddle fragments from the Old Bering Sea culture (H. Collins 1937: 253). The Kukulik site on St. Lawrence Island, dated 200 BCE to 1879 CE, contained more than 400 boat fragments. Archaeological data leave little doubt that by the 1st century CE, skin-covered watercraft were actively and extensively employed on both sides of the Bering Strait.

This evidence becomes progressively richer toward the end of the 1st millennium CE and beyond. In Alaska, skin boat parts were recorded at the Deering site (821–1200 CE) in Kotzebue Sound and at Birnirk and other sites (500–1300 CE) in the vicinity of Point Barrow (Ford 1959: 156–60). The quantity of both umiak and kayak boat fragments at the original Birnirk site attests to the importance of maritime subsistence and transportation. Among other finds, the site yielded scores of wooden frame remains that belonged to a single umiak dating to circa 1015 CE (Anichtchenko 2013: 24–25). In the 13th century CE, the Thule migration, originating in northwestern Alaska, swept across the Canadian Arctic to Greenland and set the stage for today's distribution of Inuit people. The remarkable speed with which the Thule culture

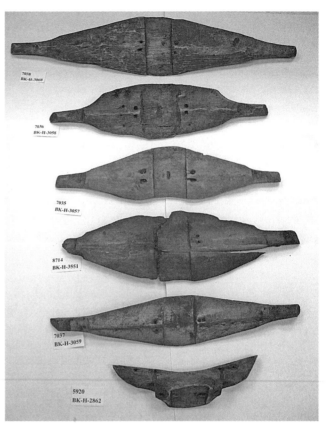

Fig. 10.12. Archaeological evidence of boats after 500 CE—especially umiaks—is plentiful in frozen Eskimo sites around Bering Strait. These crosspieces (top to bottom: NMNH 7038, 7036, 7035, 8714, 7037, 5920) from the Birkirk site near Point Barrow, Alaska, date to 500–1300 CE and are probably all from a single open skin boat. (Courtesy Smithsonian National Museum of Natural History)

covered nearly 4,000 kilometers, possibly within a single generation or two, should be attributed to these people's watercraft at least as much as to their dogsleds.

Archaeological sites in western and south-central Alaska have also yielded boat finds. The 2008–11 excavation of the Nunalleq site (dated to circa 1300–1650 CE) in the Yukon-Kuskokwim Delta uncovered a number of wooden artifacts that have been interpreted as boat remains (Britton et al. 2013). Fragments of both kayaks and umiaks were discovered in cave sites (890–1667 CE) on Kagamil and Kanaga islands in the Aleutian chain (W. Nelson and Barnett 1955: 387–92) and in a cave on Unga Island (Dall 1878: pl. 8). Skin boat remains from Karluk sites (1300–1700 CE) on Kodiak Island (Knecht 1995) and the Palutat cave (1700–1800 CE) on Prince William Sound (De Laguna 1956: 65, 239, 245–49) have provided a glimpse into the Sugpiaq boat tradition of the late precontact period.

ORIGIN, DIFFUSION, AND EVOLUTIONARY THEORIES

Given the fragmentary character and complexity of circumpolar boat data, it is not surprising that analysis has produced a wide range of hypotheses and theories, particularly in connection with the evolution of circumpolar watercraft and the relationships among bark, skin, and dugout traditions. Most researchers suggest an inland Eurasian origin for all three traditions; however, the issue of relationships and evolutionary connections among these different vessel types and their subforms has generated a wide range of opinions.

George Dyson proposed that kayaks evolved from inflated animal-skin floats used for river crossing "through a long period of step-by-step development of seagoing skin vessels, which might have developed, perhaps repeatedly, as land-based hunters faced a rising sea level and the growing temptation of sea-going prey" (1991: 262). In Dyson's interpretation, the umiak was a product of the development of the kayak. The further development of the kayak was fueled by a self-amplifying circle encompassing the kayak, the hunter, and the prey:

> One kayak was required to obtain the game to sustain and clothe the hunter while building another kayak, in its turn required to hunt down the materials to build other kayaks: thus the ingredients of kayak evolution cycled forward from year to year. The kayak competed in speed, stealth, and stamina against a wide range of amphibious vertebrates—including fellow kayaks, both in peacetime and in war. (1991: 263)

An alternative line of thinking suggests that umiaks preceded and influenced kayak development. Analyzing a 2,000-year-old kayak model from the Ekven cemetery in Chukotka (see fig. 8.11, page 168), Zimmerly pointed out that its forked gunwales at the bow and stern exhibit some umiak characteristics, suggesting that "the kayak is a descendant of the umiak" (1986: 3). Arima also believes that umiaks influenced kayak design, specifically in the case of Bering Sea kayaks and the characteristic bifid bow of Unangan (Aleut) kayaks, but does not exclude the possibility of the kayak's independent development (2004: 137–38).

The native lore of the Unangan people also supports the notion that the kayak developed from the open skin boat. According to a legend recorded by Lucien Turner in the Aleutian Islands, decked boats for a single hunter evolved from the larger open skin family boats at a time when increased warfare made seafaring unsafe (2008: 2). Similar lore exists in Greenland, where "it is said that long ago the kayak was an open vessel, without a deck, and the skin cover was hung on the frame with bone pegs stuck into the top of the sheer boards" (Petersen 1986: 15). In addition, an origin story of the Sugpiaq people states that their first boat was a two-hatch kayak (Doroshin 1866: 369–70).

The archaeologist William Laughlin postulated that the kayak originated circa 10,000 years ago in southwestern Alaska. According to him, early migrants who crossed the Bering land bridge from Eurasia used open skin boats after they arrived in America. But he demurred: "Whether only coracles or open retrieval boats were in use for exploiting the rich marine resources at the ice edge or the exposed summer coasts, or whether an ancestral form of the umiak was used, cannot yet be essayed" (Laughlin, Heath, and Arima 1991: 184). Unfortunately, he provided no explanation of how and when kayaks came to Eurasia, and the general lack of supportive evidence does not allow for further development of this idea.

James Hornell proposed that umiaks evolved from Asian coracles. According to him, the transformation occurred "when the bands of early men were driven northwards by the pressure of more powerful tribes in the south" (1970: 177). Once they emerged on the Arctic Sea coast, "the lack of timber and the unsuitable nature of the round river coracle for use on the wind-swept northern waters bred in certain tribes an inventive faculty that produced the umiak, suitable for the transport of the family and its few chattels, and later . . . for the pursuit of the whale" (177). Some scholars see the rounded stem and stern of the Koryak umiak as evidence of its evolution from coracles (Arima 2002).

The construction of the kayak, in Hornell's opinion, had no relationship to the umiak or coracle but instead grew out of the bark canoe (1946: 179). This theory is based mainly on two unrelated sets of evidence: the similarity between the ram- or sturgeon-nose canoe types of British Columbia and the Amur River, and the existence of the so-called kayak-form bark canoe. Hornell believed that sturgeon-nose canoes evolved into kayaks in a scenario similar to that of his coracle-into-umiak transformation—as a response to a treeless environment and the need to adjust from inland to open-ocean water conditions. He further pointed out that "the probability of the ancestral affinity of the Amur bark canoe to the kayak is increased by the fact that the Sakha and Nanay tribes use double paddles, so characteristic a feature of kayak propulsion" (180). It is not, however, clear from his discussion how the sturgeon-nose canoe form made it to North America as a bark boat. Following his logic, once the transformation into the skin-covered boat was complete, the boat that crossed the ocean to Alaska must have been a kayak. To preserve the similarity between the bark canoes of British Columbia and those of the Amur region, that kayak would have had to make a reverse transition to bark boat at some point in its North American afterlife.

The similarity between the kayak-form bark canoe and the skin-covered kayak is due to the way that the bark canoe's frame is constructed. Adney and Chapelle described this type of bark canoe as a "flat-bottomed, narrow canoe having nearly straight flaring sides and either a chine or a very quick turn of the bilge" (2007: 154). It was widely employed in the American Northwest, from the Yukon River to the Mackenzie Basin and British Columbia. Some regional variants had bark covers stretched from gunwale to gunwale at bow and stern, which made them partially decked and strengthened their resemblance to kayaks, particularly in their single-chined variants, such as the Greenlandic and Chukchi ethnographic types. This structural similarity seemed too strong to some researchers and moved them to suggest a genetic relationship (Mason and Hill 1901; Hornell 1946). The direction, nature, and timing of this relationship, however, remain topics of discussion. It might be more plausible that kayak-type bark boats evolved in imitation of skin kayaks, and not vice versa.

One of the difficulties in tracing kayaks to kayak-form canoes is the fact that flat-bottomed kayaks, which resemble kayak-form canoes, have not been recorded in the region where these canoes are used. All the ethnographic kayaks of Alaska and western Canada have multichined hulls with characteristic semicircular cross-sections. The only known examples of kayaks with a single pair of stringers and flattened bottoms are from eastern Canada (northern Labrador and Baffin Island) and Greenland (Adney and Chapelle 2007: 154; Kankaanpää 1989: 27).

John Heath noted an interesting similarity in the structural configuration of the kayaks of the Koryak of the Russian Far East, the inland Copper Inuit of northeastern Canada, and the Greenlandic Inuit: all three of these geographically removed Native nations had kayaks with flat decks. This observation formed the basis for his classification of all kayak types into two families: the ridged-deck type of the Bering Sea and southern Alaska, characterized by raised decks, thin gunwales, and cockpits integrated into the frame; and the flat-deck type of the rest of the Arctic and Subarctic regions.

Heath suggested that the fact that the second type was present at opposite outer fringes of the Inuit habitation "could indicate that there was an ancient archetype from which all kayaks evolved" (1978: 22). According to him, the formation of the two types occurred at the time of Eskimo migration into North America and was aided by the Seward Peninsula, which served as a "fork in the road for nomadic maritime cultures, because they would tend to go up the coast or down the coast" (20).

Jarmo Kankaanpää both refined and reassessed these observations, pointing out that Heath's classification is based on two constructional features: the deck assemblage and the longitudinal members that form the kayak hull. Kankaanpää considered both features to be configurative components—"compound structural features, which owing to their primary nature most easily become unconscious *idées fixes*, established configurative assumptions that can be changed only through strong intrusive impulses" (1989: 24). He further argued that these features can therefore provide a baseline for our understanding of watercraft development in larger geographic and temporal scopes. Based on these criteria, all historical kayaks can be divided into three main type groups:

1. flat-decked kayaks with a hull shaped by two stringers and a keel: e.g., the eastern Canadian and Greenlandic types and the Koryak type;
2. flat-decked types with multiple hull stringers: e.g., the Copper and Caribou Inuit (of the Chukchi Sea coast of Alaska Arctic) types;
3. ridge-decked types, whose camber, or sloping sides, adds hull strength and water shedding capabilities, with multiple hull stringers: e.g., the Bering Sea and South Alaskan types

Two kayak types—those of the Mackenzie and Reindeer Chukchi—are excluded as "not directly assignable to any group" (36). Based on the level of constructional complexity and geographic distribution of these types, Kankaanpää suggested that the first group represents the oldest and most original kayak type in eastern Canada. Archaeological finds, such as a kayak rib from house no. 76 of the Nunguvik site on Northern Baffin Island that has been dated to the 4th to 6th centuries CE (uncalibrated; Mary-Rousselière 1979), imply a connection to Dorset culture. This kayak type might have been developed in Canada by the Dorset people or their predecessors, or it could have evolved in Siberia—hence the Koryak variant—and been carried to North America by the Arctic Small Tool tradition, which reached Alaska circa 5000 BP and northeastern Canada and Greenland around 4000 to 4500 BP, via the earliest Pre-Dorset culture (33–34). Kankaanpää suggested an early spread—perhaps even from Cape Denbigh—of the flat-bottomed kayak to the inland peoples of the Chukchi Peninsula, where it might have been used as a reindeer-hunting boat and was later adopted by the Koryak for maritime use. In this scenario, the inland kayak of the Reindeer Chukchi might be the most archaic form of ethnographically known kayak (Kankaan-pää 1989: 37) instead of a simplified form adopted from the coastal Yupik (see chapter 8).

The second group, consisting of flat-decked kayaks with multichined hulls, according to Kankaanpää (1989: 37), is connected to the Thule culture and its spread into Canada and Greenland beginning in the 12th and 13th centuries CE. This conclusion is based largely on James Ford's analysis of kayak miniatures from the Birnirk site that appeared to have round bottoms. However, the same site produced kayak ribs that suggest a flat bottom (1959: 159).

The time and place of origin of the third group, the round-hulled kayaks with ridged decks, remain open questions. The oldest ridged-kayak deck beams discovered to date are those found on Kagamil Island in the Aleutian chain, loosely dated to 890–1667 CE (Coltrain, Hayes, and O'Rourke 2006: 540; Dall 1878: 318, pl. 8), and those from the Nukleet site in Norton Bay, circa 1400s CE (Giddings 1964: 83). The Kagamil Cave finds also included thin, rounded wooden fragments that might be bent kayak ribs. Despite these comparatively recent dates, Kankaanpää proposed that both the ridge-decked and mul-tichined kayaks "originated in the Alaska Peninsula–Kodiak Island area or the Aleutian Islands," perhaps as early as 6700 BCE. He believed this occurred in the process of adapta-tion to open-ocean hunting in this high-energy environment, "since the structural function of the ridged deck is to prevent the frame from sagging in a swell" (1989: 31). He also sug-gested that this kayak technology spread to western Alaska fairly late, probably only toward the end of the 1st millen-nium CE, and stopped at the southern margin of the Seward Peninsula because the Punuk and Thule cultures' focus on whaling made oceangoing kayaks unnecessary. Consequently, the kayaks of the Seward Peninsula and northern Alaska retained their flat decks (38).

While Kankaanpää's study of kayak typology and cul-tural history offers important insights into the connections among different kayak types, the limited archaeological and ethnographic data leave many questions unanswered. The same issue tempers the progress of indigenous boat studies in general. Despite a number of keen observations and bold ideas, most of the conclusions regarding the relationships among different indigenous boat forms of Eurasia and North America will remain speculative until more archaeological evidence is uncovered and comprehensively analyzed, along with living traditions and ethnographic, genetic, linguistic, and environmental records.

It is also important to note that morphological resem-blances between different boat types do not need to indicate "genetic" relationships. Adaptation to the same environmen-tal conditions and hunting strategies prompted similar boat-building solutions. Ridged kayak decks, for instance, were a necessity for the pursuit of prey in the open ocean, while flat decks were allowed for hunting kayaks in the icy waters and estuaries of Kamchatka, northern Alaska, Arctic Canada, and Greenland, where they did not need to shed waves. The kayak's use also determined the proportions of its hull. Longer kayaks were faster and better suited for open water; short hulls offered increased sturdiness and maneuverability. The width of the hull was connected to hunting methods: wide hulls provided a hunter with stability, needed so that he could remain still while waiting for prey to approach (Birket-Smith 1924: 318–20). Narrow hulls minimized a kayak's drag and were employed when the success of the hunt depended on a chase, as in caribou and beluga hunting (Arima 1975: 99–100; Arima 1987: 60). Multichined hulls, such as those of Ber-ing Sea and Aleutian kayaks, allowed a deeper hold and the opportunity to transport cargo and passengers (Heath 1991: 6), while flat-bottomed kayaks with fewer stringers weighed less and were better adapted for longer sea voyages. Yet while environmental factors played an important role in boat design development, very few regional differences can be explained by environmental constraints alone (Rousselot 1994: 253).

THE EVER-CHANGING BOAT: FUTURE PROSPECTS

In addition to larger data sets, the study of circumpolar indigenous watercraft is in need of an extended theoretical and methodological framework. Initially inspired by the beauty and ingenuity of indigenous practice, this research presently is focused on the full-scale boats and models pre-served in museum collections, as both the general public and researchers presume that this tradition is gone from the contemporary world. This focus consequently determines both research questions and the way they are addressed.

Skin cover fragments, although less common than boat frame pieces, do exist in both ethnographic and archaeological records, and the analysis of this material will contribute to our understanding of both local traditions and their interrelationships. However, since most kayaks in museum collections lack skins, the mainstream of skin boat research has focused on frame analysis and given little attention to covers, which contrasts sharply with the actual practice of skin boat building and use. A well-built frame could last several decades, while skins were changed every couple of years, meaning that most boat maintenance centered on securing, preparing, and sewing skins. Both kayak and umiak covers were ritualistically embedded, as they had immediate implications for the survival of the people who used these boats. "The man's life is on the tip of a woman's needle" is a saying one hears when talking to contemporary umiak-skin sewers in Barrow, Alaska (fig. 10.13). In the past, special rituals were performed in conjunction with the making of boat covers. On Nunivak Island, for instance, when the last stitch of a new kayak cover was sewn, the owner of the boat would strip off his clothes and sing a childbirth song to his new kayak (Curtis 1930: 12–15). Women sometimes gave birth over old boat skins (Blue 2007: 33–35), and kayaks often accompanied hunters' burials (Himmelheber 2000: 139). In today's practice, it is considered important that women sewing umiak covers maintain a happy attitude. While sewers of skins still play an important role in the traditional whaling communities

of Utqiagvik (Barrow) and Point Hope, the disappearance of the skin boat tradition from contemporary Arctic villages on both sides of the Bering Strait is often attributed to the lack of local skin-sewing expertise.

Another pattern in indigenous boat research is the tendency to focus on a particular form when drawing larger cross-regional analogies. The absolute majority of circumpolar indigenous boat studies are dedicated to kayaks. While some attempts have been made to link kayaks to bark boats and umiaks to dugout canoes, comprehensive analysis of the combined umiak and kayak traditions of the circumpolar north is still lacking. Such an analysis would be particularly interesting because similarities among the kayaks of different nations do not always align with long-distance relationships among umiaks. The Koryak kayak, for instance, resembles eastern Canadian and Greenlandic forms, while the Koryak umiak (see figs. 8.18–8.19, pages 176–177) shares features with the open skin boats of the Aleutian Islands. At the same time, Aleutian kayaks are similar to those of the Sugpiaq, but the open skin boats of these groups differ significantly. This situation is intriguing, as kayaks and umiaks are closely aligned in the context of the circumpolar north's indigenous history, and one might assume that similar, if not identical, processes drove the development of both the kayaks and the umiaks of the same Arctic groups. A comprehensive picture of this development will evolve only when kayaks and umiaks are considered on equal terms.

A key issue in indigenous boat research at the conceptual level is the question of change. As discussed above, many conclusions regarding the relationships among different boat forms are based on the presumed conservatism of Native boatbuilding and the (again presumed) isolation of different boat traditions from one another. Indigenous boats often are perceived as tools of local subsistence, made on an ancient pattern passed down from one generation to another and used in a fairly limited geographical area. Yet boats were made to travel, and the local lores of circumpolar peoples include many stories about long-distance voyaging. Travel allowed for contact between both neighboring and geographically remote nations. Trading voyages and military expeditions transmitted not only trade goods and the spoils of war, but also technological ideas and engineering concepts. As one of the most mobile artifacts of indigenous cultures, boats were both catalysts and objects of continual change, influenced by many factors from climatic and social shifts to the introduction of new materials and encounters with new people (fig. 10.14). As Golden eloquently

Fig. 10.13. The role of women in northern boat culture is too often overlooked. They processed birch and other bark types for canoes and tent covers and labored over hide preparation and needlework, joining skins and fitting them to boat frames. This photograph shows a Point Hope woman repairing a damaged umiak walrus hide cover in the 1930s. (Courtesy Anchorage Museum)

puts it, indigenous boats changed "both subtly and gradually, and yet also suddenly on account of new tools and materials or even by emulating a design used by a particularly successful hunter" (2006: 117). While tradition played an important part in how people built and used their boats (and continues to do so), at no given time has the development of watercraft reached a final state and become sealed in time and space.

Finally, one of the most important and urgent needs in indigenous boat research is to incorporate surviving living traditions. Some forms of watercraft are already gone from the contemporary practice of indigenous peoples; others are still present in actual practice or oral lore. The last bark canoes in Alaska were built in the 1950s; kayaks, although they disappeared from both sides of the Bering Strait about 50 years ago, are now making a comeback as educational and recreational boats. Umiaks, the most resilient form of indigenous boats in Alaska, presently are used by the Native whale hunters of Utqiagvik (Barrow), Point Hope, and Gambell, Alaska; and Sireniki, Chukotka. These communities represent the last remnants of skin boat use in Eurasia and North America. Just 50 years ago, dozens of villages engaged in the production and use of skin boats. The next 50 years might witness the complete disappearance of active skin boat traditions from North America and the circumpolar north in general. The most important task today, while some of the last tradition-bearers are still among us and old bark and skin boats still grace remote Siberian and Alaskan ocean shores and riverbanks, is to record and preserve this tradition.

Fig. 10.14. The Smithsonian National Museum of Natural History acquired the Paul Jensen angyapik (NMNH E436141), covered with split walrus hide, from the University of Oregon in 2017. The boat dates to the 1950s, when it was used for whaling on St. Lawrence Island. Later it was purchased by Jensen for his circumnavigation of St. Lawrence Island with Yupik hunters. Its design reflects mid-20th-century changes resulting from the introduction of the outboard motor, which was mounted in an inboard well, and it has bentwood ribs for added strength. The boat's exterior is painted white, which helped preserve the skin and camouflaged the boat among ice floes (see fig. 8.14). (Courtesy University of Oregon and Smithsonian National Museum of Natural History)

Appendix

LITERATURE ON EURASIAN BARK CANOES AND SKIN BOATS

Here we present a brief overview of the main sources for our history of bark canoes and skin boats in Northern Eurasia. All the material discussed here—with key content and sources grouped by geographical territories and waterways, and listed according to cultural group—is also in the "Northern Eurasian Bark and Skin Canoes" database maintained at the Smithsonian Arctic Studies Center, where it is accessible for further study.

ORIGINAL DIARIES, BOOKS, AND PAPERS

The most important sources for this book are first-hand accounts and illustrations by explorers, which present the peoples of Northern Eurasia and their boats in their original geographic locations. These early travelers—surveyors, scientists, priests, soldiers, traders, and scientists—were usually in search of furs, metals, and minerals, and they drew maps of the landscapes they traversed and the sea routes they took to reach unexplored northern waters. They described what they saw on their journeys, collecting information from the environment and, in many cases, interviewing local people and fellow travelers. Among the earliest outside visitors to Northern Eurasia were paramilitary Cossacks, who subjugated Native peoples in order to extract *yassak* (tribute) in the form of furs and convert them into future taxpayers. Their intent, like that of most early travelers in the region, was exploitation of land, water, and people.

From the 15th through the 19th centuries, furs were a highly valuable currency in international trade and were obtained first in Scandinavia and the Western Urals, and then in Western and Eastern Siberia. Fur traders' diaries, books, and papers cover nearly 450 years of canoe history, and this wealth of data offers invaluable insight into both the bark canoes and the skin boats of the Eurasian north. Yet canoes and other boats usually are not in the foreground of these accounts, and therefore the quality and quantity of information about them are variable. Most accounts these travelers recorded of their encounters with Native peoples who used skin boats and canoes are brief, although a few are quite detailed, and some even include sketches or drawings. Only a fraction of these original reports have been cited in boat literature, however. Possibly the oldest written information on skin boats may be found in Chinese sources that have not been known in the West until recently (Chen 2003). In later times, photos have proved to be the best resources on canoe and skin boat design, and they are augmented by canoes and model boats in museums.

In the old western literature, we see a regional trend that reveals how and when Northern Eurasian skin boats and bark canoes gradually became known to scientific circles and the public. One trend started in the era of maritime exploration of northwestern Eurasia, which began in the 1500s, while the other started with imperial Russian territorial expansion, led by Cossacks, from west to east to conquer new lands in Western Siberia, a process that began in the 1500s. Colonization of Eastern and Pacific Siberia, mainly by sea expeditions that reached as far as Alaska, became a major element of Russian policy in the early 1700s, and such journeys continued until the mid-1800s. In the final stage of this Great Power geographic rivalry, Russia established its presence in the Far East in the 1850s, after its border disputes with China and Japan had been settled.

Skin boats were the first to appear in historical accounts in the latter half of the 1500s, when illustrated maps and the earliest travel accounts of the Arctic Ocean coasts appeared. The English captain Stephen Burrough (1567) mentioned the Samoyed and their deerskin boats at the coast near Vaigach Island, as well as their habit of carrying boats on their shoulders to shore. The Dutch merchant Olivier Brunel, while exploring the seaway to China in 1576 (Spies 1997), reported meeting in Ob Bay some Samoyed paddling an open skin boat off the Taz Peninsula. In the 18th century, the French ship doctor Pierre Martin de La Martinère, who sailed twice to Novaya Zemlya and Vaigach islands as a member of a Danish expedition, provided the first good account (1706) of a seal skin–decked kayak and an illustration of a skin boat mentioned by Burrough. Probably the earliest information about a birch-bark canoe was included in the first written description of Siberia, recorded by A. Dobbin, a military officer. In 1673, he wrote, "At the large river the Yenisey (Jelissee) live the Tungus, who feed on fish; their boats are made from birch bark, which they know how so to tar, that in them completely does not penetrate water; they are noticeably high-speed" (1702: 301).

In those days, the area called Siberia included only the part now known as Western Siberia; the territory east of the Yenisey River was mainly unknown. Available information on Siberian skin boats and bark canoes decreased sharply during the 1700s, probably because they became rare in inland waters and along the sea coast, where explorers were most likely to see them. Later, information on these craft in Western Siberia increased suddenly when a series of trained scientists, mostly employed by the Russian Academy of Sciences (RAS) and the Russian Geographical Society, set forth to map this country, its resources, and its people. Among those scientists were Daniel G. Messerschmidt (1964), Gerhard F. Müller (1957), Dimitry and Khariton Laptev (1739), Peter S. Pallas (1776), and Johann G. Georgi (1775, 1776a,b, 1777). Their travel reports and diaries contain a rich body of data, including encounters with and information on canoes. Messerschmidt was the first trained scientist to travel in Siberia, in 1721–28, although his papers are among the least known today. He wrote a five-volume report for the RAS that mentioned the larch-bark and birch-bark canoes he had seen on the Lower Tunguska River, but it was not printed in full until 1964. As a junior scientist, Messerschmidt was forgotten, and he never was permanently employed by the RAS. Lieutenant Khariton Laptev was a Navy officer who mapped the sea route from the Lena River to the eastern Taimyr Peninsula, finding a fully maritime-adapted skin boat people of mixed origin at the Khatanga River. This information was confirmed much later in the papers of G. F. Müller. Pallas located Mansi bark canoes on the eastern slope of Ural Mountains; Georgi documented Tungus bark canoes at Lake Baikal, and his team drew a Yukagir skin kayak in the Lena River basin—the only Yukagir skin boat that ever has been illustrated.

KEY SOURCES

Georg W. Steller (2003) and Gavril A. Sarychev (1805) might have been the first to record northeastern Siberian maritime skin boats. Steller was a scientist on Bering's expedition of 1741–42, which explored the North Pacific coasts, including the Aleutian Islands, parts of southern Alaska, and Kamchatka; he wrote his diary in Kamchatka after Bering's ship was wrecked on Bering Island. Thanks to him, we know much about the Kamchatka Itelmen and Koryak and the fact that some of these Natives covered their large boats with a single skin from a large sea cow, now extinct. The Itelmen, the Koryak, and their skin boats were studied later by Karl von Dittmar (1890a,b, 2004), Waldemar Jochelson (1908), and Valentina V. Antropova (1961). Artists assigned to the naval expedition led by Captain Sarychev (1805), under the command of Commodore Billings, drafted illustrations of people and their boats on the Siberian coast, and this work provides us with more information on Eskimo kayaks around Bering Strait. The secretary of Billings's expedition, Martin Sauer (1802), produced a lively account of a Native sea bird–hunting party with canoes in an Sea of Okhotsk village where the expedition was making preparations for their voyage.

Expeditions and papers in the 1800s produced much more direct information on people and their canoes over the entire territory of Western and Eastern Siberia, as well as in the Far East, and the Amur Peninsula, Sakhalin, and the Okhotsk coast became connected to the western world for the first time. As before, the major scientists were of German origin and had sought employment with the Russian Academy of Sciences, but by this time Russian, Finnish, American, and English travelers were making contributions as well. Imperial Russia had not yet fully consolidated the new lands in the east, and China, Great Britain, Japan, and the United States also showed interest in these territories.

In Western Siberia, Frans O. Belyavsky (1833) toured the Ob River estuary and wrote an account of Ostyak (Khanty) skin boats. The Finnish linguist and ethnologist Matthias A. Castrén (1857a,b,c) covered the entire territory and visited nearly all the Samoyed (Nenets) and Yenisey Ostyak (Ket) peoples from the Yamal and Taimyr peninsulas to Lake Baikal and Mongolia, establishing the principles of their languages and compiling ethnic history and geography; he published his results in his 12-volume, 4,800-page collected works. Thanks to Castrén, we know much more about peoples who used ancient canoes in the past, and he also recorded accounts of bark canoe–using people whom he met at the Yenisey River. E. P. von Orlov (1858) and Gustav Radde (1861)

Table 4

Literature Sources on Bark and Skin Boats in Northern Eurasia

Only sources referring directly to bark canoes, skin boats, paddle finds, or boats in rock art are included. Works that include useful illustrations or photographs are italicized. References to museums in this table indicate surveyed catalogue entries and year of survey.

Century in Which Travel Occurred	Northern and Northeastern Europe	Western, Central, and Southern Siberia	Eastern and Pacific Siberia, Including Lake Baikal	Far East, Including Amur, Sakhalin, and Kamchatka
1500s	Magnus 1555 Burrough 1567 Linschoten 1598	Brunel, travel in 1576 Balak 1581	—	—
1600s	de La Martinière 1706	Dobbin 1702	—	—
1700s	Chydenius 1753	Pallas 1776	Laptev 1739 Georgi 1776a Pallas 1776 Messerschmidt 1964	Müller 1957 Krasheninnikov 1755 Sarychev 1805 Steller 2003
1800s	von Düben 1873	Belyavsky 1833 Castrén 1857b Orlov 1858 Radde 1861 Müller 1882	Wrangel 1839 Tronson 1859 Middendorff 1875 Nordenskjöld 1881 Dittmar 1890a,b Sieroszewski 1993	Sauer 1802 Reclus 1882 Orlov 1858 Przhevalsky 1869 Knox 1871 Schrenk 1881 Mason and Hill 1901
1900s	Zagoskin 1910 Reid 1912 Trebitsch 1912 Itkonen 1942 Gjessing 1944 Whitaker 1954, 1977 Foss 1948 Haavio 1952 Troyanovskiy and Petrov 2018 Johnston 1980 Westerdahl 1985a *Burov 1996* McGrail 1998	Nansen 1911 *Sushilin photograph, 1926* Naumov 1927 *Khoroshikh, Library of Congress photograph collection, 1930* Lehtisalo 1932, 1959 Donner 1933a, 1979 Chernetsov and Moszyńska 1954 Popov 1964a,b Haviland 1971 Tugolukov 1985 Starcev 1988 Golovnev and Michael 1992	Jochelson 1908, 1924 Brindley 1919a,b,c Pälsi 1929, 1983 Steiner 1939 Antropova 1961 Rudenko 1961 Adney and Chapelle 1964 Bandi 1972 Jensen 1975 Johnston 1980 *Zimmerly 1986* *Kankaanpää 1989* *Neryungri Museum of History 1997* McGrail 1998 Orekhov 1998	Antropova 1961 Levin 1984 Thiele 1984 Gumilev 1997
2000s	Burov 2000 Shutikhin 2003, 2008	Golovnev 2000 Perevalova 2003 Belgibaev 2004 Krauss 2005 Sirina 2006 Permyakova 2007 Turov 2008 Altner 2009 Irkutsk Museum 2010	Nefedkin 2003 Abakumov 2001 *Kunstkamera Museum 2009*	Chen 2003 Chepelev 2004 Noll and Shi 2004 Lee-Duffy 2005 Yanchev 2006

studied the Lake Baikal region and the Amur basin for the Russian Geographical Society in the footsteps of J. G. Georgi (1775, 1776 a,b, 1777) and gave us many accounts of Evenk (Tungus) people and their bark canoes. Lieutenant Orlov (1858) also studied the Amur and wrote a detailed description of the Negidal birch-bark canoe fabrication process. F. F. Müller (1882), working for the Russian Academy of Sciences, recorded his long inland journey by boat from Lake Baikal to the Yana River, east of the Lena River basin, a trip on which he used a birch-bark canoe as an auxiliary boat.

Eastern Siberia was well studied in the 1800s, and understanding of skin boats and their users improved greatly thanks to many outstanding explorers and scientists. Russian Navy Lieutenant Ferdinand P. von Wrangel (1839) and his companion, Midshipman F. F. Matyushkin, made an adventurous journey through the Eastern Siberia tundra and sea coast, meeting Yukagir, Evenk, and Chukchi people, and wrote a fine account of their travel. Their diary was the first major scientific report written and published in the Russian language; all major Russian reports previously had been written in German, at that time the lingua franca of European science. The Lena River estuary and Aldan River were explored by Alexander von Middendorff (1875), a German scientist who documented birch-bark canoes in drawings and tried—unsuccessfully—to launch skin boats for coastal navigation. Thanks to Swedish-Finnish N. A. E. Nordenskjöld (1881), we know much about Arctic Ocean flora and fauna and Chukchi open skin boats and kayaks in the Chukotka Peninsula. A British naval officer, Lieutenant J. M. Tronson (1859), patrolling the Okhotsk coast during the Crimean War, met some Even (Lamut) sea coast people in Ayan and wrote a rare account of their skin kayak, while a Polish political exile, Wacław Sieroszewski (1993), studied Sakha (Yakut) birch-bark, log, and planked boats and proposed that the Yakut bark canoe had a Ket origin.

In the 19th century, the Amur region was annexed to Russia, and thereafter this little-known land and its peoples gradually became better understood. E. G. Ravenstein and A. H. Keane edited Elisée Reclus's 1882 monumental *The Earth and Its Inhabitants*, whose volumes 5 and 6, on the early Russian conquest of the Far East, cast light on the boating traditions of the Tungus-Manchu, Chinese, and Ainu peoples in the Amur basin and Sakhalin Island. In the Ussuri River basin, a Russian intelligence officer, Nikolai Przhevalsky (1869), mapped the Russian border with China and wrote an account of his travels, including meetings with Ulch bark canoe builders. On a Russian Academy of Sciences mission

in the Amur, German scientist Leopold von Schrenk (1881) explored the territory and carefully documented Nanay (Gold) and other bark canoes and log boat–building traditions.

The American Thomas W. Knox (1871) traveled in Siberia and published a book about his experiences, which included a description of a Nanay bark canoe; he compared it to American Indian canoes. Finally, Otis T. Mason and Meriden S. Hill (1901) produced a paper comparing the sharp-prowed bark canoes from the Kootenai River in British Columbia to those built in the Amur River basin, noting similarities in design. Mason based his Siberian similarities on the travel diary written by von Schrenk and model canoes he borrowed from the collections of the St. Petersburg Museum of Anthropology and Ethnology, also known as the Kunstkamera. Some of the most informative descriptions of canoes and kayaks are found in the ethnography and other publications of Waldemar Bogoras and Waldemar Jochelson, Russian members of Franz Boas's Jesup North Pacific Expedition of 1897–1902, conducted by the American Museum of Natural History.

Studies Based on Multiple Sources

In the 1900s, it became much more difficult to get direct in-situ information on skin boats and bark canoes because these boats were becoming rarer, except in some small areas of Siberia and the Amur. As a result, there was a shift toward new methods of studying these watercraft, and projects began to be carried out by professionals in archaeology, ethnology, linguistics, and folklore. This change generated a wave of papers and studies drawn from multiple sources employing indirect methods, a trend that has continued to this day. As bark canoes and skin boats slowly vanished from tribal life and the role of expanded and planked boats increased, museums began to acquire more canoes. Before circa 1900, only a few Native boats were placed in museums, but soon afterward their numbers grew in major museums around the globe; one example was the 540-centimeter-long Ket bark canoe collected at the Yenisey River by Kai Donner (1915), who transported it to Helsinki (see fig. 5.10a–b, page 108). Thanks to the introduction of photography, more information on canoes and skin boats was collected in these years as well: N. Sushilin in 1926 and N. P. Naumov in 1927 provided rare photos of Western Siberian skin boats, or canoe-kayaks, which they documented between the Lower and Upper Tunguska rivers (see fig. 6.5, page 128), and P. Khoroshikh (1930) took fine photos of Evenk skin boat construction at Nepa village, the source of the Lower Tunguska River.

In archaeology—to give only a few examples—the Russian archaeologist M. E. Foss (1948) studied Neolithic settlements in the eastern Onega Lake region and along the White Sea coast and provided information on early maritime hunters of seal, walrus, and whale, whose activities were also documented in the Vyg River petroglyphs (see pages 72 and 174). Some 20 years later, Grigori Burov conducted fieldwork in the Western Urals, Vychega River, and the Komi Republic, and he found at Vis-1 a full set of hunters' tools, including bows and arrows, stone tools, and a fragment of a paddle dated to the early Holocene at circa 8,400 years ago (see page 72). Valerie N. Chernetsov (1935) discovered walrus hunters' sites and the remains of what might be a kayak at the northern end of the Yamal Peninsula, and these inspired a lively scholarly discussion about possible "Eskimo connections" in Western Siberia (W. Fitzhugh 1998).

Smithsonian Institution Canoe Studies

In 1964, the Smithsonian Institution published *The Bark Canoes and Skin Boats of North America* by Edwin Tappan Adney and Howard I. Chapelle (see fig. 0.1, page 1), which also mentioned a few Eastern Siberian boats, mainly those of the Sakha, Siberian Eskimo, Chukchi, and Koryak. This book opened an approach to the study of Native boats on all continents and established a standard for future books on Native bark canoes and skin boats. This was not the only or first contribution by the Smithsonian Institution on Northern Eurasian canoes; as noted above, Otis T. Mason and Meriden S. Hill published "Pointed Bark Canoes of the Kutenai and Amur" in 1901. An American contribution to the study of Eastern Siberian skin boats is David Zimmerly's 1986 book *Qajaq: Kayaks of Siberia and Alaska*, which outlines the history of skin kayaks and is illustrated with drawings and photos. Like the Smithsonian's 1964 Adney and Chapelle and 1901 Mason and Hill publications, Zimmerly's book suggests a common source for bark and skin canoe evolution on both continents. Recent research on the Kodiak Island Alutiiq *niĝaalaĝ* or *angyaq* (Russian: *baidara*) and St. Lawrence Island angyapik bring a modern perspective to the study of indigenous maritime technology and history (Anichtchenko 2012, 2017).

European contributions to the bark canoe and skin boat history of the Eurasian north are both rich in detail—mostly due to the many German travelers—and modest in the number of dedicated papers and books. Studies taking a general continent-wide view are absent, with only a few exceptions. One of those rare works is a 1911 paper written by the Austrian Rudolf Trebitsch, "Fellboote und Schwimsäcke" (Skin Boats and Rafts). Perhaps the first paper ever published on the global distribution of skin boats, it covers many continents and cultures. He consulted most major sources he could find, and turned over many stones to find relevant written or pictorial information on the existence of skin boats and other floating devices. Trebitsch referred to archival sources from early and modern times and discussed studies conducted around the world. He made a convincing case that many kinds of skin boats were known in the past in many European regions, as well as in Northern Asia (a tentative picture, which has come into somewhat clearer focus today), Southern Asia, North and South America, and Greenland, and he illustrated his findings with pictures and a global map, summarizing its Northern European skin boat information as follows:

> When we look at the distribution of skin boats in Europe in the past we conclude the following: . . . Skin boats were located in regions of Celtic people in Great Britain (also Ireland, Wales and Scotland), in Spain, in upper Italy, by the Lapps in Scandinavia, and by the Samoyeds in NE Russia; possibly the skin boat was also known in N. Germany and France, and in the lands along the Danube (Donau) River. (1912: 180)

Russian ethnologist Valentina V. Antropova wrote the second major European contribution to northern bark and skin canoe history, an extensive survey of Native boats that was published in 1961 as a chapter in Levin and Potapov's *Historical-Ethnographic Atlas of Siberia*. This outstanding paper—in effect a canoe history—used information that the Russian Academy of Sciences had collected from various sources. It covered all of Siberia and all the Native groups inhabiting the Lena River basin, the Chukotka Peninsula, and the Amur River and Peninsula, although it dealt with Siberia west of the Yenisey River in less detail. Antropova's paper remains the best single source on the boats that Native peoples of Siberia built and used, including birch-bark canoes, open skin boats, kayaks, and log boats. She presented this massive body of information succinctly, people by people, in region after region, giving a good picture of the diffusion of Native boats over half of Northern Eurasia and ending with summaries of bark canoe and skin boat typologies, including their regional distribution and the tribal names of various boats. Birch-bark canoes, she noted, were deeply rooted in the Siberian taiga among all peoples and were, until rather recently, used by some Amur peoples; Antropova concluded that inland skin boats or kayaks coexisted with bark canoes in more northern latitudes near the tundra. She also presented information about the skin boats of the maritime peoples of Chukotka, Kamchatka, and Sakhalin Island, their tribal customs and trade, and the differences among their skin boat construction methods.

Another European contribution was *The Seacraft of Prehistory*, a general boat history by Paul Johnston (1980). It provided important early information about skin boats in Northern Eurasia (although bark canoe information was mostly missing) and included excellent data on early skin boats collected in the northern British Isles and in Scandinavian locations since the 1400s, which are assumed to be of North American or Greenland origin. Unlike Grahame Clark and Stuart Piggott, who believed that Fennoscandian peoples and cultures derived from western Europe, Johnston saw early Saami-related cultures as originating from the east and reaching Norway via the coast of White Sea. Thus, Clark and Piggott regarded the Lake Onega, Vyg, and Karelian boat carvings as being part of the Scandinavian boat tradition. The fact that similar carvings are known from the Yenisey and Lena mouths is further evidence that the Fennoscandian images are part of a circumpolar skin boat tradition (1980: 32–33).

Johnston also wrote about skin boats in Eastern Siberia, noting that they were used primarily by the Chukchi, Koryak, Aleut, and Eskimo, but he was noncommittal about their origin. On the relationship between Eastern Siberian and Western Siberian or European skin boats, Johnston assumed that the skin boats and kayaks of the Samoyed (Nenets) and Lapps (Saami) in the western Barents Sea were a separate tradition that might or might not have been associated with bark canoe building. He also surmised that people in the west first used skin boats and later turned to bark ones. Today archaeological evidence shows that planked log boats have been made since at least middle Holocene times, when forests became well established near the northern coasts and woodworking tools such as stone gouges, axes, and adzes began to appear.

It seems appropriate that we also note one of the latest contributions, this one dealing with evidence that might support the existence of bark canoes at the Mesolithic Star Carr site in Britain. However, this paper, by Peter Rowley-Conwy (2017), largely focuses on environmental analysis rather than direct evidence of canoes. These finds reemphasize the central problem facing scholars of early boat traditions: the ephemeral nature of the evidence and the shallow database available for study and comparison. One can only marvel at the gap between the present material evidence and the fact that humans arrived in Australia 60,000 years ago and in North American 15,000 to 20,000 years ago, likely in bark or skin boats. In short, we have much to learn.

GLOSSARY

CANOE AND BOAT TERMS

See individual chapters for cultural and linguistic terms relating to specific kinds of boats.

adze: Woodworking tool with asymmetric blade mounted crossways to handle, with beveled cutting edge on distal face, making it suitable for carving interiors of log boats or planing logs and planks

aft: Toward the rear of a boat

angyapik **(Siberian Yupik):** Open skin boat (Alutiiq: *angyak*; Iñupiaq: *umiak*; Russian: *baidar*)

axe: Woodworking tool with blade edges sharpened on both sides; used to fell trees and split wood

baidar/baidara **(Russian):** Open skin boat

baidarka **(Russian):** Kayak

ballast: Weight carried low in boat to increase its stability

bast: Fibrous inner tree bark used for caulking planks and making cordage

beam: Widest dimension of a boat's hull

bilge: Lowest inner part of a boat

bow: Front end of a boat

camber: Crossways curvature of a boat's topsides that helps drain water and adds rigidity to hull

carvelle: Type of outer hull planking in which the sides of planks are butted flush and close together to form a smooth exterior

chine: Junction of side and bottom planking, or a member backing this junction. *Double-chine* hulls have an additional junction between chine and sheer (junction of side and deck or gunwale), giving the hull a more rounded look. *Hard-chine* hulls have a single distinct bottom/side planking junction. *Multichined* hulls have one or more additional plank angle changes between bottom chine and deck

chip **(Ainu):** wooden dugout boat. See also *mochip*

clinker: Type of boat in which upper plank overlaps plank below to form exterior much like house siding. Also called *lapstrake* construction

coracle: Round boat with frame of bent withies and hide cover, commonly used to cross rivers

dolblenka **(Russian):** expanded log boat

double-ended canoe: Boat whose side planks come together at both ends

draft: Distance from waterline to vessel's deepest point, or depth of water a boat can travel over without hitting bottom

dugout: Boat created by digging out one side of a tree trunk; often basis for an expanded log boat

dyav **(Evenk):** birch-bark canoe

expanded log boat: Boat made from hollowed-out log whose sides have been expanded by soaking in water, heating with hot rocks, and gradually forcing apart sides with timbers wedged in crossways

forward: Toward front end, or bow, of boat

frame: Rib of boat's hull framework

freeboard: Portion of boat's side above surface of water

garboard: Plank adjoining keel; also called *garboard plank* or *strake*

gunwale: Upper structural members running from bow to stern on each side of a boat, to which ribs attach

hogging: Describes a boat that humps upward at its middle and has a lower bow and stern; sometimes a purposeful design feature but often indicates aging and insufficient longitudinal rigidity

inwale: Part of gunwale inside canoe

kayak: Eskimo skin boat with covered deck

keel: External structure extending along bottom of a vessel that strengthens its hull; in a sailing vessel, provides upright stability and prevents side-slippage

keelson: Fore-and-aft spine at bottom of hull to which ribs attach. External keelson projects through boat's bottom and provides extra rigidity, better tracking, and less side slippage in crosswinds

knee: Crossways-angled brace or reinforcement, usually strengthening junction between hull's bottom and its sides or transom

lapstrake: Having planks whose edges are overlapped to form an irregular exterior, like siding on a house. Called *lapstrake* because upper plank overlaps next lowest plank. Also called *clinker*

lodya **(Russian):** Large planked river boat

loft: To build a boat from design plans and measurements

log boat: Boat made from a log, or whose bottom is based on a hollowed-out log whose sides were expanded and to which planks were added

longitudinal: Hull framing member running length of a boat (e.g., chine, keel, sheer, or batten)

mast step: Socketlike depression into which base of a mast or spar is inserted

matyv **(Koryak):** Open skin boat

mereke **(Even and Evenk):** Flat-bottomed birch-bark boat

mochip **(Ainu):** Dugout with stitched plank sides

oarlock: Originally one or two thole-pins (see below); more recently, a metal O- or Y-shaped pin that holds oar in place. Also called *rowlock*

omorochka **(Russian):** birch-bark canoe

outwale: Gunwale strip on outside of canoe

painter: Line made fast to bow of a boat

pitch: Fore and aft motion of a boat in heavy seas

port: Left side of a boat when one is looking forward. See also *starboard*

rocker: Fore and aft curvature of a boat's bottom

roll: Side-to-side motion of a boat in crossways seas

rowlock: Mechanism to hold oar in place on gunwale. Also called *oarlock*

rudder: Vane at stern that steers boat

sheathing: Outer planks or strips of wood fastened to a boat's ribs or frame

sheer: Side profile of boat marked by junction of sides and deck or gunwale. A boat with high sheer has its side higher at bow and stern than at center; in a low-sheer vessel, sheer arc is closer to a straight line

shoal: Shallow water

soima **(Russian):** Planked boat

spar: Mast or upright member projecting above hull

square-sterned: Having a flat rather than a pointed stern

starboard: Right side of boat when one is looking forward; term originated from Old Norse *styrbord*, steering board (rudder) attached to a Norse ship's right side, forward of stern. See also *port*

stem: Structural member that rises from keel to which side planks attach at bow or stern

stern: Rear end or part of a boat

strake: Single line of planking extending from bow to stern

stringer: Thin strip of wood running fore and aft, crossing ribs, and providing extra longitudinal rigidity in addition to keel and gunwales

strip planking: Planking method that uses strips of wood installed longitudinally outside ribs

styrbord **(Norse):** Steering board or oar positioned near stern on right side of a boat; origin of English *starboard*

thole-pin: Wood or metal pin, sometimes used in pairs, set vertically into gunwale and serving as an oarlock

thwart: Crossways structural member running from gunwale to gunwale to provide lateral rigidity

tiller: Bar or handle attached to rudder. In large boats, steering wheels replace tillers

transom: Crossways flat surface forming aft (stern) end of a boat

umiak **(North American Iñupiaq and Inuit):** Open skin boat used for voyaging and whaling (Siberian Yupik: *angyapik*)

GEOGRAPHIC, CULTURAL, AND OTHER TERMS

boreal forests: Northernmost forests in both the New and Old Worlds between temperate zone and Arctic tundra zone; consists largely of birch, aspen, pine, and spruce in North America and birch, pine, and Siberian larch in Eurasia

Chukotka: Political jurisdiction of northeastern Siberia east of Kolyma and Anadyr rivers, including Chukchi Peninsula lands

Cossacks: Russian paramilitary forces who brought Siberia under Russian rule from 16th to to 19th centuries

Dauria (Manchu): Eastern part of Inner Mongolia

Fennoscandia: Area comprising both Scandinavia and Finland

Heilong Jiang (Manchu and Chinese): Amur River

jiang **(Chinese):** river

Karafuto (Ainu and Japanese): Sakhalin Island

Kunstkamera: Original (and still popular) name of Museum of Anthropology and Ethnology, St. Petersburg, Russia

Paleo-Asiatics: Ancient Ice Age cultures of Asia

Paleolithic: Early human technology and cultures dating before the end of the Ice Ages circa 12,000 years ago

petroglyph: Carving or inscription on rock

Saami: Natives of northern Fennoscandia. Known formerly as Lapps or Laplanders, and as Lappalaiset in Finland, as Finns in Norway, and as Lapar in Russia

Siberia: Territory of northern Russian northeast of Ural Mountains

Transbaikal (Russian): Lands beyond (east of) Lake Baikal

tundra: Vegetation zone north of boreal forest where climate does not permit trees to grow, although shrubs such as willow and alder might grow there

Western Urals: European term for Russian lands west of Ural Mountains

yassak: Tribute or taxes paid to Russian Cossacks following their subjugation of Siberian Native peoples

Yezo (Early Japanese): Hokkaido (also Ezo, Yeso, and Yesso)

ACKNOWLEDGMENTS

Harri Luukkanen: It would have been impossible to prepare this study without the help of many friends and colleagues who shared their time, experience, and interest in boats and canoes. Without their generous assistance in providing information on canoe collections, locating rare and obscure archival and library sources, and commenting on early drafts, this canoe history could never have been written.

Special thanks go first to William Fitzhugh for his good company and advice during the long research and writing process. An exciting first face-to-face meeting and subsequent friendship, cooperation, and trust kept this book project on course. Christer Westerdahl, of the Norwegian University of Science and Technology in Trondheim, guided me in the early writing process and offered me an opportunity to present a summary of my canoe project at a northern maritime conference in Trondheim in 2008 honoring Norway's pioneering anthropologist Gutorm Gjessing. The late Ole Crumlin-Pedersen, an expert in Viking boats, kindly tutored me in expanded log boat research and offered his help with this bark and skin canoe study as well. Grigori Burov of Sevastopol University, Ukraine—an expert in northeastern European canoe studies—helped resolve problems arising from the interpretation of Russian sources and shared his detailed knowledge. Research scientist Mikhail Batashev, of the Krasnoyarsk Krai Museum, has an endless command of peoples and places in Western and Eastern Siberia and advised me on many points related to Native group locations and where to find photo archives and literature sources. Evguenia (Jenya) Anichtchenko, an expert on Alaskan skin boats, contributed to this study by writing the epilogue on Bering Sea skin boats on both continents. Anichtchenko also located museum specimens and archives in St. Petersburg, translated some Russian texts, photographed boats and models, and assisted in acquiring rights and permissions from Russian sources. Naturally, I owe a great debt to Carolyn Gleason, director of Smithsonian Books, for her patience during the years of manuscript preparation.

Special thanks are also due to Petr Sorokin, of the Russian Academy of Sciences in St. Petersburg, for guiding me in the difficult task of writing log boat histories of both Slavic and Finnish peoples and for sharing his knowledge of the history of Novgorod. Alexander Shutikhin, of Kotlas in the Komi Republic, has written papers on bark canoes and has been my best source on the process of working birch bark; he has also shared his experience in building and using birch-bark canoe replicas. Arthur Chubur of Bryansk University shared his interest and sources on log boat studies, as did Georgy Vizgalov of the Center for Historical and Cultural Heritage in Nefteyugansk and Oleg V. Kandash of Ekaterinburg. Taras Tjupko of Archangel, an expert on the Pomor, informed me on the peoples and boats of the White Sea region. Likewise, Aadu Must, of Tartu University, instructed me on boats in the Amur region. Director Jerzy Litwin and scientist Waldemar Ossowski, of the Polish Maritime Museum in Gdańsk, supplied me with information on log boat history in Poland.

Warm thanks go to Timm Weski, of Bayerisches Landesamt für Denkmalpflege, Munich; Diana Altner, of Humboldt University, Berlin; and chief editor Erik Hoops, of the German Maritime Museum, Bremerhavn, for their efforts to make obscure literature available. Xingcan Chen, director of the Chinese Academy of Social Sciences' Institute of Archaeology in Beijing, translated and supplied important Chinese papers and illustrations. Likewise, I thank Stephen Shennan, director of the Institute of Archaeology at University College, London, and Brian Durrans, deputy keeper of ethnography at the British Museum, London, for sharing their achives. Richard Birmingham, of Newcastle University, shared his views on wooden boat construction and design.

Peter Jordan, of Groningen University in the Netherlands, helped me obtain documents on Siberian peoples. Naval architects Dougal Harris in Tasmania and Jurgen Sass in Stockholm helped me draft 3D drawings from old photos, a task that eventually turned out to be too demanding for this book and was postponed.

During the course of the project, I have had rewarding discussions with many friends and colleagues. I am grateful to my old canoeing friend John Lind, of Copenhagen, for information on Novgorod. Patrick Henry, of Strasbourg, translated French papers, and my thanks go also to Athol Anderson, of Australian National University. My friend Marilyn Vogel, of the American Canoe Association in Philadelphia, made important suggestions on my 2007 bark and skin canoe draft. Mehmed Bulut, of Istanbul University, informed me on Turkish boat studies. My U.S. canoe friends Hugh Horton and Harvey Golden were always inspiring and generous sources.

In Finland, several people have supported this study in different ways. Helsinki University docent Tapani Salminen helped me identify many Finno-Ugrian groups. Henry Forssell, a boat history author, shared his photos of the Ket bark canoe and helped me indentify some White Sea sealing boats. Hannu Kotivuori, director of the North Finland Regional Museum in Rovaniemi, informed me about new paddle finds. I am thankful to Janne Vilkuna, of Jyväskylä University, for his information on ancient Finnish boats. Pentti Kettunen, of the Tampere University of Technology, advised me on Finland's early metal age. Andrei Kokov offered his help in clarifying Russian boat terms. Maire Aho, head librarian at the Slavic Library in the National Library, and Anna-Liisa Kristiansson, at the Institute for National Languages, helped me locate rare Russian books. I also thank archaeologist Mika Sarkkinen for sharing his knowledge; Frederik Koivusalo for his inspiring book on expanded log boats; and Lauri Pohjakallio for sharing his study on log boat finds in Finland. Helsinki University research scientist Rauno Lauhakangas (2013) and Knut Helskog, at Tromsø Museum and University, kindly shared their photos. At the National Board of Archaeology, many scientists helped with data on old paddle and canoe finds and photos. At the Finland National Board of Antiquities, I thank keepers Jaana Onatsu, Pirkko Hakala, Risto Hakomäki, Idiko Lehtinen, Kaarlo Katiskoski, Kari Varmio, and Ismo Malinen.

Finally, great thanks go to my canoe friends in Finland, who have shown a keen interest and curiosity in my canoe history and helped me in many ways. I especially thank Risto Lehtinen, who originally set me on course by encouraging me to prepare a study of ancient Finnish canoes. Risto also translated some key Russian books and papers for me, and he has taken care of my computer and communication system. Harri Mäkilä has made several fine Stone Age paddle replicas whose testing allowed us to draw conclusions about the boats with which such paddles might have been used. Tapani Pakarinen and Matti Tuunanen were excellent company in discussing findings and interpreting information in photographs and old literature. Finally, my wife, Sari, and boys, Otso and Leo, were unbelievably supportive throughout this project; they might be the people proudest of all to see the book finally in print, as well as being relieved at its successful conclusion.

William W. Fitzhugh: The conclusion of a long and difficult project is always bittersweet. After many years, a challenging chapter in one's life ends, and working relationships begin to fade and are replaced by new people, issues, and goals. This canoe book was a delightful and unanticipated excursion from my normal research routine, which grew from aspects of my personal and professional lives—a lifelong interest in boats, an explorer's wanderlust, and a career interest in Russian studies. All these elements were the ingredients that attracted me to this project when I discovered Harri Luukkanen's research into Eurasian boat history. Harri's curiosity, his research and writing skills, and his dogged determination made him the perfect partner for a book that would never have been written had it not been for our chance encounter and the Smithsonian's publication of Adney and Chapelle's book on North American Native boats. As with many things in life, chance produced an unpredictable but fortunate outcome.

I am immensely grateful for Harri's tenacity in conducting the basic research and his early drafting of this book. My role has been to contribute anthropological and archaeological data, to rewrite and edit, and to inject a degree of caution in our attempt to peer too deeply into the evolutionary past of canoe history. With so little archaeological material available, our theories about the origins of ancient canoes and kayaks are still largely theoretical. Even where rock art would seem to provide tangible deep-time history, we have little firm ground. Yet our book may be at least a baseline on the ethnographic use of bark and skin boats, with occasional dips into recent prehistory. None of this would have happened without Harri's stimulus and Adney and Chapelle's groundbreaking precedent.

Like Harri, I have been assisted by many. Jenya Anichtchenko was an invaluable partner, and her final, comparative chapter serves well to connect our story to North America and Otis T. Mason's, Waugh's, and Adney and Chapelle's work. Her research in the Smithsonian's archaeological collections from Barrow and St. Lawrence Island shows the promise of archaeological work on boat history (Anichtchenko 2017), and her scouting in the St. Petersburg museums and archives suggests that work in collections across Russia will yield many new boat finds. Anichtchenko has also contributed literature translations, interfaced with Russian museums and archives in acquiring illustrations, and helped me winnow Harri's large illustration file down to a manageable set of final selections.

My colleague Igor Krupnik is due heartfelt thanks for his encouragement of this project. He has been keenly aware of the need for a large-scale effort to produce an English-language book on the cultures of the Russian north, and Harri and I greatly appreciate his forbearance in supporting this single-themed enterprise on boats. Igor generously reviewed the manuscript and corrected many inaccuracies, recognizing that neither Harri nor I could do justice to Russian ethnography and history without Russian fluency and deeper understanding of Russian anthropology. Harri and I also benefited from reviews of sections of the manuscript by Vladimir Pitulko and Natalia Fedorova. Anthropologist Andrei Golovnev provided me with understandings about northern Russian (especially Yamal) ethnology and history. I also appreciated the help of Feng (Gilbert) Qu, who read some of the Far East materials and arranged for their review by anthropologist Zhang Minjie, a Chinese Native culture boating expert and the retired vice director of the Heilong Jiang Museum of Nationalities. Ben Fitzhugh, Masaru Kato, Koji Deriha, and Katsunori Takase helped us acquire photographs and information from Hokkaido University Natural History Museum and Botanical Museum collections. Andrei Ptashinsky facilitated a visit to the Petropavlovsk Museum collections. We underscore that none of these scholars bears any responsibility for our mistakes or shortcomings.

Most of the others who assisted me have been involved with illustrations and book production. Carolyn Gleason, Smithsonian Books director, was fascinated with the project from the beginning and provided editorial guidance throughout, assisted by editor Christina Wiginton, and offered both carrots and sticks along the way. Her coordination and the miracles produced by text editors Martin Edmunds and Juliana Froggatt of our difficult initial drafts are greatly appreciated. Laura Harger, the book's final editor, performed miracles that ensured consistency and accuracy. Thanks are also due to boat history experts David Zimmerly, Stephen Braund, and Harvey Golden for permission to use their information and illustrations.

Marcia Bakry created most of our line art and transformed many other illustrations into high-quality images, a long-term effort that she performed with gracious humor. The canoe typology drawings and some of the construction detail illustrations are Marcia's renditions of Harri's original drawings. Smithsonian cartographer Dan Cole produced the maps that introduce each of our regional chapters and determined correct place-name toponymy. The task of assembling the mass of material into a coherent package for the press fell on the worthy shoulders of a series of office assistants: Laura Flemming Sharp was followed by Meghan Mulkerin, who coordinated the submission effort with the assistance of Katherine Leo, Jordan Boggan, Cara Reeves, Margaret Litten, Mary Maisel, Gina Reitenauer, and Michael Mlyniec unscrambling bibliographic notes, finding illustration files, obtaining permissions, and serving as project coordinators. Like Harri, I relied on resourceful librarians: in my case, Maggie Dittemore and Brandee Worsham, who tracked down innumerable obscure publications. Curtis Dozier helped provide translations from ancient Latin texts. Zaborian Payne contributed by handling our accounts and spreading good cheer. Toward the end of the project, Arctic Studies Center office manager Nancy Shorey was an invaluable assistant. I give my final thanks to my wife, Lynne Fitzhugh, who saw too much of the back of my head when I should have been helping maintain our "farmhouse" on Capitol Hill in Washington, DC, and our hillside retreat in Fairlee, Vermont.

References

Abakumov, S. 2001. "Po Sledu Orla. Iz Istorii Ulusov Yakutii" [Following the Eagle: The History of the Uluses of Yakutia]. Culture and tourism website, Ministry of Culture of the Republic of Sakha. http://npeople.ucoz.ru/publ/4-1-0-50 (accessed May 9, 2018).

Ackerman, R. 1984. "Prehistory of the Asian Eskimo Zone." In D. Damas, ed., *Handbook of North American Indians*, vol. 5: *Arctic*, 106–18. Washington, DC: Smithsonian Institution Press.

Adney, E. T., and Chapelle, H. I. 1964. *The Bark Canoes and Skin Boats of North America*. Washington, DC: Smithsonian Institution Press.

———. 2007. *Bark Canoes and Skin Boats of North America*. New York: Skyhorse Publishing. Repr. 1964 ed.

Advinatee, Y. A. 1966. "Nekotorye Voprosy Izucheniya Naskal'nykh Izobrazheniy Karelii" [Some Questions in the Study of Rock Art in Karelia]. In G. A. Pankrushev, ed., *Novyye Pamyatniki Istorii Drevney Karelii* [*New Monuments in the History of Karelia*], 44–96. Leningrad: Nauka.

Ahlqvist, A. 1859. *Muistelmia Matkoilta Venäjällä Vuosina 1854–1858* [*Memories of Travels in Russia, 1854–1858*]. Helsinki: G. W. Edlund.

Aigner, J. 1977. "Anangula: An 8,500 BP Coastal Occupation in the Aleutian Islands." *Quartär Jahrbuch für Erforschung des Eiszeitalters und der Steinzeit* 27–28: 65–102.

Aikio, A. 2006. "On Germanic-Saami Contacts and Saami Prehistory." *Journale de la Société Finno-Ugrian* 91: 9–55. www.sgr.fi/susa/91/SUSA91.pdf (accessed March 26, 2018).

Ainana, L., T. Archirgina-Arsiak, and T. Tein. 1996. "Asiatic Eskimo." In V. Chaussonnet and I. Krupnik, eds., *Crossroads of Continents: Cultures of the Indigenous Peoples of the Far East and Alaska*, 22–23. Washington, DC: Arctic Studies Center, Smithsonian Institution.

Ainana, L., V. Tatyga, P. Typykhkak, and I. Zagrebin. 2003. *Umiak: The Traditional Skin Boat of the Coast Dwellers of the Chukchi Peninsula*. Trans. R. L. Bland. Anchorage: Shared Beringian Heritage Program, US National Park Service.

Albova, G. A. 1968a. *Zhizn' i byt Tungusov v 13–16 Vekakh* [*Daily Life of the Tungus in the 13th to 16th Centuries*].

www.protown.ru/information/hide/6543.html (accessed March 26, 2018).

———. 1968b. *Zhizn' Buryatov i Yeniseyskikh Kyrgyzov v 13–16 Vekakh* [*Life of the Buryats and Yenisei Kyrgyz in the 13th to 16th Centuries*]. www.protown.ru/information/hide/6541.html (accessed March 13, 2019).

———, ed. 1968c. "Zhizn' i byt Yakutov v 13–16 Vekakh" [Daily Life of the Yakuts in the 13th–16th Centuries]. In *Istopya Cibirii* [*History of Siberia*], pt.1, chap. 8. Leningrad: Nauka. www.protown.ru/information/hide/6543.html (accessed June 19, 2019).

Alekseenko, E. A. 1976. "Narodnaya Technika Obrabotki Dereva u Ketov" [Traditional Techniques in Ket Woodworking]. In I. S. Vdovin, ed., *Materialnaya Kultura Narodov Sibirii i Severa* [*Material Culture of the Peoples of Siberia and the North*], 156–72. Leningrad: Nauka.

Alenius, T., T. Mökkönen, and A. Lahelma. 2013. "Early Farming in the Northern Boreal Zone: Reassessing the History of Land Use in Southeastern Finland through High-Resolution Pollen Analysis." *Geoarchaeology* 28, no. 1: 1–24.

Alexan, N., S. Chickalusion, A. Kaloa, and B. Karp. 1981. *The Last Indian War in Tyonke and Other History*. Edited by J. Standifier and C. Chickalusion. Fairbanks: Alaska Bilingual Materials Development Center.

Altner, D. 2009. *Die Verkleinerung der Yakhautboote: Fischerkulturen in Zentral- und Südtibet im Sozioökonomischen Wandel des Modernen China* [*The Decline of Yak-Skin Boats: Fishing Cultures in Central and Southern Tibet and Socioeconomic Change in Modern China*]. Wiesbaden, Germany: Harrassowitz Verlag.

Anderson, D. G. 2007. "Mobile Architecture and Social Life: The Case of the Conical Skin Lodge in the Plutoran Plateau (S. Taimyr) Region." In S. Beyries and V. Vaté, eds., *Les civilisations du renne d'hier et d'aujourd'hui: Approches ethnohistoriques, archéologiques et anthropologiques* [*The Reindeer Civilizations of Yesterday and Today: Ethnohistorical, Archaeological, and Anthropological Approaches*], 43–63. Antibes, France: Éditions Association pour la Promotion et la Diffusion des Connaissances Archéologiques, 27th International Meeting of Archaeology and History.

Anderson, G. D. S. 2004. "The Languages of Central Siberia: Introduction and Overview." In A. Vajda, ed., *Languages and Prehistory of Central Siberia*, 1–123. Amsterdam: Benjamins. http://citeseerx.ist.psu.edu/viewdoc/download?doi=10.1.1.739.1049&rep=rep1&type=pdf (accessed May 27, 2019).

Anderson, W. B., ed. 1936. *Sidonius: Poems and Letters*. Loeb Classical Library 1. Cambridge, MA: Harvard University Press.

Anichtchenko, E. 2012. "Open Skin Boats of the Aleutians, Kodiak Island, and Prince William Sound." *Études/Studies/Inuit* 36, no. 1: 157–81.

———. 2013. "The Birnirk Umiak: A Glance at Prehistoric Arctic Boat Technology." *Arctic Studies Center Newsletter* 20: 24–25.

———. 2017. "Reconstructing the St. Lawrence Island Kayak: From Forgotten Watercraft to a Bering Sea Maritime Network." *Alaska Journal of Anthropology* 15, no. 1: 1–23.

Antropova, V. V. 1961. "Lodki" [Boats]. In M. G. Levin and L. P. Potapov, eds., *Istoriko-Etnograficheskiy Atlas Sibiri* [*Historical-Ethnographic Atlas of Siberia*], 107–29. Moscow and Leningrad: Institute of Ethnography, Russian Academy of Sciences.

———. 2005. "Boats." Edited by I. Krupnik. Trans. H. Michael from Antropova 1961. Manuscript. Arctic Studies Center Archives, Smithsonian Institution, Washington, DC; Rock Foundation, Edmund Carpenter Collection, Smithsonian National Anthropological Archives, Washington, DC.

Arbin, S. von. 2012. "Byslättsbåten är Från Bronsåldern" [Byslättsbåten in the Bronze Age]. Blog post, *Divers Community Scandinavia*. January 11. www.dykarna.nu/dyknyheter/byslattsbaten-daterad-1411.html (accessed May 18, 2018).

Arbin, S. von, and M. Lindberg. 2017. "Notes on the Byslätt Bark 'Canoe.'" In J. Litwin, ed., *Baltic and Beyond: Change and Continuity in Shipbuilding: Proceedings of the 14th International Symposium on Boat and Ship Archaeology Gdańsk 2015*, 245–50. Gdansk, Poland: National Maritime Museum.

Arima, E. Y. 1975. "A Contextual Study of the Caribou Eskimo Kayak." Canadian Ethnology Service Mercury Series Paper 25. Ottawa: National Museums of Canada.

———. 1987. "Inuit Kayaks in Canada: A Review of Historical Records and Construction." Canadian Ethnology Service Mercury Series Paper 110. Ottawa: Canadian Museum of Civilization, National Museums of Canada.

———, ed. 1991. *Contributions to Kayak Studies*. Canadian Ethnology Service Mercury Series Paper 122. Ottawa: Canadian Museum of Civilization.

———. 2002. "Building Umiaks." In J. Jennings, ed., *The Canoe: A Living Tradition*, 138–57. Toronto: Firefly Books.

———. 2004. "Barkless Barques." In J. Jennings, B. W. Hodgins, and D. Small, eds., *The Canoe in Canadian Cultures*, 43–61. Winnipeg, MB: Natural Heritage/Natural History Inc.

Armstrong, T. 1984. "In Search of a Sea Route to Siberia, 1553–1619." *Arctic* 37, no. 4: 429–40.

Arnold, B. 2014. *Les pirogues "kapepe," l'espace nautique du bassin de la rivière Malagarasi (Tanzanie) et quelques observations sur les pirogues en écorce d'Afrique orientale* ["*Kapepe" Canoes, the Nautical Space of the Malagarasi River Basin (Tanzania), and Some Observations on the Bark Canoes of East Africa*]. Paris: Le Locle, Éditions G d'Encre.

Arntzen, M. S. S. 2007. "Bilder på Sten" [Pictures in Stone]. Master's thesis. Archaeology, Faculty of Social Sciences, Tromsø University, Tromsø, Norway.

Arutiunov, S. A., and W. W. Fitzhugh. 1988. "Prehistory of Siberia and the Bering Sea." In W. W. Fitzhugh and A. L. Crowell, eds., *Crossroads of Continents: Cultures of Siberia and Alaska*, 117–29. Washington, DC: Smithsonian Institution Scholarly Press.

Arutiunov, S. A., and D. A. Sergeev. 2006. *Ethnohistory of the Bering Sea: The Ekven Cemetery*. Trans. R. L. Bland. Anchorage: Shared Beringian Program, US National Park Service.

Atwood, C. P. 2004. *Encyclopedia of Mongolia and the Mongol Empire*. New York: Facts on File Library of World History.

Austin, P., and J. Sallabank. 2015. *The Cambridge Handbook of Endangered Languages*. Cambridge: Cambridge University Press.

Autio, E. 1981. *Karjalan Kalliopimokset* [*Karelian Rock Drawings*]. Keuruu, Finland: Routledge.

Backer, W. S. 1965. "Dartmouth down the Danube." *National Geographic Magazine* 128, no. 1 (July): 34–79.

Balak, J. 1581. "Puteshestvie v Sibir na Reku Ob, Izlozhtnnoe v Pisme k Gerardu Merkatoru" [Journey into Siberia and to the River Ob, as Described in a Letter to Gerard Mercator]. Trans. M. P. Alexeeva. Blog post. www.vostlit.info/Texts/rus16/Merkator/brief_balak_20_02_1581.htm (accessed May 13, 2018).

Bandi, H.-G. 1969. *Eskimo Prehistory*. Fairbanks: University of Alaska Press.

———. 1972. "Archäologische Forschungen auf der St.-Lorenz-Insel, Alaska" [Archaeological Research on St. Lawrence Island, Alaska]. *Polarforschung* 42, no. 1: 35–41.

Bartlett, R., and R. Hale. 1916. *The Last Voyage of the* Karluk. Toronto: McLelland, Goodchild, and Stewart.

Batchelor, J. 1892. *The Ainu of Japan*. London: Religious Tract Society.

Belgibaev, E. A. 2004. "Chelkantsi Landshaft i Kul'tura" [Chelkantsi Landscape and Culture]. In M. I. Tseremisina, ed., *Yazyki Korrenykh Narodov Sibiri* [*Indigenous Languages of Siberia*], vol. 17: *Chelkan Collection*, 102–26. Novosibirsk and Barnaul, Russia: Altai State University. http://severberesta.ru/articles/313-chelkancy-landshaft-i-kultura-ea-belgibaev-barnaul-altajskij-gosudarstvennyj-universitet.html (accessed March 5, 2018).

Belov, M. I. 1956. *Arkticheskoye Moreplavanie s Drevneyshikh Vremyen do Serediny XIX Veka* [*Arctic Navigation from the Earliest Times to the Middle of the 19th Century*]. Moscow: Publishing House Morsko 1 Transport.

Belyavsky, F. O. 1833. *Poezdka k Ledovitomy Moryu* [*A Trip to the Arctic Sea*]. St. Petersburg: Lazarev Institute of Eastern Languages.

Bestuzhev-Marlinsky, A. 1838. "Russland—Sibiriens Licht- und Nacht-Seiten" [Russia—Siberia's Light and Night Sides]. In J. Lehmann, ed., *Magazin für die Literatur des Auslandes* [*Magazine of Foreign Literature*], vols. 13–14. Berlin: A. W. Hayn.

Birkely, H. 1994. *I Norge har Lapperne Først Indført Skierne* [*In Norway, the Lapps Were the First Skiers*]. Indre Billefjord, Norway: Indut.

Birket-Smith, K. 1924. "Ethnography of the Egedesminde District, with Aspects of the General Culture of West Greenland." *Report of the Fifth Thule Expedition, 1921–24.* Meddelelser om Grønland 66. Copenhagen: Gyldendalske Boghandel, Nordisk Forlag.

——. 1929. "The Caribou Eskimos: Material and Social Life and Their Cultural Position." *Report of the Fifth Thule Expedition, 1921–24*, vol. 5, pt. 2. Copenhagen: Gyldendalske Boghandel, Nordisk Forlag.

——. 1953. *The Chugach Eskimo.* Copenhagen: National Museum Publication Fund.

Black, L. 1988. "The Story of Russian America." In W. W. Fitzhugh and A. L. Crowell, eds., *Crossroads of Continents: Cultures of Siberia and Alaska*, 70–82. Washington, DC: Smithsonian Institution Scholarly Press.

Blue, L. 2003. "Maritime Ethnography: The Reality of Analogy." In C. Beltrame, ed., *Boats, Ships, and Shipyards: Proceedings of the Ninth International Symposium on Boat and Ship Archaeology, Venice, 2000*. Oxford: Oxbow Books.

Boas, F. 1903. "The Jesup North Pacific Expedition." *American Museum Journal* 3, no. 5: 72–119.

——, ed. 1904–09. *The Jesup North Pacific Expedition*, vol. 7, pts. 1–3. *Memoirs of the American Museum of Natural History* 11. Leiden, Netherlands: E. J. Brill; New York: G. E. Stechert. Repr. 1975, New York: AMS Press.

——, ed. 1957. *Handbook of American Indian Languages*, vol. 2. Washington, DC: Bureau of American Ethnology.

Boehmer, G. H. 1891. "Prehistoric Naval Architecture of the North of Europe." *Annual Report of the United States Museum*, 527–647. Washington, DC: Smithsonian Institution.

Bogojavlensky, S. 1969. *Imaangmiut Eskimo Careers: Skinboats in Bering Strait.* PhD diss. Department of Anthropology, Harvard University, Cambridge, MA.

Bogoras, W. 1904–09. "The Chuchkee." In F. Boas, ed., *The Jesup North Pacific Expedition*, vol. 7, pts. 1–3, *Memoirs of the American Museum of Natural History* 11. Leiden, Netherlands: E. J. Brill; New York: G. E. Stechert. Repr. 1975, New York: AMS Press.

——. 1913. "The Eskimo of Siberia." In F. Boas, ed., *The Jesup North Pacific Expedition*, vol. 8, pt. 3. *Memoirs of the American Museum of Natural History* 12. Leiden, Netherlands: E. J. Brill; New York: G. E. Stechert.

Bogoslovskaya, L. S. 2007. *Osnovy Morskogo Zveroboinogo Promysla* [*Handbook of Marine Mammal Hunting*]. Moscow and Anadyr: Russian Institute of Cultural and Chukotka Institute of Teacher Training and Natural Heritage.

Bogoslovskaya, L. S., I. V. Slugin, I. A. Zagrebin, and I. Krupnik, eds. 2016. *Maritime Hunting Culture of Chukotka: Traditions and Modern Practices.* Anchorage: Shared Beringian Heritage Program, US National Park Service.

Borgos, J. I., and T. Torgvaer. 1998. "Samer og Båtbygging" [The Sami and Boatbuilding]. In S. Haasum and I. Kaijser, eds., *Människor och Båtar i Norden* [*People and Boats in the Nordic Countries*], 104–15. Stockholm: State Historical Museum.

Braund, S. R. 1988. *The Skin Boats of Saint Lawrence Island, Alaska.* Seattle and London: University of Washington Press.

Brindley, H. H. 1919a. "Notes on the Boats of Siberia." *Mariner's Mirror* 5, no. 3: 66–72.

——. 1919b. "Notes on the Boats of Siberia: Part 3." *Mariner's Mirror* 5, no. 5: 130–42.

——. 1919c. "Notes on the Boats of Siberia: Part 4." *Mariner's Mirror* 5, no. 6: 184–87.

Britton, K., et al. 2013. "Maritime Adaptations and Dietary Variation in Prehistoric Western Alaska: Stable Isotope Analysis of Permafrost-Preserved Human Hair." *American Journal of Physical Anthropology* 151, no. 3: 448–61.

Broadbent, Noel. 2010. *Lapps and Labyrinths: Saami Prehistory, Colonization, and Cultural Resilience.* Washington, DC: Arctic Studies Center and Smithsonian Institution Scholarly Press.

Brøgger, A. W., and Shetelig, H. 1951. *The Viking Ships: Their Ancestry and Evolution.* Oslo: Dreyers Forlag.

Bronshtein, M., and K. A. Dneprovsky. 2009. "Archaeology at Ekven, Chukotka." In W. W. Fitzhugh, J. Hallowell, and A. L. Crowell, eds., *Gifts from the Ancestors: Ancient Ivories of Bering Strait*, 94–95. New Haven, CT, and Princeton, NJ: Yale University Press and Princeton University Art Museum.

Bronshtein, M., K. A. Dneprovsky, and A. B. Savinetsky. 2016. "Ancient Eskimo Cultures of Chukotka." In T. M. Frisen and O. K. Mason, eds., *The Oxford Handbook of the Prehistoric Arctic*, 469–88. Oxford: Oxford University Press.

Bubrikh, D. V. 1947. *Proiskhozhdenie Karelskogo Naroda* [*Origin of the Karelian People*]. Petrozavodsk, Russia: State Publishing House of the Karelian Finnish SSR.

Burov, G. M. 1989. "Some Mesolithic Wooden Artifacts from the Site of Vis-1 in the European North-East of the U.S.S.R." In C. Bonsall, ed., *The Mesolithic in Europe*, 391–401. Edinburgh: John Donald Publishers.

——. 1996. "On Mesolithic Means of Water Transportation in Northeastern Europe." *Mesolithic Miscellany* 17, no. 1: 5–15.

——. 2000. "Baltic Region Inhabitants' Inland Waterborne Trade with Communities in the Urals Area in the Mesolithic and Neo-Eneolithic." In H. von Schmettow, ed., *Schutz des Kulturerbes Unter Wasser* [*Protection of Underwater Cultural Heritage*]. *Beiträge zur Ur- und Fuhgeschichte Meclenburg-Vorpommern* 35: 21–34. Schwerin, Germany: Archäologische Landesmuseum Mecklenburg-Vorpommem.

——. 2001. "Ancient Wooden Objects and Structures in Oxbow Peat Bogs of the European Northeast (Russia)." In B. A.

Purdy, ed., *Enduring Records: The Environmental and Cultural Heritage of Wetlands*, 213–32. Oxford: Oxbow Books.

Burrough, S. 1567. "The Navigation and Discovery toward the River of Ob, Made by Master Stephen Burrough, Master of the Pinnesse Called *The Serchthrift*, with Divers Things Worth Noting, Passed in the Yere 1556." In R. Hakluyt and E. Goldsmid, eds., *The Principal Navigations, Voyages, Traffiques, and Discoveries of the English Nation*, vol. 2, 322–44. 1903 ed., Glasgow: James MacLehose and Sons. www.perseus.tufts.edu/hopper/text?doc=Perseus%3Atext%3A1999.03.0070%3Anarrative%3D73 (accessed May 18, 2018).

Burykin, A. A. 2001. "Sledy Kultury Eskimosov na Okhotskom Poberezh'e po Archeologicheskim, Etnograficheskim, Folklornim, i Lingvisticheskim Dannym" [Traces of Inuit Culture on the Coast of the Okhotsk Sea through Archaeological, Ethnographic, Folkloric, and Linguistic Data]. Blog post, *Sibirskaja Zaimka* [*History of Siberia in Scientific Publications*]. www.zaimka.ru/ethnography/burykin9.shtml (accessed June 20, 2019).

Carpelan, C. 2006. "On Archaeological Aspects of Uralic, Finno-Ugric and Finnic Societies before AD 800." *Slavica Helsingiensia* 27: 78–92.

Castrén, M. A. 1844. "Om Savolots Tsud" [About the Savoy Tsud]. In *Tidskrift i Fosterländska Ämnen Fjärde Årgången* [*Journal of Patriotic Subjects, Fourth Volume*], vol. 4, 3–22. Helsinki: Finska Litteratursällskapets Förlag.

———. 1856. *Nordische Reisen und Forschungen* [*Nordic Travel and Research*], vol. 2: *Reiseberichte und Briefe aus den Jahren 1845–1849* [*Travel Reports and Letters from the Years 1845–1849*]. St. Petersburg: Kaiserlichen Akademie der Wissenschaften.

———. 1857a. *Nordische Reisen und Forschungen* [*Nordic-Travel and Research*], vol. 4: *Ethnologische Vorlesungen über die Altaischen Völker Nebst Samojedischen Märehen und Tatarischen Heldensagen* [*Ethnological Lectures on the Altaic People along with Samoyed Stories and Tatar Heroic Legends*]. St. Petersburg: Kaiserlichen Akademie der Wissenschaften.

———. 1857b. *Nordische Reisen und Forschungen* [*Nordic Travel and Research*], vol. 10: *Versuch einer Burjatischen Sprachlehre nebst Kurzem Worterverzeichniss* [*A Buryat Language Grammar with a Small Dictionary*]. St. Petersburg: Kaiserlichen Akademie der Wissenschaften.

———. 1857c. *Nordische Reisen und Forschungen* [*Nordic Travel and Research*], vol. 11: *Versuch einer Koibalischen und Kragassischen Sprachlehre nebst Wörterverzeichnissen aus den Tatrischen Mundarten des Minussinschen Kreises* [*A Koibal and Karagas Language Grammar with Dictionaries of the Tatar Dialects*]. St. Petersburg: Kaiserlichen Akademie der Wissenschaften.

———. 1858. *Versuch Einer Jenissei-Ostjakischen und Kottischen Sprachlehre* [*A Yenisei Ostyak and Kottian Language Grammar*], vol. 8. Edited by A. Schiefner. Moscow: Russian Academy of Sciences.

———. 1967. *Tutkimusmatkoilla Pohjolassa* [*Research Trips in the Nordic Region*]. Porvoo, Finland: WSOY.

Chard, C. S. 1963. "The Nganasans: Wild Reindeer Hunters of the Taimyr Peninsula." *Arctic Anthropology* 1, no. 2, 105–21.

———. 1974. *Northeast Asia in Prehistory*. Madison: University of Wisconsin Press.

Chen, X. 2003. "Where Did Chinese Animal Skin Rafts Come From?" *Bulletin of the Museum of Far Eastern Antiquities* 75: 170–88.

Chepelev, V. R. 2004. "Traditional Means of Waterway Transportation among Aboriginal Peoples of the Lower Amur Region and Sakhalin." *Study of Maritime Archaeology* 5, no. 5: 141–61.

Chernetsov, V. N. 1935. "Drevnyaya Primorskaya Kul'tura na Poloustrove Yamal" [An Ancient Maritime Culture of the Yamal Peninsula]. *Sovetskaya Etnografiya* 4–5: 109–33.

Chernetsov, V. N., and W. I. Moszyńska. 1954. "V Poiskakh Drevney Rodiny Ugorskikh Narodov" [In Search of the Ancient Land of the Ugrian Peoples]. In G. B. Fedorov, ed., *Po Sledam Drevnikh Kultur: Ot Volgi do Tikhovo Okeana* [*On the Tracks of Ancient Cultures: From the Volga to the Pacific Ocean*], 163–92. Moscow: State Publishing House of Cultural-Educational Literature.

———. 1974. *Prehistory of Western Siberia*. Trans. H. N. Michael. Translations from Russian Sources 9. Montreal: McGill-Queens University Press; Calgary: Arctic Institute of North America.

Chernigov, H. V. 2000. "The Tracks of Ancient Boats in Karelia." Unpublished paper delivered at "Conference on Man, Nature and Society—Vital Problems." St. Petersburg. December.

Chinese Academy of Social Sciences. 2014. "Oroqen Autonomous Banner." *Hulunbuir Ethnic Cultural Relics and Archaeology Series*. Bejing: Institute of Archaeology and Scientific Press.

Christensen, A. E. 2000. "Ships and Navigation." In W. W. Fitzhugh and A. L. Crowell, eds., *Vikings: The North Atlantic Saga*, 86–97. Washington, DC: Smithsonian Books.

Christie, W. F. K. 1837. "Om Helle-Ristninger og Andre Indhugninger i Klipper, Især i Bergen Stift" [On Helle-Ristninger and Rock Art, Especially in the Bergen Region]. *Norsk Antiqvarisk-Historisk Tidskrift* 1: 91–97. Bergen, Norway: Bergen Museum.

Chydenius, A. 1753. "Den Amerikanska Näverbåten" [American Bark Boats]. Master's thesis. Åbo Akademi, Turku, Finland.

Clark, G. 1968. *Prehistoric Europe: The Economic Basis*. Stanford, CA: Stanford University Press.

Cochrane, J. D. 1829. *A Pedestrian Journey through Russia and Siberian Tartary: To the Frontiers of China, the Frozen Sea, and Kamchatka*, vol. 1. Edinburgh: Constable and Co.

Collins, H. B. 1937. "Archaeology of St. Lawrence Island, Alaska." *Smithsonian Miscellaneous Collections* 96, no. 1: n.p.

——. 1940. "Outline of Eskimo Prehistory." *Smithsonian Miscellaneous Collections* 100: 533–92. Washington, DC: Smithsonian Institution.

Collins, P. M. 1962. *Siberian Journey down the Amur to the Pacific, 1856–1857*. Edited by C. Vevier. Madison: University of Wisconsin Press.

Coltrain, J. B. M. G. Hayes, and D. H. O'Rourke. 2006. "Hrdlicka's Aleutian Population Replacement Hypothesis: A Radiometric Evaluation." *Current Anthropology* 47, no. 3: 537–48.

Cook, J. 1967. *The Journals of Captain James Cook on His Voyages of Discovery: The Voyage of the* Resolution *and* Discovery, *1776–1780*, vol. 3, pt. 2. Edited by J. C. Beaglehole. Cambridge: Cambridge University Press for the Hakluyt Society.

Cooper, H. K., et al. 2016. "Evidence of Eurasian Metal Alloys on the Alaskan Coast in Prehistory." *Journal of Archaeological Science* 74: 173–83.

Crantz, D. 1820. *The History of Greenland: Including an Account of the Mission Carried on by the United Brethren in That Country.* London: Longman, Hurst, Rees, Orme, and Brown.

Crawford, M. H., R. C. Rubicz, and M. Zlojutro. 2007. "Origins of Aleuts and the Genetic Structure of Populations of the Archipelago: Molecular and Archaeological Perspectives." *Human Biology* 82, nos. 5–6: 695–717.

Crowell, A. L., A. F. Steffian, and G. L. Pullar, eds. 2001. *Looking Both Ways: Heritage and Identity of the Alutiiq People.* Fairbanks: University of Alaska Press.

Crumlin-Pedersen, O. 1981. Introduction. In J. S. Madsen and K. Hansen, eds., *Barkbåde. Vikingeskibshallen i Roskilde* [*Bark Boats in the Roskilde Viking Ship Museum*]. Roskilde, Denmark: Viking Ship Museum.

——. 2004. "Den Udspaenda Båd" [The Expanded Boat]. Manuscript. Provided by author to HL.

——. 2010. *Archaeology and the Sea in Scandinavia and Britain: A Personal Account.* Maritime Culture of the North 3. Roskilde, Denmark: Viking Ship Museum.

Crumlin-Pedersen, O., and A. Trakadas, eds. 2003. *Hjortspring: A Pre-Roman Iron Age Warship in Context.* Maritime Culture of the North 5. Roskilde, Denmark: Viking Ship Museum.

Curtin, J. 1908. *The Mongols. A History.* Boston: Little Brown.

Curtis, E. 1930. "The Alaskan Eskimo." In *The North American Indian: Being a Series of Volumes Picturing and Describing the Indians of the United States and Alaska*, vol. 20. Cambridge: Cambridge University Press.

Dall, W. H. 1878. "On the Remains of Later Pre-Historic Man Obtained from Caves in the Catherina Archipelago, Alaska Territories and Especially from the Caves in the Aleutian Islands." *Smithsonian Contributions to Knowledge* 22, no. 318. Washington, DC: Smithsonian Institution.

Davidson, D. S. 1937. "Snowshoes." *Memoirs of the American Philosophical Society* 5. Philadelphia: American Philosophical Society.

De Laguna, F. 1956. *Chugach Prehistory: The Archaeology of Prince William Sound, Alaska.* Seattle and London: University of Washington Press.

——. 1972. *Under Mount Saint Elias: The History and Culture of the Yakutat Tlingit.* Smithsonian Contributions to Anthropology 7. 3 vols. Washington, DC: Smithsonian Institution Scholarly Press.

De Laguna, F., and DeArmond, D. 1995. *Tales from the Dena: Indian Stories from the Tanana, Koyukuk, and Yukon River.* Seattle and London: University of Washington Press.

DeLisle, J. N., and Königsfeld, T. 1768. "Extrait d'un voyage en Sibérie, M. DeLisle & journal de M. Königsfeld." In Prévost d'Exiles (Abbé) Antoine François, ed., *Histoire générale des voyages*, vol. 72, 84–217. Paris: Didot/Chez Roset.

Diiben, G. von. 1873. *Om Lappland och Lapparne* [*Lapp Country and People*]. Stockholm: P. A. Norstedt unt Söners Förlag.

Dikov, N. N. 1977. *Arkheologicheskie Pamiatniki Kamchatki, Chukotki i Verkhnei Kolymy (Aziia na Styke s Amerikoi v Drevnosti)* [*Archeological Sites of Kamchatka, Chukotka, and Upper Kolyma (Asia at the Crossroads with America in Antiquity)*]. Moscow: Nauka.

——. 1978. "Ancestors of Paleo-Indians and Proto-Eskimo-Aleuts in the Paleolithic of Kamchatka." In A. L. Bryan, ed., *Early Man in America from a Circum-Pacific Perspective*, 68–69. Occasional Papers of the Department of Anthropology 1. Edmonton: University of Alberta.

——. 1979. *Drevnie Kultury Severo-Vostochnoi Azii: Aziia na Styke s Amerikoi v Drevnosti* [*Ancient Cultures of Northeastern Asia: Asia at the Crossroads of America in Antiquity*]. Moscow: Nauka.

——. 1988. "The Earliest Sea Mammal Hunters of Wrangel Island." *Arctic Anthropology* 25, no. 1: 80–93.

——. 1996. "The Ushki Site, Kamchatka Peninsula." In F. Hadleigh-West, ed., *American Beginnings: The Prehistory and Paleoecology of Beringia*, 244–50. Chicago: University of Chicago Press.

——. 1999. *Naskalniye Zagadki Drevney Chukotki (Petroglify Pegtymelya)* [*Mysteries in the Rocks of Ancient Chukotka (Petroglyphs of Pegtymel)*]. Trans. R. L. Bland. Anchorage: Shared Beringian Heritage Program, US National Park Service.

——. 2004. *Early Cultures of Northeastern Asia.* Trans. R. L. Bland. Anchorage: Shared Beringian Heritage Program, US National Park Service.

Dittmar, K. von. 1890a. "Über die Koräken und die ihnen sehr nahe verwandten Tschuktschen [On the Koryaks and the Neighboring Chukchi]." Electronic ed. for *Siberian Studies*. Repr. from German ed. of 1858. www.siberian-studies.org/publications/PDF/Dittmar1858.pdf (accessed May 17, 2019).

——. 1890b. *Reisen und Aufenthalt in Kamtschatka in den Jahren 1851–1855.* St. Petersburg: Kaiserlichen Akademie der Wissenschaften. www.siberian-studies.org/publications/PDF/Dittmar1890.pdf (accessed April 9, 2019).

———. 2004. "Auszüge aus dem 1. Teil mit Ethnographischem Bezug" [Excerpts from Part 1 with Reference to Ethnography]. www.siberia-studies.org (accessed June 19, 2019).

Dixon, E. J. 1999. *Bones, Boats, and Bison: Archeology and the First Colonization of Western North America.* Albuquerque: University of New Mexico Press.

Dobbin, A. 1702. "Generale Beschreibung von Sibirien" [General Description of Siberia]. In J. A. Brand, ed., *Reysen Durch die Marck Brandenburg, Preussen, Churland, Lieflandt, Pleskovien, Gross-Naugardien, Tweerien und Moscovien etc. Anbei eine Seltsame und Sehr Anmerkliche Beschreibung von Siberien* [*Travels through the Marck Brandenburg, Prussia, Churland, Lieflandt, Pleskovia, Gross-Naugardia, Tweeria and Moscovia, Etc., Including a Strange and Very Remarkable Description of Siberia*], 294–302. Wesel, Germany: Heinrich Christian von Hennin. http://digital.bibliothek.uni-halle.de/hd/content/titleinfo/631402 (accessed April 7, 2019). First published 1673.

Dolgikh, B. O. 1960. "Rodovoi i Plemennoi Sostav Narodov Sibiri v XVII Veke" [Clan and Tribal Composition of the Siberian Indigenous Peoples in the 17th Century]. Moscow: Nauka.

———. 1962. "On the Origin of the Nganasans—Preliminary Remarks." In H. N. Michael, ed., *Studies in Siberian Ethnogenesis*, 220–99. Toronto: University of Toronto Press.

Donner, K. 1915. *Siperian Samojeedien Keskuudessa Vuosina 1911–1913 ja 1914* [*Among the Siberian Samoyeds in the Years 1911–1913 and 1914*]. Helsinki: Kustannusosakeyhtiö Otava.

———. 1930. *Siperia, Elämä ja Entisyys.* [*Siberia, Present and Past Life*]. Helsinki: Otava.

———. 1933a. *Ethnological Notes about the Yenisey-Ostyak (in the Turukhansk Region).* Suomalais-Ugrilaisen Seuran Toimituksia 66. Helsinki: SKS.

———. 1933b. *Siperia: Elämä ja Entisyys* [*Siberia: Present and Past Life*]. Helsinki: Kustannusosakeyhtiö Otava.

———. 1979. *Siperian Samojedien Keskuudessa 1911–1913 ja 1914* [*Among the Samoyed of Siberia 1911–1913 and 1914*]. Yale University Human Relations Area Files. Helsinki: Otava.

Doroshin, N. 1866. "Iz Zapisok Vedennyh v Russkoi Amerike" [From Notes Taken in Russian America]. *Gornyi Zhurnal* 3: 365–99.

Drake, S. 1918. *Västerbottenlapparna under Förrä Hälften av 1800–Talet* [*Västerbottens Lapps in the Later Half of the 1800s*]. Etnologiska Studier. Uppsala: Almqrist & Wiksell.

Duff, W. 1981. "Thoughts on the Nootka Canoe." In D. N. Abbot, ed., *The World Is as Sharp as a Knife: An Anthology in Honor of Wilson Duff*, 201–06. Victoria: British Columbia Provincial Museum.

Duggan, A. T., et al. 2013. "Investigating the Prehistory of Tungusic Peoples of Siberia and the Amur-Ussuri Region with Complete mtDNA Genome Sequences and Y-Chromosomal Markers." *PloS ONE* 8, no. 12: e83570. doi:10.1371/journal.pone.0083570.

Dumond, D. 1977. *The Eskimos and Aleuts.* New York: Thames and Hudson.

Dumond, D. E., and R. Bland. 1995. "Holocene Prehistory of the Northernmost North Pacific." *Journal of World Prehistory* 9: 401–52.

Durham, B. 1960. *Canoes and Kayaks of Western America.* Seattle: Copper Canoe Press.

Dyson, G. 1986. *Baidarka: The Kayak.* Edmonds: Alaska Northwest Publishing Co.

———. 1991. "Form and Function of the Baidarka: The Framework of Design." In E. Y. Arima, ed., *Contributions to Kayak Studies*, 259–317. Canadian Ethnology Service Mercury Series Paper 122. Ottawa: Canadian Museum of Civilization.

Elert, C.-C. 1997. *Språket i Södra Skandinavien under Bronsåldern: Finsk-Ugriskt, Baltiskt* [*The Language of Southern Scandinavia in the Bronze Age: Finno-Ugric and Baltic*]. PhD diss. Studier i Svensk Språkhistoria 4. Institutionen för Nordiska Spark, Stockholms Universitet, Stockholm.

Ellmers, D. 1996. "The Beginnings of Boatbuilding in Central Europe." In R. Gardiner and A. E. Christensen, eds., *The Earliest Ships: The Evolution of Boats into Ships*, 11–23. Conway's History of the Ship. London: Conway Maritime Press.

Engelhard, A. P. 1899. *A Russian Province of the North (Archangelsk).* Westminster, UK: Archibald Constable and Co.

Erichsen, M., and K. Birket-Smith. 1936. "En Gammel Kystkultur På Yamal Halvøen" [An Ancient Coastal Culture on the Yamal Peninsula]. *Geografisk Tidsskrift* 39: 164–67.

Ermolova, N. V. 1984. *Evenki Priyamurya i Sakhalina: Formirovaniye i Kulturno-Istoricheskiye Svyazy, XVII- Nachalo XX Vekov* [*The Evenks of Amur and Sakhalin: Formation and Cultural-Historical Connections: From the 17th to the Beginning of the 20th Century*]. PhD diss. Institute of Ethnography of the Soviet Academy of Sciences, Leningrad Division. www.dissercat.com/content/evenki-priamurya-i-sakhalina-formirovanie-i-kulturno-istoricheskie-svyazi-xvii-nachalo-xx-vv (accessed March 5, 2018).

Erslev, E. 1885. *Nye Oplysninger om Brødrene Zenis Rejser* [*New Information about the Travel of the Brothers Zenis*]. Copenhagen: Hoffensberg & Traps.

Eskerød, A. 1956. "Early Arctic-Nordic Boats: A Survey and Some Problems." *Arctica (Ethnographica Studia Upsaliensia)* 11: 57–87.

Evers, D. 2004. "Hunters and Planters, Prehistoric Scandinavian Rock Carvings." Blog post, *StoneWatch*. http://freemedia.ch/downloads/006.pdf (no longer online).

Fabricius, O. 1962. "Otto Fabricius' Ethnographical Works." In E. Holtved, ed., *Meddelelser om Grønland* 140, no. 2. Copenhagen: C. A. Reitzel.

Fagundes, N. J. R., et al. 2008. "Mitochondrial Population Genomics Supports a Single Pre-Clovis Origin with a Coastal Route for the Peopling of the Americas." *American Journal of Human Genetics* 82, no. 3: 583–92.

Fedorova, N. 2003. "Treasures of the Ob in the History of the Western Siberian Middle Ages." In Y. K. Chistov and T. A.

Popova, eds., *Treasures of the Ob: Western Siberia on the Medieval Trade Routes: Catalog of the Exhibition*, 19–28. Salekhard and St. Petersburg: Shemanovsky Museum and Russian Academy of Sciences, Urals Branch.

Fitzhugh, B. 2012. "Hazards, Impacts, and Resilience among Hunter-Gatherers of the Kuril Islands." In J. Cooper and P. Sheets, eds., *Surviving Sudden Environmental Change: Answers from Archaeology*, 19–42. Boulder: University of Colorado Press.

——. 2016. "The Origins and Development of Arctic Maritime Adaptations in the Western Subarctic." In T. M. Friesen and O. K. Mason, eds., *The Oxford Handbook of the Prehistoric Arctic*, 253–78. Oxford: Oxford University Press.

Fitzhugh, B., E. Gjesfjeld, W. Brown, M. J. Hudson, and J. D. Shaw. 2016. "Resilience and the Population History of the Kuril Islands, Northwest Pacific: A Study in Complex Human Ecodynamics." *Quaternary International* 419: 165–93.

Fitzhugh, B., V. O. Shubin, K. Tezuka, Y. Ishizuka, and C. A. S. Mandryk. 2002. "Archaeology in the Kuril Islands: Advances in the Study of Human Paleobiogeography and Northwest Pacific Prehistory." *Arctic Anthropology* 39, nos. 1–2: 69–94.

Fitzhugh, W. W. 1975. "A Comparative Approach to Northern Maritime Adaptations." In W. W. Fitzhugh, ed., *Prehistoric Maritime Adaptations of the Circumpolar Zone*, 339–86. International Congress of Anthropological and Ethnological Sciences. The Hague: Mouton.

——. 1994. "Crossroads of Continents: Review and Prospect." In W. W. Fitzhugh and V. Chaussonnet, eds., *Anthropology of the North Pacific Rim*, 27–51. Washington, DC: Smithsonian Institution Scholarly Press.

——. 1998. "Searching for the Grail: Virtual Archaeology in Yamal and Circumpolar Theory." In R. Gilberg and H. C. Gulløv, eds., *Fifty Years of Arctic Research: Anthropological Studies from Greenland to Siberia*, 99–118. Publications of the National Museum, Ethnographic Series 18. Copenhagen: Danish National Museum.

——. 2006. "Settlement, Social and Ceremonial Change in the Labrador Maritime Archaic." In D. Sanger and M. A. P. Renouf, eds., *The Archaic of the Far Northeast*, 47–82. Orono: University of Maine Press.

——. 2008. "Arctic and Circumpolar Regions." In D. M. Pearsall, ed., *Encyclopedia of Archaeology*, 247–71. New York: Academic Press/Elsevier.

——. 2009. "Notes on Art Styles, Cultures and Chronology." In W. W. Fitzhugh, J. Hollowell, and A. L. Crowell, eds., *Gifts from the Ancestors: Ancient Ivories from Bering Strait*, 88–93. Princeton, NJ: Princeton University Art Museum.

——. 2010. "Arctic Cultures and Global Theory: Historical Tracks along the Circumpolar Road." In C. Westerdahl, ed., *A Circumpolar Reappraisal: The Legacy of Gutorm Gjessing (1906–1979)*, 87–109. BAR International Series 2154. Oxford: Archaeopress.

——. 2016. "Solving the 'Eskimo Problem': Henry B. Collins and Arctic Archaeology." In I. Krupnik, ed., *Early Inuit Studies: Themes and Transitions, 1850s–1980s*, 165–92. Washington, DC: Smithsonian Institution Scholarly Press.

Fitzhugh, W. W., and A. L. Crowell, eds. 1988. *Crossroads of Continents: Cultures of Siberia and Alaska*. Washington, DC: Smithsonian Institution Scholarly Press.

Fitzhugh, W. W., and C. O. Dubreuil, eds. 1999. *Ainu: Spirit of a Northern People*. Seattle and Washington, DC: University of Washington Press and Smithsonian Institution Scholarly Press.

Fitzhugh, W. W., M. Rossabi, and W. Honeychurch, eds. 2013. *Genghis Khan and the Mongol Empire*. Washington, DC: Arctic Studies Center, Smithsonian Institution.

Fitzhugh, W. W., and E. Ward, eds. 2000. *Vikings: The North Atlantic Saga*. Washington, DC: Smithsonian Books.

Fladmark, K. R. 1979. "Routes: Alternative Migrations Corridors for Early Man in North America." *American Antiquity* 44, no. 1: 55–69.

Flegontov, P., et al. 2016. "Genomic Study of the Ket: A Paleo-Eskimo-related Ethnic Group with Significant Ancient North Eurasian Ancestry." *Scientific Reports* 6, no. 20768. www.nature.com/articles/srep20768 (accessed November 4, 2018).

Ford, J. A. 1959. "Eskimo Prehistory in the Vicinity of Point Barrow, Alaska." *Anthropological Papers of the American Museum of Natural History* 7, no. 1.

Forster, J. R. 1784. *Geschichte der Entdeckungen und Schiffahrten im Norden: Mit Neuen Originalkarten Versehen* [*History of the Discoveries and Seas in the Nordic Countries: With New Original Maps*]. Frankfurt: Carl Gottlieb Strauß.

Forsyth, J. 1994. *History of the Peoples of Siberia: Russia's Northern Asian Colony, 1581–1990*. Cambridge: Cambridge University Press.

Fortescue, M. 2004. "How Far West into Asia Have Eskimo Languages Been Spoken, and Which Ones?" *Études/Studies/Inuit* 28, no. 2: 159–83. www.erudit.org/en/journals/etudinuit/2004-v28-n2-etudinuit1289/013201ar (accessed June 5, 2019).

Foss, M. E. 1948. "Kulturniye Svyazy Severa Vostochnoy Evropy vo II Tysyachiletnii do Nashey Eri" [Cultural Relations of Northeastern Europe from the Turn of the Millennium until Our Era]. *Sovetskaya Etnografiya* 4: 23–35.

Friesen, T. M., and Mason, O. K., eds. 2016. *Oxford Handbook of the Prehistoric Arctic*. Oxford: Oxford University Press.

Fuentes, J. A. A. de la. 2010. "Urban Legends: Turkish Kayık 'Boat' and 'Eskimo' Qayaq 'Kayak.'" *Studia Linguistica Universitatis Iagellonicae Cracoviensis* 127: 1–24. www.wuj.pl/UserFiles/File/Studia%20Linguistica123/Studia%20Linguistica%20127/Art1.pdf (accessed June 21, 2019).

Georgi, J. G. 1775. *Bemerkungen Einer Reise im Russischen Reich im Jahre 1772*, vol. 1. St. Petersburg: Kaiserliche Academie der Wissenshaften.

——. 1776a. *Beschreibung Aller Nationen des Russischen Reichs* [*Descriptions of All Nations of the Russian Empire*], vol. 1: *Nationen vom Finnischen Stamm* [*The Finnish People*]. St. Petersburg: Schnoor, Johan Cark.

——. 1776b. *Beschreibung Aller Nationen des Russischen Reichs* [*Descriptions of All Nations of the Russian Empire*], vol. 2: *Tatarische Nationen* [*The Tatar People*]. St. Petersburg: Carl Wilhelm Muller.

——. 1777. *Beschreibung Aller Nationen des Russischen Reichs* [*Descriptions of All Nations of the Russian Empire*], vol. 3: *Samojedische, Mandshurische und Östliche Siberische Nationen* [*The Samoyed, Manchurian, and East Siberian Peoples*]. St. Petersburg: Weitbrecht und Schnoor.

Gessain, R. 1960. "Contribution à l'anthropologie des Eskimo d'Angmagssalik" [Contributions to the Anthropology of the Angmassalik Eskimo]. *Medelelser om Gronland* 161, no. 4.

Giddings, J. L. 1964. *The Archaeology of Cape Denbigh*. Providence: Brown University Press.

——. 1967. *Ancient Men of the Arctic*. New York: Alfred A. Knopf.

Gjerde, J. M. 2010. *Rock Art and Landscapes: Studies of Stone Age Rock Art from Northern Fennoscandia*. Tromsø, Norway: Tromsø Museum.

Gjessing, G. 1936. *Nordenfjelske Ristninger og Malinger av den Arktiske Gruppe* [*Rock Engraving and Painting of the Arctic People*]. Oslo: Instituttet for Sammenlignende Kulturforskning.

——. 1944. *The Circumpolar Stone Age*. Copenhagen: Ejnar Munksgaard.

Goebel, T., M. R. Waters, and M. Dikova. 2003. "The Archaeology of Ushki Lake, Kamchatka, and the Pleistocene Peopling of the Americas." *Science* 301: 501–05.

Golden, H. 2006. *The History and Development of the Greenland Hunting Kayak, 1600–2000*. Portland, OR: White Horse Grocery Press.

——. 2007. "Circum-Polar Kayak Types: An Illustration of What Is (and Was) Where." Blog post. www.traditonalkayaks.com/kayakreplicas/types.html (no longer online).

——. 2015. *Kayaks of Alaska*. Portland, OR: White Horse Grocery Press.

Golovnev, A. V. 1995. *Govorlaskchie Kul'tury: Traditsii Samodiitsev i Ugrov* [*Talking Cultures: Samoyed and Ugric Traditions*]. Ekaterinburg: Russian Academy of Sciences, Urals Branch.

——. 2000. "Wars and Chiefs among the Samoyeds and Ugrians of Western Siberia." In P. P. Schweitzer, M. Biesele, and R. K. Hitchcock, eds., *Hunter-Gatherers in the Modern World: Conflict, Resistance, and Self-Determination*, 125–49. New York and Oxford: Bergham Books.

Golovnev, A. V., and H. N. Michael. 1992. "An Ethnographic Reconstruction of the Economy of the Indigenous Maritime Culture of Northwestern Siberia." *Arctic Anthropology* 29, no. 1: 96–103.

Golovnev, A. V., and G. Osherenko. 1999. *Siberian Survival: The Nenets and Their Story*. Ithaca, NY: Cornell University Press.

Gracheva, G. N. 2012. "Nganasan." In *Countries and Their Cultures*. Trans. P. Friedrich. www.everyculture.com/Russia-Eurasia-China/Nganasan.html (accessed March 24, 2015).

Granö, J. 1886. "Suomalaisten Elämästä Siperiasta" [A Letter to Finland from Tomsk, Siberia]. *Finland's Morning Paper*, August 29. www.migrationinstitute.fi/files/pdf/suomalaiset_siperiassa/pastori_granon_kirjeita.pdf (accessed March 5, 2018).

Gray, E. G. 2007. *John Ledyard: Empire and Ambition in the Life of an Early American Traveler*. New Haven, CT: Yale University Press.

Great Britain Naval Intelligence Division. 1920. *A Handbook of Siberia and Arctic Russia*, vol. 1. London: H. M. Stationery Office.

Grenier, R., M.-A. Bernier, and W. Stevens, eds. 2007. *The Underwater Archaeology of Red Bay: Basque Shipbuilding and Whaling in the 16th Century*. 5 vols. Ottawa: Parks Canada Publishing and Depository Services.

Grinnell, G. B. 2007. *The Harriman Expediion to Alaska Encountering the Tlingit and Eskimo in 1899*. Fairbanks: University of Alaska Press.

Grønnow, B. 1994. "Qeqertasussuk—The Archaeology of a Frozen Saqqaq Site in Disko Bugt, West Greenland." In D. A. Morrison and J.-L. Pilon, eds., *Threads of Arctic Prehistory: Papers in Honor of William E. Taylor, Jr*, 197–238. Archaeological Survey of Canada, Mercury Series Paper 149. Ottawa: Canadian Museum of Civilization.

Gumilev, L. 1997. "Mongols and Mogolian Warfare: Mongolia in the First Half of the 13th Century." In L. Gumilev, ed., *History of the East: The East in the Middle of the 13th Century A.D.*, chap. 4. Online publication (Russian), http://gumilevica.kulichki.net/HE2/he2401.htm (accessed June 21, 2019).

Gurina, N. N. 1987. "Main Stages in the Cultural Development of the Population of the Kola Peninsula." *Fennoscandia Archaeologica* 4: 35–48.

Gurvich, I. 1963. "Current Ethnic Process Taking Place in Northern Yakutia." *Arctic Anthropology* 1: 86–92.

Haavio, M. 1950. *Väinämöinen: Suomalaisten Runojen Keskushahmo* [*Väinämöinen: The Central Character of Finnish Poems*]. Porvoo, Finland: WSOY.

——. 1952. *Väinämöinen Eternal Sage*. 2 vols. Folkore Fellows Communications 144. Helsinki: Suomen Tiedeakatemia.

Habu, J. 2004. *Ancient Jomon of Japan: Case Studies in Early Societies*. Cambridge: Cambridge University Press.

——. 2010. "Seafaring and the Development of Cultural Complexity in Northeast Asia: Evidence from the Japanese Archipelago." In A. Anderson, J. H. Barrett, and K. V. Boyle, eds., *The Global Origins and Development of Seafaring*, 159–70. Cambridge: McDonald Institute for Archaeological Research.

Hahn, E. 1907. "Über Entstehung und Bau der Ältesten Seeschiffe." In *Zeitschrift für Ethnologie*, 42–56. Berliner Gesellschaft für Anthropologie, Ethnologie und Urgeschichte. Berlin: Behrend & Co.

Häkkinen, J. 2010. "Johdatus Samojedikieliin" [Introduction to Samoyedic Languages]. Teaching guide, Helsinki University. www.elisanet.fi/alkupera/Samojedi.pdf (accessed June 21, 2019).

Hallström, G. 1960. *Monumental Art of Northern Sweden from the Stone Age: Nämforsen and Other Localities*. Stockholm: Almqrist & Wiksell.

Hämet-Ahti, L. A., A. Palmén, P. Alanko, and P. Tigerstedt. 1989. *Suomen Puu-Ja Pensaskasvio [Finnish Trees and Plants]*. Helsinki: Suomen Dendrologinen Seura.

Hauer, E., and O. Corff. 2007. *Handwörterbuch der Mandschusprache [Hand-Dictionary for Manchu Language]*. Wiesbaden: Harrassowitz.

Hatt, G. 1916. "Moccasins and Their Relation to Arctic Footwear." *Memoirs of the American Anthropological Association* 3, no. 3: 147–250.

Haviland, M. D. 1971. *A Summer on the Yenisey*. 2nd ed. New York: Ayer Publishing.

Hawkes, E. W. 1916. *The Labrador Eskimo*. Geological Survey Memoir 91, Anthropological Series 14. Ottawa: Canada Department of Mines.

Heath, J. 1978. "Some Comparative Notes on Kayak Form and Construction." In D. W. Zimmerly, ed., *Contextual Studies of Material Culture*, 19–26. Canadian Ethnology Service, Mercury Series Paper 43. Ottawa: National Museum of Man.

———. 1987. "Baidarka Bow Variations." In *Faces, Voices, Dreams: A Celebration of the Centennial of the Sheldon Jackson Museum, 1888–1988*, 93–96. Fairbanks: Division of Alaska State Museums.

———. 1991. "The King Island Kayak." In *Contributions to Kayak Studies*, 1–18. Canadian Ethnology Service, Mercury Series Paper 122. Ottawa: Canadian Museum of Civilization.

Helimski, E. 2001. "Samoyedic Studies: A State-of-the-Art Report." *Finnisch-Ugrische Forschungen* 56: 175–216.

———. 2006. "The 'Northwestern' Group of Finno-Ugric Languages and Its Heritage in the Place Names and Substratum Vocabulary of the Russian North." In J. Nuorluoto, ed., *The Slavicization of the Russian North: Mechanisms and Chronology*, 109–27. Slavica Helsingiensia 27.

———. 2008. *Taimyr, Lower Yenisey in the Early XVII Century: Notes of G. F. Miller in Ethnology, Ethnonyms and Toponyms in Mangazeya Country*. http://helimski.com/Muelleriana/M507-2Taimyr.rtf (no longer online).

Hellmann, I., et al. 2013. "Tracing the Origin of Arctic Driftwood." *JGR Biogeosciences* 118, no. 1: 68–76. https://doi.org/10.1002/jgrg.20022 (accessed June 5, 2019).

Helskog, K. 1985. "Boats and Meaning: A Study of Change and Continuity in the Alta Fjord, Arctic Northway, from 4200–500 Years B.C." *Journal of Anthropological Archaeology* 4: 177–205.

———. 1988. *Helleristningene i Alta. Spor Etter Ritualer og Dagligliv i Finnmarks Forhistorie. [Rock Art in Alta: Ritual and Daily Life in Finnmark Prehistory]*. Alta, Norway: Alta Museum.

Herron, R. 1998. *The Development of Asian Watercraft: From the Prehistoric to the Advent of European Colonization*. College Station: Texas A&M University Press.

Herz, O. 1898. *Reise Nach Nordost-Siberien in das Lenagebiet in Jahren 1888 und 1889 [Journey to Northeast Siberia in the Lena Region in the Years 1888 and 1889]*. Deutsche Entomologische Zeitschrift Lepidopterologische Hefte 10: 209–65.

Hiekisch, C. O. 1879. *Die Tungusen—Eine Ethnologische Monographie. [The Tungus—An Ethnographic Monograph]*. PhD diss. University of Dorpat. http://dspace.utlib.ee/dspace/bitstream/handle/10062/5862/hiekisch_tung.pdf?sequence=1 (accessed June 21, 2019).

Himmelheber, H. 2000. *Where the Echo Began and Other Oral Traditions from Southwest Alaska*. Trans. K. Vitt and E. Vitt. Edited by A. Fienup-Riordan. Fairbanks: University of Alaska Press.

Hitchcock, R. 1891. "The Ainos of Japan." In *United States National Museum Annual Report for 1889–1890*, 417–502. Washington, DC: US Government Printing Office.

Hofstra, T., and Samplonius, K. 1995. "Viking Expansion Northwards: Mediaeval Sources." *Arctic* 48, no. 3: 235–47.

Holm, B. 1987. "The Head Canoe." In P. Corey, ed., *Faces, Voices and Dreams: A Celebration of the Centennial of the Sheldon Jackson Museum*, 143–55. Sitka: Alaska State Museums.

Hornell, J. 1940. "The Genetic Relation of the Bark Canoe to Dug-Outs and Plank-Built Boats." *Man* 40: 114–19. www.jstor.org/stable/2791622 (accessed March 4, 2018).

———. 1946. *Water Transport: Origins and Early Evolution*. Cambridge: Cambridge University Press.

———. 1970. *Water Transport: Origins and Early Evolution*. Newton Abbot, UK: David & Charles.

Hornig, K. 2000. "Zum Wasserverkehr im Altertum. Quellen und Geschichtliche Anfänge." *Skyllis—Zeitschrift für Unterwasserarchäologie* 3, no. 1: 22–27.

Hyttinen, P. 2001. "Anders Chydenius och 'den Amerikanska Näverbåten" [Anders Chydenius and American Watercraft]. http://educa.kpnet.fi/kpkeko/chydeni/anders/digiluku/tuohiart/phnvborj.htm (accessed June 18, 2019).

Ides, E. Y. 1706. *Three Years' Travel over Land from Moscow to China*. Comp. and edited by Nicholas Witsen. London: W. Freeman. http://gdz.sub.uni-goettingen.de/dms/load/img/?PPN=PPN34141865X (accessed April 8, 2019).

Inukai, T. 1939. "Ainu no Yarachip" [On the Ainu Bark Canoe]. *Studies of the Research Institute for Northern and Arctic Culture* 1: 93–105.

Irimoto, T. 2012. "Northern Studies in Japan." Institute for the Studies of North Eurasian Cultures of Hokkaido University. http://d.hatena.ne.jp/irimoto/20110720 (accessed June 8, 2019).

Itkonen, T. I. 1942. *Suomen Ruuhet: 1-, 2-, 3- Ja Monipuiset Sekä Lautaruuhet Kivikaudesta Vuoteen 1940 [The Log Boats of Finland. 1-, 2-, 3-, and Multilog Boats and Planked Canoes from the Stone Age to 1940]*. Forssa, Finland: Kansantieteellinen Arkisto.

Jackson, F. G. 1895. *The Great Frozen Land (Bolshaia Zemelskija Tundra): Narrative of a Winter Journey across the Tundras and a Sojourn among the Samoyads.* Edited by Arthur Montefiore. London: Macmillan and Co.

Janhunen, J. A. 1996. "Nenets." *Encyclopedia of World Cultures.* www.encyclopedia.com/doc/1G2-3458001018.html (accessed March 20, 2015).

———. 1997. "The Languages of Manchuria in Today's China." *Senri Ethnological Studies* 44, 123–46.

Janhunen, J. A., and Salminen, T. 2000. "Northern Altai." *UNESCO Red Book on Endangered Languages.* www.helsinki.fi/~tasalmin/nasia_report.html#Naltai (no longer online).

Jasinski, M. E., and O. V. Ovsyannikov. 2010. "Maritime Culture of the White Sea Littoral: Traditional Ships and Boats of Pomorye in the First Half of the 18th Century." In C. Westerdahl, ed., *A Circumpolar Reappraisal: The Legacy of Gutorm Gjessing (1906–1979),* 149–79. Oxford: Archaeopress.

Jennings, J. 2002. "The Realm of the Birchbark Canoe." In J. Jennings, ed., *The Canoe: A Living Tradition,* 15–24. Toronto: Firefly Books.

———. 2004. *The Art and Obsession of Tappan Adney.* Toronto: Firefly Books.

Jensen, P. S. 1975. *Den Grønlandske Kajak og Dens Redskaber* [*The Greenland Kayak and Its Gear*]. Copenhagen: Nyt Nordisk Forlag.

Jochelson, W. 1905. "Religion and Myths of the Koryak." In *The Jesup North Pacific Expedition. Memoirs of the American Museum of Natural History* 10, no. 1. Leiden: E. J. Brill; New York: G. E. Stechert.

———. 1908. "The Koryak: Material Culture and Social Organization." In *The Jesup North Pacific Expedition,* vol. 6, pts. 1–2. *Memoirs of the American Museum of Natural History* 10. Leiden: E. J. Brill; New York: G. E. Stechert; repr., New York: AMS Press, 1975.

———. 1910. "The Yukaghir and the Yukaghirized Tungus." In *The Jesup North Pacific Expedition. Memoirs of the American Museum of Natural History* 9, pt. 1, 1–134. Leiden: E. J. Brill; New York: G. E. Stechert; repr., New York: AMS Press, 1975. http://digitallibrary.amnh.org/bitstream/handle/2246/26//v2/dspace/ingest/pdfSource/mem/M13Pt01.pdf?sequence=3&isAllowed=y&bcsi_scan_2687365ababd2c82=pFrT3PD0Wa5Cg2HDa9Iu4jctyLxnAAAADtjAdw==:1 (accessed March 23, 2015).

———. 1924. "The Yukaghir and the Yukaghirized Tungus." In *The Jesup North Pacific Expedition. Memoirs of the American Museum of Natural History* 13, no. 2, 135–342. Leiden: E. J. Brill; New York: G. E. Stechert; repr., New York: AMS Press, 1975. http://digitallibrary.amnh.org/bitstream/handle/2246/26//v2/dspace/ingest/pdfSource/mem/M13Pt02.pdf?sequence=2&isAllowed=y&bcsi_scan_2687365ababd2c82=H7riveRDJbOnc/CtzkmMKDzsTD5nAAAAQji+dw==:1 (accessed March 23, 2015).

———. 1926. "The Yukaghir and the Yukaghirized Tungus." In *The Jesup North Pacific Expedition,* vol. 9, pts. 1–3, 343–469. *Memoirs of the American Museum of Natural History* 13. Leiden: E. J. Brill; New York: G. E. Stechert; repr., New York:

AMS Press, 1975. http://digitallibrary.amnh.org/bitstream/handle/2246/26/v2/dspace/ingest/pdfSource/mem/M13Pt03.pdf?sequence=1&isAllowed=y (accessed March 23, 2015).

———. 1928. *Peoples of Asiatic Russia.* New York: American Museum of Natural History.

———. 1933. "The Yakut." *Anthropological Papers of the American Museum of Natural History* 33, no. 2: 35–225. http://digitallibrary.amnh.org/dspace/handle/2246/138 (accessed March 25, 2015).

———. 1993. *The Kamchadals.* Typescript prepared from original unpublished Jochelson manuscripts in Jochelson Papers, New York Public Library, by Ingrid Summers and David Koester, University of Alaska. 2005 ed.: http://digitallibrary.amnh.org/bitstream/handle/2246/26//v2/dspace/ingest/pdfSource/mem/M13Pt03.pdf?sequence=1&isAllowed=y (accessed November 4, 2018).

Johnston, P. F. 1980. *The Seacraft of Prehistory.* Edited by Sean McGrail. Cambridge, MA: Harvard University Press.

Kalm, P. 1772. *Travels into North America,* 2nd ed., vols. 1–. Trans. J. R. Forster. London: T. Lowndes. www.americanjourneys.org/pdf/AJ-117a.pdf (accessed April 4, 2019).

Kankaanpää, J. 1989. *Kajakki. Typologinen ja Etnohistoriallinen Tutkielma* [*The Kayak: A Study in Typology and Ethnohistory*]. Master's thesis. Helsingin Yliopiston Kansatieteen Laitoksen Tutkimuksia 15. Department of History, University of Helsinki. English ed.: http://greenlandpaddle.com//images/stories/dokumenter/the_kayak.kompressed.doc (accessed November 4, 2018).

Kardash, O. V. 2011. *Gorodok Sikhirtya v Bukhte Nakhodka* [*The Sihirtia Hillfort in Nakhodka Bight*]. Ekaterinburg, Russia: Nefteyugansk.

Kari, J., and J. A. Fall. 2003. *Shem Pete's Alaska: The Territory of the Upper Cook Inlet Dena'ina.* Fairbanks: University of Alaska Press.

Kari, J., B. A. Potter, and E. J. Vajda, eds. 2011. *The Dene-Yeniseian Connection.* Fairbanks: University of Alaska Press.

Kashina, E. A. and N. M. Charckina. 2017. "Wooden Paddles from Trans-Urals and from Eastern and Western Europe Peat Bog Sites." *Archaeology, Ethnology, and Anthropology of Eurasia,* 45(2) 97–106.

Kaul, F. 2003. "The Hjortspring Boat and Ship Iconography of the Bronze Age and Early Pre-Roman Iron Age." In O. Crumlin-Pedersen and A. Trakadas, eds., *Hjortspring: A Pre-Roman Iron-Age Warship in Context,* 187–207. Ships and Boats of the North 5. Roskile, Denmark: Viking Ship Museum.

Kaverzneva, E. D. 2012 "Pogrebenie s Lad'ei-kolybel'yu iz Shagarskogo Mogil'nika Epokhi Bronzy" [A Boat Cradle Burial from the Bronze Age Shagara Site]. In I. V. Belotzerkovskaya, ed., *Obrazy Vremeni. Iz Istorii Drevnego Iskusstva* [*Images of Time from the History of Ancient Art*], 57–63, 189. Moscow: Federal Historical Museum.

Kemp, B. M., et al. 2007. "Genetic Analysis of Early Holocene Skeletal Remains from Alaska and Its Implications for the

Settlement of the Americas." *American Journal of Physical Anthropology* 132, no. 4: 605–21.

Kerttula, A. 2000. *Antler on the Sea: The Yupik and Chukchi of the Russian Far East*. Ithaca, NY: Cornell University Press.

Khanturgayeva, N. T., L. N. Khankhunova, and I. V. Zhilkina, eds. 2003. *Istoriya Kultury Buryatii [History of the Buryatian Culture]*. Ulan-Ude, Russia: Eastern Siberian State Technological University.

Khlobystin, L. P. 1990. "Drevniye Svyatilisha Ostrova Vaygach" [Ancient Shrines of Vaigach Island]. In I. P. V. Boyarsky, ed., *Pamiatnikovedenie. Problemy Izucheniia Istoriko-Kulturnoi Sredy Arktiki [Monument Studies: Problems in the Study of the Historical-Cultural Environment of the Arctic]*, 120–35. Moscow: Nauka.

———. 2005. *Taymyr: The Archaeology of Northernmost Eurasia*. Edited by W. W. Fitzhugh and V. V. Pitulko. Trans. L. Vishniatski and B. Grudinko. Contributions to Circumpolar Anthropology 5. Washington, DC: Arctic Studies Center, Smithsonian Institution.

Khomich, L. 1995. "Gipotezy o Proiskhozhdeniya Nentsev" [Hypotheses about the Origins of the Nenets]. In L. Khomich, ed., *Nentsy: Ocherky Traditsionoi Kultury [Nentsy: Descriptions of Traditional Culture]*, 34–41. St. Petersburg: Russian Court.

Kiriak, M. A. 1993. *Archaeologiya Zapadnoy Chukotky v Svyazy s Yukagirskoy Problemoy [Archaeology of Western Chukotka in Connection with the Yukagir Problem]*. Moscow: Nauka.

———. 2007. *Early Art of the Northern Far East: The Stone Age*. Trans. R. L. Bland. Anchorage: Shared Beringian Heritage Program, US National Park Service.

Kivikoski, E. 1944. "Ita-Karjalan Eshhistorialliset Muistot [East Karelian Prehistoric Remains]." In *Muinaista ja Vanhaa Itä-Karjalaa [Ancient and Old Eastern Karelia]*, 28–54. Tutkielmia Ita-Karjalan Esihistorian, Kulttuuri-Historian ja Kansankulttuurin Alalta. Helsinki: Suomen Muinaismuistoyhdistys.

Klaproth, J. von. 1823. *Asia Polyglotta*. Paris: A. Schubart.

Klem, P. G. 2010. *Study of Boat Figures in Alta Rock Art and Other Scandinavian Locations*. Master's thesis. Department of Archaeology, University of Oslo.

Klimenko, V. V. 2010. "A Composite Reconstruction of the Russian Arctic Climate back to AD 1435." In R. Przybylak, ed., *The Polish Climate in the European Context: An Historical Overview*, 295–326. New York: Springer.

Klingstädt, T. M. von. 1769. *Historische Nachricht von den Samojeden und den Lappländern [History of the Samoyeds and Lapplanders]*. St. Petersburg: Hartknoch.

Knecht, R. A. 1995. *The Late Prehistory of the Alutiiq People: Culture Change on the Kodiak Archipelago from 1200–1750 AD*. PhD diss., Bryn Mawr College, PA.

———. 2019. "Nunalleq Kayaks." Blog post, April 6. nunalleq .wordpress.com (accessed June 5, 2019).

Knox, T. W. 1871. *Overland through Asia: Pictures of Siberian, Chinese, and Tatar Life*. New York: Arno Press. www .gutenberg.org/files/13806/13806-h/13806-h.htm (accessed June 21, 2019).

Knutsson, H. ed. 2004. *Pioneer Settlements and Colonization Processes in the Barents Region*. Vuollerim, Sweden: Vuollerim 6000 år.

Koch, G. 1984. *Boote aus aller Welt [Boats of the World]*. Berlin: Museum für Völkerkunde.

Koivulehto, J. 1983. "Suomalaisten Maahanmuutto Indoeuroopalaisten Lainasanojen Valossa" [Finnish Immigration in the Light of Loans]. *Suomalais-Ugrilaisen Seuran Aikakauskirja* 78: 107–32.

Komi People. 2014. *Academic Dictionaries and Encyclopedias*. http://partners.academic.ru/dic.nsf/enwiki/268667 (accessed March 7, 2018).

Korsakov, G. 1939. *Koryaksko-Russki Slovar [Koryak-Russian Dictionary and Concise Koryak Grammar]*. Moscow: Russian Academy of Sciences.

Koshkarova, V. L., and A. D. Koshkarov. 2004. "Regional Signatures of Changing Landscape and Climate of Northern Central Siberia in the Holocene." *Geologiya i Geofizika* 45, no. 6 (June): 717–29.

Kosintsev, P. A., and N. V. Fedorova. 2001. "Nenets i Sikhirtiya" [Nenets and Sihirtia]. In *Kulturnoe Naslediye Narodov Zapadnoy Sibiri [Cultural Heritage of the Peoples of Western Siberia]*, 51–53. Tobolsk-Omsk: Russian Academy of Sciences.

Kotivuori, H. 2006. "Savukosken Kivikautinen Mela" [Savukoski Stone Age Paddle]. *Raito Newsletter*. Rovaniemi, Finland: Provincial Museum of Lapland.

Kovalev, R. K. 2002. *The Infrastructure of the Novgorodian Fur Trade in the Pre-Mongol Era (ca. 900–ca. 1240)*. PhD diss. Department of History, University of Minnesota.

Kradin, N. N., Y. G. Nikitin, and N. A. Kliuev. 2009. "Hunting, Fishing and Early Agriculture in Northern Primor'e in the Russian Far East." In S. Sasaki, ed., *Human-Nature Relations and the Historical Backgrounds of Hunter-Gatherer Cultures in Northeast Asian Forests*, 15–24. Senri Ethnological Studies. Osaka: National Museum of Ethnology. http://citeseerx.ist .psu.edu/viewdoc/download?doi=10.1.1.612.1476&rep=rep1 &type=pdf (accessed February 25, 2018).

Krasheninnikov, S. 1755. *Opisanie Zemli Kamchatki [A Description of the Land of Kamchatka]*. Trans. E. A. P. Crownhart-Vaughan. St. Petersburg: Russian Imperial Academy of Science. 1972 ed.: *Exploration of Kamchatka*. Portland: Oregon Historical Society.

Krauss, M. 2005. "Eskimo Languages in Asia—1791 On, and the Wrangel Island–Point Hope Connection." *Études/Inuit/Studies* 29, nos. 1–2: 163–85.

Krichko, K. 2017. "China's Stone Age Skiers and History's Harsh Lessons." *New York Times*, April 19. www.nytimes .com/2017/04/19/sports/skiing/skiing-china-cave-paintings .html (accessed June 6, 2019).

Kriiska, A. 1996. "Stone Age Settlements in the Lower Reaches of the Narva River, North-Eastern Estonia." In T. Hackens et al., eds., *Coastal Estonia: Recent Advances in Environmental* and Cultural History, 359–69. Strasbourg: Council of Europe. http://ethesis.helsinki.fi/julkaisut/hum/kultt/vk/kriiska/tekstid/02.html (accessed March 5, 2018).

Kriiska, A., A. Tarasov, and J. Kirs. 2013. "Wood-Chopping Tools of the Russian-Karelian Type in Estonia." In K. Johanson and M. Tõrv, eds., Man, His Time, Artefacts, and Paces, 317–45. Tartu, Estonia: Department of History and Archaeology, University of Tartu.

Krupnik, I. 1993. Arctic Adaptations: Native Whalers and Reindeer Herders of Northern Eurasia. Hanover, NH: University Press of New England.

———. 2019. "Chuvans." In Encyclopedia of World Cultures. Moscow: Gale Group. www.encyclopedia.com/doc/1G2-3458000966.html (accessed June 21, 2019).

———, ed. 2016. Early Inuit Studies: Themes and Transitions, 1850s–1980s. Washington, DC: Smithsonian Institution Scholarly Press.

Krupnik, I., and M. Chlenov. 2013. Yupik Transitions: Change and Survival at Bering Strait, 1900–1960. Fairbanks: University of Alaska Press.

Kulemzin, V. M., and N. V. Lukina. 1992. Znakom'tes': Khanty [Introducing the Khanty]. Novosibirsk, Russia: Nauka.

Kuusi, P., and A. Pertti. 1985. Kalevala Lipas. Helsinki: Suomalaisen Kirjallisuuden Seura.

Kuzmin, Y., et al. 2004. "Chronology of Prehistoric Cultural Complexes of Sakhalin Island." Radiocarbon 46, no. 1: 353–62.

Lagus, J. J. W. 1880. Erik Laxman, Hans Lefnad, Resor, Forskningar och Brefvexling [Erik Laxman, His Life, Travel, Research and Correspondence]. Finska Litteratur-Sällskapets Trycheri [Contributions of the Finnish Research Society] 34. Helsinki: Finska Litteratur-Sällskapets.

Laptev, K. 1739. "His Narrative of Sailing to Khatanga Bay and Exploring E. Taimyr." Cited in N. A. E. Nordenskjöld, 1881, The Voyage of the Vega round Asia and Europe: With a Historical Review of Previous Journeys along the North Coast of the Old World, vol. 1. Trans. A. Leslie. London: MacMillan and Co.

Lashuk, L. P. 1968. "Sirtya: Dreniye Obitateliy Subarktiki" [Sihirtia: Ancient People of the Subarctic]. In V. P. Alekseev and I. S. Gurvich, eds., Problemiy Antropologiiy i Istoricheskoy Etnografii Azii [Problems of Anthropology and Historical Enthnography of Asia], 178–93. Moscow: Nauka.

Lattimore, O. 1962. "The Gold Tribe, 'Fishskin Tatars' of the Lower Sungari." In O. Lattimore, ed., Studies in Frontier History: Collected Papers 1928–1958, 339–402. Oxford: Oxford University Press.

Laufer, B. 1898. "Einige Lingnistische Bemerkungen zu Grabowsky's Giljakischen Studien" [Some Linguistic Remarks on Grabowsky's Gilyak Studies]. Internationales Archiv für Ethnographie 11: 19–23.

———. 1900. "Preliminary Notes on Explorations among the Amoor Tribes." American Anthropologist 2, no. 2: 297–338.

———. 1917. "The Reindeer and Its Domestication." Memoirs of the American Anthropological Association 4: 91–147.

Laughlin, W. S. 1963. "Eskimos and Aleuts: Their Origins and Evolution." Science 142, no. 3593: 633–45.

Laughlin, W. S., J. D. Heath, and E. Y. Arima. 1991. "Two Nikolski Aleut Kayaks: Iqyax and Uluxtax." In E. Y. Arima, ed., Contributions to Kayak Studies, 163–210. Canadian Ethnology Service Mercury Series Paper 122. Ottawa: Canadian Museum of Civilization.

Lauhakangas, R. 2013. Veneaiheisia Kalliopiirustuksia ja Kaiverruksia Karjalassa ja Kuolassa [Boat-Inspired Stone Age Paintings and Engravings in Karelia and the Kola Peninsula]. Estonian Centre of Ancient Art. Tallinn, Estonia: Virukoda-arkisto.

Laushkin, K. D. 1959. Onezhskoe Sviatilishche 1–2 [Onega Sanctuary 1-2]. Scandinavia Collection 4–5. Tallinn, Estonia.

Laxman, E. 1793. "Sibirische Briefe" [Siberian Letters]. In Neue Nordische Beyträge 1781–1796 [New Nordic Interpretations 1781–1796], vol. 5. St. Petersburg: Russian Academy of Sciences.

Lebedintsev, A. I. 1998. "Maritime Cultures of the North Coast of the Sea of Okhotsk." Arctic Anthropology 35, no. 1: 296–320.

Lee-Duffy, J. 2005. "How the Last Hunters in China Became an Endangered Species." South China Morning Post, August 15. Repr., Southern Mongolia Human Rights Information Center. www.smhric.org/news_89.htm (accessed February 25, 2018).

Legends of Altai. 2010. "Folklore Ensemble AltaiKai—Altai Throat Singing and Traditional Music." Blog post, Legends of Altai. www.legendsofaltai.com/pages/about_altai.php (accessed March 4, 2018).

Lehrberg, A. C. 1816. "Über die Geographische Lage und Geschichte des im Russischen-Kaiserlichen Titel Genanten Jugrishen Landes" [About the Geographical Location and History of the Russian-Imperial Name Called Ugric Lands]. In P. H. Krug, ed., Undersuchungen zur Erläuterung der Älteren Ust-Ilimsk Russlands [Approaching an Understanding of the Old Ust-Ilimsk Russia], pt. 1, 1–101. St. Petersburg: Imperial Academy of Sciences.

Lehtisalo, T. V. 1932. Beiträge zur Kenntnis der Renntierzucht Beim uen Juraksamojeden [Contributions to Knowledge of Reindeer-Breeding of the Yurak Samoyeds]. Trans. F. Schmidt. Instituttet for Sammenlignende Kulturforskning, ser. B, vol. 16. Oslo: Aschehoug.

———. 1959. Tundralta ja Taigasta: Muistelmia Puolen Vuosisadan Taka [Tundra to Taiga: Memoirs of the Past Half-Century]. Porvoo and Helsinki: WSOY.

Leikola, M. 2001. Runolaulu Tuohiveneestä—Yritys Juurruttaa Tuohikanoottikulttuuria Suomeen 1700-Luvun Puolimaissa [Poetry Songs from Tuohivene—Root and Birch-Bark Canoe Culture in Finland from the Middle Ages to the 1700s]. Vammala, Finland: Vuosilusto.

Lepehkin, I. 1774. Tagebuch der Reise Durch Verschiedenen Provinzen des Russischen Reiches im Jahr 1768–1769 [Diary of a Journey through Different Provinces of the Russian Empire in 1768–1769]. Altenburg, Germany: Richterische Buchhandlung.

——. 1964. *The Peoples of Siberia.* Chicago: University of Chicago Press.

——. 1984. "The Orochen Birch Bark Canoe in Amur." In P. Thiele, ed., *Boote aus Northasien, Gerd Koch,* 169–77. Berlin: Museum für Völkerkunde. Originally published 1927.

Levin, M. G., and L. P. Potapov, eds. 1961. *Istoriko-Etnograficheskiy Atlas Sibiri* [*Historical-Ethnographic Atlas of Siberia*]. Moscow and Leningrad: Institute of Ethnography, Russian Academy of Sciences.

——, eds. 1964. *The Peoples of Siberia.* Trans. S. Dunn and E. Dunn. Chicago and London: University of Chicago Press.

Levin, M. G., and B. A. Vasilyev. 1964. "The Evens." In M. G. Levin and L. P. Potapov, eds., *The Peoples of Siberia,* 670–84. Trans. S. Dunn and E. Dunn. Chicago and London: University of Chicago Press.

Liapunova, R. 1975. *Ocherki po Etnografii Aleutov* [*Essays on Aleutian Ethnography*]. Leningrad: Izdatel'stvo, Nauka.

Lind, J. H. 2004. "Varangians in Europe's Eastern and Northern Periphery: The Christianization of North and Eastern Europe, ca. 950–1050 — A Plea for a Comparative Study." *Ennen Ja Nyt* 4: 1–18. www.ennenjanyt.net/4-04/lind.pdf (accessed November 4, 2018).

Lindau, Y. 1983. *Opisanie Narodov Sibiri: Pervaya Polovina 18-go Veka* [*Description of the Peoples of Siberia in the First Half of the 18th Century*]. Magadan, Russia: Magadanskoe knizhnoe izdatel'stvo. Orig. pub. 1743.

Lindberg, M. 2012. "The Byslätt Bronze Age Boat: A Swedish Bark Canoe." Master's thesis. Marine Archaeology Programme, University of Southern Denmark, Odense.

Ling, C. 1934. *Songhua Jiang Xia You de Hezhe Zu: Shang Xi Ace* [*The Goldi (Hezhe) Tribe of the Lower Sungari River*]. Nanjing: Institute of History and Lnguages, National Research Academy.

Linschoten, J. H. van. 1598. *John Huighen van Linschoten, His Discours of Voyages into Ye Easte and West Indies: Deuided into Foure Bookes.* London: John Wolfe.

Lintrop, Aado. 1999. "The Mansi: History and Present Day." Blog post, Institute of Estonian Language. www.folklore.ee/~aado/rahvad/masuingl.GIF (accessed June 18, 2019).

Linevski, A. M. 1939. *Petroglifõ Karelii* [*Petroglyphs of Karelia*]. Tsh. 1. Karelia: Petrozavodsk.

Lönnrot, E. 1853. *Om det Nord-Tschudiska Språket* [*On the Northern Chud Language*]. Helsinki: Alexander Universitet.

Łuczynski, E. 1986. *Staropolskie Slownictwo Zwiazane Z Zegluga XV i XVI Wiek* [*Old Polish Words Associated with Shipping in the 15th and 16th Centuries*]. Gdansk, Poland: Wydawnictwo Morskie.

Luukkanen, H. 1985. "Canoe Building in Finland and the History of Paddling, 1885–1985." In M. Melojatry, ed., *Marjaniemen Melojat 50 Vuotta — Melontaa Suomessa 100 Vuotta* [*Marjaniem Paddlers, 50 Years — Canoeing in Finland, 100 Years*], 105–60. Helsinki: Yliopistopaino.

——. 2005a. *Finnic Canoe History,* pt. 1: *A Short History of Canoeing in Finland: An Introduction.* Helsinki: Eco-Intelli Ltd.

——. 2005b. *Finnic Canoe History,* pt. 2: *From Makeshift Log Rafts to Inflatable Rubber Boats.* Helsinki: Eco-Intelli Ltd.

——. 2005c. *Finnic Canoe History,* pt. 3: *When Stone Age Men Made Skin Boats.* Helsinki: Eco-Intelli Ltd.

——. 2005d. *Finnic Canoe History,* pt. 4: *Paddles Which Propelled Stone Age Canoes.* Helsinki: Eco-Intelli Ltd.

——. 2005e. *Finnic Canoe History,* pt. 5: *From One-Log Canoes to Two- and Three-Log Dug-Out Canoes.* Helsinki: Eco-Intelli Ltd.

——. 2005f. *Finnic Canoe History,* pt. 6: *A Short History of Canoeing and Canoe Building in Finland: The Origin of Canoes from the Stone Age to the Present.* Helsinki: Eco-Intelli Ltd.

——. 2006a. *Finnic Canoe History,* pt. 7: *Volga-Finnic Canoe Cultures: The Bronze Age and Trade in Eastern Europe: How Finland Became Finnic.* Helsinki: Eco-Intelli Ltd.

——. 2006b. *Finnic Canoe History,* pt. 8: *Expanded Dug-Out Canoes: Technical Innovation in Karelia, the Volga, and the Baltic.* Helsinki: Eco-Intelli Ltd.

——. 2007. *Finnic Canoe History,* pt. 9: *The Bark Canoes and Skin Boats of the Eurasian North — How the East Meets the West in Western Siberia.* Helsinki: Eco-Intelli Ltd.

——. 2010. "On the Diffusion of Bark Canoes, Skin Boats, and Expanded Log Boats in the Eurasian North." In C. Westerdahl, ed., *A Circumpolar Reappraisal: The Legacy of Gutorm Gjessing (1906–1979),* 189–217. BAR International Series 2154. Oxford: Archaeopress.

Lyon, G. F. 1825. *A Brief Narrative of an Unsuccessful Attempt to Reach Repulse Bay: Through Sir Thomas Rowe's "Welcome," in His Majesty's Ship* Griper, *in the Year MDCCCXXIV.* London: John Murray.

Maak, R. O. 1859. *Travels on the Amur River Coinducted by Order of the Siberian Department of the Emperor's Russian Geographical Society in 1855.* St. Petersburg: S. F. Soloviev.

MacDonald, G. M., K. V. Kremenetski, and D. W. Beilman. 2007. "Climate Change and the Northern Russian Treeline Zone." *Philosophical Transactions of the Royal Society of London B Biological Sciences* 363, no. 1501: 2285–99. http://rstb.royalsocietypublishing.org/content/363/1501/2283 (accessed March 7, 2018).

MacRitchie, D. 1890. "Notes on a Finnish Boat Preserved in Edinburg." *Proceedings of the Society for Antiquities of Scotland* 24: 353–69.

——. 1912. "The Aberdeen Kayak and Its Congeners." *Journal of the Royal Anthropological Institute of Great Britain and Ireland* 42: 493–510. http://ads.ahds.ac.uk/catalogue/adsdata/PSAS_2002/pdf/vol_046/46_213_241.pdf.

Madsen, J. S., and K. Hansen, eds. 1981. *Barkbåde. Vikingeskibshallen i Roskilde* [*Bark Boats in the Roskilde Viking Ship Museum*]. Roskilde, Denmark: Viking Ship Museum.

Magnus, O. 1555. *Historia om de Nordiska Folken* (*A History of the Nordic Peoples*), vols. 1–4. Stockholm: Gidlundsfôrlag. Repr., 1976, *A Description of the Northern Peoples*. Edited by Peter Foote. Hakluyt Society 2nd series 182, 187, 188. London: Hakluyt Society.

———. 1939. *Carta Marina et Descriptio Septemtrionalium Terrarum . . . Anno Dui 1539* [*A Description of the Northern World . . . in the Year 1539*]. Pienennetty Näköispainos Uppsalan Yliopiston Kirjastossa Olevasta Alkuperäiskartasta. Helsinki: Karttakeskus.

Makarov, N. P., and M. S. Batashev. 2004. "Cultural Origins of the Taiga-Dwelling Peoples of the Middle Yenisey." In E. J. Vadja and A. P. Dulzon, eds., *Languages and Prehistory of Central Siberia*, 233–48. Amsterdam and Philadelphia: John Benjamin Publishing.

Mäkelä, E., and H. Hyvärinen. 2000. "Holocene Vegetation History at Vätsäri, Inari Lapland, Northeastern Finland, with Special Reference to Betula." *Holocene* 10, no. 1: 75–85.

Mangin, A. 1869. *The Desert World.* London: T. Nelson and Sons.

Manker, E. 1947. "The Study and Preservation of the Ancient Lapp Culture: Sweden's Contribution since 1939." *Man* 47: 98–100.

Marstrander, S. 1963. *Østfolds Jordbruksristninger, Skjeberg, Bd. I–II.* Oslo: Universitetgsforlaget.

———. 1986. *De Skjulte Skipene* [*The Skjulte Ship*]. Oslo: Gyldendal Norsk Forlag.

Martin, F. R. 1895. Die Samlung F R Martin. Ein Betrag zur Kenntnis der Vorgeschichte und Kultur Sibirischen Völker [The F. R. Martin Collections: An Account of the Prehistory and Culture of the Siberian Peoples]. Stockholm: Swedish Museum of Ethnography.

Martin, J. 1978. "The Land of Darkness and the Golden Horde—The Fur Trade under the Mongols, 18th to 19th Centuries." *Cahiers du monde russe et sovietique* 19, no. 4: 401–21.

———. 1983. "Muscovy's Northeastern Expansion: The Context and a Cause." *Cahiers du monde russe et sovietique* 24, no. 4: 459–70.

Martinière, P. M. de La. 1706. *A New Voyage to the North.* London: T. Hodgson and A. Barker.

Martynov, A. 2012. "The Islands of the White Sea, from the Mesolithic to the Middle Ages: The Ancient Development of the White Sea Islands on Archaeological Data." *Arctic and the North* 5, 1–37. http://narfu.ru/upload/iblock/b34/11.pdf (accessed November 4, 2018).

Mary-Rousseliere, G. 1979. "The Thule Culture on North Baffin Island: Early Thule Characteristics and the Survival of the Thule Tradition." In A. P. McCartney, ed., *Thule Eskimo Culture: An Anthropological Retrospective*, 54–75. Archaeology Survey of Canada, Mercury Series Paper 88. Ottawa: National Museum of Man.

Mason, O. K. 2009. "Flight from the Bering Strait: Did Siberian Punuk/Thule Military Cadres Conquer Northwest Alaska?" In H. Maschner, O. K. Mason, and R. McGhee, eds., *The Northern World, AD 900–1400*, 76–128. Salt Lake City: University of Utah Press.

Mason, O. T., and M. S. Hill. 1901. "Pointed Bark Canoes of the Kutenai and Amur." In *Report of the U.S. National Museum for 1899*, 525–37. Washington, DC: Government Printing Office.

Maydell, G. 1896. "Der Sibirische Kahn Oder die Wjetka" [The Siberian Khan or Wjetka]. In *Reisen und Forschungen im Jakutskischen Gebiet Ostsibiriens in den Jahren 1861–1871* [*Travels and Research in the Yakutsk Region of Eastern Siberia in the Years 1861–1871*], 621–23. St. Petersburg: Russian Academy of Sciences. https://archive.org/stream/reisenundforsch00maydgoog/reisenundforsch00maydgoog_djvu.txt (accessed March 4, 2018).

McGrail, S. 1998. *Ancient Boats in North-West Europe: The Archaeology of Water Transport to AD 1500.* New York: Addison Wesley Longman.

McPhee, J. 1975. *The Survival of the Bark Canoe.* New York: Farrar, Straus and Giroux.

Menzies, G. 2003. *1421—The Year China Discovered the World.* London: Bantam Books.

Messerschmidt, D. G. 1964. *Forschungsreise Durch Sibirien 1720–1725* [*Research Trip through Siberia, 1720–1725*], vol. 2 of 5. Berlin: Akademi-Verlag.

Michael, H. N., ed. 1962. *Studies in Siberian Ethnogenesis.* Toronto: University of Toronto Press.

Middendorff, A. T. von. 1856. *Reise Durch Sibierien* [*Travels in Siberia*], vol. 4, pt. 2. St. Petersburg: Eggers & Company.

———. 1867. *Reise inden äussersten Norden und Osten Siberiens. [Journey to the Extreme North and East of Siberia],* St. Petersburg: Kaiserliche Akademie der Wissenschaften, vol. 4, pt 1.

———. 1875. *Übersicht Natur Nord- und Ost-Sibiriens: Die Thierwelt Sibiriens. Die Eingeborenen Sibiriens*, vols. 2–4: *Reise in den Äußersten Norden und Osten Sibiriens* [*Overview of Northern and Eastern Siberia: The Animal World of Siberia. The Natives of Siberia*, vols. 2–4: *Journey to the Extreme North and East of Siberia*]. St. Petersburg: Buchdruckerei der Kaiserlichen Akademie der Wissenschaften.

Mills, W. J. 2003. *Exploring Polar Frontiers: A Historical Encyclopedia.* Oxford: ABC CLIO.

Moberg, C.-A. 1975. "Circumpolar Adaptation Zones East-West and Cross-Economy Contacts North-South: An Outsider's Query, Especially on Ust-Poluj." In W. W. Fitzhugh, ed., *Prehistoric Maritime Adaptations of the Circumpolar Zone*, 101–12. The Hague: Mouton.

Monnier, F. R. von. 1882. *Die Verbreitung der Menschheit. Vortrag Gehalten* [*The Spread of Humanity: A Lecture*]. Vienna: Geographische Gesellschaft.

Mozhinskaya, W. 1953. "Material'naia Kul'tura i Khoziaistvo Ust'-Poluia" [The Material Culture and Economy of Ust'-Polui]. In *Materialy i Issledovaniia Poarkheologii* [*Materials and Studies in Archaeology*]. SSR 35, 72–109. Moscow: Russian Academy of Sciences.

Mulk, I.-M., and T. Bayliss-Smith. 1998. "The Representation of Sámi Cultural Identity in the Cultural Landscapes of Northern Sweden: The Use and Misuse of Archaeological Evidence." In P. J. Ucko and J. Layton, eds., *The Archaeology and Anthropology of Landscape*, 358–96. London: Routledge.

———. 2006. *Rock Art and Sami Sacred Geography in Badjelánnda, Laponia, Sweden*. Kungl., Skytteanska Samfundet 58. Umea, Sweden: Department of Archaeology and Sámi Studies, University of Umea.

Müller, F. F. 1882. *Unter Tungusen und Jakuten: Erlebnisse und Ergebnisse der Olenék-Expedition der Kaiserlich Russischen Geographischen Gesellschaft in St. Petersburg* [*On the Tungus and Yakuts: Experiences and Results of the Olenék Expedition of the Imperial Russian Geographical Society in St. Petersburg*]. Leipzig: F. A. Brockhaus.

Müller, G. F. 1957. "Description of the Siberian Peoples." Manuscript from Great Northern Expedition, 1733–42, in L. P. Potapov, ed., *Proiskhozhdeniye i Formirovanie Khakasskoy Narodnosti* [*The Origin and Formation of the Khakas Nation*], 219–20. Abakan: Russian Academy of Sciences. Original ms. 1730–40.

———. 2010. "Beschreibung der Sibirischen Völker, 1736–1747" [Description of the Siberian Peoples, 1736–1747]. In W. Hintzsche and A. Christianovich, eds., *Ethnographische Schriften I* [*Ethnographic Studies I*]. Sources on the History of Siberia and Alaska from Russian Archives VIII 1. Halle, Germany: Verlag der Franckeschen Stiftungen zu Halle, Harrassowitz. Originally published ca. 1730–40.

Müller, G. F., and P. S. Pallas. 1842. *Conquest of Siberia*. London: Smith, Elder, and Co.

Mysak, L. A. 2001. "Patterns of Arctic Circulation." *Science* 293, no. 5533: 1269–70.

Na, M. 2011. "Huashupi Chuan Zhizuo Jiyi Chuanchengren: Guo Baolin" [Tree Bark Craftsmanship of Guo Baolin]. In Feng J. and Gengsheng B., eds., *Zhongguo Minjian Wenhua Jiechu Jichengren* [*A Folk Culture Heritage Treasure*]. Outstanding Heritage of People, Chinese Folk Culture Series. Beijing: Minzu Chubanshe.

Nansen, F. 1911. "Eskimo and the Skraeling." In *In Northern Mists: Arctic Exploration in Early Times*, vol. 2, 66–94. Trans. A. G. Chater. New York: Frederick A. Stokes Co.

Naumov, N. P. 1927. "Vetki: Small Boats near the Upper Uchami." In Polar Census Photo Album, www.abdn.ac.uk/polarcensus/list_25/7930-1-25-08/7930_1_25_08.htm (accessed April 4, 2019).

Needham, J., and G.-D. Lu. 1962. "Comparative Morphology and Evolution of Sailing Craft." In J. Needham, ed., *Science and Civiliation in China: Physics and Physical Technology*, 383–87. Cambridge: Cambridge University Press.

Nefedkin, A. K. 2003. *Voennoye Delo Chukchey (Seredina XVII–Nachalo XX vv)* [*Military Affairs of the Chukchi from the Mid-17th to the Beginning of the 20th Century*]. St. Petersburg: Peterburgskoe Vostokovedenie.

Nelson, R. 1969. *Hunters of the Northern Ice*. Chicago: University of Chicago Press.

Nelson, S. M., ed. 2006. *Archaeology of the Russian Far East: Essays in Stone Age Prehistory*. BAR International Series 1540. Oxford: Archaeopress.

Nelson, W. H., and F. Barnett. 1955. "A Burial Cave on Kanaga Island, Aleutian Islands." *American Antiquity* 20, no. 4: 387–92.

Nesheim, A. 1967. "Eastern and Western Elements in Lapp Culture." In I. Hoff, ed., *Lapps and Norsemen in Olden Times*, 104–68. Instituttet for Sammenlignende Kulturforskning. Series A, 26. Oslo: Universitetsforlaget.

Nikolaeva, I., and M. Tolskaya. 2001. *A Grammar of Udihe*. Berlin: Mouton de Gruyter.

Nishimura, S. 1931. *A Study of Ancient Ships of Japan*, pt. 4: *Skin Boats*. Tokyo: Society of Naval Architects.

Noll, R., and K. Shi. 2004. "Chuonnasuan (Meng Jin Fu): The Last Shaman of the Oroqen of Northeast China." *Journal of Korean Religions* 6: 135–62.

Nooter, G. 1971. "Old Kayaks in the Netherlands." In *Mededelingen van het Rijksmuseum voor Volkenkunde*, 10–11. Leiden: E. J. Brill.

Nordenskjöld, N. A. E. 1881. *The Voyage of the* Vega *round Asia and Europe: With a Historical Review of Previous Journeys along the North Coast of the Old World*, vol. 1. Trans. A. Leslie. London: MacMillan and Co.

Nordmann, A. 1867. "Zoologische Beobachtungen in Amurlande. Ueber den Fishfang und Jagd der Am Amur Wohnenden Giljaken" [Zoological Observations on the Fishing and Hunting of the Amur Gilyak]. In A. Erman, ed., *Archiv für Wissenschaftliche Kunde von Russland* [*Archive for the Scientific Study of the Russian Peoples*], 331–64. Berlin: Adolf Erman.

Nordqvist, K., and O. Seitsonen. 2008. "Finnish Archaeological Activities in Present-Day Karelian Republic until 1944." *Fennoscandia Archaeologica* 25: 27–60.

Norwegian Polar Institute. 2006. "Ethnic Groups." http://ansipra.npolar.no/english/Indexpages/Ethnic_groups.html (accessed March 4, 2018).

Ohtsuka, K. 1999. "Itaomachip: Reviving a Boat-Building and Trading Tradition." In W. W. Fitzhugh and C. Dubreuil, eds., *Ainu: Spirit of a Northern Culture*, 374–76. Seattle and Washington, DC: University of Washington Press and Smithsonian Arctic Studies Center.

Okladnikov, A. P. 1957. *Drevnee Proshloe Primor'e* [*The Ancient Past of the Pacific Coastal Region*]. Vladivostok: Nauka.

Okladnikov, A. P., and N. A. Beregovaya. 2008. *The Early Sites of Cape Baranov*. Trans. R. L. Bland. Anchorage: Shared Beringian Heritage Program, US National Park Service. Originally published 1971.

Okladnikova, E. 1998. "Traditional Cartography in Arctic and Subarctic Eurasia." In D. Woodward and G. M. Lewis, eds., *History of Cartography: Cartography in Traditional African,*

American, Arctic, Australian, and Pacific Societies, 329–49. Chicago: University of Chicago Press.

Orekhov, A. A. 1998. *An Early Culture of the Northwest Bering Sea.* Trans. R. L. Bland from 1987 Russian ed. Anchorage: Shared Beringian Heritage Program, US National Park Service.

Orlov, E. P. von. 1858. "Die Nomadischen Tungusen von Bauntowsk und der (Obere) Angara" [The Nomadic Tungusen of Bauntowsk and the (Upper) Angara]. In K. Neumann, ed., *Zeitschrift fur Algemaine Erdkunde. Der Gesellschaft fur Erdkunde in Berlin* [*Journal of Geography: The Geographic Society of Berlin*], 43–88. Berlin: Verlag von Dietrich Reimer.

Pakendorf, B. 2007. *Contact in the Prehistory of the Sakha (Yakuts): Linguistic and Genetic Perspectives.* PhD diss. Faculty of Letters, University of Leiden, Netherlands. https://openaccess.leidenuniv.nl/bitstream/handle/1887/12492/Thesis.pdf (accessed March 4, 2018).

Pallas, P. S. 1776. *Reise Durch Verschiedene Provinzen des Rußischen Reichs vom Jahren 1772–73* [*Journeys through Various Parts of the Russian Empire in 1772–73*], vol. 3. St. Petersburg: Kaiserlichen Akademie der Wissenschaften.

Pälsi, S. 1929. *Merillä ja Erämaissa* [*On the Sea and in the Wilderness*]. Helsinki: Otava.

———. 1983. *Arktisia Kuvia 1914–17* [*Arctic Pictures 1914–17*]. Keuruu, Finland: Otava.

Parpola, A. 2012. "Formation of the Indo-European and Uralic (Finno-Ugric) Language Families in Light of Archaeology: Revised and Integrated 'Total' Correlations." In R. Grünthal and P. Kallio, eds., *A Linguistic Map of Prehistoric Northern Europe*, 119–84. *Mémoires de la société finno-ougrienne* 266. Helsinki: Société Suomalais-Ugrilaisen.

Pelikh, G. I. 1972. *Proiskhozhdenie Sel'kupov* [*The Origins of the Sel'kup*]. Tomsk, Russia: Tomsk University.

Perevalova, E. V. 2003. *Obdorskiye Khanty (Khaby): K Voprosu o Formirovanii Gruppy* [*The Obdorsk Khanty: On the Formation of the Group*]. Yamal Archaeology Paper 19. Salekhard, Russia: Arctic Studies Center, Archaeology Section. www.yamalarchaeology.ru/index.php/texts/etnograph/105-perevalova-e-v-2003-obdorskie-khanty-khabi-k-voprosu-o-formirovanii-gruppy (accessed March 4, 2018).

Permyakova, A. D. 2007. *Primitive Cattle Breeders of Siberia.* Tomsk University, Ilim College, Russia. MS in HL possession.

Petersen, H.-C. 1986. *Skin Boats of Greenland.* Roskilde, Denmark: Viking Ship Museum.

Petrov, I. V., and M. I. Petrov. 2008. "A Brief History of the Karelian People." Kurkijoki, Russia: Kiryazh Regional Study Center.

Pitulko, V. V. 1991. "Archaeological Data on the Maritime Cultures of the West Arctic." *Fennoscandia Archaeologica* 8: 23–34.

———. 2016. "The Arctic Was and Remains an Archaeological Enigma." *The Arctic* (July 4). http://arctic.ru/analitic/20160704/386534.html (accessed November 5, 2018).

Pitulko, V. V., A. E. Basilyan, P. Nikolskiy, and E. Girya. 2004. "The Yana RHS Site: Humans in the Arctic before the Last Glacial Maximum." *Science* 303, no. 5654: 52–56.

Pitulko, V. V., et al. 2016. "Early Human Presence in the Arctic: Evidence from 45,000-Year-Old Mammoth Remains." *Science* 351, no. 6270: 260–63. doi:10.1126/science.aad0554.

Plastinin, A. N. 2008. "Lod'ya-Ushkuy-Verkhneuftyugskii Struzhok" [Boats, Shallops, and Small Boats from the Upper Uftyugskaya River]. *Podosinovets News.* www.podosinovets.ru/podosinovetsnews/muzey/561-lodja-ushkujj-verkhneuftjugskijj.html (HL copy).

Poikalainen, V. 1999. "Some Statistics about Rock-Carvings of Lake Onega." *Folklore* 11: 60–69. www.researchgate.net/publication/26428182_Some_Statistics_About_Rock-Carvings_of_Lake_Onega (accessed June 23, 2019).

Poikalainen, V., and E. Ernits. 1998. *Rock Carvings of Lake Onega.* Tartu: Estonian Society of Prehistoric Art.

Popov, A. A. 1937. "Okhota i Rybolovstvo u Dolgan" [Hunting and Fishing among the Dolgan]. In *Pamyati V. G. Bogoraza 1865–1936* [*Essays in Honor of W. G. Bogoras 1865–1936*], 147–206. Moscow: Akademii Nauka.

———. 1964a. "The Dolgans." In M. G. Levin and L. P. Potapov, eds., *The Peoples of Siberia*, 655–719. Trans. E. Dunn. Chicago: University of Chicago Press.

———. 1964b. "The Nganasans." In M. G. Levin and L. P. Potapov, eds., *The Peoples of Siberia*, 571–86. Trans. E. Dunn. Chicago: University of Chicago Press.

———. 1966. *The Nganasan: Material Culture of the Tavgi Samoyeds.* Uralic and Altaic Series. Bloomington: Indiana University Press. Originally published in Russian in 1937.

Popov, A. N., and D. R. Yesner. 2006. "Early Maritime Adaptation on the Southern Coast of the Far East of Russia in Ancient Times." In D. L. Peterson, L. M. Popova, and A. T. Smith, eds., *Beyond the Steppe and the Sown*, 469–76. Colloquia Pontica 13. Leiden and Boston: Brill.

Potapov, L. P. 1936. *Ocherki po Istorii Shorii* [*Essays on the History of the Shoriiy*]. *Trudy Instituta Vostokovedeniya* [*Proceedings of the Institute of Oriental Studies*] 15. Moscow and Leningrad: Russian Academy of Sciences of the USSR.

———. 1957. *Proiskhozhdenie i formirovanie Khakasskoy Narodnosti* [*The Original and Formation of the Khakas People*]. Abakan: Russian Academy of Sciences.

———. 1969. *Etnicheskiy Sostav i Proiskhozhdeniye Altaytsev: Istoriko-Etnograficheskiy Ocherk* [*Ethnic Composition and the Origin of the Altaians: Historical-Ethnographical Work*]. Leningrad: Nauka. http://s155239215.onlinehome.us/turkic/20Roots/201Altaians/Potapov-AltaiansEthnPart1Ru.htm (accessed May 8, 2018).

Potter, B. A. 2010. "The Dene-Yeniseian Connection: Bridging Asia and North America." In J. Kari and B. A. Potter, eds., *The Dene-Yeniseian Connection*, 1–24. *Anthropological Papers of the University of Alaska,* new ser. 5, nos. 1–2. Fairbanks:

Department of Anthropology and Alaska Native Language Center, University of Alaska.

Price, T. D. 2015. *Ancient Scandinavia: An Archaeological History from the First Humans to the Vikings*. Oxford and New York: Oxford University Press.

Przhevalsky, N. 1869. "Travels on the Ussuri River 1867–1869." *Journey through Time*. www.geografia.ru/prjeval1.html (accessed November 5, 2018).

Purchas, S. 1625. *Purchas His Pilgrim: Microcosmus, or the Historie of Man*. London: William Stansby for Henrie Fetherstone.

Quimby, G. I. 1947. "The Sadiron Lamp of Kamchatka as a Clue to the Chronology of the Aleut." *American Antiquity* 11, no. 3: 202–03.

Radde, G. 1861. *Berichte Uber Reisen in S Ost-Siberien im Autrage der Keiserlichen Russischen Geographischen Gesellschaft, Ausgefuhrt in den Jahren 1855 bis Incl. 1859* [*Reports on Travel in Eastern Siberia on Behalf of the Russian Geographical Society, Carried Out in the Years 1855 to 1859*]. St. Petersburg: Russian Academy of Sciences.

Ravdonika, V. 1936. *Naskal'nye Izobrazhenia Onezhskogo Ozera* [*Naskal'nye Images from Lake Onega*] 1. Moscow and Leningrad: Nauka.

Ravenstein, E., and A. H. Keane, eds. 1905. *The Earth and Its Inhabitants*, vol. 5: *The North-East Atlantic, Islands of the North Atlantic, Scandinavia, Islands of the Arctic Ocean, Russia in Europe*. New York: D. Appleton and Co. http://ia600304.us.archive.org/22/items/earthitsinhabita05recl/earthitsinhabita05recl.pdf (accessed June 5, 2019).

Reclus, E. 1882. *The Earth and Its Inhabitants*, vol. 5: *Europe and Russia*. Edited by E. G. Ravenstein and A. H. Keane. New York: D. Appleton.

Reid, R. W. 1912. "Description of Kayak Preserved in the Anthropological Museum of the University of Aberdeen." *Journal of the Anthropological Institute of Great Britain and Ireland* 42: 511–14.

Ritzenthaler, R. E. 1950. "The Building of a Chippewa Indian Birch-Bark Canoe." *Bulletin of the Public Museum of the City of Milwaukee* 19, no. 2: 59–98.

Rousselot, J.-L. 1983. *Die Ausruestung zur Westlichen Eskimo, Untersucht in Ihrem Kulturellen Kontext* [*Western Eskimo Sea Hunting Equipment: A Contextual Study*]. Munchner Beitrage zur Amerikanistik, Band 11. Munich: Klaus Renner Verlag.

———. 1994. "Watercraft in the North Pacific: A Comparative View." In W. W. Fitzhugh and V. Chaussonnet, eds., *Anthropology of the North Pacific Rim*, 243–58. Washington, DC: Smithsonian Institution Scholarly Press.

Rousselot, J.-L., W. W. Fitzhugh, and A. L. Crowell. 1988. "Maritime Economics of the North Pacific Rim." In W. W. Fitzhugh and A. L. Crowell, eds., *Crossroads of Continents: Cultures of Siberia and Alaska*, 151–72. Washington, DC: Smithsonian Institution Scholarly Press.

Rowley-Conwy, P. 2017. "To the Upper Lake: Star Carr Revisited—by Birchbark Canoe." In P. Rowley-Conwy,

D. Serjeanston, and P. Halstead, eds., *Economic Zooarchaeology: Studies in Hunting, Herding, and Early Agriculture*, chap. 23. Oxford: Oxbow Books.

Royal Historical Society. 1914. *The Chronicle of Novgorod, 1016–1417*. Trans. R. C. Beazley. Camden Society, 3rd ser., 25. London: Royal Historical Society.

Rubicz, R. C., and Crawford, M. H. 2016. "Molecular Genetic Evidence from Contemporary Populations for the Origins of Native North Americans." In T. M. Friesen and O. K. Mason, eds., *The Oxford Handbook of the Prehistoric Arctic*, 27–50. Oxford: Oxford University Press.

Rudenko, S. I. 1947. "Drevniye Nakonechniki Garpunov Aziatskikh Eskimosov" [Early Harpoon Heads of the Asiatic Eskimo]. *Sovetskaya Etnografiya* n.s., no. 2: 233–56.

———. 1961. *The Ancient Culture of the Bering Sea and the Eskimo Problem*. Edited by H. N. Michael. Trans. P. Tolstoy. Anthropology of the North: Translations from Russian Sources 1. Toronto: Arctic Institute of North America and University of Toronto Press.

Saarikivi, J. 2006. *Substrata Uralica—Studies of the Finno-Ugrian Substrate in Northern Russian Dialects*. PhD diss. Faculty of the Arts, Department of Finno-Ugrian Studies, Helsinki University. http://ethesis.helsinki.fi/julkaisut/hum/suoma/vk/saarikivi (accessed February 25, 2018).

Saint-Pierre, J.-H. B. de. 1836. *The Studies of Nature*, vol. 2. London: Printed for C. Dilly.

Salminen, T. 2001. "The Rise of the Finno-Ugric Language Family." In C. Carpelan, A. Parpola, and P. Koskikallio, eds., *Early Contacts between Uralic and Indo-European: Linguistic and Archaeological Considerations*. *Mémoires de la société finno-ougrienne* 242: 385–96. Helsinki: Mémoires de la société finno-ougrienne.

———. 2003. *Uralic (Fenno-Ugrian) Languages: Classification of the Uralic Languages, with Present Numbers of Speakers and Areas of Distribution*. Helsinki: Helsinki University.

———. 2006. "Genuine and Confused Information about Central Siberian Languages." Review of *Languages and Prehistory of Central Siberia*, edited by E. J. Vajda. *Finnisch-Ugrische Forschungen* 59: 142–49.

Sarychev, G. A. 1805. *Achtjärige Reise im Nördöstlichen Sibirien 1785–1790, auf dem Eismeere und dem Nordöstlichen Ozean* [*Account of a Voyage of Discovery to the Northeast of Siberia, the Frozen Ocean, and the Northeast Sea*]. Leipzig: Wilhelm Rein und Company.

Sauer, M. 1802. *An Account of a Geographical and Astronomical Expedition to the Northern Parts of Russia: For Ascertaining the Degrees of Latitude of the Mouth of the River Kolyma, of the Whole Coast of the Tshutski to East Cape, and of the Islands in the Eastern Ocean, Stretching to the American Coast: Performed by Commodore Joseph Billings, in the Years 1785 to 1794*. London: T. Cadell, Jun. and W. Davies.

Savateev, Y. A. 1991. "Rybolovstvo i Morskoy Promysel v Karelii" [Fishing and Marine Craft in Karelia]. In N. N. Gurina, ed., *Rybolovstvo i Morskoy Promysel v Epochu*

Mezolita- Rannevo Metalla [*Fishing and Marine Trades in the Mesolithic–Early Iron Age*], 182–202. Leningrad: Nauka.

Savinetsky, A. B. 2002. "Mammals and Birds Harvested by Early Eskimos of Bering Strait." In D. E. Dumond, ed., *Archaeology in the Bering Strait Region: Research on Two Continents*. Trans. R. L. Bland. University of Oregon Anthropological Papers 59: 275–305. Eugene: University of Oregon.

Savvinov, A. I. 2011. *Siberian Ethnography in German Museum Collections: The History of Collection and Research*. Institute of Humanitarian Studies and Issues of the Indigenous Peoples of the North, RAS, Yakutsk. http://docs.exdat.com/docs/index-100277.html (accessed November 28, 2018).

Sbignew, A. 1867. "Ueber die Tungusen der Kustenprovinze on Ostsiberien" [About the Tungus of the Coastal Province of Eastern Siberia]. *Archiv für Wissenschaftliche Kunde von Russland* 21: 18–27.

Schiefner, A. 1969. Introduction to M. A. Castrén, *Grammatik der Samojedischen Sprachen* [*Grammar of Samoyed Languages*]. In M. A. Castrén, *Nordische Reisen und Forschungen* 7. Leipzig and Berlin: Zentralantiquariat der Deutschen Demokratischen Republik.

Schnepper, H., and M. Hörnes. 1908. *Die Namen der Schiffe und Schiffsteile im Altenglischen*. Kiel, Germany: Druck von H. Feincke.

Schrenk, A. G. 1848. *Reise Nach dem Nordosten der Europäischen Russlands, Durch die Tundren der Samojeden, zum Arktischen Uralgebirge* [*Travels to Northeastn European Russia through the Tundras of the Samoyeds to the Northern Ural Mountains*]. Dorpat (Tartu), Estonia: Laakmann.

Schrenk, L. von. 1881. *Reisen und Forschungen im Amur-Lande*, vol. 3: *Die Völker des Amur-Landes* [*Travels and Research in the Amur*, vol. 3: *People of the Amur*]. St. Petersburg: Russian Academy of Sciences. https://ia600402.us.archive.org/3/items/reisenundforschu31schr/reisenundforschu31schr.pdf (accessed March 1, 2018).

Schurr, T., R. Sukernik, E. B. Starikovskaya, and D. C. Wallace. 1999. "Mitochondrial DNA Variation in Koryaki and Itelmen: Population Replacement in the Okhotsk Sea–Bering Sea Region during the Neolithic." *American Journal of Physical Anthropology* 108: 1–39.

Scott, G. R. and D. H. O'Rourke. 2010. "Genes across Beringia: A Physical Anthropological Perspective on the Dene-Yeniseian Hypothesis." *Anthropological Papers of the University of Alaska* 5, nos. 1–2: 119–32.

Shakhnovich, M. M. 2007. *Mezolit Severnoy i Zapadnoy Karelii* [*Mesolithic North and West Karelia*]. PhD diss. Department of Archaeology, St. Petersburg University. www.dissercat.com/content/mezolit-severnoi-i-zapadnoi-karelii (accessed March 1, 2018).

Shetelig, H. 1903. "Fragments of an Old Boat from Halsnø (Notes from the Antiquarian Collection)." *Bergens Museums Årbok* 7: 8–21.

Shimkin, D. 1996. "Countries and Their Cultures: Ket." In *Encyclopedia of World Cultures*, 1. www.everyculture.com/Russia -Eurasia-China/Ket-History-and-Cultural-Relations.html (accessed March 1, 2018).

Shirokogorov, S. M. 2010. "Migrations." In *Psychomental Complex of the Tungus*, vol. 1, sec. 27. London: Kegan Paul, Trench, Trubner and Co. www.shirokogorov.ru/s-m -shirokogorov/publications/psychomental-complex-tungus -01/27 (accessed March 1, 2018).

Shrader, T. 2002. "Pomorskiye Lotsiy- Istochnik Izucheniya Istorii Plavaniya Russkikh v Severnuyu Norvegiyu" [Pomorsky Sailing: A Scholarly Study of the History of Russian Sailing in Northern Norway], 129–34. Edited by Y. Krivosheyeva and M. Khodyakova. St. Petersburg: Mavrodinskiye Readings. http://qwercus.narod.ru/schrader_2002.htm (accessed June 23, 2019).

Shternberg, L. 1933. *Gilyaks, Orochs, Golds, Negitals, Ainu*. Khabarovsk, Russia: Dalgiz; Human Relations Area Files, Yale University, New Haven, CT.

Shubin, V. O. 1994. "Aleuts in the Kurile Islands: 1820–1870." In W. W. Fitzhugh and V. Chaussonet, eds., *Anthropology of the North Pacific Rim*, 337–46. Washington, DC: Smithsonian Institution Scholarly Press.

Shutikhin, A. 2003. "Istoriya Berestyanikh Remyosel" [Toward a History of Birch Bark Handicrafts]. Blog post, *Northern Birch Bark*. www.tues.narod.ru/statyi/9/9.html (accessed March 1, 2018).

——. 2008. "Istoricheskaya Rekonstruktsiya Drevney Karkasnoy Lodki iz Beresty" [Historical Reconstruction of a Birch-Bark Frame Boat]. Manuscript in HL possession; copy of paper from conference "Problemy Razvitiya Transportnoy Infrastruktury Evropeyskovo Severa Rossii" [Problems in the Development of Transport Infrastructure in the European North of Russia], Kotlas/St. Petersburg State University, March 2008. Kotlas/St. Petersburg State University.

Sieroszewski, W. 1993. *Yakuty: Opyt Etnograficheskovo Issledovaniya* [*The Yakut: An Experiment in Ethnographic Research*]. Moscow: Nauka. Originally published Moscow: Nauka, 1896.

Sillanpää, L. 2008. *Awakening Siberia: From Marginalization to Self-Determination: The Small Indigenous Nations of Northern Russia on the Eve of the Millennium*. Acta Politica 33. Helsinki: Department of Political Science, Helsinki University.

Simchenko, Y. B. 1976a. "Nganasans." *Narody i Kul'tury* XXIII: 35–37.

——. 1976b. *Kul'tura Okhotnikov na Oleney Severnoy Evrazii* [*The Culture of Reindeer Hunters of Northern Eurasia*]. Moscow: Nauka.

Sinor, D. 1961. "On Water Transport in Central Eurasia." *Ural-Altaische Jahrbücher* 33: 156–79.

Sirelius, U. T. 1904. "Die Handarbeiten der Ostjaken und Wogulen" [Handicrafts of the Ostyak and Vogul]. *Journal de la société finno-ougrienne* 22.

——. 1906. *Über die Sperrfischerei Bei den Finnisch-Ugrischen Völkern* [*On Fishing among the Finno-Ugric People*]. Helsinki: Finsk-Ugriska Sällskapet.

Sirina, A. A. 2006. *Katanga Evenkis in the 20th Century and the Order of Their Life-World*. Northern Hunter-Gatherers Research Series 2. Edmonton: Canadian Circumpolar Institute Press.

Sjögren, A. J. 1828. *Anteckningar om Församlingarne i Kemi-Lappmark* [*Notes on the Parishes of Kemi-Lapland*]. Helsinki: Simelii Enka.

Smith, K. 1995. "Landnam: The Settlement of Iceland in Archaeological and Historical Perspective." *World Archaeology* 26, no. 3: 319–47.

Snow, H. J. 1897. *Notes on the Kuril Islands*. London: John Murray.

Sokolova, Z. P. 1979. "K Proiskhozhdeniyu Sovremennykh Mansi" [On the Origins of the Modern Mansi]. *Sovetskaya Etnografiya* 6: 46–58.

——. 1983. *The Mansi*. Moscow: Nauka.

Sorokin, P. 1997. *Waterways and Shipbuilding in Northwestern Russia in the Middle Ages*. St. Petersburg: Institute of the History of Material Culture, Russian Academy of Sciences.

Spaulding, A. 1946. "Northeastern Archaeology and General Trends in the Northern Forest Zone." In F. Johnson, ed., *Man in Northeast North America*. Papers of the Robert S. Peabody Foundation for Archaeology 3, 143–67. Andover, NH: Phillips Academy.

Spies, M. 1997. *Arctic Routes to Fabled Lands: Olivier Brunel and the Passage to China and Cathay in the Sixteenth Century*. Amsterdam: Amsterdam University Press.

Spörer, J. 1867. *Novaja Semlä in Geographischer, Naturhistorischer und Volkwirthschftlicher Beziehung* [*Novaya Zemblya and Its Natural History and Ethnological Relationships*]. Petermanns Geographische Mitteilungen 21. Gotha, Germany: Justus Perthes.

Spranz, B., ed. 1984. *Boots, Technik und Symbolik* [*Boats, Technique and Symbolism*]. Freiburg, Germany: Museum für Völkerkund.

Stang, H. 1980. "Rysslands Uppkomst—En Tredje Ståndpunkt" [The Rise of Russia: A Third Position]. *Svensk-Sovjetiska Historiesymposiet Vid Lunds Universitet*, 154-198. Lund: Sweden. www.scandia.hist.lu.se (accessed June 24, 2019)

Starcev, G. 1988. *Die Ostjaken: Sozial-Ethnographische Skizze. Aus dem Russischen Übertragen von Katharina Oestreich-Geib* [*The Ostyaks: Social-Ethnographic Sketch, Translated from the Russian by Katharina Oestreich-Geib*]. Trans. K. Oestreich-Geib. Munich: Veröffentlichungen der Congregatio Ob-Ugrica.

Steiner, F. B. 1939. "Skinboats and the Yakut 'Xayik.'" *Ethnos* 4, nos. 3–4: 177–83.

Steller, G. W. 2003. *Steller's History of Kamchatka*. Fairbanks: University of Alaska Press. Originally published 1774.

——. 2013. *Beschreibung von dem Lande Kamtschatka* [*A Description of Kamchatka*], vol. 2. Edited by E. Kasten and M. Dürr. Klassiker der Deutschsprachigen Ethnograhie. Bonn: Holos Verlag.

Stralenberg, P. J. 1738. *An Historico-Geographical Description of the Northern and Eastern Parts of Europe and Asia; but More Especially of Russia, Siberia, and Great Tartary*. Trans. W. Innys and R. Manby. London: W. Innys and R. Manby.

Tajima, A., M. Hayami, K. Tokunaga, and T. Juji. 2004. "Genetic Origins of the Ainu Inferred from Combined DNA Analyses of Maternal and Paternal Lineages." *Journal of Human Genetics* 49, no. 4: 187–93.

Takakura, H. 2012. "The Shift from Herding to Hunting among the Siberian Evenki: Indigenous Knowledge and Subsistence Change in Northwestern Yakutia." *Asian Ethnology* 71, no. 1: 31–47.

Takase, K. 2016. "Archaeology along the Coast of the Okhotsk Sea: Achievements, Problems, and Perspectives." In *Proceedings of the 30th International Abashiri Symposium*, 39–46. Abashiri, Japan: Association for the Promotion of Northern Cultures.

Tallgren, A. M. 1931a. *Suomen Muinaisuus* [*Ancient Finland*]. Porvoo, Finland: WSOY.

——. 1931b. "Luoteis-Siperian Kulttuurikosketuksista Kr. Syntymän Aikaan" [Culture Contacts in Northwest Siberia c. 0 AD]. *Kalevalaseuran Vuosikirja* 11: 104–24.

——. 1934. "Die 'Altpermische' Pelzenwareperiode an der Pecora" [The "Altpermische" Fur Trade at the Pechora]. In *Muinaismuistoyhdistyksen Vuosikirja 1934*, 152–81. Helsinki: Otava.

——. 1938. "Kauko-Karjalan Muinaismuistot Ja Esihistoriallinen Asutus" [Russian Karelian Archaeological Finds and Prehistoric Inhabitation]. In A. M. Tallgren, ed., *Karjalan Historiaa* [*History of Karelia*], 9–20. Jyväskylä, Finland: Gummerus.

Tambets, K., et al. 2004. "The Western and Eastern Roots of the Saami—The Story of Genetic 'Outliers' Told by Mitochondrial DNA and Y Chromosomes." *American Journal of Human Genetics* 74, no. 4: 661–82.

Tengengren, H. 1952. *En Utdöd Lappkultur i Kemi Lappmark. Studier i Nordfinlands Kolonisationshistoria* [*An Extinct Lapp Culture in Kemi Lappmark: Studies in Northern Finland's Colonization History*]. Acta Academiae Aboensis, Humaniora 19, no. 4. Åbo: Åbo Akademi.

——. 1965. "Hunters and Amazons: Seasonal Migrations in the Older Hunting and Fishing Communities." In H. Harald, ed., *Hunting and Fishing: Nordic Symposium on Life in a Traditional Hunting and Fishing Milieu in Prehistoric Times and Up to the Present Day*, 427–92. Lulea, Sweden: Norrbottens Museum.

Thiele, P. 1984. "Boote aus Westasien" [Boats of Western Asia]. In G. Koch, H. Hartmann, and K. Helfrich, eds., *Boote aus Aller Welt*, 169–77. Berlin: Museum für Völkerkunde.

Timofeev, A. I. ed. 1882. *Pamyatniki Sibirskoi Istorii XVIII Veka* [*Monuments of 18th-Century Siberian History*], vol. 1. St. Petersburg: Tipografiya Ministerstvo Vnutrennykh Del.

Tomilov, N. A. 2000. "Ethnic Processes within the Turkic Population of the West Siberian Plain from the 16th to the 20th

Centuries." Trans. from Russian by A. J. Frank. *Cahiers du monde russe* 41, nos. 2–3: 221–32. http://monderusse.revues.org/docannexe/4402tomilov-cmr-2-3-2000.pdf (accessed November 9, 2018).

——. 2012a. "Chulymsy." Blog post, *The Peoples of Russia.* www.narodru.ru/peoples1299.html (accessed November 9, 2018).

——. 2012b. "The Ethnic Composition of the Omsk Region: On the Life of the Siberian Tatars, Kazakhs, Russian, Ukrainians, and Germans." Blog post (no longer online).

Tomilov, N. A., and P. Friedrich. 1996. "Siberian Tatars." In *Encyclopedia of World Cultures*, vol. 6: *Russia and Eurasia/ China*, 340–42. http://1.droppdf.com/files/BuapW/encyclopedia-of-world-cultures-volume-6-russia-and-eurasia-china-1994-.pdf (accessed March 3, 2018).

Torvinen, M. 2000. "Säräisniemi 1 Ware." *Fennoscandia Archaeologica* 16, no. 1: 3–35.

Trebitsch, R. 1912. "Fellboote und Schwimsäcke und Ihre Geographische Verbreitung in der Vergangenheit und Gegenwart" [Leather and Skin-Covered Boats and Their Distribution in the Past]. In German Archiev für Anthropologie, new ser. 11, 161–84. Braunschweig: Friendrich Vieweg & Sohn.

Trevor-Battye, A. 1895. *Ice-Bound on Kolguev*. London: Archibald Constable and Co.

Tronson, J. M. 1859. *Personal Narrative of a Voyage to Japan, Kamtchatka, Siberia, Tartary, and Various Parts of Coast of China in HMS* Barracouta. London: Smith, Elder and Co.

Troyanovskiy, S. V., and M. I. Petrov. 2018. "The XI Century Boat from Novgorod Tower." Internet report Nauchnoe Naslediya, *Soviet Archaeology* 2: 1–7. https://historicaldis.ru/blog/43991598325/Ladya-XI-v.-iz-Novgoroda, http://arc.novgorod.ru/aleshk/ind.php3?file=article/ship.txt&menu=./util/art#r1 (accessed March 3, 2018).

Tsubaki, R. 2011. *Pehr Kalm, Suomalainen Amerikan Löytäjä* [*Pehr Kalm, the Finnish Discoverer of America*]. Trans. A. Leikola. Helsinki: Terra Cognita.

Tugolukov, V. A. 1963. "The Vitim-Olekma Evenki." *Sovetskaya Etnografia* 2, no. 2: 15–40.

——. 1985. *Tungusy (Evenki i Eveny)* [*Tungus (Evenk and Even)*]. Moskow: Nauka.

Turner, L. 2008. *An Aleutian Ethnography*. Fairbanks: University of Alaska Press.

Turov, M. G. 2008. *Economy of Evenkis in the Central Siberian Taiga at the Turn of the 20th Century*. Northern Hunter-Gatherers Research Series 5. Edmonton, AL: Canadian Circumpolar Institute Press.

University of Alaska, Fairbanks. 2008. "Prehistoric Cultures Were Hunting Whales at Least 3,000 Years Ago." *Science-Daily*. April 8. www.sciencedaily.com/releases/2008/04/080404160335.htm (accessed June 6, 2019).

Ushnitsky, V. V. 2008a. "Vsya Pravda o Tungusakh i Ikh Istorii" [The Whole Truth about Tungus and Their History]. Blog post, *All the Truth about Tungus and Their History*. June 6. http://merkit.livejournal.com/ (accessed March 3, 2018).

——. 2008b. "Sistema Vospitania u Narodov Yakutii" [The Child-Rearing System among the People of Yakutia]. Blog post, *All the Truth about Tungus and Their History*. June. http://merkit.livejournal.com/1418.html (accessed November 9, 2018).

——. 2015. "Legendarniye Plemena Yakutii XVII Veka" [Legendary 17th-Century Tribes of Yakutia]. *Nauchnoye Obozrenie Sayano-Altaya* 4, no. 12: 15–20.

——. 2016. "Problema Etnogeneza Sakha: Novyi Vzglyad" [The Problem of the Sakha People's Ethnogenesis: A New Approach]. *Zhurnal Sibirskovo Federalnovo Universita: Gumanitarniye Nauki* 8, no. 9: 1822–40.

Utagawa, H. 1887. *Dai-Nippon Busson Zue* [*Products of Greater Japan*]. Tokyo: Ōkura Magobei.

Vainshtein, S. 1980. *Nomads of South Siberia: The Pastoral Economies of Tuva*. Edited by Caroline Humphrey. Trans. M. Colenso. Cambridge: Cambridge University Press.

Vajda, E. 2010. "A Siberian Link with the Na-Dene." *Anthropological Papers of the University of Alaska*, new ser. 5, no. 2: 31–99.

Vajda, E. J., and A. P. Dulzon, eds. 2004. *Languages and Prehistory of Central Siberia*. Philadelphia: John Benjamin Publishing Company.

VanStone, J. W., ed. 1959. "An Early Account of Russian Discoveries in the North Pacific." *Anthropological Papers of the University of Alaska* 7, no. 2: 91–106.

——. 1985. *An Ethnographic Collection from Northern Sakhalin Island*. Chicago: Field Museum of Natural History.

Vartanyan, S. I., V. E. Garutt, and A. V. Sher. 1993. "Holocene Dwarf Mammoths from Wrangel Island in the Siberian Arctic." *Nature* 362: 337–40.

Vasilevich, G. M. 1969. *Evenki: Istoriko-Etnograficheskiye Ocherki (XVIII- Nachalo XX vv)* [*The Evenks: Historico-Ethnographic Essays (From the 18th to the Beginning of the 20th Centuries)*]. Leningrad: Nauka.

Vasilevsky, A. A., and O. A. Shubina. 2006. "Neolithic of Southern Sakhalin and Southern Kuril Islands." In S. M. Nelson, A. P. Derevianko, Y. V. Kuzmin, and R. I. Bland, eds., *Archaeology of the Russian Far East: Essays in Stone Age Prehistory*, 151–66. BAR International Series. Oxford: Archaeopress.

Vasil'evsky, R. S., and C. S. Chard. 1969. "The Origin of the Ancient Koryak Culture on the Northern Okhotsk Coast." *Arctic Anthropology* 6, no. 1: 150–64.

Vasiliev, V. I. 1979. *Problemy Formirovaniya Severo-Samodiyskikh Narodnostey* [*Problems in the Formation of the Northern Samoyedic Peoples*]. Moscow: Nauka.

Vdovin, I. S. 1965. *Ocherki Istorii i Etnografii Chukchey* [*Essays on the History and Ethnography of the Chukchi*]. Moscow and Leningrad: Nauka.

Veltre, D. 1998. "Prehistoric Maritime Adaptations in the Western and Central Aleutian Islands, Alaska." *Arctic Anthropology* 35, no. 1: 223–33.

Vermeulen, H. S. 2016. "Ethnography and Empire: G. F. Müller and the Description of Siberian Peoples." In H. F. Vermeulen, ed., *Before Boas: The Genesis of Ethnography and Ethnology in the German Enlightenment*, 131–58. Lincoln and London: University of Nebraska Press.

Verner, G. K. 1977. "Aktsentirovannye Sravnitel'nye Slovarnye Materialy po Sovremennym Enisejskim Dialektam" [Accented Comparative Lexical Materials on the Modern Yeniseic Dialects]. *Jazyki i Toponimija* 4: 131–95.

Vilkuna, K., and E. Mäkinen. 1976. *Haapio Isien Työ* [*Aspen Canoe Thesis*], 3rd ed. Helsinki: Otava.

Vitenkova, I. 2003. *Pozdniy Neolit Karelii: Pamytaniki s Grebenchato-Yamochnoy Keramikoy* [*Late Neolithic Karelia: Monuments with Pit Comb Ware Ceramics*]. PhD diss. Department of History, Petrozavodsk University. www.dslib.net/arxeologia/pozdnij-neolit-karelii.html (accessed March 3, 2018).

Vizgalov, G. P. 2005. "Russkaya Mangazeya, ili Zapolyarnoe 'El Dorado'—Sekrety Strannovo Goroda" [Russian Mangazeya, or the Polar "El Dorado"—Secrets of a Strange City]. *Argumenty i Fakti v Zapadnoy Sibiri* [*Arguments and Facts in Western Siberia, Tyumen Region*] 559, no. 52: 115–20.

———. 2006. *Transportniye Sredstva Zhiteley Goroda Mangazeya* [*Transport of the Inhabitants of Mangazeya*]. Nefteyugansk, Russia: Center of Historico-Cultural Heritage.

Vogel, W. von. 1912. "Von den Anfängen Deutscher Schiffahrt" [The Beginnings of German Ships]. *Praehistorische Zeitschrift* 4: 1–16. www.degruyter.com/view/j/prhz.1912.4.issue-1-2/prhz.1912.4.1-2.1/prhz.1912.4.1-2.1.xml (accessed March 3, 2018).

Volodko, N. V., N. P. Eltsov, E. B. Starikovskaya, and R. I. Sukernik. 2009. "Analysis of the Mitochondrial DNA Diversity in Yukaghirs in Evolutionary Context." *Genetika* 45, no. 7: 992–96.

Walsh, W. ed. 1948. "The Chronicle of Novgorod, 1016–1417." In *Medieval Sourcebook: The Novgorod Chronicle: Selected Annals*. Department of History, Fordham University. Syracuse: Syracuse University Press. http://legacy.fordham.edu/halsall/source/novgorod1.asp (accessed June 24, 2019).

Watanabe, Y. 2013. "Beluga Hunting Practices of the Indigenous People of Kamchatka: Characterization of Sea Mammal Hunting in Northeastern Asia." *Senri Ethnological Studies* 84: 177–94.

Waugh, F. W. 1919. "Canadian Aboriginal Canoes." *Canadian Field-Naturalist* 33: 23–33.

Weber, A., M. A. Katzenberg, and T. G. Schurr, eds. 2011. *Prehistoric Hunter-Gatherers of the Baikal Region, Siberia: Bioarchaeological Studies of Past Life Ways*. University of Pennsylvania Museum of Archaeology and Anthropology Series. Philadelphia: University of Pennsylvania Press.

Weinstock, J. 2005. "The Role of Skis and Skiing in the Settlement of Early Scandinavia." *Northern Review* 25–26: 172–96.

Westerdahl, C. 1979. "Är Verkligen Byslättfyndet en Barkkanot?" [Is the Byslätt Find Really a Bark Canoe?]. *Meddelanden frå Marinarkeologiska Sällskapet* 3, no. 79: 30–31.

———. 1985a. "Sewn Boats of the North: A Preliminary Catalogue with Introductory Comments. Part I." *International Journal of Nautical Archaeology and Underwater Exploration* 14, no. 1: 33–62.

———. 1985b. "Sewn Boats of the North: A Preliminary Catalogue with Introductory Comments, Part II." *International Journal of Nautical Archaeology and Underwater Exploration* 14, no. 2: 119–42.

———. 1987. "*Et Sätt Som Liknar Them Utitheras Öfriga Lefnadsart.*" *Om Äldre Samiskt Båtbyggeoch Samisk Båthantering* [*"A Way Similar to the Utitheras Second Life Style": About Early Saami Boat Building and Boat Management*]. Johan Nordlander Sällskapet 11. Umeå, Sweden: Umeå University.

———. 1995. "Samischer Bootsbau" [Saami Boat-Building], part 1. *Deutsches Schiffahrtsarchiv* 18: 233–60.

———. 1999. "Samischer Bootsbau" [Saami Boat-Building], part 4. *Deutsches Schiffahrtsarchiv* 22: 285–314.

———, ed. 2010. *A Circumpolar Reappraisal: The Legacy of Gutorm Gjessing (1906–1979)*. Edited by C. Westerdahl. BAR International Series 2154. Oxford: Archaeopress.

Wetterhoff, O. 2004. *Bergön Pyyntimiehet: O. Helanderin Arvostelu* [*Bergön Catchers: O. Helander's Review*]. Helsinki: Suomalaisen Kirjallisuuden Seura.

Whitaker, I. 1954. "The Scottish Kayaks and the Finnmen." *Antiquity* 28, no. 110: 99–104.

———. 1977. "The Scottish Kayaks Reconsidered." *Antiquity* 51, no. 201: 41–45.

Wickler, S. 2010. "Visualizing Sami Waterscapes in Northern Norway from an Archaeological Perspective." In C. Westerdahl, ed., *A Circumpolar Reappraisal: The Legacy of Gutorm Gjessing (1906–1979)*, 349–61. BAR International Series 2154. Oxford: Archaeopress.

Wiklund, K. B. 1947. *Nordisk Kultur. Samlingsverk, Saame* [*Nordic Culture: Saami Collection Work*], 10. Stockholm: Bonnier.

Willerslev, R. 2007. *Soul Hunters: Hunting, Animism, and Personhood among the Siberian Yukaghirs*. Berkeley: University of California Press.

Witze, A. 2008. "Whaling Scene Found in a 3000-Year-Old Picture." *Nature* (March 31). doi:10.1038/news.2008.714.

Wixman, R. 1984. *The Peoples of the U.S.S.R.: An Ethnographic Handbook*. London: Macmillan and Co.

Woss, C. F. 1779. *Neuere Geschichte der Polar-Länder* [*Modern History of the Polar Regions*], vol. 4. Berlin: den Christian Fredrich Boss.

Wrangel, F. P. von 1839. *Reise Laengs der Nordküste von Sibirien und auf dem Eismeere in den Jahren 1820–1824* [*Traveling along the Northern Coast of Siberia and on the Frozen Sea in the Years 1820–1824*]. 2 vols. Berlin: Voss'schen Buchhandlung. English trans., 1944. *Wrangel's Expedition to the Polar Sea*, 2 vols. London: J. Madden and Co.

——. 1948. *Travels along the Northern Shores of Siberia and the Arctic Sea Committed in 1820, 1821, 1822, 1823, and 1824.* Ed. E. Shvede. Moscow: NSRA, http://az.lib.ru/w/wrangelx_f_p (accessed June 4, 2019).

Yamaura, K. 1978. "On the Development Process of Toggle Harpoon Heads around the Bering Strait." *Journal of the Archaeological Society of Nippon* 64, no. 4: 23–50.

——. 1998. "The Sea Mammal Hunting Cultures of the Okhotsk Sea, with Special Reference to Hokkaido Prehistory." *Arctic Anthropology* 35, no. 1: 321–34.

Yanchev, D. V. 2006. *The Economy and Material Culture of the Negital.* PhD diss. Department of History, Ethnography, Ethnology, and Anthropology, Far Eastern State University, Vladivostok. www.ihaefe.org/26-27126/yanchev.pdf (accessed February 25, 2012).

Zagoskin, N. P. 1910. *Russkie Vodnie Puti i Sudovoye Delo v Do-Petrovskoy Rossi [Russian Waterways and Shipping in Pre-Petrine Russia],* 371–80. Edited by I. N. K. Khartonova. Russia: Litetipografiya.

Zarisovski, A. I. 1949. "Sibirskiye Zarisovki Pervoy Poloviny XVIII Veka" [Siberian Sketches of the First Half of the Eighteenth Century]. In A. I. Andreev et al., eds., *Letopis' Severa [Chronicles of the North],* vol. 1, 123–35. Moscow and Leningrad: Glavsevmorputi Publishing.

Zeeberg, J. 2005. *Into the Ice Sea: Barents' Wintering on Novaya Zemlya—A Renaissance Voyage of Discovery.* West Lafayette, IN: Purdue University Press.

——. 2007. *Terugkeer naar Nova Zembla. De Laatste en Tragische Reis van Willem Barents [Return to Nova Zemblya: The Last and Tragic Journey of Willem Barents].* www.researchgate.net/publication/315677723 (accessed June 18, 2019).

Zimmerly, D. W. 1986. *Qajaq: Kayaks of Siberia and Alaska.* Fairbanks: University of Alaska Press.

——. 2000. *Qajaq: Kayaks of Siberia and Alaska,* 2nd ed. Fairbanks: University of Alaska Press.

——. 2010. "Annotated Bibliography of Arctic Kayaks." Blog post, *Arctic Kayaks.* www.arctickayaks.com/Bibliography/biblioA-C.htm (accessed February 27, 2018).

Zlojutro, M., R. Rubicz, E. J. Devor, and V. A. Spitsyn. 2006. "Genetic Structure of the Aleuts and Circumpolar Populations Based on Mitochondrial DNA Sequences: A Synthesis." *American Journal of Physical Anthropology* 129, no. 3: 446–64.

Zuev, A. 2012. *Russkiye i Aborigeny na Kraynem Severo-Vostoke vo Vtoroy Polovine XVII- Pervoy Chetverti XVIII vv [Russians and Natives in Far Northeastern Siberia in the Second Half of the 17th and the First Quarter of the 18th Centuries].* Novosibirsk, Russia: Novosibrisk State University. http://zaimka.ru/zuev-aborigines (accessed March 3, 2018).

INDEX

Page numbers followed by *f* and *t* refer to figures and tables, respectively.